gings

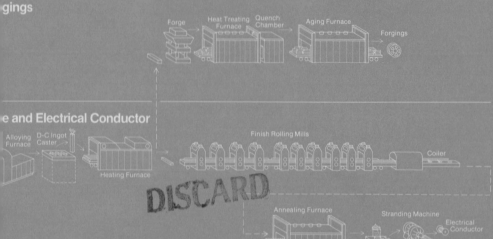

e and Electrical Conductor

DISCARD

wn Bar and Rod

ruded Shapes and Tube

D0872240

wn Tube

From monopoly to competition

C. M. HALL.
PROCESS OF REDUCING ALUMINIUM BY ELECTROLYSIS.

No. 400,766.   Patented Apr. 2, 1889.

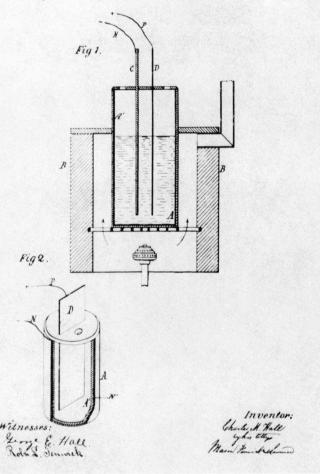

Witnesses:
George E. Hall.
Roln S. Simmah.

Inventor:
Charles M. Hall
by his atty
Mason Foulwick

Patent 400,766: Sectional drawing of Charles Martin Hall's idea for an electrolytic reduction process for making aluminum. Figure 1 illustrates an iron or steel melting pot (A) with a protective carbon lining (A′) placed in a furnace (B). In the crucible, alumina (oxide of aluminum) is added to a fused bath of the fluoride of aluminum, the fluoride of sodium potassium, and cryolite. An electric current is passed through the solution by means of electrodes (C and D), which are connected to an electric power source by wires (N and P). By action of the electric current, oxygen is released at the positive electrode and aluminum is reduced at the negative electrode. Figure 2 represents a modified form of the apparatus in which the carbon lining (A′) is employed as the negative electrode.

From monopoly
to competition

The Transformations of Alcoa,
1888–1986

George David Smith

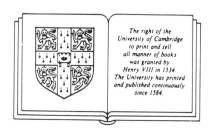

The right of the
University of Cambridge
to print and sell
all manner of books
was granted by
Henry VIII in 1534.
The University has printed
and published continuously
since 1584.

CAMBRIDGE UNIVERSITY PRESS
Cambridge
New York   New Rochelle   Melbourne   Sydney

Published by the Press Syndicate of the University of Cambridge
The Pitt Building, Trumpington Street, Cambridge CB2 1RP
32 East 57th Street, New York, NY 10022, USA
10 Stamford Road, Oakleigh, Melbourne 3166, Australia

First published 1988

Printed in the United States of America

All photographs, except where noted in the text, are reproduced by permission of Aluminum Company of America.

Table 4.1. *Comparison of world consumption of principal nonferrous metals, 1921–38.* Reproduced by permission of the Brookings Institution.

Table 5.2. *Alcoa's market share in the major products of the aluminum industry on the eve of World War II.* Reproduced by permission of McGraw-Hill Publishing Company.

Table 6.1. *Leadership pattern of list-price changes of pig aluminum, 1944–58.* Reproduced by permission of Harvard University Press.

LIBRARY OF CONGRESS
Library of Congress Cataloging-in-Publication Data

Smith, George David.
    From monopoly to competition : the transformations of Alcoa.
1888–1986 / George David Smith.
      p.   cm.
    Bibliography: p.
    Includes index.
    ISBN 0-521-35261-4
    1. Aluminum Company of America—History. 2. Aluminum industry and trade—United States—History. I. Title.
HD9539.A64A74 1988
338.7'669722'097—dc19   88-17049
                                       CIP

For Betty

Contents

List of charts

End papers
> Representation of Alcoa's aluminum operations.

Frontispiece
> Patent 400,766: Sectional drawing of Charles Martin Hall's idea for an electrolytic reduction process for making aluminum

List of Tables

List of photographs

Editor's preface

Throughout the world today, government officials, educators, administrators, and other informed citizens are concerned about the sources of efficiency and innovation in the private and public sectors. So concerned, in fact, that equity has for a time been forced into the backseat of social discourse in many countries. Whether a nation is capitalist, socialist, or communist, the same questions have pushed forward: How do you ensure that the means of production and distribution will be flexible enough to respond to a rapidly changing environment and effective enough to provide the goods and services society needs at reasonable prices? As a truly global economy emerges, the necessity of finding answers to these questions has become all the more pressing.

In the United States, much of the discussion about efficiency and innovation has been focused on the nation's largest firms. On those that have encountered problems meeting competition from abroad. On those that have been successful. Never has there been more interest in the business system and in the particular manner in which America's large corporations have evolved in the past century. These business giants provide most of our goods and services. To a significant degree, their fate is the fate of the American economy today and in future years.

It is thus especially important that George David Smith has written and the Cambridge University Press published a history of Alcoa, the Aluminum Company of America.* *From Monopoly to Competition* focuses on questions of efficiency and innovation over the long term, in this case from 1888 to 1986. As Smith makes clear, the aluminum business was small potatoes when it began. Charles Martin Hall successfully patented the basic invention, an electrical process for smelting the metal, in 1886, but it was at that time far from self-evident that the new technology would become a business success. There were problems involving the technology that had to be solved. Large amounts of capital had to be raised and a workforce trained to handle the production process. But the most pressing entrepreneurial dilemma was the need to develop markets for what was then considered to be a novelty product.

One of the most intriguing aspects of this volume is its description and analysis of the manner in which Alcoa's leaders solved that basic problem of innovation. One part of their answer involved technological progress and economies of scale that sharply reduced costs and made aluminum competitive with a broad range of other materials. Equally important in the early years were the firm's moves via vertical integration into finished products. Market development – like the other modes of innovation – was an uneven process, but over the long run Alcoa succeeded and by 1916 had sales of almost $145 million. Backward integration into raw materials and electrical power also eliminated transactions costs and improved efficiency. As a result, economies of scale and scope protected the firm's domestic markets long after the original patents on aluminum smelting had expired. Alcoa was an efficient and innovative monopoly – and thus an anomaly to many economic theorists – and it is this dimension of Smith's history that speaks with particular force to our present-day concerns.

Over the past century, Alcoa's style of innovation has changed. In the early years, Alcoa's technical progress was largely a result of hands-on management and shop-floor tinkering; the most important early advances in production and in new products stemmed from the mundane tasks of development rather than scientific research. After World War I, however, Alcoa created a formal R&D program, with substantial emphasis on fundamental research. By 1928, the annual R&D budget was $700,000. By that time, too, Alcoa had adopted the functionally departmentalized structure common to most manufacturing companies in the United States. Top man-

*The firm adopted this name in 1907 and Alcoa was coined three years later, but I have throughout used these names for the business.

agement and ownership were still synonomous, but the foundations for a modern organization with professional management had been laid.

Smith gives his readers a good sense of the team of business leaders that guided Alcoa to the front ranks of American industry. Alfred E. Hunt brought to the enterprise technical and engineering training; the Mellons – Andrew W. and Richard Beatty – provided the risk capital the young firm needed; Arthur Vining Davis, who would remain in the business for an unbelievable sixty-five years, contributed aggressive business leadership and a full knowledge of the new product's unfolding markets. Davis was the personal symbol of what became in his lifetime one of the nation's largest and most successful industrial firms. Davis and the rest of the managerial team ran Alcoa in an informal, highly personalized style. The company was in their heyday paternalistic toward its labor force. Authority was centralized in a few hands. Decision-making was still a relatively simple process in a firm that by 1928 had over half of the world's capacity to produce primary aluminum.

Even though innovative and efficient, Alcoa's powerful monopoly status was bound to come in conflict with the U.S. antitrust laws. Smith recounts in an evenhanded style the business' ongoing struggles with the Department of Justice. Particularly interesting and important was the landmark 1945 court decision that undid the monopoly, creating an oligolistic market dominated for a time by three large producers: Alcoa, Reynolds, and Kaiser.

The new structure did not result in the price competition that economists and the Department of Justice might have anticipated. Prices continued to be administered and remained relatively stable, as they had long been under the monopoly. If anything, prices may have been kept high by Alcoa's efforts to protect its competitors and thereby avoid further confrontations on the antitrust front. Competition in this new setting, nevertheless, put pressure on Alcoa, and the firm did not always deal successfully with this challenge. As Smith notes, Reynolds was more innovative in distribution, using brand names and advertising more effectively than Alcoa. The edge that kept Alcoa successful during this period of growing demand was its R&D organization and the new products and processes that the firm was able to develop. Particularly important was rigid container sheet, which enabled the aluminum producers to take over the market for cans, including the ubiquitous six-pak.

The shifting patterns of Alcoa's R&D program provide an interesting subplot to this company's history. In the early years, Smith explains, research was always closely tied to production and marketing. Most of the resulting innovations reflected this influence; they included new fabricating technologies, new ways of dealing with corrosion, new forms of process metallurgy, and new alloys. In the 1930s, when the company organized the Aluminum Research Laboratory, the tie between R&D and operations was loosened, fostering more fundamental scientific research. But after World War II, Alcoa again tightened the bonds between research and the firm's short-term operational needs. A series of successful innovations followed that kept Alcoa at the forefront of primary metal production; but as Smith explains, the price was a company that was eventually not very well-positioned when those markets began to change in a dramatic fashion.

In the years following World War II, Alcoa also returned to the international operations it had abandoned in the late 1920s in order to concentrate on the domestic market. The corporation invested heavily overseas, especially in Australia and Brazil. Alcoa also diversified during these years. It backed into the real estate business as a result of its role in the construction of large, modern buildings, and by the early 1970s, real estate was providing over half of the company's net income. Multinational and diversified operations strained the firm's centralized structure, and belatedly, management adopted the multidivisional style (the M-form) of organization that most large U.S. corporations had been using since the 1940s.

Smith carefully analyzes the manner in which foreign competitors have in recent years cut into the domestic market, forcing Alcoa and the other U.S. companies to revamp their organizations and to reconsider their business strategies. Competition has also pressed Alcoa to look closely for ways to improve its operations by changing its labor–management relations. Unlike most business histories, *From Monopoly to Competition* presents a full description of the company's evolving labor policies. Smith follows this trail from the early days of nonunion operations, through the 1920s' efforts to forestall unionization by means of welfare capitalism, to the 1930s' struggles that led to a curious mixture of industrial and craft unionism under government auspices. This New Deal settlement – framed in terms of equity more than economic efficiency – lasted in aluminum and other industries through the Second World War, the prosperous 1950s, and the beginnings of the Great Inflation in the sixties. The unions gradually strengthened their positions. In the "golden age" of aluminum during the postwar years, Alcoa's management yielded to the union demands for higher wages and greater fringe benefits in order to prevent strikes. Alcoa wanted to maintain its position of world leadership in the production of basic metal by buying industrial peace. When demand leveled off and competition became more intense, however, Alcoa found itself locked into expensive agreements and work rules it could no longer afford.

It was during this important transition – during the 1970s and 1980s – that equity concerns began to yield to the need for efficiency and innovation. Smith provides an especially interesting description and evaluation of Alcoa's experience with this wrenching transition. Workers were faced with a choice between yielding concessions on wages and work rules or watching the company close their plants. Alcoa had no choice but to meet the prices set in this intensely competitive market; the company could no longer afford the wages and restrictive work rules it had lived with so comfortably in the golden years. When Alcoa could not get the concessions it needed in Pennsylvania, Texas, and Alabama, it closed the plants involved. And as competition became more global, white-collar employees began to suffer as well. Alcoa, like so many other American companies, began to slice the size of its staffs in order to cut costs.

The firm meanwhile attempted to get its workforce directly and progressively engaged in the process of revamping the business. Like many other American corporations, Alcoa wanted its workers to participate along with management in the effort to improve operations and meet foreign competition. By cutting the number of grievances filed and by reducing absenteeism, Alcoa again improved the efficiency of its operations. But this was a difficult and complex transition to manage. As Smith leaves the company in the eighties, it is unclear whether either labor or management will be able to shuck off the strongly intrenched tradition of adversarial relations. But it is evident that the competitive pressure that made a new style of labor–management relations necessary is not going to subside in the foreseeable future.

By the eighties, Alcoa was becoming a new style of firm. The leaders who had built the business were gone and their families no longer in control of the company. A new breed of professional managers was steering Alcoa toward further diversification, toward involvement in plastics and chemicals, toward production of various forms of packaging in addition to those made of aluminum. If that future seems problematical in the late 1980s, it is certainly far more predictable than was the original venture of the 1880s. The accomplishments and the problems of those early years and the changes that Alcoa has experienced in the past century deserved to be recounted as they have been by George David Smith in this perceptive and carefully analyzed volume. This is a history that should be of interest to everyone who wants to understand the U.S. business system and its role in American society.

Louis Galambos
Department of History
The Johns Hopkins University

Author's preface

There was an air of crisis at Alcoa in the spring of 1983, when I and two of my colleagues at The Winthrop Group, Inc., arrived in Pittsburgh to begin a proprietary study of the company's "corporate culture." Alcoa had reported its first annual loss in net income since the Great Depression, and was laying off large numbers of managers, engineers, and workers. High energy costs, excess capacity, labor problems, low earnings, and gloomy demand forecasts were taking their toll on corporate morale. W. H. Krome George had just retired as chairman of the board, but not before he had made public his conviction that the "golden years" of Alcoa's basic product, primary aluminum, were past. George warned that Alcoa, which for so long had thrived as the leading producer of aluminum, would have to adapt to "a world quite different from the one we have known." "Or languish and die" was the unspoken message that almost everyone we talked to thought they had heard.

The company was in the throes of a strategic and structural change that insiders experienced as a revolutionary upheaval. George's successor, Charles W. Parry, was moving swiftly to bring his giant, multinational corporation into alignment with the economic challenges of the 1980s. The major threats to the business were posed by exogenous technological developments and foreign competition. In this regard, Alcoa was experiencing many of the same problems that confronted many other American corporations in basic, capital-intensive industries.

After five months of interviewing and reading in the history of the business, Davis Dyer, Margaret Graham, and I produced a report, some findings of which have since been published in an article by Alcoa manager John E. Wright and me in *Across the Board* (September, 1986). Alcoa, we found, was a proud company of strong and self-conscious traditions; most of the managers and workers we had spoken with had well-articulated views of the company's history. We came to understand that not only tradition in the broad sense but also some very specific events in Alcoa's past – some verifiable, some mythical – were shaping its views of the future and would continue to condition the ways in which it would conceive and implement new policies and strategies.

The dual notion of history as both a source of strength and a constraint on the corporation's ability to adapt to changing circumstances became popular very quickly at Alcoa. The company was looking forward to an industry centennial in 1986 and a corporate centennial in 1988, both of which the management wanted to commemorate in a creative fashion. Thus, I was commissioned to write a formal history of the company – in the style of an analytical narrative – that would serve as a bedrock of knowledge for managers and employees on Alcoa's evolution. That the book might be useful to significant audiences outside the company, such as industry analysts, professional students of business, government officials, customers, and even competitors was also desirable, but the main purpose was to educate the corporations.

The idea, by early 1984, was to focus a history of the company mainly on the "postmonopoly" period, that is, on the years from the end of World War II to the present. As I began the research, however, I soon became convinced that underlying the persistent concerns of the corporation since the war was a particular set of themes that had their roots in an earlier period. In the first place, there were so many institutional values and belief systems that seemed to be a legacy of the company's prewar experience as a closely held monopoly run by owner-managers whose tenure as executive managers of the company spanned not just many years but many decades. Alcoa also possessed unique attributes (when compared with the other producers in aluminum as well as most capital-intensive industries) that could only be explained by a longer-term perspective. The basic outlines of most areas of Alcoa's modern business were shaped to some degree under monopoly conditions and were only gradually transformed by increasing competition.

Moreover, the technological and strategic visions of the founders,

Charles Martin Hall and Alfred E. Hunt, had achieved mythical stature and were enduring, if not well-understood, parts of the corporate mentality. And such men as Arthur Vining Davis, Roy Hunt, and I. W. Wilson, whose leadership of Alcoa extended from its early beginnings to well after World War II, had left deep imprints on Alcoa's management structure and style. The idiosyncratic influence of their personalities is felt at Alcoa even to this day.

I had also become fascinated by some surface anomalies in Alcoa's culture. For example, in 1983, Alcoa was a huge and complex bureaucracy, and yet its managers operated in ways that were highly collegial, informal, and reminiscent of a much smaller, familial firm. Alcoa was, until recently, highly centralized in its decision-making structure, and yet it also had strong traditions of managerial autonomy. Alcoa was also full of tradition that placed great value on the mastery of basic science, and yet its research organization had long been dominated by immediate and practical engineering priorities. I wanted very much to understand these seeming contradictions. But how was I to penetrate the surface in order to explain these and other paradoxes without tracing the origins of each problem back to its beginnings?

These intriguing questions edged me toward the conclusion that it would be useful to write a more elaborate history of this interesting institution. Alcoa seemed so different in several key respects from the large corporations I had studied. I wanted to develop a living tapestry of Alcoa's entire evolution, weaving together portraits of important personalities, depictions of events both large and small, and recurrent patterns of important themes. My wish was well-received by Alcoa's managers, who were good enough to let me have my way.

A comprehensive plan for the book then unfolded in consultation with managers assigned as liaisons to me and with an "advisory committee" that was established to review drafts of the manuscript, with the proviso that I alone retained the right of final interpretation. (The makeup and role of that committee is described in the acknowledgments.) Because my primary audience was internal and consisted mainly of people who were sophisticated readers but were largely unexposed to business history, it was important to provide some background on the larger historical contexts in which Alcoa emerged as a complex corporation. This explains Chapter 2, which is devoted to a synthesis of recent literature in business history as it is relevant to Alcoa. The company must, after all, not simply be understood in its uniqueness; Alcoa was part of and was shaped by a more general development encompassing the rise of big business in the world's foremost capitalist economy. In subsequent chapters, I have provided historical and comparative contexts where I thought they would better anchor Alcoa in time and place.

In writing history, the historian ought to have an overriding perspective, a strategic orientation to the narrative. The orientation I have chosen is that of the executive manager. But while most of the book looks at the corporation from the top down, I have occasionally sent down shafts into the structure of the corporation to get a deeper and more varied perspective on particular aspects of Alcoa's experience. Several long-term themes run through the book relating to corporate strategy and structure, technological innovation, labor relations, international development, and regulation. The emphasis given to each of these themes ebbs and flows at different points in the narrative, depending upon the historical circumstances.

Without revealing too much, a brief preview of the chapters is in order. The first deals mainly with the founding stories and with the problem of moving an invention into commercial production through the establishment of Alcoa's corporate predecessor, The Pittsburgh Reduction Company. Chapter 2, as mentioned, provides the contexts for the formative period of the modern complex corporation. Then in Chapter 3, the technological and market characteristics of aluminum and the corporate strategies that led to Alcoa's becoming a powerful monopoly are treated in detail, along with discussions of the company's early antitrust problems and managerial and technical practices. Chapter 4 covers the turbulent period between the wars, which entailed years of rapid growth followed by years of economic depression. Here I focus mainly on the problems Alcoa's managers confronted as they tried to implement more systematic approaches to administration and innovation, as they expanded and then withdrew from international markets, and as they were confronted by the rise of organized labor. The ways in which Alcoa dealt with all these challenges had important long-term implications.

In World War II, Alcoa lost its monopoly, even as aluminum reached its apogee as a "strategic metal." Chapter 5 deals with Alcoa's role in the war and its inability to meet the sharply increased demand for aluminum – a problem which resulted in the massive infusion of government funds for the construction of new plants. I also discuss the consolidation of power by labor unions in the company's plants and revisit one of the great legal battles in the history of business, *U.S. v. Alcoa*, which culminated in a landmark antitrust ruling that held Alcoa to be an illegal monopoly because of its sheer market power.

Following the sale of Government aluminum plants to Kaiser and Reynolds, I analyze in Chapter 6 the details of Alcoa's responses to a complex set of strategic, marketing, administrative, and technological problems posed by oligopolistic competition under continuing Government pressure. Chapter 7 is organized around the contributions of three important executives, Frank Magee, Fritz Close, and John Harper, who did much to shape the modern Alcoa. In the period from 1958 to 1970, the company moved back into international markets and developed new strategies for entering into higher-volume and higher-margin markets in semifinished products. Meanwhile, tensions between the centrifugal and centripetal forces in Alcoa's managerial structure were exposed during a series of administrative reforms. In this period, too, we see the maturing of Alcoa as a more socially sensitive institution and the erosion of the North American oligopoly. A truly international industry began to emerge.

The eighth and last chapter brings us virtually to the present day. In covering the years from 1971 to 1986, my main concern is to account for the radical strategic and structural reforms that have only recently taken shape, reforms that seemingly defy many of Alcoa's most durable assumptions about its technology, markets, and management. Some themes in this chapter will seem familiar to anyone who follows the contemporary business press: intensifying competition, especially from abroad; the rise of a new breed of top managers; a loosening of ties between ownership and management; the breakdown of long-standing patterns of labor–management relations; the disintegration of technical and economic functions; the downsizing of corporate staffs and decentralization of control over operations; crises in research and development.

Indeed, it is the final chapter and concluding remarks that are the least historical and most speculative, and yet the attention to current issues will no doubt be of greatest interest to many readers. Thus, I will issue a caveat: the particular emphases in my discussion of current and future issues will be difficult to appreciate unless the reader knows something about Alcoa's earlier history. Even during an era of change, it is in the unfolding tapestry of history where the manager will discover the vital threads that bind the corporation's past to its future.

*　　*　　*

In producing this book, I have enjoyed the cooperation and assistance of Alcoans at all levels of the corporate organization. Scores of managers and workers, both current and retired, were interviewed – most on tape, some not. Transcriptions or notes of those interviews are on file in the corporate archives at Pittsburgh (see Appendix E). Countless others provided me with informal but important background on all manner of problems – technological, administrative, financial, and characterological – that I have treated in the text. Everywhere I went, busy plant personnel were hospitable and unflaggingly patient in showing me the details of aluminum processes and products and in discussing their views on plant technologies, labor relations, and the larger corporation.

As drafts of chapters were produced, many Alcoans were good enough to offer their ideas on points of interpretation, corrections on points of fact, and verifications of specific passages in the text that were not easy to document through conventional sources. While I am grateful to them all, it would be a futile (and risky) exercise for me to try to account by name for everyone who helped. Yet there are a few whose indispensable support merits special acknowledgment. It was Jack Nettles, a senior manager of Alcoa's public relations, who first discussed with me the possibility of doing a corporate history of Alcoa, which the company would underwrite. He made it clear from the outset that his company wanted a history that was rigorously researched and independent in its conclusions. Once we all agreed that to go forward, Alcoa's chairman, Charles W. Parry, put the full weight of his authority behind my primary demands: that I be granted access to all records and people in the corporation and that I be given complete freedom of interpretation. Dana Friedman, an Alcoa attorney, was wonderfully flexible in accommodating the corporation to a contract that protected my intellectual freedom on all matters historical, while I agreed to ensure the confidentiality of *present-day* proprietary or competitive secrets. The late Alfred E. Hunt lent his gracious and crucial blessing to a project that he understood might alter many long-standing beliefs and assumptions that had been a part of the culture of his very tradition-conscious corporation. I regret that he did not live to see the finished work.

Richard Schalk was my first liaison, and he guided me nimbly through the Alcoa system until his retirement in 1986. He was a constant source of good humor and companionship. He was succeeded by John Wright, who, with his remarkably subtle grasp of corporate culture and politics, helped me thread my way through the more arcane nooks and crannies of Alcoa's bureaucracy in the difficult, final stages of research. Both men are endowed with the openness and sophisticated skepticism that I soon came to realize were highly valued attributes at Alcoa headquarters.

For primary records and photographs, I leaned on Norman Belt, Kristen Hensen, and their overworked staffs in Pittsburgh and on Philip Morton, Virgie Jo Sapp, and their colleagues at the Alcoa Laboratories. Robert Washburn and his staff at the *Alcoa News* ran a series of biographical sketches (which I spun out of research in progress) that elicited all kinds of useful responses from both currently active and retired employees. Elinore Thomas in Pittsburgh read the text with an excellent eye for facts and style, and William Frank at Alcoa Laboratories provided critical commentary on technical matters. Correspondence from Edward B. Foote and Howard Dunn, late of the Alcoa Laboratories, were especially useful. Karen Rafalko did long and hard work on the artistic design of charts and graphs. Linda Graf and Barbara Yuhasz made sure that I got lodged, fed, and paid and were themselves valuable repositories of more Alcoa history than I could possibly include in this book.

Outside Alcoa, Mary E. Curry and David B. Sicilia of The Winthrop Group, Inc., helped with research in the public record, while Alan Gardner, a historian living in New York, gathered some useful materials on the labor history. John Smith, a graduate student at Carnegie Mellon helped isolate and compute data for the charts and graphs in the appendices. Forrest Reinhart, a graduate student at the Harvard Business School, brought to my attention an important source I would have otherwise overlooked in my discussion of the sale of the aluminum defense plants in Chapter 5.

Correspondence from Norman Craig, Professor of Chemistry at Oberlin College, had a transforming influence on my perception of Charles Martin Hall as a research scientist. He and Geoffrey Blodgett, a historian at the same institution, informed me about the sources relating to Charles Martin Hall's will and Arthur Vining Davis's difficulties with the college's trustees in the late 1920s. William Bigglestone then gave me access to the voluminous records on Alcoa at the Oberlin College Archives.

At my request, an "Advisory Committee" was established to read and comment on the manuscript at various stages of its development. The committee's members were as follows: Alfred D. Chandler, Jr., of Harvard University; Joel A. Tarr of Carnegie Mellon University; Richard A. Hunt of Harvard, who also is a member of Alcoa's founding family; Arnold Kramer, a Nashville, Tennessee, attorney, who is former general counsel to Alcoa; Jack Morber, former vice president of labor relations at Alcoa; and William Shepard, former vice president of public relations at Alcoa. The committee had authority to make recommendations and suggestions but no power to order any alterations in the text, unless it could be established that I had made an error in fact. Even though Richard Schalk and I had originally conceived of the committee as a way to help allay any "political" problems that might develop in reaction to the emerging text, no such problems surfaced; nevertheless, each member of the committee made vital contributions to the intellectual process. I commend such an arrangement to any professional who would write a company history as a way to bring a broad range of theoretical and practical perspectives to bear on the subject, from conceptualization to final presentation.

I owe a lot to Louis Galambos of Johns Hopkins University, who did a deft and sensitive job in his general editorial criticism of the manuscript. Frank Smith managed the arrangements for publication by the Cambridge University Press with a steady hand, and Ernest Haim shepherded the manuscript through design and typesetting with consummate skill.

Finally, I wish to thank the principals and managers of The Winthrop Group, Inc., for their unflagging support and good cheer. David G. Allen played an important role in drafting the agreement with Alcoa. Davis Dyer and Margaret B.W. Graham helped with the formulation of issues early on, and Graham and Bettye Pruitt, who are completing a more specialized history of Alcoa's research and development, offered keen observations on the penultimate draft. Their criticism was of the rigorous high quality that I have come to take for granted from all my Winthrop colleagues.

Brooklyn, New York
March, 1988

Note on the corporate name

The business of Aluminum Company of America was first charted as The Pittsburgh Reduction Company on October 1, 1888.

The modern legal name, Aluminum Company of America, was adopted in 1907. According to Edwin S. Fickes, the company's chief engineer, "The Pittsburgh Reduction Company . . . did not indicate the business in which the company was engaged [by1907]; moreover, the name of the company was often confused in Pittsburgh with the name of the American Reduction Company, a local concern engaged in garbage collection and disposal, to the great annoyance of telephone operators and mail clerks."*

Alcoa, which today is the commonly used name for the company, was coined in 1910 by Lucy M. Rickey, wife of the company's chief hydraulic engineer. Mrs. Rickey suggested the name to company president Arthur Vining Davis to designate a village that had sprung up in eastern Tennessee in support of the development of power sites in the area. In 1919, that village was renamed Calderwood, but Alcoa was quickly revived to designate another settlement that was forming around Alcoa's smelter located near Maryville, Tennessee.

*Edwin S. Fickes, "History of the Growth & Development of the Aluminum Company of America," a typescript bound in Volume 17 of the *Histories of the Manufacturing Properties of the Aluminum Company of America . . .*, Alcoa Archives, p. 62.

In the late 1920s, Alcoa was registered as a company trademark for ingot and became the telegraph address for the company's New York and Pittsburgh offices. It was also incorporated into the company's logo. In the late 1930s and 1940s, Alcoa was often used by the courts, the press, and the company itself as a convenient shorthand for the legal corporate name. Internally, the corporation was often referred to as "ACOA" in correspondence and as "The Aluminum Company" in discourse.

After the war, Alcoa came into common usage both within and without the company, as the company's experience with antitrust rendered common usage of "The Aluminum Company" increasingly problematic from a public relations standpoint. Today, one almost never hears the name Aluminum in the company's Pittsburgh headquarters.

1

Invention and entrepreneurship: the electrolytic process and the establishment of The Pittsburgh Reduction Company

Few inventions are successfully commercialized. This is a history of one that was. On February 23, 1886, while experimenting in the woodshed of his kitchen in Oberlin, Ohio, Charles Martin Hall discovered an inexpensive way to smelt aluminum. Nearly five months later, in accordance with legal custom, he applied for a patent. For seventeen years, as the owner of a patent, he could sue others who attempted to copy his invention without his permission. This gave him, in effect, a legal monopoly right to transform his discovery into a useful commercial process. Hall's patent, U.S. No. 400,766, was not actually issued until April 2, 1889, but the claim to it had already become the principal asset of a little experimental shop known as The Pittsburgh Reduction Company, Alcoa's corporate predecessor.[1]

It was on a summer day in Pittsburgh, on July, 31, 1888, when a small group of entrepreneurs gathered at the home of Alfred Hunt to discuss their potential interest in Hall's patent claim. These budding aluminum entrepreneurs were experts in steel, all connected, one way or another, with an industry that was enjoying spectacular growth, fast becoming the linchpin of Pittsburgh's industrial development. Nonetheless, they had some spare funds and were attracted to the technical and commercial possibilities of the lighter, nonferrous metal, about which they knew very little. There is no detailed record of the meeting, but Hunt no doubt explained to them what he had found out about Hall's process. It was as yet undeveloped; it had not been proven to be technically or commercially feasible. Nevertheless, its potential was worth considering: If the process could be made to work, if a market could be found for its product, then one of earth's most common (yet theretofore inaccessible) elements could be mass produced under patents for great profit. Eight days later, a smaller group of six agreed to stake $20,000 to support a trial development of the new aluminum process.[2]

The entrepreneurs won their bet. Within months, Hall's invention was developed into commercial production. The enterprise grew rapidly, and by the mid-1890s, The Pittsburgh Reduction Company was operating a large smelting complex in Niagara Falls, New York, and a fabricating plant in New Kensington, Pennsylvania, making aluminum and aluminum shapes for an emerging national market. By the time the firm was renamed the Aluminum Company of America in 1907, it had become one of America's larger industrial enterprises with a secure patent monopoly on its main line of business. The investors who stayed with the business became rich, and Hall himself would leave an estate that, on the basis of a single discovery, made him the wealthiest inventor in the United States.

The technical and commercial background

Aluminum, or "aluminium," as it is known outside the United States, is an abundant element comprising about eight percent of the earth's crust. And yet for most of the nineteenth century, it was a precious metal few people wanted and even fewer could afford. In the midnineteenth century, the cost of aluminum exceeded $500 per pound, more than twice the value of gold or platinum.[3] After the great English chemist Sir Humphry Davy had identified "alumium" in 1807, interest in the metal was limited to the curiosity of a few scientists and to the Court of France, where in the 1850s it adorned the banquet table in the form of finely crafted eating utensils and became a fashionable substance for jewelry, more fashionable at times than either gold or silver. Aesthetically pleasing in its silvery color, incredibly light but strong, and resistant to corrosion, aluminum was envisioned by Napoleon III as an untapped resource with great military potential. The Emperor, hoping to outfit his *cuirassiers* in light helmets and armor, joined the French Academy in financing the experiments of Henri Sainte-Claire Deville, who had discovered a promising process to reduce aluminum in large quantities from the chemical compounds that imprisoned it in nature.[4]

Fig. 1.1. Napoleonic baby rattle made of aluminum, circa 1850.

The seeming economic paradox of aluminum – its natural abundance and high price – arose from the technical difficulty in separating it from other elements to which it is bonded. In the earth, aluminum appears almost always as an oxide known as "alumina," which is found in nearly all common rocks. Occurring mainly in the form of silicates such as feldspars, micas, and various clays, aluminum came to be known in the nineteenth century as the "metal of clay." This was a revelation. While metals such as iron, bronze, and copper had been used by humanity since antiquity, aluminum, at least in its metallic form, had remained elusive. Uses of aluminum silicates for pottery and "alums" for vegetable dyes and medicines had been traced back to ancient Egypt and Persia. However, no one recognized aluminum as an element until 1782, when Antoine Lavoisier postulated its existence as "the oxide of a metal whose affinity for oxygen is so strong that it cannot be overcome either by carbon or any other known reducing agent."[5]

The reduction, or smelting, of pure, metallic aluminum from its oxide-bound state confounded some of the best scientific minds of the nineteenth century. Lavoisier had not acted upon his speculation, and not until some twenty-five years later did Davy succeed in isolating aluminum for barely an instant. By fusing iron with alumina in an electric arc, Davy freed the element from its oxide only to have it join immediately with the iron as an alloy.[6] Between Davy and Deville, who was the first to bring aluminum to market, at least two significant steps toward the isolation of aluminum by chemical means were taken. In 1825, Danish physicist H. C. Oersted produced the first small amount of aluminum by heating potassium amalgam with aluminum chloride, which he had first made by passing dry chlorine over a heated mixture of alumina and carbon. This process yielded potassium chloride and an aluminum amalgam, which once distilled "without contact with the atmosphere...forms a lump of metal which in color and luster somewhat resembles tin" showing "remarkable qualities." Friedrich Wöhler in Berlin repeated Oersted's experiments, but to no avail; however, he then substituted metallic potassium for the potassium amalgam and was able to produce metallic aluminum in the form of gray powder. By 1845, after eighteen years of painstaking research, Wöhler managed to make aluminum in large enough amounts for study when he hammered out two metal globules from particles the size of pinheads and then measured their specific gravity at somewhere between 2.50 and 2.67. In addition to its remarkable lightness (about a third of the density of copper), Wöhler confirmed some of the metal's other important qualities: it was "ductile" (easy to work when cold), "stable in air," and "can be melted with the heat of a laboratory blowpipe." Wöhler, however, could not melt his tiny particles together into a coherent mass. An oxide film that formed on the metal particles (and incidentally protected them from corroding influences) prevented their coalescence.[7]

Laboratory research in aluminum was an indulgent and expensive undertaking for curious scientists. Deville, a more entrepreneurial researcher than his predecessors, addressed the problem left by Wöhler's experiments by using sodium instead of potassium to react with aluminum chloride. Deville observed that sodium chloride formed in the reduction of the aluminum chloride acted as a flux, enabling the particles to fuse together. This was the discovery that excited the French Academy and the Emperor.[8]

Because sodium was far less expensive than potassium, Deville's process held out hope for making aluminum at a reasonable cost. Beginning with a grant from the Academy and support from the

Fig. 1.2. Henri Sainte-Claire Deville.

state, Deville conducted developmental work on his process with the aid of several French scientists at the Javel Chemical Works. In 1855, bars, or "ingots," of aluminum were exhibited at the Paris Exposition, as Deville began commercial production with Debray, Morin, and Rousseau Frères at Glacière at a selling price of 300 francs per kilo. The work at Glacière gave way to a new facility at Nanterre built specifically for the production of aluminum in 1857. At Nanterre, Deville introduced some changes in the chemistry, the most significant of which involved the introduction of fluorides, such as fluorspar and cryolite, as fluxes. Ten parts of crushed aluminum-sodium chloride were mixed with five parts fluorspar and two parts sodium in a closed reverberatory furnace. Aluminum, ninety-seven percent pure, was tapped out of the furnace in a stream and then formed in a solid body under the cover of a slag that flowed out last.

Through production economies of scale and technique, the price of aluminum was reduced to 200 francs per kilo, or $17 per pound, in 1859.[9]

Deville, whose ambition was to make aluminum for a handsome profit, tried to postulate a market niche for the metal. He thought that aluminum was best regarded as an "intermediate metal standing between the precious and base metals." The markets for such a material were predictably confined to ornamental uses, whether applied in pure form or as an alloy in combination with other metals. Still, he knew that for even such limited markets, the price would have to come down. He attacked that problem by producing the sodium used in the reduction process himself in an attempt to lower its cost.[10]

Innovative activity accelerates as expectations for future profits rise. Accordingly, Deville's improvements in the cost structure of aluminum production aroused the interest of many free-lance inventors and also brought many new commercial enterprises into the business. By 1888, several aluminum concerns in England, France, and Germany, employing a variety of methods, had made dramatic strides in reducing the price of sodium and in improving its utilization. An American, Hamilton Castner, discovered a means for producing sodium from caustic soda, bringing sodium's cost down to twenty-five cents per pound at a time when one pound of aluminum required three times that amount of sodium in the furnace. Castner's method was adopted in 1886 by a British firm, the Aluminium Company, Ltd. at Oldbury, which was the low-cost producer of both sodium and aluminum for three years. Elsewhere in England, advances were made in the reduction of cryolite. One German company formed around a patented process using aluminum fluoride as the source of aluminum and sodium as the reducing agent. The utilization of sodium reached as high as ninety-percent efficiency in this process, which also yielded aluminum of more than 99.5-percent purity.[11]

Despite these technical improvements and their corresponding reductions in costs, aluminum remained a craftsman's material, luxurious and semiprecious. Remarkable advances in sodium reduction processes helped bring the American price of the metal down to eight dollars per pound by the end of 1887. But this was still too high a price for mass consumption. The accumulated total of worldwide aluminum production since 1854 was probably under 140,000 pounds, mostly produced in the 1880s.[12] Applications ranged from jewelry and other small personal items to more functional but still

Fig. 1.3. The aluminum capitol atop the Washington Monument.

luxurious uses in navigation instruments, balances, and clocks. Napoleon had purchased a breastplate, but no aluminum products were produced in volume for military purposes or otherwise. Some artists found aluminum-copper or -silver alloys desirable for statuary: the image of Eros in Piccadilly Circus was a Deville-Process cast, and 100 ounces of aluminum found a lofty perch atop the Washington Monument, where the metal served as both ornament and lightning rod in 1884, at a cost of $225.[13]

Between 1854 (when Deville had begun his work) and 1859, the price of aluminum plunged from about $550 to about $17 per pound, making it about equal in value to silver. By 1888, as sodium reduction techniques reached their apogee, the world price of aluminum had continued to drop to about $4. The decrease had not been enough to render aluminum a "base metal," but it was sufficient for a number of small firms to bring it to market for specialized and profitable applications. A number of aluminum alloys that could be produced without making aluminum first had also come onto the market. In 1886, an American company operated by the prominent metallurgists Alfred and Eugene Cowles patented an electrothermal process for reducing mixtures of alumina, carbon, and some other heavy metal to produce light alloys with up to forty-percent aluminum content. Then, suddenly, a technological revolution occurred, displacing sodium methods of making pure aluminum by cheaper and radically different means of production, that would make the earth's commonest metal available for a mass market.

This technological revolution occurred in November 1888, when the pilot plant of The Pittsburgh Reduction Company became the first commercial enterprise to smelt aluminum by electrolysis. Just seven years later (and four years after the last of the sodium reduction works was closed), some 920,000 pounds of aluminum produced by electrolysis were sold in the United States for about fifty-four cents per pound.[14]

Invention: The electrolytic process

The advent of a fundamental technological innovation, such as the Hall Process for smelting alumium, depends on at least two prior conditions: an accumulated body of knowledge that establishes strong scientific or empirical foundation for the decisive insight, and a well-perceived commercial opportunity for the exploitation of the invention. Inventions such as Hall's also arise in a cultural climate favorable to specific kinds of scientific inquiry. In the industrializing societies of Western Europe and America in the late nineteenth century, there was a high value placed on the application of science to economic production. It is hard to imagine Hall, or anyone else for that matter, devoting himself to a problem as scientifically complex as the smelting of aluminum in the absence of the prevailing ethos of industrial progress. Given the context, it is not surprising to see that Hall was but one of several curious explorers into the chemistry of aluminum and was not the only one to find an answer to its most intriguing problem within a very short span of time.

In fact, the discovery of the modern process of smelting aluminum is one of many famous cases of simultaneous invention, in which people working independently make substantially the same discoveries based on equivalent understandings of the state of an art. Working continents apart and in complete ignorance of each other, Charles Martin Hall and a French citizen, Paul L. T. Héroult, each devised a commercially plausible way to produce aluminum electrolytically and thereby ushered in a new era in man's use of metals. That the two men arrived at the same means for making aluminum at almost the same time resulted from a concatenation of technological developments in metallurgy and in the new science of electricity.

In the late nineteenth century, metallurgy was less a modern science than a raw empirical discipline. Systematic knowledge about the nature of metals and their behavior under different conditions was the accumulated wisdom of centuries of slow, sporadic trial and error. This was true even of ferrous metals, which had been smelted since the third millennium B.C. and from which highly successful hardened products had been developed over the centuries. There existed no fundamental understanding of the properties of cast iron, wrought iron, and steel until the late eighteenth century. An oxide-bound, nonferrous metal, aluminum was, by comparison, a complete enigma.[15]

Davy's attempts to reduce aluminum proceeded from his crude understanding of molecular structures and his interest in the nascent science of electricity. He tried but failed to reduce aluminum with a current from a battery. Any chance of success with electrolytic methods awaited more intense sources of power. In the meantime, an alternative path of chemically based experiments was taken by Oersted, Wöhler, and Deville. By 1854, Robert Bunsen and Deville independently produced aluminum by electrolysis of aluminum chloride, but contemporary batteries were still inadequate for generating the power required to make the process economically feasible. Other technical problems, including the high volatility of aluminum compounds under electrolysis, defeated numerous experiments. Nevertheless, inventors persisted in the belief that electrolysis – as it has been applied to the plating of silver, gold, copper, and nickel – held the key to cheap aluminum reduction. This belief was justified when the development in the 1870s of practical dynamos made possible the continuous generation of the large amounts of electric power required to reduce aluminum at a reasonable cost.[16]

If anyone seemed destined to find a way to transform aluminum into a "common metal," it was the young Charles Martin Hall, the third son and sixth child of a Congregational missionary who had settled in Oberlin, Ohio. Little is known about his early years other

Fig. 1.4. Frank Fanning Jewett, Charles Martin Hall's chemistry professor at Oberlin.

than that he was intellectually precocious and that his imagination was seized by chemistry more than by ordinary childhood pastimes. According to his principal biographer, he became interested in books at an age when most children could not yet read, and among his readings was a well-worn chemistry textbook he found in his father's library. By the age of twelve, he was performing makeshift chemical experiments at home.[17]

Tradition has it that Hall was inspired by a remark of his Oberlin chemistry professor, Frank Fanning Jewett, to the effect that fame and fortune awaited the man who could find a cheap way to reduce aluminum. Jewett, who had been quick to recognize Hall as a gifted student, "took him into my private laboratory and gave him a place by my side – discussing his problems with him from day to day."

> Possibly [said Jewett years later] a remark of mine in the laboratory one day led him to turn his especial attention to aluminum. Speaking to my students, I said that if anyone should invent a process by which aluminum could be produced on a commercial scale, not only would he be a great benefactor to the world but would also be able to lay up for himself a great fortune. Turning to a classmate, Charles Hall said, "I'm going for that metal." And he went for it.[18]

It has been established by others that Hall, "even before he entered college" at age sixteen had been fascinated "by the subject of the extraction of aluminum from its ores." What Hall encountered in Jewett was a strong mentor, one of the first important American academic professionals in chemistry. Having studied at Yale, Harvard, Göttingen (where he had met Wöhler), and Tokyo, Jewett offered as advanced instruction in chemistry as might be found in undergraduate education. His own education reflected the growing international character of the chemical sciences in the midnineteenth century, when Germany was the undisputed mecca of the discipline. It was from Germany, no doubt, that Jewett brought home his knowledge of electrochemistry in particular. Along with Hall's other studies in science and mathematics, Jewett's chemistry course offered the young, aspiring chemist a formal methodological framework within which he could transform his boyhood hobby into an adult calling.[19]

The technological and economic environment was favorable to Hall's scientific ambition. As Hall came of age, he was living in a nation that was just in the process of being linked by railroads and by telegraph and telephone wires. He was part of that generation that was the first to benefit from electrical power, steel, mechanized farm equipment, heavy and light machinery, and even a countless array of machines that made parts for other machines – all of which were transforming an agrarian landscape into an urban and affluent nation. Technology was driving the American industrial revolution, and men like Samuel F. B. Morse, Silas McCormick, Elias Howe, Alexander Graham Bell, and Thomas Edison, whose inventions had been capitalized into major industrial enterprises, were national heroes. It was perfectly plausible to believe that the discover of an inexpensive process for making a light metal to serve the new industrial age might join the American pantheon of inventor-entrepreneurs – and get rich, too.

Though Hall's quest to join the ranks of such luminaries was no irrational boyhood dream, it was a prospect with a low probability. Discovering something significant for which one could become universally recognized was unlikely; being the first to market with a new invention was even less likely; and developing a new technology into a profitable industrial enterprise was a very long shot. Imagination, skill, and luck at every stage were required, and only a few of the countless thousands who had ever tried to convert invention into enterprise had managed to succeed on a grand scale. Hall,

Fig. 1.5. Charles Martin Hall in 1885, when he began
working in earnest on his aluminum experiments.

blessed with luck and helpful friends, had also the imagination and
skill required to succeed.

At that stage of his life, Hall was more akin, as an inventor, to
Bell, the dedicated amateur, than to Edison, the expert professional
who presided over a highly organized laboratory of scientists and
engineers and contracted for industrial research. While at Oberlin,
Hall had experimented on copper alloys, read about patent applications, and tinkered with ideas for a novel form of electric battery
and new kinds of electric-light filaments, all in addition to his formal
and informal courses of study under Jewett. The same year the
Washington Monument was capped with aluminum, Hall set up a
makeshift laboratory in the woodshed adjoining the kitchen of his
parents' house. There he pursued several projects before he decided

Fig. 1.6. Julia Brainerd Hall, who assisted her brother
Charles in his aluminum experiments at their home in
Oberlin, Ohio.

to concentrate on aluminum. Upon graduating from Oberlin in 1885,
he turned to his aluminum project full time.

Hall used some equipment he had borrowed from Jewett and was
assisted in his efforts by his older sister, Julia, who had also taken
the chemistry course four years earlier at Oberlin. Julia's role was
important. By the time of their mother's death in the spring of 1885,
she had already become the head of household matters and served
as an important influence on Charles and two of their sisters. For
her shy younger brother, she had become something of a surrogate
mother as well as an intellectual sounding board, the closest woman
in his life. Whether or not she contributed anything substantial to
the ideas underlying Charles's great invention is impossible to know,
but it is evident that she served her brother as a knowledgeable
alter ego and helped him to keep a careful record of the work.[20]

Hall worked assiduously in accordance with the then (by modern
standards) crudely empirical methods common to chemical research.

One must bear in mind that Mendeleev's periodic table of the elements had been published as recently as 1869, and there were few scientific journals conveying state-of-the-art knowledge. Hall's family lived in a kind of genteel poverty, and so he could afford precious little in the way of laboratory resources. He relied instead on his limited knowledge of the experiments of others, his skills in devising homemade laboratory equipment, and his boundless degree of patient self-discipline. By making incremental adjustments in the temperature, quantities, and mix of ingredients, and observing the results of each attempt, Hall explored several alternatives to the conventional chemical smelting process before finally taking the fateful leap of imagination into his successful discovery.

Hall had tried, in college, to employ chemical methods common to obtaining iron and other metals. Failing that, he turned to electrolysis. After constructing a sufficiently powerful battery, Hall tried electrolyzing aluminum fluoride (earlier attempts had involved aluminum chloride) in water in 1884–5 in Jewett's laboratory. The products were hydrogen gas and aluminum hydroxide at the battery's cathode. After June 1885, Hall worked in his little woodshed laboratory at home, where he turned to experimentation with fused salts of fluorides in a homemade furnace capable of sustaining high temperatures. After trying calcium fluoride, aluminum fluoride, and magnesium fluoride, Hall turned to synthetic cryolite, the double fluoride of sodium and aluminum, which he discovered on February 9, 1886 to have a lower melting point and to be a good solvent for aluminum oxide.[21]

The nub of Hall's discovery was to dissolve alumina in a fused salt more stable than aluminum oxide so that the alumina could be decomposed electrochemically without reacting with the solvent. "I [had earlier] tried," he later explained, "to electrolyze a solution of aluminum salt in water, but found nothing but a deposit of [aluminum] hydroxide on the negative electrode." Over time, through innumerable trials and errors, an "idea formed itself in my mind that if I could get a solution of alumina in something which contained no water, and in a solvent which was more chemically stable than alumina . . . , aluminum could be obtained by electrolysis."[22]

Electrolytic reduction had been tried, of course, by both Davy and Deville, who had abandoned the technique.[23] Hall was working with essentially the same type of Bunsen cell batteries that had been available to experimenters before the advent of the dynamo. But even under the most parsimonious laboratory conditions ("Hall," notes a modern chemist, "had to fashion his own apparatus, prepare chemicals, and make batteries afresh for each experiment"), [24] he arrived at a workable process on February 23, 1886. What he had finally discovered was that cryolite, a double fluoride of sodium and aluminum, melted easily and could dissólve alumina "in large proportions." After rigging "a little electric battery," Hall "melted some [synthesized] cryolite in a clay crucible, dissolved alumina in it and passed an electric current through the molten mass for about two hours." No aluminum formed, but that, he reasoned, was due to the dissolution of silica from the clay crucible, which interfered with the process. When he substituted a carbon crucible, which unlike the clay would not dissolve (this he did by lining his clay crucible with a smaller crucible of graphite), Hall repeated his experiment and poured out, in Julia's presence, his first "small globules" of the nearly pure metal.[25]

Jubilation reigned in the Hall household until it was learned in October that one Paul L. T. Héroult had applied for an American patent for a process similar to Hall's. Héroult had also electrolyzed alumina successfully, for which he received a French patent on April 23, 1886. It is likely that Héroult did not grasp the commercial possibilities of the aluminum process as clearly as Hall, sharing perhaps the opinion of most metals experts that the future lay in aluminum alloys. It was on a different process for making alloys that Héroult concentrated his immediate attention, while Hall, the single-minded amateur, quickly put his process into practice.[26] But the French inventor did file for an American patent in May, more than a month before Hall filed his claim, and thus Hall was presented with a serious legal challenge. The two applications were held to be in interference in June 1887, and it took many months of litigation to clear up the matter. In fact, Héroult may have discovered his process before Hall did his, but Héroult could not establish priority of invention under American patent law, which recognized only his filing date.[27]

The differences between the young Hall and his French counterpart were as striking as their similarities. Héroult, the genial, bourgeois son of a Norman leather tanner had already become well-traveled, bilingual, married, and worldly. Hall was a somewhat reserved man; Héroult was naturally gregarious. While Hall drew recreational pleasure from playing the piano and reading, Héroult preferred the camaraderie of Parisian cafes and their billiard tables. Hall shunned tobacco and alcohol and was decidedly straitlaced, whereas Héroult developed a reputation for indulging in all manners of amusement. In research, Hall kept meticulous records. Héroult

Fig. 1.7. Paul L.T. Héroult.

was more casual about recording the processes or costs of his work. What Héroult shared completely with his American counterpart was his peculiar fascination with aluminum, which he had picked up from a chance reading of Deville's famous treatise *De l'Aluminium*.

Observing that Deville had tried to electrolyze sodium-aluminum chloride with batteries, Héroult reasoned that the advent of the dynamo presented an unbounded opportunity for the cheap production of aluminum. He entered the Ecole des Mines, where his mentor was Henri le Chatelier, who encouraged the young student's interest in aluminum reduction. This was Héroult's only interest, academically; he failed in his other courses. He returned to Normandy without completing his studies in order to take over his deceased father's firm, where he ignored the business in order to pursue his researches. To the family tannery, he attracted some students from the Ecole de Mines, including Louis Merle, whose family had founded a profitable aluminum business. Using a dynamo (he was much better equipped than Hall), Héroult and his young research group electrolyzed aluminum successfully by April 23, 1886.[28] Héroult described his discovery, which

> ... consists in decomposing alumina dissolved in a bath of molten cryolite by means of an electric current connected to the bath on the one hand by means of an electrode in contact with the crucible of charcoal containing the cryolite, and on the other by a similar sintered electrode charcoal which dips into the bath. Using a low-tension current this results in the decomposition of the alumina. Oxygen is liberated at the anode and burns up with it; the aluminum is deposited on the walls of the crucible which constitutes the cathode and is precipitated as a residue on the bottom of the crucible. The bath remains constant and serves indefinitely if fed with alumina. The anode has to be replaced after combustion but the combustion prevents polarization and ensures constant power and stability in the action of the electric current.[29]

An important difference between Héroult's process, as it became applied, and Hall's is worth noting. Héroult's method rendered alumina fluid by use of an electric arc with a carbon anode and a layer of molten metal as the cathode, whereas Hall's was more purely electrolytic (that is, it relied more on electricity as part of the chemical process) in its suspension of alumina in a bath of fused salts. The Héroult method was better for making alloys, whereas Hall's was geared more to the production of pure aluminum. The practical effects for commercial manufacture, however, were much the same, and the discoveries of both men have been refined over a century as the "Hall-Héroult Process," which remains to this day the only viable means for smelting aluminum commercially.

In the years following their landmark discoveries, Hall and Héroult's careers diverged. Héroult virtually abandoned his interest in aluminum, turning instead to the development of electric arc furnaces for making high-quality steel. Hall remained professionally consumed by the business he helped create, continuing active research for as long as he lived. Their paths finally crossed in 1911, when Héroult traveled to New York to congratulate his American counterpart on being awarded the Perkin Medal for contributions to chemistry. Three years later, their lives connected again when both men, in the prime of their professional maturity, were struck down by disease. Héroult died of typhoid, while Hall, whose once remarkably boyish appearance had been ravaged in the wake of a virulent typhoid attack in 1908, gradually and painfully succumbed to leukemia.[30]

At least Hall died having achieved his personal dream of inventing an inexpensive aluminum process and striking it rich. By 1910, his stock in the aluminum enterprise provided him with a hefty annual dividend income of more than $150,000 (today's equivalent would be in the millions). At the end, his stock alone was worth about $5 million at its stated par value. The actual value of his estate has been estimated as high as $45 million, an unprecedented fortune for an inventor.

In his mature years, Charles Martin Hall had become a powerful public symbol of his industry, leading a busy professional and public life as a founder of the American Electrochemical Society, as an Oberlin trustee, and as an active participant in the civic affairs of Niagara, where he helped organize the YMCA and served as trustee and president of a local hospital. Taking advantage of his business travels throughout the United States and Europe, Hall acquired a taste for the fine arts and amassed a private collection of paintings, chinese porcelains, and oriental rugs. Much of this collection he left to Oberlin, which also became the leading beneficiary of his ample estate. The sum of Hall's gifts has appreciated to about half that college's present-day endowment. Oberlin, said his older brother, had been to Hall the equivalent of "wife, child, and all – his life." After providing for his close relatives and friends, such as Arthur Vining Davis, who at Hall's death was the president of Alcoa, the inventor left the "residue" to educational enterprises in the form of Alcoa stock that was to be held in trust for fifteen years. This stock was divided so that one-third went to Oberlin, one-sixth to the American Missionary Association for its work in the education of southern blacks, and one-sixth to Berea College for nonreligious purposes. The remaining third was used to establish The Charles Martin Hall Educational Fund, which sponsored endowments for twenty educational institutions in Europe, the mid-East, and Asia and provided the funds to found the Harvard-Yenching Institute in Cambridge, Massachusetts.[31]

Within the company, Hall had a mixed reputation. On the one hand, he inspired respect as a man of simple piety who took pains to worry about the well-being of his company's workers. He held the warm regard of his closest friends, who admired him for his insatiable curiosity, moral integrity, and generosity. Arthur Vining Davis was steadfastly loyal to Hall, who had taught him the technical side of the aluminum process when it was first being developed into full-scale production. On the other hand, Hall appeared to many of his contemporaries as more than a bit odd. At a time when scientific curiosity seemed quaintly academic to men enmeshed in the day-to-day rigors of applied engineering, he was regarded somewhat disdainfully by other Alcoa managers as a "research man," obsessed with scientific inquiries that got in the way of useful work. And despite his many public associations, Hall was by temperament a loner and impressed those who knew him well "as a very reticent man with a very peculiar disposition," "very much preoccupied," an eccentric. Though once engaged to his college sweetheart, he never married; though wealthy, he chose to live a life that was almost ostentatiously frugal, residing in boardinghouses until he was thirty-nine years old. Strictly temperate – "clean living and thinking" in all respects according to his secretary – Hall once thought of striking his bequest to Oberlin out of fear that the college might one day relax its prohibition on smoking. In his youth, Hall had enjoyed dancing – "we liked the girls and we were always open for a good time," Davis recalled a half century later. But as a mature adult, he turned to more sedate activities, taking his greatest pleasure, apart from his work, in playing the piano on which he liked to regale a captive audience with long and, as Junius Edwards implied, boring recitals.[32]

Hall awaits a good biography. There is enough in the record of his life and correspondence to reveal a man more textured and interesting than either history or company mythology has made him out to be. Suffice it to say here that his quiet eccentricities were more than offset by his legacy to technology and society. He was a major personna in the emerging scientific communities of metallurgists and electrochemists, and, despite his failure to achieve another great breakthrough in his advancing years, he had in his youth, in one great stroke, achieved more than most scientists achieve in a lifetime. Even today, he shares with his French colleague Héroult the remarkable distinction of having devised a process of production that remains the basis of a major industry after 100 years.

Entrepreneurs

"Nothing," Deville had warned, "is more difficult than to introduce into the pattern of men's lives and to get them to accept, a new material, however useful it may be."[33] Nevertheless, Hall and Héroult believed there would be a great market for inexpensive aluminum. Still, moving an invention – however well-conceived and tested – out of the laboratory, through the manufacturing plant, and into the hands of paying customers is a problem of considerable risk and complexity. No single person could hope to engineer a new industrial technology into commercial production without the kinds of resources – financial, technical, and managerial – that can only be joined in a corporate enterprise. In the late nineteenth century, the private business corporation – in which many investors could pool their funds under conditions of limited liability – was fast becoming society's entrepreneurial vehicle for the exploitation of "high technologies."

Inventors with patentable ideas thought to have profit-making potential could either sell or license their inventions to others or form their own businesses around the patents. In the case of radical departures from existing technologies, inventors were likely to find potential buyers skeptical and so often had to share both the risks and the labor of development with any backers that could be found. Some inventors, such as Cyrus McCormick or Elisha Gray, enjoyed the entrepreneurial role of establishing businesses based on their discoveries. Even an inventor with little taste for business, such as Alexander Graham Bell, found that he had to participate in the early phases of corporate development of his invention in order to render it practical. In the cases of Héroult and Hall, both sought corporate backing to help them bring their aluminum processes to market.

Héroult at first tried to interest the French capitalist A. R. Pechiney, who controlled the Merle Chemical Aluminum Company, in sponsoring the new aluminum process. According to tradition, Héroult rather untactfully trounced Pechiney in a game of billiards, after which the latter declared that aluminum would never find applications beyond its limited luxury markets, even with a reduction in price. As Pechiney explained it, Héroult remembered later, "aluminum was a metal ... for opera-glasses; and whether the kilogram [sold] for 10 or 100 francs, I would not be able to dispose of one kilogram more." Aluminum would find its best markets, Héroult was told, as an alloy of aluminum bronze, a product in which Pechiney simply was not interested.[34]

Later, after failing to secure financing from the Rothschild Bank, Héroult was overheard in a cafe complaining about his misfortune by a sympathetic and well-connected gentleman who put the young inventor in touch with some powerful German steel interests led by Emil Rathenau. At first, they tried to establish the Héroult process in Germany for the production of aluminum bronze, but ran up against prior patent claims of the Cowles Company, a Cleveland concern, about which more will be said later. The Germans looked to Switzerland, where there were no patent laws yet in effect. In 1887, the Swiss Metallurgical Company (the corporate forerunner to the modern Alusuisse) was created at Neuhausen to develop Héroult's method for the production of aluminum and aluminum bronze. Shortly thereafter, a French concern, the Societé Electrometallurgique, was formed, where Héroult advanced his work in aluminum.

Early development work on Héroult's process focused less on pure aluminum than on the production of aluminum alloys. Heeding the advice of Pechiney, Héroult laid aside for the time being the production of pure aluminum and turned to a series of new researches in the electrothermal reduction of metals resulting in an 1887 patent for a "system of electric furnaces and a process . . . which made possible a continuous production of alloys of aluminum and particularly of all metals difficult to melt and reduce." The development of Héroult's electrolytic process to a successful result fell to others in the Swiss company in the 1890s. Gradually, Héroult's growing interest in electrothermal processes led him to shift his concentration to ferrous metals, where he made important contributions in the development of electric-arc furnaces for making high-quality steel.[35]

Charles Martin Hall, on the other hand, was wholeheartedly determined from the start to use his electrolytic process to make pure aluminum for the market. This is exactly what he had in mind when he searched for the financial support to transform his invention into a business. In the wake of his great discovery, Julia and other members of his family helped introduce him to potential backers. Quite aside from his limited financial means, Hall also apparently understood the limits of his talents beyond science. Having no experience in business, he willingly relied on others for support in organizing the affairs of business around his invention.[36] Yet like Héroult, Hall at first had to struggle to find support. After filing his patent application on July 9, 1886, he made some preliminary attempts at financing his invention in Boston through his older brother George, and in Cleveland, through his uncle, a prominent physician. Finally, in October, through the good graces of his uncle, he found backers in the Cowles brothers, Alfred and Eugene, who had done as much as anyone to introduce the electric furnace to the industrial world.[37]

The Cowles Electric Smelting and Aluminum Company was head-quartered in Cleveland, which in the 1880s was an important center of electrochemical activity. Since 1885, Cowles had been manufacturing aluminum bronze (an alloy made mainly of copper) electrothermally[38] at Lockport, New York, drawing upon a drop from the Erie Canal for cheap power for their dynamos. Their activities at Lockport presaged the development of a great industrial center at Niagara Falls, where, by 1910, cheap hydropower fueled some twenty-five plants of the nation's principal electrochemicals manufacturers.

Soon after his arrival at Lockport, Hall became convinced that Alfred Cowles "did not seem particularly interested" in his patent. In fact, the Cowles brothers had been alert to the potential threat to their process from Hall's invention and so took a six-month option on Hall's patent in exchange for a small salary and modest research facilities, which they put at his disposal.[39] But in a year's time, Hall was unable to develop a process for aluminum production that seemed to have commercial potential. At one point, after trying to use Cowles's internal heating method for the production of aluminum in a cryolite bath only to fail, he turned to a series of experiments that employed external heat, copper (rather than carbon) anodes, and a bath consisting of aluminum and potassium fluorides. In this, Hall was trying to develop a second patent, filed in January 1887, which would prove to be worthless. On none of his nearly 125 production runs did he produce any aluminum of more than ninety-three-percent purity in quantities of more than twelve ounces.

Impatient with his progress and perhaps satisfied with their own growing business in the well-established market for aluminum bronze, the Cowleses failed to renew their option. Hall was deeply frustrated over what he felt was an utter lack of support for his work, and he later claimed that he would have stayed on had the Cowleses made good on their promise of a bonus of $750. After demonstrating that he could make pure aluminum for 24.5 horse-power-hours per pound at bench scale (when it required Cowles 35 horsepower-hours to produce aluminum alloys), he reasoned that it was time to seek funds elsewhere for a plant-sized pilot test of his process. Thus, for a pittance, the Cowles Company forfeited the opportunity of a lifetime – an opportunity it would in time try to reclaim.[40]

Hall left Cowles in July 1888. Through the good offices of Romaine C. Cole, the young general manager at Cowles, who apparently felt that his employers had given up on the young inventor too soon, he was introduced to Alfred E. Hunt, a thirty-three-year-old metallurgist.[41] Hunt was the offspring of a pair of pioneering Massachusetts families. His mother, Mary Hanchett, was a schoolteacher who instilled in him a love for science. His father, Leander Hunt, ran an axe factory, where the young Fred acquired an early interest in the shaping of metals. Together his parents steered him through a rigorous Boston education, which he capped by graduating from MIT as a Bachelor of Science in Mining Engineering in 1876. He worked for two New England steel companies as a chemist and mining engineer before migrating in 1881 to Pittsburgh, where some of the most exciting developments in the emerging American steel industry were taking place.

Pittsburgh in the 1880s was a hotbed of industrial activity. It had become established as a manufacturing center, specializing in iron fabrication, even before the Civil War. Between 1860 and 1880, its core population had jumped from some 84,000 to nearly a quarter million. By 1865, it produced about forty percent of the nation's iron. More than sixty percent of its 55,000 workers in 1879 were employed by firms making and dealing in metal and metal products.[42] It was not the most pleasant of sites. Despite its location on one of the most beautiful natural sites in the United States – snug in the confluence of the Monongahela and Allegheny rivers as they meet to form the Ohio – Pittsburgh was a tough, dirty city. Its reputation for smoky air had been established early in the nineteenth century, when city residents already relied on local deposits of bituminous coal for heating and fuel. In 1868, a writer called it "Hell with the Lid Taken Off," which held alternatively positive and negative connotations.[43] Noisy, crowded, and polluted, Pittsburgh was vital, exciting, and brimming with opportunities for capitalists, workers, and entreprenuerial metallurgists.

Hunt had strong entrepreneurial yearnings. After two years of managing the open-hearth and heavy-forging department of the Black Diamond Company, he left to go into the technical consulting business with George H. Clapp, his metallurgical assistant. The two men took over the newly formed Pittsburgh Testing Laboratory in 1887. Together, they built the Laboratory into a preeminent firm in the fields of chemical testing, analysis, and inspection, primarily for steel applications.

That, for most men, would have been an ample calling, but Hunt was busy on several fronts. He had always been fascinated by military discipline and had joined the local militia wherever he had lived. In Pittsburgh, he organized and became the commanding of-

Fig. 1.8.   Alfred E. Hunt in his military uniform, in 1898.

ficer of a light-artillery battery in the Pennsylvania National Guard
(more of an honor then than now), from which he took his sobriquet,
"Captain," into civilian life. A man with a strong sense of civic duty,
Captain Hunt became a prominent citizen of Pittsburgh, active in
its public affairs, not the least of which were his attempts to promote
filtration of the city's contaminated water supply. He would have
run for mayor had he lived long enough. Instead, it was his destiny
to lead Battery B on a combat mission to Puerto Rico, where he
contracted malaria, which in combination with other health com-
plications led to his death in 1899.[44]

By then, Captain Hunt had guided the business development of
Hall's aluminum process through the most critical years of its sur-

vival. A fine chemist, an ambitious entrepreneur, and a stickler for discipline, Hunt foresaw great opportunity in the Hall Process if it could be harnessed to productive ends. At the Testing Laboratory, he had become interested in aluminum's potential for treating molten steel and had directed his young assistant, Romaine Cole (before Cole went to work for the Cowles brothers), in experiments on reducing aluminum oxide with carbon, just as iron was smelted from iron oxide with carbon. Upon meeting Hall, he immediately proposed the formation of a company to bring aluminum to market.

The organizational meeting for a "Pittsburgh Aluminium Company" was held at Hunt's home on Shady Lane at the end of July, and on August 8, a total of 200 shares of stock were issued at $100 per share to Hunt, Clapp, and four other men[45] whose professional and personal friendship Hunt, "a man of great personal charm," had taken the pains to cultivate. All held important positions in the Pittsburgh steel industry. R. J. Scott was superintendent of the Union Mills of Carnegie, Phipps & Co., whose offices would serve as the informal headquarters for the budding aluminum enterprise. Howard Lash was president of the Carbon Steel Company. Millard H. Hunsiker was Carbon Steel's general sales agent. Winfield S. Sample was the chief chemist at the Pittsburgh Testing Laboratory. Together they brought to Hall's patent a broad range of experience in chemistry, engineering, and management of metals, although the development of aluminum would prove to involve technical problems very different from those of steel.[46]

Equally important, they brought money. The six partners paid a total of $20,000 in capital, five percent at a time, on call. The money was devoted to the construction of what "we fondly conceived to be a plant" on the corner of 32nd and Smallman streets, where a 125-horsepower engine, with two direct-current dynamos, was installed. Hall was not required to make a financial investment, but he and Romaine Cole were put to work on developing a commercially feasible aluminum smelting process by mid-October. On October 1, 1888, the enterprise was officially chartered as The Pittsburgh Reduction Company.[47]

Although staffing began with a false start, the pilot plant moved quickly into production. Cole and Hall were unable to work together, even though Cole's business sense had served them both well. (It was Cole who had negotiated the contract with the company's capitalists in July 1888 that established the basis for the grant to him and Hall of forty-seven percent of the common stock, when the company's capital structure was changed in October 1889.[48]) Hall was

Fig. 1.9. The 125-horsepower steam engine and twin dynamos used to power the aluminum smelter at Smallman Street in 1888.

named superintendent of the plant, and in September, after Cole's departure, he teamed up with the young Arthur Vining Davis, the son of a Congregational minister in Hyde Park, Massachusetts. A graduate of Amherst College, Davis had come to work for Hunt and Clapp at his father's bidding (his family had been friends to the Hunts in Massachusetts). He and Hall lived in the same boarding house, where each paid $5 a week for room and board. By the time the Smallman Street plant was ready to go into production, Davis was assigned to work with Hall full-time. The two men began operations on Thanksgiving Day, a little more than a month behind the original schedule set by the company's directors.

The work was difficult and production erratic, as technical problems plagued the operation. By early 1889, Hall and Davis were dividing twelve-hour shifts between them. Hall wrote, to his chagrin, that he was forced to work on Sundays (the crucibles could not be allowed to freeze) in "Satan's Church," where it took a good "deal of ability as well as grit to stand...the dirt, soot and worse the fumes...." A night superintendent was hired to help keep the current flowing through the bath of molten cryolite and alumina around the clock. At some point, two "furnace men" were hired to help tend the "reduction pots," as the crucibles that contained the electrolytic bath came to be called, and a laborer was hired to perform odd jobs around the plant. But the original process was "handicapped by the inadequacy of our machinery," making it "a gamble from hour to hour whether the electrical apparatus would continue to function." Meanwhile, the owners became "shaky" in their resolve to stay with the business, according to Hall, but through backbreaking labor in the plant's hot, smoky, and choking atmosphere, he and Davis were soon able to make about thirty to fifty pounds of aluminum per day. This, however, was far short of a projected production of 250 pounds per day. These small amounts sold at $8 a pound and were kept in an office safe. The first reduction pots were crude, made of cast iron – twenty-four by sixteen by twenty inches – and lined with three inches of baked carbon and capable of holding at least 200 pounds of bath. At least six carbon anodes were suspended by thin copper rods from an overhead copper bus. Arranged in series, two pots were charged with up to 1,800 amperes at sixteen volts of direct current while also being heated from below with a gas flame. The carbon lining served as a cathode and a carbon anode was suspended above the cell.[49]

Energy to power the operation and the need for constant monitoring were problems from the begining. It took extraordinary amounts of electricity to pass from anode to cathode, depositing aluminum on the cathode. (Indeed, the availability of electrical power was to become the main determinant of the location of production facilities.) Oxygen from the alumina was released at the anode, uniting with the carbon to form carbon dioxide, eroding the anode in the process. And the cryolite would break down unless enough alumina were maintained in the bath. Thus the process had to be attended to constantly, around the clock, lest the bath freeze or the cryolite electrolyze. The aluminum was periodically removed while more cryolite and alumina were added, and the anodes were frequently replaced. Also, bringing the cost of production down at this experimental stage required constant tinkering with the electrolytic process to fine-tune the relationships among the size of the pots, the constituents of the bath, and the voltage and resistance of the electrical current. As larger pots were introduced, Hall and Davis found not only that larger crucibles required less electricity per unit volume of the bath, but also that the heating effect of the electric current could maintain the bath liquid, eliminating the need for external heating by a gas flame.[50]

Fig. 1.10. Drawing of the original Hall electrolytic cells, depicting the cast-iron crucibles, or "pots" (each 24 × 16 × 20 inches), and carbon anodes suspended by copper rods from an overhead copper bus, and ingot molds.

As primitive as the Smallman Street operation was by modern standards, the fundamental technology of commercial smelting has not changed since. Then, as now, aluminum production was a continuous process, requiring constant attention from well-trained potroom attendants. The Smallman Street plant's primitive conditions, however, were reflected in what might be regarded as the company's earliest labor problems. The company's first potroom crew was neither diligent nor skilled, though by no means lacking in cleverness. Those who remember the mature Davis as an extremely intimidating boss may be surprised to learn that in his youth he was overmatched by the wiles of his first crew of workers. "Whenever the employees desired to have a little vacation, the engineers would announce that the fly-wheel needed painting or something else like that and Mr. Hall and I, neither of us, knew enough to gainsay." Davis was especially upset at the technical ignorance of the "furnace men," one of whom described his work as "taking one volt out of one furnace and putting it into another." The laborer ("our prize package") worked "intermittently . . . when he was sober" and never on Mondays. One of his jobs was to mix aluminum fluoride with alumina (purchased in fixed amounts) and hydrofluoric acid, which he did without weighing the latter to the detriment of the result. "When I asked him why he was not weighing it," related Davis, "he said that it was not necessary . . . , for he had discovered that there was a pound for every gurgle and a gurgle for every pound."[51]

In retrospect, Davis judged that he and Hall were simply too ignorant of "manufacturing technique" to train and manage a workforce. They had taken the problem of staffing for granted, but when things went wrong, they were prone to blame their workers, the first of whom seem to have been treated as little more than temporary hired hands. The workers behaved accordingly.[52] It quickly became apparent that, apart from the developmental tinkering Hall and Davis themselves performed on their new process, even routine labor in the potroom required some skill and experience to monitor the chemistry of the bath and regulate the electrical voltage and resistance. In time, Davis came to realize that "labor enters relatively into the cost of aluminum much more than into the cost of any other metal whatsoever," and that recognition would enable aluminum workers to command a premium in wages.[53]

The start-up of business suffered from the part-time involvement of the owners who, with the exception of Hall, were generally out of touch with operations. Hunt and Clapp were preoccupied in their downtown office with the testing business, and Hunt spent a good part of 1889 in Europe as part of a traveling delegation of American engineering societies (during which tour he tried to raise funds for the aluminum business through the sale of foreign patent rights). This situation would have to change if the company were to prosper. But it was not until June 1889 that some action with regard to the management of operations was ordered by the board of directors. After Robert Scott (one of the stockholders) found the night superintendent "asleep behind the engine and was able to awaken him only after striking him four times with his umbrella," the owners resolved to "take immediate steps to disinfect the disgraceful state of affairs and to procure a manager to look after the plant and improve the morale of the employees." Winfield Sample was made the first general manager, a function which, soon afterward, Hunt himself took over.[54]

Despite the looseness of its operations in the first year, Hall and Davis had developed the Smallman Street plant into a viable commercial proposition with remarkable speed. In about six months after start-up, Pittsburgh Reduction was able to sell an average daily output of fifty pounds of aluminum at $5 a pound. By the fall of

1889, as the price skittered down to $2, the pilot plant was deemed a success. The owners increased the firm's nominal capitalization to $1 million, the par value of 10,000 shares of common stock. Within another nine months, although a small loss was reported on the books, anticipation of greater demand warranted expanding operations; the plant was enlarged and two new, more powerful dynamos were installed. By September, the company produced 475 pounds per day. Even though production was below capacity, the owners were already planning a new plant at New Kensington, Pennsylvania, where the company could take advantage of natural gas and cheap coal deposits for power.[55]

Expanded operations in underdeveloped markets compelled the owners to seek new sources of funds. The Pittsburgh Reduction Company found itself at times perilously short of cash to meet its current liabilities. During his trip to Europe in 1889, Hunt had sold Hall's foreign patent rights in hopes that operations based on them would help solve some the the cash problems of his company. But the foreign patents had yielded little, and so the company, whose requirements for capital seemed insatiable as production was scaled up, had to look for new sources of outside funds. The directors turned to Pittsburgh businessmen, such as David L. Gillespie, a prosperous lumber dealer, and William Thaw, whose family had become rich in the coke and railroad businesses.[56] Their loans to Pittsburgh Reduction were repaid, at least in part, with stock. More important was the firm's new association with the banking house of T. Mellon & Sons, which on January 16, 1890, acquired sixty shares of stock from Charles Martin Hall at par value.[57]

The bank was run by Andrew W. and Richard Beatty Mellon, the third and fourth sons of a Scotch-Irish immigrant who had founded T. Mellon & Sons in 1869. Thomas Mellon had been a lawyer who had served as a county judge, but he had also dabbled in real estate ventures and had become wealthy in the expanding Pittsburgh real estate market. He used his surplus capital to make money on high-interest loans in the booming postwar demand for capital. He brought up his sons to have a healthy respect, if not love, for the power of money. Of all his sons, Thomas regarded the shy, physically frail, but canny Andrew as having the best judgment and executive ability. In 1874, Andrew, only twenty, was brought into the business.[58]

When Thomas retired in 1882, he gave the entire bank to Andrew, who then gave half to his younger brother, Richard. Thus began one of the most intimate partnerships in American business history.

Fig. 1.11.   The T. Mellon & Sons Bank building, circa 1880. *Courtesy of Mellon Bank.*

A. W. and R. B. Mellon were never known to quarrel, spoke always as a couple – "my brother and I," – accepted each other's business decisions without question, and maintained a joint bank account. While A. W. was clearly the more creative, more powerful intellect, R. B. was a stalwart alter ego, a true and equal partner. According to Charles J. V. Murphy, "for forty years it was their all but automatic practice, as a principle of brotherly action, to take equal shares, which is to say equal risk and responsibility, in any business or property venture that looked good."[59]

There was a time, however, when the Mellons had shown relatively little interest in corporate finance. Aside from taking deposits and making loans, before 1889, they had been primarily involved in real estate, although they had entered the insurance and trust fields and had taken stock in some small firms. But A. W. became convinced that greater opportunities lay in moving beyond conventional banking functions to finance fledgling enterprises more aggressively.

In fact, A. W. was ripe for a speculative venture when Alfred Hunt, Arthur Vining Davis, and George Clapp, woefully short of funds to operate their little aluminum plant on Smallman Street, came to him in 1889 to seek a $4,000 loan. He talked them into taking $25,000. Soon afterward, the Mellons advanced them the funds for their move to New Kensington. Through their real estate connections, the Mellons were able to secure for the company a favorable deal on land along the Allegheny River along with a loan to finance the relocation. For their pains, the Mellons took stock (the initial offering was for 500 shares of stock at $60 per share) and seats on the board of directors. A. W. replaced George Clapp as the company's treasurer, as the board recognized "that in the course of the next year, a business experience and financial reputation in the executive position of Treasurer . . . will be very greatly to the interests of the Pittsburgh Reduction Company."[60] Two years later, the Mellons would take a strong position in the bonds issued to finance the development of smelting operations at Niagara Falls, the key move that resulted in production economies that would bring the price of the metal down sufficiently to open a mass market.

The Pittsburgh Reduction Company was the first major investment for the Mellons in their promotion of new ventures. During the 1890s, they displayed a remarkable ability to spot good men with promising ideas to whom they granted loans for equity positions in their businesses. By the turn of the century, they were at the center of capital formation in Pittsburgh, where some 155,000 workers were employed by an increasingly diverse industrial economy that had blossomed into such basic businesses as steel, electricity and electrical machinery, glass, carborundum, oil, coke, shipbuilding, and, of course, aluminum. The Mellons acquired positions in these industries, and others, and became men of staggering wealth and power. They took positions on boards of directors where it was their policy to advocate plowing back profits to increase the long-run value of the enterprises in which they had a stake. By the end of World War I, A. W. served as an officer or director of more than sixty corporations, including the four that formed the cornerstone of their industrial empire: Gulf Oil, Koppers, Carborundum, and Alcoa.[61]

With the advent of the Mellons, the company became more formally organized. Captain Hunt, in addition to being president, would become general manager in 1893, taking more direct responsibility for overseeing sales and operations. By that time, Hunt had determined that he would have to devote himself to the aluminum business, and he left the direction of the Testing Laboratory to George Clapp. Hall, temporarily in Europe to shore up his applications for foreign patents, was designated to continue his work as vice president of technical operations. Meanwhile, A. V. Davis, who in Hall's absence was managing the plant, had become so indispensable to operations that the stockholders voted him 104 shares of stock (Davis could not afford to purchase stock on his own account) in March 1890. In 1893, he would became the firm's assistant general manager.[62]

It was the triumvirate of Hunt, Davis, and Hall who were to pioneer the markets for the "metal from clay" beyond the limited uses to which aluminum, usually in the form of aluminum-copper alloys, had been put. They had their work cut out for them, because the major markets for aluminum were as yet undefined and most of the techniques for its fabrication were as yet largely unknown. The Scovill Manufacturing Company of Waterbury, Connecticut, had taken up much of the company's production in 1890 and converted it into novelties of all kinds, but the public's initial fascination with the metal's lightness proved to be little more than a fad. In November 1891, Hall virtually echoed Pechiney's warning to Héroult when he wrote to Romaine Cole explaining:

> The mention of $2 in 1,000-pound lots didn't seem to interest anyone. I know a good many people look at it as a big buy, and they have reason to do so, as they know that the total consumption of aluminum in the U.S. has hardly been 1,000 pounds a year. People have said we didn't have 1,000 pounds. They were wrong, but they might have said, that so far as the users of aluminum were concerned, practically no one wanted 1,000 pounds.[63]

By that time the price of aluminum had been brought down to $1.21 per pound, but applications for aluminum had extended beyond the traditional luxury markets in only one important respect. The biggest customer for the company's output was the steel industry, which used small quantities of aluminum – with its affinity for oxygen – to remedy the problem of "blow holes," or pock marks on steel ingots caused by the presence of excessive oxygen in the open-hearth furnaces. Otherwise, small quantities were taken by cus-

Table 1.1. *Select prices of aluminum, 1852–97 (dollars per pound)*

Year	Country	Price
1852	France	$545.00
1854	France	272.00
1855	France	113.00
1856	France (Deville Process)	34.00
1862	France	11.75
1885	France	11.33
1886	France	12.00
1887	Switzerland	8.00
1888	U.S.	8.00
1888	England	4.84
1889	U.S. (Hall Process)	4.08
1890	U.S.	2.00
1891	U.S.	1.21
1892	U.S.	0.86
1893	U.S.	0.78
1894	U.S.	0.61
1895	U.S.	0.54
1896	U.S.	0.48
1897	U.S.	0.36

Sources: U.S. v. Alcoa, Exhibits and Testimony, passim; Pittsburgh Reduction Company, Minutes of the Board of Directors, 1888–97, passim.

tomers for experimental purposes. An aluminum tea kettle, some cooking utensils, and an electrical conductor had been produced at Smallman Street, but The Pittsburgh Reduction Company was as yet a smelter of pure aluminum, not a fabricator of aluminum products.[64]

The Pittsburgh Reduction Company looked toward the future almost entirely as the master of its own fate. There was virtually no competition in the pure aluminum market in the United States after mid-1893, by which time the firm's development of the electrolytic smelting process rendered its pure aluminum less expensive than aluminum produced by other means. One significant improvement stemmed from Hall's realization that as he scaled up his technology, he could maintain the bath in its molten state in the crucible with internal, rather than external, heat, much in the manner of the electric-furnace technology he had seen at the Cowles Company. This improvement was a necessary adjunct to larger-scale production and it would soon embroil him in legal trouble when Cowles began to produce pure aluminum by a similar method in January 1891. But, as we shall see, Cowles was forced to withdraw, never again to become a serious commercial threat.[65]

Protecting the Hall patent

So rarely has a business been able to sustain a controlling patent position for a long period of time that it is not surprising that there would be a challenge to Hall's claims. It was the opinion of one contemporary expert that Charles Martin Hall himself may not have immediately understood that apart from the particular apparatus he devised in his experiments, the underlying conception of the electrolytic process was in itself a "broad and valuable invention."[66] But Hall's patent, after it was given priority in the United States over Héroult's competing application, proved remarkably strong as a fundamental idea. Once conceived, the electrolytic process was so simple, yet so nearly comprehensive in its elements, that its patenting foreclosed all but one competing claim to a viable commercial process. That competing claim was based on the Cowles's furnace technology on which a key patent had been filed in 1885. This patent became the crux of a protracted litigation between The Pittsburgh Reduction Company and the Cowles Electric Smelting and Aluminum Company.

The Pittsburgh Reduction Company's success in marketing its output at increasingly lower prices alarmed the company that had so casually forsaken Hall and his early attempts to develop the electrolytic process. By 1890, it was becoming apparent to the Cowles brothers that they could not produce their aluminum alloys by their electrothermal process as cheaply as alloys could be made from pure aluminum. At the same time, it had become apparent to Hall that he would have to employ an internal-heating technique in his aluminum pots in order to keep the bath in fusion in anything larger than a small, uneconomical scale of operation. Thus, each company was finding it necessary to employ the technologies of the other. Neither Hall nor Héroult had originally understood the technical and economic importance of internal heating for the fusion of the bath, just as the Cowles brothers had failed to appreciate Hall's method for dissolving alumina in a suitable bath. If both techniques could be shown to be essential to the commercial production of aluminum, then there would be a standoff between the two parties.

After failing in an attempt to negotiate a merging of patent rights

Fig. 1.12.   Arthur Vining Davis as he appeared at about the time he joined The Pittsburgh Reduction Company.

with George Clapp, the Cowles Company hired away one of Pittsburgh Reduction's furnace operators, John Hobbs. This seemed fair
enough, since Hobbs had previously served as a furnace foreman in
the Cowles Company's Lockport, New York, plant before being lured
to Pittsburgh in 1889. In January 1891, Cowles offered pure aluminum for sale at a price undercutting Pittsburgh Reduction's, triggering a price war and a lawsuit charging that Pittsburgh was
infringing on Cowles's patented electrothermal technology. Shortly
thereafter, A. V. Davis slipped into Lockport incognito and sneaked
onto the little island where the Cowles factory was located. Davis
was only a little over five feet tall, but by hoisting himself atop a
pile of bricks, he managed to peer through a window to ascertain
that from all appearances, the Cowles operation was employing the
Hall Process. The Pittsburgh Reduction Company immediately filed
suit.[67]

Depositions were taken amidst charges that the Cowles Company, offering aluminum for sale at $0.50 per pound, was pricing well below cost. A preliminary injunction restrained Cowles from increasing production or lowering its price below Pittsburgh Reduction's (which for 1892 averaged about $0.86). Hall testified to the lack of support he had received from the Cowles brothers while in their employ. Alfred Cowles, in turn, belittled the priority of Hall's claims and testified that Hall's experiments at their facilities were insubstantial. A year and a half later, William Howard Taft of the Circuit Court of the Northern District of Ohio ruled decisively in favor of Hall and ordered Cowles to pay $292,000 in damages.[68]

The Cowles Company delayed payment and eventually won the right to reopen the case on the grounds that the commercial success of Hall's process in fact hinged on the adoption of internal heating, a method on which Cowles claimed a prior invention. If so, it would have put both companies in the position of infringing the other's patents. However, no trial was held to rule on that claim, because Cowles filed a more potent suit against Pittsburgh Reduction based on internal-heating experiments conducted in the early 1880s by Charles Bradley.[69]

Like the Cowles brothers, Bradley had devised a means for separating metals, including aluminum, from highly refractory, nonconducting ores by the use of an electric arc, the current for which was then passed through the molten mass to maintain the metal in a fused and conducting state. His patent application was initially rejected by the Patent Office in 1883 as too broad a claim. Bradley, in any case, had not worked toward bringing his idea into commercial application, an important criterion in pretwentieth-century patent law. Nevertheless, the Cowles brothers, in a precautionary move, purchased all of Bradley's "interest in any and all discoveries and inventions relating to electric smelting processes and furnaces" that might interfere with their own claims. In 1891, a shrewd patent attorney named Grosvenor P. Lowrey, an old associate of Thomas Edison's, helped Bradley procure a pair of patents based on rewritten claims in return for the assignment of those claims to Lowrey. In the legal tangle that followed, the conveyance to Lowrey was voided, allowing the Cowles interests to file a new suit against Pittsburgh Reduction in 1897. Through all that followed, Bradley was left fuming on the sidelines, shorn of any opportunity to profit directly from the outcome.[70]

The Cowles Company contended that the simultaneous fusion and electrolysis of the molten bath by the electric current was necessary for commercial production. Hall's patent had been based on heating the bath from an external source. Hall himself recognized the threat of the Bradley patents and tried at first to intervene "to prevent the Cowles Co. from buying him up."[71] Having failed in that, he suggested technical arguments against Bradley's claims. Hall's arguments contended that Bradley's original applications indicated extraordinary amounts of voltage to both electrolyze and fuse the molten bath, and that Bradley's insight, in any case, was not original but could be traced back to experiments of Sir Humphry Davy, who had used electrolyzing currents to maintain fusion of the electrolytes. Bradley, who had performed his experiments casually while serving as an electrician at the Pearl Street Station of the Edison Company in New York, had produced only negligible quantities of aluminum. Hall claimed that Bradley "was occupied on the matter not over two or three days" and neither appreciated nor developed the commercial possibilities. The District Court once again ruled in favor of Pittsburgh Reduction in 1901, though not necessarily on Hall's grounds. Bradley's patent was simply given a narrow interpretation. Without much appreciation for the complex electrochemical issues involved, the court seems to have been persuaded that a practicable electrolytic process rested only on Hall's discovery that alumina dissolved freely in cryolite.[72]

Dauntless, Cowles appealed, and the decision was reversed. Writing for the Circuit Court of Appeals in October 1903, Judge Coxe held that The Pittsburgh Reduction Company had infringed the Bradley patents. Noting that before Bradley the efforts of inventors to produce aluminum had been by the use of external heat, the Court granted Bradley's invention, as described in one of his patents, a liberal construction as "a fundamental discovery," on which Hall's achievement was, at least in part, an improvement.[73]

Whatever the legal merits, there was, by common-sense standards, some injustice in the 1903 ruling. It is true that Hall had achieved a practical application of internal heating only after increasing the size of his pot and scale of his operations so that the heat generated by higher voltages became sufficient to keep the bath melted. (This explains why Hall had not thought of internal heating in conjunction with his patent application, which was based on a much smaller-scale operation.) Hall's process as commercially developed could not avoid using internal heat in accordance with Bradley's prior claim. That notwithstanding, the court could have found that the beneficial consequence of internal heat proved to be an inevitable and inextricable by-product of the electrolytic process when applied on a large scale. Under this construction, it is questionable whether a distinct act of inventive genius should even have been recognized in connection with the phenomenon. In fact, maintaining the right amount of internal heat in large pots was highly problematic, requiring considerable experimentation as to the lining and positioning of the pot, the mix of the bath, and the regulation of voltage and resistance. That kind of process development had been undertaken by The Pittsburgh Reduction Company, whose technology was then appropriated by Cowles.[74]

But the appeals court did not see it that way: the Bradley claim was upheld, and Pittsburgh Reduction was ordered to pay Electric Smelting about $3 million in damages. If anything, the outcome was a stalemate, not unusual in the history of patent law. As a contemporary trade journal put it:

> It will be noted that the above decision does not affect the validity of the Hall patent for the use of cryolite as a solvent for alumina. On the contrary, it more firmly establishes it. Nor can there be any doubt that it was the Hall invention whose successful exploitation made aluminum a commercial metal. The situation is simply one which constantly recurs in the history of inventions, in which an inventor whose work reaches commercial success finds that he must settle with the owner of some earlier pioneer patent whose claims are entitled to a broad construction.[75]

Settle they must and settle they did. At the Pittsburgh Reduction Company, all capital expansion programs came to an abrupt halt. Panic must have seized the other side as well because, under the conflicting patents ruling, neither company could stay in the aluminum business without an agreement. Terms were struck in a matter of days. In return for a license to produce aluminum under the Bradley patent, Pittsburgh Reduction paid Electric Smelting $250,000 in back damages and agreed to pay an additional rate of $120,000 per annum until the expiration of the patent. Electric Smelting was also to receive a $0.01 per pound royalty for each pound of aluminum over eight million pounds produced by Pittsburgh Reduction. The latter also agreed to sell the former 146,000 pounds per annum of aluminum for the life of the license at a ten-percent discount from list price. Under the terms of the agreement, companies controlled by the Cowles interests were forbidden to manufacture pure aluminum while remaining free to buy and sell all grades of aluminum.[76]

Just why the Cowles interests, with all their technical know-how, chose not to reenter the aluminum smelting business is one of the more intriguing questions in the annals of business strategy. According to antitrust testimony offered on behalf of Alcoa in 1938, it appears that Alfred Cowles, having shut down his smelting operations in 1893, had been able to make money "purchasing scrap and doing a general jobbing aluminum business." With the Bradley patent, he was then able to extract a discount on Pittsburgh's aluminum that was about five percent greater than the discount granted to any other middleman in the business, so that "relations between the Aluminum Company and the Cowles Company very soon became again friendly." Thus, Electric Smelting wound up with a total of $1,136,000 by 1909 for its trouble along with a healthy jobbing business in the discounted aluminum that it purchased from Pittsburgh. When the Bradley patent expired, the relationship continued substantially the same, apparently dampening any desire the Cowles interests may have harbored to reenter the smelting business directly, even if, by that time, they could have raised the capital required to compete with Pittsburgh's vastly expanded scale of operations. To raise the capital, it would have been no mean feat "to persuade bankers to underwrite new ventures in the aluminum industry, where volume of production, costs, and profit margins were jealously regarded trade secrets known only to The Pittsburgh Reduction Company."[77]

The effect of the settlement on Pittsburgh Reduction, therefore, was to prolong its controlling patent position for three years beyond the expiration of the Hall patent. The three extra years, extending to seventeen years from the issuing of the Bradley patent in 1892, better enabled the company to integrate vertically and to increase its investment in anticipation of postpatent competition.

Strategic issues for the fledgling enterprise

Beyond their hopes of exploiting Hall's patent, it is hard to say just what the owners of The Pittsburgh Reduction Company anticipated when they made their initial investments between 1888 and 1892. Some inferences can be made, however. The founders had been associated with the steel industry and so were familiar with the high capital-intensiveness involved in the production of metals and their alloys. Any commercialization of aluminum, assuming a feasible production process were devised, would certainly require a commitment of large sums to build the facilities required for production on an economical scale. Moreover, it was not clear, beyond the existing markets, what the demand for inexpensive aluminum might be. If one assumed that a large, latent market existed (and that was precisely the assumption that brought Alfred Hunt and his cronies into the business), it was obvious that sales of aluminum would increase beyond existing applications only as the price came down. If the company could develop new applications for aluminum at a competitive price with other common metals, then a single firm with a controlling patent in a low-cost process could dominate a growing American market for at least seventeen years.

Still, there was no guarantee that demand for aluminum actually would be great. And though we know in retrospect that the company's patent control over aluminum technology gave it the time to establish its monopoly power over the long term, contemporary businessmen were certainly aware that patents were both legally and technologically fragile documents. Investment in a capital-intensive business of this nature was risky, and to realize a long-term payoff from their investment, the owners of The Pittsburgh Reduction Company had to consider strategies that anticipated the loss of its patent position.

From the start, they knew that they would have to risk precious time and money on the refinement of Hall's only partially developed process. This required faith. They also understood that the technology supported a very large scale of production, much of which, given industrial society's experience with sharp business cycles, would have to be carried through periods of slackened demand. This required a commitment to substantial growth in capacity over the long term. That commitment had to be made in advance of well-established demand for the metal, because only through economies of scale in production could the price of aluminum be brought down sufficiently to cultivate demand on a mass scale. They knew, too, that the material inputs and power to produce aluminum were scattered and expensive. Power needs, especially, required a willingness to site and build operations in distant locations near inexpensive sources of energy.

Other long-term realities of the business, not apparent at the outset, would become manifest by the time the patents controlling the basic smelting process had expired. The owners and managers of Alcoa would learn that the health of their business ultimately rested not on the proprietary control of a patented technology, but on an entire system of technology that linked the various phases of production from bauxite to aluminum to the manufacture and distribution of semifinished and finished products. They would learn that they could not rely forever, as they first did, solely on outside sources of supply for alumina and bauxite. Nor would they be able to sell most of their output in primary aluminum without first transforming it into useable shapes. Integration of these sources and outlets would become imperative.

Moreover, the establishment of sizeable markets would require pioneering work in new applications and production techniques and research into the properties of aluminum and its alloys. At the same time, the company's management had to be alert to external technological events that might pose competitive threats. These requirements would then trigger more concerted efforts to expand the company's scientific base and its technical know-how. The establishment of in-house research and engineering capabilities, along with large-scale growth and vertical integration, would have complex financial, organizational, economic, and legal implications. In the process, the entrepreneurial venture that had begun as a small pilot plant, manned by two young novice engineers, would evolve into a full-fledged, complex corporate bureaucracy by World War I.

In retrospect, we know that the Hall Process and Alcoa's mastery of it, both, proved remarkably durable. Alcoa continued its spectacular growth and sustained its U.S. monopoly in primary aluminum until the Second World War. Aside from the telephone, there was no technology that had been as successfully parlayed into one firm's dominance of a business for so long a time.[78] And even today, in a much more competitive world, Hall's discovery remains the basis of an entire industry. But before we run too far ahead of our story, we ought first to consider the larger patterns of American industrial development in which Alcoa's particular history unfolded. The strategic and organizational problems facing Alcoa's early owners and managers were part of a phenomemon that is often referred to as the rise of big business. It is to the rise of big business, which transformed the United States from a set of regional, predominantly agrarian economies into a modern industrial state, that we now turn.

2

Alcoa in context:
the rise of the complex corporation

Once Charles Martin Hall discovered a way of producing aluminum in large quantities at low cost, the business that formed around his invention became part of America's "second industrial revolution." Spanning the era from the 1870s to World War I, the second industrial revolution was characterized by the rise of a new breed of capital-intensive, technology-based industries in which the means of production and distribution were becoming consolidated in a few very large "managerial corporations." Those managerial corporations that established themselves as the leaders of their industries also became central to the nation's economic growth and prosperity in the twentieth century and were known collectively, sometimes pejoratively, as "big business."[1]

There is no doubt that Alcoa ranks as one of the more durably successful big business enterprises. It became that way by establishing and protecting new markets over a wide geographic area through the achievement of economies of scale and scope. In its early years, it grew large quickly, secured control over its critical sources of supply, and developed effective outlets and channels of distribution for its basic product, primary aluminum. Then, to sustain its growth, it developed bureaucratic administrative structures, staffed with professional managers, to coordinate its increasingly diverse products and functions. It continued to adapt to new opportunities and threats in the marketplace by constantly innovating and by investing in new technologies, plant, and personnel. And it accom-

43

modated, albeit grudgingly, to the countervailing forces of government and organized labor. Had Alcoa not done all these things
reasonably well and consistently over time, it might no longer exist
today; most certainly it would not still be a major industrial power.

Big business

In 1888, when The Pittsburgh Reduction Company was founded, big
business was already a dramatically evolving phenomenon. An essentially rural and fragmented American economy was rapidly
being transformed by the appearance of large, complex corporations
that could control the consolidated assets of productive units over
wide territories serving national markets. The complex corporation
was fast becoming the driving force in the growth of American industry, if not its most typical form. In a short space of time, just
since the Civil War, comparatively few great manufacturing and
utility firms operating railroads, telegraph and telephone services,
electrical power stations, and oil and steel producers had already
established themselves as linchpins of an emerging national
economy.

Merely a generation earlier things had been very different. The
antebellum United States was little more than a collection of regional economies dominated by agriculture and serviced by thousands of small shops and factories. Before the Civil War, foreign
visitors who traversed America's agrarian landscapes[2] were impressed by the vast expanse of the American countryside, its abundant natural resources, the rugged independence of its people, and
the modesty of its political and economic institutions. What struck
that most perceptive of foreign visitors Alexis de Tocqueville was
not only the apparent "absence of government" that seemed to characterize this, the most democratic of modern societies, but also the
modest scale of its business enterprises. America's "productive industry," he wrote, was characterized "not so much by the marvelous
grandeur of some undertakings, as the innumerable multitudes of
small ones."[3]

In antebellum America, the markets for manufactured products
were local or regional; factories were small, requiring little financing
to get started. Manufacturing firms were generally unincorporated
properties of individuals, families, or small partnerships. Even the
largest producers were capitalized at less than a million dollars.
Although a modern "factory system" employing mass-production

techniques based on interchangeable parts was emerging in certain pockets of American industry (most notably in the manufacture of firearms), American production techniques, even in the larger firms, remained, by and large, those of a handicraft culture.[4]

Manufacturing firms were almost always single-function enterprises – purchasing rather than making their inputs and distributing their products through independent factors. A producer of pig iron, for example, purchased raw materials and then sold the castings through a commission merchant to equally specialized bloomers or processors whose products, in turn, were distributed through independent agents. This was possible as long as the technology remained simple, production unintegrated, and markets unconcentrated.[5] Prospects for mass or high-volume production were bound by a number of constraints: fragmentary and isolated markets, discontinuous transportation systems, slow communications, small and informal distribution networks, few sources of energy for highly concentrated generation of motive power, and limited sources of massed capital. There were also legal and social impediments to growth in the size of firms. State laws made incorporation difficult, set upper limits on capitalization, and restricted the ability of firms to hold stock in other companies. And large corporate organizations were anathema to the small, egalitarian island communities that typified the America of Jefferson and Jackson, the latter of whom brought down the Second Bank of the United States with the approbation of a public hostile to institutionalized concentrations of wealth and power.

Neither were the administrative problems of unitary, specialized producers great nor their organizations complex. Owners of antebellum manufactories supervised their businesses personally. Factories were less subject to bureaucratic rules than to understandings based on custom. To foreign observers, both casual and official, American manufacturing was remarkable for its absence of rigid class structure, a high degree of personal mobility and organizational flexibility, and by progressive notions of technology and social welfare.

Yet forces that would irrevocably alter the face of American industry were already quietly at work. By the 1880s, these forces surfaced and coalesced with full impact, establishing an environment in which big business emerged with astonishing suddenness. Urbanization, the development of an interregional infrastructure in transportation (railroads) and telecommunications (a telegraph network), the harnessing of electrical power, a general rise in domestic savings and increasing investment from abroad, a tendency toward economic liberalism in public attitudes and political theory, the evolution of a legal climate increasingly favorable to the formation of business corporations with limited liability – all these trends that had begun to develop in antebellum America now accelerated and converged, auguring well for the marriage of an emerging mass market to the technological potential for mass production.

By the late 1880s, several large business firms capitalized in the many millions of dollars had become a familiar part of the American economy. The new infrastructure industries, railroad and telegraph, which had their entrepreneurial origins in the 1840s, spawned elaborate corporate organizations to finance and administer complex and far-flung operations. An electric-power-transmission industry emerged in the wake of the invention of the electric light and advances in power generation. The trend toward bigness was followed in manufacturing industries, beginning in the deflationary years of the 1870s, when chronic overcapacity drove many producers into association for the purposes of controlling prices and output. Some producers began to organize and consolidate their manufacturing and distributing operations on a large scale and capitalized on the latent opportunities presented by the rise of national, urban markets, new product and production technologies, and availability of mass transportation and high-speed communications.[6]

For Alcoa, as for all the successful pioneers in big business, sustained growth almost invariably required substantial control over competitive forces. Many companies attempted to achieve this through horizontal integration, the consolidation of firms in the same line of business, which began as an effort to diminish "ruinous competition" in times of overcapacity. Numerous trade associations were formed in the wake of the depression of 1873 in attempts to stem declining prices in industries with overcapacity. But such cartel-like arrangements failed to sustain their objectives in the face of legal hostility and lack of enforcement powers. Some firms found alternative solutions, first through the "trust" and then through the holding company. The exemplar of this evolution was John D. Rockefeller's Standard Oil Company, which during the 1870s and 80s successfully brought ninety percent of the refining capacity in the United States under its control. Rockefeller and his associates – sometimes by persuasion, sometimes by intimidation – brought refiners together by exchanging trust certificates for the common stock of participating firms, whose policies were then dictated by Standard Oil as trustee. After 1889, New Jersey's novel general incorporation law became the means by which a holding company could be formed to purchase the stock of other corporations on an unrestricted basis. (The word "trust" persisted as a popular term to describe not only the large holding company but all forms of big business.[7])

Similar consolidations took place before 1890 in other industries involving continuous-process production, such as sugar refining, whiskey, linseed oil, cottonseed oil, and lead processing. During the next fifteen years, a great wave of merger activity engulfed corporate America. From 1897–1904, some 4,227 firms merged into 257 corporations. By the end of this period, 318 trusts were believed to control two-fifths of the country's manufacturing assets.[8] Horizontal integration became a widespread device among producers to control output and prices and to limit new entry into an industry. But while monopoly through merger and acquisition may have been a producer's dream, it turned out that a less-drastic solution was required to have a good measure of control over prices. Indeed, prices could be controlled reasonably well by a few players in a single field, as the emerging oligopoly in sugar demonstrated.[9]

Alcoa, as we shall see, relied much more on internally generated growth than on acquisition to expand its business and to keep competition in check. But whether a company grew through merger and acquisition or through direct investment in new plant and equipment, it required enormous amounts of capital. Relative to smaller companies, a large, capital-intensive corporation must retain large portions of its earnings in the business in order to replenish and expand operations. But retained earnings were not enough. Balancing the near-term desire of stockholders to enjoy strong returns on their investments with the long-term needs of a capital-intensive business for enormous infusions of capital became a tricky problem for many companies. Even the most conservative owners of big business soon discovered that growth could not be achieved through internally generated capital alone. Expanding assets had to be offset by expanding issues of equity and debt. Important enabling factors were the rise of national capital markets in which various forms of securities were traded, and the emergence of investment bankers who served as intermediaries between supplies of capital and corporate demand for it. Such investment bankers, like the great J. P. Morgan in New York, became vital sources of venture capital in good times and of rescue capital in economic downturns. It was the Mellon family who performed this function in Pittsburgh for a number of that city's nascent big business enterprises, including The Pittsburgh Reduction Company, Gulf Oil, Carborundum, and Kop-

Fig. 2.1.   Group portrait of Thomas Mellon's wife, Sarah Jane Negley, and his sons, photographed sometime in the 1880s. From left to right are Richard B., James, Andrew W., George, Mrs. Mellon, and Thomas A. Mellon. Richard and Andrew became directors of The Pittsburgh Reduction Company in 1892. *Courtesy of Mellon Bank.*

pers. The development of large-scale financial services was as revolutionary as the rise of the big corporation itself and made it possible for capitalists to reach well beyond their own resources, to tap ever-larger sources of savings in a prospering economy.[10]

Like other corporations, Alcoa became increasingly dependent upon the financial intermediaries who underwrote new stock issues, made loans, or placed debt in the hands of third parties. By the early twentieth century, financiers had assumed important, sometimes controlling, positions on the boards of directors of companies whose debt they had converted into voting stock. What came to be called "finance capitalism" was a distinct historical phase of development between traditional family or owner-managed enterprise and modern bureaucratic, managerial enterprise. In the early twentieth century, investment bankers often played dominant roles in the strategic and policy decisions of the firms in which they became interested and helped reorganize in expansionary times. In some cases, like AT&T, U.S. Steel, or General Motors, financiers actually displaced the capitalists who had originally controlled the business.

At Alcoa, the role played by the Mellon brothers was more like that of partners with the other directors of the business, a role circumscribed by the Mellons' own restraint and by the determination of the company's owner-managers to keep as much control of the business in their own hands as possible.

Large-scale growth, either though direct investment or by acquisition, was attempted in most sectors of American manufacturing. But companies that became large stayed large only if substantial gains in productive efficiency were realized. The economic reality supporting the rise of big business was the potential for achieving "economies of scale" – or the lowering of costs per unit of production as output increases – that could be derived through the exploitation of size.

Some important facts were already known about various forms of production economies. In the late eighteenth century, Adam Smith had explained that economies could be achieved through a "division of labor": in larger shops, more specialized machines and human tasks could be devised, resulting in more efficient production due to an increased dexterity of the workers, reduced time in "passing from one species of work to another," and increased capacity of machines to "facilitate and abridge labor, and enable one man to do the work of many." Andrew Carnegie, the prevailing genius of the nineteenth-century American steel industry, described economies derived from large-scale organization in simple terms: "the larger the scale of operation, the cheaper the product."[11]

Economies of scale could be purely physical, as both theorists and practical men had observed. From his seat in the library of the British Museum, Karl Marx had calculated such things as in the application of energy, the cost of transmission equipment "does not grow in the same ratio as the total number of working machines which it sets in motion." Carnegie found that "the huge steamship of twenty thousand tons burden carries its ton of freight at less cost" than smaller vessels.[12] In the continuous-process production involved in such industries as oil refining, glass manufacturing, or metals reduction, output (again within limits) was found to increase in favorable proportion to the costs of building or operating larger-volume processing units. A simple example involves the doubling of the radius of an oil pipeline, which quadruples the amount of oil flowing through it. The sheer size of a manufacturing space bore with it economies of scale in its initial capital costs.[13] All that may have been obvious enough, but physical economies also came in more subtle and specific forms, which could only be grasped through the accumulation of experience. We have already seen that in the early phases of aluminum smelting, it was discovered through trial and error that larger containers for the fused chemical bath being electrolyzed to make the metal required less electricity per unit volume of the bath.

Economies of scale could also be derived from the increased ability of large firms to devote smaller proportions of capacity and labor in reserve to cover breakdowns or routine servicing in operations and to adapt to sudden fluctuations in demand. As companies grew larger, overhead costs generally could be spread over wider spheres of activity. This was as true for many functions at the corporate level in a complex enterprise as it was within a single plant. Alcoa, like other large corporations with multiple operations, would discover that the "centralization" of treasury, research, and marketing activities could service its growing network of production facilities more efficiently than would have been possible had each plant undertaken those functions for itself.

Bear in mind that economies of scale were not achieved in all industries. They applied to a special kind of industry, one that was capital-intensive and technologically suited to large-batch or continuous-process production by machine for mass markets. In such industries there existed a high ratio of fixed costs (e.g., land, capital, and plant) to variable costs (raw materials and labor). Both alumina refining and smelting were highly capital-intensive technologies for which large investments were required to achieve reasonably economical scales of production. An established capital-intensive enterprise – as Alcoa had become by the time its smelting patents expired in 1909 – could enjoy a long lead over its potential competitors in capital investment, market position (in both supplies and distribution), management experience, and technical know-how. On the other hand, in labor-intensive industries, such as printing or furniture making, increasing size might simply pose more expensive administrative complexities without offsetting increases in output per unit of input. Many combinations of firms in low-technology, labor-intensive industries, moreover, proved pointless, because there were neither economies of scale nor barriers to entry posed by high capital requirements nor any necessity to integrate vertically. This helps explain why giants like Standard Oil, U.S. Steel, and American Tobacco became and stayed dominant over a long period, while others like National Cordage (rope and twine), National Salt, and the United Button Company did not.[14]

Even though capital-intensive industries enjoyed scale economies, they bore heavy risks associated with their necessarily high ratio of fixed costs to variable costs. When in his early days as an aluminum smelting operator, Arthur Vining Davis discovered that even his relatively small plant had to run "steady and full" to sustain low unit production costs, he was encountering what Carnegie had recently described in discussing capital-intensive industry generally:

> ...in enormous establishments with five or ten millions of dollars of capital invested, and with thousands of workers, it costs the manufacturer much less to run at a loss per ton or per yard than to check his production. Stoppage would be serious indeed. ...Therefore the article is produced for months [or] for years... without profit or without interest on capital.[15]

Indeed, the high fixed costs of investment made capital-intensive business far more sensitive to downturns in demand than traditionally smaller manufacturing establishments had been. As recessions occurred in the normal course of business cycles, small operators could cut back or suspend operations altogether with much less pain than could large manufacturers who still had to pay interest charges, taxes, and other costs associated with maintaining the basic plant, even in an idle condition. The more complex technologies of big business, moreover, made experienced labor more precious (therefore less a variable cost) and, in some cases, made stoppages in operations precarious for technical reasons. An interruption of electrical power in the smelting of aluminum, for instance, led to a "freezing," or solidification of the metal and bath. This resulted not only in unproductive expense to restart operations (it could take a day to bring operations back to normal under the best of circumstances), it could also cause serious damage to the various components used in the process.[16]

Thus, the extraordinary risks associated with capital-intensive industry and the need to sustain operations through hard times furthered the tendency toward horizontal mergers in the hope that consolidation would bring costs down through the realization of scale economies and keep prices from deteriorating to destructive levels during times of slack demand. Insofar as the formation of big business resulted in lower costs and price stability, it performed a worthwhile socioeconomic function, even as it lined the pockets of the great "tycoons" whose machinations made it happen with unparalleled fortunes.

However achieved, growth in no capital-intensive industry was likely to succeed unless accompanied by some degree of vertical integration. Like most large industrial corporations, Alcoa found that growth required consolidation under common ownership of inputs and intermediate outputs from the extraction or procurement of raw materials to the delivery of finished products. Integration "forward," or "downstream," by manufacturers occurred in industries seeking to combine mass distribution with their capacity for mass production. Often this occurred in response to needs for larger networks and more specialized expertise in the handling or selling of products than could be expected of independent wholesalers. Entrepreneurs, such as Gustavus Swift (Swift and Company), Philip Armour (Armour & Company), and Andrew W. Preston (United Fruit), promoted the development of new refrigeration and heating techniques with which they moved downstream. This enabled them to coordinate the slaughtering or harvesting of perishables with transportation and wholesale distribution in distant urban markets. In the production of costly electrical equipment, such corporations as General Electric and Westinghouse, McCormick, and Babcock & Wilcox discovered that they themselves had to provide credit to customers and demonstrate, install, and service sophisticated machinery. Distribution of high-volume, standardized machines, as Singer Sewing Machine learned, required the control of sales offices.[17] All of these enterprises thus tapped latent markets for their goods that might otherwise have gone unexploited. We shall see that Alcoa's forward integration into "fabricated products" would be spurred by the need to demonstrate aluminum's usefulness in markets that were serviced by other materials.

"Backward" or "upstream" integration was less common among companies, occurring only when serious problems arose in procuring materials at the quantity, quality, or price desired. Marx had rightly predicted that once the factory was organized to take advantage of sophisticated machine technology, "sudden extension by leaps and bounds" of "the modern industrial system . . . finds no hindrance except in the supply of raw material and the distribution of the produce."[18] Real-life practitioners, as it turned out, were quick to recognize the dangers posed by lack of control over resources and markets and applied this knowledge to their own firms. Backward integration did more than protect large companies from fluctuations in supply and grease the wheels of distribution. It also created opportunities for savings derived from the substitution of internal organization for multiple dealings in external markets.[19] After American Bell Telephone Company, for example, acquired Western

Electric in 1882 and then consolidated its telephone operating agencies, the company gained more effective control over the development, quantity, quality, price, and distribution of its proprietary technology. Then as Bell found ways to coordinate research, development, and manufacturing with the provision of telephone service, it was possible to achieve great savings in transactions costs.[20] We shall see that when Alcoa first integrated backward after the turn of the century, it did so to gain logistical and technological control over bauxite, alumina, and power, the indispensable ingredients in aluminum production. From there it could then exploit its integrated structure to achieve considerable control over technology and costs.

Alcoa's moves upstream into mining, refining, power generation, other inputs, and to some extent transportation, followed the general pattern of the steel industry. Andrew Carnegie had integrated backward into pig iron production in order to eliminate the dependency of his bessemer converters on fluctuating sources of supply. Henry Clay Frick went further in the 1890s, as he expanded the Carnegie steel empire, buying up iron mines and sources of fuel and transporting raw materials in company steamships and rails. The company thus insulated itself from the vagaries of the marketplace. As a veteran of the company observed, "from the moment ... crude stuffs were dug out of the earth until they flowed in a stream of liquid steel in the ladles, there was never a price, profit, or royalty paid to an outsider."[21] Likewise, Alcoa was to become throughly integrated upstream, providing for almost all its major supply needs internally.

Sustaining large, vertically integrated enterprises required the development of managerial systems to regulate the speed, volume, and combination of "throughput," or the flow of materials through the production process. Modern managerial systems originated in the railroads, where the activities of salaried managers were organized around specialized "line" and "staff" functions in bureaucratic hierarchies of responsibility. The railroad experience was adapted to other industries, and where management was efficiently deployed, growing companies found that they could both increase the scale and scope of operations and substantially lower their costs. Again, the classic case is Standard Oil. As Rockefeller organized his "trust" in the late 1870s, he moved backward into shipping. By 1882, he was building long-distance pipelines through which oil could be pumped at a far lower cost than shipping by rail. This, then, supported further consolidation of refineries. As the organization swelled, administration was centralized and managerial and technical positions became more specialized. Specialized management enabled further integration, forward into wholesaling and backward into drilling. A large central office was established in New York to allocate the flow of petroleum from the oil fields to the refineries and to coordinate the output of worldwide markets. Layers of middle managers supervised the myriad business and technical functions and routines of labor throughout the enterprise in accordance with policies set by executive managers. Integration assured the refineries a more rapid flow of high-volume output into the market while guaranteeing a steady and predictable inflow of supplies, protecting the refineries against a possible combination of external suppliers. Specialists coordinated throughput at every stage, so that production could be safely and efficiently regulated at high capacity. The result was remarkable: the average cost of refining a gallon of oil plunged from 1.5¢ to 0.5¢ between 1882 and 1885.[22]

Electrochemicals manufacturers and metals producers, especially, benefitted from vertical integration and from the centralized management of specialized functions in order to maximize the quality and quantity of throughput. Electrochemical businesses were organized around, and ultimately dependent upon, very sophisticated processes (as distinct from products). Therefore, purely from a technological standpoint, it became necessary to develop sound chemical engineering "systems" to integrate the flow and quality of inputs into the core manufacturing process. Metals were not only subject to scale economies, they were also more difficult to shape than other materials, requiring finer tolerances and specifications in their production. Minor variations in quality at each stage of production could have major effects on production at succeeding stages. Thus, the coordinated integration of vertical production functions in furnace and foundry industries – as raw materials were converted into basic metals that were then alloyed and transformed into semifinished and finished shapes – was a problem both of sustaining high volume and of assuring quality. In iron and steel, the integration of blast furnaces with rolling mills and finishing mills, along with technological breakthroughs in steel alloys, greatly increased the potential for high-speed throughput. This, then, required better coordination of personnel, more systematic scheduling, better quality control, and more specialized assignment of tasks on the shop floor.

For an electrochemically based metals producer, it became a matter of considerable complexity to develop integrated systems of engineering and management to coordinate the flow of bauxite to the refinery and of alumina to the smelter over great distances and then to channel primary aluminum into a proliferating variety of specialized products, with due diligence for the quality at each stage. As the company grew in size and complexity, the specialized job descriptions of managers and technicians alike required increasing bureaucratic elaboration.

It was, in the last analysis, the development of modern managerial bureaucracy that made large-scale enterprise tick. As Alfred D. Chandler, Jr., has explained it, big business had to substitute the "visible hand" of management for Adam Smith's "invisible hand" of the marketplace, lest the large, multifunctional enterprise fall of its own weight. The great corporations out of necessity developed "managerial hierarchies" – business bureaucracies with specialized functions and orderly routines – "to coordinate a high-volume flow of materials through the processes of production and distribution, from the suppliers of raw materials to the ultimate consumers." As business organization became more complex, the trend was for salaried executive managers to succeed owners and entrepreneurs who lacked the administrative skills necessary to plan and operate an ongoing enterprise of great scale and complexity.[23] By 1920, an identifiable "technic of administration" was a widely recognized fact of American corporate life. The long-term survival of big business was determined by the degree to which administrators at all levels of the large corporation could coordinate an efficient system of throughput and effectiveness with which general managers could allocate resources, stimulate innovation, find new markets, and assess future prospects. Management became increasingly systematic in its attempts to link the technical problems of production to the social and economic realities of corporate life and the marketplace. Big business came to rely increasingly on schools of engineering and business administration to supply them with formally trained technical and managerial talent. Management thus became a kind of profession with interests and functions identifiably distinct from those of "capital" and "labor."[24] In one large firm after another, the managerial capitalist replaced the finance capitalist, who had in turn replaced the family capitalist, as the controlling agent of big business enterprise.

At Alcoa, we shall see that the progression toward bureaucratic management was remarkably slow, though nonetheless inexorable. Like all successful big business enterprises, Alcoa underwent a necessary transition from an enterpreneurial, owner-managed venture into a more formally structured corporation that was administered by career professionals. A correlative process was the dispersion of ownership control out of the hands of a few owner-directors to stockholders who were far removed from, even ignorant of, the technical aspects of the business whose stock they held. In most large corporations, demands for capital were too high for the original owners to meet, and founding entrepreneurs proved temperamentally ill-suited to administer the complexities of the large businesses they created. It was for these reasons, for example, that a frenetic empire builder like William Durant not only had to give up ownership control of General Motors to "outsiders," but also had to relinquish managerial control of his company to the more systematic, analytical Alfred Sloan. Once those kinds of transitions occurred in any company, the progression toward formal managerial bureaucracy was swift. But Alcoa's experience was unusual in that it remained closely held by a handful of owners among whom were men who managed the company through successive phases of development over a very long period of time. Arthur Vining Davis and Roy Hunt, in particular, were with the company for more than sixty-five years each, their boards of directors were stable and long-lived, and the key men who reported to them enjoyed lengthy careers as senior managers. Under such circumstances, Alcoa's structure remained intensely personal and informal, and despite rapid changes in the scale and scope of its business, the company's bureaucracy was slow to evolve.

This is not to say that Alcoa's management structure was ineffective. The company's ability to bring, and keep, the price of its products down depended, first, on its achievement of economies of scale, and, then, on its ability to coordinate its production and marketing efficiently. Over the long run, Alcoa proved especially adept at managing innovation to meet changing market needs and competitive threats.

Indeed, Alcoa's management of research and development forms a vital part of our history. A crucial occurrence for all companies engaged in new technologies was the rise of industrial research and development as specific managerial functions of the enterprise. Corporate innovation was defined by the strategic imperatives of new products and markets: the need to scale up and perfect basic processes of production, the need to educate customers on the characteristics and uses of new products, the need to disseminate advancing technical knowledge within the vertically integrated corporation, and the need to minimize the threat from outside sources of innovation.

For a time, such needs could be met *ad hoc*, in the context of the

Fig. 2.2. Arthur Vining Davis in 1903.

workaday routines of production. As problems were identified, they were solved through trial-and-error experience and testing. If fundamental or theoretical problems arose, help could be solicited from outside scientific and engineering consultants. In-house research or patent departments were set up to monitor outside scientific developments and to conduct experiments on particularly important problems. Yet it was not until technical problems began to stretch the outer limits of contemporary scientific knowledge that full-fledged corporate "R&D" organizations – with large staffs of technical specialists pursuing the advancement and application of scientific knowledge on a systematic, long-term basis – came into being.

The industrial research laboratory signified an evolutionary advance over the inventor-entrepreneur, as the complex corporation came to require a more complex, organized response to the scientific and technical problems of its business.[25] As companies formed around new and dynamic technologies, they failed to institutionalize research at their peril. Alcoa was not alone in recognizing the necessity for formal R&D in World War I; in 1921, some 350 firms claimed to have their own R&D facilities. Only a few were as yet very large or distinguished, and most concentrated more on product and process testing than on innovative research. Nonetheless, the industrial laboratory was fast becoming a major market for scientists and engineers with advanced degrees and as a source of new scientific knowledge.[26]

The scientists recruited by Alcoa after World War I quickly found that corporate needs for product and process innovation took precedence over the researcher's freedom to choose what problems to work on or what methods to employ. Industrial scientists and engineers were better paid and more lavishly equipped than their academic counterparts, but they were also tied to the practical demands of the marketplace and of the corporation's need to control costs. As David Noble has put it, industrial science "became essentially a management problem," and the industrial scientist "a soldier under management command, participating with others in a collective attack on scientific truth."[27] But at Alcoa, the institutional subservience of the researcher was softened not merely by material rewards, but by psychic and professional rewards as well. Like progressive companies, such as General Electric, AT&T, DuPont, and Standard Oil of Indiana, Alcoa made a good home for first-rate scientific researchers by satisfying professional longings for recognition, publication, and opportunities to work on basic, as well as applied, problems. In return, its cadre of scientists buttressed the company's essentially empirical methods of innovation with the kind of fundamental and theoretical knowledge that often led to important technological and commercial breakthroughs. At Alcoa, science was most assuredly a handmaiden to corporate strategy, but as such, it yielded new basic knowledge about the structure and composition of metals – knowledge that might not have been cultivated elsewhere.

In addition to achieving growth through scale, scope, and technological innovation, Alcoa strove for as wide a geographic expansion as it could manage. In this regard, the company was conforming to a general trend in American business that was curtailed sharply in the 1930s by economic depression and a rising tide of protectionism. Historically, the United States had traditionally been a target rather than source of international investment, but after the Civil War, the technologies of the steamship and telegraph cable made it easier for companies to look abroad for additional markets. I. M.

Singer established sales offices in Europe and then built sewing machine factories in Canada and Scotland to achieve control over foreign patents and independent merchants, so that by 1874, half of its sales were offshore. This pioneering experience was followed by companies in electrical apparatus, chemicals, petroleum, and insurance. Companies like General Electric, Standard Oil, Western Electric, and Eastman Kodak both made and sold goods abroad, often (because of their great economies) at cheaper prices and at higher quality than local firms could achieve. American firms seeking raw materials and crops went abroad to establish mines, ranches, and farms in Canada, Latin America, and the Caribbean (which also proved to be ripe territories for investments in railroads, power, and timber), and overseas to Europe and China. By World War I, the value of American investments abroad accounted for seven percent of the gross national product.[28]

Before the war, Alcoa went abroad in pursuit of energy and raw materials: hydropower in Canada and bauxite in the Caribbean. Later, the company expanded into Europe and even Asia, broadening its interest overseas to include refineries, smelters, and fabricating facilities. But like many American multinationals, Alcoa found that it could not effectively manage its foreign operations. Some companies reorganized their operations as separate entities; others eliminated them altogether. In 1929, Alcoa divested virtually everything but its Caribbean bauxite. It was not until after the dust cleared from World War II that American corporations would once again find international expansion attractive. Alcoa waited until the late 1950s to reestablish overseas operations on any meaningful scale.

In sum, by the 1920s, Alcoa had taken its place as one of a durable core of large, complex corporations at the center of the American economy. Alcoa had achieved significant economies of scale through the consolidation of capital-intensive operations. Continuing growth and success were assured through the achievement of control over material inputs into production, over scientific and innovative activities related to both process and products, and over distribution into markets. Such control enabled the company not only to become national in its markets and operations, but also to go abroad, at least for a time, in search of raw materials, labor, and markets. Alcoa's scale, scope, administrative systems, and scientific and technical sophistication all constituted formidable barriers to the entry of would-be competitors, who, for more than half a century, could not crack Alcoa's American monopoly in primary aluminum. What was true for all capital-intensive industries – where the first com-

panies to grow large, integrate vertically, develop managerial hierarchies, and internalize innovation became and stayed dominant in
their industries for years to come – was true in spades for aluminum.

Antitrust

Like all large, complex corporations, Alcoa had to learn to live with
evolving social and political constraints on its freedom. Some of those
constraints were absorbed by the company as part of larger evolutionary patterns of social and political change; others involved actions taken by the Government against the company that were more
specific and traumatic in their effects. One such action was the great
antitrust case of 1937, the single thing for which the company is
best remembered in graduate schools of law and business. Judge
Learned Hand's 1945 opinion that Alcoa wrongfully held its monopoly in primary aluminum by virtue of its sheer dominance of the
market was a climactic point in the public history of the large
corporation.

Yet, the simple fact that Alcoa held a monopoly in the production
of primary aluminum for so long a time is remarkable in the annals
of American business. At the end of World War I, which marked the
end of what historians commonly think was the formative period in
the rise of big business in America, Alcoa was firmly ensconced as
one of the nation's more important corporations, ranking 48th
among American industrials. It was still modest in size when compared to the very largest manufacturers of that time – U.S. Steel,
Standard Oil of New Jersey, Armour, Swift, and General Motors[29]
– but no other American corporation had developed its own industry's markets any more dramatically and then dominated them any
more completely.

Thereafter, Alcoa became widely recognized as the very model of
monopoly enterprise, having taken the concentration of large-scale,
capital-intensive production to its logical conclusion. To appreciate
what that means, think of American Tobacco, Standard Oil, or
AT&T, the companies most commonly remembered as great monopolies. Unlike the first two, which were dismembered by Supreme
Court decisions in 1911, Alcoa had been able to sustain virtually
absolute control of its basic market and would continue to do so until
World War II. Unlike AT&T, which was successively wrapped in
layers of regulation at the local, state, and federal levels, Alcoa
remained free to set its own prices and plan its investments without

regulatory approval. It was not until 1941 that political circumstances enabled Reynolds Metals to put the first chink in Alcoa's protective armor. And it was not until 1946 when, in the aftermath of a novel antitrust ruling, Alcoa irrevocably lost its nearly complete hold on the American aluminum market.

Alcoa's status as a monopolistic enterprise and its reputation as a property of one of America's best-known financiers, Andrew W. Mellon, made it a choice target of populist politics and antitrust. Neither public sentiment, nor politics, nor the aspirations of potential competitors favored monopoly enterprise, and eventually all three would conspire to break Alcoa's monopoly in primary aluminum. Even after the most thorough investigations by agencies of the Federal Government could not demonstrate any significant violations of antitrust law, the company's dominance of the aluminum market would ultimately be condemned as illegal, and after World War II, it was forced to accept competition by virtual Government fiat. That such an outcome was more or less inevitable is at least partly explained by the historic nature of American attitudes toward big business.

The rise of the capital-intensive corporation attended a dramatic improvement in the welfare of society as a whole. The prosperous, urban, and diverse economy that the United States became in the twentieth century owed much to the presence of big business. From 1870 to 1930, the population of the United States exploded from fewer than 40 million to nearly 123 million souls, among whom were more than 30 million immigrants who came in search of the economic opportunities provided by America's great industrial boom. At the same time, real per-capita gross national product increased from $531 to $1,671 (in 1958 dollars). The nation, still predominantly rural in 1870, when seventy-four percent of the population lived in places of fewer than 2,500 people, had officially become an urban society by 1920, almost entirely as a consequence of large-scale industrialization. New technologies, such as household electricity, the telephone, the automobile, and even the airplane, appeared, transforming the very structure and patterns of everyday life. The great center corporations and the countless peripheral firms that sprang up to supply the needs or take the products of big business made possible the mass production of a growing array of consumer goods and provided jobs for the rapidly expanding workforce, as the nation's labor pool swelled from 12.5 million to 48.8 million.[30] The transforming effects of big business were readily apparent to contemporaries, and its advent was not altogether welcome.

Unsettling and worrisome was the transition of the American landscape from a loose collection of quiet and familiar rural communities, where livings were related primarily to the land, to an interconnected web of sprawling and impersonal cities, where people worked in noisy and gloomy factories. Moreover, the giant corporations who ran the factories were concentrated repositories of wealth and power, and nothing could have been more disturbing to basic American individualistic and democratic sensibilities. Various shades of anticorporate populism became the broad emotional reaction against the erosion of agrarian and small-town values, providing strong ideological support for the creation of Government agencies and antitrust (which in and of themselves were not necessarily populist in their origins) as "regulatory" controls on the seemingly wanton power of corporate interests.

It is not that these responses were unreasonable. There had simply been too much suddenness and callousness with which a few businessmen had amassed great resources to build their large organizations. Big business had spawned a new kind of noble caste, sheltered from personal responsibility for the misdeeds of their companies. The apparently unbridled greed, and "public-be-damned" attitudes of such well-known railroad era magnates as Commodore Vanderbilt, Jay Gould, Daniel Drew, and Jim Fisk had already fixed in the public mind an image of the corporate tycoon as robber baron. Over the years, cynical manipulations of stocks and bonds in the railroad and utilities industries, extortionate practices in the consolidation of the oil and tobacco industries, unhealthy products in the food and drug industries, degraded conditions of labor in coal mines and steel factories, and ill-concealed bribery of public officials formed a litany of horrors reported regularly in the nation's newspapers, magazines, and best-selling books.[31]

No less problematic were the perceived organizational consequences of big business. The development of impersonal, bureaucratic, managerial hierarchies, and the emergence of "scientific" principles of factory management (which promised to engineer workers into perfect harmony with their machines), only added to the general discomfort. Most striking were the sheer size and vast resources of large corporations, especially when compared to the organizations of local and state governments. Corporations, like governments, wielded power, but they did so in secrecy, subject to no checks and balances. And though corporations were chartered by the state and often benefitted from nurturing policies of the state (for example, on the federal level in the form of stiff tariff protection), companies with large blocks of publicly traded stocks could refrain from any public reporting about their finances or operations. Even in the liberal, *laissez-faire* climate of late nineteenth-century capitalism, big business seemed unaccountable to the extreme.[32]

Attacks on big business were launched from all directions. Labor organizers, farmers, urban populists, small businessmen, intellectuals, and muckraking journalists alike assailed the "trusts." Revelations of specific wrongdoings focused a more generalized fear that concentrated corporate power might deprive ordinary citizens of their livings, their familiar landscapes, their social mobility, and their individuality. Consortia of large producers could drive small producers out, fix prices and wages, and close off economic opportunities for entrepreneurs of modest means. The issue of the "trusts" dominated political debate from the 1880s to World War I. Following the loosely organized populist movements of the 1880s and 90s, a national, "Progressive" consensus emerged, acknowledging a need to impose some checks on unbridled free enterprise. This consensus, which encapsulated a wide range of opinions as to how business/ government relations ought to be structured, reflected deeply ambivalent feelings about the new order being wrought by industrialization, an ambivalence that remains deeply rooted in the American psyche to the present day.

Near the center of the consensus stood politicians like Theodore Roosevelt, who on the one hand accepted the economic and technological premises of the new industrial order, but on the other hand, feared the "real and grave evils" of trusts. Even though the "captains of industry . . . have on the whole done great good," he said, their corporations had "tendencies hurtful to the general welfare." No less a pillar of American business attitudes than *The Banker's Magazine* openly fretted about the potential subversiveness of big business to the body politic: "That [government is not] entirely controlled by these interests is due to the fact that business organization has not yet reached full perfection." Thus, it became the "sincere conviction" of basically conservative men like Roosevelt that "combination and concentration should be, not prohibited, but supervised and within reasonable limits controlled."[33]

Big business, in other words, was at once a welcome development that contained within it threatening implications. So, as markets and corporations became national in scope, the focus of business regulation widened from cities and states to include the Federal Government. As business grew in power and organization, governments responded with powers and organizations of their own, laying

Fig. 2.3. An idealized drawing of The Pittsburgh Reduction Company's pilot plant on Smallman Street with Pittsburgh's "North Side" in the background.

Fig. 2.4. A 1906 photograph offers a more sobering view of Pittsburgh's turn-of-the-century industrial development in the area around Smallman Street, again looking north. *Courtesy of Carnegie Library.*

the foundations of the modern administrative state. At the federal level, the Interstate Commerce Commission was created in 1887 to regulate railroads, the first of a series of acts aimed at controlling rates and certain business practices in transportation and telecommunications. By World War I, several federal agencies or commissions had been empowered to monitor activities in banking as well as in corporations more directly concerned with production. The latter were brought under closer scrutiny by the establishment of the Federal Trade Commission in 1914, which was initially empowered to demand information from corporations, to issue cease and desist orders, and to bring offending companies to trial.[34]

Equally important was the development of judicial authority over business. The Sherman Act of 1890 crystallized a trend, growing out of common-law principles, toward restraining price fixing and monopolization. The act outlawed cartels and "every contract, combination in the form of trust or otherwise, or conspiracy, in restraint of trade or commerce." One immediate, unanticipated effect of the Sherman Act was to hasten business consolidation by formal merger. Mergers as a way of reducing competition increased in popularity when the earliest prosecutions under the act were brought mainly against small company associations and labor unions. Ironically, as the pace of government antitrust prosecutions quickened under Presidents Roosevelt and Taft, the vast majority of antitrust actions were directed at loose horizontal associations and cartels of peripheral firms. This emphasis reinforced the drive toward formal consolidation and vertical integration in capital-intensive industries. However, as the Department of Justice became more and more a vehicle for monitoring the behavior of business, consolidated corporations, Alcoa among them, became increasingly subject to the provisions of the Sherman Act.[35]

Large-scale consolidations remained a matter of judicial and public ambivalence. It was an especially nettlesome problem for large corporations that bigness *per se* could be regarded as bad. A formidable body of opinion held that great size could not be achieved honestly, nor, once achieved, operated efficiently, nor once established, reconciled with the spirit of competitive, "free" enterprise. Such "prejudice existing against corporations," an Alcoa engineer noted in private correspondence, inhibited even those corporate activities that might be perfectly reasonable, even humane, in their intent.[36]

Outright monopoly control of an industrial market was an especially unsettling prospect for a society traditionally hostile to concentrations of power. Alcoa's A. V. Davis argued with some justification that "a beneficent, wise, fair monopoly at the inception of an infant industry might well be more beneficial to the public than cutthroat competition between two rivals who cared nothing about the public and only about themselves."[37] (Alcoa, of course, enjoyed the protection of patent laws in its establishment of a monopoly at the inception of its own "infant industry." The continuation of its monopoly after the expiration of its patents was at the mercy, at least in part, of public tolerance.) Yet it was simply too much to believe that any businessman of the day, if left entirely to his own devices, could properly serve the public welfare. And a monopolist was too extreme a case of unchecked power to be trusted. Given the climate of public opinion, firms successful enough to achieve overwhelming market dominance in their industries had reason to feel defensive. Combinations exerting "monopoly control" in the railroads were brought to heel by the Supreme Court in a series of decisions between 1897 and 1903. In 1911, the Court expanded its application of the Sherman Act to consolidations in manufacturing when it ordered the dissolution of the Standard Oil Company and American Tobacco. They were not, the Court ruled, "reasonable" combines. To businessmen, this seemed vague; it appeared that the Court, like President Theodore Roosevelt, was trying to make a distinction between "good" and "bad" trusts.[38]

Imprecise as this kind of legal reasoning was, it could only have rendered the leaders of big business more cautious, at least about what they said if not always about what they did. The political tide against large corporations reached a peak in the first Wilson administration, culminating in the passage of the Clayton Antitrust and Federal Trade Commission (FTC) Acts of 1914. The Clayton Act went farther than the Sherman Act in defining anticompetitive conduct in an attempt to refine the Government's means for checking tendencies toward monopoly power. The public mood was perhaps best captured in the studied ambivalence of Woodrow Wilson – "I am for big business, and I am against the trusts," he once remarked[39] – which actually made him a bit more conservative than the thrust of his own administration's regulatory policy.

To mainstream policy makers under Roosevelt and Taft, the control of an industry by a few large companies had seemed a perfectly reasonable form of organization for the orderly planning of enterprise, so long as conspiracies to fix prices or limit output could be prevented. Liberal Wilsonians, on the other hand, held "that competition [among many firms] can be and should be maintained in every branch of private industry...." No one believed this more fervently than the guiding intellect of Wilson's economic program, business attorney Louis Brandeis, who could not understand why the market structure of the oil industry should be any different from that of the shoe industry. Brandeis was far from alone in his aversion to (and ignorance about) big business, an aversion based more on visceral and nostalgic notions of competitive individualism than on any rational comprehension of the economic and technological imperatives driving capital-intensive enterprise.[40]

Wiser counsels prevailed as more became known about the special nature of capital-intensive industry. The superior efficiency of many large, vertically integrated, and professionally managed firms was becoming much better understood by economists, and for a younger generation of influential liberal thinkers, like Walter Lippman, size and power were no longer necessarily equated with greed. Lippman, and others, began to notice one especially striking characteristic of the large corporation that rendered it more responsible: professional management that could deal efficiently with large-scale industrial organization for positive social ends. "The real news about business," wrote the young Lippman in 1914, "is that it is being managed by men who are not profiteers. The managers are on salary, divorced from ownership and from bargaining.... The motive of profit is not their motive. That is an astounding change."[41] Perception of this change apparently reached the Supreme Court by 1920, when it ruled, "The law does not make mere size an offense."[42]

Meanwhile, World War I had pushed the problems of big business out of the headlines while creating conditions for more cooperative relationships between industrial leaders and government officials. For a decade after the war, the existence of the dominant center firms was generally accepted by the mainstream political establishment. Those were the halcyon days of corporate capitalism, when the business of America, Calvin Coolidge proclaimed, was business. In the boom years of the 1920s, giant corporations became the cherished engines of growth and prosperity, achieving an estimable stature in popular opinion that they have not enjoyed since. Still, antitrust would continue to be an important factor in national economic policy, and it was on this battlefront that Alcoa would fight a defensive struggle for power over its hard-won markets for decades after its controlling patents expired.

Indeed, antitrust was destined to become Alcoa's nemesis. So successful had Alcoa been in dominating the industry it had spawned that it was first charged in 1911, the year of the oil and tobacco decisions, with violating the Sherman Act on the presumption that it could not have achieved its position without resort to nefarious business practices. Alcoa, as we shall see in greater detail later, survived its first encounter with antitrust virtually unscathed, and during the next five years, it not only held a monopoly on North American primary aluminum production, it produced more than sixty-three percent of the entire world's output. But from the end of World War I until the late 1960s, there was hardly a year when the company was not under some form of antitrust pressure. A round of FTC investigations dogged Alcoa during the 1920s. Private antitrust suits posed major threats to the company through the early 1930s before administrators in Franklin Roosevelt's second term revived antitrust as a major regulatory weapon against concentrated market power. Amidst all the publicity given to large corporations during the hearings of the Temporary National Economic Committee between 1938 and 1940, bigness in industry once again became bad. By virtue of its monopoly in primary aluminum production and its ties to the Mellons – symbols as they were of a bygone era of free-wheeling capitalism, Alcoa became a prime target of this shift in political sentiment. Even after the final resolution of the great case that began in 1937, and then lasted through various court proceedings for twenty years, the company remained beset by antitrust problems into the 1960s.

Beyond antitrust, of course, lay other regulatory concerns with a wide range of corporate behavior. After the Great Depression had thoroughly soured public attitudes toward big business, the New Deal decisively subordinated a variety of private business activities – from labor practices to financial reporting – to government regulation. From the 1930s forward, regulation would be extended to more and more areas of business activity, culminating in recent years in the proliferation of laws and agencies for environmental controls, equal employment opportunity, and employee health and safety. Compared to its long and bitter experience with antitrust, Alcoa's adjustment to these kinds of political constraints was relatively painless.

Big labor

Seen in a larger perspective, Federal Government regulation of big business was but one aspect of the bureaucratization of other important sectors of the economy, each making its own bid for power in the national economy – including small-business associations, business, state and local governments, the professions, and ultimately the consumer. In time, these other sectors of the economy became better organized and exercised their own corporate power, often in opposition to the aspirations of big business. No movement to organize was more feared and resisted by big business than the rise of the industrial labor union.

The mass organization of labor as a countervailing force to big business lagged by a full generation. It was not until the Great Depression of the 1930s that the industrial union became a significant force in the center corporations of American industry. We have come to take labor unions for granted, but at the time of Alcoa's founding a century ago, the formal organization of labor in the American economy involved a little more than one percent of the entire workforce. During the course of the Industrial Revolution, workers – as distinct from slaves and servants, on the one hand, and masters, manufacturers, and merchants, on the other – evolved in the American economy as a distinct economic class, but their labor as a distinct property was ill-defined vis-à-vis real estate, chattel, and capital. Aside from the mechanic liens that defined the rights of hired workers to claim wages against the assets of a bankrupt master's customers, there was scant recognition in law or custom of economic rights peculiar to labor. Moreover, there was no strong body of custom or law that allowed workers to organize as a corporate class in order to extract rents from the owners of capital: that is, to win wages higher than those that could be achieved by workers contracting through foremen or as individual hired hands.[43]

Before the advent of big business, the organization of unions in the United States had been sporadic, small-scale, and local – the most enduring organizations being fairly traditional forms of skilled journeyman's associations, or small craft unions. With the emergence of a national economy after the Civil War, national political and social movements arose to carry the banner for labor as a distinct socioeconomic class. But such attempts at large organization as the National Labor Union and the Knights of Labor quickly fell by the wayside. The conservative political and liberal economic climates of the late nineteenth century could not sustain strong labor movements that combined the quest for better wages and working conditions with broader agendas for "radical" social reform. The law, which had always looked askance at organized "conspiracies" to restrain trade by workers through strikes and other job actions, made unionization tough enough. And those who tried had to face sharp resistance from companies that employed strikebreakers, spies, and other forms of intimidation.[44]

In 1886, the head of the New York union of cigar makers, Samuel Gompers, organized the American Federation of Labor (AFL), a national association of craft unions dedicated to "pure and simple unionism," or the control by workers of wages, hours, and working conditions through organized coercion. With a well-administered and conservative program, Gompers was able to succeed where other, more utopian national labor movements had failed. The weapon of the AFL was the strike, backed by careful, business-like administration of dues and union discipline. By eschewing fundamental social reform, by concentrating on crafts (as opposed to industries), by attending to local issues (relative to national), by building a well-coordinated organization, and by carefully marshalling its financial resources, the AFL became a durable, if conservative, force in American labor.

For some fifty years, the AFL dominated the labor movement in both numbers and spirit as other, more inclusive and political ventures, notably the International Workers of the World (IWW), flamed, flickered, and ultimately suffocated in an atmosphere hostile to "foreign" influences and "socialist" ideas. A radical organization such as the IWW, which imbibed heavily of the ideological programs of international socialist movements, could not muster a meaningful base of popular support and was easily crushed by public authorities in the patriotic frenzy of the war. Except for such groups as the United Mine Workers and the International Ladies Garment Workers Union, industrial unionism remained a weak force in the American economy until the 1930s.

Like most industrial corporations engaged in mass production, Alcoa experienced little difficulty in breaking nascent craft union movements in its plants before the Depression. Even during World War I, when "patriotic" unions were afforded substantial Government protection in exchange for labor peace, Alcoa management's treatment of labor was benign enough to forestall any significant attempts at unionization. The company enjoyed virtually unchecked control over nonmanagement employees and was able to stay the advent of unionism without resorting to the kinds of violence and intimidation employed by many other industrial corporations.

Before the Great Depression, Alcoa conformed to the general pattern of labor relations in that hiring, firing, wages, promotion, allocation of work, and treatment of individual workers were arbitrarily administered, often at the sole and capricious discretion of foremen on the production line. Throughout American industry, labor was a commodity, and not a particularly well-managed one at that. Employment was insecure (even in a good year like 1909, the industrial average for employment fluctuated by about fourteen percent), and layoffs had no basis in seniority or performance. Employment – its compensation, duration, and conditions – was strictly a matter of an arbitrary employer's will. Circumstances changed somewhat with the outbreak of war, when the twin pressures of manpower shortages and rising military demand created opportunities for workers to extract premium wages. The National War Labor Board forced industrial companies to comply with the eight-hour workday, and the Government explicitly recognized employees' rights to organize and bargain collectively through chosen representatives. Even so, workers at Alcoa, like workers in steel, automobiles, rubber, and radio, emerged from the war virtually unorganized. After the war, when public fears of "radical" social causes that were identified with "alien" immigrants at home and "bolshevist" revolution abroad swept the country, unions became identified with an array of "subversive" forces that seemingly threatened "native," middle-class virtues. National trade union membership, which had exceeded 5,000,000 at the end of the war, fell precipitously to 3,600,000 by 1921 amidst intensive resistance to unions by employers. As the first postwar depression set in, wages fell sharply, and powerless workers were laid off in droves.

During the 1920s, Federal Government policy also took a decisively antilabor turn under probusiness Republican administrations. Labor was also hurt by promanagement Supreme Court rulings, one of which sanctioned "yellow-dog contracts," a device legal in most states allowing companies to make contracts with individual workers that required them not to join unions. The economy also helped dampen enthusiasm for organized labor. A decade of prosperity reinforced the image of the American corporation as the engine of plenty, as the domestication of such technologies as electric power, central heating, home appliances, the automobile and the telephone improved the standards of living for ordinary Americans.[45] Under such conditions, Alcoa, like most other major American industrials, was able to maintain union-free plants with little trouble.

Yet neither the external environment nor the coercive powers of management could have turned back the tide of unionization without some measure of corporate reform. "Welfare capitalism" and its creed of managerial paternalism underpinned an earnest attempt by companies in the center industries to develop a more rational and stable labor policy. The underlying motives were both humane and practical: attention to the welfare of workers, said U.S. Steel's Elbert Gary, was "a simple duty that industry owes to labor"; it was also, said General Electric's Gerard Swope, a way of getting men to increase output. Fostered by a number of leading businessmen (such as Swope and Bethlehem Steel's Charles Schwab), business academics, and a new breed of professional personnel directors who were just beginning to make their presence felt in the larger corporate bureaucracies, welfare capitalism became a powerful counterforce to unionism.

But not all large corporations formally embraced the welfare capitalism. Alcoa, for example, had no formal personnel function as such until the mid-1930s, and relied on fairly traditional methods of hiring and maintaining its workforce. Health clinics, recreational programs, housing, and educational facilities were established at various plants by the 1920s, all of which efforts helped promote morale and loyalty. Alcoa also attempted to provide some form of pensions and tried to find ways to stabilize terms of employment, at least through short-term fluctuations in business conditions. But there was little articulation of corporate policy on labor welfare as such beyond some expression of the paternalistic sentiments of its top management.[46]

When the full force of the Great Depression struck, however, no amount of paternalistic good will could sustain the company's most important commitment to its workforce, the implicit promise of job security that grew out of the boom years of the 1920s. In the bleak years of the 1930s, capitalism writ large went on the defensive, as the popular image of business leadership fell thoroughly into disrepute. Conservative Republicans lost control of Congress, and prolabor Democrats were able to pass national legislation that created a positive legal basis for industrial organization. Under these conditions, the sleepy American labor movement awakened with renewed vigor. For the first time, American unions were able to organize the great industrial corporations where semiskilled labor on mass-production lines did not easily fit into conventional trade union categories. Propelled by hard times, greased by rage against the discredited industrial order, and sustained by more favorable Government policy, industrial unionism arrived with the same remarkable speed that the industrial corporation had a half century earlier.

The shift in Government policy was especially important. In 1932,

the Norris-LaGuardia Act made explicit the worker's right to freedom of association without employer interference, outlawed yellow-
dog contracts, and restricted conditions under which courts could
issue injunctions in labor-management disputes.[47] In the following
year, Congress passed the National Industrial Recovery Act (NIRA),
the Roosevelt administration's ambitious experiment in economic
control, which contained in Section 7A provisions granting workers
the right to collective bargaining through representatives of their
own choosing and enabling industries to set maximum hours and
minimum wages. It was, declared Gomper's successor, William
Green, "a charter of industrial freedom" for millions of unorganized
workers.

Union membership in the unorganized mass-production industries
surged nationally in the early months of the NIRA, but employers
either ignored Section 7A or, like Alcoa, denied its full implications
while counting on the inability of the unions to mount effective
organizing campaigns. New union recruits in the major industrials
fell away until the political process once again intervened in a
strange twist of events. In May 1935, NIRA was invalidated by the
Supreme Court as an unconstitutional usurpation of power by Congress. Out of the congressional scramble to restore many of the pieces
of the NIRA emerged the National Labor Relations Act, the cornerstone of modern labor legislation. Commonly known as the Wagner Act, this legislation rewrote Section 7A to render the principle
of collective bargaining less ambiguous and less susceptible to company interpretation. The act reaffirmed the right of employees to
organize, outlawed the imposition of company unions, and explicitly
forbade employer interference, coercion, or influence on the process
of unionization. A key provision lodged exclusive collective bargaining rights for all nonmanagement workers in whatever representatives were designated by a majority of workers in an election
monitored and certified by a new National Labor Relations Board.

In the spate of aggressive union activity that followed passage of
the Wagner Act (which in 1937 withstood a test in the Supreme
Court), the Committee (later Congress) of Industrial Organizations
(CIO) was born. This new national union was the brainchild of John
L. Lewis of the United Mine Workers, who in 1935 led a large coterie
of reform-minded trade union leaders out of the AFL to concentrate
on the broad-scale organization of industrial workers. At the end of
1937, the CIO had mounted successful organizing drives in steel and
autos as strikes swept through the American economy. This goaded
the AFL, which had been trying to incorporate many semiskilled

and unskilled workers into its ranks, into action. A bitter rivalry emerged between the two nationals, a rivalry that was fanned by the mutual animosity of its two leaders and by the AFL's aversion to communist and socialist unionists who found the CIO to be a useful outlet for their ideological fervor and organizational skills. Struggles between the unions for control of local members were often as intense and violent as those between labor and management. In the aluminum industry, labor rivalry would ultimately lead to a fragmented union structure, which today is divided among three major national organizations and a number of smaller craft unions.

As World War I had marked the ripening of the large managerial corporation, World War II marked the flowering of the industrial labor movement in the United States. Despite considerable resistance from many employers, organized labor had already secured at least a foothold in all the important mass-production sectors of the economy. Now, unions could extend their sway and consolidate their gains under the emergency, labor-short conditions of war; often they did so by launching crippling strikes. The major national unions also could begin to make their collective power felt in both local and national politics by devoting money and manpower to the election of candidates committed to labor's agenda. This served only to harden the identification of the Republican Party with big business, on the one hand, and the Democratic Party with "the common man," on the other. And Alcoa, through its Mellon connections, was one of the most conspicuously "Republican" big businesses.

In 1947, the passage by a Republican Congress of the Taft-Hartley Act clapped restraints on labor's ability to strike without due process; outlawed the closed shop, secondary boycotts, and jurisdictional strikes; made it possible for states to pass "right-to-work laws"; stopped the use of union funds in political campaigns; and forced union officials to foreswear any affiliation with the Communist Party. But Taft-Hartley, which placed some constraints on the behavior of unions as had the Wagner Act on the behavior of corporations, was ironic testimony to the power of "Big Labor," whose role in the American economy was secure. Nationally, unions covered about two-thirds of the manufacturing workforce. In basic industries dominated by the center firms of the economy, union organization was nearly complete. Thus, out of the ebb and flow of American politics, unions had finally won the right to serve as bargaining agents for workers. No longer would the industrial corporation be able to combine its capital with labor for profit without first negotiating the costs and conditions of labor with the organized power of the workers themselves.

first negotiating the costs and conditions of labor with the organized power of the workers themselves.

We shall see that unionization at Alcoa followed the general pattern after 1935. By the end of World War II, the labor union had become yet another large, bureaucratic entity that demanded the aluminum worker's allegiance, defined the work, and either limited or expanded freedom and compensation – hopefully in the worker's best interest. For management, the union became yet another formally organized, corporate stakeholder in the business. But unionization was not the entire story. The internal evolution of the corporation was also important in the realignment of power between workers and managers. Even before unions took hold, Alcoa had begun to develop personnel policies that reduced the arbitrary power of the shop foreman. The threat of unionization helped stimulate and direct this process, but the rationalization of labor policy and practice was also in the interest of a company that wanted nothing more than peaceful and productive workers. Over time, Alcoa's labor relations moved toward greater stabilization of wages, more equitable treatment of individual employees, improved job security, and the demise of a tradition that regarded labor strictly as a commodity to be bought in the open market. The result was a rule-bound, "internal labor market"[48] in which the relationships between managers and workers became subject to well-defined laws, principles, and procedures.

Alcoa

In the chapters ahead, we shall see that Alcoa's strategic, structural, regulatory, and labor histories corresponded in their main outlines to the general patterns of big business in America. Like other large, complex business enterprises, Alcoa passed through definable stages of organization and administrative control that transformed it from an owner-managed, "family" firm, with relatively informal methods of administration, into a more professionally managed, "public" corporation, characterized by bureaucratic systems of control. Like all such corporations, Alcoa increasingly became subject to external constraints on its business behavior in deference to larger social interests. And like all great industrial concerns, Alcoa became subject to the unionization of its nonmanagerial workforce, which transformed the free-market relationship between owner and employee into more formally administered processes of negotiation and arbitration.

This is not to say, however, that Alcoa's experience was merely derivative or mimetic. In several crucial respects – and not merely in details – Alcoa's experience was profoundly peculiar, *sui generis*, dictated by the special nature of its markets, its technology, its circumstances, and its leadership. What makes Alcoa's particular story significant, in fact, are the many unique ways in which the company managed its opportunities and constraints over time. Alcoa's evolution into a modern bureaucratic enterprise proved to be an unusually protracted process. Its antitrust experience was extraordinarily problematic, and at one point almost disastrous. On the other hand, its labor relations, though sometimes stormy, were relatively easy over the long haul, when compared to the experience of other sectors of heavy industry.

What is perhaps most significant about Alcoa is its durability in a world where most businesses emerge, grow, then flicker and vanish after relatively short periods of time. Throughout its nearly one hundred years, Alcoa has been constantly vulnerable to serious challenges – to changes in the political and social environments, to shifts in market structure, to new forms of technology, to internal stultification. Every year that it has been in business, it has had ample opportunities to fail. And so, as we return to our more detailed discussion of the corporate history, keep in mind that we are dealing with the history of a venerable enterprise that has successfully adapted itself to the major challenges confronting it, time and again.

3

Building a big business:
markets, strategy, and structure
through the First World War

"While it was a great and wonderful thing to invent the process for making aluminum," said Arthur Vining Davis, "it was a totally different and as it actually turned out an infinitely more difficult problem to make aluminum commercially, and a still greater problem to utilize the aluminum when made."[1] The great challenges for the owners of the Hall and, later, Bradley processes extended beyond raising seed capital, developing the basic techniques of manufacture, and defending the company's patents. From 1891 to World War I, the transformation of The Pittsburgh Reduction Company from a small producer of a proprietary product for limited markets into a center industry of the national economy required strategic imagination, a broad conception of markets, a willingness to invest huge sums of capital, and the development of expertise along a chain of specialized functions – from the extraction of raw materials to the sale and servicing of final products.

It was Charles Martin Hall's vision and his backers' intention to transform the market status of aluminum into a common metal. Accomplishing this goal during the life of the patents required active cultivation of the market through demonstration and promotion of aluminum as a substitute for more familiar materials. A strategy of rapid expansion of productive capacity was supported by a policy, from the beginning, of plowing back earnings. The directors were far more interested in building their business than in milking their patent monopoly. Only twice, during the company's first decade of business, were dividends on the company's stock paid out, and in the years before World War I, dividends were kept generally at levels well below ten percent of the company's authorized capital.[2]

Once the owners and managers of The Pittsburgh Reduction Company established their core business in aluminum smelting, they developed strategies for vertical integration, moving forward into fabrications, which were vital to the creation of new markets, and backward into the extraction and manufacture of raw materials, which ensured a reliable flow of inputs to the ever-expanding productive capacity. Integration also served to extend and protect the company's long-term position as the major American factor in the industry after the expiration of the Hall-Bradley patents. In the process, the company was careful to exploit its claim as a nascent industry to achieve tariff protection against potential foreign competition. Once its patents expired, the company managed to emerge from its first major encounter with federal antitrust action by foregoing some restrictive contractual agreements with potential competitors. The result, by World War I, was the creation of a major new industry in which there was only one basic producer, a company that had gone far to secure itself from competition and to establish itself as one of the world's largest and most thoroughly integrated manufacturers.

Developing the markets

Finding markets for aluminum was problematic in the early years. By the time The Pittsburgh Reduction Company moved from its experimental operation on Smallman Street to full-scale production at New Kensington, aluminum had very limited and somewhat exotic uses. The electrolytic process had lowered the costs of aluminum production, but the metal was still expensive at a base price of $1.21 per pound, and its vaunted applications were largely unproven. For other basic materials, such as iron, steel, and wood, mass-production techniques had been developed to meet rising demand in a national market. For aluminum, markets would have to be "made" in order to realize the light metal's potential for mass production. It was not immediately obvious that aluminum was a viable replacement for other materials generally, nor that it might become a superior alternative to some metal in particular, such as copper, against which aluminum would later compete for electrical transmission applications. Nor was it apparent that aluminum would find important uses in areas where its inherent qualities would be essential to the development of new technologies, such as aircraft. The major markets for aluminum were latent and would have to be cultivated like so many strange seeds whose mature plants were as yet unknown.

Lowering production costs and increasing output to bring the price of aluminum down was the major challenge facing the company during the 1890s. To make a significant market for aluminum at all, its price would have to come down substantially. Hall and Davis therefore concentrated their technical efforts on process improvements during the first few years of the business. As assistant general manager, Davis kept close watch over the development of all phases of production, which in the early 1890s ranged from the calcining (high-temperature drying) of alumina to smelting to the production of a limited number of sheet products and castings. Throughout the decade, he made "almost daily visits" from the general office in Pittsburgh to New Kensington, where "he got into his old clothes" and "kept everybody awake on the job."[3] But even as he toiled in the factory alongside his employees, he knew that mastering the techniques of production alone would not make the business a success.

Writing to Hunt from the factory, Davis explained that the company could bring down its costs of production dramatically "if we can run full month in and month out" and increase the ratio of reduction pots to inputs of electrical power. But higher capacity also greatly increased the cost of partial shutdowns. Davis had recognized a basic truth about large-scale, capital-intensive enterprise: that to realize economies from higher capacity, it was "cheaper" to "run full," even in slack times. But, at some point, the market would have to absorb the output, and that, Davis feared, might be more than the market could bear. It was, of course, possible to continue production on a small scale for limited markets and make a profit, but if the company were determined to grow through high-volume sales, then "our sales are going to regulate our costs."[4] More sales would support more capacity, which, in turn, would yield greater economies of scale.

In order to establish the strongest possible market position before the expiration of the patent monopoly, it became imperative to expand capacity as rapidly as possible. That the sponsors of the Hall Process were determined to transform aluminum into a mass-produced, common metal was obvious from the money they and their backers were pouring into the expansion of higher-volume, lower-cost operations at New Kensington.[5] During the critical period of transition from pilot-scale to full-scale operations, the company lost money and went deeper into debt, but the stockholders, for the most part, were prepared to be patient. In early 1892, Hunt was confident that major expansions in capacity would find support in the marketplace. During the early phases of his company's litigation with Cowles, Hunt rationalized the board of directors' quest for new sources of debt capital as follows:

> If the suit goes against us and the art becomes a free one, The Pittsburgh Reduction Co. would then be the largest manufacturers [sic] in the world and practically holding the trade in the [American] market; and having this once in our hands, we would be in a stronger position than our competitors. If we succeed in our suit, we are just that much further advanced; and if the money will earn a satisfactory return (as the Board are confident it will), we have considered it advisable to make the investment.[6]

Hunt's optimism was justified by rising sales. Just a glance at the statistics indicates that revenues swelled during a series of dramatic drops in the price of aluminum. Production jumped from around 4,000 pounds per month in 1891 to 1,000 pounds per day in 1893, when the company earned $139,726 after interest charges (or 13.58 percent on an average equity investment of $1,028,605), all of which earnings were retained in the business.

Cheaper energy, lower overhead, and production economies were derived from larger-scale operations at New Kensington, where four generators were driven by a single Westinghouse steam engine supplying electricity for up to twenty reduction pots. By the end of 1892, the price of a pound of pure aluminum ingot had come down to $0.85. The lower price helped stimulate an increase in sales in one year from 58,604 pounds to 138,307. In June 1893, Pittsburgh Reduction was the first customer of the new Niagara Falls Power Company with which it negotiated a 1,500-horsepower contract (expandable to 5,000 hp) in order to secure an even cheaper source of electricity than the coal and gas at New Kensington. By 1895, a plant at Niagara was in operation, based on a plan that would quickly allow for a doubling of capacity as the markets grew. The Board reported:

> Due to the much cheaper cost of electrical power, which is one of the leading costs in the manufacture of aluminum by the Hall process, as well as by decreasing the general costs per pound by the larger output, we can confidently look forward to a very marked decrease in the cost of manufacture and increased profit to the company from the operation of our Niagara plant.[7]

Fig. 3.1. Drawing of the upper and lower smelting works of The Pittsburgh Reduction Company at Niagara Falls, circa 1900.

The Pittsburgh Reduction Company was the first in a wave of metals and chemicals producers to begin operations at Niagara Falls between 1895 and 1910. Diverse concerns – Carborundum, United Barium, Electrical Lead, Auto-lite Battery, Union Carbide, North American Cyanamid, to name a few – followed in the aluminum producer's wake, to create a great complex of industrial concerns organized around electrochemistry. Charles Martin Hall moved to Niagara in 1895, where he became a pillar of the lively community of scientific and engineering professionals whose meetings, formal and informal, advanced both the theory and techniques of their common scientific discipline. Over the long term, everyone benefitted.[8]

In the shorter term, the move to Niagara Falls was motivated by the desire to find a cheaper source of energy, better to realize aluminum's potential for economies of scale through high-volume production. But the move itself was expensive. The high initial cost of building the Niagara Works, which, by 1907, included three large potlines (the connection in series of smelting pots sharing a common source of electricity), required taking on more debt, arranged by the Mellons. By late 1897, the company showed capital stock valued at $1,000,000 (an arbitrary figure since it was scarcely traded),

$200,000 in funded debt (through the sale of bonds), and $110,000 in mortgages. The mortgages were retired by late 1898, and then in 1899, after Alfred Hunt's death, the funded debt was retired through the sale of an unusual form of dividend-bearing preferred stock to the company's shareholders.[9]

Dramatic increases in the scale of production – accompanied by steady improvements in the smelting process and by the move to Niagara Falls to secure even cheaper energy sources – brought the cost of pure aluminum steadily downward. Thus, the price could also fall and still leave a wide enough margin for the company to extract a healthy profit. The directors felt it imperative to keep the price of aluminum low enough not only to compete favorably with "other common metals," but also to generate the high-volume sales so necessary to the company's long-term health. In 1895, the board of directors recorded that "the selling price for the year has been a gradually downing one, not on account of competition but on account of our own voluntary wish to encourage new customers for our very much larger output for aluminum which we intend to produce." In 1898, Hall stated flatly that given the company's intention to expand capacity, there was a continuing "necessity to increase [the] volume of business. This means lower prices."[10]

This strategy, the lowering of price through the achievement of scale economies, enabled The Pittsburgh Reduction Company to establish its early markets. Although inventories often became a problem, the long-term trend in sales was sharply upward. By 1894, the firm had not only turned profitable, but it was also able, that year, to weather a general business depression that spelled the demise of many capital-intensive firms. In September, the directors of The Pittsburgh Reduction Company reported a seven-percent return on capital investment and noted that "the company has been . . . in easy financial circumstances during the entire year."[11]

By 1900, annual American aluminum production was in the neighborhood of seven million pounds, while the American price had dropped to $0.33 per pound.[12] Meanwhile, economies of scale enabled the company to improve its profit rate – that is, its net earnings after interest and taxes as a rate on capital plus owner's equity – from somewhere in the neighborhood of 3.7 percent, from 1890 through 1894, to 5.9 percent, during the next five-year period. Then, at the turn of the century, The Pittsburgh Reduction Company shifted its pricing strategy in favor of stabilization. For several years thereafter, the average American price (protected by a tariff wall and international cartel agreement, which will be discussed later) hovered at $0.33 per pound, and the company's profit rate increased to about sixteen percent, on average, from 1900 through 1904.[13] Future sales, and profits, now depended on the company's ability to cultivate large-scale demand and therefore grow larger in a predictable pricing environment.

Increased sales of aluminum, however, were never a function of pricing alone. New applications had continually to be fostered, according to Davis, lest, "much to our disgust, we [remain] dependent upon novelties." It was important, he said,

> to find places where aluminum would really fit in. Aluminum in rolled steel and steel castings, aluminum alloyed with copper for making copper bronze, and aluminum sheet and castings for certain specific purposes were gradually developed until in the course of time we built up a consumption which had some merit and stability to it. To do this was really one of our most difficult jobs and as I look back upon it now, one which presented the greatest opportunity for catastrophe in the event of not finding these permanent uses.[14]

The "difficult job" of finding high-volume applications for aluminum had begun in earnest in 1892. Hunt made it a point to visit his company's customers and noted some sixteen "larger" applications for his company's product. At least half these uses for aluminum were due to its specific technical advantages. It was necessary for making aluminum bronze and was becoming established as a deoxidizing agent in the manufacture of steel castings. But other uses were being discovered in light-machinery parts, in the alloying of other metals, in architectural uses, and even horseshoes, where light weight and corrosion resistance were important advantages.[15]

Every new application involved the substitution of aluminum for other metals. Because metals are not interchangeable in their properties or performance, The Pittsburgh Reduction Company had to demonstrate that aluminum was a superior material for many specific applications, even where it may have enjoyed a price advantage. This was especially difficult to accomplish in the absence of a well-defined body of knowledge about the specific behavior of aluminum under various conditions of fabrication. There was no accumulation of empirical rules for rolling or casting the metal. Established foundries, rolling mills, or wire-drawing plants with investments tied up in better-known metals had little incentive to experiment. Lacking large-scale fabricators for its increasing capacity to produce aluminum ingot, The Pittsburgh Reduction Company moved its own activities "downstream" by adding foundry, wire-drawing, tubing,

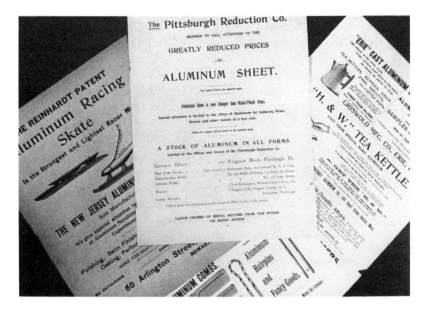

Fig. 3.2. Early advertisements for semifinished aluminum stock and finished products.

and other fabricating facilities to its plant at New Kensington. Within a few years, the company had become its own largest customer for aluminum, which it then transformed into a multitude of products for industrial, end consumer, and even military uses.[16]

The Pittsburgh Reduction Company introduced new products via aggressive campaigns of demonstration and education. Before his death in 1899, Hunt, along with other company officials, spoke and published widely on the properties and uses of the metal. Attempts by more venturesome fabricators to apply aluminum to a variety of products caused the company considerable anxiety, as skepticism arose in many quarters as a result of exaggerated claims or inappropriate applications. Recognizing the danger, Hunt took pains to publicize the limitations as well as virtues of aluminum in exhibitions and through publications in trade journals, scientific forums, and metals industry associations.[17]

From the mid-1890s into the first decade of the twentieth century, the fastest growing application of aluminum was in cooking utensils. According to one company official, before the Second World War, aluminum was best-known (often only known) to the general public through kitchenware. Entry into this important market illustrates

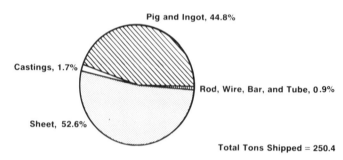

Chart 3.1. The Pittsburgh Reduction Company shipments by product/technology class, 1895 (percent total tonnage). *Source: Alcoa Plant Histories.*

the process by which The Pittsburgh Reduction Company extended its business forward from reduction to fabrication to marketing. In 1899, the company had tried to sell aluminum to a manufacturer who would then cast it into teakettles. Upon discovering that there was no strong market among light manufacturers for making castings from ingot, the company had then attempted to sell rolled aluminum sheet to stamped cooking-utensil manufacturers after persuading them of the merits of the shiny, lightweight, highly conductive, acid-resistant metal. But the markets for aluminum utensils developed unevenly. Consumers were often discouraged by problems arising from poor handling or cleaning and by the poor-quality manufacture of finished pots and pans. The company found the solution to that problem by acquiring the necessary expertise.

It happened that in 1901, Hill, Whitney & Wood, a Massachusetts producer of aluminum "thickware" utensils went bankrupt. Technically, it was a good operation; its failure was attributed to its having been undersold by manufacturers of lower-quality "thinware." The Pittsburgh Reduction Company, anxious to maintain high-quality utensils in the market, decided to operate the business. It took over Hill, Whitney & Wood's assets in settlement for its unpaid obligations. The utensils machines and dies were moved to New Kensington along with its former owner, who became supervisor of the company's new utensil department.

Among the former customers of Hill, Whitney & Wood was a small central Pennsylvania partnership that assembled kettles and coffee pots for door-to-door sales with noteworthy success. The two partners, John H. Wilson and Charles Ziegler, were recruited by The Pittsburgh Reduction Company, and a wholly owned subsidiary, The Aluminum Cooking Utensil Company was organized. The new company adopted a successful direct-marketing strategy by developing a door-to-door sales force composed mainly of college students as "an educational campaign to housewives . . . which would probably pay its own way in sales." While this was not considered to be "a dignified or ethical way to sell a high-grade line of goods," according to Wilson, it was certainly effective. The program was expanded when retailers showed little initial interest. In 1938, long after the company's "Wear-Ever" utensils were marketed through retail stores, canvassers still accounted for about half the line's sales.[18]

The production of cooking utensils did not involve economies of scale; it was a naturally competitive field for many producers. In 1909, the company was only the third largest manufacturer of aluminum cooking utensils in the country, but it subsequently expanded production through the Aluminum Goods Manufacturing Company, a partially controlled subsidiary. In 1912, Alcoa's kitchen utensils had more than seventy-five percent of the burgeoning American aluminum utensils market. Following Hill, Whitney & Wood's policy, Alcoa manufactured its utensils from a thicker sheet than normally used by independent fabricators, and its products were branded. By controlling the quality as well as distribution of cooking utensils, the company was able to secure a dominant hold on this important end market while expanding the outlets for its expanding capacity to produce ingot.[19]

On other fronts, the company was developing an impressive catalogue of small products, including such items as bicycle parts, semaphores, cameras, shoe eyelets, horseshoes, locomotive headlight reflectors, and lithographic stones. These were not high-weight applications, but as such products proliferated, they provided the company with important experience in the nuances of aluminum fabricating methods. The learning process inside the company was transmitted to outside communities of metal fabricators through trade association publications, academic treatises, expositions, and Alcoa salesmen. By 1900, the substantially lowered price of aluminum and a growing consumer acceptance for a wide range of small aluminum products had rendered the light metal a viable substitute for brass, zinc, tin, and iron in machine parts, electrical apparatus, containers, utensils, and novelties.[20]

Exogenous technological advances spurred new aluminum applications: the development of the oxyacetylene torch, for instance, made it possible to weld and solder aluminum more reliably (aluminum is an inherently difficult metal to join). A combination of ammonium nitrate and aluminum powder was discovered in 1901

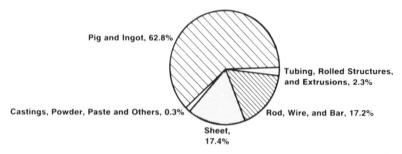

Total Tons Shipped = 19,000 (approx.)

Chart 3.2. Alcoa shipments by product/technology class, 1911 (percent total tonnage). *Source: Alcoa Plant Histories.*

to produce a powerful explosive. By World War I, either in response to external discoveries (coming mainly from Europe) or as a result of its own development work, Alcoa produced aluminum alloys in sheet, wire, rod and bar, tubing, extruded shapes, forgings, castings, powder, and paste for producers in a broad array of markets, which well before the war even included some automotive and aircraft applications. The progress of aluminum in the marketplace was summarized in 1909 by Joseph W. Richards, the country's leading academic authority on the metal:

> ... aluminum seems finally to have attained a position among commercial metals where it is treated entirely on its merits. In the early days of the industry the claims for aluminum with regard to its noncorrosive qualities, lightness and other distinguishing characteristics, were so exaggerated that it failed to measure up to expectations thus created. It was tried in many uses to which it was not suited, and a reaction occurred, so that the real merits which the metal possesses have been somewhat discounted for a number of years. This condition no longer exists and today aluminum is ranked among metals according to its value.[21]

The growing market in cooking utensils, of course, helped establish aluminum as a common metal. With the establishment of that line of business, The Pittsburgh Reduction Company was no longer entirely dependent on specialty products for numerous small consumers. But the great future for aluminum as a ubiquitous staple product lay in the high-volume markets of the transportation, electrical transmission, architectural, and general engineering fields. By the early twentieth century, the electrification of American cities

Table 3.1. *Alcoa production of pig aluminum and sales of
aluminum products, 1889–1909 (pounds)*

Fiscal year	Pig production (lb)	Product sales (lb)[a]
11/88–		
12/31/89	10,440	6,943
12/31/90	44,854	42,692
12/31/91	47,594	59,604
8/81/92 (8 mos.)	83,293	87,335
8/31/93	215,517	147,152
8/31/94	494,459	361,257
8/31/95	500,732	612,360
8/31/96	1,001,780	833,785
8/31/97	2,371,345	1,551,882
8/31/98	2,992,511	2,805,966
8/31/99	3,261,775	4,025,718
8/31/00	5,061,695	4,525,394
8/31/01	5,738,256	5,808,607
8/31/02	7,477,581	5,970,706
8/31/03	8,311,453	6,462,965
8/31/04	10,261,643	7,534,951
8/31/05	13,276,596	10,236,017
8/31/06 (16 mos.)	25,183,015	20,439,889
8/31/07	22,245,852	13,707,443
8/31/08	11,651,518	12,795,005
8/31/09	35,164,853	30,003,704

[a]Includes consumption within Alcoa companies.
Source: Alcoa Plant Histories, Vol. 17.

in both telecommunications and power was well under way. The
automobile was no longer a mere curiosity as the development of
the internal-combustion engine and production techniques were
promising to make it an affordable and reliable means of mass transportation. The company recognized the potential for aluminum in
these new basic industries.

Penetrating these lucrative industrial markets depended on the
solution of technical problems, on aggressive and specialized selling
techniques, and on price. The marketing of aluminum electrical wire
and cable are good cases in point. Electrical wire was one of the
earliest products of The Pittsburgh Reduction Company and was
installed in the company's own potrooms in the early 1890s. A vivid
piece of company folklore is the story of how A. V. Davis, in 1899,

sold electrical cable conductors to a utilities syndicate in San Francisco before he had any facilities to produce the goods. After failing to find any existing wire or cable manufacturer willing to try, Davis hastily installed a rod mill along with wire and cable machinery in the New Kensington plant.[22] But having the capacity to produce did not ensure that the product would be bought.

Indeed, neither wire nor cable found significant markets right away. For wire, price was the main factor. There could be no external demand for aluminum wire unless a rising trend in the price of copper continued until it met the falling price of aluminum. In 1898, prices had drawn close enough so that the company felt that it could introduce aluminum conductors at a "development price" of $0.29 per pound as compared with $0.14 for copper. This price, given the trade-off between aluminum's density (30 percent that of copper) and its inferior conductivity (65 percent that of copper), yielded a slight cost advantage to users of aluminum. Alvah K. Lawrie, the company's general sales manager, touted the advantages of aluminum wire to the American Electrochemical Society:

> ... aluminum wire for electrical conductors has an advantage of being considerably lighter in weight, having the same conductivity and efficiency; that is aluminum wire of equal conductivity to copper wire should have a cross section of 160 for aluminum as against 100 for copper, but notwithstanding this increased cross section the weight of an aluminum cable of equal conductivity would weigh but 47% of that of the copper. Besides the lightness in weight, which is an advantage both in ease and economy of erecting and stringing the wire, there are incidental economies in the number of poles, insulators, etc., which are required, which are inducements to the purchase of aluminum wire outside of its characteristic of weight. In other words, aluminum can be furnished with no greater Ohmic resistance per thousand feet or per mile than a copper cable of given capacity, but of less than half the weight and at a saving in cost.[23]

By 1908, aluminum conductor wire was well-established, but the development of a market for cable was more complex. In cable, as in wire, the weight of aluminum held out promise for economies, primarily through the use of fewer and lighter supports for transmission cable, thus reducing construction costs for utilities employing the light metal. Yet aluminum was handicapped in the cable market by the metal's lack of strength for very-high-tension uses until that problem was solved in 1908 by William Hoopes, an electrical engineer at Alcoa, by an ingenious application of a composite material. Hoopes devised a cable consisting of a galvanized steel core around which he wrapped six aluminum strands, producing a composite cable that weighed twenty percent less and possessed fifty-seven percent more strength than an equally conductive copper medium.

Still, many technical problems had to be solved. Aluminum cable was weak, compared to copper, and had to be sold at a reduced price. The market for it, said Magee, was a virtual "dumping ground." According to Alcoa's chief engineer, aluminum cable simply "could not be made and used like copper; new methods of manufacturing, testing, handling, erection, splicing, all had to be developed without delay, or else the company would have to leave the electrical transmission business to the copper people." Again, much had to be learned about the special properties of an unfamiliar metal, mainly through empirical experiments. Within a few years the various problems were brought under control. By 1912, Hoopes's aluminum cable, steel reinforced (ACSR) had gained a firm toehold in the market for cable transmission, and the electrical conductor market, in toto, consumed about twenty percent of all aluminum sold in the United States.[24]

ACSR could be sold at prices higher than all-aluminum cable, offering utilities considerable savings, compared with equivalent lines of copper, in the number of transmission-line supports required to bear the load. Still, there remained the task of selling aluminum cable to customers reluctant to turn away from familiar technologies. Former company chairman Frank Magee (who had originally joined the firm in 1917) remembered the marketing problem from his vantage point as a young sales apprentice. Despite the technical advantages of ACSR, "there was a lot of skepticism," from both the purchasing agents of electrical utilities and electric trolley companies and "engineers who were stuck in their ways...." It was difficult, at first, to attract utilities customers to aluminum on its "engineering merits." Instead, prices were gutted. In order to penetrate new markets, promotional prices were justified by future prospects for higher-volume sales.

Alcoa salesmen tried to circumvent the engineers by going directly to the executives of utility companies. On one occasion, while carousing at an electrical association convention in Toledo, Magee was locked into a hotel room by his cronies, left in the company of an inebriated executive of a small northern Ohio utility "with the idea of, by God, I either sold it [cable] to him or else!" He did, and "it was the first order for [aluminum] electrical conductors in Ohio."[25]

Initially, price was the only factor in a cable sale. Only after a protracted period of education and experience did the inherent engineering merits of aluminum cable become a significant factor, relative to price, in holding the market. Thus, once an order was secured on the basis of a "developed price" (pitting "one foot of copper against one foot of aluminum"), the work had only begun. It was crucial, in order to close a sale, to offer substantial technical assistance. Because aluminum presented an unfamiliar set of construction problems, it was up to Alcoa engineers to analyze the topography, work with the suppliers of tower structures, and "practically lay out that line for them [the customers]."

The requirements for technical support proved to be ongoing. Early customers for cable "had some bad experiences . . . , largely because the fellows in those days didn't know how to handle it. . . . If they handled it like copper we were dead. Some guy got a prejudice against us and we couldn't get back in." And so specialized "cable supervisors" – engineers who assisted in the selling – were then assigned to help customers maintain the line and to perform occasional troubleshooting. In the process, innovation became a necessary adjunct to the service-support relationship. Clamps had to devised "to hold both the steel and aluminum," or to tie ACSR in with copper so as not to get "electrolytic action." Such accessories became "a very important and profitable part of the line." Vibration problems arising from the tension of the steel required novel dampening techniques, the development of which spawned a small research and testing facility at the Massena, New York, plant where wire and cable had been made since 1904. Over time, as utilities customers became more accustomed to working with aluminum conductors and with Alcoa engineers, aluminum took the market from copper.[26]

In the emerging automotive market, on the other hand, the inherent qualities of aluminum were immediately perceived as important. The development of copper- and zinc-aluminum alloys possessing far more strength, hardness, and elasticity than the pure metals made aluminum attractive to the makers of automobiles before the turn of the century. Aluminum's light weight and the easy machinability of its castings made the metal useful for many automobile parts despite the lower cost of iron and bronze castings. In 1904, according to the company's chief engineer, "demand was growing for sheet and castings for automobile bodies, and the Company was not only making fenders and other parts, but was trying its hand [no doubt a formidable undertaking] at building bodies at

Fig. 3.3.   Aluminum automobile carriages and workers at New Kensington, circa 1904.

New Kensington." Four years later, it was reported that "aluminum castings have been used for the engine bed, gear case, rear axle housing, and numerous other parts" of the automobile.[27]

By World War I, as much as twenty-five percent of annual aluminum production was sold in harder-alloy form, mainly to automobile manufacturers. Castings were especially important: By 1914, about eighty percent of American automobiles employed aluminum crankcases and gearcases, although, given the extremely limited development in hard alloys, a satisfactory substitute had to be developed to replace the cast-iron piston. The development of permanent-mold castings in 1912 made possible stronger, harder, and more machinable aluminum pistons, which found increasing markets in aircraft and truck engines in subsequent years. An opportunity to move permanently into the automotive market with aluminum sheet flared hopefully for a few years after the depression of 1908, when, Davis explained, aluminum prices plunged to a point that encouraged "the adoption of sheet aluminum for the manufacture of automobile bodies." In the long run, however, Alcoa was unable to sustain its early success in auto bodies. High-quality, deep-drawn steel (ironically made possible by the addition of small quantities of aluminum to steel ingot molds) proved much less expensive for the mass production of low-cost "pleasure vehicles." As Magee lamented, "we sold a modest amount of aluminum to the steel companies, but they took the market."[28]

Thus, the quest for high-volume markets was subject to technical threats as well as opportunities. But to capitalize on the opportunities, Alcoa had to learn to become much more than a primary aluminum producer. The case of aluminum cable, for instance, demonstrates a kind of linkage of technical functions along a chain from product innovation to introduction in the market to customer service that became crucial to the marketing of aluminum for high-technology applications. In order to develop and keep customers in such important markets, the company had not only to offer a good product at a competitive price, but also to participate directly in demonstrating its application and improving its performance.

More broadly speaking, there are three basic ways to expand the market for a technology: through the creation of new products, through additional sales to established customers, and through expansion of the customer base for established products. Alcoa pushed on all three fronts to develop the market for aluminum before World War I. In the beginning, the company's main problem had been to establish uses for aluminum, which required the development of novel techniques in fabrication and aggressive marketing to break down customer resistance to abandoning more familiar materials. Additional sales required attention to quality and careful consumer education, so that the actual performance of aluminum products would fall in line with expectations. Expansion of the customer base took place mainly within the United States market, where, because of initial resistance from customers, the company often found it necessary to make its own finished products. The American market was protected by tariffs for most of the period before World War I. At the same time, Alcoa expanded overseas in the export of aluminum from its Canadian works, the Northern Aluminum Company, Ltd., and of sheet and finished goods from its American operations (especially after 1910). A growing Canadian market for cooking utensils was met after 1914 in competition with European suppliers.[29]

Vertical integration

To support its expanding markets, The Pittsburgh Reduction Company integrated backward to secure a reliable supply of raw materials and energy. Making, rather than buying, certain basic material inputs for the production of aluminum was a simple solution to the problem of meeting highly specialized needs. Acquiring control over the inputs into the production of aluminum – alumina, cryolite, carbon, and electricity – arose from strategic as well as technical considerations. Although they provide little direct evidence on the decision-making process, we can get a glimpse of the strategic motives driving vertical integration from the board's minutes of 1895. By that time, the directors were

> looking forward with the larger output which we shall have in the future, to the necessity of putting in our own plant for the manufacture of alumina from the bauxite on, and also for manufacturing our own carbon anodes....
>
> With the use of aluminum metal itself as conductors for the electric current, in the future ... at a cost which will be an economy to us over the use of copper conductors as used in the past, with our own plant for the manufacture of alumina, and with direct connection with our bauxite ore supplies, the company will be in a position to manufacture the metal at the most favorable rates – more favorable than any other concern, which might start with any other process, could possible [sic] arrange in the future."

Thus, seven years into the business, the directors of The Pittsburgh Reduction Company had grasped the necessity of supporting growth with backward integration not only as a technical matter, but also as a barrier to entry. Moreover, as economies of scale reached their limits (when "the proportion of fixed charges to be distributed to the cost per pound could not be further reduced"), vertical integration would become increasingly important as a means for reducing costs.[30]

Some important steps toward self-sufficiency had already been taken. Facilities for the industry-specific production of carbon anodes and furnace linings were installed at New Kensington before 1894, and at Niagara, their production became an integral part of the smelting operations. The production of anodes required careful attention to the problems of size and capacity with relation to the changing capacities of pots – too small an amperage carried less than economically efficient amounts of current, whereas too large an amperage created other technical problems. Carbon pot linings required a high degree of precision in their manufacture as well, with respect to both strength and conductivity, lest they disintegrate in use from stress or overheating. In either case, faulty production could lead to shutdowns in pot operations, resulting in wasted labor and materials. Self-sufficiency became important with respect to other raw materials, cryolite and, of course, alumina.[31]

The process of backward integration was tied to a complex set of strategic concerns that were raised in an 1897 letter to Hall from Captain Hunt. Hunt raised two vital long-term issues, patents and tariffs, which he knew would affect the long-term strategic position of the company in its American markets, once the company's control of its patent monopoly had expired. At the time Hunt wrote his letter, the Hall patent (assuming it could be defended against infringement) afforded the company only nine more years to exploit its position as the sole American producer of aluminum. As for the tariff protection that the company enjoyed as a new industry, and that insulated the company from lower-priced metal from Europe, Hunt was sensitive to important shifts in the larger economic and political climate. As he saw it, there were clear signs that the Government's protection of major industries against foreign competition was becoming less popular among more-established corporations and the then dominant Republican Party. Therefore, Hunt surmised, the company "will have to be looking forward to the time when the Hall patents [sic] will have expired, and it must be our policy now for the next few years to strengthen and solidify the position of The Pittsburgh Reduction Co. that we shall be independent of both the tariff and the patent situation."[32] The way to achieve such independence was through continuing expansion of the company's fabricating facilities, on the one hand, and taking greater control of electrical power and mineral resources on the other.

Near-term cost considerations were also important. It was the Hall Process requirement for extraordinary quantities of electrical power that had piqued the company's interest in the pioneering developments of hydroelectric power under way at Niagara Falls. The Niagara turbine shafts provided "mechanical horsepower" to the smelting plant generators for conversion to electrical energy. In late 1896, all smelting operations were transferred from New Kensington, where the production of steam power from coal and gas operated at a distinct cost disadvantage, to the company's second plant at Niagara Falls.[33]

From that time on, the availability of inexpensive power became the major determinant in the siting of Alcoa smelters. Thus it was a matter of great strategic importance to lay claim to desirable hydro sites before the patents expired. Accordingly, The Pittsburgh Reduction Company began to acquire its own hydropower sites, the first, in 1899, at Shawinigan Falls on the Saint Maurice River in Quebec. This move across the northern border to where cheap water power was abundant had been planned as early as 1896, when the board's minutes noted that it would be necessary "to occupy the [Canadian] field to preclude the establishment in the future of works to manufacture aluminum at some of the Canadian waterpowers."[34]

The high cost of power made it only a matter of time before the company sought to free itself, as much as possible, from dependence on outside sources of supply. In 1906, The Pittsburgh Reduction Company built its own power plant on the American side of Niagara Falls to support the operations of a third company plant at that location. In the same year, the company acquired the power plant, canal, and riparian rights of the financially distressed St. Lawrence Power Company, which had been sending power under contract to the Massena, New York, works since 1903. The acquisition of the St. Lawrence Company brought with it the ownership of other concerns involved in local real estate, railway transportation, city lighting, and water supply. This was followed by an aggressive program of purchasing riparian rights along the Long Sault section of the St. Lawrence, but plans for the construction of a company-owned and -operated hydro project were defeated by the failure to obtain joint Canadian-American Government approval. Subsequent attempts to develop the water power for commercial production were thwarted by the opposition of conservationists who were politically powerful in New York and Pennsylvania.[35] In 1909, Alcoa (as the company had come to be called in 1907) shifted its attention to the Little Tennessee River, where it subsequently gathered up almost all power and riparian rights for a forty-mile stretch in the Great Smoky Mountains by purchasing the Knoxville Power Company and the Union Development Company (in Tennessee) and the Tallassee Power Company (in North Carolina). The company built its own dams and power stations to supply energy for its new smelting plant at Alcoa, Tennessee, in 1914. In 1915, a failing French venture known as the Southern Aluminum Company sold its assets in North Carolina to Alcoa. Those assets included, in addition to a partially completed smelter, a waterpower site on the Yadkin River. Alcoa's construction group, by now a formidable civil-engineering organization, built a dam and power plant to supply energy for the new

Badin Reduction Works, which, in the meantime, had begun smelting operations using purchased power.[36]

The acquisition, development, and expansion of hydroelectric power were paralleled by Alcoa's moves into mining and refining of mineral resources. The basic mineral resource in aluminum production, then as now, was bauxite, a common name for ores of varying colors and physical texture that are particularly rich in alumina, the direct material input into the aluminum smelting process. Alumina (aluminum oxide) is in fact found in all varieties of clay, but the best source in nature is bauxite, which carries a high percentage of alumina (more than fifty percent) chemically combined with water (as monohydrate or trihydrate) and "contaminated" with quantities of silica, ferric oxide, and titanium oxide. Bauxite was first identified in 1821 near the village of Baux by P. Berthier, a French chemist. Its native abundance was later exploited by the emerging French aluminum industry, which enjoyed some cost advantage in having a fruitful and conveniently located source of high-grade ore. In North America, a modest deposit of bauxite was found in 1883, in Rome County, Georgia. From there, the ore was shipped to independent refiners, who sold alumina for various chemical and abrasive applications. Within a few years, more substantial bauxite deposits were discovered in Alabama and Arkansas, where production began in 1891 and 1899, respectively. Bauxite deposits were first acquired by the company in 1894 through a small venture known as the Georgia Bauxite Company, but it was not until the late 1890s that major steps were taken toward the full integration of bauxite.[37]

Integration into bauxite occurred as follows. Hunt made an inspection tour of the Arkansas bauxite fields just as they went into production in 1899, when reserves in Alabama and Georgia were known to be approaching exhaustion. Anxious to secure better control over his sources of supply, Hunt purchased "for $60,000 a substantial acreage of bauxite reserves" in Arkansas, but that, too, soon proved inadequate. Thus, in 1906, the company acquired the General Bauxite Company of Arkansas, which held 15,000 acres in mineral rights, and three years later (just as its patent monopoly on the aluminum smelting process expired), Alcoa purchased the Republic Mining & Manufacturing Company from the Norton Company and entered directly into mining operations. Thereafter, Alcoa became a net seller, rather than purchaser, of bauxite, which it used to tactical advantage. Surplus bauxite and alumina were shipped to such chemical concerns as Pennsylvania Salt, Norton, and General

Chemical companies under contracts that prohibited the buyers from making aluminum.[38]

Bauxite supply continued to be a problem for the company, nonetheless. Reserves of high-grade ore in the United States were believed to be low, and the company frequently dispatched representatives to Europe to look into the prospects for securing sources of French, Austrian, and Italian ores. In 1915, the company went to the British and Dutch Guianas to explore their rich bauxite lands, and in December 1916, Alcoa organized the Surinaamsche Bauxite Maatchappij. Thereafter, all significant additions to Alcoa's bauxite reserves would come from overseas.[39]

Alumina posed a different set of problems, more technical than logistical. By the turn of the century, Hall had already turned his attention to the refining stage of production and had became convinced that aluminum could be manufactured by calcining and grinding high-grade bauxite and then feeding it directly into the electrolytic pots. It took about two pounds of alumina to smelt one pound of aluminum, and because the price of alumina at that time constituted about one-half the total cost of producing aluminum, Hunt became excited by Hall's idea. If "we can make as much aluminum per unit of horsepower from bauxite... as from pure alumina," he reasoned, "then it would seem that this is the field which is now ripest for us to investigate for increasing the economy of manufacturing." But no way was found to remove the silicon, iron, and titanium from "the bauxite-made aluminum," so Alcoa turned instead to refining its own alumina while increasing its bauxite reserves.[40]

In the 1890s, the company had relied almost wholly on the Pennsylvania Salt Manufacturing Company for its alumina. Not surprisingly, that arrangement came to be recognized as an undesirable dependency, and during the last year of his life, Captain Hunt devoted considerable efforts toward gaining more control over alumina, as well as bauxite supplies. In 1899, an experimental plant for refining bauxite was established at New Kensington. Three years later, a huge, six-acre plant was erected at East St. Louis, Illinois. The distance from mining operations was justified by access to cheap Illinois coal to power the refining operation, by a more available supply of labor, and by the strategic location of St. Louis as a shipping point. There, The Pittsburgh Reduction Company received bauxite, which had been shipped from Arkansas on the company's own railroad trunk lines and river boats, and then transformed it into alumina at a peak rate of some 30,000 pounds per day.[41]

At first, the company's refining methods were both inefficient and expensive. In 1905, rights were obtained to a process devised by an Austrian chemist, Karl Josef Bayer, whose patent would not expire until 1911. The Bayer Process, which is still used by Alcoa in modified form, involved the digestion of bauxite under pressure with caustic soda to form a solution of sodium aluminate. Filtering operations removed the impurities, which formed a highly alkaline residue known as "red mud" (the careful containment and disposal of which was the company's first conscious attempt at environmental controls), along with a dissolved alumina precipitated as aluminum trihydroxide. The trihydroxide was then washed and calcined to produce aluminum oxide. The entire refining process involved a complex of chemical and physical interactions and required monumental-sized digesting cylinders, pressure-reducing tanks, thickeners, and filter presses, all connected by a maze of pipes spanning acres of land.[42]

But the Bayer Process, which was Alcoa's first major attempt to adapt a "borrowed" technology into the chain of aluminum production, was not implemented expeditiously. Indeed, for several years, the refining process remained a bottleneck in the production of aluminum. (Even after opening its own refinery, Alcoa still had to rely on the Pennsylvania Salt Company for much of its supply for years to come.) It was not until 1909–10 that the ailing but still active Charles Martin Hall awakened to the full significance of the Bayer Process. In a series of letters to company managers and engineers, Hall carried on detailed discussions about the development of the Bayer Process at East St. Louis, where development, he thought, had become hindered by attempts to preserve and advance Alcoa's existing methods. "The Bayer process as practised at East St. Louis," he wrote, "is a hybrid between that and the [company's existing] process." Perhaps it was time to become humble enough "to investigate the [Bayer] process to its fullest extent," not only "very carefully, and at once, in the laboratory," but also "in the form in which it is used by other manufacturers." In a stern admonishment to the East St. Louis plant superintendent (which was equally a confession of the inventor's own myopia), Hall concluded:

> I do not want to see us make again the mistake which we did before – i.e. of underestimating the advantages of the process which our [European] competitors were using. We really ought to have known all about the Bayer process...five or six years ago, and not have gone along working our own process with the idea that it was superior, without really knowing....[43]

Fig. 3.4.   Interior of the powerhouse at the Massena, New York, smelter, circa 1903.

As Alcoa mastered the Bayer Process, a marked differential in the quality of internal and external sources quickly became apparent. In July 1911, the superintendent of the East St. Louis Works, Charles B. Fox, suggested that "we would be money in pocket if the Reduction Plants were to depend entirely on the East St. Louis Works, because we are now making alumina at a lower price than what we are paying the Penn Salt Company" and at higher quality. Fox recommended that Alcoa "suspend all further shipments [from Penn Salt] until such time as they can produce an ore equal of that which is being made at our plant." It would take several more years before East St. Louis could bring its rate of production abreast with the growing demand of Alcoa's smelters, but by 1915, the refinery's capacity was up to 700,000 pounds per day "on the same plot of land at which we originally made 30,000 pounds per day."[44]

The Pennsylvania Salt Company had also been The Pittsburgh Reduction Company's principal source of cryolite, the solvent for alumina in the smelting bath. This, however, was a highly risky arrangement. Cryolite was mined by the Danish Government from a fjord in Greenland from which it was shipped to America under exclusive contract to Pennsylvania Salt. By 1910, the aluminum company found it less expensive to produce its own synthetic version.[45]

Thus, Alcoa became a highly self-sufficient enterprise upstream. This was of crucial importance at the primary phases of production, where the coordination of throughput from mine to metal depended on reliable and adjustable flows of materials. Though no records have been found in which the economics of production were discussed before World War I, there can be little doubt that the refining operation had become the linchpin of economic aluminum production. The high operating cost of alumina production was, during the first two decades of the twentieth century, the focal point of Alcoa research, insofar as it existed, before the war. Moreover, as a future generation of economists would explain (see Chapter 7), the minimum efficient scale of production for a refining plant was much greater than that of a smelter. Several smelters, in other words, had to be built to take the optimal production of one alumina refinery. By World War I, the ore from Alcoa mines was crushed, ground, and dried by a beneficiation plant built at the mines near the company town, Bauxite, Arkansas. The ore was shipped on Alcoa transport to the East St. Louis refinery, which then shipped alumina to Alcoa smelters at Niagara Falls and Massena, New York; Shawinigan Falls, Canada; Alcoa, Tennessee; and Badin, North Carolina.

That was by no means the full extent of Alcoa's integration upstream. Most of the electricity consumed in the reduction process was converted by Alcoa generators, many of which were supplied by Alcoa water power. The company even built its own railroad lines, sometimes with a brash confidence in its own ability to get things done. For example, Calderwood, Tennessee, the site of an Alcoa dam, was linked to the nearest terminus of the Southern Railway in six weeks by the company, after Southern had offered to cover the six miles of rugged terrain in six months. When war broke out in Europe, causing the diversion of many American rail cars to the shipment of supplies for America's allies, the company purchased waterfront property across from Memphis from which it loaded ore onto its own fleet of barges. To mount all these capital-intensive activities, the company developed its own corps of civil and hydraulic engineers. After initially relying on outside consultants, an "engineering staff" was in place as early as 1906.[46]

Fig. 3.5. The smelting potroom at Massena, New York, in 1914.

Alcoa, of course, was also moving downstream into various lines of fabricated products. As an integrated enterprise, Alcoa was its own major customer for the aluminum ingot produced by its smelters, as fabricating facilities at New Kensington, Niagara, Massena, and Edgewater turned out sheets, rods, wire, cable, tubes, castings, and finished utensils for industrial and household customers. What ingot the company did not use was shipped to other fabricators. Such external markets would become increasingly important over time, and at the end of the Hall-Bradley patent period, Alcoa began to become more directly concerned with the state of its principal downstream markets.

As sole supplier of ingot, Alcoa had powerful leverage to organize and bring outside segments of the fabricating business under more direct control. In 1909, Alcoa chartered the Aluminum Goods Manufacturing Company in Newark, New Jersey, in order to consolidate three independent aluminum utensils fabricators. Part of Alcoa's plan was to improve the credit position and capital base of the firms to "properly promote the rapid growth of their business for which the future held great promise." The company also wanted to mitigate

Figs. 3.6 and 3.7. Aluminum sand casting (top) and permanent-mold casting operations (bottom), probably at Cleveland, circa 1910.

Fig. 3.8. Aluminum sheet production at New Kensington in 1912.

the effects of competition among the firms – to reduce the "petty quarrels" that often resulted in price wars, which "threatened the growth of the aluminum novelty business and thereby to diminish [sic] the Company's market for sheet and ingot aluminum...." For its pains in arbitrating the dispute and organizing the merger, Alcoa took a twenty-five-percent interest in the new company.[47]

Soon thereafter, in response to "a growing demoralization in the aluminum foundry industry" caused by competitive rivalry among several independent producers, Alcoa organized major foundries in Ohio, Michigan, and New York into the Aluminum Castings Company. The New Kensington foundry was folded into this new organization at Cleveland, where an impressive acquired staff of metallurgical scientists performed research and development in castings technology. Alcoa at first took forty percent of the new company's stock and later increased its share to half ownership. One hesitant target for the consolidation recounted years later the lengths to which he believed Alcoa had gone to bring the castings sector of the industry under control. According to Isadore Freud, part owner of the Michigan Aluminum Foundry Company, Alcoa had at first asked him to sell out his company. When he refused, he suffered damaging delays in ingot shipments, material thefts, and a loss of crucial employees to Aluminum Castings, all of which he attributed to the machinations of Alcoa. Finally, when his profits declined, he decided to sell out after all. Government allegations that the castings combination was formed so that Alcoa could discriminate in ingot prices so as to drive competitors of Aluminum Castings out of business were never adjudicated, but it is clear that, however it was achieved, consolidation helped Alcoa rationalize production, stabilize prices, and ensure a reliable market for its ingot. Contemporary estimates had the combination producing half the nation's output of aluminum castings by 1912, and so stock participation also meant handsome profits in this fast-growing market for aluminum applications.[48]

Among the world's other aluminum companies, only British Aluminium was fully integrated through all stages of production, though on a much smaller scale than Alcoa. In the absence of cartel arrangements or Government protection, integration conferred important strategic benefits vis-à-vis potential competitors. With the expiration of the company's patent monopoly, vertical and horizontal integration solidified Alcoa's dominance of the primary aluminum market in North America by improving its control over costs, technical know-how, and distribution. The most important barrier to entry to the production of primary aluminum was Alcoa's size and, by dint of its investment in huge production facilities, economies of scale that could not be achieved by potential entrants lacking the capital to match Alcoa's extensive operations. But large-scale production of aluminum required reliable fabricating outlets for the metal and reliable sources of power and bauxite, so that smelters could operate at high enough capacities to enjoy economies of scale.

That vertical integration also generated significant economies in its own right was an important conclusion arrived at by both defenders and critics of Alcoa's corporate structure in later years. Donald H. Wallace's critical study of Alcoa's dominance of the American aluminum industry before the Second World War credits the company's vertically integrated structure for having resulted in cheaper power, better quantitative and qualitative control of throughput, closer touch with markets, and therefore lower-cost production and distribution than would have been possible in an unintegrated industry. Yet, despite these economic benefits, in the eyes of a society fearful of corporate power, Alcoa's ability to sustain its monopoly control of smelting operations while extending its span of control over downstream fabricating operations as well, was something less than an unalloyed blessing.[49]

Market control and antitrust

Between 1900 and America's entry into World War I, capital investment in Alcoa grew from $2.3 million to more than $90 million. Growth occurred along all parts of the vertical chain and was financed principally out of retained earnings. Earnings were high in part because the company was able to command a closed American market. Fortune was with Alcoa. Exogenous forces – first, cyclical fluctuations in the economy, and later, the outbreak of war in Europe – always seemed to favor its market position, securing it against the incursions of competitors both foreign and domestic. In 1906, the Bradley patent, which had come to the company as a consequence of its legal tangles with the Cowles interests, bought Alcoa three additional years of patent protection in which to expand its operations and sales. 1905–7 were especially strong years for the economy and the industry, and by a conventional calculation the company enjoyed profits at a rate of 29.5 percent overall from 1905 and 1909. Profit rates fell after the expiration of the patents, to an average of 17.6 percent, until the outbreak of war in Europe, which then spurred Alcoa's sales and profits even higher, to 22.01 percent, from 1915 through 1919.[50]

Both before and after its controlling patents expired, the company's small group of stockholders preferred capital gains to dividends and plowed their profits back into the business to support an aggressive program of expansion.[51] The life of the Bradley patent ended in 1909 in the middle of a business recession (a hangover from the Panic of 1907), and in the slow recovery that followed, the American market for aluminum did not grow so quickly as to attract immediate entry. A positive side effect of the recession (from Alcoa's standpoint) was a dampening of incentive for others to invest capital in the aluminum field. Meanwhile, Alcoa continued to expand, thus constantly raising the ante for competitive entry. Every year that passed saw an improvement in Alcoa's economies of scale, its managerial and technical experience, and its markets for both primary aluminum and fabricated products.

Before 1909, when Alcoa was protected against the rise of competing domestic smelters by the Hall and Bradley patents, there were well-established producers of aluminum ingot in Switzerland, France, and England. Thus, in a global context, competition was formidable. The major European producers were The Aluminium Industrie A. G. of Neuhausen, Switzerland (founded in 1889 to exploit Héroult's patent), with holdings in France, Germany, and

Austria; the Societé Electrometallurgique Française (founded in 1888); Compagnie Alais (formed in 1894 to exploit the Hall Process and taken over by Pechiney – now finally convinced that the electrolytic process was a viable commercial proposition – in 1896); and the British Aluminium Company (1896), smaller but more highly integrated than the other three. Before World War I, additional aluminum producers were organized in England, France, Norway, and Italy. By 1909, the European aluminum companies produced more than sixty percent of the world's primary ingot, and had great potential to export large quantities of aluminum to the United States, which was the world's leading national aluminum consumer.[52]

Yet for many years, while it established and extended its sway in the American market, Alcoa was blissfully free from the threat of imports. Before the close of the Hall-Bradley patent period, protection against imports was achieved through high tariffs and, much more important, participation in international cartel agreements. Tariff protection, at least in the early years, supported Pittsburgh's hold on the American market because of the lower-cost operations of the major European producers, who had good access to high-grade bauxite reserves, cheap labor, and well-located sources of hydroelectric power. The European selling price, moreover, was held down by competitive conditions and by the tendency of European plants toward excess production. These facts worried the directors of The Pittsburgh Reduction Company who, even as they strove to reduce their costs, wanted to sustain as high margins as possible in the American market. They recognized the strategic importance of import duties on even lower-cost European metal and so lobbied hard for them. During the patent period, tariff protection for aluminum was strong. The 1890 import duty on ingot was a staggering $0.15 per pound. The duty was nearly halved to $0.08 by 1897, but, given the plunge in the price of aluminum, this figure was actually proportionally greater in relation to the costs of production. Despite Alfred Hunt's concern that this highly protective situation would soon disappear, the aluminum tariff was revised downward only once (to $0.07) before 1909.[53]

Tariff protection extended beyond aluminum ingot to fabricated products. Indeed, duties on semifinished products were even higher than on ingot; throughout the period, the tariff on finished goods ranged from a high of $0.13 to a low of $0.035 per pound between 1897 and 1913. Whether or not foreign producers would have chosen to sell aluminum in the American market below Alcoa's cost is unclear, but the world price for aluminum prior to 1909 was low enough to lend credence to A. V. Davis's claims in congressional tariff hearings that the Europeans enjoyed a decided cost advantage over Alcoa, even after accounting for the costs of shipping aluminum overseas.[54]

Not content to rely wholly on tariff protection, Pittsburgh found ways to participate, at least indirectly, in a series of cartel arrangements that had been formed by European producers between 1896 and 1908. The Pittsburgh Reduction Company entered into an agreement with the Swiss (the most important producers in the European market at that time) in 1896, but the agreement worried company attorneys in light of the Sherman Act's proscription of cartels. Therefore, in 1901, when the company entered an arrangement with the major aluminum producers in France, England, and Switzerland, it did so indirectly through its newly formed Canadian subsidiary, the Northern Aluminum Company. In this way, by making the arrangement entirely one of foreign entities, the company hoped to avoid charges that it had illegally participated in a cartel. Under the terms of the agreement, each national producer was allotted the market of its own country as a "closed" market with prices fixed at about one cent per pound higher than for sales in the "open market." Intermarket transfers were regulated by quotas. The United States was treated as a closed market, the needs of which, under the formal terms of the agreement, were to be supplied by Northern Aluminum. In practice, Pittsburgh supplied the American market, and any exports it made of fabricated goods, which it was free to do at less than the cartel price, were charged against Northern Aluminum's quotas. This arrangement, in the absence of clearly defined judicial interpretations of the Sherman Act, was regarded by The Pittsburgh Reduction Company as technically correct, and Alcoa's de facto membership in the cartel was maintained through the signing of a new convention in 1906 and through Alcoa's explicit involvement in a division of markets and control of prices in 1908.[55]

It is impossible to ascertain with precision the effects of the aluminum producers' cartel (which took various forms over the years), but it seems at least to have served its main purpose of protecting the territories of the various producers until the depression year of 1908. One unintended effect of the cartel was to buoy world prices sufficiently to encourage rapid expansions in world productive capacity. At the same time, higher prices in closed world markets boosted Alcoa's position in the United States. All this worked as long as capacity did not exceed demand. But the very success of the cartel worldwide led to its undoing, as high prices whetted the expansive appetites of primary aluminum producers and encouraged the entry of newcomers. A world shortage of aluminum, in 1906–7, triggered a boom in plant construction in North America and Europe, which in turn ignited intracartel disputes on pricing strategies.[56] Once the business depression of 1907–8 struck with full force, prices collapsed and the cartel disbanded.[57]

The end of the international cartel posed serious problems for Alcoa in its American market. The number of European producers between 1901 and 1908 had increased from four to thirteen under the umbrella of the cartel price. Now, mounting inventories from overproduction led to a rapid decline in prices, which, according to one expert, fell "to a level definitely below the costs of all producers."[58] In the absence of any agreement on market territories, European producers began to dump their surplus metal in the United States, where demand was relatively strong and competition relatively weak. Lehigh College Professor Joseph W. Richards signaled Davis in April 1908 that foreign metal was being quoted in the United States at "some 10 cents per lb. below your present quotations" and that it would be advisable "to slash deeply into the price of aluminum . . . to discourage competition."[59]

Indeed, after 1909, rising imports provided the only direct threat to Alcoa's market position in primary aluminum. From 1909 to 1912, the average American price for a pound of aluminum sank to about $0.22, while the average European price stood even lower at $0.14. During that period, imports of European ingot increased from a negligible amount in 1908 to 10,324 metric tons in 1912, an amount equal to more than half Alcoa's own output. With the election of Woodrow Wilson, a strong, national protectionist policy that had been sustained through every administration since the Civil War was decisively reversed by the Underwood Tariff of 1913. Not persuaded by Davis's contention that a lower tariff would ruin Alcoa (and thereby the American industry), Congress slashed the duty on aluminum ingot to $0.02. But after a temporary reduction in revenues, which was attributed at least in part to the effect of imports, Alcoa's earnings once again shot up with the outbreak of war in Europe. Imports plunged rapidly after 1914, as overseas producers became but a negligible factor in the American market.[60]

One would think that by World War I there would have emerged other producers in the American aluminum industry. But even after its patents had expired, Alcoa's head start in primary aluminum had reached almost unchallengeable lengths. In the markets for

Fig. 3.9. Construction of the narrows dam for Alcoa's hydropower development on the Yadkin River near Badin, North Carolina, in 1916.

semifinished and finished aluminum goods, small fabricators sprung up on the periphery wherever technologies of production did not offer significant economies of scale (in castings or utensils, for example). But Alcoa was a major player in every aluminum market it chose to enter, and as a fabricator, it uniquely enjoyed the benefits of full integration.

Between 1891, when the Cowles Company had tried to expropriate the Hall Process, and World War II, there was only one significant attempt to compete with Alcoa in the production of primary aluminum in the United States. In 1912, a well-heeled group of European entrepreneurs launched a project to develop hydroelectric power for aluminum smelting in North Carolina. The Southern Aluminum Company was formed and headed by experienced promoters from the French industry equipped with both technical know-how and access to excellent sources of French bauxite. The project, however, foundered on the inability of the backers to procure further financing once war had broken out in Europe. Alcoa purchased the site and developed a large hydropower complex and smelter at Badin,

North Carolina. Because no comparably endowed or experienced group existed on the North American continent, Alcoa faced no other domestic challenge to its primary aluminum business.[61]

Alcoa's leaders had done everything well by business standards. They had cut the cost of their basic product substantially and developed markets with remarkable success in a short period of time. Its directors had wisely nurtured its capital, reinvesting substantial profits in the business, generally avoiding the temptation to milk the business for all it was worth in the shorter term. As managerial capitalists, the leaders of the company were striving to build a business, not simply to realize an immediate return on their personal investments. In the process, they were contributing significantly to the financial and technological wealth of the society at large. Yet, had they thought about it, they must have realized that sooner or later their dominance of the American aluminum industry had to arouse the skeptical scrutiny of the Federal Government.

During the Taft administration, no important business was free from scrutiny, as antitrust suits and congressional investigations dominated the political headlines. In May 1911, the Department of Justice filed a complaint charging Alcoa with illegal participation in foreign cartels, with making restrictive covenants in the purchase of alumina and bauxite, and with undertaking unfair competitive practices in some of its downstream markets.[62] Anxious to avoid a confrontation, the directors of the company ordered complete cooperation with the investigators, and the matter was settled within a year without going to trial. In the end, Alcoa was not judged to have built its "substantial monopoly of the production and sale of aluminum in the United States" illegally, but it was enjoined from some specific practices pending the rise of greater competition in the industry.[63]

At stake was the Government's desire to limit anticompetitive business practices that derived from the existing market power of the firm, albeit those practices from the company's standpoint may have seemed eminently reasonable in the normal course of competitive enterprise. The terms of a "consent decree" signed by Judge James M. Young of the District Court of Western Pennsylvania, in June 1912, spelled out how Alcoa used both its patent position and market power to head off competition in the United States. The decree forbade the company to enter into any cartel agreement through any subsidiary or agent that would restrain imports or affect prices of bauxite, alumina, or aluminum. It struck down provisions of exclusionary agreements made in the patent period (but continuing beyond it) between Alcoa and other companies involved in bauxite and alumina (the General Chemical Company, the Norton Company, and the Pennsylvania Salt Company) that limited their rights to make aluminum or to sell bauxite to third parties for ultimate conversion to aluminum. Alfred Cowles testified in a later proceeding that it was Alcoa's continuing control of bauxite and alumina, after its patents had expired, that had dissuaded him from trying to reenter the aluminum business.[64]

Voided also was an agreement with an independent aluminum utensils manufacturer that limited its markets geographically. In addition, the decree issued a laundry list of injunctions that stemmed mainly from concern over Alcoa's relationship to such entities as the Aluminum Castings Company and the Aluminum Goods Manufacturing Company. The company was enjoined from combining in any way with other manufacturers to control output, delaying or cutting off shipments without good cause, discriminating in prices or conditions of sale between independent firms and firms in which the company held an interest, demanding information on customers' plans to use metal purchased from the company, making any intimations that aluminum supplies from Alcoa depended on restraints by customers either with regard to their own growth in the aluminum business or with regard to their dealings with Alcoa's competitors.[65]

The speed of the settlement and the absence of any penalties imply that the ship of state had merely intended to fire a warning shot across the company's bow. There were to be no drastic remedies such as had been applied to Standard Oil or American Tobacco, which had suffered dismemberment at the hands of the Federal Government. Yet, as much as Alcoa would have preferred to grow unfettered by serious competition, its future now depended on its officers' sensitivity to limits placed on their behavior in the marketplace by a growing presence of extramarket regulatory forces. In acquiring the assets of the Southern Aluminum Company in 1915, for instance, Alcoa was careful to consult with the Justice Department in advance. And from 1912 forward, Alcoa's prices and behavior toward its competitors were tempered by a healthy fear of the Sherman Act. Ironically, it was this fear that kept the company from trying to extract the level of monopoly profits that might have provided the necessary incentive for competitors to enter the smelting business.[66]

Alcoa enjoyed a respite from serious legal and political pressure until World War I, but was thereafter to be dogged by a continuing round of Government investigations and antitrust litigation from both private and public antagonists. Testifying before the War Industries Board in 1918, Davis freely acknowledged that "we are a monopoly," as he explained his company's position on pricing.

> I suppose it has always been our aim to foster this industry. We started in this industry many years ago, making 30 pounds of aluminum a day; we have built it up and we consider ourselves, with some pride, the father as well as creator of this industry; it has always been our conception that the stability of price was the basis on which to build the industry.[67]

But what A. V. Davis considered to be a matter of pride was precisely what worried others: Alcoa was indeed a monopoly and, as such, had virtually complete discretion (at least in the short run) over the price and output of aluminum. Again and again, this simple fact, buttressed by the memory of the strategies and tactics of the company's early years, was to be cited as evidence of excessive corporate power.

Management and structure before World War I

On the eve of America's entry into the Great War, Alcoa was more than a large company; it was evolving into an elaborate business and technological network. In little more than a quarter century, the company had acquired a range of technical functions that rippled like a set of concentric waves from the core of the smelting business. From its initial focus on producing pure aluminum on a high-volume, low-price basis, Alcoa had become involved in the fabrication and use of semifinished and finished goods in order to establish a large market for the basic product. Then, as we have seen, it moved backward into the extraction and manufacture of raw materials and energy, acquiring capabilities in mining, hydro and electric power construction, and transportation. It took vigorous management to coordinate the increasing scale and complexity of the company's various parts over a wide geographic area.

By World War I, Aluminum Company of America was both an operating and a holding company. From its Pittsburgh headquarters, Alcoa maintained its control over the country's entire capacity in primary aluminum production directly under its own corporate name. Major bauxite and alumina sources and most of its fabricating facilities were grouped under wholly owned subsidiaries operating in the manner of "incorporated departments." Power and transportation requirements were met through a variety of arrangements ranging from direct ownership and operation (either through Alcoa or subsidiary corporate charters) to outright purchase from independent suppliers. For many years, the coordination and operation of the various parts of the business were achieved through rather informal relationships. There was no organization chart – the first would be drawn up in 1919, when the company first established a central office along functional lines – and no systematic bureaucracy.

At top and center of Alcoa's aluminum empire stood the board of directors, comprised of the men who owned the lion's share of the business. Several small blocks of stock had been granted to management employees under a profit-sharing plan begun in 1904. But the board remained one that was essentially representing the interests of its own membership which, by 1917, was a small group of men, some of whom simply owned, others who both owned and managed the company.

As owners, the Mellons controlled as much as a third of Alcoa's stock by World War I,[68] although they left the management of the company to others. It was a cornerstone of their business philosophy to separate finance from management. This is not to say that they were always content to be minority shareholders in Alcoa. Indeed, on at least one occasion, they had hoped to seize control of the board. In 1899, when R. B. Mellon became president upon Alfred Hunt's death, the company's funded debt was retired through the sale of an unusual form of dividend-bearing preferred stock to the shareholders. Because the preferred stock was to have voting power, it was A. W.'s hope to take a majority share, but he confessed to a correspondent that "the other side [the company's management] have been alert and may continue to dominate the business." That is exactly what happened when the board voted to issue the new stock on a pro rata basis. Thereafter, until the 1920s, both ownership and administrative control lay on the side of the company's owner-managers.[69] Indeed, since February 1910, the board had been led by owner-manager Arthur Vining Davis as company president. It is hard to ascertain with precision the relative holdings of the principal stockholders in the business (so confidential was the matter that no formal records were kept on their holdings), but it is clear that by World War I, basic policy and strategic decisions were approved by Davis, who was in effect the company's chief executive officer.

Davis had actually taken charge of the company's operations at the turn of the century after Alfred Hunt's death. He continued to serve as general manager under the presidency of Richard B. Mellon, but even before Mellon yielded the presidency to him, Davis was making important strategic decisions. He derived much of his power from Hall. The two men, who had labored together in the little Smallman Street plant, remained very close friends over the years, and on the board, they were a powerful tandem. Before Hall died, Davis appears to have held about twenty-five percent of the total outstanding common stock in his own right, and according to a knowledgable contemporary, he and Hall together held "a little more than one half" the company's common stock.[70]

A. V. Davis's authority was enhanced by a brilliant intellect, a fierce dedication to perfection, and a vivid though quarrelsome personality. Despite his small physical stature, Davis possessed charismatic qualities: intense eyes, a quick wit, a genuine self-assurance, and requisite amounts of manipulative charm and intimidating temper. It was his voice, one journalist wrote, that most commanded attention: "it calls to mind the rushing of a heavy freight train through a long tunnel." It was also said that he possessed a smile that could in one instant transform his apparently grave and chilly demeanor into a warm beam of light. But all too often, he preferred to make his presence felt in the manner of a blunt weapon. When excited or angry – Davis was prone to sharp bursts of temper – his eruptions of thumping and screaming could leave bystanders shaken to the core. Yet he could remain remarkably controlled and calm in times of stress and, somehow, the combination of his attributes managed to inspire immense confidence in his leadership of the enterprise among his colleagues and subordinates.[71]

By 1914, Davis had disengaged from the operating administration of Alcoa. At some point (it is not clear when), he had moved to New York, although the company's headquarters remained in Pittsburgh. Roy Hunt remained in Pittsburgh, and as the senior ranking operating manager, he became Alcoa's principal day-to-day administrative officer. He and Alcoa's other managers got used to shuttling between their facilities and New York on an overnight train. One who no doubt spent a lot of time on the train was A. V.'s younger brother, Edward K. Davis, who had joined the company in 1901 on a part-time basis and had, like Roy Hunt, worked his way up through the ranks in both operating and staff capacities. Not yet an officer (in 1913, he had been made the company's general manager of sales), Edward Davis worked assiduously to develop a highly trained sales force for an expanding network of district sales offices.[72] Having his brother in such a key position no doubt helped A. V. Davis sustain his authority in Pittsburgh. In New York, Davis remained concerned with strategy and finance, and he liked to keep an eye on marketing, which he could do easily enough at the New York district sales office. New York was also the headquarters for bauxite and shipping, and it was from New York that Davis would develop his postwar plans for international development.

Upon Hall's death, Davis's position was further enhanced by a provision in the inventor's will. Hall, according to John R. Rogers, an Oberlin trustee, had "felt and often said that the success of his enterprise was very largely due to the business judgment and executive ability of Mr. Arthur V. Davis ... ," [73] and the provisions of Hall's will reflected the sentiment. Davis and Homer H. Johnson, the lawyer who had drawn up the will, were named co-trustees of the part of Hall's estate that he had left in the form of Alcoa stock. That amounted to 48,905 shares, or about twenty-six percent of the 187,000 shares of Alcoa common stock outstanding at the time. [74] "Mr. Hall," Rogers explained, "was very anxious that the control [of Alcoa] should be kept in the hand of Mr. Davis, and provided in his will that his [Hall's] stock should not be distributed to the beneficiaries, but held in escrow" for fifteen years with "only the income [dividends] paid to the beneficiaries," thus leaving Davis "the power of voting this stock and thereby controlling the company." [75]

Responsibility for managing day-to-day operations fell increasingly to Roy Arthur Hunt, son of the company founder. The younger Hunt had first worked for the company in 1902, when after his junior year at Yale, he applied for a summer job with The Pittsburgh Reduction Company, offering to do anything, "from digging a hole to emptying paper baskets." What he got was a job as a machinist's helper at the New Kensington Plant. A year later, after graduating, he went to work full time for the company as a "mill clerk." Though it may have been a foregone conclusion that the young man would eventually hold an important position in the company (he was, after all, principal heir to his father's stock), he learned the business from the ground up. His career progressed steadily. His managerial skills were nurtured carefully by Davis, who let him work his way through the ranks to become New Kensington plant superintendent in 1908. In 1914, Hunt was named general superintendent of all fabricating operations, and in 1915, just after Hall's death, he was elected to the board. [76]

With Davis firmly ensconced as its head, Alcoa's board of directors was a bastion of continuity. Its composition, after having seen twenty-one members come and sixteen members go during the first eleven years of the company's existence, had been very stable since the turn of the century, and by 1916, it was comprised entirely of old hands. In addition to Davis and the Mellon brothers, George Clapp and David L. Gillespie had served on the board since the early 1890s. Alvah K. Lawrie was a former sales manager, and George Gibbons, the one relative newcomer to the company, had been elected to the board in 1910, following the acquisition of his bauxite holdings. Roy A. Hunt, the newest director, was, of course, a major stockholder, as well as an experienced senior manager. Thus, by World War I, Alcoa's board was composed of a group of men most of whom had helped nurture the business for a quarter century or more, planning its expansion, securing and allocating its funds, appraising its performance, and dividing its profits. Longevity, ownership, and familiarity with the business helped ensure continuing agreement on one basic policy underlying the expansion of the business since the turn of the century – that earnings were to be plowed back to finance continuing growth.[77]

The board ruled over a strikingly simple company organization, electing only three corporate officers. Two of the three served as staff, not line, managers. George Gibbons, who had originally controlled the Georgia Bauxite and Mining Company, was both vice president and secretary of the corporation. Robert Withers, who started as clerk of The Pittsburgh Reduction Company, was treasurer. (No officer-rank replacement had been named for Hall who had also been a vice president.) These men appear to have worked closely with the board in the overall planning and appraisal of the business.[78]

Rapid growth had an impact on the structure of management. During the patent period, the firm grew to a size of about 4,000 employees in seven locations with more than a quarter of the work force located at New Kensington, site of the company's headquarters. Sales, including transactions within Alcoa's system of companies, increased to about $35,500,000. Between 1910, when Davis became president, and 1916, the company's sales more than quadrupled to nearly $145,000,000, while its workforce swelled to 14,000 employees in eleven locations.[79]

With the proliferation of operating sites, the old general manager's responsibility for day-to-day operations devolved upon the various heads of the subsidiary companies and the superintendents of Alcoa corporate plants. In 1911, Davis and his staff relocated their headquarters in Pittsburgh in order to disengage from the operational concerns of the New Kensington Works. At Pittsburgh, the general management of the company dealt with business policy, made fundamental strategic decisions, allocated capital resources, issued guidelines for uniform accounting procedures, and monitored the flows of materials and information between its many and varied operations. Otherwise, managerial authority was highly decentralized. Even though Davis made it a point to interview every candidate for a managerial position in the Alcoa system, he left internal operating authority to the plant superintendents, who were left to organize their own facilities and to run them, according to company tradition, like "little fiefdoms."[80]

Geographically dispersed enterprise gave superintendents of local plants considerable power and prestige. Because most of its operations were located in predominantly rural areas near supplies of raw material, fuel, or water power, Alcoa was a highly visible concern in locales that came to expect much from the company in support of their economic well-being. In such environments, plant superintendents played crucial roles in maintaining the kinds of social and political relationships that were vital to the company's economic health. A range of problems – from rights of way to riparian rights, from tax rates to labor relations – were bound up in the company's good will with state and regional authorities and with local public opinion.[81]

Generally, Alcoa's labor situation followed the norm for major industries before the 1920s. Labor relations were entirely a local matter. Hiring practices and wages for nonmanagerial employees differed markedly from place to place, depending on regional demographic, social, and economic conditions. Although Davis testified in 1908 that the corporation had established an eight-hour working day sometime in the early part of the century, there is evidence that in many operations a twelve-hour shift continued to be the practice. Alcoa was exceptional in some regards. For example, aluminum workers in the potrooms received higher than average wages for industrial employment. This was due to an extraordinary demand for skills that took from two to four years to acquire.[82]

In its two company towns – Bauxite, Arkansas, and Alcoa, Tennessee – the company built and maintained communities that have been fondly recalled by retired employees as supporting pleasant and intimate familial societies. Alcoa's management adopted a highly paternalistic posture toward its workforce, and by its own lights, pursued a "policy of always providing, in backward or isolated communities, excellent schools and medical care, supplemented by hospital facilities, for the benefit of its employees."[83] Alcoa, Tennessee, was designed by the company with parks and playgrounds and a clear separation between residential and industrial buildings. There, and at Bauxite, there is neither record nor memory of anything approaching the squalid, inhumane conditions of company towns that characterized other contemporary manufacturing and mining industries.

The work itself, especially in the mines, refineries, and potrooms, was often unpleasant, dirty, arduous, and, given the potential for explosions, electrocutions, and exposure to toxic chemicals, dangerous. Aluminum workers were unorganized, having no collective power to represent their interests to management. Alcoa staunchly resisted unions of any kind. A modest American Federation of Labor attempt to build a union of wire mill workers in New Kensington following a short strike, the company's first, in 1900, was modestly successful until the depression of 1908, when management refused to renegotiate a scale of wages and declared Alcoa an open shop. When a strike was called, Alcoa obtained an injunction, which broke the back of the union. An attempt by the International Workers of the World in 1913 to organize Eastern European immigrant workers in New Kensington was squelched with the help of city authorities. Two years later a miner's strike at Bauxite was thwarted by imports of "scab" labor from Alabama. Later in the decade, an effort by the American Federation of Labor to organize Alcoa, Tennessee, resulted in the firing of prospective members.[84] Management felt it could fairly dispense to the needs of workers through modest programs, such as a voluntary "employment fund," established in 1908, in which the company set aside a sum equal to 2.5 percent of an employee's wages on which one could draw after two years' service, and a "sick fund" that provided financial assistance, at the discretion of a company committee, to "deserving employees" at times of illness.[85]

Alcoa's absolute control over labor was at least tempered by the paternalistic values of the management, by the threat of occasional wildcat strikes, and by economic and social realities. In good economic years, plants found that concessions in wages or working conditions had to be granted to attract workers to dirty jobs in the refineries or potrooms. In rural areas of Tennessee or Arkansas, local populations of small farmers provided an often less-than-reliable, independently minded workforce. Everywhere, plant superintendents looked to newly arrived Eastern and Southern Europeans, Mexicans, and Southern blacks for especially tough jobs

Fig. 3.10. "Uncle Jesse" Smith (third from right), a blacksmith, with his coworkers who constructed machinery at the Badin Works, circa 1916.

(such as the hot, miserable labor of potrooms in the summertime) that were unattractive to more established citizens in the nation's labor force.[86]

Managing technology

In advancing understanding of aluminum and its alloys, Alcoa began to devote resources to scientific research very slowly and hesitantly. Initially, The Pittsburgh Reduction Company drew on the personnel and facilities of the Pittsburgh Testing Laboratory. The main concern during the start-up period, of course, was to improve the chemistry and operating control of the basic smelting process, so sensitive was the aluminum process to slight chemical and physical alterations. At New Kensington, a small laboratory was set up to enable Charles Martin Hall to pursue some problems in research that were not immediately tied to the management of day-to-day production.

Leaving A. V. Davis to tend to operations, Hall became more devoted to research, and in this capacity, he directed some experiments in alloy composition and the tempering of aluminum.[87] Most of the company's internal research work in this early period focused on process and product development and metalworking techniques, and Hall's approach to these problems was consciously systematic and scientific.

At the turn of the century, Alcoa's sponsorship of scientific research was limited to problems in the refining of alumina, wherein lay the greatest single cost of the production of aluminum. In 1900, a one-man laboratory at New Kensington was at work on a series of what proved to be unsuccessful "dry" processes for producing alumina from bauxite. Hall himself took out four patents on a "dry" process for the electrothermal smelting of alumina from a mixture of bauxite and coke. This work was carried out "on a considerable scale" at Niagara until 1910, when it became clear that the alumina produced was not pure enough to make high-grade aluminum. Thereafter, Hall went to work on the "Serpek Process," for which Alcoa had bought the patent rights, whereby alumina could be extracted from aluminum nitride derived by heating bauxite with carbon at high temperatures. That, too, was unsuccessful.[88]

Meanwhile, the New Kensington laboratory was placed under the control of Earl Blough, a PhD in chemistry, who expanded operations from six people in 1906 to twenty by 1913. Blough served as the company's chief chemist and metallurgist, while William Hoopes, who had joined the company in 1899, served as chief electrical engineer. By 1915, these men were the principals of a "Research and Laboratory Department" at New Kensington, which was divided into an "Analytical Laboratory" (for the analysis of alloys) and a "Testing Laboratory" (for the monitoring of fabricated materials). Fundamental scientific inquiries continued to be devoted to finding cheaper alternatives to the Bayer refining process (this effort was suspended in 1919) and, in a small way, to the reclamation of scrap in fabrications. Inquiries into the composition and behavior of alloys, which would later become the focal point of fundamental research at Alcoa, were limited to empirical measures of performance in conjunction with manufacturing operations.[89]

All through the prewar period, Alcoa relied very little on outside expertise. The company did retain Joseph W. Richards, an accomplished electrochemist and metallurgist and the country's foremost academic expert on aluminum. Known affectionately as "Plug" to his students at Lehigh, Richards was probably most valuable to

Alcoa for his students, many of whom came to Alcoa fresh from his metallurgy program. From as early as 1891, he also provided expert testimony in patent cases and served as a conduit for technical publicity on the industry through his publications (he was president of the American Electrochemical Society). But in truth, his academic expertise in aluminum, or for that matter metallurgy, was no greater than Alcoa's own, and when the Bradley patent expired, A. V. Davis grudgingly paid Richards a princely $5,000 per annum for just twenty days labor in order to keep the professor's knowledge of proprietary technology under wraps. As the expiration date on Alcoa's controlling patents approached, Richards himself appears to have understood that by that time, the main purpose of the company's retainer was to keep him "on the shelf."[90]

Technological innovation was treated mainly as a set of incremental and empirical problems to be dealt with on the production line. The management of production was essentially a local matter, but in order to relate technical improvements in any one part of the production chain, from mining to fabrication, to all the other parts, Pittsburgh had to find ways to coordinate and advise on technical changes. Before World War I, the task of coordinating technical information was defined more in terms of people than systems. Before illness slowed him down, Hall himself visited production sites to give advice on carbon and refining processes. Gradually, other staff officers and engineers traveled more and more frequently to plants to inspect operations, troubleshoot, and disseminate information on a wide range of problems. At the head of a small "engineering department" was Edwin S. Fickes, a civil engineer whose correspondence and memoirs provide rich detail on the myriad problems involved in coordinating the development of aluminum technology.

Fickes's first job was as a consulting engineer, during the winter of 1899–1900, when he was called upon to design the smelter at Shawinigan Falls, a task made more difficult than necessary by the intense secrecy that surrounded the aluminum business at the time. To Fickes's astonishment, Hall had refused him entrance to the Niagara operations to see how an aluminum plant actually functioned. But he soon gained the company's trust and took on regular employment, siting and designing the company's new facilities. As the company's chief engineer, Fickes traveled widely and became immersed in all manner of problems relating to the business: from the analysis of specific material requirements to the measurement of operating performance, from the management of labor relations to the engineering of fire protection, from the erection of bridges to the planning of company towns, from the mediation of internal disputes to the negotiation of freight rates. By World War I, Davis had called upon him to travel to Western Europe, Russia, and Japan to investigate bauxite resources and possibilities for overseas aluminum operations.[91]

Fickes's correspondence with the plants and the East St. Louis refinery reveal his importance to the company on matters great and small, managerial as well as technical. Indeed, by World War I, Fickes had succeeded Hall as Alcoa's central repository of technical intelligence. However, the technical experience he acquired was based on information that was more random than systematic, and the networks of technical communication he established were more personal than institutional. Before World War I, his engineering department was but a small, minimal structure for the dissemination and coordination of technical information on a corporate-wide basis. Research and development at all phases of production were randomly conducted and loosely coordinated. This was not a problem during the early, entrepreneurial phases of the company's growth, but at the close of the patent period, Alcoa was becoming too large, too complex, and too diverse an enterprise for informal technical administration. No one understood the problem better than Fickes himself.

To a large degree, the absence of a technical bureaucracy at Alcoa can be traced back to Charles Martin Hall's personal dominance of technical matters. After 1900, too many of Alcoa's experiments were increasingly defined by Hall's idiosyncratic interests. At Niagara, he hired a "personal chemist" to work with him in a "plant laboratory which was located by the No. 1 potroom." There, he concerned himself with problems in refining and smelting technology almost up until the time of his death. But his drift into fruitless experiments aimed at transmuting base metals into rhodium, platinum, or gold[92] seemed downright alchemical to Alcoa's managers, and his tendency to disrupt operations for the sake of his experiments made it hard for production managers to appreciate his efforts. "Mr. Hall," explained his secretary, "was a *research man*" and as such "was not properly understood by many people." Before long, the great inventor of the of the aluminum process became a source of irritation to the Niagara plant superintendent, who of course was utterly helpless to do anything about it.[93]

Properly understood or not, Hall's status as a principal owner and officer of the corporation left him free to establish his own priorities.

Fig. 3.11.   Charles Martin Hall (standing at right rear) relaxing with friends, including Alcoa manager Safford K. Colby (lying in foreground), during a day's rest from work at Niagara Falls in 1902.

We should not underestimate his role in stimulating important advances in smelting and refining techniques, in particular, and his importance in developing the field of electrochemistry, in general. At Alcoa, he kept tabs on technical problems in all the plants and was the principal voice for technological innovation on Alcoa's board of directors. Still, Hall lent little if any support to fundamental inquiries into problems that did not suit his own interests and displayed little sensitivity toward the long-term *institutional* requirements of research and development. And we have evidence that he was decidedly opposed to the idea of a strong, central technical organization.

It was 1909 when Fickes and Hoopes proposed the establishment of "an independent and competent research organization" that could clarify and arbitrate technical problems as they arose between the related technical functions of different parts of the organization. But

Hall rejected the idea, as Fickes explained it, because he had "decided that such an organization would be very expensive, that it might not do all we hoped, and might even do more harm than good." Davis, who thought well of the plan, nevertheless deferred to Hall, without whose approval no important policy decisions were implemented during his lifetime. And "thus the matter rested," Fickes lamented, "since we were never able to convince Mr. Hall that such a scheme would return more than it would cost.[94]

Hall was wrong. There were already ominous signs that a condition of functional disintegration was beginning to develop at Alcoa – a condition described by Fickes in a striking passage well worth quoting at length:

> From the time I first became familiar with the company's potroom records and operations in 1902 and had become intimate with its operating superintendents, I had noted great and variable differences in output per unit, in the quality of metal produced in different works, and in the same works at different times; there were even greater opinions and theories as to the causes. There was no consensus of opinion about the causes of trouble, or reasons for success, and as time went on, fabricating plant men became convinced that the reduction plant operators were indifferent to their complaints, or worse; the reduction plant heads were convinced not only that East St. Louis ore was poor and variable, but also that any carbons other than those made at their plants, were uncertain in quality and troublemakers; or, if their own make was unquestionably bad, they were apt to blame the quality of the pitch or petroleum coke; at East St. Louis it was held that the reduction plant superintendents didn't know good ore from bad, and that their troubles certainly were due to something else, probably their own folly. Nor was East St. Louis satisfied with its bauxite; [Bauxite, Arkansas] was sure that if folks at East St. Louis really would devote their undoubted energy and ability to making alumina, instead of finding fault with bauxite, great profit would accrue to the stockholders. As between the works superintendents, the habit of buck-passing and the writing of acrid and somewhat useless correspondence, even before 1909, was a growing evil.[95]

The lack of a strong, centralized technical organization – to perform "independent research" and coordinate technical development – was a serious weakness in Alcoa's structure. Along the vertical chain, there was no independent way to isolate problems in one area that might impact on the performance of any other. Nor were there adequate means for reconciling differences in technical performance in separate facilities with like functions. How could the company arrive at general standards for the output and quality of products and assure these standards on a corporate-wide basis without a central mechanism to consider technology outside the context of the workaday production process? And though Fickes and Hoopes may not yet have seen it, there was also a need to conduct fundamental scientific research on a more coordinated basis. Soon, the war would make demands for aluminum alloys that were higher in strength than anything in the company's manufacturing experience. There was no adequate store of fundamental knowledge to support the development of new alloys.

To summarize the problem, Alcoa, by World War I, had become a much more complex creature since its founding as a small, undifferentiated enterprise. It was highly diverse in both its technical functions and products. It had become a huge complex of operations scattered over a wide landscape. Its management had become increasingly specialized and differentiated. The company's officers were necessarily becoming more concerned with the overall planning and resource allocation and less involved in the quotidian technical and managerial problems of production. Yet, amidst all this growth and change, the principles underlying the managerial organization of the company had remained static. Alcoa had coped with the problem of scale simply through de facto decentralization – by allowing authority for the management of operations to devolve upon the heads of plants and subsidiary firms. In the process, Alcoa had become a cluster of nineteenth-century firms writ large: a small holding company presiding over a set of other companies, or company-like units, lacking strong institutional means for integrating their diverse but ultimately related technical functions. Obviously, this arrangement had sufficed for a time, but eventually the increasingly complex demands of technology would have to be met by a more integrated organizational response or Alcoa would suffer in greater measure the sort of functional disintegration so readily perceived by its staff engineer.

The impact of war

War was good to Alcoa. Its outbreak in Europe in 1914 ended the threat of aluminum imports into the United States. Alcoa became an exporter. Production from 1915 through 1918 increased from 109 million to 152 million pounds as America's British, French and Italian allies bought nearly 90 million pounds of Alcoa's primary output. Domestic sales took off. From less than 30 million pounds in 1914, Alcoa's shipments of pig and ingot soared to a high of 108,349,656 pounds in 1917 (a volume that would not be surpassed until 1928) as American military needs stretched the company's capacity to the limit. Plant facilities were hastily expanded to meet demand, and shipments of bauxite from the company's new mines in South America began in earnest.[96]

By the time of America's entry into the war, some ninety percent of Alcoa's production was being taken up for military apparatus and supplies. Numerous new applications were found in high-technology military equipment, ranging from aircraft and automobile parts to electrical supplies and screw machine products. Ammonal, a powerful high explosive made of ammonium nitrate and aluminum powder, normally used in mining, was applied to a less benign use. In 1918, the manufacture of cooking utensils at New Kensington was virtually suspended so that production could be shifted to such items as mess kits, canteens, helmets, gas masks, identification tags, and other light equipment for combat personnel. Once established in these areas, aluminum became a strategic material.[97]

The surge in military orders was less prosperous for Alcoa than it would have been had prices been allowed to rise to their free-market levels. But aluminum, like all critical industries, became part of the regulated command economy of the second Wilson administration. A. V. Davis was called to serve as his industry's advisor to Bernard Baruch's War Industries Board, established in the summer of 1917, to help determine production priorities, coordinate purchasing, and fix pricing. Alcoa voluntarily delivered some eight million pounds of aluminum to the Government at $0.275 per pound in the spring and summer of 1917. However, Alcoa's status as the only producer of primary aluminum attracted suspicion. When the Secretary of the Navy testified in the Senate that Alcoa was selling canteens produced at $0.275 per pound for more than twice that amount, Alcoa's prices were placed under strict Government control. From late 1917 to early 1919, the price of aluminum, then fixed at a base price of $0.38 per pound, was lowered in the wake of an FTC investigation to $0.32 (later raised to $0.33), substantially less than the sixty cents charged to "outside" customers.[98] Davis's publicized protests about his labor and production costs did not win Alcoa much sympathy.

In the short run, the war seemed only a temporary deviation from the normal trajectory of Alcoa's business. The cessation of hostilities was followed by a precipitous decline in demand, a resurgence of imports, a lifting of price controls, and in a day of minimal peacetime military establishments, a return to predominantly civilian markets. Alcoa faced the peace with capacity that was much greater in relation to demand than had been the case since 1907, and the company's rate of return would fall off sharply in the early 1920s. Wartime inflation also conspired with wartime labor shortages to drive up wages and shorten hours (the Government rigidly enforced the eight-hour day), benefits to workers that would have to be largely rescinded in the postwar contraction.

But in many long-term respects, the company's business was profoundly altered by the war. The wide scope of military uses of aluminum spilled over into civilian uses. The establishment of the metal as a strategic resource heightened the Government's sense of responsibility for ensuring the industry's well being. The war affected Alcoa in at least two other important ways. First, it signaled a major new market in both war and peace, as the potential for aluminum in aircraft structures was revealed. Second, the quest to develop an alloy necessary for high-tonnage applications in aircraft structures exposed a critical weakness in Alcoa's scientific capabilities.

Aluminum for aircraft construction had been imagined as early as 1898, when one Thomas M. Crepar wrote to Alfred Hunt proposing a collaborative effort on a "Crepar Palace Air-Ship," a fabulously preposterous vessel to be borne aloft by a propeller-driven blimp. Its fanciful purpose was to provide transportation over mountainous terrain to the gold fields of Alaska. Other aspiring aviationists requested large quantities of aluminum, often on credit secured by their self-professed ability to get their would-be contraptions off the ground. Success in aviation, one supplicant explained to the company, "would multiply the demand for your product ... [so that the] cost of construction would be insignificant in view of the profits that accrue from it."[99]

The company was not especially captivated by these schemes, but aluminum did gradually find applications in flight. Aluminum alloyed with copper was used in the engine crankcase and waterjackets of the first successful machine-powered airplane at Kitty Hawk.[100] By World War I, the metal accounted for up to a third of the total weight of aircraft engines and was beginning to replace wood and other materials for propellers and other parts. During the war, aluminum was used in numerous engine parts and in auxiliary apparatus to the airplane, including fuel tanks, fuselage, hoods, cowling, seat backs, aileron frames, navigation instruments, and communi-

Fig. 3.12. The Crepar Palace Air-Ship, a fanciful design for the application of aluminum to aviation.

cations devices.[101] And if aviation were to progress beyond the small-scale and dangerous state of its primitive beginnings, the wood and canvas structures of contemporary aircraft would have to be replaced by a light metal.

The Germans had already developed an aluminum alloy both light and strong enough to support large structures in flight, and they applied it in their lighter-than-air Zeppelins. The requisite hard metal had come from a breakthrough in aluminum metallurgy made in 1908, when Alfred Wilm patented an aluminum-copper-magnesium alloy along with a process of heat treatment and spontaneous age-hardening at room temperature by which the metal assumed the strength of a "mild steel." The alloy was called "Duralumin" and its importance cannot be overstated: it was to aluminum what steel was to iron. The only American concern licensed to use Duralumin was the Electric Boat Company of Connecticut, which showed little interest in developing it.

Alcoa, without any systematic effort in alloy research, tried in

Fig. 3.13.　A flying wing of Curtis JN4-D "Jennys," early aluminum-skinned training aircraft, in 1918.

vain before the war to develop a Duralumin substitute. With the advent of armed conflict in Europe, the Navy became keenly interested in the development of a hard alloy for rigid airships in which Germany had advanced technology and therefore pressed Alcoa to step up its efforts to make Duralumin (the patents for which had been appropriated by a wartime Alien Property Custodian). The patents, however, proved to be vague, and Alcoa metallurgists were frustrated by their inability to understand enough about the basic properties of high-strength alloys to make them on any large scale. Metallurgists, much like cooks who concoct recipes, could barely explain the theoretical bases for the results of many of their experiments. Wilm himself could not explain the results of his great discovery, and so his "recipe" was hard to translate into a product without a clear grasp of the underlying metallurgical processes involved in the various stages of development and production.[102]

At Alcoa, where alloy development had always been somewhat random and undirected, no easy solution to the Duralumin problem was found until Paul Merica of the National Bureau of Standards and other Government researchers proposed a theory for the mechanism by which heat treatment, rapid cooling, and aging at room temperature caused aluminum-copper-magnesium alloys to develop extraordinarily high strength. Prior to that time, seemingly successful experiments in the laboratory could not subsequently be scaled up for good-quality production. At the continuing urgings of the Navy, which in those days was the Government's most sophisticated consumer of technology, Alcoa chemist Earl Blough led the company's finally successful effort to produce a Duralumin-type alloy, 17S, that could be produced on a large scale.[103]

The impact of the Duralumin program on Alcoa's research and development was profound. Before the war, Alcoa had been more interested in the processes of production than in what was being produced. The war exposed serious weaknesses in Alcoa's coordination of product innovation and manufacture, as the company was unable to produce satisfactory sheet and components for the Navy's airship program. Blough's view from the laboratory was that Aloca's "facilities for experimental work were practically non-existent or at best primitive ... and lack of trained staff made the work go by very slowly." But by the end of the war, "the whole scene changed. We realized that the production of strong alloys was a very highly technical matter and that we must do it with more equipment, more men and more precision than we ever presumed in any of our work before."[104] Having discovered that aluminum development could no longer rest on empirical tinkering, Alcoa would not only have to improve the coordination of its development and production operations, it would also have to develop the capability to probe deeper and more systematically into the mysteries of the element on which its business was built.

4

Alcoa comes of age: organization, innovation, and labor from the Roaring 20s through the Great Depression

The end of World War I was a watershed for Alcoa. Rapid growth had brought with it increasing complexity, which in turn required more sophisticated systems of administration. In 1918, Alcoa's management designed a new corporate structure. A second, related order of business was to define more clearly an organizational basis for technological innovation. The creation of an administrative structure based on functional principles of organization and, within it, cadres of managers responsible for scientific research and technological development would better equip Alcoa to defend its markets, to open new ones, and to continue growing.

Alcoa's growth between the two World Wars proceeded through two phases: a decade of rapid expansion to a pinnacle of size and earnings followed by years of slow recovery from a sharp retrenchment in assets. First came the good years, the "Roaring 20s," which, despite one deep recession and some cyclical fluctuations, was a decade of prosperity unprecedented in the history of industrial society. In 1920, the census reported that the United States had officially become an urban nation; trade and manufacturing, not farming, had for the first time become the primary means of livelihood for ordinary citizens. In this "New Era," farmers did not fare very well, but a new class of industrial workers, so long as they held their jobs, could expect to amass surplus cash for savings and for consumption well beyond the bare necessities of life. The modern mass-consumer society was dawning. Luxuries, like the telephone and automobile, were transformed into everyday "necessities"; stoves, refrigerators, and radios appeared in most American homes. As the real gross national product (GNP) increased by thirty percent between 1920 and 1930, common citizens bought stock in America's center firms. In doing so, they were buying into the dreams and aspirations of the capitalist order. All of this was good for Alcoa, which saw demand for its aluminum rise at an even faster rate than the economy. Having already established a range of viable markets for aluminum and having sustained its monopoly well past the expiration of its controlling patents, Alcoa entered a new phase of its development. It benefitted from a strong economy and a favorable political climate, which made monopoly growth not only possible but almost respectable. Then came the bad years. Like everyone else in business, Alcoa suffered sharp reversals after the stock-market crash of 1929. But after its worst year, 1932, the company rebounded, and its sales climbed steadily toward a new high in 1937. Overall, from 1919 through 1937, Alcoa's assets swelled from about 120 to 223 million dollars and the number of its employees increased by about 11,000.[1]

Alcoa grew through territorial expansion and by continuing to promote aluminum as a substitute for other materials. Throughout the industrial world, aluminum grew far more rapidly than other nonferrous metals between the World Wars, as manufacturers of semifinished and finished goods became more familiar with its properties. Aluminum seized collapsible tube and foil markets from tin and truck bodies from steel while losing ground to cast iron in automotive engine applications.[2] Alcoa developed new products through the exploitation of new fabricating and alloy technologies. Novel techniques for the manufacture of collapsible tubing, die castings, impact extrusions, rolled structural shapes, and press forgings made possible a wider range of applications in military, industrial, and domestic life. One important postwar application developed in screw machine products, and the development of heat-treatable alloys of extraordinary strength elevated aluminum to the status of a strategic material with indispensable uses in aviation. Alcoa's reliance on the automotive industry (which, in 1915, had taken sixty-five percent of all new aluminum) declined rapidly,[3] but transportation as a broad category remained the biggest outlet for aluminum produced in the United States, surpassing tonnages taken for electrical transmission and cooking utensils.

Alcoa continued to develop new product ideas during the Depression. Aluminum was used for the tower and spandrels in the Empire

Table 4.1. Comparison of world consumption of principal nonferrous metals, 1921–38
(thousands of metric tons)

Year	Aluminum Tons	Aluminum Index	Copper Tons	Copper Index	Zinc Tons	Zinc Index	Lead Tons	Lead Index	Tin Tons	Tin Index	Year
1921	71.2	100	621.9	100	478.0	100	840.6	100	81.7	100	1921
1922	97.9	140	891.0	142	794.7	166	1,044.3	123	131.8	151	1922
1923	138.2	195	1,178.8	190	950.3	200	1,152.4	137	137.0	168	1923
1924	169.5	240	1,322.8	210	1,031.5	215	1,304.4	156	136.2	166	1924
1925	183.1	256	1,447.3	230	1,176.6	246	1,496.9	177	154.6	189	1925
1926	190.4	275	1,480.0	238	1,228.5	257	1,561.2	186	151.4	185	1926
1927	180.9	365	1,525.2	244	1,308.2	275	1,604.3	191	156.9	192	1927
1928	236.3	330	1,725.0	277	1,416.7	295	1,654.6	196	175.3	214	1928
1929	268.8	380	1,984.8	320	1,442.5	300	1,708.1	202	184.3	226	1929
1930	209.4	294	1,639.4	262	1,232.6	260	1,524.9	181	161.1	197	1930
1931	175.0	245	1,372.7	220	1,027.1	215	1,300.5	154	134.3	161	1931
1932	150.0	210	1,074.2	172	842.0	177	1,117.3	133	116.8	143	1932
1933	155.0	219	1,271.5	205	1,008.7	210	1,198.1	142	144.6	177	1933
1934	210.0	295	1,515.2	240	1,158.8	241	1,369.2	163	139.9	171	1934
1935	307.0	430	1,805.7	290	1,371.6	287	1,458.4	174	162.4	198	1935
1936	407.4	575	2,000.2	338	1,514.9	315	1,586.7	188	174.6	214	1936
1937	501.7	705	2,378.6	380	1,605.6	337	1,732.4	206	192.5	235	1937
1938	515.0	725	2,143.8	342	1,426.7	300	1,607.3	192	164.6	215	1938

Source: Louis Marlio, The Aluminum Cartel (The Brookings Institution: Washington, DC, 1947), p. 127.

Table 4.2. *Alcoa's share of major markets for aluminum in the United States, 1931*

Market	% Share
Transportation (automobile, railroad, traction, aircraft, marine)	38
Electrical transmission	16
Cooking utensils	14
Machinery	9
Iron and steel metallurgy	8
Foundry and metalworking	4
Building trades	4
Chemicals	2
Food containers	1
General miscellaneous	4

Source: John Leeds Kerr, "A Comprehensive Report of the Aluminum Industry: A Survey Prepared under the Supervision of Young & Otley, Inc." (New York, 1931), ms. on file in the Alcoa Archives, env. 161.

State Building and for window sills in Rockefeller Center, the first major building construction applications. In mass-consumer markets, aluminum appeared increasingly in screens, furniture, packaging, and high-fashion gift ware. Alcoa also established some exotic markets for aluminum and its by-products in such areas as "alumilite products" (colored finishes) and fluorides for use in lumber treatments. In end products, such as furniture, Alcoa simply hoped to stimulate demand for aluminum before leaving the finished manufacturing and distribution to others. In semifinished products, Alcoa generally entered markets to stay.[4]

Alcoa expanded operations in the United States as aluminum became more widely established in its prewar applications. More dramatic was the company's abortive attempt to go abroad. Few today remember that by the late 1920s, Alcoa had become a multinational corporation, having acquired not only raw materials abroad but also smelting, fabricating, and distributing capabilities. International manufacturing operations were sited mainly in Canada, where the company already had sprouted deep roots, feeding on the northland's abundant and cheap water power. But in 1928, a combination of logistical, organizational, and legal constraints led Alcoa's management to sever the company's foreign holdings and markets. The divestiture of the company's foreign holdings (with a

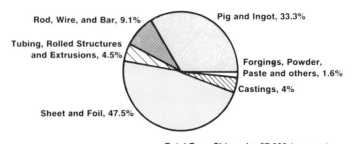

Total Tons Shipped = 67,000 (approx.)

Chart 4.1. Alcoa shipments by product/technology class, 1922 (percent total tonnage). *Source: Alcoa Plant Histories.*

notable exception of its Dutch Guiana bauxite) resulted in the birth of the Canadian company known today as Alcan.

Even though aluminum was a major growth industry, Alcoa remained the only producer of primary aluminum and the major producer of most fabricated aluminum products in the United States. The market structure of the industry will be discussed in the next chapter; suffice it to say here that major firms, such as General Electric, DuPont, and Ford, all explored the possibility of entering the smelting business in the 1920s, but decided not to take the risk. Smaller entrepreneurs fared no better. In 1932, the Bohn Aluminum and Brass Corporation investigated the use of an alternative ore for alumina production, but balked amid the depressed state of American business.[5] Competition existed in fabricated products, but Alcoa sustained its predominance in the more capital-intensive, high-tonnage applications.

Organizational reform and technological innovation helped sustain the company's position. Following World War I, administrative and incremental technical improvements were undertaken simultaneously with commitments of large resources to fundamental research and development. Organizational and productive efficiency on the one hand and innovation on the other – often conflicting goals in corporate management – proceeded in tandem. Alcoa's great economies of scale, its integrated structure, and its technological superiority were thus reinforced, making attempts by rivals to enter major product/technology markets surpassingly difficult.

Dominance of its industry notwithstanding, the period between the wars was not always easy for Alcoa. Demand was uneven; peacetime civilian markets proved to be highly sensitive to economic cycles. Immediately after the war, Alcoa could not meet the surge

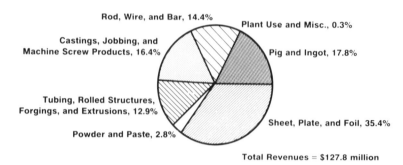

Rod, Wire, and Bar, 14.4%

Plant Use and Misc., 0.3%

Castings, Jobbing, and Machine Screw Products, 16.4%

Pig and Ingot, 17.8%

Tubing, Rolled Structures, Forgings, and Extrusions, 12.9%

Sheet, Plate, and Foil, 35.4%

Powder and Paste, 2.8%

Total Revenues = $127.8 million

Chart 4.2. Alcoa shipments by product/technology class, 1937 (percent total sales and operating revenues). *Source: Alcoa Plant Histories.*

in demand from domestic aluminum customers. Then, suddenly, the company found itself with far too much capacity as cancellations of large orders were rampant in the deep, albeit brief, depression of 1920–1.[6] Alcoa did not make a full recovery until 1923, but enjoyed great prosperity for the rest of the decade while operating, for the most part, at full capacity. At times, Alcoa even had to import metal to meet growing demand. In 1925, an aggressive program was launched to double primary capacity, so optimistic were the forecasts for sustained growth.[7]

Optimism turned to trepidation in the Great Depression. For nearly five years after the 1929 stock-market crash, aluminum sales and profits were badly hurt. Hourly rated workers were laid off in droves, as gross revenues dipped from $34.4 million in 1929 to $11.1 million in 1932. The number of employees fell to 13,652 from 24,857 in the same period. Salaried professionals were far from immune from the disaster. Engineers were dismissed and even the sales force was pared back, so gloomy was the outlook in the dark years between 1929 and 1933. Former chairman Fritz Close remembers that his monthly salesman's salary in New York was slashed from $175 to $131.50 in the early 1930s, while Frank Magee in the Atlanta district sales office eked out a living for himself and his wife, who was dying of cancer at a time when there was no medical insurance to pay the bills.[8] Alcoa's engineering staff was sharply reduced as new plant construction came to a virtual standstill. By 1936, however, pent-up demand for aluminum burst into a new round of orders and the company enjoyed a generally good recovery until 1939, when, once again, a global war spurred a quantum increase in aluminum production.[9]

Between the wars, aluminum became more solidly established as a common metal in a wider range of applications. On the other hand, for employees, managers, and owners alike, the business remained fraught with uncertainty; production and sales remained sensitive to general business cycles. Despite Alcoa's strong market position, the company's managers grew chronically anxious, worried that they would always have to struggle to survive, if not against other aluminum producers, against the adverse fortunes of the economy. And the Depression brought in its wake yet another constraint on management. Workers at Alcoa, no longer confident in the company's ability to look after their interests, formed industrial unions. Alcoa's traditional labor paternalism went awash in the rising tide of organized labor.

Expansion overseas and retrenchment

The Great War had interrupted the flow of European metal into North America and provided lucrative markets for Alcoa's aluminum overseas. For the year 1919, the total tonnage of metal imported from European producers, pure and alloyed (including recycled scrap), was 2,360 metric tons, as compared with 5,643 metric tons from Alcoa's Canadian operations.[10] After the war, Alcoa took both defensive and offensive measures to protect its markets at home and to expand its business abroad. Although Alcoa's foreign investments in the 1920s did not constitute a major part of its overall business in financial terms, its moves overseas were strategically significant.

One way in which Alcoa might have dampened the influx of imported metal was to have its interest looked after through its Canadian subsidiary's membership in a new European cartel. However, the 1912 consent decree prohibiting Alcoa's participation in any agreement that would restrict imports from any part of the world had "shattered for all time the pattern by which Alcoa had participated in the European markets either through multi-party cartels or agreements with individual companies, such as the Swiss."[11] Alcoa took the position that the Northern Aluminum Company remained free to enter cartels governing the aluminum market so long as the American market was deemed to be unaffected by the agreement. Indeed, in 1913, the Canadian company participated in the international Aluminium Association so that it could do business "in the European way." The Justice Department, which had been consulted on the matter, acquiesced.[12] After the Association's demise in 1915, no international cartel formed again until late 1923, and neither Alcoa nor Northern participated.[13]

Instead, Alcoa resorted to the tariff. The return of the Republican Party to the White House and Congress saw a restoration of economic nationalism. Andrew W. Mellon was installed as Secretary of the Treasury (one of Warren G. Harding's few competent cabinet appointments), a post he would hold until Herbert Hoover's defeat at the hands of Franklin Delano Roosevelt. Mellon was often accused of using his public office to further his business interests, but in reality it was his conservative economic philosophy – which emphasized low taxes, a balanced budget (a possible combination in those days of relatively small government), and minimal government regulation – that determined public policy. He also favored stronger protection against foreign competition, as did Congress, which passed the Fordney-McCumber Act in 1922. Even though the bill had been intended mainly to appease the Farm Bloc, the new industrial product schedules under the act as passed were revised upward from the low levels of the 1913 tariff. Aluminum rates were raised as follows: from $0.02 to $0.05 per pound on ingot; from $0.05 to $0.09 cents on sheet.[14]

Historically, Fordney-McCumber fit squarely within a revived "Hamiltonian" approach to the sheltering of American industrial enterprise. It worked wonders in aluminum; European producers, especially the Germans, who were rebuilding their aluminum industry rapidly, were unable to establish a strong market for their metal in the United States. Between 1923 and 1928, aluminum imports (including those from Canada and from smaller Alcoa smelters in Norway) were less than fifteen percent of the total of all sales of virgin aluminum in the United States. Imports from Europe reached a high of 18,400 metric tons in 1926 (a year in which Alcoa was forced to purchase some aluminum from Germany to service its own customers), but then tailed off sharply. Foreign metal sold in the U.S. was not substantially discounted from the Alcoa list price (from which Alcoa often discounted) and seems not to have exceeded the amount needed to make up for Alcoa's own shortfalls in meeting demand. In 1930, Alcoa gained no further benefit from the ultra-protectionist Hawley-Smoot tariff, which actually lowered aluminum rates by a penny on ingot and two cents on sheet. But the onset of the Depression kept imports down.[15]

Meanwhile, between 1920 and 1928, Alcoa pursued a small-scale but multifaceted strategy for foreign expansion. The company set up sales offices and established operations, from ore deposits to fab-

ricating facilities, in Europe as well as in the more familiar territories of Canada and the Caribbean. In its ventures abroad, Alcoa
was participating in the more general flow of American corporate
investment overseas that had been increasing rapidly since the onset
of World War I, and it was helped in this regard by a favorable
political climate, as administrations from Wilson to Hoover encouraged overseas investment, providing favorable tax breaks, diplomatic aid, and foreign intelligence.[16]

Entry into Europe involved a complex of considerations. First,
European producers had great surplus manufacturing capacity after
the war. In 1921, European capacity was about 129,000 metric tons
per annum compared to Alcoa's 83,000, and Germany would build
even more, practically from scratch. For Alcoa, this meant (in addition to protecting its home markets from the dumping of European
surpluses) that many European facilities, including those for raw
materials and power, were being offered at bargain prices. French
producers with foreign holdings were especially handicapped in that
they were unable to increase their investments in their holdings
outside French borders reflecting postwar French Government policy. The weakening of European currencies, moreover, lowered the
price of already cheaper European labor and materials. Alcoa could
also look forward to manufacturing some of its output overseas at
lower cost.

Second, the erection of tariff walls and a rising spirit of economic
nationalism made it imperative to locate the manufacture of products for sale overseas, where they were to be sold. A. V. Davis believed that Alcoa could penetrate European markets and compete
with foreign producers on their home turfs. His search for ore and
water power was also relentless, and in the postwar American economy, domestic water power, especially, was becoming more expensive for Alcoa to purchase. Finally, there was the unspoken threat
that an increase of European exports to the United States might be
met with an increase of Alcoa's own capacity in Europe. This last
factor, however, was not as important as the others, and certainly,
given the capital investment required, not an easy threat on which
to make good.[17]

Alcoa sometimes bought foreign properties and facilities outright,
but usually preferred to take a partial interest in companies that
were either already in operation or were created as joint ventures.
Upstream, Alcoa had already acquired bauxite in Southern France
in 1912 under the rubric of Bauxites du Midi. In 1921, the company
purchased bauxite rights in Yugoslavia and Italy, the former out-

right, the latter with local partners. French bauxite holdings were reorganized in 1927, when Alcoa joined a consortium of European companies in the creation of the Carrières de l'Arboussas.[18] In addition to bauxite, Alcoa purchased almost all the stock in Prodotti Chimici Napoli, an Italian venture that proposed to make alumina from leucite, a silicate of potassium and aluminum, by leaching it with hydrochloric acid.[19]

The leucite venture was one of Alcoa's more awkward blunders. In 1928, A. V. Davis, who was not immune to occasional lapses of judgment, became enchanted by one Count G. Cippico. The Count had arrived in New York to promote the interests of another noble worthy, his countryman the Baron Gian C. Blanc, who held patent rights to the leucite refining process. Despite skepticism among technical experts as to the commercial feasibility of the process, Davis was persuaded to buy eighty-five percent of Prodotti Chimici before any study could be made of its prospects. Davis, it appears, was lured into the deal on the basis of a cablegram that warned of a competitive bid. Then, without so much as a pilot test by the Italian management, he acquiesced in a switch to a nitric acid process. He continued to throw good money after bad, trying to salvage the venture, and dispatched a consulting chemist to rescue the operation, in vain. The property, a white elephant, eventually passed into the hands of Aluminium Limited, which tried unsuccessfully to convert the plant into a Bayer refinery. The entire episode, mused Duncan Campbell, who studied it closely, could be attributed to Davis's "penchant for things Italian – good food, fine wines and polished gentlemen bearing titles of nobility." But it also suggests the kind of difficulty inexperienced American companies faced in trying to assess and manage overseas opportunities.[20]

Alcoa acquired water power sites in Norway and France and the Elektrokemisk carbon plant in Norway, which held the so-called Soderberg patents. These patents covered a continuous-process method for producing anodes in the smelting pots, a process that sharply reduced the need for labor to replace the anodes individually.[21] These acquisitions were intended to give the company the capacity to operate in Europe on a full-scale, vertically integrated basis. It was in Norway where Alcoa made its most serious effort to produce aluminum outside North America. In 1923, after three years' negotiations, the company bought half the stock of Norsk Aluminum Company, an unintegrated concern that had been losing money. Norsk was to compete with French and English operations in Norway that exported to the United States. At about the same time, Alcoa took a third interest in the closed plant of Det Norsk Nitrid from its French and English owners. Alcoa also bought a third interest in Aluminio Espagnol, which did no exporting, from its Spanish operators and half of Societa dell'Alluminio Italiano from its French owners. The combined Alcoa capacities of these smelters was about 10,500 metric tons per annum, a modest but hopeful beginning.[22]

Downstream, Alcoa bought interests in foundries in England, France, and Germany, and a share of a French cable manufacturer. These purchases, made between 1923 and 1927, might have been tactical ploys to keep European companies from investing in North America, but they were also opportunistic attempts to revivify languishing or undercapitalized operations. Davis, drawing upon the domestic experience of his enterprise, assumed that Alcoa's progress in European markets must be supplemented by the production of aluminum in finished form. To sell Alcoa aluminum abroad, he established sales companies in Europe as well as in Latin America and Asia.[23] Upstream, he developed Alcoa's holdings in Surinam, which would become the company's major source of bauxite by mid-century, as domestic ore was depleted rapidly.

The most significant foreign expansion occurred in the more familiar territories of Canada. Northern Aluminum's Shawinigan Works contained the largest smelting operation in the British Empire, drawing its power from its namesake falls on the St. Maurice River. Shawinigan had to cut back production after the war, but after 1922 ran up to its capacity of about 15,000 metric tons and also enjoyed a healthy cable fabricating business for the Canadian power industry.[24] The success of Canadian operations combined with the constraints of British Commonwealth economic policy and the lure of Canadian water encouraged expansion north of the border.

In 1916, Alcoa had leased bauxite-rich lands in British Guiana through a subsidiary, the Demerara Bauxite Company. A binding covenant to the leases specified that the company build an alumina refinery somewhere in the British Empire, the deadline for which Alcoa managed to extend to 1929. The Saguenay River, where a refinery could be reached by deep-water vessels, was an ideal location for an alumina plant. Even more compelling was Alcoa's interest in water-power developments along the Saguenay River, which were being undertaken by James B. Duke, the erstwhile tobacco magnate, and his minority Canadian partners. Duke, was approached briefly by the Uihlein family of Milwaukee (owners of Schlitz Brewery) and by George Haskell of the Baush Machine Tool

Fig. 4.1. An Alcoa steamer on the Paranam River in Surinam, circa 1921.

Company, who for a while was in partnership with Henry Ford in the latter's desire to explore ways to get aluminum for his automobiles more cheaply. Alcoa, aroused by the interest potential competitors were showing in the Saguenay and concerned that prime American water-power sources were growing scarce, entered the bidding for Duke's Canadian developments.[25]

Davis's negotiations with Duke to obtain power from the latter's planned hydro plants at Isle Maligne and Chute à Caron limped along until 1924, when Davis accepted a dramatic proposal. The Saguenay power developments were advanced and magnificent ventures that reflected all the expertise, money, and passion that Duke, who had been pioneering hydro developments in the United States since 1906, could bring to bear on such an enterprise. Alcoa wanted participation in the Saguenay properties badly enough so that Davis brought in A. W. Mellon to help with the negotiations. (Mellon was off Alcoa's board while in the Cabinet, but he was still willing to use his prestige and influence to further the interests of an enterprise in which he remained a major stockholder.) A tentative agreement was finally reached, whereby Alcoa would merge with the Lower

Development at Chute à Caron, granting the Duke interests one-ninth share in the new corporation. The new firm would also take rights to water from the Upper Development, which was otherwise left in Duke's hands.[26]

When the merger was struck in July 1925, the Duke interests agreed to take about $16 million of preferred stock at par value and a full fifteen percent of no-par common stock of the new firm. James B. Duke's death just three months later gave Alcoa the opportunity to buy a controlling interest in the Upper Development in order to help the Duke executors pay his estate taxes.[27] Much of the Duke estate passed into a charitable trust, and what remained to his family became a passive investment insofar as Alcoa's board of directors was concerned.[28]

Once Alcoa had gained control over Duke's Canadian developments, it hastened to put this new power to use. Fickes was dispatched to the Saguenay in the spring of 1925 along with I. W. Wilson, the head of Alcoa's primary production. The two men chose a site for an aluminum works five miles between Jonquière and Chicoutimi near Ha! Ha! Bay, which offered a deep-water port for major shipping. In this isolated territory (an overnight train ride from Montreal), where winter temperatures sank to shuddering depths, the town of Arvida was built, named in honor of Arthur Vining Davis. A power plant was built on the Lower Development, a smelter of 27,000 metric tons was in operation by 1927, and a refinery for a "dry process" would soon follow. Arvida was a prideful indulgence for Davis, who spent considerable time on the site, offering not always welcome advice, and who called in prominent New York architects and construction engineers to plan and erect recreational, religious, educational, and medical facilities as well as housing. Arvida was chartered for a city governed by a mayor and aldermen. Built as a company town, it was intended ultimately to become an independent city.[29]

In 1928, Alcoa had over half the total world capacity in primary aluminum, 150,000 metric tons: 90,000 in the United States, 45,000 in Canada, and as much as another 15,000 in Europe. But, just as the company was becoming a multinational power in the integrated production and distribution of aluminum, there was a change of heart. On June 4, 1928, Alcoa divested its ownership or interest in some thirty-four companies worldwide, transferring them to the newly created Aluminium Limited of Canada. Alcoa shareholders received one share of stock in the Canadian corporation for every three Alcoa shares held. As a corporation, Alcoa kept to itself only

some temporary interest in Canadian power and a permanent interest in its bauxite mines in Dutch Guiana.[30]

This retrenchment from multinational business was the handi-
work of A. V. Davis, whose motives were complex and to some extent,
highly personal. He had found that managing overseas operations,
especially in sales, was a problem, and by 1928, he concluded that
Alcoa was "simply not a foreign organization; our people naturally
preferred to sell in large quantities in the United States rather than
to bother, as they perhaps may have considered it, with smaller
quantities abroad." That salesmen were neglecting foreign markets
in favor of selling larger tonnages at home was attested to by Edwin
Mejia, who moved to Aluminium Limited in 1929. "[We] had become
a bunch of Friday afternoon exporters," he said. "We worked terribly
hard all week on domestic sales – then about 2 o'clock on Friday
afternoon, somebody would say 'My Gawd, what have we done about
exports,'... and that's no way to develop a world business."

> Furthermore [explained Davis], very few of our people could
> speak foreign languages, and very few were familiar with for-
> eign business customs. I considered that it was necessary for the
> advancement of the business in Italy to do it by Italians in an
> Italian manner, and to do it in Germany by Germans in a Ger-
> man manner, and so on. I don't mean that the German, Italian
> and other branches of the company were to be entirely divorced
> from jurisdiction on this side, but the various active selling
> officers, particularly, and also to a somewhat less extent the
> manufacturing operations, I conceived should be nationalized to
> a very much greater extent than we had so far done.[31]

Another critical factor in the decision was a perception that there
had been a progressive hardening of nationalist feelings since the
war, especially in the British Commonwealth. "Sentimentally," said
Edward Davis, "a company in the British Empire employing British
people, using British materials and paying British taxes enjoys quite
a notable... preference... as compared with foreign companies." Alcoa executives Roy Hunt and George Gibbons were convinced that
the greatest prospects for aluminum expansion lay in the British
empire and that a Canadian company would be in a prime position
to exploit that opportunity. The two men agreed that the management of foreign operations had to be segregated from Alcoa to operate
on its own principles and on a priority basis.[32]

There was an antiregulatory rationale for the divestiture as well.
Alcoa's corporate secretary George Gibbons explained not long after
the event that "continual persecution by Legislative Bodies and

Commissions...based on allegations that we were endeavoring to control the prices of aluminum throughout the world" was a principal reason for the retrenchment from international operations. An independent Canadian corporation could participate freely in foreign cartels – to do business, as Davis put it, "in the European way" – without implicating Alcoa in American antitrust problems.[33]

One final factor contributed to the timing, if not the substance, of the divestiture. A. V. Davis, now sixty-one, had begun to think about lightening his duties – stepping up, as it were, into semiretirement. Spinning off the foreign operations into a separate company would resolve his "little personal problem," the hard choice between his younger brother, Edward, and his long-time colleague and friend, Roy Hunt, as his successor at the helm. Edward and Roy had come to work at Alcoa "at the same time,...and they had each of them gone along in a successful, satisfactory manner until one of them had become the head of the selling department and the other head of the manufacturing department." Edward was sent north with a small band of Alcoa technical experts and salesmen to become head of Aluminium Limited, while Roy Hunt remained in Pittsburgh to become president of the firm his father had founded.[34]

In sum, from the standpoint of Alcoa's senior managers, who were also among its principal stockholders, the divestiture of foreign operations made perfect sense on several counts. Alcoa's stockholders had nothing to lose and everything to gain. The interests of management and stockholders were virtually identical, and Roy Hunt avowed in court testimony that even if he and his associates had nothing to do with the management of the foreign business, "we would all get our share."[35]

Alcoa's retrenchment from foreign operations, like its earlier decision to go abroad, moved in tandem with a larger trend in corporate policy among American companies. Multinational growth generally would be sharply curtailed in the Great Depression. But even beforehand, prospects for sales abroad were dimming in the rising tide of nationalistic economic policies, which increasingly limited foreign investments and stockholders' rights. Like Alcoa, many American companies discovered that they could not effectively manage their foreign operations. Thus, they reorganized those operations as separate entities or got rid of them altogether. American multinational operations that persisted through the lean years were doomed to go under in World War II and its confusing political aftermath.[36] It was unfortunate, because considerable learning was lost. In the post-World War II era, American companies that ventured overseas had to learn anew about joint-venturing overseas investments to share risks, assessing political risks, taking on national partners, negotiating favorable terms with host governments, and coming to terms with wide cultural differences in order to establish and manage their enterprises abroad effectively. Despite shrinking power resources at home and notwithstanding growing markets overseas, more than a quarter century would pass before Alcoa itself would again pursue opportunities abroad, save for its ongoing stake in a reliable source of foreign bauxite. But there was a unique factor in Alcoa's case: the status of the company's principal stockholders as owners and directors of Aluminium Limited. Notwithstanding the two companies' denials of any plan to this effect, Limited acted virtually as the foreign arm of the joint stockholders' business, generally refraining from entry into American markets.

Of course, one unforeseen short-term benefit to Alcoa's balance sheet was that it had been relieved of its foreign liabilities in the nick of time. In the first few years of the Depression, Aluminium Limited barely survived, muddling through by going deeply into debt and by drawing upon considerable technical help from Alcoa and upon the use of some of its alumina and rolling facilities. Limited's fortunes improved, and by 1937, it was out of debt and prospering, having increased its payroll from 4,000 to 12,000 employees and having more than doubled its capacity at Arvida.[37] Thus, in the longer run, the principals benefitted financially, but the arrangement was ultimately to become the most effective charge in the Federal Government's assault on Alcoa's corporate power.

The quest for efficiency: functional organization

Even before World War I, Alcoa's operations had outgrown the loosely bound structure through which the company conducted its diverse and far-flung business. Senior managers with small staffs had neither the ability nor the time to oversee day-to-day operations, while also planning growth, allocating resources, and monitoring the performance of the entire business. The vertical integration of Alcoa's enterprise required increasingly specialized expertise in the management of the various technical and business functions. Such major line and staff activities as mining, refining, smelting, fabricating, sales, research, engineering, accounting, and personnel were carried out by the subsidiary and directly owned plants of the company. And yet there existed no institutional mechanism for integrating these highly differentiated functions across institutional boundaries. Under Alcoa's rather simple organization, there were no consistent means for identifying the sources of problems in the throughput process, imposing standard operating procedures, eliminating waste or duplication of effort, sharing state-of-the-art information, evaluating performance, or scheduling the volume and flow of production in accordance with the general conditions of the economy and the state of the markets. As we have seen, the company's chief engineer, Edwin S. Fickes, had already sensed the problem, even if he did not fully articulate it.[38] If the company were to grow any larger and more complex, it would have to devise a better way of structuring the administration of its business and technical functions lest there be great confusion of managerial roles and inefficient coordination of the enterprise as a whole.

At the end of the war, most large American companies persisted in managing vertically integrated operations through traditional, but administratively awkward, holding-company structures. Many large industrial corporations had moved to a higher stage of bureaucratic sophistication, successfully departmentalizing their activities along functional plans of organization that were highly efficient for vertically integrated enterprises. However, in the other nonferrous metals – copper, nickel, zinc – the dominant firms integrated upstream in mining, refining, and smelting, but downstream they sold relatively undifferentiated products to few customers. Under the relatively stable market, technological, and competitive conditions that characterized those industries, there was little pressure for organizational reform.[39]

Aluminum was actually more like the ferrous metal steel in its business characteristics. Although the markets for semifinished steel products were not as varied as those for aluminum, contemporary steel firms had become highly integrated concerns. By World War I, many large steel concerns had consolidated their operations into departmentalized structures organized around technical and business functions, and at least one, the Republic Iron & Steel Company, had moved to an even more modern-looking divisional form of organization along geographic lines. On the other hand, Pittsburgh's own United States Steel Corporation demonstrated how a dominant firm in a market could persist in a condition of structural stasis. U.S. Steel was not only a thoroughly integrated concern along the vertical axis, dealing in many products for many customers, it was also the country's largest industrial corporation. The coordination of its throughput was an immense and complicated problem, and yet under Judge Elbert Gary, U.S. Steel had barely progressed beyond the loose holding-company structure created at the time of its founding. In 1901, when Andrew Carnegie's enterprise was merged with two other major steel companies by J. P. Morgan, it became "a federation of independent companies ... each with its own distinct government, officers, sphere of influence, and particular products."[40] Content with its leading position in an expansive era for steel products, U.S. Steel was an even less coherently managed enterprise than Alcoa and offered little to emulate.

Therefore, when Alcoa began to recast its structure along functional lines in World War I, there were few relevant examples and no well-defined body of organizational wisdom to inform the process. Pressures of the aluminum business had simply mounted so that organizational change had become a necessity. The company's new structure was to be shaped along common-sense lines with respect to the company's underlying technologies and markets.

Lacking direct evidence of the reasoning that drove the reorganization, we can logically infer that the impetus to reform sprang from several sources. The increasing scale of the business was a factor. Aluminum, in its drive to take markets from other materials, was very price-sensitive, and so it was crucial to keep production costs at levels that could not be easily undercut by the more established metals. Because Alcoa had always maintained a policy of pricing aluminum internally to Alcoa fabricating operations at the same price as to external markets (the one exception to this policy was in the pricing of electric cable vis-à-vis copper), there was constant pressure to make operations more efficient via technological improvements and well-coordinated management of throughput. As the organization grew, it became more difficult to coordinate without more explicit specialization of duties among the company's officers and clearer channels of communication between Pittsburgh and outlying operations.

Aluminum technology was growing more complex, not only as a result of coordination and improvement of production processes, but also due to changes in the science of aluminum. With the advent of hard alloys and new techniques in metallurgical research, systematic research and development became more important. Selling aluminum products had also become more complicated, as applications spread to highly technical and sophisticated markets. The financial and accounting problems of a business that involved so many different kinds of activities spread over a wide geographic area required careful monitoring and controls. Research and development, the

Fig. 4.2. Alcoa executives at Alcoa, Tennessee, circa 1919. From left to right are I. W. Calderwood, superintendent of construction; James W. Rickey, chief hydraulic engineer; Edward S. Fickes, chief engineer; Arthur Vining Davis, president; Charles B. Fox, manager of alumina; Roy A. Hunt, manager of fabricating; Judge H. Bart Lindsay, a local company attorney from Knoxville; and Charles H. Moritz, manager of smelting.

management and coordination of production, financial controls, and marketing had always been full-time concerns of the executive officers of the company, but both size and complexity had so differentiated them in their managerial requirements that some way had to be found to administer them on a more specialized basis.

It is hard to pinpoint the exact timing of the reorganization, except to say that it was in the planning stages during the war and was in place by 1919. Fragments of an organization chart for 1919, probably the company's first, show the establishment of a central office at Pittsburgh divided into six functional departments, each having specific responsibility for production, engineering, finance, purchasing, sales, and technical development. The new Engineering Department incorporated many of the major siting and heavy-construction activities that had already been centralized at Pittsburgh under Fickes. The new Finance Department was the outcome of a process that appears already to have begun in attempts by the central office to prescribe uniform standards of accounting for all its constituent operations. Centralization of purchasing functions would help Alcoa realize important economies both from the better coordination of inputs across the system and from block buying power of the company for standardized items. A new Sales Department assumed the functions of a discrete operation of the company that had been located at Pittsburgh since the turn of the century. Unlike the other departments, Sales included not only functions located at operating sites, but also in several major cities in North America and overseas, where regional and local sales offices had been established for both general and specialized markets. The Technical Department, the activities of which will be described later, brought together the company's scientific functions under central control at New Kensington. It was Alcoa's practice to charter its operations as wholly owned subsidiaries – whether organized around established fabricated products, like the U.S. Aluminum Company (after 1922); or newly acquired, like the American Magnesium Corporation; or newly created, like the Aluminum Screw Machine Product Company – to exploit particular markets or to manage specialized technologies and channels of distribution. But these separate legal entities fell entirely within the scope of central office administration.[41]

There was an abortive attempt to bring corporate executives into closer contact with local works superintendents by the establishment of an "Alcoa Operating Committee," which was supposed "to meet from time to time at the company's various works and offices." This plan proved unworkable. Instead, the Production Department, which encompassed three "divisions" – Ore, Reduction, and Rolling and Fabrication – became the heart of corporate-wide operations. The Production Department as such had no manager: the three managers of the production divisions, Charles B. Fox (Ore), Charles H. Moritz (Reduction), and Roy Hunt (Rolling and Fabrication) sat as a committee, also known as the Operating Committee. Roy Hunt had senior status, and, as the only board member with operating duties, was the closest thing to a modern chief operating officer.[42]

Each new department had responsibility for coordinate functions within the plants, both directly owned or subsidiary, of the corporation. Local plant organization, however, did not mirror the central office structure – each plant was organized in accordance with its own principles of operations and occupational specialties. But the new central office structure at least made it possible for like functions and tasks to communicate directly across intra-Alcoa boundaries. In accordance with "line and staff" divisions of management responsibilities, the plant superintendents reported directly to the heads of the Production Department divisions while their specialized subordinates could communicate with the heads of Engineering, Finance, Purchasing, Sales, and Technical. All this was a marked improvement over the old company structure in which there had been no formal channels for communication except through the heads of local operations. Wholly owned but legally separate corporate entities, such as The Aluminum Cooking Utensil Company, appear to have stood in relation to the central office much like a plant.[43]

Even though A. V. Davis maintained a strong interest in operations and remained remarkably familiar with the technical details of the enterprise for years to come, the organizational reform reflected a recognition that neither the board of directors nor its president was in any position to monitor day-to-day activities. The new structure not only made possible the kind of centralized coordination of vertical functions that had been difficult under the ill-defined reporting relationships of the prewar structure, it also conferred greater status on three of the company's most valuable and experienced hands. Fox, Moritz, and Fickes – senior managers whose careers had progressed without ties to the board or to the families of the founders – were elevated along with Hunt to vice presidencies. The heads of two other departments also became vice presidents. Robert E. Withers, already company treasurer and long-time member of the board, became head of the new Financial Department. Edward K. Davis became vice president of Sales. Only in Purchasing and Technical do we find men – J. S. Murray and William Hoopes, respectively – who were neither officers of the corporation nor members of the closed circle of substantial stockholders.[44]

Alcoa's functionally based organization remained essentially unchanged in basic principle well into the 1960s. But before World War II, the functional organization underwent at least two important modifications, in 1929, with the divestiture of Alcoa's foreign operations, and again in the late 1930s. It is ironic that the problems with Alcoa's overseas operations might have well been solved through the decentralization of its management. In any case, one organizational upshot of the divestiture and its consequent reshuffling of key personnel was the creation of the Office of the Chairman of the Board for A. V. Davis. The new president's office, which reported to the chairman, replaced the Production Department's committee of three. Reporting to Hunt were five vice presidents responsible for Production, Technology, Ore, Finance, and Sales and Publicity. The head of this last department was George R. Gibbons, corporate secretary since 1910, under whom Sales and Publicity had been divided into separate divisions. (No one had yet risen to succeed Edward Davis as vice president of sales.) The appearance of a Publicity and Development Division reflected the increasing sophistication of marketing aluminum through broader-based efforts to promote and defend the company's good will.[45]

After 1929, there was a gradual attentuation of the functional structure until 1938, when three senior vice presidencies (under Gibbons, Fickes, and Withers) were constituted. In the organization charts for that year, we see some substantial alteration in functional definitions. A more general grouping of central office functions was due to the growth and elaboration of middle-management positions. Under Gibbons were grouped vice presidents for Sales and Public Relations; under Fickes, a vice president for Alumina and managers for Research, Hydraulic and Electrical Engineering, and Purchasing. Vice presidents for production (Reduction and Fabricating), Bauxite, Auditing, and Pittsburgh office management reported directly to President Hunt. Also reporting to Hunt were the heads of key subsidiary concerns, The Aluminum Cooking Utensil Company, the Aluminum Seal Company, and the Nantahala Power and Light Company (a North Carolina subsidiary formed for the purpose of meeting state requirements) as did managers for Castings, Die Castings, and Personnel.[46]

Owner-managers and loose controls

The growth of Alcoa's central office occasioned the removal of the company's headquarters from the Oliver Building to the Gulf Building in 1933.[47] This move not only gave the company more room for its increasing staff, it also reinforced the public identification of the firm with the Mellon Family. Indeed, the influence of the Mellons, whose Alcoa stock had increased to about thirty-seven percent of the total, remained powerful. Alcoa was still dominated by its traditional family stockholders and bankers, and A. V. Davis's grip on management remained as firm as ever. When he relinquished the presidency in 1929 to become chairman of the board, it did not mean what it signified in many corporations of that era – that he had been kicked upstairs or that he had simply drifted into semiretirement. Little happened at Alcoa in policy or general practice that did not bear his stamp of approval, and by 1938, the seventy-year-old chairman was still in charge. His critical faculties were as keen as ever, a fact he proved impressively in the course of his stunningly detailed testimonies on the business and its operations in antitrust proceedings.[48]

It might seem surprising that there had ever been a day when Davis doubted his ability to maintain his grip. And yet there had been just such a time in 1925, when the reorganization of Alcoa in its merger with Duke posed a threat to Davis's effective control of the board of directors. Davis, remember, was coexecutor of Charles Martin Hall's estate and had the power to vote the Hall Trust beneficiaries' common stock through 1929.[49] With the Duke-Alcoa merger in the works, Davis approached Oberlin College, Berea College, and the American Missionary Association with a clever but incredibly ill-advised scheme to improve his position in the reorganized company.[50] After some informal meetings, Davis formally proposed on May 5, 1925 that the trustees of the three institutions authorize the sale of "a substantial block of common stock" from the Hall Estate to "a syndicate" of Alcoa managers headed by Alcoa secretary George Gibbons "in which," Davis avowed, "I am interested." Davis outlined the terms of a Duke-Alcoa merger:

> [T]he new corporation will have an authorized capital stock of 1,500,000 shares of 6% cumulative preferred stock and 1,500,000 shares of no par common stock. The present plan contemplates that the assets of the Aluminum Company shall be acquired on the basis of 7 shares of the 6% preferred stock and 6 shares of no par common stock of the new corporation for each outstanding share of stock in the Aluminum Company. The new preferred stock is to be issued, one half effective as of the first day of July, 1925, and the other half in the form of transferable warrants exchangeable on the first day of January, 1927, for preferred stock, but meantime entitled to receive neither interest nor dividends.[51]

A problem was that Duke decided to ask for "a larger percentage of the common stock" for a merger between Alcoa and his properties "than his pro rata share thereof would be, based on the assets turned over by himself and associates." Davis, of course, wanted to end the threat Duke's hydropower posed to Alcoa's aluminum monopoly, but he was also concerned about his own stock position. He wanted a substantial improvement in his holdings of Alcoa common, or else the merger, which would surely benefit the institutional stockholders, might not be consummated.[52]

Davis proposed that two-thirds of the stock of the Hall estate to which the three institutions were entitled be sold to the Gibbons

Syndicate "at the price of $730 per share, payable as follows: $25 per share in cash; $5 buys one share of common stock in the new corporation, and $700, at the option of the purchaser, either in cash or in preferred stock in the new corporation, at par." (The remaining third of the stock would be sold to a second syndicate from which Davis, himself, would be excluded.) Upon conclusion of the transaction, the Hall Estate trusteeship was to be terminated, more than four years before it need be under the terms of the will. The principal of the trust fund could then be distributed to the beneficiaries.[53]

The Hall Estate's cotrustee, Homer Johnson (who stood to gain none of the stock sold to the Davis syndicate), rendered his advice that the merger and the terms of Davis's proposal would result in a "much higher present return to the [Hall Estate] beneficiaries." The three boards of trustees met in New York to consider the proposal. A couple of doubts were voiced but were quickly dispelled by Johnson's advocacy of the plan, and "after a rather desultory discussion" (and with no independent examination of Alcoa's financial position), "the respective Boards of Trustees ... adopted the resolutions, thereby approving the plan of reorganization." It was acknowledged in the meeting's minutes that "Mr. Davis will probably profit thereby through his interests in the Syndicate." The plan was approved on June 6 by the Surrogate Court.[54] This was nothing, Davis claimed later, but a deal made in everyone's best interests based on a candid and full disclosure. If that is what he thought at the time of the transaction, he was mistaken. Both he and the institutional trustees would rue the day.

The trustees had strong incentives to accept Davis's plan. Oberlin's trustees in particular felt that Alcoa's policy of retaining earnings had "been good for the Company but ... has made it hard for the beneficiaries who have been looking forward to making use of the income. ... " And now Davis in his presentation was implying that this policy might become more stringent, that dividends might even be suspended for a few years. The preferred stock would, of course, pay a reliable rate of interest. Then too, the distribution of the principal from the Hall estate would give the beneficiaries an opportunity to dispose of Alcoa stock to finance some immediate projects. Most of the Oberlin trustees and their financial advisers felt that it was important for the college to diversify its holdings and that the opportunity was ripe to take the profits from the sale of large blocks of Alcoa common. Finally, Davis posed the risk that should his common voting power weaken too much, he could be dislodged as head of the reorganized Alcoa. Everyone agreed that Alcoa's stockholders would be better served if Davis continued "as a director and officer of such new company."[55]

What went wrong is that both Alcoa and Davis flourished. When Alcoa common was listed on the New York Curb Exchange on July 31, 1925, it sold for $34 per share. By April 1926, the stock was quoted at $65. Trading was slow, and Davis and his allies may have been supporting the price (the institutions were having trouble placing their stock for sale in large blocks), but as the Berea trustees noted, "Mr. Davis made a very handsome thing out of buying our common stock at $5 a share." A year later, Alcoa common was reportedly trading at $125 per share, and in 1929, the stock sold for as much as $197.75. Davis argued "that there was no basis whatever for the present exorbitant price..., except the fact that there was little in the market and speculators knew that neither Mellons nor himself would sell."[56] It was doubtful that a large volume of stock could command such a high price. Besides, Davis maintained, the $5 per share he had paid for the Hall Estate's stock was an honest price at the time. He could not foresee that the stock would do as spectacularly well as it appeared to have done by 1929. Nonetheless, suspicions that Davis had originally misrepresented Alcoa's position as well as his own were in full bloom. The Oberlin trustees were already soliciting legal opinions in order to build a case against Davis and Johnson for fraud.[57]

Davis, a man "accustomed to draw his own papers," had unwittingly wounded himself in his 1925 presentation to the trustees by not consulting with his attorneys on the language of his letter.[58] There was a presumption that Davis, simply by taking the action he did, had violated his fiduciary responsibility to the Hall Estate. For their part, Oberlin officials were loath to enter into litigation, lest they come to be regarded by potential benefactors "as an uncomfortable group to deal with." The president of Oberlin considered the risk that the college would lose substantial good will. Davis and Johnson, moreover, were old friends of the college.[59] But the harder sentiments prevailed. The Oberlin trustees informed Davis and Johnson that they would charge them with "a most serious breach of trust," which should render the 1925 transaction void. Oberlin, Berea, and the American Missionary Association turned aside Davis's suggestion that the dispute be arbitrated by no less a jurist than Charles Evans Hughes.[60] Instead, they unleashed their lawyers on Davis, who could ill afford the publicity, driving him to a quick and confidential settlement.

Davis's only hope was for a discreet resolution of the matter by which he would admit no guilt and would thereby salvage his reputation, his "business honor." It was by no means certain that he would lose in litigation; there was enough solid legal opinion on his side to enable him to build a stout defense. But the very process of a trial would bring him into ill repute. Alternatively, he and Johnson did not want to risk a judgment that might conceivably, "upon a technicality of law, ruin them both financially." Over a period of five months, Davis made his case in conferences with attorneys, as the two sides haggled over how much of Davis's stock should be returned. Davis, it was calculated, had received 61,285 shares of the new Alcoa from the Gibbons Syndicate, on the basis of which he was later able to subscribe to at least a third that many of Aluminium, Limited, when it was spun off in 1928.[61] He thought it "unthinkable" that he "give up all of this stock after having carried it for five years; that . . . it [was] very unjust that the institutions should come around . . . after the stock had apparently gone up in price, and seek its return." He at first offered to turn back 12,000 and then 30,000 shares,[62] but the Oberlin attorneys pressed for much more, and in an agreement signed on January 21, 1930, Davis finally acceded 45,000 shares of Alcoa and 15,000 shares of Limited to the three institutions in exchange for their abandonment of claims against him, Johnson, and other Alcoa directors, officers, and shareholders. (The stock was later estimated by Johnson to have a combined value of approximately $3 million.) Oberlin attorneys gloated over their triumph. They had, after all, gotten the better of a shrewd businessman at his own game.[63]

Davis was deeply hurt and angered by allegations that he had misled the beneficiaries of the Hall Estate. "Nothing in his entire life," he was reported to have said, "had disturbed him so much as the present situation in which his good faith and fair dealing had been questioned." As for Homer Johnson, himself a former Oberlin trustee, he was nervous, furious, and mortified.[64]

Six years later, a young assistant dean at Oberlin dined with Johnson and was so struck by a story Johnson related to him after dinner that he recorded it in a handwritten memo. Under the rubric of *The Inside Story*, Donald M. Love recorded Johnson's recollection of the Davis-Oberlin stock incident. Davis's purpose, according to the memo, had been to get "a crucial 5% of stock . . . *to keep the majority of votes out of Mr. Mellon's hands*." That was something that Davis could not afford to have revealed. Knowing that, the Oberlin trustees "then pinched Mr. Davis when he couldn't do anything but hand over the transferred stock or reveal the primary purpose which had been to freeze Mellon out of a controlling interest in the Aluminum Company."[65]

In the absence of records, we cannot verify what portion of the common stock was controlled by the Mellons in 1925, when Davis hatched his ill-fated scheme. Assuming that the Mellons had more than thirty-five percent (it was unlikely that the proportion of their holdings had slipped since the end of the war from its level of thirty-seven percent), they and Duke combined would have a majority of the common stock following the merger. This would place overwhelming financial control of Alcoa in the hands of men who were not themselves managers and could have a serious impact on company policy. Davis seems to have regarded this as a threat to his position, and he was no doubt looking ahead to 1929, when his powers of trusteeship over Hall's stock would lapse. Whether there had been any friction between the Mellons and Davis or any serious disagreement over policy, we simply do not know. We only know that Davis made some representation to the Hall beneficiaries of the potential for a change in the managerial status quo, a change which they apparently feared.

As it turned out, with Duke dead and Davis's power over the Hall Estate lapsed, the Mellons' shareholdings were sufficient to give them effective control of the board of directors. But any fears that they might restructure Alcoa's management were never realized. The Mellons were in for the long haul and seemed content, as always, to share power with Davis and Hunt. After both senior Mellons had gone by the end of 1937, representation of their family's stake in Alcoa passed on primarily to Richard's son, Richard King Mellon, who attentively watched over his interest as a member of the board through the following three decades.[66]

Another outgrowth of the Duke-Alcoa merger was "a very radical change in policy" regarding financial reporting. In 1927, the company began to issue public financial statements, a consequence of "the drift on to the stock exchanges of the country" of the reorganized company's "huge capital stock." Alcoa, explained George Gibbons, had ceased to be "closely held by a mere handful of closely associated stockholders . . . , a private corporation."[67] Gibbons was right about the direction of things, but we must be careful not to take his words at face value. Alcoa was still a very "private" concern, still under the control by a durable handful of owners – most of whom had been with the company for decades. In 1938, the year of its fiftieth anniversary, Alcoa remained a firm in which the principal managers were also principal owners. First-generation owners and their off-spring, like Roy Hunt, held the preponderance of executive offices. Of the senior vice presidents, Gibbons was the son of the head of the Arkansas bauxite mines that had been merged into Alcoa in 1909. Withers had been a major stockholder and company treasurer since 1898. Only Fickes had attained the rank of senior officer (and director) of the company on the basis of professional, that is, bureaucratic, criteria.[68]

There was an important relationship between Alcoa's tradition of owner-management and what everyone agreed was its weak central bureaucracy. In a company where the continuities of command and the association of family and person with office were strong, formal structure did not loom as a major instrument of control. This was especially true at the top, where the tone of the enterprise was set. Alcoa's veteran managers dwelled little on the subject of organization as a matter of philosophical or theoretical concern. At Alcoa, there were no students of structure equivalent to General Motors' Alfred Sloan or DuPont's cadre of bureaucratic innovators. A. V. Davis had been used to wielding authority by the force of his personality. Roy Hunt believed that formality in organization inhibited enterprise. Between them, they tried to maintain a somewhat loose system of governance characteristic of a much smaller, more personal association of like-minded businessmen.

Thus, on the one hand, the formal structure clarified reporting channels along functional lines, which was especially important for the sharing of technical information, and it better enabled Pittsburgh to keep itself informed about the business as a whole. But behind the formal structure were underlying attitudes about corporate governance that were decidely unbureaucratic and that weakened the thrusts toward centralization and toward rigid hierarchical chains of command that one would normally expect from functionally based administration. Operating units of the business continued to enjoy a high degree of independence. The foundries at Cleveland, for example, were organized as the Aluminum Castings Company and managed their own sales. "Powerful fellows" like Charles "Alumina" Fox and Winthrop "Bauxite" Nielson ran their departments (organized as subsidiary companies) with iron hands and brooked no interference (as they would have interpreted it) from Pittsburgh. This was true as well of such operations as the fluorspar mines, the steamship line, cooking utensils, and even automobile bodies, the last of which existed for three years as the American Body Company under Stafford K. Colby (until Alcoa concluded that it could not compete with steel in that business). Even where local plant managers reported to departments whose heads resided in Pittsburgh, they remained lords of their local domains, exercising nearly complete operational discretion over production and in the hiring and firing of subordinates. Likewise, regional sales had considerable freedom to develop and manage their territories. Ambitious young men could aspire to few positions in the corporate world that offered more authority and autonomy than those of Alcoa plant superintendent and district sales manager.[69]

The aborted Alcoa Operating Committee of 1919 reveals some of the difficulty the central office had in providing mechanisms for corporate-wide control. The Committee included the various works superintendents and central office executives and sought to make them "better acquainted with each other and with the company's different plants and activities." It was felt that "the rush of work and growth of the company during the war period . . . left little time for its executives and superintendents to do anything more than to attend to routine duties." This attempt to provide local operators a better appreciation for the overall conduct of the business and to keep executives current with local operations was doomed to failure. Time, the ultimate constraint on all business activity, simply did not permit it. Davis himself chaired the meetings, which between March and July of 1919 took place at seven different sites in Pennsylvania, Tennessee, and New York. The travel alone was enough to make it difficult for superintendents to direct their operations, vice presidents to manage their departments, and senior executives to coordinate the enterprise as a whole[70]

None of this meant that central controls were unachievable; it was just that control worked better as it seemed less intrusive. Local superintendents were brought into harmony with the overall goals of the enterprise through consensus techniques. A more formal technique was the linking of like operations in a kind of network of mutual assessment, wherein each superintendent kept a close watch on his production costs, which were then measured against the costs of comparable operations in other plants. It is not known when this practice began, but it was certainly routine by the late 1920s. As a former engineer at Niagara explained it, "every reduction plant kept very minute costs of every item and these were circulated [among] the plants" who would then "criticize" each other's performance "on a competitive basis."[71]

Only when crises erupted between two or more functional areas of the business, or between a plant and customers, did Pittsburgh intervene decisively. Such intervention sometimes required extraordinary measures. From his vantage point in Sales, Frank Magee recounted his own involvement in a case in which substandard forgings and sheets were being shipped from Aluminum Castings to the American Body Company sometime in the late 1920s. The Sales Department had received serious complaints from customers about the delivery and quality of American Body products, a problem that was traced, at least in part, to the manufacture and delivery of forging stock and sheet from Massena, New Kensington, and Edgewater. The head of the Fabricating Department was Robert L. Streeter, a former army ordnance officer and Rensselaer professor who, as Magee tells it, had been recruited by Hunt only to be undone by the younger Davis. "Colonel" Streeter's reputation for fast cars, wild parties, and the ladies did not sit well with the more straitlaced Alcoa senior managers. His graver fault lay in his attempt to shield his operations from corporate scrutiny. The younger Davis, whose salesmen began to complain, recruited three "ambassadors" from his department to go to the offending plants in order to find out what was going on. In this "delicate" matter of sending Edward Davis's salesmen into Roy Hunt's operations, Magee was dispatched to Massena.

The troubles between the Sales Department and production managers at New Kensington and Edgewater were smoothed over, once their causes had become known and explained. At Massena, the plant superintendent, Arthur Vail, was an obstacle to reform. The plant superintendent remained stubbornly unconvinced about the need for improvements in quality control and shipping. Vail, said Magee, "was not a guy to run a plant that was being run for customers," who would attribute bad products to Alcoa's "damn monopoly." More to the point, no one was coordinating a solution to the metallurgical and engineering problems that were involved in defective materials. By the time the situation was restored to normal, both Vail and the Colonel were sacked and replaced by men who hopefully had greater appreciation for the overall demands of the company's business.[72]

The story illustrates the brute facts of power that enabled Pittsburgh to contain the centrifugal forces of its loosely bound structure. The power to hire and fire the heads of local operations could always bring local operations reasonably back into line with corporate policy. Pittsburgh also controlled the sources of funds vital to plant maintenance and growth and the scheduling of overall production, which, of course, could be shifted among plants depending on their efficiency. But beyond those attributes of corporate power, Pittsburgh could rely normally on the sense of common identity throughout the system that welded diverse and scattered operations into a kind of cultural whole, a single company of people engaged in a single enterprise, "The Aluminum Company."

The production and distribution of aluminum was a role in society that belonged to no one else but the people of Alcoa. Company employees at all levels of the hierarchy commonly referred to their corporate "family," an ideal that supported the formation of consensus on its ways of doing business. This ideal, which permeated all areas of the corporation and gave it much of its cohesion, was based on some very durable sentiments of the family firm and of respect for modes of corporate association that were more traditional than modern, more paternal than bureaucratic. At its most benign, Alcoa was a company that valued its people more than its capital. The exercise of authority and power could be highly arbitrary under such circumstances, but interpersonal relationships mattered more than regulated arrangements. Roy Hunt liked to relate a dream he had in which Alcoa faced imminent catastrophe. He thought that if only he could keep his men, "we will build new plants." The simple articulation of such sentiments in a capital-intensive enterprise was a powerful incentive to corporate loyalty and morale.[73]

Alcoa thus remained a hybrid of family and finance capitalism in which the owners who managed continued to hold sway on the board of directors. Taking a strong managerial point of view, the board continued to emphasize retained earnings. And though like any large capital-intensive business, Alcoa had to raise large sums over and above its retained earnings to finance expansion; preferred stock and debt were employed in preference to public offerings of common.[74] The close relation of ownership to management also accounts for the slow process by which new blood rose to the top. In the fullness of time, Alcoa's leading families would inevitably have to cede control to younger professionals drawn from the ranks. In the organization chart for 1938, we can spot the rising star of Irving W. Wilson as vice president of Reduction and Fabricating. A fine electrochemical engineer with strong managerial capabilities, Wilson had joined the Niagara Works in 1911, upon his graduation from MIT. He had not expected to stay, worried at the time that he had already missed the aluminum boom.[75] He worked his way up through the smelting side of the business and became general superintendent of smelting in 1921. In 1931, he became Alcoa's youngest vice president as head of operations. Now he was on the verge of joining the company's top ranks, and in time, he would become Alcoa's chief executive, the first with neither old-family ties nor a substantial block of stock.

Innovation and the organization of research

When ill health forced Edwin Fickes into retirement in 1938, he could draw satisfaction from the internal empire of technical functions he had helped Alcoa fashion. In the course of his company career, Fickes had been involved in mining, refining, construction, traffic, water power, electrical systems, and research. He wound up as the prince of one of Alcoa's major fiefdoms, the Engineering Department. The jewel in his crown was the Aluminum Research Laboratories. Formed as a "Research Bureau" in 1919, the Laboratories had brought Alcoa into the mainstream of industrial research and development.

Before the war, remember, innovation at Alcoa had had little basis in formal research except for Charles Martin Hall's projects. Although research on the alumina refining process had received considerable attention, the company had invested little in the way of exploration into the fundamental nature of aluminum, its alloys, or the theoretical basis of their fabrication and application. Research projects, as former public relations director Charles C. Carr put it, had been "informally organized and frequently had to be put aside for more pressing production problems." There had been little progress toward organizing research and development on a permanent institutional footing – a fact that we can ascribe to Hall's own attitude in the matter.[76]

But after the war, the company could no longer afford to ignore the more fundamental problems of metallurgy. As we have seen, the war highlighted the problems the company was having not with its processes but with its products, especially in the area of hard alloys. There had arisen a distinct possibility that an outside invention, such as Wilm's Duralumin, could threaten a major segment of Alcoa's business. Without the in-house capability of responding to, or anticipating, such technological events, Alcoa might not be able to replicate an important new technology, find a reasonable substitute, or bring key patents under its control. Like other large firms whose technology operated on the frontiers of contemporary knowledge, Alcoa finally found it necessary to finance fundamental research and development in order to defend its own business base.

The quest for a research director after Hall's death was organized around Alcoa's ongoing concern for process development. There is a letter from William Hoopes to Joseph W. Richards at Lehigh, written in the spring of 1917, seeking a "resourceful chemical engineer with considerable experience and originality" to "start a research laboratory." Its primary purpose would be to investigate problems in the manufacture of alumina, still the high-cost bottleneck in the integrated system of production. Hoopes explained that this laboratory was to have an extended life as a "general research laboratory" in order to "work on any problem which gives promise of making improvement in any of the company's existing processes."[77]

The man recommended to head Alcoa's new research efforts was a thirty-three-year-old research chemist from the University of Minnesota, Francis C. Frary. Frary had spent several years teaching industrial chemistry, having been educated at Minnesota and Berlin. A fine figure of a man, Frary had a reputation for great physical strength, athletic prowess, and boundless energy, which last quality spilled over into his work. He was endowed with a wide-ranging curiosity and a prodigious memory, which in addition to his precise and correct manners, aversion to alcohol, piety, and gentle sense of humor would make him seem larger than life to his colleagues and employees. At Minnesota, he was a whirlwind of activity. He taught no fewer than fifteen courses in at least nine discrete subjects in one academic year while conducting experiments in electrometallurgy. By 1915, he had patented and sold six of his own inventions – five hard-lead alloys, which he marketed through the United Lead Company, and a safe method for producing phosphorus sesquisulfide, the incendiary substance used on matcheads. He then left the academy to find more lucrative work at the Oldbury Chemical Company in Niagara Falls, where he studied potassium and caustic compounds and became an expert on the production of phosgene, a toxic gas. By the time Alcoa found him, he had earned his spurs as a business scientist, production engineer, and "pipe-fitting chemist." He could read technical journals in several languages and was a self-taught expert on patents. These qualities were rare in a scientist who was not only skilled in rigorous fundamental research, but who had also achieved the stature of a generalist with credentials spanning the fields of chemistry, chemical engineering, and metallurgy.[78]

When interviewed by the superintendent of the Niagara Works, Frary expressed enthusiasm "about handling work of an original nature, but not in solving problems that arise from time to time at the Works relating to process control." He was reassured on this point, saying that it was the company's intention "to establish a general research laboratory, somewhat along the lines of those established by the General Electric and other companies, and that the work that would be carried on there was of an investigating nature and did not pertain to troubles of various kinds relating to Works' operations." No doubt this was confirmed in his interviews with a committee of the board of directors who interviewed him twice.[79]

One cannot overstate the importance of Frary's arrival on the scene for the future of Alcoa research. Frary's reputation as a scientist set the tone, if not the precise conditions, for his employment. He was hired in the fall at a premium salary, a fact that quickly became known, causing something of a stir among other company technical personnel who clamored for a transfer to the proposed new laboratory in New Kensington. He was given carte blanche to select his own research staff from candidates both within and outside Alcoa. Unfortunately, his start was delayed by the army, which drafted him for work in toxic chemicals. It was not until December 1918 that Frary arrived at New Kensington, where the new Research Bureau was to commence operations.[80]

Originally, the Research Bureau had been set up as one of two branches of the new Technical Department. The other branch, the Technical Direction Bureau, was responsible for functions related to process improvements and quality control under the guidance of chief chemist Earl Blough.[81] The Research Bureau, by contrast, was intended to operate without regard to the "routine work" of the company, and as a mark of its independence, was to be lead by an outsider whose background and interests were not tied to aluminum production.[82]

Frary did not find what he had expected. The Research and Technical Bureaus shared the third floor of the New Kensington Works clockhouse, with the men's locker room above and the restaurant below. Support staffing was inadequate. Fickes and Hoopes had pressed Davis for a site away from operations, lest they "become a dominant factor in determining a research policy that would neglect other problems of the business that might be of far greater importance to the Company than those of the single works where the laboratory was located." But "this idea had little support" among the executives, whose tight purse strings kept Dr. Frary "in cramped and inadequate quarters" during the first few years. The decision not to build a laboratory right away resulted in a scattering of research operations at major operating sites, a phenomenon that had lasting effects.[83]

Undaunted, Frary built a staff from the bottom up. He drew heavily on his outside associations from teaching and from his involvement in professional organizations. In 1920, Alcoa took over the Lynite Laboratories, a division of the financially troubled Aluminum Castings Company of Cleveland that was offered as payment for primary metal purchased on credit during the war. With the Cleveland facility came a number of young PhDs, including Robert S. Archer and Zay Jeffries, already luminaries in aluminum science and future coauthors, in 1924, of the then definitive *Science of Metals*. The prestige of his growing corps of scientists made it possible for Frary to attract other talented metallurgists.[84]

While its sister organization, the Technical Direction Bureau, attended to workaday process improvements and quality control, the Research Bureau delved into more basic problems on a wide front. Frary had strong control over the research agenda. Almost immediately after his arrival at Alcoa, he put his authority to a test by cancelling a project on alumina refining that was a longtime favorite within the corporation and reviving an idea of William Hoopes's that had failed to get management support. Working with Hoopes at Badin, Frary built an experimental pot in which the two scientists floated a molten fluoride electrolyte under a layer of pure aluminum (which served as a cathode) upon a heavier aluminum-copper alloy (which served as an anode). Pure aluminum was then dissolved from the heavier anode alloy and deposited in the cathode layer of molten aluminum. The result was the production of aluminum more pure than could be made by the conventional Hall Process, an improvement from 97.75 to 99.99 percent, which greatly enchanced the Research Bureau's ability to determine with precision the properties and behavior of aluminum alloys. The success of the Hoopes Process depended upon precise knowledge of the physical and chemical properties of the electrolyte, the pure aluminum, and the alloy – properties such as density and melting points – to permit exact control of the process. The relevant data had to be determined by research chemists in a laboratory.[85] It was the absence of this kind of research that had made such ideas as Hoopes's impossible to achieve before the war; it was the presence of this kind of research that would drive Alcoa's innovation in the future.

What guaranteed Frary's success (and his organization's independence) was his sensitivity to corporate requirements. Frary structured his organization around recognizable problems of an evolving aluminum technology. During the 1920s, he set up a Division of Physical Metallurgy to perform both fundamental research, directed at explaining the phenomenon of age-hardening in high-strength alloys, and applied research, devoted to making improvements in fabricating technologies. This division also undertook research on corrosion and developed the technology for high-magnification photography necessary to the study of microstructure. Carbon, Engineering, and Development Divisions were also established, the last of which specialized in process metallurgy. A Physical Chemistry Division worked on developing new products, such as paints and lubricants, while an "Experimental Laboratory" was devoted to problems in alumina refining. He set up a library based on the best models he could find and incorporated the newest research technologies, striving always to emulate best practice in the larger scientific community.

If science at Alcoa was driven by business requirements, it can also be said that the postwar requirements of the business were pushing Alcoa into new and more scientific areas of endeavor. The need to find a product to sustain the company's aluminum powder plant at Logan's Ferry, for example, was met by the Research Bureau's discovery that powder could be used as a paint pigment. The company's acquisition of the American Magnesium Corporation in 1920 could only be justified by fundamental research into efficient means of producing magnesium – a potential threat to aluminum – and into new ways of casting and working it. The most demanding technological, hence research, problems centered on the development of new alloys. The pure aluminum developed by Hoopes and Frary proved crucial to the creation of many new alloys, and fundamental research into the structure and behavior of metals was applied to a proliferation of new aluminum applications, from building materials to aircraft propulsion and body construction, from beer barrels to screw machine products.[86]

Such activities were costly and required strong top-management support. Budgets steadily increased as Alcoa's executives came to regard research as a main line of defense against competition. The young Kent Van Horn, who would one day succeed Frary as head of Alcoa Research, remembered his first impression of Alcoa's expensive and modern facilities, and of the company's pioneering efforts in X-ray diffraction techniques and fundamental research into the structure of metals. In 1928, the research budget stood at about $700,000. A. V. Davis was now willing to do better than that; following a personal tour of the Research Bureau, he condemned it as "a slop hole of a Laboratory" and ordered a new facility to be built. In 1930, the Aluminum Research Laboratory, a beautiful structure

Fig. 4.3.   The Aluminum Research Laboratories building at New Kensington.

replete with marble and aluminum trimmings, was erected high on a hill overlooking the New Kensington Works.[87]

The new building helped give research a distinctive status in the company. Frary's core group of scientists were now physically separated – literally as well as figuratively elevated – from operations. But research could not and did not function in isolation. When Earl Blough departed for Aluminium Limited, Frary found it necessary to take on more responsibility for the technical functions of the corporation as a whole following the merger of the Research Bureau with the Technical Direction Bureau. Having assumed Blough's responsibilities for process improvements and quality, Frary was obligated to devote more of his attention to the development and implementation of new technologies and to coordinate his activities with the day-to-day requirements of the enterprise. His organization's activities accordingly broadened beyond research to deal with immediate and ongoing technical problems.

The building of the New Kensington laboratory was not a prelude to further centralization of corporate research activities. In fact, research remained geographically decentralized throughout Frary's tenure, and his organization became known in the plural, the Laboratories. At New Kensington, research focused mainly on the development of hard alloys, new products, and smelting and fabricating processes. Cleveland maintained its own laboratory under a director who reported to Frary, concentrating specifically on problems in forgings and in castings (both sand and permanent-mold) that emerged in the course of production. Specialized research was also conducted at Massena, on problems of electrical transmission, and at East St. Louis, in conjunction with refining processes. These outlying research facilities had considerable autonomy in practice, even though their projects were funded under a central budget. Frary did nothing to disturb this decentralized structure, feeling that work on the Bayer Process, in particular, required "daily contact with the technical personnel in the operating department."[88]

Research budgets declined during the worst years of the Depression ("total research expense" fell to $445,000 in 1932), but the company took pains to defend its program at a time when investment in industrial research was coming under heavy criticism in the country at large. By the late 1930s, it was clear to Fritz Close, a young salesman, that the Laboratories were "the big deal" at Alcoa, which could boast that twenty-three of twenty-seven basic alloys and seventeen of twenty wrought alloys in use had been developed through its own research efforts. A. V. Davis considered the Laboratories one of his proudest achievements, putting it forth as one of the social benefits of industrial monopoly. By 1940, Frary had a core staff of 220 with advanced technical degrees and allocated as much as twenty-five percent of his budget to fundamental research performed by men who were prominent in their fields. In the Alcoa system that year, there were eighteen chemical laboratories, eleven physical testing laboratories, and one motor laboratory, altogether employing 554 people and commanding a $1.75 million annual operating budget, of which some $868,000 qualified as "research expense."[89]

During the 1930s, process improvements continued to receive high priority in research, especially upstream, where refining costs had always been problematic. Laboratory-based innovations were introduced in the beneficiation of ores and in the development of a "Combination Process." This latter technique involved sintering the red mud produced in the refining process, and then returning a recovered sodium-aluminate solution to the Bayer digesters so that commercially feasible amounts of alumina could be retained from low-grade, high-silica bauxites. Between 1930 and 1935, the East St. Louis laboratory achieved a major breakthrough in developing a process "for the continuous digestion of bauxite," in lieu of the batch method that had been employed since 1903. A new refinery at Mobile opened in 1939, based on a continuous-process method that saved a substantial amount of fuel and labor.[90]

Like refining, smelting was a perennial research-and-development priority. There were no fundamental breakthroughs in the basic technology, but development of the Hall Process proceeded apace. One way in which Alcoa achieved improvements was in the control of the composition of the bath in the smelting cell. Before 1925, this part of the process had been largely a matter of trial and error and experience, whereby crew foremen, much like chefs, adjusted the mix from time to time. After 1925, more systematic scientific techniques were employed for maintaining the bath (though the process remained, by modern standards, remarkably judgmental)[91] and for better control of what is known as the "anode effect," an interruption of electrolyzing current caused by the formation of gas between the anode and the bath. This was especially important because any stoppage resulted in a costly process of restarting or worse, the cracking of the pot itself.[92]

It would be a mistake to attribute all Alcoa's technological progress during this period (or any period) to the existence of a research laboratory. As always, systematic and creative work by production engineers continued to bear fruit, sometimes leading to innovations of great significance. For example, the "Direct Chill" Process for ingot casting – which one engineer called "metallurgically and mechanically one of the most inspiring" technical developments in all of Alcoa's operations – was developed at Massena by plant metallurgist William C. Ennor. Ennor's work overcame a serious bottleneck in Alcoa's chain of production following the building of large blooming and structural mills in 1929. First tried in December 1934, the Direct Chill Process made possible the production of very large ingots for semifinishing into sheet, plate, and large rolled sections. By mid-1937, about half of all alloy rolling-ingot production was made by this new method. Though he would later join the Laboratories as assistant director of research, Ennor was, at the time of his important work on ingot casting, not even a development engineer.[93]

Whether accomplished in the Laboratories or on the production line, there were substiantial gains in labor-saving technologies between the wars. A series of incremental improvements raised the yield of the standard reduction pot up to 250 pounds per day by 1940.

Moreover, the average price of primary aluminum, which had fallen to less than \$0.20 from around \$0.27 per pound in 1926, reflected greater efficiency in power consumption and in the reduction of labor required to man the pots. But a single pound of aluminum still required some twelve kilowatt-hours of electricity, enough to keep a forty-watt bulb lit for twelve and a half days, and Alcoa consumed enough electricity in a single day to supply 17,000 homes for an entire year. Thus, smelting would continue to be a major concern of the Laboratories. By World War II, Alcoa was devoting "considerable research" into an alternative to the Hall Process.[94]

The discovery of new materials and primary process improvements were strategically important, but equally important to Alcoa's competitive position was the ability to make incremental improvements in the manufacture of fabricated products. A key case in point was the development of a hard-aluminum, Duralumin-type alloy. As we have already seen, the war helped Alcoa to develop a hard alloy, which it called 17S, a viable substitute for the German Duralumin. After the war, the Baush Machine Tool Company of Springfield, Massachusetts, was the most successful of three independent firms to start aluminum sheet-rolling operations in the United States. Baush, which had developed a Duralumin-type alloy known as 2S, acquired a nearby brass and iron foundry and converted it for aluminum fabrications, especially sheet.[95] Baush's entry into the sheet business presented a threat to Alcoa in a fabricating sector where competition was historically negligible and where the future of high-tonnage sales, especially for aircraft, undoubtedly lay. Baush's challenge was met and turned back primarily because of Alcoa's habits of innovation.

Baush's challenge began in 1919, when its president, George Haskell, discovered that he could buy aluminum from foreign sources at one to two cents below the Alcoa price. He installed a single, eighteen-inch rolling mill (with six pairs of rolls for the breakdown of preheated ingots, roughing, and finishing) operating at a speed of seventy-eight feet per minute. Alcoa had larger mills with higher operating capacity, but Baush's sheet was of high quality and enjoyed a good reception among automobile and aircraft producers. Baush's sales of 2S Duralumin sheet – stimulated by low penetration prices[96] – grew nicely until 1925, but then fell off so that Alcoa's sales in its equivalent sheet surpassed Baush's in 1927, the year, incidentally, when Charles Lindbergh flew from New Jersey to Paris, an event that gave new impetus to aircraft construction. Even with the market so narrowly defined to include only Duralumin-

Fig. 4.4.   Charles A. Lindbergh and the aluminum-sheathed "Spirit of St. Louis" in 1927.

type sheet of eighteen or less inches in width, Baush had only a 7.3-percent share by 1931. In reality, there was a market for sizes of hard-alloy sheet, which Baush did not make. After investing little more than fifty thousand dollars in improvements in its rolling equipment over a decade, and having made no effort at new product development, and having failed to reduce its production costs, Baush abandoned its aluminum sheet business. By mid-1935, all of its fabricating operations, including tubing, rod, and wire, were shut down.[97]

Because Baush's lack of success in hard-alloy sheet became the subject of lengthy private litigation from 1931 until 1935, the precise conditions for Alcoa's victory are confused by the ambiguous outcome of the legal proceeding, which is discussed in the next chapter. In fact, much of Baush's problem was due to poor planning and management. Charles Carr rightly observed that Haskell was "an entrepreneur rather than an industrialist, manufacturer, or salesman," with neither the financial, nor organizational, nor human resources, nor the interest to make the investment necessary to achieve the volume and quality to compete over the long run.[98] Haskell, not surprisingly, felt otherwise, contending that Alcoa had forced him out of the market by entering into collusive agreements with foreign suppliers of aluminum ingot and by squeezing the differentials between the prices of ingot and semifabrication. But Alcoa need not have done anything illegal; it need only to have produced Duralumin at comparable quality and at lower cost. Alcoa's rolling capacity alone – its sheet width was expanded from 60 to 120 inches – was much larger than Baush's and its investment in its sheet mill exceeded $7 million. That there would be substantially proportional savings in labor and scrap costs in wider sheets rolled at higher speeds is obvious.

Alcoa also had working in its favor a commitment to innovation that the much smaller operation simply could not afford, even had it been so inclined. Baush did little over the years to improve its aluminum plant, its processes, or its products.[99] By contrast, Alcoa's research and development on hard alloys yielded knowledge on how to roll wider sheet and improve its quality and also generated new hard-alloy products. The company's original commercial-grade Duralumin-type alloy, 17S, was but a starting point. After ironing out the bugs in its manufacture, the Research Bureau developed other hard alloys, 25S and 24S – the former with superior qualities in heat treatment used principally for forging; the latter with significantly higher tensile strength. In 1926, an Alcoa researcher, Edgar H. Dix, Jr., developed a method for "cladding" sheet alloys with a thin aluminum surface, which electrolytically protected the strong core against corrosion, an especially important innovation for aircraft construction. By World War II, a wide range of both unclad and "Alclad" alloys were on the market. In 1938, Alcoa produced some seventeen wrought and twenty-seven casting alloys, the vast majority developed since the war through a "tremendous expenditure of scientific effort."[100]

The manufacture of Alcoa's hard alloys was improved through analysis and engineering far more sophisticated than could be achieved by tinkering on the production line. The replacement of cast-iron sheet rolls with those of forged steel, the use of different rolls for making flat and coiled sheet, and the scaling up of ingot-remelting furnaces were all process improvements in which laboratory personnel brought their formal methods of testing and experimentation to bear on immediate problems of quality and costs.[101]

In assessing Alcoa's competitive technological advantage, consider

Fig. 4.5.   Loading ingot into a remelt furnace at Alcoa, Tennessee, in the 1920s.

for a moment the perfectly mundane matter of remelt furnaces. Conrad F. Nagel, Alcoa's chief metallurgist at the time of the development of its first Duralumin-type alloy, testified that Alcoa at first installed several 100-pound-capacity furnaces in an experimental mill in order to study methods of remelting 17S. Furnaces were then redesigned to capacities of 350 pounds. By 1924, a 3,000-pound-capacity furnace had been designed and progressive improvements led eventually to a working capacity of 20,000 pounds in 1931. (Baush employed 90- and 380-pound crucibles throughout.) Large-scale remelting made it possible to analyze fewer samples from larger batches and to maintain more uniform temperatures, easing composition control and the monitoring of product quality. In addition, more efficient sampling economies were derived from a reduction in labor force to charge and maintain fewer furnaces during operation, from reductions in heat loss (small and large furnaces required the same-sized doors), and from continuous remelting, because metal in a large furnace could be added at about the same rate it was extracted without disturbing the composition of the molten contents.[102]

By World War II, Alcoa's research activities encompassed three general areas: new alloys with varying physical and chemical properties, process innovation, and new product design. Work in all three areas reflected both offensive and defensive strategic concerns. The Laboratories had become an indispensable force in the company's evolving technology: a well-funded, well-managed, and well-motivated community of scientists who, in the process of serving the business needs of the firm, had ample opportunities to do fundamental science, to attend conferences, to publish, and to work under a director who understood their deepest professional longings. Frary admonished his researchers to think freely, to avoid preconceived ideas, to be unafraid of the facts, and to feel intellectually independent of their organizational superiors. In a tribute to Frary, Webster Jones, the Director of Engineering at the Carnegie Institute during World War II, could think of no industrial laboratory with a reputation better than Alcoa's or "more harmoniously knitted, integrated, and effective [as an] organization of management and research." If that is how Alcoa's research organization appeared, it was due very largely to the strength of one man's personality and his stature inside the corporation. Insiders attributed the scientific rigor, intellectual intensity, and high morale of the Laboratories to Frary's leadership. Frary himself, in addition to his administrative duties, remained an active researcher. Between 1919 and 1946, when he became Alcoa's second recipient of the Perkin Medal, Frary coauthored one book, wrote another (on glassblowing!), published numerous articles, and patented several inventions.[103]

The rise of Alcoa research along with the increasing coordination of the company's technical functions was a response to the growth of the industry and the increasing complexity of its technology. By World War II, research had become essential to continuing growth, the protection of markets, and the control of costs. The company was still small enough so that it was possible for a strong leader to direct all these activities and then to ensure a good flow of information among the Laboratories, the production divisions, and customers of sophisticated applications without much bureaucratic elaboration or formality.[104] When war came, the Laboratories would continue to make important strides in hard but light alloys as well as in the development of new consumer products; in the years to follow, continued growth and complexity would require more highly structured forms of coordination among Alcoa's decentralized laboratories, as well as between research and the other technical functions of the enterprise.

Organizing aluminum workers

Far less harmonious, integrated, and effective were the relations between labor and management. Before the Depression, Alcoa had enjoyed a long period of labor peace. This was due largely to the aluminum worker's paycheck. At the end of World War I, the average yearly wage of an aluminum worker was $1,169 compared with $1,141 for all manufacturing in the United States. By 1929, the numbers were $1,400 and $1,301, respectively, making aluminum wages 107.6 percent of the all-manufacturing average.[105]

Aluminum plants of the early 1930s were hardly models of secure or pleasant working conditions. Individual workers were hired and fired on solely arbitrary bases, and the labor was often as hazardous as it was unclean. In smelters, the potential for explosions and electrocution was particularly high in addition to the normal run of careless accidents. Exposure to chemical agents (especially fluorides and carcinogens and, to a lesser degree, airborne alumina dusts and asbestos insulating materials) and to physical agents (such as excessive heat and noise) were also problems. The company's top management may genuinely have cared about the safety of workers (the effects of fluoride emissions was a particular concern of Frary's in his work at the Laboratories), but there seems to have been no strong company policy. Local superintendents were left to their own devices in matters of health and safety. When a sensitive young graduate of MIT, Arthur Johnson, went to Niagara in 1926, he was dismayed by the hazards he found and by local management's apparent lack of concern for workers' health.[106]

On the other hand, aluminum was not as subject to the mind-numbing boredom of the lock-step, assembly-line production that had become commonplace in many mass-production industries. Low turnover and stable management mitigated some of the impersonal and alienating tendencies of mass-production work. By the standards of the day, working conditions were generally accepted as adequate. Pre-Depression aluminum workers demanded little, and sometimes accepted less than they were offered. Early company attempts to start pension programs for unsalaried workers had been met with lack of interest. Of all Alcoa's major plants, only New

Kensington employed an essentially "urban" workforce; most Alcoa's operations were located in rural areas, where both union activities and urban pressures were weak and where agricultural depression made the relatively high pay of industrial employment seem luxurious.

Alcoa had always experienced sporadic labor problems at New Kensington, situated as it was in the "Black Valley" west of the Alleghenies, which had a bitter history of labor uprisings in the coal and steel industries. New Kensington's management tried, with some success, to blunt the alienation of its largely immigrant workforce through "Americanization" programs in films, lectures, and classroom instruction. Elsewhere in Alcoa plants, labor was more placid. Immigrants were enticed to Massena "by the trainload" from New York City, joining indigenous country boys and French Canadians to sweat gratefully in the potrooms and in the carbon, rod, wire, and bar plants.

New arrivals also found their way to the rural backwaters of Saline County, Arkansas, where they joined poor, rural natives to labor in the mines and dwell in the neat, peaceful little town that had been designed and built by the company. At Alcoa, Tennessee, rural local farmers and small-town residents labored hard, though not always steadily (it was difficult to maintain a stable workforce during harvest time or hunting season), for wages that were high by the region's standards. Over time, increasing numbers of black workers were imported to toil in the oppressive heat and dust of the Tennessee potrooms, which required constant attention from men who were not otherwise distracted by the concerns of the family farm. In the town of Alcoa, which had been largely built and designed by the company, management took pains to see that workers had decent housing, health care, and educational facilities for their children.[107]

The written record is skimpy, but in interviews, some surviving Alcoa workers of that period harbored considerable nostalgia for Alcoa's regime of labor paternalism. Consider Bauxite, Arkansas, where the work of mining was especially arduous and the pay especially low. Old-timers recall the relatively meager southern wages of the 1920s ($0.225 per hour before 1933), the backbreaking labor of the pick and shovel, and the long unbroken hours in a day when complaints about even the most unhealthy working conditions were considered to be audacious. In the informal atmosphere of unregulated hiring practices, an underage boy could plead for and win a job in the strip mines for under-the-table compensation, but few self-respecting Arkansans would enter the deep mines – that was left to hungrier, poorer Mexicans who were imported for the work.

Hardships were exacerbated by layoffs due to general economic conditions and to Alcoa's increasing reliance on superior ore and cheaper labor in Surinam. Yet, in the nostalgic memories of elderly men, it was an era of good feeling in which workers accepted management's premises that the company had the power to determine all decisions affecting labor – including working conditions, wages, and job security – as a matter of right. There were few foremen and supervisors – "workers just knew what to do." Survivors of Depression-era Bauxite remember the efforts of the mine superintendent to avoid layoffs, the company's matching-funds program for unemployed workers, and the "neat" and "perfect" close-knit community in which they lived "like one big family" in company-subsidized housing.[108]

Pre-Depression labor-management relations at Alcoa have been characterized by one labor leader as a kind of benign master-servant relationship.[109] Perhaps, but it was certainly not a secure relationship. When the Depression came, the constant threat of unemployment hastened the demise of the old paternalistic order. By the time World War II pushed levels of employment and wages to unparalleled heights, it was too late to restore the old order. The basic premise of labor relations had been transformed in the interim. The traditional, lopsided social contract between the hourly worker and the paternalistic firm had been replaced by collective bargaining and the organized industrial union.

It all began in the wake of company-wide reductions of wages (and salaries) in 1931, a year when employment in the company fell off almost twenty-three percent from the previous year's total of 22,481. Though not as disastrous as the sharp reduction in force that had taken place in the postwar recession of 1921–2, when Alcoa's employment was halved from 20,952 to 10,007, the 1931 reduction in force marked the second of three consecutive years of abrupt declines in personnel. Fearful of losing its investment in experienced workers, Alcoa tried to hold as many employees as it could through part-time employment and through the speculative stockpiling of ore and ingot. Between 1926 and 1933, the aluminum industry kept its employment rolls high relative to American industry as a whole. Wage reductions continued through 1933, and it was not until 1936 that Alcoa rebounded to the level of employment it had achieved in the

Figs. 4.6. and 4.7. Mining bauxite underground and on the surface at Bauxite, Arkansas, in the 1920s.

late 1920s.[110] Meanwhile, Alcoa's workers began to organize to secure higher pay, job security, and better working conditions.

When Section 7A of the National Industrial Recovery Act (NIRA) spurred the organization of labor in the major mass-production industries, Alcoa's first response was to resist. The company's official position was that it stood ready, under the terms of the Act, to negotiate with its employees and their representatives about wages and working conditions. But the full implications of Section 7A went far beyond what management was willing to accept. As unions advanced their arguments for closed shops under the legislation, they violated a fundamental assumption of management: that it had an inherent right to contract and negotiate with its workers as free agents.

On August 2, 1933, Roy Hunt convened the first meeting of what was to become the Aluminum Association in order to "formulate a code of fair competition under the provisions of . . . the National Industrial Recovery Act," and he placed labor first on the agenda. With Alcoa clearly in command of its proceedings, the Association sought to establish a national scale of wages higher than prevailing industry rates but significantly lower than amounts workers were beginning to seek. The scale, which discriminated between northern and southern plants and between male and female employees in the north, was as follows:

Bauxite mining	$0.25/hour
Refining	0.30
Smelting and fabrication	0.35 (northern male)
Smelting and fabrication	0.30 (northern female)
Smelting and fabrication	0.30 (southern male and female)

Hours were limited to forty per week for noncontinuous and to forty-two for continuous-process labor. Objections from the National Recovery Administration (NRA) Policy Board to the $0.25 rate for mining (which Alcoa argued was performed by largely unskilled workers, who frequently left the mines to tend their farms) soon forced the hourly wage at Bauxite up another nickel. The immediate effect of these changes was to provide more jobs through the reduction of work weeks, but not necessarily at better pay, as the NRA-sanctioned minimum wages were used to undercut the wages of many employees who had been making more before the reform.[111]

Wages paled in importance compared to the question of control over employee representation. Because some organization of workers under the NRA was regarded as inevitable, however undesirable, management devised a Plan of Employee Representation for non-salaried workers that would effectively have brought the collective organization of labor under company control. The terms of the Plan provided for elective worker representation on local plant councils that would include management officials. An elaborate, chain-of-command grievance procedure was established that relied on final adjudication by management. But amidst a groundswell of independent union activity, Alcoa was unable to use the NRA to co-opt the process of labor-management relations. The promise of a company union was insufficient to stem a pent-up tide of workers' frustration over their inability to negotiate in force with the management. In a secret ballot taken in early September, workers at New Kensington overwhelmingly rejected the company's plan, thus dooming its implementation throughout the Alcoa system. When NRA head Hugh Johnson declared his intention to "impose" rigorous labor regulation on the aluminum industry, unionization began in earnest.[112]

Management dug in its heels, firmly resisting attempts to form unions independent of the company. Organization began at New Kensington, where a local aluminum union was chartered in August 1933 by the AFL (which had moved quickly to bring aluminum under its purview). The company nominally recognized Local 18356, which it was required to do to be in compliance with the NIRA's guarantee of employees' rights to establish their own bargaining units. But management flatly rejected the union's crucial demands for a contract and an enforced checkoff for union dues. One female organizer was fired and preferential work treatment was given to those workers who would subscribe to the company's Plan. Alcoa enjoyed strong political clout in the community, and many union workers soon found themselves up against the hostility of local merchants and the Catholic clergy. All this, however, served only to stiffen the spines of local organizers as they inveighed against "the predatory wealth of the Mellons" and called the first of many Depression-era strikes in October to demand wages of $0.40 and $0.35 for male and female employees, respectively.[113]

Meanwhile, growing fears of economic privation spurred sentiments for unionization in Alcoa's other operations. Within months, AFL organizers formed unions at New Kensington, Arnold, Alcoa, Garwood, Logan's Ferry, Massena, Badin, and East St. Louis. But the progress of unionization beyond this first step was made difficult by internal dissension and mismanagement. Lacking a coherent program for the aluminum industry, the AFL was unable to bring the company to terms on such fundamental issues as the closed shop and the enforced checkoff of union dues by the company – both conditions essential to the maintenance of the union as bargaining agent for aluminum workers. Led by the cautious William Green, the national AFL did not support the more aggressive demands of many of its locals. At New Kensington, where the AFL had organized some 6,000 workers in thirty-seven crafts, the Pittsburgh district office had difficulty keeping its membership in line after the national organization withheld financial backing for a strike in March 1934. Rivalries erupted between local union officials and Pittsburgh district union office representatives.[114]

Most workers were interested in wages and regarded the union as a device to achieve higher pay. For activists, the priority was to achieve union recognition. The AFL's strategy was to work slowly, first by consolidating its membership, by filling its national coffers with dues, and only then by confronting management at the local levels as bargaining agent for employees. The strike was regarded as a crucial but last-resort weapon in the arsenal, to be used only after negotiations were exhausted. To frustrated workers, on the other hand, a strike for wages was long overdue, and local union organizers mobilized this sentiment to launch the first major strike in Alcoa's history. A ten-day "wildcat holiday" took place in Alcoa's Pennsylvania plants in March 1934. Five thousand workers, mostly from New Kensington, walked out, but as pickets marched in freezing snow, the strike received only lip service from the AFL national union. The workers came away with an eleven-percent across-the-board increase in wages, but AFL negotiators failed to capitalize on the opportunity to fight for the fundamentally more important demands of local organizers for recognition and collective bargaining.

Management was acutely aware of the unfocused and factional structure of union politics and was therefore willing to concede no more than necessary to keep production lines operating. Alcoa simply refused to accede to union demands for universal wage rates (a thorny issue in the southern plants) and layoffs by seniority. More important, it refused even to acknowledge the union's right to act as a collective bargaining agent. Demands for a wage checkoff to assure the union its dues were rejected by Roy Hunt on the grounds that they were not "a natural or necessary function of the company. . . ." Alcoa's president maintained "the right of the company to enter into agreements or contracts with *any* of its employees." That any agency be allowed to negotiate collectively on behalf of Alcoa's workers was, he declared, "contrary to the spirit and letter of the NRA."[115]

Alcoa's adamant resistance to recognition forced the AFL to acquiesce, albeit reluctantly, in the first general strike of its aluminum industry members. On August 10, 1934, six plants were closed: New Kensington, Arnold, Logan's Ferry, Alcoa, Massena, and East St. Louis. "An orphan from the beginning," in the words of one historian, the strike lasted for five weeks, causing hardship among the workers while gaining them little in the way of immediate results. Management personnel virtually imprisoned themselves in the plants to safeguard production facilities (in Tennessee, a metallurgist had his three-year-old daughter mailed to him for a visit behind the picket lines), but no attempt was made to sustain operations.

Alcoa had the resources with which to withstand a strike, and its practice of stockpiling inventories (done partly to protect its workers) had given it a cushion on which it could rest during a shutdown. Thus, by refraining from overt actions to break the strike, the company kept the peace, while the financial resources of the strikers dwindled. As restive workers mounted a "back-to-work movement," AFL district representatives were unable to get any satisfaction on union demands for a checkoff, layoffs by seniority, and universal wage rates. They achieved modest gains through the mediation of the Federal Labor Department, but only after management refused to accept arbitration by the National Labor Relations Board (a path preferred by the union). For all practical purposes, the strike had failed.

What the workers had "won" was an agreement whereby the company agreed only to what it had already been prepared to give up, namely: to accept the principle of collective bargaining without recognizing an exclusive union agent, to hold wages constant but not raise them, to refrain from discriminating against union members, and to establish a grievance procedure that would be effectively controlled by management. Roy Hunt said only that Alcoa "will continue to meet at any time with any of its employees or representatives of its employees for the purpose of discussing wages, hours and working conditions." National union officials declared themselves satisfied with these limited gains, which they asserted would "greatly improve the workers' bargaining position through the unqualified recognition by the company of the fundamental principles and methods of collective bargaining...."[116]

For many of the New Kensington rank and file, the union had let the company get away with too much. Embittered workers turned against their union. Membership in Local 18356 withered from "thousands" to a "small band" amid fractious squabblings of local, district, and national union officials over policy and personalities. Out of the confusion emerged a small but cohesive group of militant workers, many of whom were imbued with socialist ideals of industrial organization and were determined to organize a movement that would be far more aggressive in challenging the company.

This new phase of the struggle began when the local militants petitioned the AFL for an international charter that would confer upon aluminum workers the status of a full-fledged industrial union. Such a demand was treated as seditious by the AFL district representative who, apparently repelled by the socialist rhetoric of the militants, complained that the New Kensington plant was being taken over by "a bunch of damn Communists," whose quest for a "wild industrial organization" would undermine the AFL's program. That kind of response served only to inflame local leaders, who complained that they had been reduced to little more than "a dues-collecting agency" for the AFL, which had only proven its tendency to withhold critical financial support in times of trouble.[17]

In fact, the growing rebellion at New Kensington was much more than a local dispute. It paralleled union struggles in other major industries, where the AFL's conservative craft traditions were challenged by first- and second-generation immigrant workers, many of whose notions about union organization were no doubt drawn from the more inclusive socialist and communist workers' movements of Europe. In 1937, the rival Committee of Industrial Organizations (CIO), already outpacing AFL organizers in auto and steel, took advantage of the AFL's problems in the aluminum industry. Though the AFL had been able to secure from Alcoa an agreement that for the first time explicitly recognized the Aluminum Workers as bargaining agent, New Kensington workers bolted. An organizer from the newly formed CIO was embraced by an overtly anti-AFL faction of Local 18356. The AFL's unwillingness to issue a full-fledged international charter (long sought by the local as a matter of principle) and the red-baiting rhetoric of the district representative alienated even the more moderate heads in the local. In April 1937, at a convention convened for the purpose, a resolution was adopted proclaiming:

> The organized aluminum workers have long suffered from inadequate organizational set-up, as Federal locals of the American Federation of Labor, resulting in uncertainty about the future, constant fear of craft raids and jurisdictional disputes.
>
> This set-up had been ruled in a high-handed and dictatorial fashion by appointees of the A. F. of L.

Figs. 4.8 and 4.9. Two methods for making aluminum tube in the 1920s. Above, tubes are made by drawing the metal through a die; bottom, tube blooms are made by extrusion.

> The industrial form of organization is the only form adapted
> to reach the needs of a modern mass-production industry, un-
> iting all the workers in a single union to give them the maximum
> unity and bargaining power.

AFL Local 18356 was then voted out and replaced by Local 2, International Union, Aluminum Workers of America, CIO. Despite
bitter protests and threats of litigation, the new union was certified
by the National Labor Relations Board (NLRB) as the sole bargaining agent for the plant's workers under the terms of the Wagner
Act. Alcoa's management had no choice but to accept the principle
as well as the reality of the outcome.[118]
It would be all too easy to attribute the struggles between contending factions among aluminum workers to differences in ideology
along conservative and socialist lines. The rebellious New Kensington convention, which had been attended by a number of AFL Aluminum Workers unions from other Alcoa operations, was notably
shunned by the politically conservative locals from Massena and
East St. Louis. And Nick Zonarich, the New Kensington aluminum
worker who became the AWA's first president, was a socialist disciple of Norman Thomas. But as the struggle for power between
contending organizations (usually the AFL and CIO) proceeded, political orientation was generally less of a factor in local struggles
for power than more practical concerns about which union would
best serve workers' demands for higher wages and job security. A
good case in point is Alcoa, Tennessee, where the AFL's problems
in industrial organization were much more clearly strategic and
tactical than ideological.
By all accounts, Alcoa, Tennessee, was a pleasant and peaceful
company town operating under "an efficient, businesslike form of
government" that had been designed by Edwin Fickes and administered by a company-recruited city manager. City services and
schools were considered to be as good or better than in the neighboring towns, and company employment by farm standards was
lucrative. Unionism took root in the Depression, and by 1937, AFL
Local 19104 had become firmly established. At that time, like other
organized workers in the Alcoa system, Local 19104 enjoyed explicit
recognition as a union, rights to collective bargaining, and a grievance procedure that provided some limited terms for independent
arbitration. It was the result of pressure from the union that Alcoa's
southern minimum wage had risen from about $0.35 to $0.45 per
hour since 1934.
Still, there remained fundamental dissatisfaction over what

amounted to an eighteen-percent difference in the hourly rate between southern and northern workers. The desire of the Local to strike in response to the company's position that wages be pegged to regional economic conditions was opposed by the AFL district representative, whose attempts to negotiate with the company came to nought. When the AFL finally consented to back a strike, a selective walkout in the fabricating plant was called on May 18, with an explicit threat of violence should the company attempt to operate the mill. At some point, a company transmission tower was dynamited, and tensions escalated quickly as the company, through its control of the city government, recruited police from neighboring counties to supplement the local force, ostensibly to prevent the strike from spreading to the Reduction Plant. The company weaned a number of employees from the union by offering temporary work in smelting, but on July 7, while the local union president was away on business, the works manager invited disaster by reopening the fabricating plant with "scab" labor, despite last-minute attempts at settlement by the Department of Labor.[119]

What then happened was the only fatal encounter between Alcoa and its workers in the company's history. As picketers attempted to block special police from escorting rehired workers into the plant, a skirmish erupted in which someone fired a gun. Some two hundred bullets later, two men – one a special policeman, the other a young union member – lay dead, and fourteen others on both sides were wounded. The company appealed to the State for the National Guard, four companies of which were dispatched to the scene, and the strike was broken. Alcoa's management refused to accept any mediation of the dispute by a federal conciliator who had been sent after a union appeal to the NLRB. Instead, an aide to AFL President Green arrived and pressured the Local president to resign as part of the process of officially ending the strike.[120]

Feeling utterly betrayed by the AFL, a number of local union leaders invited AWA president Nick Zonarich to come to Tennessee in order to launch a CIO organization drive. Local 9 of the CIO was born and grew quickly in membership (due in part to its willingness to recruit blacks) only to become locked in furious competition for membership with the stalwarts of Local 19104 and a new company-sponsored group known as the Aluminum Employees Association. The Association actually received a substantial amount of support and was initially larger than either the AFL or CIO unions, feeding as it did on the basic conservatism of native employees and their hostility to "outside" influ-

ences. Through considerable harassment and red-baiting prop-
aganda from its rivals, the CIO weathered four NLRB elections
to determine the sole bargaining agent for the Alcoa Works.
In the end, it was the result of superior organization and tactical
work in the election process that enabled the CIO finally to win
the clear majority necessary for certification.[121] From there, the
struggle for power between the AFL and CIO spread to other Alcoa plants until the latter won about as many local elections as
the former. Local conditions determined local outcomes, and the
CIO was unable to achieve its goal of a single industrial union
that would provide aluminum workers with "maximum unity
and bargaining power." In later years, the United Auto Workers
would become a major third power in Alcoa's foundries, while a
variety of smaller unions organized various craft specialties in
many plants.

Fragmented and contentious as it was in its origins, unionism
had triumphed at Alcoa. With their rights to bargain collectively, both sanctioned by the law and recognized by the company, Alcoa's workers could now command far higher wages
than would have been possible had they remained unorganized.
Across the board, wages in aluminum manufacturing between
1936 and 1939 increased from \$0.57 to \$0.70 per hour, an increase that can be directly attributed to the strength of the
union movement. Even at Bauxite, where wages had improved to
\$0.45 per hour in the mining boom that followed the 1937 recov-
ery, the advent of the CIO in October 1941 would bring another
immediate hike of \$0.10 per hour.[122] It would take several more
years for aluminum unions to bring other important concerns
under their purview, such as layoffs by seniority, work rules,
and the company-enforced checkoff of wages that would assure
union coffers a regular flow of dues, but by World War II, Alcoa
was well on its way to becoming a union shop.

Thus, it happened that within a few short years following the
depths of the Depression, aluminum's labor relations were unal-
terably transformed by the collectivization of the aluminum labor market. Management always resisted attempts to organize
workers as those attempts spread from one plant to the next, but
in the end, always lost. No longer could management, even with
the best of intentions, expect to make unilateral decisions about
pay, job security, health and safety, discipline, or even output. In
the decades to come, all these things were to be governed in-

creasingly by negotiations between labor and management as adversarial, yet mutually dependent, institutional subsets of the industrial corporation.

State of the company in 1938

In 1938, Alcoa turned fifty. The company was suffering a bit from a drop in net earnings following the sharp recession of 1937, but the trajectory of its business was decidedly upward.[123] It had survived the depths of the Great Depression to become a much larger and more sophisticated business than it had been at the end of World War I. It was also a stronger company, having reformed its technical and managerial structure and having reaped many benefits from its organized efforts in research and development. It had weathered the lean years reasonably well, largely because the country did not suffer from the extent of aluminum overcapacity that it might have obtained under more competitive conditions. All in all, Alcoa was a healthy, half-century-old monopoly.

But there were also problems. Alcoa faced ongoing struggles over the rights and prerogatives of unions and mounting competition, if not from other primary producers, at least from fabricators. There was also the continuing threat posed by alternative technologies. In 1938, Alcoa's research laboratories were tracking developments in plastics, stainless steel, nickel alloys, and magnesium, which might "decidedly limit the scope of aluminum," perhaps "depriving aluminum of some market which it already has."[124] One problem that lay just beyond the horizon was that another war would make capacity demands on the company that it simply could not meet. That alone would prove sufficient to end Alcoa's monopoly. A more obvious threat was the old nemesis of antitrust. Federal investigations and private lawsuits had kept Alcoa continually at bay throughout the 1920s and 30s. Great time and expense had been devoted to defending the company from a litany of accusations – some ridiculous, some plausible – the most serious focusing on Alcoa's power to "squeeze" the margins of competing fabricators. In 1938, Alcoa was mounting a defense for what would become the greatest legal proceeding in history, after the Government brought suit against the company for monopolizing the American aluminum industry. The penalty upon conviction could be a wholesale divestiture. Thus, even as prosperity loomed on the horizon, Alcoa fell into a struggle for its very existence – a struggle not with the more familiar threats of economic downturns, competition, or unions, but with the even more potent and less comprehensible machinations of the Department of Justice.

5

Undoing the monopoly:
the Second World War
and Learned Hand

Whereas the First World War had been a powerful stimulus to the American aluminum industry, the Second World War transformed it. The consolidation of extraordinary military and economic power in the hands of the Federal Government (to a far greater degree than had been the case in World War I) became the means for mobilizing American industrial strength in global conflict. An economic boom, spurred by the demands of war, propelled Americans out of the lingering depression they had come almost to take for granted. As federal spending jumped from $9.1 billion in 1940 to $95.1 billion in 1944 (accounting for forty-five percent of GNP),[1] the fortunes of big business became inescapably intertwined with the strategic and economic concerns of big government. In tandem were carried the concerns of organized labor, which used the return to full employment as leverage to improve its position. The aluminum industry in particular became an indispensable part of the war effort, which required thousands of tons of the light metal for the air power necessary to win the peace. Alcoa, as a consequence, grew large and profited handsomely, but in the process it lost its monopoly.

In the late 1930s, as the world moved inexorably toward its second global war, Alcoa scarcely perceived what opportunities and threats that mobilization would bring in its train. But once it had become clear that the Third Reich had resurrected the once shattered German aluminum capacity to a scale unparalleled in the industry's history (by 1938 Germany was the world's largest producer),[2] Amer-

191

Table 5.1. *Comparison of primary aluminum production by*
country, 1939–44 (thousands of metric tons)

Country	1939	1940	1941	1942	1943	1944	Total
United Kingdom	25.4	19.3	23.1	47.6	56.6	36.1	208.1
Canada	75.1	99.0	194.0	290.8	449.7	419.2	1,527.8
U.S.	148.4	187.1	280.4	472.4	834.8	695.3	2,618.4
Germany	199.5	211.3	233.6	264.0	250.1	244.2	1,402.7
France	52.5	61.7	63.9	45.2	46.2	26.2	295.7
Switzerland	27.0	28.0	26.0	24.0	19.0	10.0	134.0

Source: United Nations Statistical Yearbook, 1954 (New York: United Nations Productions, 1954), p. 241.

ican and Allied military orders soared to dizzying heights. Because Alcoa could neither fully comprehend nor fully afford to mobilize the capacity necessary to respond to the emergency demands of the Allied powers, it fell to the Federal Government to finance most of what amounted to more than a doubling of American aluminum capacity. This simple fact – an unprecedented increase in demand and the company's inability to meet it – threw the door wide open for competitive entry into the business of making aluminum.

Alcoa was already under siege on another front. It had become embroiled in what was becoming the largest proceeding in the history of Anglo–American law. In April 1937, Alcoa, Aluminium Limited, and sixty-one related corporate and individual defendants were sued under Sections 1 and 2 of the Sherman Act for restraint of interstate and foreign trade and for monopolization of the aluminum industry. The charges covered almost every aspect of Alcoa's business. The proposed remedy was both radical and threatening: "to create substantial competition in the industry by rearranging the plants and properties of the Aluminum Company and its subsidiaries under several separate and independent corporations" along with "a divorcement of the Aluminum Company and Aluminium Limited, a Canadian corporation through whom it is alleged that the Aluminum Company has conspired with other world producers to restrain imports and preserve the Aluminum Company's monopoly in the United States."[3] Just how the properties of Alcoa were to be divided and just how the industry might be structured was left unspecified, but should the Government succeed, Alcoa might be left, if not dead, severely wounded and amputated, no longer anything like the self-sufficient and powerful corporation it had become in a half century of business.

The case was still undecided when Japan bombed Pearl Harbor. Thus, Alcoa went to war on two fronts: one in the service of its country, the other against the Department of Justice. The company emerged from these struggles in a prosperous condition larger than ever, but with its industrial environment altered forever. By the war's end, Alcoa had won commendations from the War Production Board and the Truman Committee,[4] no mean compliment for a large corporation. But it also stood convicted by a Court of Appeals of monopolizing the ingot market. When, finally, as a matter of public policy, the War Surplus Property Board (SPB) sold most of the com-Government aluminum plants to competing enterprises, Alcoa was forced to accept the establishment of competition from integrated domestic producers.

The great antitrust case

"If we are a monopoly," said Alcoa's corporate secretary, George Gibbons, "it is not of our own choosing." Nor was it inadvertance that had put Alcoa in its "monopolistic disposition"; it was the reluctance of others to risk the "enormous investments" required to compete.[5] But in the United States, no monopoly can live in peace, even if it has attained its position through its own efficient achievement. There are too many forces at work in American society that are hostile to size and power – forces that when activated, can turn against even the most productive large-scale enterprise. Such forces include a traditional American fear of large institutions, hostility toward concentrated power, free-market ideologies, populist politics, and a strong body of antitrust law. At any time when the political climate is especially unfavorable for big business, all it takes to galvanize these forces are the thwarted ambitions of competing businessmen or the aspiring ambitions of antitrust attorneys. The late 1930s were such a time.

Alcoa's antitrust woes harkened back to its first encounter with the Justice Department in 1911. The 1912 consent decree, which barred the company from participating in foreign cartels and from entering into restrictive contracts, far from settled the matter. After World War I, the company came under renewed scrutiny from the Federal Government. In the first significant action under Section 11 of the Clayton Act (empowering the FTC to order a divestiture of an acquisition that is deemed to restrain commerce), the Federal Trade Commission moved against Alcoa's attempt to purchase a controlling interest in the Cleveland Metals Company (reorganized as Aluminum Rolling Mills Corporation), which at the time was "the only competitor of any consequence" in the sheet-rolling business.[6] In 1922, the FTC launched what was to be an eight-year-long investigation of Alcoa. Acting on complaints from manufacturers, especially those of the Charles B. Bohn Foundry Company of Detroit, the FTC developed a long list of anticompetitive practices with which it charged Alcoa in a partial complaint in 1924 and a full one in 1925. The investigation, which the company called "biased and unfair to the last degree," focused mainly on the cooking utensil business; it alleged price discrimination, defective or delayed shipments, and the cancellation of quotas to independent producers. The complaint was broadened to include charges of monopolization of the sheet and sand casting businesses, of the secondary scrap market, of ingot, and of raw materials. Allegations that Alcoa had violated the terms of the 1912 consent decree and had conspired over time to control the world's water power and aluminum trade were thrown in for good measure.[7]

The FTC was a weak agency, but it was endowed with the power to subpoena documents and take testimony and then to refer its findings to the Justice Department, sometimes with great effect. Special agents of the DOJ set up office at Alcoa headquarters in 1925 to undertake a detailed investigation of the company's records. In the end, neither the DOJ findings (known as "The Benham Report") nor the FTC investigation led to any significant action. In 1930, the FTC, then laboring under the embarrassingly incompetent leadership of its egregiously probusiness chairman, William E. Humphrey, dismissed the complaint, finding that charges against Alcoa were unsupported by numerous exhibits and by some 5,000 pages of testimony taken in nine cities over seven years.[8]

Exoneration by the FTC was a tepid blessing. Friends and foes of big business alike did not take the agency seriously, and so after reams of unfavorable publicity, the FTC's clean bill of health did little to restore Alcoa's image. Moreover, the investigation emboldened several smaller firms to initiate private antitrust suits against Alcoa. The most important of these suits was brought by the Baush Machine Tool Company.[9] After Baush's aluminum plant closed down in 1931, company president George Haskell filed suit in the Connecticut District Court seeking $3 million in antitrust damages. Haskell had already brought three unsuccessful suits against Alcoa and the Duke interests, claiming that he had been unfairly excluded from participation in the Saguenay water power projects. This new action, based on Baush's failure to sustain its markets in Duralumin forgings and sheet, had the earmarks of a nuisance suit. But it was a big nuisance. With the triple-damage requirements of the law, $9 million was more than 80 percent of the firm's revenues for that year and more than double its net income.

Baush's attorneys pursued two major lines of attack. They accused Alcoa of undercutting Baush's prices for forgings and sheet by reducing the differentials between the prices of its ingot and its semifabricated products below the true costs of production by an independent fabricator. Such "price squeezing" by an integrated firm was deemed anticompetitive under the antitrust laws. Alcoa was also accused of conspiring with and coercing foreign producers to keep their metal out of the American market. The fact that Aluminium Limited and Alcoa were controlled by the same stockholders allegedly contributed to the high prices of pure aluminum for independent producers. The case did not reach trial until the fall of 1933, and after ten weeks of testimony, Alcoa was cleared by a Connecticut jury. A federal appeals court then ordered a new trial after finding that the judge's instructions to the jury had been too narrowly framed and that evidence had been erroneously excluded. The appeals court, moreover, implied that there need be no direct evidence of control of importation of aluminum by Alcoa if the condition of monopolization of the domestic market was found to exist. A second trial in 1935 resulted in a verdict for Baush. The jury, operating on more liberal instructions, awarded the plaintiff $2,868,900 in treble damages plus attorney's fees.[10]

Alcoa won its second appeal. Two arguments made by the company's attorneys were of great legal significance from the company's point of view. First, Alcoa contended that uniformity of price and/ or high prices on ingot charged by Alcoa and importers should not be construed as violations of the antitrust law if they resulted from the independent action of the producers (that is, through oligopolistic pricing behavior). Second, the company argued that price spreads that did not cover the conversion costs at every stage of a vertically integrated enterprise were not unlawful. Since few antitrust cases had ever been instituted, let alone decided, on the basis of vertical integration, Alcoa's attorneys seemed to be standing on fairly firm ground.[11] However, Alcoa's legal arguments were not fully adjudicated, as the court ruled in favor of Alcoa largely on technical grounds. Thus, when Baush made more rumbling noises, Alcoa, rather than suffer yet another suit from Haskell, agreed to settle. The final agreement was conditioned upon a letter from the Attorney General that the settlement would not be used as a basis for any future action.[12]

Yet the underlying issues in the Baush case bubbled up once again in the accusations brought by the DOJ in its 1937 antitrust suit. Some 140 charges were made, accusing Alcoa of monopolizing sixteen markets and entering conspiracies with foreign producers to keep competing aluminum out of the United States. All the old charges of the 1912 suit were resurrected along with the more recent history of the firm's behavior and its ties, through its directors, to Aluminium Limited. Not only was Alcoa's horizontal control of production facilities in various product lines attacked, but also its vertical control of bauxite, water power, alumina, and, of course, virgin aluminum. Alcoa was even accused of monopolizing the secondary aluminum (scrap) market and of engaging in specific forms of intimidation to drive competitors out of business or into Alcoa's effective control. In this case, the remedy sought was not a financial settlement, but a divestiture that would break the company up into competing enterprises.[13]

To Alcoa's management it seemed sinister that U.S. Attorney General Homer Cummings's firm had served as counsel for Baush. Whatever Cummings's influence (he took care formally, at least, to disengage himself from the matter),[14] *U.S. v. Alcoa* was far more than a mere sequel to a private suit, more than a single attorney's crusade. There were forces at work in the larger political and economic environment driving the Government's attack.

Alcoa's antitrust problem was partly a matter of image. Among all major industries where concentrated economic power existed, aluminum was most clearly a monopoly and Alcoa a monopolist. Alcoa had become the very model of industrial concentration, and its principal owners had become exemplars of the kind of corporate barony that seemed distant, powerful, and dangerous to the popular mind. In the public prints, the company was widely known as "the aluminum trust," having, noted *The New Yorker's* "Reporter at Large," "all the Lombroso stigmata of an octopus." Alcoa's vulnerability to antitrust was heightened by its reputation as a "Mellon Company" and by A. V. Davis's insouciance about, if not thorough distaste for, public relations.[15]

Alcoa's ties to the Mellon interests had come to appear downright nefarious. Former Treasury Secretary Andrew Mellon was a great financier, a philanthropist, and a dedicated public servant. But he

Fig. 5.1.   Andrew W. Mellon and his aluminum Pierce Arrow. *Courtesy of Mellon Bank.*

had also become a personified symbol of corporate America at a time when that was decidedly not a good thing to be. Even before he had become a favorite whipping boy of New Dealers, Mellon was a marked man. In the mid-1920s, firms controlled by or connected to the Mellons had come under a highly publicized Senate investigation into corporate tax abuses, an investigation that probed into the Secretary's conduct in office and his personal finances. Attempts by Calvin Coolidge to head off the more ardent Mellon-baiters in Congress had served only to fan the fire. Populist democrats took off after Mellon at every opportunity, and it was they, according to George Gibbons, who had embroiled the company in the FTC investigation that had cost Alcoa more than a million dollars.[16]

The Mellon family was, of course, one of the richest in the world, and A. W., in particular, a lion among capitalists. Though reticent and reclusive, he was a brilliant financier, widely respected in business circles for his ability to master the finanical problems of an extraordinary range of enterprises. In his role as public servant, he had become the greatest Secretary, some said, since Alexander Hamilton. In that position, which he held through Herbert Hoover's presidency, Secretary Mellon was a strict fiscal conservative. He cut federal expenditures, engineered a sharp reduction in corporate and personal income taxes, and opposed public works, veterans' bonuses, and regulation. None of that made him popular. Instead, he became a choice target for his political opponents, who vilified him as a corrupt man of wealth insensitive to the needs of all but the nation's richest. All this played well at a time when statistics showed that the nation's 60,000 wealthiest families had as much money as the twenty-five million poorest. The head of one of those wealthy families, New York Governor Franklin Delano Roosevelt, excoriated Mellon as "the master mind among the malefactors of great wealth." By 1930, when Senator George Norris, the great Nebraska populist, assailed Mellon as "head and front of the aluminum trust," Alcoa was easily identified as yet another link in the chain that bound government to big business with all the hidden evils that such a relationship had come to imply. The Secretary of the Treasury's protestations that he himself did not run Alcoa fell on deaf ears, and *Fortune* observed that the company was "commonly regarded as a monopoly, and therefore bad; and as a Mellon monopoly, and therefore worse." When Mellon left office in the wake of the Democratic victory, he hoped to return to a quiet life in Pittsburgh. But he was not to be left alone.[17]

As the nation plunged into the depths of depression, A. W. Mellon became a leading scapegoat for what many saw as the failure of the American business system. His gaunt and slightly disheveled appearance, his old-fashioned black suits, black tie, and black cigarettes subjected him to ridicule in the press, which turned him into a dour personification of the political and social bankruptcy of corporate capitalism. The failure of his coal enterprises in Western Pennsylvania made "Uncle Andy" a focus for working-class rage. When the Democrats took power, his business reputation for integrity could not forestall yet more politically motivated investigations into his personal affairs and a humiliating grand-jury proceeding (in which he was cleared) on flimsy charges of income-tax evasion.[18] There was perhaps some mercy in the timing of Mellon's death just before the great antitrust suit went to trial.[19]

With A. V. Davis, the problem was a bit different. More sheltered from the slings and arrows of Washington politics, he was more openly arrogant about his business success than Mellon, who was, if anything, self-effacing. A minister's son, Davis suffered his share of the sin of pride. Over the years, Davis had become known to his subordinates (who were both bemused and intimidated by his imperious and blunt demeanor) as a "Napoleonic" figure who had become a bit too infatuated with his monopoly.[20] Though meticulously careful in his business correspondence and legal testimonies, his public behavior was less than discreet. One day in 1933, while his firm was locking horns in court with the Baush Machine Tool Company, Davis was reported to be in typically fine fettle at a Washington gala. *The Pittsburgh Press* clipping speaks volumes:

> A new kind of performance was given in the great ballroom of the Willard Hotel. The cast was the NRA and the Mellon-controlled Aluminum Company of America.
>
> Presidents [of the company's subsidiaries], first vice presidents, third and fourth vice presidents, and every kind of official took part.
>
> Diminutive, immaculately-tailored Arthur V. Davis, chairman of the board of the Aluminum Company (once described by ex-ambassador James W. Gerard as "one of the 100 most powerful men in the world") led the aluminum ballet.
>
> Fidgeting with his rimless nose glasses, Mr. Davis stood below the orchestra stand and answered rapid questions.
>
> Sometimes, dapper Mr. Davis turned his head an inch and piped: "Do we own that company?"
>
> Whereupon the presidents and vice presidents would chorus: "Yes."
>
> Once Mr. Davis was asked how much virgin aluminum his company controls in the United States.
>
> "How much do we control?" queried Mr. Davis, slightly turning his head.
>
> From the back of the room a bass voice boomed:
>
> "One hundred per cent."[21]

Suffice it to say that in public relations terms, Alcoa was a sitting duck for the New Deal attorneys who marched into Federal Court with their sweeping indictment in April 1937.

Shifts in the political arena determined both the timing and the nature of the suit. After first trying to stabilize depressed American industry through Government-sponsored cartelization (the NRA) and through suspension of antitrust pressure on matters of production, price setting, and employment, the Roosevelt administration veered toward antitrust as a political tool for controlling industry. The initiation of the Alcoa suit preceded by several months the arrival of the vigorous trustbuster, Thurman Arnold, at the Justice Department. The DOJ, with the influential Brandeis disciple, Robert Jackson, serving a brief tenure as head of the Antitrust Division, was planning a renewed assault on what it saw as the power of big business to control markets and prices.[22]

The outlawing of the NRA by the Supreme Court in 1935 and an

Table 5.2. *Alcoa's market share in the major products of the aluminum industry on the eve of World War II*

Product	Percentage produced by Alcoa[a]
Bauxite, for aluminum	100
Alumina	100
Aluminum, primary	100
Fabricated Aluminum Products	
Sheet	60
Extruded shapes	40
Forgings	40
Tubing, rod, wire, and bar	60
Foil	50
Pistons	22
Aluminum bronze powder	50
Cooking utensils	50

[a]The statistics were drawn from Government estimates and from data filed by Alcoa in 1937. It is assumed that market shares for aluminum products were relatively static through the latter part of the 1930s.
Source: E. B. Alderfer and H. E. Michl, *Economics of American Industry* (New York: McGraw-Hill, 1942), p. 103.

increasing loss of faith in the ability of business to regulate its own affairs had given greater influence to administration antimonopolists like Jackson, Harold Ickes, and Leon Henderson, who advocated the restoration of "free markets" and "price competition" in the highly concentrated center industries. Believing that the interests of small businessmen, farmers, and workers were collectively distinct from those of big business, the antimonopolists wanted to ensure that business maintained high levels of investment without resorting to higher prices under conditions of monetary expansion. When a sharp recession occurred in 1937 after a few years of incremental recovery from the depths of the Great Depression, the antimonopoly wing of the New Deal accused big business of deliberately dampening the recovery through niggardly investment and excessive prices.[23]

Today, we know a good deal more about the reasons for the prolonged duration of the Great Depression than the people who struggled with it at the time. Conservative (by modern standards) fiscal policies of the Federal Government and tight money policies of the Federal Reserve Bank had a far more negative impact on the economy than any imaginable conspiracy of big business could possibly have achieved. Yet, the views of the antimonopolists gained the ascendancy by the end of 1937, just as a serious economic contraction interrupted what had been a gradual recovery from the depths of the Depression, which made it more convenient for the Roosevelt administration to blame its party's traditional political enemies for the failure to achieve prosperity. Under Thurman Arnold, the Antitrust Division, which had been a mere "corporal's guard" during Roosevelt's first term, would greatly expand its resources and personnel in order to promote reforms in industry structure. Government antitrust suits and consent decrees, more than ever before, became viewed as appropriate tools in the management of the economy.

The Alcoa case became tied up in legal maneuverings for several months after its filing, but then heated up after Arnold's appointment in early 1938. To those inured to the obscene proportions of modern antitrust proceedings, it is interesting to recall the astonishment of contemporary lawyers and laymen alike with the magnitude of the Alcoa case. The DOJ took strange pride in the length of the proceedings, which, from filing to verdict, lasted longer than the American Civil War. It was 176 days longer in its six and one-half months of actual trial days than the notorious case of the Tichborne claimant in 1874, the reigning champion in the history of Anglo-Saxon litigation. Before its trial was over, Alcoa would spend more than $2 million to defend itself (the Government spent a half million), and, as it would turn out, this was only the first round in a proceeding that would wind through various stages of appeal until 1956.[24]

The trial itself began in June of 1938 and lasted until 1940, when new briefs were produced, and some more time passed while the judge considered his verdict. Considerable publicity was given to the case in the press, almost all of it unfavorable to Alcoa, a result of skillful news management by the DOJ and the ill-advised reticence of the company.[25] Yet, despite its worsening public image, Alcoa won the first round in March 1942. In a stunning verdict, the venerable Francis G. Caffey of the United States District Court for the Southern District of New York (after sitting through twenty-six months of testimony, countless motions and procedural hagglings, and some 58,000 pages of trial record) found the defendants not guilty on every one of the over 130 charges.

Judge Caffey's ruling, which he read aloud over a period of nine days, fell squarely within the dominant strain of antitrust law. For

Caffey, it was necessary to show proof of intent to monopolize in the accumulation and concentration of resources and/or the actual commission of unlawful acts in order to be held guilty of illegal monopolization. In charge after charge, he found that Alcoa's success had been the result of sound business practice and acceptable competitive behavior, and in most cases, no monopoly could be said to exist. There was no monopoly of bauxite, not even in the United States, where Alcoa was held to control about fifty percent. Alcoa's hydroelectric power, by then only 0.0003 percent of the entire power capacity of the United States, paled by comparison to other developments, especially those of the Government in the Tennessee Valley and the Pacific Northwest.[26]

Charges of monopolization in the downstream side of the business – in aluminum cooking utensils, foil, pistons, and other products – fell away in the face of evidence of actual or potential competition. Each product/technology line went to different markets and had different economic and technical characteristics, posing lesser or greater barriers to entry. The picture presented to the judge was complex and often imprecise, but in such relatively easy to enter fields as castings, where neither capital requirements nor reliance on Alcoa's primary ingot were great, it was clear that Alcoa faced competition (from hundreds of producers in the case of sand castings) both large and small. Alcoa did dominate in the sale of extrusions, especially in large structural shapes, through its pioneering and command of relevant technologies; but the cost of entry into this still new, rapidly evolving field was not prohibitive, and evidence existed that here, as in some other cases of semifabricated products, Alcoa encouraged, even assisted the development of outside extruders who would become customers for Alcoa's ingot. In the case of one exotic specialty, aluminum foil, Alcoa had ample competition and was surpassed by Reynolds Metals, which had specialized in the business since the mid-1920s. Alcoa's lone position in aluminum cable could be largely attributed to the still dominant power of copper producers to establish the market price for electrical cable. The company's once nearly complete dominance of the combined aluminum and alloyed sheet markets was seen to be declining (Alcoa had but 71.2 percent of the combined markets in 1938), and again competition had emerged as competitors' technologies had improved, often with the aid and advice of Alcoa engineers.[27]

It might reasonably have been expected that Alcoa could restrain competition in especially lucrative lines of business by seeking control of key competitors. But Caffey found otherwise. For example,

Figs. 5.2. and 5.3. Alcoa's Calderwood, Tennessee, dam (top) and its "Wear-Ever" cooking utensils plant in New Kensington, Pennsylvania (bottom), signify the span of integrated control the company enjoyed over virtually every phase of aluminum production – a control that the Department of Justice wanted to bring to an end.

in the case of the long-watched utensils field, where Alcoa held a substantial interest in the Aluminum Goods Manufacturing Company, the judge found that the latter firm had always competed vigorously with Alcoa's own 100-percent-controlled "Wear-Ever" subsidiary.[28] It might also be expected that Alcoa could hurt competitors through a price squeeze. But while the judge did find that the margin between Alcoa's ingot and sheet prices was narrow enough to cause potential harm to competitors between 1925 and 1932, the spread had widened afterward. In any case, Alcoa was caught between the conflicting desires of two classes of customers – of mill operators for wider, and of final fabricators for narrower, price spreads.[29] It did not help the prosecution's case that independent fabricators of aluminum testified eloquently on behalf of Alcoa's helpfulness in developing their lines of production. Nor did it help that George Haskell, the best-known "victim" of Alcoa's prices, swore he had "never testified that the Aluminum Company was intentionally trying to injure the Baush Machine Tool Company or to put anyone else out of business."[30]

The nub of the matter was Alcoa's historic position in primary aluminum. Yet, even though Alcoa had clearly enjoyed a monopoly in the production of alumina and virgin aluminum in the United States, this did not, in Caffey's view, constitute illegal monopolization in the absence of specific proof that Alcoa had sought to exclude competition. For the years between 1929 and 1938, Caffey accepted the company's arguments that it faced substantial competition from foreign producers and especially from recycled "secondary" aluminum. Caffey was not disturbed by Davis's forthright testimony that "it was always our idea to carry on the business in such a manner that the inducement to go into the aluminum business would not be inordinately great." If a monopoly was that efficient, why not? In the last analysis, the judge estimated Alcoa's share of the American aluminum market at about thirty-three percent after including secondary and excluding that part of "Alcoa's own production which it fabricated and did not therefore sell as ingot." Including Alcoa's own used production, its market share was estimated at sixty-four percent.[31]

Caffey dismissed the Government's substantial efforts to recall Alcoa's turn-of-the-century cartel arrangements as evidence of a systematic, ongoing attempt to conspire with foreign producers. Nor did he believe the vague and imprecise (and largely hearsay) testimony of Government witnesses that Alcoa had engaged in tacit agreements with foreign producers since 1915. As for Aluminium Limited, the judge established a rigorous test: it was not enough to show that the Canadian company had participated in European cartels and had otherwise struck agreements with certain foreign producers that would be illegal in the United States. It was necessary to show that there had been a specific conspiracy between Aluminium Limited and Alcoa.[32] Indeed, with regard to the Alcoa–Aluminium Limited connection, where the board-level and top-management personal relationships were so clearly intimate and business interests so clearly intertwined, the judge was remarkably unconcerned. This, in retrospect, seems to have been a serious weakness in his grasp of the competitive realities of the North American industry.

But Caffey's findings elsewhere reflected a solid understanding of the technological and business constraints on Alcoa's ability to exercise monopoly power. Given his judicial outlook, which required strict tests of evidence of wrongdoing, Caffey wrote a sophisticated and well-reasoned, if somewhat injudiciously partial, opinion. It was quite reasonable, for example, to conclude that Alcoa passed the 1911 Supreme Court's test of an acceptable trust. The judge's partiality showed up in his unabashed admiration for the company and its management. After alluding to the "bias" and "wishful thinking" of many of the Government's witnesses, Caffey referred to "the great number of . . . competitors as well as customers of Alcoa, who have completely exculpated Alcoa from blame and have praised its fairness as well as its helpfulness in the aluminum industry." He then heaped accolades upon Arthur Vining Davis who, he noted, had begun his career in aluminum virtually "as a laborer . . . not infrequently forced to whistle for his pay." By dint of hard work and excellent business judgment, Davis rose to become the man "who chiefly and primarily, has built up and made Alcoa what it is today." The judge pointed to one of Davis's self-advertised achievements, the company's well-funded research laboratory, as one of the great benefits bestowed by the firm upon industry and society. His conclusion: "it would be greatly contrary to the public interest either to dissolve or to enjoin Alcoa."[33]

Having rendered his opinion, Judge Caffey confessed his fatigue with the matter. He had presided over the lengthiest and most ponderous legal proceeding in the nation's history. When Arnold asked if he might begin the inevitable appeal before the judge's decision was revised into final draft, Caffey responded, "If there is any legal way for me to get rid of this case, I'll do it so quick that it'll make your head swim." The judge was more than ready to "welcome an appeal,... recognizing, as I do, my own fallibility."[34]

According to one partisan, it was precisely the good judge's fallibility and the defense's ability to play on it that had lost the Government its case. Irving Lipkowitz, who had served as the economist for the Department of Justice during the trial, recalled the deep disappointment the Antitrust Division felt after failing utterly to impress the court, a failure he ascribed largely to Alcoa's superior courtroom presence. The Government could muster no witness as powerful or impressive as Davis, who spent thirty days on the stand and whose mastery of detail and command of concepts was one of "the two pleasures, and I really mean pleasures, that I had in that courtroom." The second was watching Alcoa's lead attorney, William Watson Smith, who had "learned his law in a law office" and whose courtroom psychology was "marvelous." Smith, according to Lipkowitz, deftly played on the difference between the generations of the young attorneys in the Antitrust Division and the septuagenarian Woodrow Wilson appointee on the bench. "The judge and [Smith] were the old guys. They had wisdom. They had judgment. And we had a bunch of kids over here, scurrying around...." Smith was "able to refer to us as Boy Scouts, and not be reprimanded by the court. He had built it up gradually, to the point where this was the atmosphere." To compound matters, the Government could not turn up a single document of "smoking-gun" quality after an intensive culling of Alcoa's files (A. V. Davis, said Lipkowitz, who had conducted a search of Alcoa's records, "ran a marvelous correspondence school"). Under such circumstances, as the defense attorneys picked away at the Government's charges one by one, "the judge did not grasp what we were trying to say about the overwhelming influence of a monopoly in stultifying the emergence of new ideas."[35]

In nonlegal terms, the Government's case rested on a bedrock notion that free enterprise always implied vigorous competition. To a New Deal liberal like Lipkowitz, arguments about business conduct under monopoly conditions were irrelevant. No elaborate economic theory was required; monopoly was just plain wrong. The objection to monopoly could be stated in terms of a desire to preserve an unfettered flow of business intelligence in a democratic society. "We don't know whether a new idea is a better idea or not, but if you don't get new ideas, you know you're going to be deprived of better ideas. You have to take that risk... in competition."[36] Others would have stated the case differently, but the main point for Alcoa's adversaries in the Government, even as they piled charge upon charge of specific violations of the law, was that a monopoly was a social evil, too powerful and monolithic to be allowed to exist in a society in which free enterprise depended upon the existence of vigorous competition and the absence of concentrated power.

This fundamental ideological point, that monopoly was an inherent social evil, had indeed been obscured, not as much by Alcoa's superior lawyering as by the Government's own inept handling of its case. By focusing on specific acts of wrongdoing, the Government lawyers lost everything, as their charges dissolved one by one in the face of contrary evidence and sympathetic testimony from Alcoa's customers and competitors. Judge Caffey was plainly annoyed by the newspaper publicity given to the case and seemed determined all the more not to be swayed by it ("I don't trust anything I see in the newspapers about anything," he declared at one point while taking testimony). Before the decision was rendered, Walter Rice, the Government's lead litigating attorney, had apparently learned enough about the business to accept an offer from Reynolds Metals to help it negotiate a federal loan for a smelting facility. By the time the trial was over, Arnold himself was beginning to look a bit silly, if not downright antisocial, as the onset of war was already dictating a more cooperative approach between Government and big business.[37]

The Government's appeal led to a different result – one that vindicated the DOJ's underlying moral and philosophical position, if not all its substantive charges. After a long delay, arguments were heard by the Second Circuit Court. The Supreme Court, where the appeal should have been heard, had been unable to mount a quorum. Four of its justices had previously been involved in Government antitrust actions against Alcoa. It took an act of Congress in June 1944 to provide that this kind of case could be certified to the lower appeals court. After hearing arguments in January 1945, the tribunal of Learned Hand, Augustus Hand, and Thomas Swan rendered their decision, written by the first of the three.[38]

In March 1945, Learned Hand set forth his famous, pathbreaking opinion that would have profound influence on antitrust law for years to come. Hand leaned heavily on Section 2 of the Sherman Act, which related to monopolization, rather than Section 1, which prohibited restraint of trade.[39] His opinion grew out of one important strain of reasoning in certain antitrust decisions since 1911. Chief Justice White in *U.S. v. Standard Oil* had distinguished "monopolization" from "monopoly" by looking for an intent to achieve monopoly power. White had first established the existence of market power and then looked at the purpose behind it.[40] Hand went further in deciding that it was not relevant whether the power, once established, is abused, or not.

Alcoa, he found, had illegally monopolized the ingot market, not because of any specifically proven acts of misconduct (at least since the 1912 consent decree), but because the company was, first, in a position of monopoly power, and, second (and this is key), had not been merely a passive beneficiary of its position. Instead, the company had engaged in a "positive drive" to expand its business, a drive that resulted in the maintenance of its monopoly. "We need charge it [Alcoa] with no moral derelictions after 1912," said Hand; "we may assume all it claims for itself is true." All that mattered was

> whether [Alcoa] falls within the exception established in favor of those who do not seek, but cannot avoid, the control of a market. It seems to us that question scarcely survives its statement. It was not inevitable that it should always anticipate increases in the demand for ingot and be prepared to supply them. Nothing compelled it to keep doubling and redoubling its capacity before others entered the field. It insists that it never excluded competitors; but we can think of no more effective exclusion than progressively to embrace every opportunity as it opened, and to face every newcomer with new capacity already geared into a great organization, having the advantage of experience, trade connections and the elite of personnel.[41]

This was harsh doctrine, virtually foreclosing any claim that the company might legally achieve monopoly through good management or indeed through good, competitive business practice. In establishing Alcoa's monopoly in aluminum ingot, Hand took a close look at Alcoa's claim that it faced substantial competition from secondary scrap, which was produced by some seventeen firms in the United States. Alcoa, he reasoned, could regulate the long-run supply of secondary by adjusting its own output of primary aluminum. "The competition of 'secondary' must therefore be disregarded." That done, he then weighed Alcoa's output against imports and concluded that the company's "control over the ingot market must be reckoned at over ninety per cent." This, he opined in his now famous dictum, was enough to constitute a monopoly, while it was "doubtful whether sixty per cent would be enough."[42]

Hand felt no need to find that Alcoa had either conspired to keep foreign ingot out of the American market or had extracted exorbitant profits.

> Having proved [Judge Hand wrote] that "Alcoa" had a monopoly of the domestic ingot market, the plaintiff had gone far enough; if it was an excuse, that "Alcoa" had not abused its power, it lay upon "Alcoa" to prove that it had not. But the whole exercise is irrelevant anyway, for it is no excuse for "monopolizing" a market that the monopoly has not been used to extract from the consumer more than a "fair" profit. The [Sherman] Act has wider purposes.... Congress ... did not condone "good trusts" and condemn "bad" ones; it forbade all. Moreover, in doing so it was not necessarily actuated by economic motives alone. It is possible, because of its indirect social or moral effect, to prefer a system of small producers, each dependent for his success upon his own skill and character, to one in which the great mass of those engaged must accept the direction of the few. These considerations, which we have suggested only as possible purposes of the Act, we think the decisions prove to have been in fact its purposes.[43]

Hand swept aside mitigating arguments made by the defense. Alcoa's claim that its net return on capital, calculated at ten percent historically (the Government had calculated the return at fifty-five percent),[44] had been modest and fair was irrelevant. "The mere fact that a producer having command of the domestic market has not been able to make more than a 'fair' profit is not evidence that 'fair' profit could not have been made at lower prices." In any case, Alcoa possessed the power to fix prices, and that was sufficient. The court also reconsidered the DOJ's charges relating to bauxite, water power, fabricated products, and cartels. It found in the last instance that there may well have been more than innocent discussions between Alcoa and foreign producers and intent to use the European cartel to restrict imports to the United States. Limited's participation in the 1936 Alliance was a violation of the Sherman Act in that the agreement covered imports into the United States. But what really disturbed the court was the common ownership and control of Limited and Alcoa.[45]

Nevertheless, the court opted for restraint in the matter of Limited and Alcoa and did not go so far as to demand a severance of ties between the two firms. The court also refused to go along with the DOJ's request for a dissolution of Alcoa. Noting that the industry had changed greatly since the closing of the evidence in 1940 and that the issue of the wartime plants was unresolved, Judge Hand reasoned that "it would be particularly fatuous to prepare a plan now, even if we could be sure that some form of dissolution will be proper." Then, showing remarkable leniency toward the company whose defense he had just savaged, he declared, "if the industry will not need it for its protection, it will be a disservice to break up an aggregation which has for so long demonstrated its efficiency."[46] Given Hand's restraint, an appropriate remedy for the appellate court's findings would be a very tricky matter. That problem was first referred back to Judge Caffey (who was still on the bench), and it would keep the lawyers busy for years to come.

While Learned Hand's decision has become a landmark, with the full stature of a Supreme Court ruling, it has always been controversial. In recent years, as the judicial tide has turned once again toward the application of a "rule of reason" in antitrust cases, it has made more plausible the argument of a conservative judicial theorist like Robert H. Bork that Hand's opinion was "a thoroughly perverse judicial tour de force." To Bork's thinking, which today is fairly congenial to even moderate views on the subject, the 1945 Alcoa ruling did untold damage to both the intent of the Sherman Act and "the entire spirit of antitrust." What has bothered so many students of the decision over the years is the seemingly antisocial logic of the decision, which, according to another eminent legal scholar, A. D. Neale, "would impute illegal intent to a firm with monopoly power *even on account of its very efficiency*, if exclusionary effects were shown to result." Indeed, in retrospect, we can see that Hand's ruling did not consider the aluminum industry's market structure primarily in terms of its impact on the consumer.[47]

Yet while the Alcoa appellate decision has been deplored over the years by some scholars as deeply flawed in its economic reasoning and by some legal commentators as an unwarranted attempt by judges to transcend both the issues of the case and the intent of the law in order to make public policy, others have praised the decision on precisely the same grounds. One pair of economists appealed to a doctrine of original intent, going so far as to praise Hand's decision as a *conservative* triumph for the "original meaning" of the Sherman Act "that had been whittled away by earlier Supreme Court decisions."[48]

The "intent" of Congress when it passed the Act, of course, is not so easy to fathom. Fears of populists and conservatives, of rural and urban constituencies, of Republicans and Democrats, all, were reflected in the legislation. Thus, while nineteenth-century legislatures might have been surprised by the wide judicial discretion taken by Hand in interpreting the Act, they might well have appreciated that insofar as his opinion was rooted in a general aversion to concentrated power, it was true to the spirit of the political and social climate in which the law was passed.

But in the final analysis, the 1945 Alcoa decision reflected the antimonopoly sentiments of the mid-twentieth century, and as such, Hand's opinion was neither pristine nor conventional law. It was law based on a fairly young judicial tradition, an activist philosophy that had been gathering force since the late nineteenth century and had gained respectability in the opinions of such legal giants as Brandeis, Oliver Wendell Holmes, and Felix Frankfurter. These modern "legal realists" understood the law to exist as more than a system of specific acts of legislation and judicial precedent. To them, the law was a mutable and positive force that must take into account the social and institutional contexts of particular cases. For such progressive jurists, among whom we must count Learned Hand, a legal decision could become an instrument of public policy, and the law "a working social tool."[49]

Leon Hickman, who had been William Watson Smith's right-hand man during the trial, was among many who saw the result as a contrived, reductionist application of law in order to arrive at the Government's preordained view of public policy.

> I can see [said Hickman] why Judge Hand felt that no matter how we got where we were, that it wasn't in the public interest that we be in such a dominant position. If you kept that in mind, then you worked back from that. "What do I pin on them?" Well, he principally pinned on us the fact that we were the first in every market that opened up. But actually, look at the reverse of that. Suppose that we had acted as a monopoly is supposed to act and we simply sat back and took our profits and hadn't developed the market. You would say now there is a monopoly of action. There is a great need for new markets and new uses for aluminum and you aren't meeting it. So, in a way, from his approach, we had no escape. He'd get us either way.[50]

Hickman was right: Alcoa was whipsawed by Judge Hand's reasoning. The judge had rationalized mightily to make his point. In his attempt to align the court's decision with the politically powerful antimonopoly sentiments of his own day, his reasoning was often weak. His decision to eliminate secondary aluminum from the consideration of Alcoa's market share, for example, was flatly incorrect. Hand's surmisal that Alcoa would try to manipulate its primary production for the sake of controlling secondary aluminum output contradicted his own observation that the company had always responded to every opportunity to expand its capacity. In arguing that the firm had been able to foreclose markets through capacity expansion, he seems to have ignored the very evidence offered by the current war, as well as the most damning contemporary criticism of the firm that it had not (or could not) expand sufficiently to meet demand opportunities.[51] But again, none of this mattered. The conclusion was foreordained by the demands of public policy.

As for the Government's view that enforced competition in aluminum would bring any further economic benefits to society, it was based less on historical fact than on faith. If other businessmen had not made serious efforts to mount competition against Alcoa's large, efficient, integrated system of bauxite mines, alumina refineries, and aluminum smelters, it was because the investment was too great, the risk too high, and not because Alcoa had simply sewed up the markets or the sources of supply. The court certainly did not find otherwise. Moreover, both the substance and logic of Judge Hand's opinion argued that Alcoa had done well historically by its products and markets. With the possible exception of some price squeezing on sheet products in the late 1920s, there was no evidence that Alcoa had used its market power unfairly or in ways that directly violated the antitrust laws. Nor had Alcoa been prone to charging monopoly prices. The company had followed a long-term practice of bringing the cost of aluminum down to compete with other materials. Although its management always preferred price stability to adjusting prices with every fluctuation in demand, one could still argue plausibly that Alcoa, among all potential entrants into the business, may have been not only the low-cost producer but the legitimate low-price producer, also. If there were no direct competitors in aluminum, it was only because Alcoa had competed too well. "I think," said Roy Hunt simply enough, "we are being penalized for our successful free enterprise."[52] But neither corporate efficiency nor consumer welfare was an overriding concern for Learned Hand's court.

That the Government won its case against Alcoa was far less the result of economic rationality than it was the triumph of a conception of judicial activism based on a progressive ideal of the use of law as a "social tool." Yet it was a judicial activism rooted in a nostalgic, if not retrogressive, vision of economic organization. Hand was determined to promote competition in the aluminum industry as a matter of public good. But the public good in the Alcoa case was implicitly defined in a way that harked back to a world long since past, in which the economic order of Adam Smith made literal sense. It was in that world, the still predominantly self-sufficient, agrarian culture of the first industrial revolution, where one could justifiably "prefer a system of small producers" without regard for the constraints imposed by the complex, interlocking technologies of capital-intensive industries operating in widespread, interdependent markets. It was in that simpler world where business success was the outcome of the "skill and character" of each of a multitude of small producers and not, as Hand put it, by the collective labor of a "great mass" who "must accept the direction of the few."[53]

In other words, the 1945 Alcoa decision, which changed the whole focus of antitrust law for more than three decades, appears to have been quite unsophisticated by today's standards. Now we expect more rigorous economic analysis in antitrust proceedings. Judge Hand's decision, like Judge Caffey's, rested more on sentiments about what was right and fair than on rational analyses of industry structure and consumer welfare. Yet Caffey's decision had been predicated mainly on a narrow interpretation of past behavior, and by that standard, he had judged Alcoa to be a good corporate citizen, while Hand, who believed in the efficacy of competition, was looking to the future. But Hand did not fully grasp the nature of aluminum production technologies, nor did he fully understand that their inherent logic required an extraordinary degree of vertical integration and concentration in refining, smelting, and certain classes of semifabricated products.

We shall see that in its effects, Hand's decision led quickly to only a very limited form of oligopolistic competition among a handful of large, integrated producers. Nonetheless, the practical results of the antitrust case proved beneficial over time. The oligopoly that emerged in the aluminum industry in the war's aftermath enlivened the industry and spurred the development of new markets well beyond what Alcoa alone might have been able to accomplish. In the postwar industrial nation, hungry as it was for aluminum, it is unlikely that one producer would have met the demand as quickly and with as many new products as did four major North American rivals. As Leon Hickman looked back some years after finishing his career with Alcoa as executive vice president and general counsel, he conceded that Learned Hand had produced bad law, perhaps, but had also produced a good outcome. In a 1984 interview, Hickman summed up the outcome as follows:

L. H. I think in the end it was in the interest of Alcoa that we have competition.
Q. Do you think it was in the interest of society?
L. H. Definitely. Definitely. I think it was in everybody's interest that we have it. The question all along was – and I'm not sure that at that time Alcoa wouldn't have become more comfortable with some competition – but how do you get it?[54]

Indeed, how? – without breaking up the enterprise. That crucial question would be decided not by the courts but by the political and economic realities of the Second World War.

Wartime pressures: capacity

By 1937, world aluminum consumption had reached an all-time high of 499,666 metric tons. Recovering from the Depression, Alcoa began laying plans for the expansion of its business. In the spring of the year, the company sited a second mining operation in Surinam, and by summer, it added several steamships to the corporate fleet for the transportation of bauxite. A new alumina refinery was located in the port town of Mobile, Alabama, more power was purchased from the TVA (expanding an agreement made with the agency in 1936), and aluminum production at the company's four smelting locations was cranked up toward full capacity. In addition to providing for expansion of its basic aluminum production, Alcoa opened a fabricating plant at Lafayette, Indiana, to meet growing demand for aluminum tubing and expanded its aluminum-rivet capacity at Massena. It was expected that any near-term growth in demand for other semifabricated and finished products could be met by the company's existing capacity, much of which had been in excess during the Depression, and since fabricated products operated in more or less competitive environments, it was well to guard against over-expansion in those areas.[55] But in general, Alcoa was doing exactly what Learned Hand observed it had always done: it was responding to every reasonable opportunity to increase capacity. The response to anticipated demand, however, was predicated on a peacetime economy. Nothing could prepare the company for the almost incredible expansion that would be required by a second global war.

Pressure to increase capacity to a wartime footing was already mounting as Germany, where Hitler, in defiance of the Versailles treaty's prohibition on the resurrection of a German air force, was building his Luftwaffe. Germany alone accounted for thirty percent of the 1937 increase in world consumption. With liberal state subsidies and no regard to production costs, the German aluminum industry mushroomed, and by 1938, the Third Reich was the largest aluminum producer in the world. The European cartel had already collapsed under the weight of German expansion, and the head of the French industry, along with a few political leaders, most notably Winston Churchill, had been crying for counterpreparedness. But the Allied governments remained sanguine until it became painfully clear what German aluminum was all about. Aluminium Limited had already been laying plans for some increase in primary capacity, but much of that was to supplement Alcoa's requirements for the American market during cyclical upturns. By the end of 1937, Great Britain began to signal Limited that it would need more aluminum to expand the Royal Air Force. After the September Munich crisis, there could be no doubt about the German threat, and Alcoa began to study the potential requirements of England and France.[56]

After consultation with domestic and foreign aircraft producers, military agencies, and Government officials, Alcoa beefed up its facilities for hard alloy sheet, forgings, and extrusions. Sales, however, remained well below capacity through the first half of 1939. Business forecasts indicated no further need for expansion. But by early fall with the invasion of Poland, it became clear that war conditions abroad and domestic demand, both, would require more smelting capacity. Alcoa, therefore, made a long-term power contract with Bonneville Power Authority to operate a smelter at Vancouver, Washington. On October 17, 1940, in response to the United States Military Aircraft Program as recently presented to Congress, Alcoa embarked on the construction of a five-million-pound-per-month capacity sheet mill at Alcoa, Tennessee. Yet neither of these developments, nor the expansion of other fabricating facilities would be enough. As the war spread in Europe and as American lend-lease to the Allies expanded, experts both outside and within the company believed that capacity was more than sufficient for projected aircraft requirements.[57] They were wrong.

More than any other factor, it was its shortage of capacity for a major war that broke Alcoa's absolute monopoly in primary aluminum. Repeated assurances from A. V. Davis and operations vice president I. W. Wilson that Alcoa would be able to supply all the aluminum needed were soon belied by the overwhelming scale of the conflict and its demands. It is not hard to understand the company's myopia. Alcoa had begun 1940 with some 215 million pounds of ingot in inventory, and neither experience nor the best forecasts had provided any clue as to the magnitude of the impending requirements. In January, the Army and Navy Munitions Board downgraded aluminum from a strategic to a "critical" commodity, "anticipating no major problem" in supply. As late as November, Edward Stettinius of the National Defense Advisory Commission reported that aluminum was in surplus. But within a few weeks, Northrop Aircraft, Inc., complained of insufficient aluminum for its production requirements, and it was from that point that Alcoa's monopoly position began to unravel.[58]

By early 1941, military needs were fast displacing civilian requirements for aluminum, and Alcoa was being pilloried for the apparent shortfall. A representative of the Federal Government's Office of Production and Management testified before the Truman Committee (which had been set up to investigate defense program problems and abuses), saying that "our sights haven't been high enough." The Committee responded by chiding the OPM for relying on "Alcoa as a source of information as to the availability of aluminum," which information, they said, was calculated "to avoid the possibility that anyone else would go into the field...." Bad information or not, the problem was compounded, according to the OPM, by the increased working inventories of aircraft plants, increased military requirements for small aluminum items, hoarding of secondary aluminum, a fall in Canadian imports, and bottlenecks at the finishing end. By the time Wilson had testified that the company had not been preparing to increase its managerial personnel (George Gibbons confessed his own "error in forecasting"), Alcoa was deeply embarrassed. The Government's predilection for relying on Alcoa's expertise in lieu of supporting alternative means of production was seen by many as yet another evil stemming from the existence of a monopoly. Even the decline in price of primary ingot from twenty to fifteen cents per pound between 1938 and 1942 might be (and was) interpreted as an attempt to engage in public relations to counter the publicity of antitrust on the one hand (production costs had been estimated at ten cents per pound), and to warn off new entrants into the field on the other.[59]

But now, finally, a rival firm was able to enter with the first competitive smelter since that of the Cowles Company in 1892. In 1939, Reynolds Metals, which had been making aluminum powder and paste and aluminum foil for cigarettes and other packagings since the late 1920s, had found itself cut off by Alcoa from its supply of ingot. When that company's president, Richard S. Reynolds, went to Europe in search of alternative sources, he grasped firsthand the magnitude of the German military buildup. Upon returning (Reynolds later claimed), he urged A. V. Davis to *triple* aluminum capacity for aircraft production. But Alcoa failed to grasp the enormity of the problem, Reynolds charged, by paying too much attention to the more sanguine projections of the War and Navy Departments and not enough to the threat posed by the German aluminum industry.[60] (This criticism would be echoed and reechoed by others throughout the crisis.) Sensing an opportunity to expand his own business, Reynolds then tried to get some aid from the National Defense Advisory Commission, but the Government was simply not interested in proposals from non-Alcoa sources. Finally, he plumbed his political connections (Reynolds was a Virginia Democrat), and with the aid of Senator Lister Hill of Alabama was put in touch with the Reconstruction Finance Corporation. The RFC then granted Reynolds loans secured by a mortgage on his eighteen plants to construct a smelter in Washington State and a smelter and sheet mill located, not surprisingly, at the newly christened Listerhill, Alabama.[61]

Meanwhile, the Truman Committee was prodding the Government to enter the aluminum business directly. Some senators thought the only way to ascertain if more production could be achieved at lower prices than Alcoa's was either for the Government to sponsor other companies or to build its own plants. As evidence of a shortage mounted through the spring and summer of 1941, the OPM was taken to task by the Committee, at which hearings Interior Secretary Harold Ickes scolded I. W. Wilson for Alcoa's "recalcitrance" in failing to meet the urgent demand. In a not very veiled threat, Ickes suggested that in the event that the Government take on the burden of financing new capacity (which by now seemed inevitable), it should be done "upon terms that won't make it possible for the Aluminum Co. to put on any financial or other screws at the end of the emergency."[62] It was no longer expected that Alcoa (which was well on its way to increasing its net investment from $236.6 million on January 1, 1937 to $427 million by the end of 1941) could afford the costs of wartime expansion.[63] Despite the hostility of the Administration, the Government would have to rely mostly on Alcoa's self-contained expertise and good will throughout the war; and it was Alcoa's seasoned Engineering Department that performed the feat of building more than twenty new plants between 1941 and 1943. Only one Government license was granted to a competing private concern, and that to Olin Corporation, to operate a smelter in Tacoma, Washington.

The contract to Olin was but one small item on the aluminum agenda of the RFC, which through a new subsidiary, the Defense Plant Corporation, had begun to finance a huge increase in aluminum production with federal funds. Because of its unique ability to provide the manpower and expertise for DPC-owned plants, Alcoa was in a good position to receive the lion's share of the Government contracts. The company built and operated all but a handful of the DPC plants under multiyear leases. In August 1941, Alcoa contracted for work that led to the building of eight smelters, eleven fabricating facilities, and four alumina refineries (two of which were never activated).[64] A refinery at Hurricane Creek, Arkansas, was of special strategic importance. There, Alcoa installed the first full-scale operation of the Alcoa Combination Process, which made possible the use of low-grade American ores that theretofore had been economically and technically unsuitable for good-quality aluminum. This was vital in the short run, because in the late summer of 1941, shipping in the Caribbean sea lanes began to falter under the threat of German submarines. By the war's end, scores of torpedoed bauxite carriers and hundreds of merchant seaman would go under in the service of American and Canadian aluminum.[65]

As in the previous war, management of industrial output was left in the hands of private enterprise, but production policy became subject to the dictates of Government. For aluminum, the DPC followed instructions from the War Production Board specifying the siting of plants and production schedules. Under amendments to the original agreement in December, the DPC determined the price of bauxite to leased alumina plants, the allocation of alumina output, the price of aluminum, and the rates of operation at all leased plants. Alcoa insisted on leases that provided for the Government to retain eighty-five percent of net profits from the DPC plants, while standing for any loss. In turn, the company agreed to build the Government plants at cost and without fee. By the end of 1943, Alcoa's combined DPC and directly owned production of alumina equalled ninety-six percent of total output (Reynolds made the balance at Listerhill) and of aluminium, ninety-three percent.[66]

Production was shifted almost entirely away from civilian markets to meet military demands. The kitchen utensils business shut down so that its plants could be turned to the production of wartime goods. Aluminum was used for all manner of metal war materials where lightness was important, including a wide range of weapons. Most annual output was dedicated to one crucial application that had barely existed in World War I: aircraft. In five and one-half

Figs. 5.4. and 5.5. Aluminum pots (or cells) in use during the war give an impression of the increasing scale and productivity of the smelting process. Despite some automation, monitoring the process continued to require manual labor. Here workers are breaking the crust of the bath in a pre-World War I-vintage Hall pot at Badin and in a more modern "horizontal-stud Soderberg pot" at Alcoa, Tennessee.

Facility	State	Primary Function
Alcoa Research Laboratories	Pennsylvania	Research
Alcoa	Tennessee	Reduction and Fabrication (Sheet and Plate)
Baden	North Carolina	Reduction
Bauxite Works	Arkansas	Ore
Bridgeport-Fairfield	Connecticut	Fabrication (Castings)
Buffalo	New York	Fabrication (Magnesium)
Cleveland	Ohio	Fabrication and Research (Forgings, Castings, Magnesium)
Detroit	Michigan	Fabrication
East St. Louis	Illinois	Alumina and Research
Edgewater	New Jersey	Fabrication
Garwood	New Jersey	Fabrication
Lafayette	Indiana	Fabrication
Massena	New York	Fabrication and Reduction
Mobile	Alabama	Alumina
Moengo, Paranam	Surinam	Ore
New Kensington	Pennsylvania	Fabrication
Niagara	New York	Reduction
Rosiclare	Kentucky	Fluorspar
Vancouver	Washington	Reduction

DPC Facilities	State	Primary Function
Baton Rouge	Louisianna	Alumina
Burlington	New Jersey	Reduction
Canonsburg	Pennsylvania	Fabrication (Forgings)
Chicago	Illinois	Fabrication (Sheet and Plate)
Cressona	Pennsylvania	Fabrication (Extrusion and Tubing)
East St. Louis	Illinois	Alumina
Hurricane Creek	Arkansas	Alumina
Jones Mills	Arkansas	Reduction
Kansas City	Missouri	Fabrication (Cylinder Heads)
Los Angeles	California	Reduction
Mead	Washington	Reduction
Mobile	Alabama	Alumina
Monroe	Michigan	Fabrication (Cylinder Heads)
Newark	Ohio	Fabrication (Bar and Rods)
New Castle	Pennsylvania	Fabrication (Forgings)
Phoenix	Arizona	Fabrication (Extrusion and Tubing)
Queens	New York	Reduction
Riverbank	California	Reduction
St. Lawrence	New York	Reduction
St. Paul	Minnesota	Fabrication (Castings)
Trentwood	Washington	Fabrication (Sheet)
Troutdale	Oregon	Reduction

Chart 5.1.   Alcoa operations in 1943.

Fig. 5.6. Continuous sheet-coil production at New Kensington during World War II.

years, some 3.5 billion pounds went into the manufacture of 304,000 military airplanes, mainly in the form of hard alloys that had been developed by Alcoa in the 1930s. Alcoa received one kind of testament to its productive prowess when eight German saboteurs were captured in 1942, armed with instructions to destroy company plants in Tennessee, New York, and East St. Louis. More flattering were the paeans of praise showered upon Alcoa from the military services, the Truman Committee, and even its antitrust adversaries in the Justice Department.[67]

Although Alcoa's bauxite-laden ships proved tragically vulnerable to German U-Boats, although its plants were under threat of sabotage, although its personnel were drafted and production deflected, war was lucrative. Under liberal amortization allowances, the company turned healthy profits and expanded its directly owned operations on a magnificent scale. Alcoa's annual reports exulted in the accelerated development of improved processes and materials and noted (accurately as it turned out) that aluminum would become a better known and more widely disseminated industrial material because of the pressure to use it in wartime.[68]

Management, however, was taxed to its limits. The company's annual payroll swelled to a high of $251.2 million in 1943, as compared with just $44.5 million in 1939. That same year, 1943, which marked the peak year of wartime production, the company's average number of employees was 95,044, up from 26,179 just four years earlier. With many workers being drafted into the military (25,844 by 1945) and many dollar-a-year technicians being called for government service, the company's ability to recruit and manage so many new and inexperienced employees (thousands of them women who had never worked outside the home) is testimony to extraordinary logistical work in staffing the new operations with adequate technical and administrative personnel. As management was stretched thin, salesmen were called in to operate and manage, and some departmental duties were expanded. That so many new people could be integrated so quickly into operations across the board suggests the degree to which basic refining, smelting, and fabricating operations had become routinized since the early days of the business.[69]

To a contemporary manager, however, wartime production seemed anything but routine. John F. Clark, a potroom supervisor, recalled the confusion of the day at the DPC plant in Riverbank, California. Copper shortages required the company to borrow silver from the U.S. Treasury to make into bus bars (electrical conductors) for new potrooms. (Aluminum was too precious to substitute for copper.) The plant was crawling with Treasury guards who, "not overly endowed with ambition or intelligence," became the butts of practical jokes. Women were another alien presence, mostly relegated to the shipping department, where "young girls from the local ranches . . . handled the fork trucks as if they were riding horses in the rodeo." "Old men" (nearly half the local labor force was over sixty-five) "worked slowly [but] they accomplished what had to be done and could be counted upon to show up for their next shift" unlike the "Okies, Arkies, and Winos," who constituted a "transient labor" force. Bonuses were established for the ingot crew to step up production, and men worked so hard that machines were taxed to their limits. Quality was monitored carefully; substandard products would lead to grueling inquisitions of crew foremen. That the plants could operate

Table 5.3. *U.S. production of strategic metals for the World War II effort: aluminum, copper, and steel*

Year	U.S. production (thousands of short tons)			% change on previous year			Indexed production (1938 = 100)		
	Aluminum	Copper	Steel	Aluminum	Copper	Steel	Aluminum	Copper	Steel
1936	112	803	53,500	30	34	6	78	99	168
1937	146	1,080	56,637	(2)	(25)	(44)	102	133	178
1938	143	814	31,752	15	19	66	100	100	100
1939	164	971	52,799	26	31	27	115	119	166
1940	206	1,268	66,983	50	9	24	144	156	211
1941	309	1,378	82,839	69	3	4	216	169	261
1942	521	1,421	86,032	77	(1)	3	364	175	271
1943	920	1,411	88,837	(16)	(13)	1	643	173	280
1944	776	1,221	89,642				543	150	282

Source: War Surplus Property Board, *Aluminum Plants and Facilities* (Washington, DC, 1945).

at all was a tribute to "the foremen and journeymen who moved to these temporary plants," where they mobilized and trained local labor forces from scratch.[70]

Wartime pressures: labor

A new round of labor problems surfaced in the war. Or, to address it from another perspective, the urgency of war provided the major industrial unions an opportunity to establish their bargaining power and to extend their control over labor issues beyond the basic rights they had already won to achieve recognition. The reimposition of Federal Government command over the economy in wartime worked in favor of the unions, just as it had done in the previous war.

Prior to American entry into the war, the AFL and CIO had been fighting battles with each other, skirmishing from plant to plant in a struggle over workers' allegiance and dues. By 1942, the CIO had won the bargaining rights in New Kensington, Alcoa, Badin, Detroit, Cleveland, Edgewater, Garwood, and even Bauxite, which had remained union-free throughout the Depression. A series of strikes, especially at New Kensington, had led to a comprehensive CIO union contract in 1939. The AFL held its ground in East St. Louis and Massena and successfully organized the company's new refinery in Mobile. Local conditions were important and experiences varied, but a pattern was clear: the AFL was successful in the more conservative regions of the country, so long as no crisis emerged, as it had in Tennessee, to discredit its more cautious approach to organization and negotiation. By 1944, CIO-related unions held sway in sixteen of thirty Alcoa-owned and -operated plants. The CIO was more at home in the urban industrial centers of the Northeast, where strong, prounion frustrations spilled over from other industries and where organizers armed with more radical social theories were able to fan antibusiness sentiments. Where it enjoyed success in the rural backwaters of Alcoa, Tennessee, Badin, and Bauxite, the CIO had simply outorganized the AFL after demonstrating its greater willingness to confront the company. The CIO's "more enterprising spirit," according to one contemporary study of the industry, enabled it to organize most of Alcoa's Government plants.[71]

In 1944, Nick Zonarich merged the Aluminum Workers of America with the United Steelworkers of America. The AWA had always struggled for financial and organizational support, and Zonarich, who supported the idea of a merger as early as 1936, knew that the

USWA had both the numbers and resources to make the "temporary" gains labor had been able to extract under Government auspices stick in peacetime. For months thereafter, the USWA had to defend its turf against rival attempts to organize aluminum workers by the more militant Mine, Mill and Smelter unions and by John L. Lewis's United Mineworkers. But the Steelworkers prevailed. With its strongly centralized organization, its rigorous labor discipline, its inclusive recruiting policies, its growing commitment to organized politics, and its persecution of communist members, the USWA would force the AFL branch of the industry to become more assertive. There was a gradual convergence of approach, if not entirely of interest, as the AFL's aluminum workers began to behave more like an industrial union and the USWA's aluminum workers became more politically moderate.[72]

Communism had become a heated issue among aluminum workers in the 1940s. Amid the rising patriotic heat of the early war years, the House Un-American Activities Committee (HUAC) focused attention on the present or former communist party affiliations of union leaders around the country. At Cleveland, where the Die Casters local led 6,000 workers out on an eight-day walkout from five Alcoa plants in June 1941, great controversy arose over the political ties of local union officials. The final citizenship papers of the Cleveland local organizer were held up by the Government, prompting union accusations that Alcoa, because of its alleged "Nazi" and "fascist" sympathies, was trying to sabotage the war effort, while the company's public relations spokesman, in an unusual departure from Alcoa's usual restraint, inveighed against what he saw as "communism" run rampant in the unions. Anticommunism among many rank and file workers served to dampen the more militant left-wing forces within the AWA. At New Kensington, where the specter of communism offended the Roman Catholic sensibilities of many workers, Nick Zonarich found it prudent to purge his local of radicals. In Cleveland, company workers proudly burned copies of *The Daily Worker* for the benefit of news photographers, while some of their number became friendly informants for HUAC. Even though the Cleveland workers won their 1941 strike for higher wages, which brought them into parity with other major Alcoa plants, the lingering effects of the communist controversy made the union more solicitous of the "national interest." After a pair of small strikes by furnace tenders, the Cleveland local, now the Mine, Mill and Smelter Workers of the CIO, negotiated a novel and widely hailed agreement with the company in July 1943. The Mine, Mill leadership lavished the company with a show of patriotism and accepted responsibility for using "their own methods" to curb absenteeism.[73]

National union organizations risked both opprobrium and legal sanctions by striking in wartime; only John L. Lewis had that kind of audacity. But Alcoa was hit by several small strikes from 1940 to 1945, as local unions used their leverage in the emergency to great advantage. Most strikes were tactical affairs of few days' duration, focusing on bread-and-butter issues such as wages, work schedules, and overtime, and isolated safety conditions: at Bridgeport, Connecticut, for instance, molders wanted the company to provide gloves for the handling of hot metal. Not until after the war did locals show much interest in fundamental matters of union prerogatives such as seniority job protection (at Detroit, the issue pitted older workers against returning war veterans) and control over discipline (at New Kensington, Logan's Ferry, and Arnold, a walkout occurred protesting company actions against a slowdown).[74]

During the war, there were few publicly recorded conflicts over shop-floor discipline as workers and company alike were generally swept up in an effort to get the metal out the door. The tone was set early at Edgewater during a strike of 3,000 workers in March 1941: men were permitted by the union to help the Navy load metal, gratis, proclaiming, "We are on strike against the Aluminum Company of America, not against the Government, and we will not be outdone by no one in cooperation with national defense." In 1942, when the CIO was pressing for a general strike, the powerful New Kensington local balked, noting the debilitating effect that the shutting down of potlines would have on the war effort. Nick Zonarich was well aware of the bad public relations arising from strikes in wartime; on one occasion, he appealed to a government official to help him persuade a group of disgruntled workers at Cressona to keep the production lines moving.[75]

Intervention by the National War Labor Board quelled the threat of general strikes by the CIO in 1941 and 1942. In the first instance, the NWLB decreased the differentials between southern and northern plants while making it clear that the company would gradually have to move toward wage parity throughout the system.[76] In 1942, the NWLB, while tempering union demands for wage increases, forced company acceptance of a "maintenance of membership" policy in union contracts.[77] Maintenance of membership did not compel individual workers to join established unions, but it did prevent existing union employees from relinquishing their memberships for the duration of a contract. Rank-and-file members chafed under no-strike commitments of national labor leaders (commitments made to help hold the line on wages) and in their concern to keep pace with the upwardly spiraling cost of living in the inflationary war years, they often pressed the issue to the verge of a strike. In response, the NWLB focused on nonwage concessions, such as the maintenance of membership requirement.

On balance, while wartime pressures for uninterrupted production moderated the militancy of aluminum workers, it did even more to weaken management's ability to resist the union shop. Aluminum was spared much of the bitterness that characterized labor–management conflicts in the steel, auto, and coal industries. Alcoa's traditional paternalism may have been a factor, but USWA negotiator Ben Fischer remembers that the company's personnel manager, Minton M. Anderson, was especially bitter about the situation during the war; negotiations were far from friendly, the company far from accommodating. Alcoa resisted organization with its share of strikebreakers, threats, and public relations campaigns designed to discredit the unions. John Harper spent the war years as an engineer at Alcoa, Tennessee, where most of the Allies' aircraft sheet was rolled, and observed that the company's management "had as tough a time accepting [unions] as anybody." But because of Alcoa's peculiar sensitivity to its strategic role in the war – a sensitivity heightened, no doubt, by the atmospherics of antitrust – "we didn't have quite the alternatives that some other people had." With "the Government looking down our throats," it was "an absolute critical necessity to keep these plants going." It was "a period where you only had one answer [for the unions] and that was 'Yes' on everything – you couldn't do anything else."[78]

In other ways, Alcoa's labor experience reflected the general wartime trend in the nation's major, mass-production industries. Aluminum wages from the depths of the Depression through 1943 had at least doubled, as was true of all manufacturing in the United States. If anything, aluminum workers had done better than their counterparts in both ferrous and nonferrous metals.[79] To Alcoa this meant that labor was coming to be a substantially higher portion of the costs of production in the upstream areas of the business, despite some economies in the improved and larger pots of newer potrooms. On the other hand, improvements in casting and rolling techniques helped greatly improve the ratio of man-hours to production downstream.[80]

The progress of organized labor in nonwage areas was also important. Time and again, the NWLB pressured Alcoa and its unions

Figs. 5.7 and 5.8. A five-stand rolling mill (top) and a worker shearing aluminum plate (bottom) at the Defense Plant Corporation facility at Trentwood, Washington.

into constructive agreements. In the process, the company grew more accustomed to negotiating, and some important irreversible trends were established in the closing of regional wage differentials, the liberalization of vacations and other benefits, and growing acceptance of binding arbitration and collective bargaining. The "check-off" of union dues from employee wages by the company, a long-standing goal of the unions, was finally conceded in an agreement with the CIO on June 6, 1945.[81] Union demands for guaranteed annual wages, group insurance, sick leave, and the union shop, on the other hand, went begging into the future.

With the war's end, the national aluminum unions moved quickly to consolidate their gains, triggering a new round of strikes. This resulted in a movement toward pattern bargaining, which would have lasting consequences for the industry's labor–management relations in the postwar era. It all began in mid-1944, when the AWA gave way to the United Steelworkers union as the CIO organization for aluminum. The USWA placed far greater stock in centralized authority than had the AWA, and effectively subordinated the interests of its aluminum locals to its strategy for steel. This, then, gave a large portion of the aluminum industry a stake in the outcome of the great steel strike of January 1946, which was the grandest in scale, if not in scope, in American labor history.

On its surface, the steel strike was nothing more than a simple wage dispute, but in reality it was an important part of USWA head Philip Murray's strategy to move decisively to improve his union's bargaining strength outside the context of a command economy. This time, there would be no backsliding in the determination of organized labor to consolidate its gains as had happened after World War I. The action affected 750,000 workers, including 16,000 at eight Alcoa plants. After President Truman relaxed price controls, which made it easier for the affected companies to increase wages, Alcoa employees were granted a nineteen-cent-per-hour raise in accordance with the overall terms for steel. Thereafter, pattern bargaining, by which the wages of aluminum workers became pegged to the rate granted to steel workers, would become the norm in labor–management negotiations for the aluminum industry.[82]

Anticipating the peace

While organized labor flourished, so did the company. The 1944 *Annual Report* reported that net income after taxes for the years following 1939 had averaged $38.6 million on revenues of $620.3 million. The war had also provided "a tremendous stimulus" to a theretofore small but promising sideline for Alcoa in magnesium, which held promise as the company's first major venture outside its basic technology.[83] But here, too, the company's fortunes were clouded with controversy.

Magnesium had long seemed a promising line of technology for the company, given its expertise in light-metals manufacture. Alcoa's direct involvement in magnesium had begun in 1919, when the company bought out the stock of the American Magnesium Corporation, doubtless as a defensive measure. Soon, Alcoa became the largest American consumer for the metal, which had important uses in making hard aluminum alloys. The company hoped also that this very light metal might be developed for light structural uses. But the magnesium smelting method employed by Alcoa proved costly, and when Dow Chemical Company demonstrated that it could produce the metal more cheaply, Alcoa ceased primary manufacture. Continuing attempts to gain a strong business position in magnesium fabrications embroiled the company in yet more legal and public relations problems.

In 1931, Alcoa entered into a joint-venture agreement with I. G. Farbenindustrie to create the Magnesium Development Corporation. In Germany, where the relative price of magnesium had been more favorable to its exploitation, superior means for its production and semifabrication had been developed. IG's contribution, therefore, lay mainly in its superior technology, which was vested in the joint venture in the form of the German company's American patents. For its participation, IG took a third interest in American Magnesium, and within a few years, Dow, reliant as it was on Alcoa for much of its sales in magnesium ingot (which Alcoa purchased under long-term, preferential contracts), was pressured to join in a new arrangement, whereby a complicated cross-licensing agreement was struck by the three firms. Subsequently, the price of magnesium ingot plunged from $0.965 per pound in 1927 to $0.25, while the average price on fabrications dropped from $1.59 to $0.63. But magnesium remained relatively expensive and hard to sell against considerable consumer resistance, and up to 1941, American Magnesium fabricated relatively small amounts of mill products at a net loss of $1,142,200.[84]

When demands of war opened up the possibility of using magnesium in unstressed aircraft parts, it suddenly became a critical metal, enough so that Alcoa became embroiled in another DOJ suit.

Figs. 5.9 and 5.10. Most of American aluminum production during World War II was shipped to aircraft manufacturing plants. Shown are the assembly of "Corsair" aircraft carrier fighter planes (top) and of bombers (bottom). *Courtesy of the Bettmann Archive.*

In 1941, the Government accused the company of conspiring with Dow and IG to limit domestic magnesium production. The charges were at least partly belied by the dramatic decline in price of magnesium (though its price remained high relative to aluminum's) and by IG and Alcoa's steady investment in the business. But the agreement, on the face of it, had indeed given the participants a cartel-like control over output so that IG could keep American metal out of the European market and Alcoa could limit the too-rapid development of magnesium as an aluminum substitute. And so rather than fight the case, which they most probably would have lost, the firms agreed to a plea of *nolo contendere*, fines, and a consent decree cancelling existing patent agreements.[85]

That done, the business of American Magnesium, once again wholly owned by Alcoa, prospered. In 1943, the company sold more than 18.5 million pounds of magnesium products at a healthy profit. Alcoa's output represented only a small portion of the 370 million pounds of magnesium products produced nationwide, mainly by Government-sponsored facilities; yet, notwithstanding its low market share, Alcoa could look forward to a postwar magnesium business, believing that the metal had become well-established and that the company was well-poised to exploit its peacetime applications. In the meantime, however, the Alcoa–IG–Dow connection took on unpatriotic overtones, while the United States scrambled to develop magnesium production for its defense requirements.[86]

Meanwhile, aluminum production peaked in 1943, after which Alcoa began to cut back production and liquidate inventories. Anticipating the restoration of peacetime conditions, Alcoa moved quickly to pare its payroll (while preparing to restore jobs to its drafted employees), divest a power subsidiary, and reduce a substantial amount of long-term debt it had taken on to finance its own expansion. By the end of 1944, the company's assets stood at a hefty $474 million, which would be further reduced, partly by major readjustments in accounting provisions for amortization of plant and equipment.[87]

If during the war, a "military–industrial complex" can be said to have come into being, some fifteen years before Dwight Eisenhower coined the phrase, the aluminum industry was a major player. Over its active lifetime, by some measures, the Federal Government's aluminum program added some 511 thousand metric tons to the nation's capacity, as aluminum output increased from 148.3 thousand metric tons to 834.1 thousand tons between 1939 and 1944. All this was augmented by total purchases of 628 thousand metric tons of Canadian metal and far outstripped anything the Axis Powers could produce.[88] Nearly all of this capacity was under the managerial auspices of a single company. After the war, *Fortune* wrote that "Aluminum and Alcoa may not be quite so synonymous as they once were, but if U.S. air power won the war, they, too, may be said to have won it." Perhaps so. But as much as Alcoa had contributed to the war effort, there was also the worrisome problem of the Government's nearly total reliance on a single company for a strategic commodity. War had brought Alcoa some good will as a counterpoint to its antitrust problems. But war had also brought the nation's dependency on Alcoa into high relief.[89]

The company was confident about its postwar prospects despite well-reasoned fears of a recession and overcapacity. Funds were allocated to new fabricating facilities at Alcoa, Tennessee, Cleveland, Massena, Lafayette and Vernon, California. Rather than cut back sharply in such areas as forgings and hard alloy sheet, which had been greatly expanded for the war, the company hoped to find new markets in automobiles, heavy transportation, and building materials. To support the reconversion to peacetime markets, Alcoa expanded its sales force and installed new R&D laboratories at East St. Louis and Cleveland, while Francis Frary's main facility at New Kensington was expanded. No one could yet see just how much more the focus of research was to shift in the postwar era toward the development of new products and toward the short-term problems of productive efficiency, but it was already well understood that innovation would be crucial to the impending struggle for markets, not only among metals, but also among new aluminum producers. But before Alcoa could devote all its energies to peacetime conversion, it would first have to deal with the Government's latest, and this time successful, attempt to restructure the American aluminum industry.

Disposal of the defense plants

Although the Second Circuit Court had ruled on the illegality of Alcoa's monopoly in primary aluminum production, the remedy was to come from elsewhere, from the temporary administrative apparatus the Federal Government set up for the postwar return to industrial normalcy. In 1944, Congress established a War Surplus Property Board (SPB), which was to dispose of government-owned facilities that had been built for the war. The mandate of the SPB

Fig. 5.11. Francis B. Frary, head of Alcoa's research and development, working at his aluminum rolltop desk during World War II.

was mixed. The Surplus Property Act was a compromise between conflicting House and Senate objectives. The House bill had emphasized speedy disposal to the highest bidder; the Senate's, the fostering of competition. Ultimately, the Act was intended to facilitate the transition from wartime to peacetime production in a way that promoted free enterprise and discouraged the concentration of industry.[90]

By the time the SPB was functioning in January 1945, it was staffed by men dedicated to the sentiments of the Sherman Act, men who took seriously the new congressional mandate to discourage monopolies. Because the Government had some $672 million in assets in its fifty aluminum plants (compared to Alcoa's $474 million), and because the Government owned more than half the nation's primary smelting capacity, the disposal of aluminum plants became a major problem for the Board. In 1944, Alcoa, between what it owned and what it leased from the Government, managed about 91 percent of the nation's aluminum capacity and nearly 96 percent of its alumina capacity. In 1945, the structure of the industry, skewed

Table 5.4. *Alumina production capacity of U.S. producers, 1944 (thousands of short tons)*

Company	Facility	Capacity	% of total capacity
Alcoa	E. St. Louis, MO	420	
	Mobile, AL	650	
	Total	1,070	43.7
Alcoa DPC	Hurricane Creek, AR	778	
	Baton Rouge, LA	500	
	Total	1,278	52.2
Reynolds	Listerhill, AL	100	4.1
Grand Total		2,448	100.0

Source: War Surplus Property Board, *Aluminum Plants and Facilities* (Washington, DC, 1945).

as it was by the existence of federally financed facilities that would not be efficient to operate in peacetime, was still overwhelmingly dominated by Alcoa. In addition to its more than ninety-percent smelting capacity, the company managed as much as ninety-one percent of alumina refining capacity, ninety percent of aluminum rod and bar, over eighty percent of sheet and tubing, over sixty percent of extrusions, and nearly half the nation's capacity for forgings.[91]

The SPB grappled with competing proposals on restructuring the aluminum industry to make it more competitive. Two proposals, solicited from expert consultants, were tendered just in the wake of the appellate court's ruling on the Government antitrust suit, a ruling in which Learned Hand had alluded specifically to the Surplus Property Act as part of the court's problem in seeking a remedy for the antitrust conviction. Gordon W. Reed, a businessman who had worked on the Aluminum Division of the War Production Board, advocated placing half the Government's smelting capacity under Alcoa's control, which would make the company's market share in primary aluminum seventy-five percent (he later suggested sixty percent). Sam Moment, an economist who had served at the Department of Agriculture, the Temporary National Economic Committee, and the Bonneville Power Authority, along with Irving Lipkowitz, who was back in the Antitrust Division after a stint on the War Production Board, felt otherwise. Moment's proposal was

Table 5.5. *Aluminum production capacity of U.S. producers, 1944*
(thousands of short tons)

Company	Capacity[a]	% of total capacity
Alcoa	415	38.0
Alcoa DPC	576	52.7
Reynolds	81	7.4
Olin DPC	21	1.9
Total U.S.	1,093	100.0

[a]Includes plant capacity that would not be efficient to operate in peacetime.
Source: War Surplus Property Board, *Aluminum Plants and Facilities* (Washington, DC, 1945).

that Alcoa be prohibited from buying any of the plants and that the Government provide both plants and liberal subsidies to new entrants.[92]

But even Gordon Reed's approach was less than wholly palatable to Alcoa, conditioned as it was upon the company's agreement to average its production across its plants and to accept a tariff cut. Alcoa, after all, had provided the expertise to build and manage four-fifths of the Government's capacity and had managed its plants effectively. Alcoa also held leases on the vast majority of Government plants, extending into 1948, and was certain to offer the best price for their disposal. Reynolds and Olin, moreover, were upstarts, relatively inexperienced, and lacked the technological expertise and the patent rights to operate modern refineries and smelters. Reynolds had less than seven percent of the nation's smelting capacity by the end of the war and had not made any money on ingot. Olin's little plant at Tacoma had also failed to turn a profit and discouraged that company from staying in the business.[93]

All this notwithstanding, the key administrator of the SPB, Stuart Symington, found Reed's approach politically difficult to support, despite its initial appeal. By mid-1945, Symington was under pressure to find buyers other than Alcoa for the Government aluminum facilities. Within days after the surrender of Japan, Alcoa's leases on alumina and aluminum plants were cancelled by the Reconstruction Finance Corporation on a dubious contractual pretext.[94] The SPB still hoped to arrive at some accommodation with Alcoa to continue operating the plants on short-term leases pending final disposition of the properties. On the other hand, Alcoa executives felt that both morality and the law were on their side, and in any case, they did not want to plan production schedules under such uncertain, short-term conditions. But when an angry A. V. Davis threatened to challenge the Government's decision, Symington, who had been vacillating, reacted sharply by moving foursquare into Sam Moment's camp.[95]

Alcoa's position worsened when the control of surplus property passed from an unwieldy three-man board to Symington as sole administrator in September 1946. A Truman appointee from Missouri, Symington had been the CEO of Emerson Electric and had managed that company's conversion to defense production. As a businessman in an industry where price-fixing was not uncommon, he had earned a reputation for hostility to antitrust. But he secured his confirmation to the SPB from a skeptical Senate subcommittee by voicing a strong personal opposition to monopoly.[96] In fact, he was prepared to take a middle road. Just as he began a search for buyers from among 227 companies in the metalworking industries, Attorney General Tom Clark weighed in with a report to Congress in September, urging legislation to reorganize and subdivide Alcoa in order to satisfy the 1945 antitrust verdict. Failing that, the Attorney General argued, subsidies could be provided to competing aluminum newcomers, an idea already endorsed by a earlier report of the SPB and one that Symington was prepared to endorse.[97]

By this time, aluminum competition at any cost had become a byword of the Truman administration. Symington himself had come to see the political wisdom of working hand in glove with the DOJ. Together, the SPB chief and the Attorney General strove to impose competition on the aluminum industry via the plant disposal program. Echoing Clark's report, Symington stressed two factors: that competitive prices be established in the aluminum industry to spur enough peacetime demand to replace that for military aircraft; and that competitors, in order to enter, be granted substantial incentives "under terms of outright subsidy, with a guarantee against all loss." Buttressing these sentiments was the lingering memory, however unjustified in its conspiratorial overtones, of Alcoa's inability to meet wartime production needs. A simple (and simplistic) theory of monopoly power was all that was necessary to make the point to Congress. As Clark put it,

> Monopoly conditions were the main reason for the absence of a safety margin in aluminum. Alcoa ... was able to keep its capacity closely geared to immediate demand, since it did not have

to compete with other producers for its market. In a competitive
industry, there is of necessity more capacity than demand. Right
from the start, therefore, the aluminum situation was more serious than it would have been had there been competition.

No longer could the nation afford to place its reliance on a single
source of supply for a strategic product.[98]

Outright subsidies to foster competition proved to be an unpopular
idea. After hearings before the Senate Small Business Committee
and a bitter outcry from Alcoa's management, the idea of providing
long-term government aid to newcomers in the industry was jettisoned. A fundamental faith in private enterprise conflated with a
more pragmatic hope that disposal of the plants could be achieved
without extraordinary Federal Government supports and guarantees. As *The New York Times* editorialized:

> The Department of Justice has been seeking to break up this
> company for some time. Assistant Attorney General McGranery
> told the Congressional Committees that "competition will be
> established within the industry no matter what it takes." We
> have had a long history of trust busting. But throughout that
> history we have not adopted a national policy of subsidizing
> competitors. . . .
>
> If it is established that undesirable effects upon our economy
> flow from the aluminum situation, we have the means of cor-
> recting them through the anti-trust acts. Government subsidies
> would be an unfortunate alternative which inevitably would
> lead to a steadily larger drain on the Treasury and would fur-
> nish another form of Government competition with private
> industry.[99]

Despite the emerging consensus on the impropriety of subsidies,
Alcoa's back was against the wall. A. V. Davis fumed while his
company's leases on fabricating plants were cancelled. Inside the
company, however, management was coming to accept the idea of
some form of the SPB's disposal program as a kind of *de facto* antitrust remedy. As Hickman, who was present at many of the discussions, recalled it, "the general view was that we'd find life a lot
easier and a lot more satisfactory if we had some competition."[100]

While Judge Caffey continued to grapple with the problem of a
remedy for the antitrust suit, the disposal program offered a potential solution to the company's own problem. Symington, to his credit,
seized the opportunity to act decisively. Again, Hickman:

> I will say, that through a combination of circumstances, I think
> they came out of it with a very constructive way to create com-

petition. That is, basically, they took these wartime plants that we had built and operated, and the Government owned – now those, we'll sell to Reynolds and Kaiser who were in the wings wanting to get in, in order to create the competition. That required some negotiation and a little arm twisting.... But ultimately we wound up with Reynolds and Kaiser in the business without raping Alcoa in the process.[101]

The "little arm twisting" involved overcoming the final barrier to the effective operation of plants by competing firms. On January 6, 1946, in the midst of negotiations with Alcoa about the licensing of some of its more important technology to competitors, Symington complained to the Senate subcommittee on surplus property that Alcoa was obstructing the sale of aluminum plants by withholding the use of critical patents. "The time has come," he declared, "to say frankly to Congress that it may well be that no disposal of any of the plants to competitors will be possible unless Alcoa changes its attitude, or unless the courts, acting under the Sherman Act, reorganize Alcoa so that its monopolistic power is broken." Symington, in a widely published letter, accused the company of trying to "keep the plants tied up until 1948" and ultimately bring the more desirable Government operations under its own permanent control. Jolted by this latest accusation, the company responded in a missive signed by I. W. Wilson, contending that Alcoa had placed no conditions on the licensing of its patents and resenting deeply the mountain of antitrust allegations attached in appendices to Symington's broadside.[102]

The impasse surfaced in the attempt by Reynolds Metals to purchase the huge alumina refinery at Hurricane Creek, Arkansas. Reynolds could not continue to operate the refinery without access to the Alcoa Combination Process and other proprietary techniques for processing low-grade bauxite economically. Unless Hurricane Creek could be made to operate efficiently, there could be no effective competition to Alcoa from a fully integrated producer. Under such conditions, it was hard to imagine anyone, including Reynolds, taking the risk necessary to enter the smelting business.[103]

Symington's decision to go public had arisen out of frustration. He had been unable to find willing buyers for his surplus aluminum plants because all the potential entrants lacked Alcoa's state-of-the-art technology in alumina processing. He had also grown impatient with contradictory advice he was getting from his own advisors on just how to manage the problem. As Lipkowitz related it, Symington finally "decided to take the bull by the horns," and scheduled an audience with A. V. Davis. But the smooth Missouri politician, who had great confidence in his reputation for charm, was entirely unprepared for the distinctly uncharmed response he got from the gritty little Alcoa chairman. After regaling Davis at length with all the wonderful public service benefits of coming to terms with the needs of competitors, Davis reportedly replied in words much like the following: "My father was a Congregational minister, and we were taught that if we feel we're doing the right thing that we don't have to take the shirt off our back and give it to somebody else." That was the end of the meeting; Symington left in a rage, "boiling mad." It took much careful soothing from his staff to keep the SPB administrator negotiating.[104]

On Alcoa's side, negotiations were taken over by Wilson and Hickman, who were more apt than their disgruntled chairman to accept the SPB's conditions. Two days after Symington had gone public with his complaint about Alcoa's intransigence, Wilson and Hickman, with Davis in tow, arrived at the Attorney General's office in Washington. Davis, himself, had become convinced that an opportunity was at hand to create "a great bulwark" against the threat of a court-imposed antitrust remedy. But, according to *Fortune*, Alcoa's management was unable to get the assurances it wanted from Symington or Clark that a deal on the patents would: (1) close the antitrust case, (2) open the door for Alcoa to buy Government plants, and (3) clear the way for Alcoa to finance its own continuing expansion. The replies to the first two terms were emphatically negative and to the third, a comment that Alcoa would have to proceed at its own risk. Now, Davis was furious.[105]

But Symington was ready for hardball. He proposed that the Government close a deal with Reynolds and be prepared to wait for the inevitable patent suit from Alcoa. Facing the prospect of another round of complex litigation with the Government, Alcoa surrendered. The very next morning, Alcoa returned with an offer to grant a license for the operation of Hurricane Creek for up to twenty-five percent of its rated capacity, above which the royalty of $1 per ton would be levied. But after some discussion, the Government argued that such an agreement might put a ceiling on Reynolds' production. In the afternoon, Wilson and Hickman met with Symington, voiced their objections, and then finally acquiesced in a plan to offer patent licenses free to the Government to grant to whoever acquired the alumina plant. Alcoa, in turn, would have the right to receive royalty-free licenses to any improvements made by Reynolds at

Hurricane Creek, a provision which many DOJ attorneys found objectionable.

Davis acquiesced by telephone. A press conference was convened at which Symington, ever the politician, heaped praise on Alcoa for its patriotic service during the war and its public spiritedness in contributing to "the establishing of real competition in the aluminum industry . . . entirely in line" with the objectives of the antitrust decision. Alcoa basked in its first favorable round of publicity in years, as congratulatory letters were passed all around, from Symington, from Clark, and finally from Davis, who wrote somewhat grudgingly:

> Except for the public considerations which you have presented to us so effectively, we could not consider a royalty-free license under such a valuable asset. However, we are glad to accede to these considerations and if by so doing we have contributed in any substantial way to a solution of the complex problems of surplus property disposal . . . , we are well repaid.[106]

Well repaid or not, Alcoa had little to do but sit on the sidelines and watch the fire sale of the plants it had built and operated for the war. To this day, the story is told at Alcoa that the DPC plants were sold to would-be competitors for "ten cents on the dollar." It was not nearly that bad, but it was a bargain, nonetheless. Through short-term leases that were gradually converted to purchase agreements, Reynolds acquired Hurricane Creek, the nearby smelter at Jones Mills, Arkansas, a smelter in Troutdale, Oregon, and three fabricating plants, all for $57,582,000, as compared with the total original construction costs of $170 million.

The bargain was too good to pass up for the great industrial entrepreneur Henry Kaiser, who had made his fortune as a highway contractor, shipbuilder, and steelmaker. Kaiser had founded the Permanente Metals Corporation in 1942 in order to operate Government magnesium plants with the help of a hefty loan from the RFC. Based on that experience and on his experience in steel, he felt he could manage the production of an integrated aluminum business.[107] Kaiser then made a successful bid for the alumina plant at Baton Rouge, Louisiana, smelters at Spokane and Tacoma, Washington, and two fabricating plants for $43.5 million as compared with their original cost of $120 million.[108]

Within a few years, Reynolds Aluminum and Kaiser Aluminum (as Permanente came to be called) became fully integrated producers after purchasing diversified fabricating facilities. Reynolds moved aggressively forward, acquiring sheet mills at Chicago and Lister-hill, Alabama, forging facilities at Louisville, and extrusion works at Phoenix and Grand Rapids. Kaiser took a sheet mill near Spokane and a blooming mill in Ohio. Eventually, Harvey Machine Tool and Apex Smelting Company would purchase potlines for production in Montana and Oklahoma, and most of the remaining viable fabricating facilities would pass on to a number of concerns. Alcoa was allowed to purchase only one Government smelter, the St. Lawrence reduction works near Massena, New York, and one small fabricating facility, the extrusion plant at Cressona, Pennsylvania.

Thus, it happened that a temporary agency of the Federal Government established competition in an industry where free-market forces and federal courts had failed to do so. It was a stunning event in the history of American business–government relations, an event which had profound and (by public policy standards) effective results on the market. Within five years after the Learned Hand decision, competition existed in every phase of aluminum production, the production of primary aluminum having taken on a distinctively oligopolistic industry structure. The capacities of the three major U.S. producers were set by the Second Circuit Court in 1950 as follows: Alcoa with 50.86 percent, Reynolds with 30.94 percent, and Kaiser Aluminum & Chemical Corporation with 18.20 percent.[109]

Postmonopoly prospects: Alcoa in 1946

As American industry returned to normal in 1946, the outlook for aluminum was good. Despite reasonable fears of a postwar recession which prompted a scaling down of aluminum capacity to half the wartime peak, capacity remained at 3.9 times prewar peak consumption. A confidential memorandum from Alcoa's Investment Research Department noted that while the "economic capacities" for castings, rod and bar, forgings, extrusions, powder, and tubing had fallen off sharply from wartime capacity, sheet and foil remained at 97 and 100 percent of wartime capacity, "presumably reflect[ing] industry belief that metal in these forms will meet strong demand." A single new product, roofing sheet, which had been developed in 1945, was believed to have "a potential market measured in several millions of *tons*, rather than *pounds*" (industry output was still commonly described in terms of pounds). Roy Hunt had estimated in 1945 that annual consumption would reach 1,250 million pounds by

1950, a figure similar to that projected by the U.S. Tariff Commission, assuming that national income would increase by seventy-five percent. Although in the spring of 1946, productive capacity and inventories were in excess of current demand, by the end of the year, the "pent-up demand for civilian goods" had suddenly put ferrous and nonferrous metals in short supply.

Luckily, aluminum was in greater supply than other metals, and so many manufacturers, eager to respond to demand pressures immediately, turned to aluminum as a substitute. By the summer, Alcoa was oversold.[110] Making the necessary allowance for the vagaries of the business cycle, Alcoa, according to its own intelligence, could look ahead to increasing its output "by every available means" and to capitalize on the present opportunity in a seller's market "to strengthen its position in new applications, and to continue aggressive research activities." I. W. Wilson, who in 1911 had thought the aluminum boom was over, was now betting heavily on a postwar boom, contrary to the expectations of industry analysts. All during 1946, he was laying plans for capacity "for the bigger markets that were, for us, five and ten years away."[111]

A key element of aluminum's strong potential was its price. Since 1924, the price of primary ingot had not once gone up, dropping steadily since 1933 against a trend of rising wholesale prices. In the next ten years, the price of a pound of primary metal decreased by a third (in constant dollars nearly sixty percent) while wholesale prices rose by fifty percent. The relative price of aluminum vis-à-vis its major competing metals, copper and steel, had improved since 1937. By late 1946, pig aluminum was quoted at $0.14 compared with copper at $0.143. Given the growth of aluminum scrap, which cost even less to produce than primary metal, aluminum looked forward to its "best competitive position in history."[112]

Alcoa's prospects were bolstered further by the stability of its financial structure and leadership. There would, of course, have to be some changes in response to the changing environment, and signs of change were already beginning to manifest themselves quite apart from external pressures on the company. The firm was still closely held, but there was a perceptible trend toward more dispersed ownership. By 1942, five years after the death of Andrew Mellon, two-thirds of the common stock and over half the preferred stock were in the hands of twenty shareholders, mainly from six families: Mellon, Davis, Duke, Hunt, Clapp, and Gillespie. New stock issues, retirements, and deaths were constantly diminishing the portion of the firm held by the company's directorate and management, and the Mellon family's own share had declined to a still hefty twenty-five percent. The Temporary National Economic Committee reported that the directors and officers of the company combined held but fourteen percent of the total assets of the corporation. Alcoa had continued to issue new stock to finance its expansion, and by 1945, the number of outstanding shares had increased from 1.47 to 4.89 million. Thus, while the concentrated ownership remained, the capitalization of the company had changed in composition. Preferred stock had become less important in the total capitalization, declining from sixty-four percent in 1938 to just twenty-five percent in 1945. Funded debt had increased to twenty-two percent, while common stock made up the balance. The firm, without dispersing the ownership of its assets too widely, was healthy in 1946, having cut in half the long-term debt the company took on in the early phases of the war to finance expansion. Current assets stood at 1.8 times current liabilities, boding well for additional investment in new plant and equipment.[113]

Managerial power at Alcoa was also shifting quietly but decisively. The company's structure remained substantially the same as before the war, although the number of its central corporate officers had increased. Gone from the senior managerial ranks were the familiar names of Fickes, Fox, and Withers (the latter two retired in 1946). George Gibbons remained the lone senior vice president. Davis, now eighty, could still imbibe a pitcher a day of his cherished martinis with no apparent ill effects. He remained as chairman, but following the antitrust suit, his full-time involvement with Alcoa came to an end. He was an old man, well past the age when most executives would have retired, and he may have been less than enthusiastic about confronting a new era in which his beloved company would have to share the glory and the profits of the American aluminum industry.

Davis moved to Florida, where after surviving two wives and all his close friends, he lived with a young companion, Evelyn Mitchell, on whom he became very dependent for both his personal comforts and business support. With her assistance, he applied his still considerable energy to the development of real estate in which he would amass a second fortune, even larger, by some accounts, than the one he had made in aluminum. As the years passed, Davis became ever more a caricature of the eccentric, aging tycoon. He sometimes borrowed Alcoa managers to tend to his personal affairs as he dabbled in ventures ranging from chicken farming to dairy cattle. Fritz Close on occasion served as Davis's errand-boy and

remembered being "fired" by the old man on at least three occasions
– for laying out a pineapple orchard in Texas that failed, for recruiting the contractor who built Davis a house in Boca Raton that
displeased him, and for refusing to leave the premises of the 21 Club
in New York when Davis, on a whim, decided he did not care to
dine in the presence of a subordinate.[114] In the decade following the
war, Davis continued to travel to his office in New York City, where
he intimidated the young salesmen stationed there. His mere arrival
in Pittsburgh is said to have been sufficient to tense the air in the
Alcoa headquarters.

And his ego remained unbounded. Former Oberlin College president William Stevenson recalled visiting Coral Gables sometime
in the 1950s, where he encountered Davis, "a gnome-like little fellow" with a "rasping little voice" who

> would take you up in a tower he had there, sort of like a Biblical
> prophet, and point to some water, and say, "you see that over
> there, that used to be hills," and he'd point over here to some
> hills, and he'd say, "I'm going to take that down and put water
> here." He was sort of playing God.[115]

Rearranging the South Florida landscape must have seemed easy
enough to the old man who in his youth had helped parlay a little-
known metal into an indispensable industrial commodity.

Sitting with Davis on the board in 1946 was the venerable George
H. Clapp (Captain Alfred Hunt's original business partner!), Roy
Hunt (the company's president), Gibbons, R. K. Mellon, Withers,
George Stanley (head of sales), and I. W. Wilson (executive vice
president). Davis was still the chairman, but that position had become somewhat honorific. After the war, his presence in the affairs
of the company would be felt less and less. The younger Mellon, no
mere shadow of his forebears, was beginning to exert his own strong
influence as the company's lead banker. In the years to come, the
board met mainly for Mellon's sake (and to meet its legal obligations), because its other important members were managers who,
except for Davis, saw each other all the time. It is difficult to ascertain the relationships among the principal officers, except to say
that decision making was highly collegial. Roy Hunt, though deeply
hurt by the antitrust decision that gnawed at him for years to come,
continued to exert a powerful influence on policy. But Wilson, whom
everyone called "Chief," was fast emerging as Alcoa's de facto chief
executive.[116]

It is fair to say that by war's end, Hunt and Wilson were acting much like partners with informally divided responsibilities for top-level tasks. They shared responsibility (though Wilson got more credit) for directing Alcoa's wartime expansion, with Wilson more concerned with technical matters and Hunt more with finance. Otherwise, their roles in the firm were partly functions of their personalities. Roy Hunt, slight in stature, reserved, shy, and gentle, was, said his son, Alfred, "Mr. Inside." During the appeals process, while Davis and Wilson increasingly took charge of affairs in Washington and New York, Hunt remained in Pittsburgh. He was most comfortable when he was dealing with problems of finance and internal organization. On the latter, he was a stickler for structural simplicity, an antibureaucrat in a bureaucratic world. In a technical environment, he was admired for his loyalty to the ideal of the corporate "family" and his paternal regard for its people. Otherwise, he was uncomfortable with public dealings, speechmaking, and conflict, and kept a low profile outside the company. He was uncompromisingly principled (some would say rigid) and "lived more in a world of black and whites than the others," according to Leon Hickman. Unlike Davis, whose gruff exterior belied a strong instinct for accommodation (Davis was "at heart a great compromiser", said Hickman), Hunt was clearly not the man to accommodate Alcoa's adversaries.

Wilson, therefore, became the authority in Alcoa's external affairs during the politically charged aftermath of Learned Hand's decision. He was, in Alfred Hunt's terms, "Mr. Outside." Like Roy Hunt, Chief Wilson was a very proper gentleman of the old school, but he was somewhat less inclined than Hunt to view issues affecting the company in moral terms. It was Wilson who had taken charge of the negotiations with the Government in the plant disposal proceedings. Davis, who for so long had relied on the soft-spoken southern gentleman, George Gibbons, for advice and support in company affairs, had come increasingly, in Alcoa's time of crisis, to lean on Wilson, the rigorous "technician."

Highly regarded within the company as a master of technical problems, Chief Wilson was a perfectionist. Physically imposing at six feet, with blue eyes and a solemn, aristocratic demeanor, he enjoyed a towering reputation as "a flesh and blood computer," with the emphasis on the qualifying adjectives. "His mind was a book," said Frank Magee, who remembered his mentor as "a fact man," enthralled with the minutiae of science and technology. Yet at the same time, Wilson was a strong "people manager," relatively comfortable with human conflict, tolerant of debate, and flexible in his approach to administration. Outwardly austere and conservative, Wilson was actually quite informal in his manners, a scotch drinker and an excellent bridge player, who enjoyed lively discussions with his subordinates. Over the years, he would gain a reputation for his ingratiating modesty, his moral and intellectual integrity, and his easy accessibility to younger managers who remembered him fondly – a man "dearly loved" by John Harper, an "old shoe" to Fritz Close. A hands-on executive, he could overwhelm his juniors with his photographic command of data and rigorous attention to detail, but he was sufficiently diplomatic (and shrewd enough) to allow his subordinates the final decisions in their areas of authority.[117]

As management gradually changed hands, the company's formal administrative structure changed even more slowly. Since the creation of a centralized, functional organization at the end of World War I, Alcoa's bureaucracy had remained remarkably static, despite the increased scale and scope of the company's operations. Roy Hunt's distaste for organization charts was so strong that only one had been drawn up since 1938, and then only because the Wage Stabilization Act of 1942 had demanded it in order to fix job classifications and salary ranges. The chart reveals no significant changes in organizational principle. But the centralized structure existed more in principle than in reality. By the end of World War II, there were growing signs of unhealthy gaps in communication among various corporate functions.

This was confirmed by a third-generation Hunt, Alfred Mortimer, who had taken up the family labor in the potrooms at Massena in 1943. The younger Hunt recalled that upon his transfer to Pittsburgh in 1946, the enterprise operated (as it long had) like a collection of "little empires – headed up by a very strong man in each case [who] didn't . . . cooperate sometimes any too well." Aside from consolidating the accounts, and making major strategic decisions, the central office at Pittsburgh still functioned largely as arbiter among the various entities and corporations that comprised Alcoa's business.[118]

During the war, Chief Wilson had tried to establish some mechanism for centralizing control of operations without disturbing the formal structure. The sheer pressures of wartime production enhanced the spirit of cooperation among managers responsible for the vertical functions of the business. Out of sheer necessity, they were spending more time in Pittsburgh, planning and coordinating the flow of materials through all states of production. The problem was how to manage the relationships among "one-man powerhouses" like

Winthrop Nielson (bauxite), Charles Fox (alumina), Victor Doerschuck (aluminum), R. R. Stevenson (mill fabrications), and Allen Norton (castings) – not to mention the managers of other semiautonomous bastions such as the steamship and railway operations. In 1943, Frank Magee was plucked out of Sales and made Wilson's assistant as "general production manager." For Magee it was "a delicate water treading job" to win the confidence of other, more senior managers who were not used to strongly centralized controls. Although he got plenty of cooperation during the war, it would take several more years, under peacetime conditions, before Pittsburgh would effectively centralize its control over operations.[119]

In the meantime, the company had to cope with the shock of competition, which, among other things, weakened the allegiance of its employees. In addition to union activities, which had unraveled management's paternalistic ties to its workers, Pittsburgh discovered that it could no longer count on the unswerving loyalty of its middle managers. With the closing of uneconomical Government facilities, many of the company's plant managers and technical personnel left to expand their careers with Kaiser and Reynolds.[120] Some had little choice, having worked in plants that the Government dealt away to Alcoa's competitors; either they went with their operations or faced transfer and possible demotion. Others simply saw opportunities to rise more quickly in the newer companies. Those who stayed regarded those who left as traitors. One Alcoa engineer who went to work for Reynolds at its Troutdale, Washington, plant recalled the bitter acrimony surrounding his departure. There, Alcoa loyalists made off with the pipeline and electrical blueprints, which, more than a little, complicated Reynolds' start-up operations.[121]

There was no loss in the company's continuity of vision, however. If anyone in 1946 had bothered to ask an "Alcoan" what his business was all about, the answer would have been much the same as it had been for the company's founders. Alcoa, explained the thick source book on company policy and activities maintained by the Public Relations Department, was a producer of a new metal, "primary" aluminum, with "secondary" markets in fabricated products. Its entry into fabrications, shipments of which after 1940 accounted for most of the company's earnings, had been forced by circumstances, by the need to create markets for its basic element. To this end, the firm had invested millions at great risk in plant and equipment all along the vertical chain, from the extraction of bauxite to the production of consumer goods, in order to realize its founder's vision of establishing aluminum as a useful common metal. Everything, including Alcoa's investment in scientific research, was directed to that simple and hopefully profitable end.[122]

Thus, while the company's business expanded steadily downstream, its heart remained lodged among "the flashing lights in a quiet potroom." It was from there that everything else radiated and to there that everything else was connected: "a mine in far-off Surinam; a whirring generator by a river in North Carolina; ... a clamorous rolling mill atop a Tennessee hill; a seething furnace in a Cleveland foundry; a long transmission line beside the St. Lawrence. All these things are Aluminum."[123] To be sure, Alcoa had withdrawn from some secondary markets and had come increasingly to share others with competitors. Yet, it alone among all the American companies in the industry could lay claim to having created and nurtured the industry. In the common parlance of its managers, employees, and customers, Alcoa was still *The* Aluminum Company.

6

Alcoa's "splendid retreat": the rise of the aluminum oligopoly, 1947–1957

"Everybody [at Alcoa] was down in the mouth," said Fritz Close, following the sale of the Government wartime aluminum plants to Reynolds and Kaiser. "But there it was. We had to accept it." Close, who had just been reassigned from his job as manager of forging production in Cleveland to the Sales Department in Pittsburgh, traveled to the various sales districts on a morale-boosting mission and passed out party horns. That was Close; he stood out in a firm that was more generally known to its regional and lower-level personnel – and to the public – for its staid and reserved corporate style. "I said the hell with Reynolds. Blow your own horn now. Let's get on with this job!"[1]

In truth, there turned out to be little need for Alcoa to bewail the loss of its monopoly. A "golden age" for aluminum was dawning. By 1947, the company was entering into an era of expansion that would more than compensate for what was certain to be a precipitous decline in market share. As the nation's economic fortunes wafted on a long wave of prosperity (real gross national product increased from around $470 to $700 billion between 1947 and 1958), Alcoa and its new rivals rode the crest, actually outperforming the economy.[2] Competition spurred the expansion of old as well as the successful development of new applications, as aluminum producers turned to more aggressive product development, marketing, and promotion. Per-capita consumption of the metal doubled. Contributing to the industry's prosperity were Government tax, loan, and purchasing policies, occasioned by yet another major war, this time in Korea. Indeed, aluminum's prosperity in the 1950s, according to the principal economic study of that era in the industry's history, has been attributed largely to the effects of Government defense policy.[3] Just how much the company might have grown in the absence of the Korean War is a matter of speculation, although it was not military but civilian demand that became the mainstay of the business.

During World War II, legions of manufacturers had been introduced for the first time to the metal's qualities and to techniques for its fabrication, uses for which were then transferred to peacetime applications. Wartime experience with high-performance alloys and new joining and finishing techniques developed for military aircraft was transferred to civilian transportation and architecture. Supply helped create demand. The availability of inexpensive surplus aluminum at the end of the war spurred a burst of civilian consumption on which the company could build in future years. On the supply side, both capacity and personnel for civilian production had been greatly increased by the Government aluminum program. Thousands of men and women had been trained under the pressures of war in the casting, forming, and assembling of aluminum structures.[4] Many of the 90,000 employees that Alcoa had employed at the peak of wartime production had gone to find other work or had returned (in the case of many women) to domestic labors, but as it converted to civilian production, the aluminum industry, including Alcoa's new rivals, was able to draw on an ample supply of experienced labor.

The major postwar threat to Alcoa came from its new competitors. Reynolds and Kaiser (and later, Alcan) had fully integrated systems of production, and more competition in primary aluminum loomed on the horizon. By 1958, Harvey, Anaconda, and Ormet established smelters in the United States, so that there were seven primary aluminum producers vying for shares of the North American market. Yet increased demand for aluminum products more than offset Alcoa's loss of market share. In a booming market, Alcoa broadened its product and technology bases and expanded its metallurgical expertise into the fabrication of other light metals. It developed a flourishing new business in monumental architecture, office buildings, and apartment housing. However, Alcoa's rate of growth was slower than that of its major competitors, and younger managers, John Harper and Krome George, thought that their superiors' preoccupation with antitrust – the company remained under court supervision until 1957 – retarded strategic initiatives into acquisitions at home and expansion overseas.[5]

Perhaps, but Alcoa was growing from a bigger base than its competitors, and by contemporary standards, the company's performance was impressive. In 1958, Alcoa had four times the primary production capacity it had in 1939, the final year of its absolute monopoly. From 1946 to 1958, its gross revenues trebled, from $298 to $869 million, while its net income soared to a period high of $89.6 million, a healthy ten percent of gross sales.[6] Writing in 1955, William B. Harris marveled at Alcoa's "splendid retreat" from the monopoly position it had been forced to abandon only a decade earlier.[7]

Growth in the postwar era

Alcoa had been somewhat demoralized, following the SPB's decision to sell the Government aluminum plants to Reynolds and Kaiser, but it clung to the hope that postwar demand for aluminum would offset the loss of its monopoly. Although the company's projections for sales seemed to many observers to be downright unrealistic (given near-term expectations for a postwar recession while there remained substantial government inventories of primary and scrap aluminum), there was a sound basis for optimism. Even though wartime inflation and union power had pushed wages upward, economies of production had improved through the introduction of labor- and energy-saving techniques. Aluminum had greatly improved its comparative advantages over other materials and had already surpassed lead and zinc in civilian consumption. It was well on a trajectory to passing copper, which in fact happened by 1952. Its relative price continued to drop, so that by 1958, the cost of aluminum compared with copper on a volume basis stood at a ratio of two to one. Copper would no longer be able to compete on price alone.[8]

Accordingly, Alcoa invested in new capacity. The first phase of the company's postwar expansion, at a cost of about $300 million, ran its course through 1949. A new smelter at Point Comfort, Texas, was powered by natural gas. A large commitment of capital at an uncertain time, Point Comfort replaced outmoded capacity at Alcoa's aging facilities (the ancient smelter at Niagara had been closed and dismantled earlier in the year), and its siting illustrates a new determination to diversify Alcoa's power sources. New fabricating facilities – for sheet and plate in Davenport, Iowa, and for rod, wire, and cable in Vancouver, Washington – were in production in 1949.

Fig. 6.1. One of two engine rooms containing natural-gas-fired, 12-cylinder Nordberg radial engines powering the smelter at Point Comfort, Texas.

These facilities were based on plans that had been hatched at least three years earlier, the minimum cycle for such major capital investment to reach fulfillment.[9] The second, and much greater, surge of postwar investment occurred between 1950 and 1956. The invasion of South Korea by Communist forces prompted a new round of military purchases of aluminum, as the United States entered the fray. Under the "Controlled Materials Plan" announced by the Office of Defense Mobilization in December 1950, primary aluminum producers were authorized to increase capacity under accelerated five-year amortization certificates covering eighty-five percent of the investment costs. All primary output that could not be sold commercially was to be purchased for a Government stockpile at published prices; the companies, in turn, had to meet Government requirements before selling in commercial markets.[10]

The immediate need for aluminum for conventional war applications was pressing enough to strain Alcoa's capacity to serve its

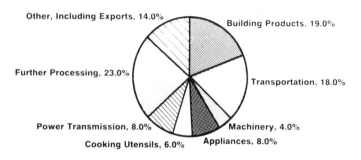

Total Sales = $476.2 million

Chart 6.1. Alcoa shipments by Market, 1950 (percent total sales and operating revenues). *Source: Alcoa Annual Report, 1962.*

domestic markets, but as Leon Hickman recalled it, one impetus behind the Government's aluminum policy, which posed even further strains on capacity, was a gruesomely naive scenario for a five-year nuclear war. In a meeting with a member of President Eisenhower's Cabinet (Hickman did not say which member), Hickman and Chief Wilson were told in effect that "some towns like Washington might be put out of business, or Pittsburgh would, but the rest would go on and they'd use this aluminum to manufacture planes and defend themselves."[11] That is what aluminum executives were told when the nuclear age was young.

But capacity expanded apace, and once again, the aluminum industry benefitted, at least in the short term, from Government defense policy. Stockpiling provided a guaranteed market for primary metal, and a countercyclical one at that, because the Government tried to time its purchases to take up the slack in "soft" markets. Accelerated amortization enabled the industry to finance more than half its expansion internally. Alcoa expanded by taking on large amounts of debt, which it then swiftly retired with cash from retained earnings and depreciation, after paying out about thirty percent of its profits in dividends.[12] With its superior credit rating, Alcoa could afford new debt without incurring the degree of risks that accrued to its major rivals. High earnings and lower taxes so greatly increased the availability of funds for investment that, even with the lapse of the Government program in the latter part of 1953, the company was in good position to continue financing a high rate of growth.[13]

While its competitors generally bought power for their smelters from commercial power stations, Alcoa continued to own and operate

Fig. 6.2.   A dragline and power shovel at Alcoa's lignite mine, providing fuel for
Alcoa's operations at Rockdale, Texas.

most of its own sources of power. The purchase of large blocks of
long-term power supplies and the erection of generating facilities
were costly, but the strategy, carried over from the monopoly days,
was maintained in the belief that the integration of power resources
would provide a long-term cost advantage. At the same time, I. W.
Wilson was anticipating the day that hydroelectric power would
have to be supplemented by other sources of energy. Alcoa leased
new oil and gas rights along the Gulf Coast and coal reserves in
Kentucky. A new dam and power station were completed in Chil-
howee, Tennessee; a fifty-year license for hydroelectric development
on the Yadkin River in North Carolina was secured from the Federal
Power Commission; arrangements were made for more power along
the Columbia River in Washington. "We could make more money,
short-term, by buying power," Chief Wilson later explained, "but
we think of power as an ingredient of aluminum, and we want to
control our own raw materials."[14]

Alcoa's reduction plants were older than the facilities that had
been sold by the Government to Reynolds and Kaiser, and so considerable resources were devoted to the replacement and upgrading
of the system's smelters. Begining with a $360 million wartime

expansion program in 1951, Alcoa increased the size of its operations at Point Comfort, opened a new smelter in Wenatchee, Washington, powered in large part by a regional hydropower source, supplemented by the federal Bonneville hydroelectric development. A revolutionary plant was erected at Rockdale, Texas, where steam–electric generators burned lignite fuel in well-guarded secrecy. In 1956, Alcoa announced a new five-year capital expenditure program totaling $600 million, devoted largely to primary production. Potlines were added to new facilities and to Massena, where Alcoa closed its own hydroelectric station and entered into contracts with the New York Power Authority to tap power from its St. Lawrence project. By 1957, Alcoa's smelting capacity approached a million tons when construction was begun on yet another new smelter near Evansville, Indiana, which was to obtain electric energy from a generating station fueled with coal from local deposits. All this primary capacity would require additional sources of bauxite for which Alcoa got concessions in Surinam and in the Dominican Republic. A new alumina refinery was built at Point Comfort to replace the alumina plant at East St. Louis, which terminated production after fifty-four years of operation.[15]

Yet, high as its levels of investment were, Alcoa grew less aggressively than either Kaiser or Reynolds and its market share fell accordingly. Determined to increase market share, those companies took on even larger proportions of debt. Reynolds financed *all* its expansion through debt between 1951 and 1954, while Kaiser issued new common and preferred stock.[16] From 1949 through 1958, Alcoa increased its primary capacity 2.7 times, compared to 3.6 times for the industry overall. Its share of the total U.S. capacity declined to thirty-eight percent, compared with twenty-seven percent for Reynolds, twenty-four percent for Kaiser, and eleven percent for three much smaller newcomers.[17] Wilson was unperturbed. "There is nothing sacrosanct about our getting forty to forty-five percent of the market," he said in 1955. "I would be just as happy provided that the market continued to expand, and provided our participation was vigorous and our contribution broad."[18]

Alcoa's concession of market share was to a large degree forced by antitrust considerations. But by the mid-1950s, Wilson was growing more cautious about the market. Younger managers exulted in the postwar boom (to them shortfalls in the industry's capacity seemed like a normal state of affairs), their seniors had not forgotten the fundamentally cyclical nature of the business. Alcoa was, moreover, conservative in its accounts. While its major rivals were anxious to show strong profits in the short term, Alcoa preferred to keep its balance sheets "clean" as a buffer to harder times. Reynolds and Kaiser "normalized" the depreciation of plant built under Government certificates of necessity in their published reports, even as they took fast tax write-offs under liberal depreciation allowances. This enabled them to overstate short-term profits and plant values relative to Alcoa, whose "tremendous undervaluation" of new facilities was reflected in the company's stock price, which was four times book value in 1955.[19]

New managers

In the wake of World War II, Alcoa underwent its first major realignment in top management since 1929 in a process that was as smooth as it was inevitable. Roy Hunt "retired" at the end of 1951, passing the president's baton to Chief Wilson almost without a break in stride. Wilson (quite contrary to lingering public perceptions that A. V. Davis was still running the company) had already been functioning since the war as a quasi chief executive. His ascension to the presidency had some symbolic importance as a new departure. Wilson was, after all, neither a member of one of Alcoa's "founding" families nor a major stockholder. On the other hand, he enjoyed R. K. Mellon's support as well as the respect of Alcoa's officers. He had long been a familiar figure at Pittsburgh's Duquesne Club (Alcoa never has had an executive dining room), where the city's industrial elite gathered for lunch, and he was a member in good standing at the Rolling Rock Club, R. K. Mellon's opulent riding and hunting retreat in the Ligonier Valley. He was, in short, the perfect bridge between the new and old eras of the company's history.[20]

He was also the right man at the right time. Quicker than either Davis or Hunt to accept the realities of Alcoa's antitrust misfortunes, Wilson was determined to adapt Alcoa to its new industry environment. Outside the company, he was widely regarded as the industry's "statesman." Dubbed "Mr. Aluminum" by the press, Wilson had earned respect for his determination to drive Alcoa's expansion in the face of great uncertainty at the end of the war. Within the company, his skills as a "diplomatic" executive enabled him to lead a restoration of corporate morale, which had flagged in the period immediately following the war. By temperament – he was both flexible and patient – Wilson was well-equipped to cope with the changes that had been wrought by the Government decrees. Under his leadership, Alcoa grew more comfortable with competition and with the society around it.[21]

Wilson became president in the same year that the company registered with the New York Stock Exchange, an event that confirmed a long-term process by which Alcoa was becoming less a "family firm" and more a "public corporation." At the time, the Mellon, Hunt, Davis, and Duke families (and their trustees) controlled (by Alcoa's own count) as much as 2.34 of 4.89 million shares of common stock. What remained was still mostly in the hands of relatively few families who, like Charles Martin Hall's heirs, had some relative with ownership or managerial ties to the company. But the trend away from family control was inexorable. In the next few years, ownership diffused rapidly through institutional and individual purchases in the stock market. A two-for-one split in 1955 helped make the company's common stock more accessible to small buyers, as the absolute number of shareholders increased from 11, 625 to 16,209 during that year alone. By 1960, the largest twenty-two shareholding families held 2.41 of 21.31 million shares.[22]

There was considerable turnover of executive personnel following the war, as a new generation of vice presidents emerged on the cusp of the Hunt–Wilson regimes. By 1949, venerable members of the old guard, Charles B. Fox, Robert E. Withers, George Stanley, Stafford K. Colby, and George Gibbons – all of whom had endured through the war years – faded into retirement. New men were also stepping up to the management of the operating units. When the 1951 *Annual Report* announced the retirement of the giant of aluminum science, Francis Frary, its management roster contained not a single name of an Alcoa vice president or subordinate officer from the monopoly days.[23]

It is important to recognize that this transfer of managerial power was more a function of time than of changes in the structure of the industry. More durable were some of the old-timers on the board of directors. When Chief Wilson became president, Roy Hunt stepped up to become chairman of the board's Executive Committee. Hunt was not content to go quietly into retirement. He revitalized what had been a moribund committee and continued to have an important impact on executive management in at least three respects. Matters for the board were usually settled by conversations between Hunt and Mellon, the company's major shareholder. Hunt's distaste for international ventures served as a damper to Wilson's more expansive ambitions. And because Wilson personally paid little attention to matters of formal structure, Hunt was able to impress his own

Fig. 6.3. An oil portrait of Richard K. Mellon.

distinctly nonbureaucratic values of organization on the company, values which, in fact, Wilson shared. Roy Hunt's impact on corporate governance and style continued to be felt for years to come.

R. K. Mellon, in the meantime, continued to make his family's influence felt. He liked to be called "General," after his rank as a retired lieutenant general in the National Guard. A pretentious affectation, it was nonetheless honored by all who knew him, and it had the virtue of reflecting his status on Alcoa's board, which meetings, according to Alfred Hunt, were short, sweet, and tailored mainly to keep Mellon informed. Important details were discussed over the phone. The Hunt family's influence was reinforced by Roy's eldest son, Alfred, who joined the board in 1949, when the ninety-one-year-old George Clapp, the last of The Pittsburgh Reduction Company's charter members, passed away. When Robert Withers died in 1952, he was replaced by Frank Magee, who had been with the company since World War I. George Stanley remained from the prewar era as did A. V. Davis, who by all accounts could still be a force to be reckoned with when the spirit moved him, though, to be sure, the spirit moved him less and less. For the most part, the nonmanagement directors remained aloof from operational concerns, but the board remained a powerful symbol of continuity and a conduit for Hunt's and Mellon's concerns.[24]

Frank Magee's appointment to the board was a prelude to his ascension to the presidency. A protege of Wilson's, Magee had become head of operations (as general production manager) during the war. Other managers who rose to the vice-presidential ranks were given titles that reflected the movement toward more centralized coordination of the Alcoa empire by Pittsburgh, where new central office functions were emerging. The modern Legal Department, for example, was established in 1951, when A. V. Davis asked Leon Hickman to join Alcoa to help the company cope with what had become a permanent preoccupation with antitrust matters. It was a measure of Hickman's love for the enterprise that he was able to brook an insult from Davis (who blamed the lawyers for the antitrust case) and to accept a cut in salary (when he left his more lucrative private law practice) to join Alcoa as its first general counsel. He was given a seat on the board of directors, and under the press of business, his small staff evolved by the end of the decade into a full-fledged department with eighteen full-time attorneys.[25]

Upper-level positions were also created for managers of Public Relations and Advertising and of Personnel and Industrial Relations. Those departments became forces for the development of more centralized corporate policies and practices. Arthur P. Hall was made a full vice president in 1951 and developed high-visibility programs for Alcoa's dealings with the outside world. Minton M. Anderson, who had been hired in 1931 to help organize college recruiting, had bootstrapped his way to a vice presidency by 1942. After the war, his department was busy recruiting new blood to fill new positions as well as old ones that had been vacated by the exodus of middle-level managers who had gone to Reynolds and Kaiser. By the mid-1950s, Personnel had become a highly professional operation by that day's standards, with an elaborate set of procedures for hiring, salary structures, performance reviews, plant foreman training, and management conferences. Anderson, not always liked by his colleagues, would not have been able to sell his programs to department, division, and works managers without the support of top management. His success had many of his peers believing that a personnel director might actually become company president.[26]

One of the most important new appointments occurred at a much lower level, in 1952, when Kent Van Horn succeeded Frary as director of research. A metallurgist who had spent a long career at the Cleveland laboratory before being transferred to New Kensington, Van Horn personified the postwar shift in both the labors and spirit of Alcoa R&D. Although he had gained some reputation as a researcher, he was valued far more for his managerial skills. Unlike his predecessor, he would eventually rise to a corporate vice presidency. Van Horn was not always patient with the leisurely pace of research scientists; under his leadership, the work of the Laboratories became more attuned to the quotidian rhythms of production engineering and the demands of marketing.[27]

Undercurrents flowing from the war influenced both the course and consequences of Van Horn's regime. The war had spurred a shift in the emphasis of research, as trained researchers had become scarce and as leisure to pursue long-term fundamental problems became a luxury. Creative minds were forced to turn to timely problems, such as work for the Manhattan Project, encasing uranium pellets in aluminum. One effect of the war had been to lash research ever more tightly to short-term considerations of production and demand. Work on lighter but stronger alloys and on processes to exploit low-grade bauxite had been undertaken in anticipation of quick results. War had also stimulated explorations into substitute materials and into substitute power sources. Although there was no conscious decision to change the Laboratories' traditional modes of research, according to historian of technology Margaret Graham, new and inexorable "trends had taken hold that would reassert themselves" in the years to come.[28]

Alcoa had also emerged from the war with a strong backlog of fundamental knowledge in aluminum science, a base that was deemed sufficient to provide the company with a solid platform for new applications. It was on this platform that the company intended to rest, while turning new research more toward the near-term needs of the marketplace.[29] Its backlog in fundamental knowledge served the company well. During the 1950s, a wide variety of new products continued to appear, based on work that had begun even before the 1940s: some successful – monumental architecture and aerospace alloys, for example – some unsuccessful – cast bearings and foil wrappings, for example. The heightened pace of wartime activity had turned the Laboratories into a hothouse of ideas for practical peacetime applications. Alcoa's annual reports for the 1950s read like a series of explosions of new applications for aluminum, its alloys, and even combinant materials such as the composite sheet of aluminum and boron carbide announced in 1957 for nuclear radiation shielding. Research and development into nonaluminum areas also continued, as significant efforts were devoted to magnesium, beryllium, gallium, and, by the mid-1950s, titanium.

Thus, the postwar pressures of competition reinforced patterns of short-term research and development with a strong emphasis on new product applications. The center of gravity of Alcoa's research program shifted decisively toward product development and its manufacturing processes and away from primary aluminum processes. Where long-term research projects continued in such key areas as the development of joining techniques and structures, they were increasingly justified in terms of near-term, commercial payoffs. One effect was that Alcoa's research budget swelled from $2.2 million in 1945 to $6 million by 1955. Another, more lasting effect was a profound change in the culture of the Laboratories. Key researchers now got expense accounts with which they could entertain marketing and sales people. And the Laboratories began to hire technical personnel, who by temperament and training were more likely to function as "team players" and less prone to hanker after external, professional rewards. Middle- and lower-level researchers were often discouraged from publishing, attending conferences, and maintaining close ties with academic institutions. Pragmatic concern that the fruits of research might too quickly pass into the hands of the company's new competitors drove Van Horn to make the Laboratories more secretive, more isolated from the scientific community, and more subject to corporate controls.[30]

All that notwithstanding, the Laboratories remained the one place in the corporation in which long-term considerations were important. Any new development project required long lead times, careful planning, and sustained commitments. Development of power generators that could make efficient use of natural gas, for example, continued on a long-term basis after the war, in recognition of the fact that domestic, low-cost, hydropower sites were a luxury of the past. Fundamental work on basic processes, though reduced in overall emphasis, was not abandoned. As early as 1952, projections were being made for a long-range inquiry into a radical alternative to the Hall smelting process. Even projects that had clearly defined market benefits involved long-term investments with no clear promise of success.[31]

Consider, in this vein, Alcoa's development of titanium forgings. On the surface, titanium would seem to parallel Alcoa's earlier experience with magnesium, which, remember, was lighter than aluminum and thus had been thought to pose a significant threat as an aluminum substitute, especially for aircraft applications. Production and fabricating techniques could be easily adapted from aluminum. However, the manufacture of the metal remained expensive and extremely fire-hazardous, and by the mid-1950s, the aircraft industry was demanding stronger materials. Titanium became a hot prospect for supersonic aircraft applications because of its much greater strength-to-weight ratio than aluminum and its combination of resistance to corrosion and good mechanical properties at high temperatures. But, unlike magnesium, titanium required novel and untested methods of production. (The difference in aluminum and titanium forging techniques, said one plant engineer, was like the difference "between a rhinoceros and a cat.") It would take a decade of highly uncertain development before Alcoa could build titanium forging facilities at its Cleveland Works. The investment reflected a fundamental appreciation of the opportunities (and threats) in untried fields of technology.[32]

Otherwise, the tenor of the company's R&D activities in the 1950s bespoke the heightened importance that marketing and sales had under more competitive conditions. Before World War II, a young man with ambition to rise in the corporation was best advised to get a job on the production line. Now, one might well be steered to the Sales Department, where young sales apprentices were exposed to the gamut of Alcoa's products and processes as they circulated through the research laboratories and the plants in a rigorous course of basic training. After some six months of apprenticeship, young salesmen stepped forth as evangelists for aluminum, fully indoctrinated in the gospel according to Alcoa. They were taught to preach the superiority of aluminum over other materials. The message was familiar, but the zeal behind it had increased since the war.

Alcoa's most zealous salesman was Fritz Close, who moved unprecedented amounts of metal into the hands of architects and developers. Brimming full of faith in an aluminum age that was only beginning to dawn, Close liked to claim that God – who in his wisdom had made aluminum light, abundant, lustrous, ductile and almost boundless in its applications – was on the side of the aluminum peddler. Barring the limits of a man's imagination, there was no more opportune calling for any salesman on the face of the earth. Young Alcoans who were not seized by the spirit of this message, said vice president for product sales Donald Wilmot, "are not compatible with our thinking and should not be in the aluminum business."[33]

New images

Meanwhile, the aluminum business was becoming a far more visible one, and it became almost as important to "sell the corporation" as the metal it manufactured. Antitrust had pushed Alcoa into the spotlight, and now competition would keep it there. Uncomfortable with publicity (which had always been bad) and accustomed to secrecy (which had always been deemed necessary), Alcoa had to learn to maneuver in new arenas, where mass advertising and public relations were vital to corporate success.

In a 1949 survey, Alcoa had determined that its major customers – not end consumers but other manufacturers – had little sense of the corporation behind the salesmen with whom they routinely came into contact. Alcoa also suffered from that debilitating scourge of all industry leaders – the stigma of size and power. Before the blows of war and antitrust had brought its monopoly down, Alcoa had only occasionally to worry about outside opinion. But both the industry and political climate had changed, so that Alcoa, no less than AT&T, General Motors, DuPont, and General Electric, had to be concerned about the attitudes of the Government, the press, and, as we shall see, broadening groups of stockholders, customers, and interest groups. As *Business Week* put it, "The opinions of these vast publics make a great deal of difference ... in court action, in legislation and in sales."[34]

Insiders had to learn to refer to their company as "Alcoa" rather than "the Aluminum Company," and in 1949, a huge "Alcoa" logo was placed on top of the plant in Edgewater, New Jersey, on the shores of the Hudson across from Manhattan. Whether it enhanced the view from the city's skyscrapers is a matter of opinion, but the event signaled the sprouting of signs on the company's theretofore anonymous factories throughout the country. Institutional and product advertising played ever more frequently in mass-distribution publications, as the company's advertising budget swelled to $3 million in 1950. In 1951, Alcoa entered the new popular medium of television, where it won sponsorship of Edward R. Murrow's CBS news program, "See It Now."[35] In the following year, the Alcoa Foundation was established as a charitable trust endowed with $3.9 million in cash and securities in order to service the company's "social responsibilities to the communities in which it operates." Local community relations had always been important to the company, but the Alcoa Foundation made it possible to disburse company largess more systematically – and more conspicuously – on the national level in both good and bad years.[36]

Nothing more symbolized Alcoa's cultivation of a new public image (and new markets) than the erection of its new corporate headquarters. Despite some misgivings, the company erected a thirty-story, aluminum building in the center of Pittsburgh's downtown triangle – a structure that stood as a beacon to urban renewal amid an ongoing, public–corporate movement to clean up Pittsburgh's badly polluted air and water and to revitalize its aging urban landscape. As participants in the civic revival, in which General Mellon played a prominent role, Alcoa's management wanted to make a statement with its new home office.[37]

Alcoa's architect, Wallace Harrison, had sized up his clients as a conservative lot. He originally submitted a design for a "sedate building made of limestone with, of course, aluminum windows and other aluminum gadgets." Indeed, Roy Hunt's first thought had been to build a structure of granite, but after some discussion, Fritz Close's instincts for promotion and General Mellon's interests in civic reform inspired the directors to settle on a radical "all-aluminum" structure which, they hoped, might serve not only as a monument to civic pride, but also a prototype for aluminum-intensive monumental architecture. As ground was broken,

> there probably was never a more nervous group of corporate executives – it was aluminum, all right . . . , and it was modern, maybe too damned modern. What would shareholders think whose names were not Davis, Hunt, or Mellon? How would ordinary builders react – or other executives, like themselves, who needed a new office building? Long before the thing was finished the awful thought crossed nearly every officer's mind that they had laid an egg.[38]

Finished in 1952, the Alcoa building was a technical triumph, if not an architectural masterpiece, a gleaming monument to aluminum in the "iron city," perched on a hill on a corner of what is now called Mellon Square. Its shimmer cut through the characteristic gloom of the city, whose industrial plants, despite considerable improvements in environmental controls, still spewed forth enough soot to compel the fastidious to change shirts twice a day. Today, in

Figs. 6.4 and 6.5. Views of Pittsburgh before and after progress was made in reducing air pollution. Fifth Avenue, in the heart of Pittsburgh's downtown triangle, at 11 A.M., on a typical day in 1945 (top). The Pittsburgh skyline in March 1952 (bottom), as the Alcoa building (left center) neared completion. *Courtesy of Carnegie Library.*

Fig. 6.6. A fisheye view of the Alcoa building rising above the Harvard–Yale–Princeton Club (right foreground) and the Smithfield Street Congregational Church, which is topped by an aluminum spire.

the pristine daylight of a clean city, the Alcoa Building remains noteworthy for its lavish display of the metal for elevators, ceiling, doors, thresholds, lighting fixtures, windows, blinds, baseboards, trim, furnishings, and even water pipes. The dazzling exterior curtain–wall introduced an "Alumilite" color finish and required neither painting, caulking, nor other exterior maintenance. This use of aluminum on such a large scale had been made possible by innovations in metalworking and building techniques, which resulted in a claimed savings of more than 3,000 tons of structural steel. The results made such an impression that Alcoa soon found itself immersed in the business of monumental architecture. By 1957, scores of buildings were erected with aluminum skins, and more than half of all commercial building starts used aluminum windows. By then, building products had become aluminum's major market, with sales surpassing older markets in transportation (including military aircraft), consumer durables, and electrical products.[39]

Even more indicative of Alcoa's determination to combine public relations with promotion of its products was its sponsorship of television. It began with Murrow, who had made his reputation reporting back from London during the Luftwaffe's air raids and had since become the country's most respected television journalist. Alcoa's Public Relations vice president hoped that through Murrow the company would then reach the "high-brow" audience that included Alcoa's major customers; and "humanize" the corporation in the eyes of opinion leaders who were sure to watch the show. Murrow – no less than the Alcoa Foundation, Wilson's press conferences, the company logo, and institutional advertising (aimed at teaching the public about how bauxite was mined, how aluminum was smelted, how alloys were rolled, extruded, and cast) – was a vehicle to a more open, more accessible corporate reputation.

There was a price to pay for openness. "See It Now" brought Alcoa into the uncomfortable realm of civic controversy. This was an arena American corporations normally avoided, then as now, and Alcoa's sponsorship of Murrow puzzled at least one business reporter, who asked how the company could become interested in a man whose "televiewing audience [included] an unusually high percentage of the corporation's natural critics." There is a story that when Murrow, who was clearly identified with liberal political opinion, first met with Alcoa executives, he chafed at questions about his political views. "Gentlemen," he is reported to have responded, "that is none of your business."[40] In fact, "See It Now" had a strong attraction for political liberals, who found in the program a willingness to tackle such touchy matters as violations of civil liberties, segregation, and the great political cancer of the day, Senator Joseph McCarthy's communist witch hunt.[41]

Chief Wilson, himself a staunch conservative Republican and outspoken anticommunist, stood fast behind the journalist who became the nation's most conspicuous voice of outraged reason during the height of the McCarthyite hysteria. In 1953, the company allowed Murrow to eliminate a commercial in order to expand his coverage of the persecution of Lt. Milo Radulovich, who had gained notoriety upon his discharge from the Air Force on the flimsy grounds that his sister and father had "Communist leanings." The Radulovich documentary caused considerable nervousness at CBS and among its affiliate stations as the controversy following the show grew noisy. Wilson took pains to praise the program for its integrity (hoping, however, that "See It Now" would not dwell exclusively on "civil liberty broadcasts in the future"). When Murrow turned full force on Joe McCarthy in a famous broadcast on March 9, 1954, the two antagonists became embroiled in a running battle. The Senator did all he could to discredit the journalist, but Alcoa kept "an impassive public stance." Finally, when McCarthy, in a calculated move to embarrass the company, submitted an invoice to Alcoa to cover the costs of his filmed reply to Murrow, Wilson simply returned it unpaid.[42]

Alcoa renewed its contract with CBS in November and remained Murrow's sponsor until after McCarthy's political influence drowned in its own backwash of hysteria. But the company had been uneasy, to say the least, through the whole affair and its grit was gradually worn down by growing complaints from influential customers. One of Murrow's programs dwelled on a land scandal in Texas, seriously straining Alcoa's goodwill with that state's public officials. In July 1955, Murrow was dropped, ostensibly for business reasons. Television households had trebled since 1950, and changing tastes had to be considered; the company was simply seeking a wider consumer audience, and a mass viewing audience, on the whole, preferred entertainment to enlightenment. *The New York Times* wrote a passing tribute to Alcoa's corporate courage, while CBS officials, on the other hand, chafed quietly over what they thought was Alcoa's loss of nerve. Murrow himself thought that Wilson had grown weary of the pressure from stockholders.[43] Alcoa picked up sponsorship of the "Alcoa Hour," a more sedate and much more popular vehicle for its advertising.

Judge Knox and the antitrust remedy

Although no one would characterize the decade following World War II as a politically bad time for big business, Government continued to loom large in the affairs of corporate America and of the aluminum industry in particular. Alcoa's ability to do business was still subject to the constraints of antitrust. Its management had to tread a fine line between the necessity of combatting competition in both its center and peripheral markets and the wisdom of steering a careful course to avoid the shoals of public hostility. The political pressures were great. With Congress and the Justice Department constantly watching, Alcoa was inhibited in both strategy and tactics. The company had become "gun-shy," said *Forbes*, and fearing Government threats, chose a course of expanding from within, eschewing acquisitions, keeping its market share in primary aluminum well within tolerable limits.[44] In its decisions on output and pricing, Alcoa management was concerned to avoid even the appearance of behavior that might be interpreted to harm the well-being of its competitors.

Legal problems continued to reverberate from the Learned Hand ruling of 1945. Alcoa had managed to avoid the worst – it was spared the usual and radical remedy of divestiture, but it remained under court jurisdiction for more than a decade. In 1946, the District Court ruled in effect that the company must take into account the costs of competitors before pricing its products (which, if Alcoa remained the low-cost producer, would enhance its profits). In 1950, the Court ordered the major shareholders of Alcoa and Aluminium Limited to divest their holdings in one or the other company, thus severing once and for all the ties of ownership between them. Not until 1957 was the book finally closed on the great antitrust suit that had begun twenty years earlier.[45]

The screws of antitrust were further tightened by congressional legislation and administration policy. The Celler–Kefauver Act of 1950 placed prior restraints on any horizontal and vertical mergers that might tend to reduce competition. This amendment to the Clayton Act of 1914 was then vigorously enforced by the Eisenhower administration. Among the nation's large corporations, Alcoa remained a special source of concern to economists, Government lawyers, and politicians alike. In a 1955 report on the aluminum industry, a subcommittee of the House Select Committee on Small Business declared that "monopoly control by private industry ... is an evil which must be recognized as equal to threat of socialism." The FTC was charged with monitoring pricing and selling by the primary producers in order to assure the survival of smaller firms in the aluminum industry.[46] The most serious problem for Alcoa, however, was that it had to labor under a continuing Court jurisdiction, the reasons for which bear closer analysis.

At the end of 1946, Alcoa's executives had hoped that their acquiescence in the decision of the War Surplus Property Board would satisfy the intent of Learned Hand. (Hand's ruling, remember, had begged the question of remedies – especially any that might require dissolution.) Nonetheless, the Department of Justice pressed ahead for a substantial divestiture of many of Alcoa's holdings along both the horizontal and vertical axes. When Alcoa petitioned in 1947 for a ruling that it no longer monopolized the primary aluminum market, the Government countered with a petition of its own, contending that Alcoa not only continued to hold monopoly power, but that it was still striving to extend its monopoly position. Back in the U.S. District Court of New York, where John C. Knox had succeeded Francis Caffey as Chief Judge, petitions and arguments by attorneys on both sides dragged on until the end of 1949. On June 2, 1950, Judge Knox handed down his lengthy and – once again befitting this most remarkable case – novel decision.

By then, the "Cold War" was heating up, and the hot one in Korea was about to draw the United States into another armed conflict. The policy problem before Judge Knox's court was how to ensure the ability of Alcoa's competitors to survive in a manner consistent with the national welfare abroad as well as at home. First, the judge disposed of the Government's principal contentions. Market shares in smelting capacity were set as follows: Alcoa at fifty-one percent, Reynolds at thirty-one percent, and Kaiser at eighteen percent. Such "relative market positions," he determined contrary to the Government's charge, "do not show prima facie monopoly power for Alcoa," and in any case, market structure alone was not the most important criterion. Monopoly power was no more than the ability to control prices, which, with the advent of Reynolds and Kaiser, was no longer within Alcoa's means. There had been no evidence of anticompetitive pricing by Alcoa in fabricated products (where he thought competition among the three companies ultimately lay), and Knox took into account secondary aluminum scrap and competition from non-ferrous metals as further evidence of Alcoa's inability to control prices. As for Alcoa's monopoly "strivings," Knox found only that it had "yielded its unlawful market position reluctantly." Under such circumstances, divestiture was not warranted and would be difficult in any case because of the highly integrated nature of the corporation. Most important, in the judge's opinion, it would be unwise to disrupt "economic and industrial forces from which the public has reaped substantial benefits" and that were vital "in these times of international tension."[47]

Knox reached instead for a principle of "effective competition" based on the performance of the firms in the industry. It was important to enable Kaiser and Reynolds to grow and prosper in a market where, for the present at least, Alcoa maintained important advantages. As "an impressive industrial power," Alcoa's "properties are far more extensive than those of Reynolds and Kaiser. Its financial strength enables it, if such be its desire, to take advantage of its trade opportunities and expand disproportionately its current share of the market." Alcoa, in other words, still possessed "impressive industrial power," with "*monopoly potential.*" And key to that potential was "its ties to Aluminium Limited."[48]

There was no question in the judge's mind that common ownership of Alcoa and Limited could be used to the anticompetitive advantage of the former, "no matter how lawful the relations with Limited may have been in the past." In 1950, the court calculated that the Davis brothers, Roy Hunt, and six members of the Mellon family owned 46.43 percent of Alcoa's common stock and 44.65 percent of Aluminium Limited's. Adding the stakes of Doris Duke and the trustees of the Duke Endowment would place the two companies under absolute majority control of eleven stockholders. Thus, reasoned Knox, there was good reason for concern.

> In view of the long association [of the nine principal stockholders] and their close connection with the aluminum industry, together with the widespread distribution of the remaining stock interests, the concerted action of the nine, if the occasion arises, may reasonably be anticipated, whereas concerted action on the part of other stockholders is unlikely.[49]

It was hard to gainsay the judge on this point. Though there was no interlocking directorate, and though there had been no legal finding that dual ownership had restrained competition between the two companies, the perception of an unholy business alliance was strong. "Blood," recalled Alcoa's Krome George, "was a hell of a lot thicker than water," and everyone knew it.[50]

Reynolds and Kaiser had good prospects for development, having been endowed with "excellent properties, low investments, and safeguards for their future stability" by the Government's disposal program. But their future was clouded by the "shadow" of "Alcoa's potential control of Aluminium Limited," whose smelting costs, even allowing for the 1948 $0.02 per pound tariff schedule, were the lowest in the industry. Alcoa's power to turn the Canadian spigot on and off at will was deemed anticompetitive.

It is inevitable [he declared] that investments are deterred, expansion retarded, and stability impaired by the power in Alcoa's controlling stockholders, if they choose to exercise it, to overwhelm, and put to naught, the best efforts of both Reynolds and Kaiser. Such power, whether or not exercised, and whether or not likely of execution, is omnipresent.[51]

It was the first time in history that American investors were ordered to relinquish their control of a foreign company.[50] Specifically, large shareholders in the two companies were ordered to dispose of their holdings in one or the other company within ten years, while the affected voting rights in Limited were held in a court-appointed trust. The decree was almost upset by the refusal of the Duke interests to sell, but given their passive history as investors, the judge allowed for alternative measures. In a complicated settlement, some family-related stockholders agreed to sell their shares in Limited, and the shares of some deceased defendants named in the 1937 suit (i.e., George Clapp, Edwin Fickes, and George Gibbons) were also sold. Only E. K. Davis, who chafed at having his voting power in Limited tied up for ten years, sold his stock in Alcoa. The result was that within six years, the number of shareholders in Limited increased from 3,559 to nearly 28,000, as control of the company shifted steadily north of the border. In 1972, fifty-five percent of Alcan's (as Limited has since become known) common stock was in the hands of Canadian investors.[53]

Another result – one which Knox anticipated with some anxiety – was the creation of yet another major source of competition in the domestic aluminum markets. Aluminium Limited could be expected henceforth to look upon the United States as another export market for its enormous, low-cost smelters. This posed a delicate problem because a novel aspect of the court's ruling was that it would retain jurisdiction over the case for yet another five years should competition from Reynolds and Kaiser prove to be "feeble, uncertain, and ineffective." Even though the judge said that he would not consider "normal competitive activity" by Alcoa as a sign of monopolistic intent, the message was clear. As Chief Wilson interpreted it, Alcoa was obliged to take care that its competitors not "fall by the wayside."[54]

Judge Knox had the imagination to foresee that should Alcoa refrain from expanding too rapidly to discourage one set of competitors, it might also deflect investment northward, resulting in a transfer of capacity away from the United States. Such an outcome would run contrary to the national interest. Both Alcoa and the court would have to walk a fine line to promote the health of the company's rivals without diminishing the nation's strength in aluminum.

Ironies abounded in the Knox decision. For Knox, secondary aluminum and nonaluminum products, which had been deemed irrelevant by Hand, seemed important to understanding the full scope of competition in the industry. Had the wishes of more ardent antimonopolists been realized, Alcoa would have been broken up into several smaller parts. Fortunately, the preemptive action of the War Surplus Property Board set the stage for an outcome in which a few integrated aluminum producers would compete. Knox, who realized that capital-intensive technologies required large producers of "minimum effective size," was right in step with the historical development of the postwar industry when he prescribed a remedy that did not require him to carve up Alcoa. Even the Justice Department had asked only that Alcoa be divested of enough assets to create a fourth major American producer, a remedy which the judge, in the end, thought "hazardous" at worst and doubtful at best.[55] A more fundamental irony is the way in which the very concept of competition was altered by antitrust. National antitrust policy was designed to promote the kind of competition in which all sellers must set the price of their goods to "cost," to the benefit of consumers. But the best that can be said of antitrust as it had evolved by midcentury was that it created the conditions for competitive rivalry, which is not exactly the same thing.

Look at it this way. Antitrust does not allow any one company to compete too well, precisely because monopoly might be the result. It is the function (if not the logical purpose) of antitrust to prevent competitive success from running its full course, that is, to the point where an industry becomes dominated by a single low-cost producer. After Learned Hand, courts looked more to the consequences, as distinct from the intents, of dominant firm behavior, and gave effective sanction to long-term industry structures in which a few firms could achieve a stable pattern of competition on a controlled basis. In the Alcoa case, Knox understood that market power in a capital-intensive industry could be shared by only a few large entities. To ensure that Alcoa would have at least some enduring rivals in the field, he would restrain Alcoa's ability to compete, keeping its management's feet to the fire for five years, time enough for Reynolds and Kaiser to prove their mettle. To facilitate the rise of "effective competition," he revoked a "grant back" to Alcoa of improvement patents on the royalty-free technology Alcoa had been compelled to license under the terms of the Government plant disposal.[56]

Thus the court's remedy was a compromise between the positions of the Justice Department and Alcoa. Oligopoly, not competition, became the cure for monopoly in aluminum. Alcoa's management accepted this outcome as the lesser of two evils, while prominent economists inveighed at the result as antithetical to the ideal of competition. As George Stocking saw it: "The court, in effect, gave official sanction to Alcoa's holding an umbrella over the industry and encouragement to a pricing policy calculated to profit the industry rather than benefit the consumer of aluminum products."[57] Aluminum remained the most concentrated of the major American industries.

To ensure the survival of its young rivals, Alcoa's every move over the next several years was scrutinized by the Justice Department and by Congress. Two more decades would pass before Alcoa's management was able entirely to stop worrying about the legal and political repercussions of the 1937 antitrust suit. As for the suit itself, it finally came to a conclusion in June 1957, when Judge Cashin of the Second District Court of New York turned aside a request from the Department of Justice for an extension of judicial jurisdiction over Alcoa. The Government contended that it was too early to tell whether or not competition had been established in the industry, reasoning that the materials programs of the Korean War had created artificial conditions for the growth of Alcoa's competitors. The judge was new, but his court was weary, and so Cashin gave the Government's argument little weight. He could not anticipate that the next five-year period would be any more "normal" for competitive conditions in the aluminum industry and was unwilling to burden himself with the opportunity to find out.[58] One might well wonder whether the Justice Department seriously thought it was doing anything more than going through the motions. Alcoa's competitors were well-established; enough was enough. Four major integrated producers of a product in a capital-intensive industry were thriving on the North American Continent, and that was the best for which one could reasonably hope.

Who can say that the volume and applications of aluminum would have grown any more slowly under monopoly conditions? Certainly not Alcoa. Like most American businessmen, Alcoa executives subscribe to a competitive creed, even while they struggle to defend themselves from its effects. The progress of the industry under oligopoly conditions gradually dispelled their bitterness over the way in which they had been stripped of their monopoly power. Lawrence Litchfield, shortly after he became Alcoa's president in 1961, put it thus:

> [T]he industry is much further along, and the commodity much more widespread, than it would have been without this competition. Although Alcoa's shareholders may have not profited to the extent that they would have if the Government had not intervened, the appreciation in the value of their holdings has been most substantial. And there can be no doubt that the amount of competitive effort injected into the industry had stimulated all participants to greater levels of achievement and higher peaks of progress than otherwise might have been attained.[59]

Fritz Close was more succinct. The establishment of competition "was a bum deal," he said, "but basically it stimulated the company."[60]

Structure and patterns of competition

One obvious problem of oligopoly is the potential for price fixing among a few firms. Irving Lipkowitz, who after the war had left the employ of the Government to become Reynolds' economist, dismissed as improbable the notion that price fixing could have taken place in the aluminum industry. In his view, the personalities involved precluded any collusion whatsoever; the chief executives of Kaiser, Reynolds, and Alcoa simply "hated each other's guts," and would never have come together even "on a business basis."[61] But no act of collusion was required for the establishment of tendencies among a few aluminum firms to sell their products at tacitly uniform prices. Uniform prices were not only possible, but usually achievable, given the common desire of aluminum producers for price stability.

The desire for price stability originated in a simple fact of life about competition in capital-intensive industries with few producers that all have the potential to sell the same products to the same customers. In such industries, entry is difficult and expensive and each producer has some ability to influence the price for the industry's products by raising or lowering output or its own selling price. Under such conditions, the movements by one producer have to take its rivals' reactions into account. Given little difference in products or services, if any one producer were to raise prices, it would soon lose business if competitors did not also raise prices. Conversely, if one producer were to lower prices, others would certainly follow in order not to lose business. Hence, there was little practical incentive for a producer to change prices in either direction, at least in the short term, unless and until there occurred a substantial change in its production or distribution costs. Holding prices fairly constant, moreover, made it easier for a few producers to agree explicitly (which was illegal) or tacitly (by observing each other's behavior) upon a level of prices that could be charged before customers would turn to a "substitute" product.

Price stability also helped socialize producers to avoid the destructive impulse of sellers in a buyer's market, an impulse that can lead to drastic and damaging price cuts below cost. This is an especially difficult problem for capital-intensive producers for whom major downward adjustments in capacity and labor would be extremely painful. An oligopolistic industry like aluminum, moreover, was more likely to enjoy a higher degree of price discipline than one with a large number of smaller producers, but the mere desire for price stability was not enough to achieve it. The crucial enabling factor was the control of supplies that could be regulated to demand. Industries like aluminum and steel were characterized by a relatively manageable supply of their basic product (as compared with copper, for example, which traded as a commodity in world markets and was virtually immune from attempts at price discipline).

In aluminum, price stability was enhanced by several important factors, such as: the cyclical nature of demand for industrial aluminum products, which made it better for producers to strike long-term sales contracts with customers; the need for potential customers to make long-term assumptions about *their* costs should they switch from other materials to aluminum; the ever-present threat of antitrust that inhibited Alcoa from gaining too much market share. On this last point, there was not only Judge Knox's implied threat of action against Alcoa should it compete too successfully, there was an explicit prohibition set forth in a 1946 District Court injunction that required the company to price its fabricated products, particularly sheet, at a price equal to the selling price of its ingot plus the cost of making and selling the fabricated product. There was to be no repeat of the kind of price squeezing tactics that Alcoa had employed briefly in the 1920s. There were also statutory pressures from such modifications of the Clayton Act as the Robinson–Patman Act of 1936, which, in addressing its main concern with unfair practices of price discrimination, mandated "soft competition" in cases where price reductions might unduly injure competitors.

Reinforcing all this was a simple belief born of years of Alcoa's experience in the business. As Chief Wilson put it to the House Subcommittee on Monopoly Power in 1951, "We attempt to hold the price as steady as we can because we believe that it will insure the maximum development of the aluminum industry." Buyers of the metal concurred; one customer of precision castings testified that "Aluminum's remarkable record of price stability is an added incentive [to buy] of incalculable value." Aluminum managers, themselves, believed that demand for the metal was inelastic (did not fluctuate) in response to short-term changes in price, but that it was highly elastic with respect to long-term expectations about price, especially as that price compared with alternative materials. In this way, aluminum came to acquire the characteristics of an oligopolistic industry with "administered prices;" that is, an industry with a few large competitors whose known or posted prices fluctuated infrequently.[62]

The postwar aluminum industry was not unusual in that oligopoly had long been the typical form of competition in the center industries in the American economy. Under oligopolistic conditions, prices were set neither by the whim of some all-powerful monopolist nor by the "invisible hand" of a free, competitive market. It is exactly this – that oligopoly prices resulting from "tacit collusion" among a few producers tend to rise above producers' marginal costs (and therefore above the "competitive price") – that worries many economists, who argue that such behavior should be deemed illegal *per se* under antitrust law. As a practical matter, courts have been reluctant to convict oligopolistic producers of antitrust violations, unless they can be shown overtly to have colluded.

In the political world of Senator Estes Kefauver (who always stood ready to lay the ills of the economy at the feet of big business), administered prices were responsible for what had become a chronic inflationary trend in the economy, a problem he was sure would not exist if prices were determined purely by the forces of supply and demand. On the other hand, in the business world of Alcoa's economist, Stanley Malcuit, competition existed "whenever two or more people are after the customer's dollar," and wherever that was the case, price was but one of many elements in the competitive struggle. The elements of oligopolistic competition, according to Malcuit, included "costs, capital investment, the nature of the product with respect to durability, style, etc., the price of substitute products, and so on." Had Malcuit filled in the blanks, he might have added such nonprice factors as marketing, branding, advertising, customer service and credit, quality, delivery schedules, and innovation. One way in which prices clearly did not compete was in shipping costs. By 1950, it had become industry practice to append an average shipping cost (f.o.b., plant), which made customers indifferent to the distance over which their metal had to travel. This "postage stamp theory of delivery" helped the newer producers whose plants were farther removed than many of Alcoa's to the northeastern industrial markets.[63]

A marked characteristic of oligopolistic competition is the phenomenon of "price leadership," the ability of a larger company to set prices that other, smaller sellers in the industry tend to follow. In its most antisocial form, price leadership results in the establishment of something tending toward monopoly profits for a dominant, low-cost company, while keeping industry prices generally at a level far higher than they would be under optimal conditions of competition. However, as we have already noted, a strong discipline of price leadership can help prevent sellers from destructive price cutting in hard times, and it can enhance price stability.[64] In aluminum, Alcoa's price leadership was clearly established after the war, although, after 1948, the initiative in changing primary prices changed from time to time. Precisely, in fifteen changes of the list price of ingot between 1945 and 1958, Alcoa lead the way in nine cases, Kaiser in three, and Reynolds in one.[65]

List prices were not necessarily the prices customers paid, but they set the standard from which actual charges for ingot or semi-fabricated products could be discounted by salesmen in the field. While discounting would become more common after 1958, when the growth of capacity in the industry was often more than adequate to meet demand, generally capacity-short conditions (before 1958) kept discounting to a minimum. It was certainly not in the interest of producers to risk triggering a price war, and Alcoa, which increasingly monitored its district sales practices from Pittsburgh to ensure compliance with antitrust law, had to be especially careful not to risk the appearance of seeking unfair price advantages. The prices of fabricated products usually followed the price of ingot; the movement of ingot list prices, therefore, served as a reasonable barometer of all phases of the industry's production.

In setting the price of unalloyed ingot, which was generally accepted as the price of aluminum (as distinct from the price of pig aluminum[66]), Alcoa was the "low-price preference" leader. When it raised prices, the rest of the industry was sure to follow, but it did not try to raise them to their most profitable levels in the short run.

Table 6.1. *Leadership pattern of list-price changes of pig aluminum, 1944–58*

Price per pound	Dates of change and price leaders (* = leader)		
	Alcoa	Kaiser	Reynolds
$0.14	post 6/44		
0.15	6/28/48*		
0.16	10/11/48	7/7/48*	7/15/48
0.165	5/22/50*	5/25/50	5/23/50
0.18	9/25/50*	9/28/50	9/29/50
0.19	8/4/52	8/4/52	8/4/52
0.195	6/23/53	6/22/53*	6/23/53
0.20	7/15/53*	7/20/53	7/20/53
0.205	8/5/54*	8/6/54	8/6/54
0.215	6/13/55	6/12/55	6/10/55*
0.225	8/1/55*	8/2/55	8/6/55
0.24	3/29/56	3/26/56*	3/27/56
0.25	8/10/56*	8/11/56	8/14/56
0.26	7/29/57*	8/1/57	8/1/57
0.24	3/28/58*	3/30/58	3/30/58
0.247	8/1/58*	8/2/58	8/2/58

Source: Merton J. Peck, *Competition in the Aluminum Industry, 1945–1958* (Cambridge, MA, 1961), p. 42.

Alcoa had never tried to extract its full potential for profits, even during its monopoly years. It had always been an article of faith in the business that moderation in aluminum pricing stimulated sales, expanded markets, and not incidentally, helped maintain barriers to entry. Together, the oligopolists would benefit if independent investors were not given high-price "umbrellas" under which they might more easily enter the field. For Alcoa in particular, there were strong antitrust incentives to keep the price of ingot-relatively low (though not so low as to hurt Reynolds and Kaiser). From 1945 to 1948, Alcoa held the ingot price at $0.15, and as metal prices generally rose after 1948, Alcoa remained firm in its determination to moderate aluminum prices. According to Donald Wilmot, Alcoa would follow another leader upward only if an analysis of the company's own costs justified the increase.[67] Industry analysts noted that the majors generally tried to support the list prices, which were set twice a year. And the majors found that rationing ingot among customers was preferable to raising prices whenever demand surged, because it kept the price of secondary aluminum high.[68]

Historically, Alcoa had followed policies that would optimize corporate growth over an extended period of time, eschewing tactics focused merely on short-term returns. Following World War II, it held to its traditional approach to pricing. Now, Alcoa's low-price preference was reinforced by its management's continuing view of pricing as a long-term problem as distinct from its competitors' greater desire for immediate profits.[69] Kaiser and Reynolds were under pressure to build retained earnings, while Alcoa, the lowest-cost producer of the three, could afford to maintain a statesmanlike position that present profits be moderated to "insure the maximum development of the aluminum industry." Alcoa wanted to continue pricing its metal in the way it had for decades, based not on what the traffic would bear but on a cost-plus system that established a profit margin targeted to a desired rate of return. Chief Wilson accounted for Alcoa's system as follows:

> In setting our prices we set them so that if and when we have a normal expected [volume] in our plants, we will make approximately 15 to 20 percent return on the capital used in connection with operations for producing that particular aluminum commodity.
>
> Now that results after taxes – over a long period of time – in a profit to the company of about 10 percent [it was actually closer to 9.7%] on the equity capital in the business. That is the history that has been shown and litigated over in the antitrust case and I think is not disputed at all....[70]

Target returns were calculated by Alcoa for all its fabrication markets with varying degrees of emphasis and success. Although the 1946 court order was "directed only to the relationship between prices of ingot and certain gauges of aluminum sheet and aluminum alloy sheet, Alcoa has felt that the principle involved in this order was one which should be observed in all the price relationships between products...."[71] Thus, all fabricated products were priced both with regard to a reasonable return on the one hand, and a reasonable spread with respect to the price of ingot on the other. But there were other variables. Sometimes, products were priced "promotionally" (as had been the case with utensils and wire early in the century) in order to gain broad acceptance in the market. Others were kept down out of fear of competition from alternative metals. This certainly was the case with many foundry products and rolled structural shapes that competed with steel. Still other prices were regulated downward by competition from other aluminum producers, as was the case with foil, castings, and extrusions, and by falling demand, as was the case with aluminum cable. Thus, target prices were usually projected on modest expectations. Higher than average target prices could be achieved only in product areas where competition, at least for a time, was weak and where demand was strong. Such a fortunate confluence of circumstances applied in the 1950s to such products as cookware, fine-gauge screen wire, and electrical metallic tubing.

Alcoa's target pricing "system" owed its origin to E. K. Davis, who had first developed it as far back as 1921. Over the years, Alcoa had come to base the prices of fabricated products on full production costs with the primary metals out of which they were composed being valued at their market prices. Shipping costs were equalized so as not to put distant fabricators at a disadvantage. General administrative overhead and selling expenses were allocated to "total works costs" in order to arrive at total unit costs. Margins were then added based on the considerations just mentioned above. The system was simple and encouraged demand. Given these virtues, Alcoa's target pricing system achieved the stature of an industry tradition as the principle was adopted by the other major producers after World War II. Still, it is important to bear in mind that the industry's major, high-margin products were produced on a job-order basis, making it difficult in reality to price them on the basis of long-term projected averages. For Alcoa, the increasingly competitive environment was eroding its historic ability to price products to long-term average return targets, even at the level of ingot pricing.

Taking the foregoing into account, it would have been pure coincidence if the short-run price of aluminum corresponded to the real current relationship between supply and demand. For more than five years following the war, the industry was characterized by a strong excess demand that was fanned further by Alcoa's preference for low prices. This situation was sustained by conservative smelting expansion out of fear that demand would taper off. During the Korean War, capacity expansion accelerated under Government incentives, but it took time for the construction of new capacity to catch up with demand. Meanwhile, the United States producers tried to stay abreast via aluminum purchases from Canada. Producers of secondary aluminum grew rapidly under these conditions (they grew from about 70 in 1940 to some 200 in 1955), and they could often exploit the demand situation by sharply increasing their prices.[72] Not until the recession of 1957–8 did the situation reverse itself so that capacity was suddenly in excess, causing the per-pound price of primary ingot – which because of rising production costs and inflation had risen from $0.14 in 1947 to $0.215 in 1955 and then surged to $0.26 in 1957 – to be reduced by a full two cents.[73]

If competition is considered more broadly than in terms of short-term equilibrium between supply and demand, aluminum prices, though administered, can be said to have been reasonable. Pricing was not merely a matter of exploiting a situation of growing demand. One had to take into account the ongoing threat of competition from alternative materials. The long-term drop in the relative price of aluminum as against copper, steel, lead, and zinc shows that demand for aluminum had expanded not simply as a function of general economic growth but at the expense of other materials. After 1949, relative prices did not change as much as they had in the 1930s and 40s, but the growth of the aluminum industry continued at a more rapid rate than GNP, while other materials with which aluminum competed merely kept pace.[74]

The large, integrated producers were the main consumers of their own primary aluminum, which was then converted into fabricated goods.[75] The pricing of the latter was complex, reflecting a large variety of submarkets and circumstances. Fabrications fell into three basic categories of price behavior: rigid, moderately flexible, and highly flexible. Products in the first category were manufactured in the most capital-intensive plants, and their prices tended to move in concert with ingot prices; those in the latter two were more competitively produced and their prices determined by "free-market" forces of supply and demand. Large-scale, semifinished mill products, such as reroll slabs and coils, foil stock, and sheet, were characterized by rigid prices; rod, wire, bar, tubing, and electrical conductor cable fell in the second category; extrusions, powder, and castings (sand and permanent-mold) were highly competitive. Because smaller, more competitive fabricators bought metal at administered prices and sold their products at fluctuating prices, they worried about a narrowing of price differentials between ingot and fabrications by the integrated producers.[76] Antitrust, however, deterred Alcoa from engaging in price-squeezing practices. Wilmot testified in relation to sheet that Alcoa kept its margins narrow in the production of intermediate products relative to the margins it took on finished sheet "for no other reason than to allow room for that non-integrated fabricator to exist."[77]

Thus, Alcoa could do well by doing good, as it became socially responsible, as well as profitable, for the company to press for higher profits in downstream operations. "To the extent that the vertically integrated firms consume their own primary aluminum production," observed Peck, "it is a matter of indifference at what stage of production the profits occur."[78] And if good profits could be made downstream, markets could be more readily protected against entry upstream.

Meanwhile, new entry into smelting was once again (as it had been in World War II) a by-product of Government stimulation. During the Korean War, accelerated amortization made more internal funds available, while guaranteed Government contracts made credit easier to obtain in the capital markets. Between 1950 and 1955, while the Government program (which cost about $300 million) was in effect, a rapid rate of expansion was joined with high profits, as the total industry's return on investment averaged a healthy 14.8 percent. Thereafter, expansion continued because of a sustained optimism in the industry's future, bolstered by favorable economic indicators.[79]

In this climate, the major producers flourished while three new primary producers joined the fray. Harvey Machine Tool Company had begun fabricating aluminum in Oregon in 1948 and then capitalized on the Government program to integrate backward into smelting. Its smelter came on stream in 1958 with the benefit of a Government promise to purchase its output for five years. Anaconda Aluminum Company, a subsidiary of the copper giant, opened a smelter in Montana in 1955 to support a growing business in fabrications without benefit of a Government contract. Ormet, a jointly owned creature of Olin Mathieson and Revere Copper and Brass, was formed in 1956, after its parent companies had failed to get Government guarantees. Its smelter in Ohio started operations in 1958, providing its parents with metal for a variety of fabricated products. In all three cases, producers had to and did procure reliable sources of alumina and water power in order to stay in business. The costs of entry into reduction *per se* were not prohibitive, although two companies that had been allocated Government purchase contracts were unable to raise the kind of funds necessary to enter the business that were available to such corporate giants as Olin and Revere. But very high barriers to entry existed in that the durability of reduction operations depended on having a strong, vertically integrated system of inputs and buyers comparable to that of the major producers. For the new producers, alumina, especially, would always be a problem.[80]

The entry of additional smelters did not disturb the basic oligopolistic pattern of the primary aluminum industry. By the end of 1958,

Table 6.2. *Aluminum capacity of major U.S. producers, 1954–61*
(in thousands of short tons)

Year	Total U.S.	Alcoa	%	Reynolds	%	Kaiser	%
1954	1,310,700	548,000	41.8	359,500	27.4	403,200	30.8
1955	1,609,200	706,500	43.9	414,500	25.8	428,200	26.6
1956	1,775,500	792,500	44.6	488,500	27.5	434,500	24.5
1957	1,839,000	792,500	43.1	488,500	26.6	498,000	27.1
1958	2,184,250	788,250	36.1	601,000	27.5	537,000	24.6
1959	2,336,050	798,250	34.2	638,300	27.3	609,500	26.1
1960	2,468,250	853,250	34.6	701,000	28.4	609,500	24.7

Source: Compiled from American Metal Market, *Metal Statistics* (New York, 1955–61).

the three newcomers would account for only twelve percent of national primary aluminum capacity. The main effect of the now realized threat of entry was to stimulate the major players even more to invest in their own capacity expansions, which further reinforced the oligopoly.

In the mid-1950s, there were some 6,900 light-metal processing plants in the United States (in addition to smelters) that relied at least in part on aluminum that they processed for the more than 24,000 firms that used the metal. As for more direct intraindustry competition, some 200 companies and more than 300 plants fabricated aluminum mill products. Most of the sheet, plate, foil, wire, and cable continued to be produced by the major integrated corporations, but extrusions, drawn tubing, forgings, and powder and paste were increasingly the province of nonintegrated "independents." Castings had long been extremely competitive, and the market shares of independents in all sectors of mill fabrications, other than foil, were growing steadily.[81]

The welfare of independent aluminum fabricators received considerable Government attention. House committees on small business and monopoly power monitored the aluminum industry constantly, hearing complaints and taking testimony on the industry at every turn. Complaints from the independents that metal was in short supply posed political problems for the major producers, who also had to meet their obligations to meet the demands of the Government stockpile. This put added pressure on the majors to expand their primary capacities. Complaints that the integrated producers were subjecting independents to a price squeeze bloomed like hardy perennials in the halls of Congress. Adding some intellectual respectability to the populist rhetoric of hostile congressmen, a young regulatory economist, Alfred Kahn, advocated the divestiture of the fabricating facilities of the "big three" producers, which would put all aluminum ingot for sale on the open competitive market.[82]

That such sentiments might achieve even a modicum of respectability generated enormous pressure on integrated aluminum producers to keep margins from narrowing. Alcoa had an obvious political interest, in the words of Leon Hickman, "to keep the spread satisfactory."[83] Moreover, Alcoa had a strong interest in keeping all the customers for its metal well supplied at reasonable prices. At one point, in 1953, Wilson struck a long-term contract with Aluminium Limited to purchase 600,000 tons of metal over six years. The Canadian metal would enable Alcoa to meet the requirements of small fabricators in times of great demand – again, an important antitrust consideration – without losing customers directly to Limited.[84]

Also, semifabricated products yielded significantly higher profits than did the production of their inputs, and Alcoa was involved in virtually all semifabricated markets. Therefore, under conditions of growing demand, the company would have been very foolish indeed to run afoul of the Government by keeping ingot prices (over which it had more control) too high relative to prices of fabrications (over which it had less control). The ability of independent extruders to take market share from the large, integrated corporations by providing better service and prices on small runs belied complaints that reflected more the smaller producers' sense of uncertainty about the future than the reality of the present.[85]

There was also the matter of growing competition from outside the country. Aluminium Limited was fast becoming a threat with its lower power and labor costs and its ability to cross-subsidize American sales with higher per-pound revenues from overseas markets. In the war's aftermath, Limited's ability to export into the United States was hampered for a time by a strong Canadian dollar, but by the late 1940s, the Canadian Company was showing signs of becoming a low-price preference leader. Limited had a capacity roughly equal to Alcoa's and the lowest costs in the business, offset only partially by United States trade policy.[86] As tariffs were lowered, in 1948, and again, in 1951, Limited preferred to hold the line on prices rather than risk demands for higher tariffs. In 1958, Limited would lead a downward revision of ingot prices. Until then,

Canada was content to reap nice margins on U.S. sales. The Soviet Union entered the world market in 1955, and its increasing sales in markets that had once belonged to Limited ultimately put pressure on the United States producers, as capacity outgrew demand by 1958. Accusations of "economic warfare" were fired by the Canadian and American industries at the Soviets, who were willing to sell their aluminum below Limited's list price (a practice U.S. producers would emulate during the recession).[87] Even though Russian aluminum would not in the long run become a major factor in Western world markets, it portended a latent problem in the international aluminum economy: the advent of Government-owned smelters that might sell not merely below list, but below cost.

Competition did not undermine a basic article of belief that had been present since the beginning of the business, that aluminum was "essentially a displacement material." It was still necessary to adapt the aluminum in its unfinished and semifinished states to manufacturing processes that were geared to other metals and to generate products for end uses in which aluminum could be shown to have a significant advantage.[88] All aluminum producers held this basic view; in this regard, they had a common interest, just as they had a common interest in maintaining stable prices. But as they also had to compete with each other once new markets were established, they devised ways to compete without savaging their price structures. Thus, nonprice forms of competition were pursued with increasing vigor. In markets for semifabricated products, high-volume customers could hardly be expected to purchase all their requirements from a single source, unless there were some persuasive reason to prefer one source's goods over another's. The fight for market share thus came increasingly to involve improving sales and service and increasing advertising of specialized applications, wherever those applications could be made to appear to be differentiated.

Alcoa also found itself drawn more and more into competition for end consumer markets. The Reynolds brothers, with their background in consumer goods and experience in distribution and marketing, led the way in transforming aluminum into a greater variety of finished products. As a materials producer that had concentrated mainly on markets in semifabricated goods, Alcoa was being drawn into largely unfamiliar territory. Immediately after the war, the entrepreneurial "Billy" Reynolds had embarked on "a frenzy of fabrication," spinning out aluminum toys, rowboats, home freezers, golf clubs, cooking utensils, and other home products, all of which inspired other manufacturers and speeded up the process of civilian market penetration for the industry as a whole. David Reynolds, as head of his company's Sales Department, pushed steadily into industrial markets in windows, automobiles, trailers, and electrical products. Kaiser, on the other hand, operated a bit more like the traditional Alcoa, but it too had to adapt to the threat that Reynolds might not only gain a significant lead in new end-market sales, but in the process might also drive many independent customers for semifabricated products out of business.[89]

In other words, competitive pressures altered the rules of market strategy just enough so that Alcoa had to reform its approaches to the game. Alcoa had always marketed its major product lines through sales engineers, whose task was to educate industrial customers on the qualities of aluminum, to help them develop techniques for its fabrication, and to assist them in establishing and promoting end uses. In 1954, in order to stimulate consumer sales for new aluminum products, Alcoa took its cue from Reynolds and hired a small group of salesmen without technical backgrounds to sell roofing sheet on an experimental basis. A steep rise in sales of that product convinced the head of sales, R. V. Davies, that nontechnical people were better at promoting certain classes of products, and recruiting practices were altered accordingly.[90]

Pressure from Reynolds deeply affected Alcoa's approach to advertising. When the public thought of aluminum products, "Reynolds" more than "Alcoa" was likely to come to mind. The company's only well-known brand name historically was "Wear-Ever," and that had not necessarily been identified with Alcoa in the minds of consumers. Now it tried to sell products branded with some version of the corporate name, such as "Alcoa Wrap," which competed with "Reynolds Wrap" household foil. In April 1955, "See It Now" aired the company's first ads for aluminum as a brand under a new Alcoa trademark. The company even inaugurated promotions to "presell" consumers on final products that the company itself would not necessarily manufacture or distribute. $70,000 was set aside for advertisements for manufacturers of aluminum outdoor furniture with the expectation that manufacturers, in turn, would agree to purchase Alcoa metal while pressing the ads on the distributors of lawn products.[91]

In competing for new customers, Alcoa could still play a very strong suit with its superior research capabilities. But research, too, was changing under pressures to attack the market. Ever since the war, the Laboratories had been undergoing a slow but steady reorientation toward projects that promised short-term payoffs in new product development, in new product-related process inventions, in new alloys, and in production processes that promised to lower costs in high-margin areas of production.[92] Research into structural applications, for example, boosted Alcoa's thrust into monumental architecture, the most lucrative sector of the strongest market in the industry. Alcoa may not always have been first into markets with new product ideas, but its 700 technical staff members, compared (in 1955) to Kaiser's 110 and Reynolds' 100, gave it a sustained advantage in innovation across the board.[93]

In almost every aspect of corporate life, competition made business more complicated and the pursuit of new products and markets more urgent. Nevertheless, Alcoa's basic strategy was slow to change. Alcoa approached the market as a maker of metal. Its main business was what it had always been, to increase primary aluminum sales. It was a producer of "crude and semicrude aluminum," competing with a variety of other materials, with other integrated aluminum smelters, with secondary smelters, and with makers of semifinished products.[94] Every ton of aluminum that Fritz Close sold to provide skin for a new office building was a ton more production for Alcoa's smelters. The pursuit of this traditional strategy, however, was becoming less viable under conditions that allowed the price of primary aluminum to drop in a leisurely fashion while priming the markets for new applications. Now the company had to react quickly to defend its business against competition along the entire chain of production, from mine to metal to value-added aluminum products. Fortunately for Alcoa, it had pockets deep enough to sustain its leading market share through a less burdensome program of investment than could be managed by its principal rivals.

It is true that after 1948, new investment in the industry had occurred "in the abnormal context of a defense economy,"[95] but that ought not obscure the fact that investment itself had become a major form of competition. Alcoa's investment strategy, we have seen, was less aggressive than that of its principal rivals, but the company possessed a long-term advantage in having a stronger equity base than either Reynolds or Kaiser. Its interest costs were lower, and a greater proportion of its expansion could be financed internally. In hard times, it would be less exposed to the perils of leverage (the more rapid decline of income relative to sales because of ongoing interest charges). In the 1960s, a new round of even greater growth would be sustained not only by a generally favorable business climate, but also by an abiding belief that aluminum was still young, that many of its best applications lay untapped, and that an increasing number of firms could flourish in ever-widening markets.

Winning labor peace

Alcoa's postwar expansion depended heavily on its relations with organized labor, which, after World War II, entered a period of economic and political "normalcy." For its part, the company sought to enter agreements that would assure stability on the production lines and predictable patterns of bargaining. While growing rapidly under competitive conditions, the last thing the company wanted to do was to take a strike, preferring instead to trade generous wage and work-rule concessions in exchange for labor peace. The aluminum unions, for their part, consolidated their positions as bargaining agents for rank-and-file workers by institutionalizing their control over all matters relating to economic and working conditions. It was as much in the interest of the union leadership as of the company to prevent independent, "wildcat" strikes by workers. By late 1950, the company and its unions had worked out ground rules for coexistence that would last for more than two decades.

By the end of the war, the United Steelworkers of America had emerged as the main force among aluminum unions. The USWA had already absorbed the debt-ridden, 20,000-member Aluminum Workers of America, CIO, in 1944. But when Steelworker president Philip Murray failed to fulfill a promise to rename his organization to reflect aluminum's participation, Local 302 of New Kensington, already chafing under a perceived decline in services from the national, went into rebellion. A bitter struggle for control of the New Kensington Works erupted in 1948, when USWA district officials charged the local leadership with communism and malfeasance. The USWA was, in turn, accused of acquiescing in Alcoa's plans to force speedups on the production line. Democratic party and local church politics were drawn into the imbroglio. A parish priest, Casimir Orlemanski, came to the defense of local leaders against district leader John Hart, who was president of the Catholic Trade Unionists. After an inconclusive union "trial," the matter was finally resolved on behalf of the district representatives.[96] That settled, the Steelworkers consolidated its control over its most important local unit.

The formal contours of Alcoa's postwar labor relations were already being shaped by the USWA, which struck its first master agreement with the company in 1947. In it, the union and the company agreed to provisions that banned strikes and lockouts, providing instead a set of grievance procedures that were capped by arbitration. The new grievance procedures contained a mandatory "fourth step," so that representatives of the presidents of the company and the union would jointly hear grievances that could not be settled at the local level. Thereafter, arbitration would be conducted by a three-man panel, one of whom was a mutually agreed-upon disinterested party. The agreement also established seniority as the criterion for determining layoffs and the filling of new job vacancies and guaranteed minimum hours of work be provided for regular employees. Healthy wage increases were provided by the contract, befitting the bargaining power of the USWA, and the company agreed to provide group insurance for death, sickness, accidents, and hospitalization. Clauses providing for the checkoff of union dues and maintenance of membership, for which the unions had fought so strenuously during the war years, were included, though the latter could not be enforced in states with "open-shop" laws. The wage portions of the agreement could be renegotiated yearly, and in 1949, a pension plan was added to the collective bargaining agreement.[97] Subsequent contracts did not vary in basic principle from the 1947 agreement until 1956, when Alcoa and its major unions agreed to a longer cycle of three-year contracts.

Although the company might have been expected to enjoy some strategic advantage vis-à-vis a divided union structure, wages and benefits were largely determined by master contract negotiations with the USWA, who, along with the United Auto Workers constituted the elite class of American workers. Alcoa's agreements with the USWA were generally followed by the old AFL aluminum workers unions, most of which were consolidated under the leadership of the Aluminum Workers International (originating in the East St. Louis refinery) in 1952. This pattern continued after the merger of the AFL and CIO in 1955. The United Auto Workers, which, after the war, controlled company plants in four locations, also negotiated separately, but the basic outlines of its agreements also followed the general pattern set by the Steelworkers. (More than a dozen smaller unions involving several hundred workers in specialized craft areas negotiated their own agreements with the company.[98])

The USWA took the lead by virtue of its enormous bargaining power and its highly disciplined, centralized structure. By contrast, the AWI, which would eventually merge with the Brick and Glassworker unions, operated with a much looser, more democratic structure, and its national representatives had to await ratification from local affiliates, where its officers were usually drawn from the ranks of Alcoa employees. The AWI was often slow to arrive at unified courses of action, therefore, the USWA, which could move more quickly, usually set the standards for aluminum workers on a company-wide basis. As a result, complained a former Alcoa labor specialist, "We were constantly having our nose broken in steel."[99]

The evolving oligopolistic structure of the industry was reflected in a system of pattern bargaining that became the norm in labor relations after World War II. Agreements between the major aluminum unions and Kaiser and Reynolds came more or less routinely to follow the patterns set by Alcoa. In 1956, both Reynolds and Alcoa suffered shutdowns in their USWA plants until both companies agreed to pacts that followed the steel industry pattern, on the one hand, and that would be followed by the Aluminum Workers International, on the other. This general pattern of aluminum labor negotiations was not a matter of company or union policy (indeed, the unions did not communicate very well with each other), but the "rules of the game" were well understood. On a more formal basis, union and company officials worked together on standards and procedures for rationalizing wage structures for various job categories.[100]

Alcoa's unions followed the lead of their national organizations in seeking to make their influence in "external" political arenas. By the late 1940s, aluminum locals were participating in political action committees of the type that had originally emerged during the war to campaign for the reelection of President Roosevelt. Union and company officials found themselves arrayed on different sides of the civic arena as well as on different sides of the bargaining table. As a result, communities in which Alcoa had once enjoyed dominant social and political influence – such as Alcoa, Tennessee; Bauxite, Arkansas; and Massena, New York – lost their unitary, "company" character. The more traditional, "paternal" style of management, which over the years had extended beyond the boundaries of the plant into the everyday routines of local community life, was mortally wounded by the new labor structure.

Alcoa's executives accepted the new labor structure but remained uncomfortable with it. They adhered to the ideal of a unitary corporate family, and beneath the veneer of acquiescence lay a strong antipathy to unions. Attempts to organize new sectors of the workforce, such as clerical or "white collar" employees were staunchly resisted whenever they arose. Management continued to blame unions for bad worker morale and for resisting improvements in productivity.

An interesting manifestation of management attitudes exists in an unusual memorandum prepared in 1948 by a Personnel Department manager, apparently an appeal for an expanded corporate communications effort. According to Lyle Mercer, the key to high worker productivity improvements was strong morale, which in turn depended on an enlightened management's ability to reach the individual worker by communicating pertinent facts about the nature of capitalist enterprise, the economics of the aluminum industry, and the desirability of embracing technological improvements and other cost-saving measures in the workplace. In particular, management had to recognize the adverse effects of mass-production routines and unionism, both which threatened to destroy individual egos and initiative. Management also had to acknowledge the worker's right and need to know more about the business and operations of the company. Only through more cooperative efforts in employee education and communication could the company establish a genuine community of interest with its workers; otherwise (to quote a prominent steel executive), labor in a mass-production environment would continue to degenerate "from craftsmanship to rote, from pride of achievement to listless nonentity ... [,to] dissatisfaction, dissension, and willingness to be led into slowdowns and strikes."[101]

"The unions," Mercer argued, "in their attempt to promote solidarity by eliminating competition and independent thinking among employees are attacking successfully the principle that men can advance through their own ability and work." Unions also distorted reasonable company appeals to workers to increase efficiency, so that "they can benefit from improvements which decrease costs and improve quality." Mercer nonetheless believed that the individual worker, if not the union, was redeemable – that the company could instill directly in the worker a proper sense of loyalty to the firm through "knowledge that the welfare of employees, management, and stockholders is dependent upon each other." A concerted and systematic effort at employee education would ultimately "improve the efficiency of the organization, ... increase sales, ... increase the real wages of our employees, ... increase profits, and, at the same time, ... sell our products at lower prices" in a competitive environment.[102]

At first blush, it would be easy to dismiss Mercer's memorandum as an atavistic broadside, a plea for a return to pre-Depression ideals of welfare capitalism. In fact, his proposal was rooted in the fashionable contemporary wisdom of "professional" industrial relations, the position of which was moving away from the corporate paternalism that had governed labor–management relations. Implicit in the memorandum was an assumption that the worker be treated, if not as a partner in the enterprise, at least as an informed stakeholder. But this was an ideal that neither management nor labor could live up to. In years to come, a more adversarial pattern of company–union relations became institutionalized through the collective-bargaining process. To put it another way, "Labor" and "Management" became more or less permanently institutionalized classes of corporate citizens, dealing with each other in an internal labor market. Terms of employment – hiring, firing, compensation, and conditions of work – were no longer the domain of the boss and the worker, nor even the corporation and its several employees. Instead, they became subject to the collective arrangements of corporate management and corporate labor in accordance with rule-bound, bureaucratic norms.

One important norm was the routinization of adversarial conflict imposed by the Master Agreement. Disputes about economic issues were muted for long stretches of time until specified dates when both the company and the unions could make their positions known and debate them through some kind of orderly process. Both Ben Fischer, who negotiated with Alcoa for the Steelworkers during this period, and Robert Heinemann, Alcoa's chief labor relations negotiator after 1947, understood how crucial it was to "modernize and make somewhat more precise and more businesslike the contracts and the [personal] relationships" during the negotiating sessions. This helped dampen, though it did not eliminate, much of the emotionalism that had attended earlier meetings, thus turning confrontations into true negotiations.[103] On the other hand, the triennial cycles placed such do-or-die weight on the negotiations that the threat of a strike loomed for months before master agreements were settled. Hints of problems at any one company could scare off customers, and so Alcoa was determined to minimize the perception that its own labor problems might be serious.[104] As mentioned, management enjoyed some potential advantage in that neither of the two major aluminum unions, acting alone, could shut down all the company's operations. But the threat was always present. In the winter of 1951–2, as the Korean War raged on, both the Aluminum Workers and the Steelworkers exerted pressure on Alcoa and Kaiser, bringing on the intervention of the Wage Stabilization Board. It was not until late July that Alcoa was able to put the threat of a major strike to rest by offering substantial increases in wages and benefits. The Steel-workers had previously called a strike in conjunction with its de-mands for pension benefits in nine Alcoa plants in 1949 and would strike again, as noted above, in 1956, but the Aluminum Workers were, by comparison, relatively quiescent.[105]

Still, according to a veteran company labor relations officer, there was "a fair amount of confrontation" at the local plant level, where supervisors encountered ongoing resistance to changes in schedul-ing, crew sizes, work rules, and management styles. Workers grieved and occasionally walked out in response to "unfair" or "undignified" treatment from their supervisors. Not long after the war, a small wildcat strike at the north fabricating plant at Alcoa, Tennessee, illustrated how passions on the shop floor could override the letter of formal agreements on work rules. When a worker refused to move a tarpaulin in order to make way for a delivery truck (on the grounds that it was not his job), the union's plant chairman intervened and was himself suspended for refusing to return to work. This triggered a plant-wide strike. The union was able to persuade the strikers to go back to work only after the company dropped disciplinary charges against all but the plant chairman, who was reinstated only after the grievance procedure had gone through the fourth step, arbitra-tion. Similar skirmishes would be fought over and over again in Alcoa plants in the decades to come, but they were usually regarded as provincial and peculiar problems by the national union organi-zations, and so their disruptive effects on the corporation could be isolated and contained.[106]

Throughout the 1950s, most of Alcoa's labor–management dis-putes would emerge and be resolved on local turf. Within the broad parameters of the master union contracts, plant managers were given substantial freedom to work out local problems, which they did with varying degrees of success. At the corporate level, the com-pany's union relations remained harmonious by most industrial standards. Workers' wages and benefits expanded steadily, save for a period of stabilization during the Korean War, and regional wage differentials were abolished. In 1957, when faced with the threat of a major USWA strike, as the nation's economy slid into its worst slump since the Great Depression, Alcoa finally agreed to guarantee wages to employees laid off from work for the equivalent of twenty-two hours per week for a year.[107]

Alcoa's response to the recession of 1957–8 is telling. It was a wretched year for business; by late spring, industrial production was down fourteen percent from the year before, and some five million

workers were cast onto the unemployment rolls. The center industries were especially hard hit, and the aluminum companies, having
grown used to years of almost unbroken prosperity, were forcefully
reminded of the fundamentally cyclical nature of their business.
Alcoa tried to minimize layoffs, even while cutting back sharply on
capital expenditures by postponing completion of several major projects. Otherwise, the inevitable wave of cost-cutting programs aimed
at prolonging the life of equipment, increasing productivity, and
improving efficiency swept through the plants, mitigated, in the eyes
of workers, by management's willingness to implement expected
increases in compensation. Between 1946 and 1957, the average
Alcoa worker's base pay increased from $1.09 to $2.44 per hour, or
123 percent of the national manufacturing average.[108] For years
afterward, Alcoa's workers enjoyed ever-higher wages, benefits, and
standards of safety and job security. There were few challenges to
the workplace rules of law as established by the master contracts,
all in exchange for which the company gained a good measure of
labor peace. Unlike its big brothers in steel, who were shut down
in 1959 by the USWA in response to proposed work-rule changes,
Alcoa was not about to take a strike.

In the 1930s, Alcoa's workers had fought to achieve mere recognition of their rights to organize in independent unions. Through
much of the 1940s, the unions had struggled to establish their bargaining power over wages and work rules. By 1958, there was no
longer any question of the union's status in the corporate structure.
As in every major industry, the dual nature of the worker's corporate
citizenship came to be accepted as just another aspect of the American social and political condition in which membership in overlapping, even competing entities is taken for granted. Arkansan bauxite
miners who lived through the tense years of union organization
explained that the company had their loyalty, but that the union
had become a matter of economic necessity and protection. In retrospect, a veteran Cleveland forging press operator viewed the entire
problem as a matter of equal but competing interests:

> At times people will say the union is bad or the company is bad.
> That is going to go on forever. You'll never be able to change
> that but it wouldn't make any difference how good or how bad
> the union head or the company head was. It wouldn't make any
> difference! You still need that system of checks and balances.
> ... I believe that if you turn one loose – if you let them go hog
> wild – that's exactly what they'll do – go hog wild! As long as

you have the arguing going on day in and day out, it [the organized labor system] checks it and holds it in balance pretty good.[109]

From the standpoint of the rank-and-file worker, both the union and Alcoa were institutions that competed for one's loyalty, buttered one's bread, prescribed and bound one's daily labor. And though it might be in the company's interest to recognize the rank-and-file's indifference to, or alienation from, union politics, it was never wise to try to exploit it. Both institutions mattered. The company held its worker's loyalty by gaining a reputation for concern over safety in an industry with a large number of dangerous jobs; for relatively clean working conditions in an industry that generated its share of dirt, smoke, and hazardous pollutants; and for reasonable packages of wages and benefits. The unions took credit for keeping the company focused on the concerns of workers for economic security, safety, and fair treatment on the job. There remained, said former Steelworker vice president Ben Fischer, "big gobs of the master–servant relationship" that had prevailed in the more familial company of the prewar era, but it was precisely Alcoa's lingering paternalism that made labor–management relations so benign by comparison to the USWA's experience with its adversaries in the steel industry.[110]

Alcoa's structure in 1957

After World War II, many center industry firms coped with problems of increasing scale, complexity, and diversity by regrouping their operations into decentralized divisions through which different classes of products could be made and sold into different markets. They created "general offices" whose executives concentrated on overall strategic and policy matters, while short-term tactical decisions for engineering, production, and marketing were left to the divisions. Most large companies in the metals industries, on the other hand, remained functionally organized enterprises in which the coordination of tactical and operational decisions remained the responsibility of top management. The durability of the functional structure in metals was due to the specialized nature of most semi-finished product lines, where production was geared to the specifications of other manufacturerers. A case for more centralized decision-making could be supported by the highly integrated streams of production – from mine to metal, from smelting to the fabrication, sale, and distribution of specialized products – that characterized the large metals companies. This was the prevailing sentiment within Alcoa where, during the 1950s, attempts were made increasingly to centralize the coordination of capacity of various fabricating operations with the trends of the market, at one end, and the output of all production processes leading to the smelting of aluminum, at the other.

Alcoa was a more complex enterprise than companies producing other nonferrous metals or steel. Its aluminum products were more diverse; its markets were evolving more rapidly. Given the company's traditions of local autonomy, it could, at least in theory, have adopted a more divisional form of organization based on markets rather than functions. But neither growth, nor the penetration of new fields of business, nor the widening range of marketing and technical problems prompted the company to reassess its basic structure. Instead, it displayed an increasing tendency toward centralization. Only in its oldest end-consumer business did Alcoa operate an executive "division": The Aluminum Cooking Utensil Company ("Wear-Ever") functioned as a semiautonomous entity with its own specialized production and sales operations.[111]

At the same time, Alcoa's management was determined to preserve a friendly and cooperative atmosphere in the executive offices. As Alcoa trebled in size during the decade after the war, it was not so much the public reserve of Alcoa's executives as their informal and collegial behavior inside the company that impressed outside observers. "Because their responsibilities are so thoroughly intertwined with the responsibilities of their fellows," explained *Business Week* in 1953, "Alcoa officers stand on practically no formality. They walk into each other's offices freely, answer their own telephones." The highest value was placed on constant, continuing "liaison between all sections of Alcoa's executive suite." There were no rigid channels of reporting. "Each officer keeps his fellows aware of what goes on. Each does so meticulously enough to keep Alcoa's top organization both fluid and precise, unstratified yet effective." Not only did senior executives answer their own phones ("I can handle an insurance salesman just as easy as anyone else," quipped Hunt), they made a point of encouraging their core group of 1,200 middle managers to convey any important ideas to the executive suites directly.

A typical day with Frank Magee was a case in point. As production head, Magee had senior line responsibility for Alcoa's seven smelters, fifteen power stations, and seventeen fabricating facilities in fifteen states, all of which he visited at least once a year. He was also responsible for coordinating his Production Department with Sales and for promoting the company among local, state, and federal officials, a task that had become, since the antitrust case, "almost a fetish." Magee had authority to make corporate decisions for his department, and his ubiquitous presence in the offices of the other vice presidents bespoke his status as a kind of chief operating officer. But what also struck the reporter was the cooperative process through which decisions emerged. If M. M. Anderson were negotiating a basic wage contract, Magee would naturally be expected to become involved, "practically at his [Anderson's] command." When the vice president for purchasing, Thomas D. Jolly, took up a major procurement problem, Magee was just naturally expected to work closely with him.[112]

In short, Alcoa's management tried to counteract the rigidifying tendencies of formal structure with informal styles of behavior. Chief Wilson gained some notoriety for his "loose executive structure," for conducting his management meetings in the manner of "a family debating society," and for encouraging rigorous discussions of differences of opinion.[113] Wilson's style was reported to have daunted a team of Harvard Business School case writers who left Alcoa "shaking their heads" in disbelief.[114] Nonetheless, it was the nurturing of individual initiative, Wilson believed, that was vital to corporate health in an increasingly complex industry. He was concerned lest the personal strengths of the individual manager wither in the growth of bureaucracy. At the same time, it was essential to keep channels of communication open to bring the benefits of collective wisdom to manager's particular problems. As he explained it in 1955,

> The biggest danger in the way we operate is that you cannot maintain the responsibility in a specific individual if he ever feels that he hasn't got complete control of those activities for which he is responsible. But being able to use the thinking of many individuals is a tremendous asset. Ours is the exact opposite of military organization where you go to the top of one department, then across and down to someone. Here, anybody can go across. Keep it this way and any executive, big or little, can feel, and be sure, that the whole company is his oyster.[115]

Sustaining that feeling, which had been easier to promote in a much smaller firm, went far to cement the vaunted loyalty Alcoa managers felt toward their company.

It should not be surprising, then, that the basic outline of Alcoa's formal structure remained somewhat old-fashioned. The first organization chart one finds for the post-World War II era is dated May 1957 and is revealing in its simplicity.[116] Top management consisted of Davis, who in fact was virtually inactive and about to retire, Hunt, the chairman of the executive committee, Wilson, the company's president, and executive vice president Magee. The executive committee had the power to act in the stead of the entire board, even in the declaration of dividends and the election of officers. It was, however, more generally used as a convenience between quarterly board meetings to enable quick decisions on matters, such as bond issues, that required legal action. Wilson and Magee were in fact responsible for running the business, but they had no large staff, relying instead on the heads of the various line departments (even Research, Industrial Relations, and Public Relations were treated as line departments) and the heads of departmental divisions with whom they convened regularly in small, unscheduled meetings. In essence, corporate decisions were arrived at, not by fiat, but through innumerable discussions. Corporate policy evolved in the manner of an unwritten constitution: it was learned, not through written codes but through the accretions of tradition and experience. In like manner, any new idea about policy was seldom written down; instead, once agreed upon through verbal agreements among corporate executives, so it appeared to *Fortune*, "it percolates down through the corporation – *sotto voce*."[117]

It sounds almost idyllic. But from a middle-management perspective, Alcoa had to work much harder to ensure adequate communications across functional specialities. This was obvious at the plant level, where in contrast to the free-flowing dialogue that was characteristic of the Pittsburgh headquarters, managers experienced great difficulty communicating across functional lines. By 1950 at Alcoa, Tennessee, for example, there were four distinct functional groups – power, smelting, fabrication, and construction, each reporting to different organizations in Pittsburgh. When the plant had been small (by modern standards), it was possible to coordinate day-to-day activities on an informal basis through the workings of "fairly close personal relationships of people who had grown up together," according to John Harper, who had served in Tennessee as a power manager. But after the war, the plant manager could no longer achieve enough coordination among the groups to eliminate conflicts and duplication of effort. Even as reporting lines converged at the "divisional" (subdepartmental) levels at headquarters, there was precious little communication between managers. "The Smelting and Fabricating Divisions were both quite powerful," explained

Harper (whose Tennessee power group reported to the former) "and were headed by two real characters [V. C. Doerschuck and R. R. Stevenson] who really didn't have much to do with each other." At levels below top management, unpleasant struggles over power and "turf" often erupted in the absence of clearly defined channels of communication.[118]

In reality, coordinating operations at the middle levels of management, in Pittsburgh as well as at the plants, sales offices, and laboratories, required substantial improvement in channeling information across functional lines. This was achieved gradually after the war through the evolution of an "informal" system of committees, the number of which would approach 100 by 1960![119] The impetus for Alcoa's committee structure came largely from a need to improve communications between Sales Department product managers, who coordinated production and sales for particular product lines, the Engineering Department, whose Production Planning Division scheduled all orders through the plants, and the Alcoa Research Laboratories. Indeed, the only interdepartmental groups that appear on the 1957 organization chart were the Research and Technology Policy Committee (chaired by Magee as executive vice president) and its subordinate Technology Committee. These bodies were composed of functional managers from Sales, Engineering and Purchasing, Personnel, and the Research Laboratories. But beneath this formal outline of responsibilities lay an array of "subcommittees" that kept communications flowing in less formal but nonetheless highly important channels. Alcoa's committee system made informal lines of reporting more vital than the formal hierarchy.[120]

The committee system also contributed to centralization. The R&D subcommittee system, in particular, illustrates the process. By the late 1940s, the Laboratories relied largely on informal communications with the rest of the company to establish new research priorities. Of two corporate-level groups concerned with innovation, one – the "General Committee," which had emerged in the 1930s under Roy Hunt to set overall policy and direction and allocate funds for R&D – was moribund. A Technical Committee, which also had its origins in the early 1930s, was charged with carrying out the actual coordinating functions of some twenty technical subcommittees organized around the research problems of the various technical operations of the business. But the Technical Committee, which had functioned well in the days when the company was small enough so that a few senior people could grasp the totality of its technology, had become an unwieldy forum "in which many individuals, each representing a different constituency, came together to discuss and to work out compromises in the R&D agenda."[121]

In 1950, R&D was reorganized under the aegis of the Research and Technical Policy Committee, which approved the overall R&D program and budget. The new committee was "to assist in bringing the activities of Alcoa Research Laboratories into still closer relationship with the Company's overall interests." Under such conditions, there was a proliferation of technical subcommittees, which became the loci for setting the direction and funding of R&D projects. They convened three or four times a year to plan and budget research and development activities, while "task forces," subgroups of the subcommittees, dealt with more specific research areas. By 1952, one finds written reports from a "Commercial Research Department" offering analyses of market opportunities to guide research efforts – long and short-term, large and small – into the most profitable channels. Meanwhile, an interfunctional, corporate-wide Technical Committee, which by the late 1940s had come to preside over the development of some dozen laboratory subcommittees, was beginning to assert tighter control over the budgeting of diverse areas of research on a line-item basis. In a series of memos in 1951, Conrad Nagel, the head of the Technical Committee, insisted on more routine reporting from the subcommittee heads and directed them to notify Technical Committee members of meeting schedules. Working from the Laboratories, Van Horn strengthened the subcommittee system as a corporate coordinating device. Staffed with research scientists, plant engineers, and marketing personnel, the subcommittees made recommendations to a central body for the funding and management of new projects on a line-item basis. Over the next decade, the subcommittees assumed increasing responsibility not merely to coordinate, but to make basic decisions on research and development.[122]

The subcommittee system had originally been conceived as a cross-functional vehicle for coordinating development of different technologies in the plants with the Laboratories' research activities on a "bottom-up" principle. The idea, as originally sponsored by its champions in the Laboratories, was to encourage innovations on a broad front to accommodate the growing complexities of production technologies, especially in the fabricating areas. It was intended to enhance existing practice in the company whereby R&D projects were conceived and worked out by cooperative efforts between plant engineers and R&D personnel. But as the company grew larger and more complex, and as the pressures of competition weighed more heavily on the sales and operations members of the subcommittees, the subcommittees increased their authority and power more than had been anticipated. What had begun as a vehicle to gather and coordinate information on the R&D efforts of various departments and divisions was turning into a mechanism for corporate control over the funding and direction of R&D projects. By 1953, according to the chairman of the alloy development subcommittee, rather than encouraging more bottom-up innovation in the plants, the subcommittees were policing plant activities ever more tightly, stifling local initiatives. The trend toward rule by subcommittee continued; however, old-line research people bridled under it, and by 1960, the Technical Committee made it a matter of policy that only limited and controlled experiments be launched by local initiative.

One might wonder whether Alcoa's growing multitude of committees, which imposed some order on decision-making, was efficient. The sheer frequency of committee and interdepartmental meetings was cumbersome. But, as Alfred D. Chandler, Jr., discovered on a research trip to Pittsburgh, this was exactly the way Roy Hunt – who remained actively concerned with the maintenance of Alcoa's traditional structure – liked it. Managers, from top to bottom, from one department to the next, were knitted together in a network of personal relationships that perpetuated the feeling of a small, cohesive, family firm.[123]

But neither Alcoa's "open-door" style of corporate management nor its multitude of committees should obscure the basic underlying trend toward centralization – the characteristic tendency of functional organization. In addition to the company's high need for technological integration, which in turn reinforced the functional form of structure, centralization was fostered in part by the fear of antitrust – especially as it bore on output and pricing decisions. Better coordination of antitrust as well as of technological problems had become increasing obsessions of department heads at Pittsburgh, as they took on increasing responsibility during the 1950s for ensuring that uniform policies and practices were followed throughout the corporation.

Wilson and Magee had been steadily at work since the war, consolidating traditionally semiautonomous operations under Pittsburgh's corporate umbrella. Old bastions of corporate independence lost their separate legal status and, as their former heads retired, were put under the charge of younger managers who were subject to more direction from headquarters. The United States Aluminum Company was rendered inactive at the end of 1947. Within five

Fig. 6.7. Roy A. Hunt, keeper of Alcoa's "small-company" tradition, standing in front of a picture of his father Alfred E. Hunt.

years, Alcoa Mining (bauxite), Aluminum Ore (alumina), and Aluminum Seal (which had made bottle caps and seals since the 1920s) became regular corporate divisions. The American Magnesium Corporation, after years of demonstrated inability to make money, was sold. With the exception of The Aluminum Cooking Utensil Company, the only domestic operations managed as subsidiary corporations were several railway trunk lines, power-generating companies, water companies, coal properties in Indiana, and a company to manage building services in connection with some district sales offices. International subsidiaries, on the other hand, grew out of necessity, as Alcoa made some expansive moves offshore. These included the Steamship Company, three bauxite exploration concerns, a Wear-Ever foreign sales organization, and the Surinam Aluminum Company. The last had been created to replace an older subsidiary, in order to develop power and smelting operations in addition to mining and refining. Alcoa International, Inc., was established in 1957 to conduct shipping and foreign sales operations. That same year, Alcoa took options on land not far from New Kensington, Pennsylvania, where it planned to consolidate its scattered research and development activities.[124]

As Alcoa grew larger and as the major markets for aluminum became more diverse, one might have asked if centralization would further embroil senior managers overmuch in the quotidian problems of operations at the expense of long-term planning. Chandler opined that more decentralized, divisional operations would enable the company to service its markets more efficiently.[125] But, as we shall see, Alcoa's next response to the increasing scale and complexity of operations was to tighten even further the central office's control over the traditional structure.

In August 1957, A. V. Davis retired, precipitating another succession in top management. The infirmities of age had finally caught up with the man who resigned from the chairmanship after an almost incredible sixty-nine years of service. He lived on until 1962, leaving behind a fortune estimated at as much as $400 million. Twice widowed and childless, he left part of his money to Evelyn Mitchell, his close companion since 1946, and part to some collateral relatives. He also left a substantial endowment to the Arvida Foundation. Most of Davis's wealth had been amassed in his second career as head of the Arvida Corporation, a real estate company that would soon fall into the control of the corrupt and horribly mismanaged Penn Central conglomerate. Davis, who had little sufferance for foolishness, was mercifully spared that embarrasing association.

Fig. 6.8. Arthur Vining Davis as he appeared at about the time of his retirement.

With Davis gone, Chief Wilson became Alcoa's second chairman, and Frank Magee stepped up to the presidency of a much larger, more complex enterprise than the one that had come out of World War II. A former salesman, who had already been serving as an untitled chief operating officer under Wilson, Magee would do little to alter the collegial style of top management. He would prove, however, to be a bold leader. In his tenure as president, he would further centralize Alcoa's administration while piloting the company through an aggressive new phase of growth.

7

Magee, Close, and Harper: covering the world in aluminum, 1958–1970

Even today, Alcoa managers like to recall "aluminum's golden years," which spanned the period from World War II to the OPEC oil embargo of 1973–4. That time was also, not coincidentally, the golden age of American business. The United States had emerged from the war as the industrial world's only healthy, intact economy, and in the ensuing quarter century, domestic markets boomed while new international markets emerged to take a growing share of the surging output of American manufacturers. In the general climate of industrial expansion, a growing number of aluminum producers invested almost fearlessly, confident that whatever they made would be taken up by an expanding world economy. Growth was by no means uninterrupted – the industry remained susceptible as ever to cyclical fluctuations. But when Alcoa emerged from the particularly harsh recession of 1957–8, its faith in the future was bolder than ever. Those were the days, said J. Tyson Kennedy, a district sales manager, when "we were going to cover the world in aluminum."[1]

After 1958, Alcoa tried to cover the world through new strategies of international expansion and high-volume production. At the same time, corporate governance passed into the hands of executive managers whose ties of kinship and friendship to major stockholders were increasingly attenuated and whose approaches to management were increasingly formal, bureaucratic, "modern." I. W. Wilson's successor, Frank Magee, had been a self-effacing member of the inner circle of top management in Pittsburgh, but as president, from 1958 to 1960, then as chairman, until 1963, he proved to be a bold leader, leading the company back into the international arena, and refining the company's functional structure – centralizing the corporation to a degree that would have been unthinkable under his predecessors.

Magee was succeeded by Lawrence Litchfield, a somewhat transitional figure, who had spent most of his career outside Pittsburgh as a bauxite engineer. As head of Alcoa's raw materials operations during the 1950s, Litchfield had worked mostly out of New York and was not drawn into the intimate circle of the Pittsburgh executive group until his appointment as executive vice president in 1959. During Litchfield's tenure as president (1960–3), Magee's influence remained strong. Then, as chairman (a post he held through 1965), Litchfield yielded effective authority to John Harper, who had succeeded him as president. He was not unimportant, however. More cosmopolitan than the traditional Alcoa executive, Litchfield brought with him an international outlook that enhanced Alcoa's expansion abroad, and he was an effective spokesman to the financial community during a period of renewed expansion.[2]

Frank Magee was one of three executives – John Harper and Fritz Close were the others – who embodied, or at least symbolized, Alcoa's transition from a relatively insular American manufacturer with a somewhat vague public image to a more diversified multinational with a high degree of social and political presence. They also represented a revival of Alcoa's reputation as an innovative corporation. Though widely acclaimed as a growth company in the 1950s, Alcoa had lost some of its glow as a technological innovator, if only by comparison to its new rivals. In the 1960s, it would reassert its claim to leadership in the development of aluminum products and processes.

Of the three, it was Close who stood for the company's revived entrepreneurial and technological spirit. Close, who served as chairman (though never as chief executive) from 1966 to 1970, was Alcoa's best salesman. He had led the company's entry into monumental building construction during the 1950s and was the boardroom's most vigorous champion of research and development. He was also well-known throughout the company's operations as the personification of Alcoa's fluid and informal style of communication. As the company's most visible advocate of new products, he was a powerful force behind Alcoa's move into very high-volume markets, where its size, deep pockets, and technological expertise proved advantageous in a more competitive industry. Though by no means the only one responsible for it, Close was the spiritual godfather of rigid container sheet (RCS), which was to become Alcoa and the industry's most important new product of the postwar era.

While Close was the corporate cheerleader for the development of new products on a grand scale, it was John Harper who approved the strategy that would gradually take Alcoa well beyond its traditional base, primary aluminum. Harper became chief executive in 1963, only three years after being appointed assistant production manager for smelting and fabricating, a meteoric rise to the top by Alcoa standards. Harper committed Alcoa to the greatest gamble of its postwar history by investing in the development and full-scale production of RCS for aluminum cans, well in advance of the market. Under Harper, Alcoa's strategic center of gravity shifted further away from smelting toward high-volume, high-margin fabricated products.

Harper also led Alcoa through several basic reforms. He enlarged the board of directors to reflect a wider spectrum of corporate views and interests, and he reformed Alcoa's administrative structure, moving away from Alcoa's strictly functional organization toward one based more on modern divisional lines. In his public persona, he was singular among Alcoa's leaders, before and since. A man of broad social vision, he promoted corporate–government relations in ways that might have alarmed his predecessors, but through his advocacy of corporate responsibility and his sensitivity to political and social demands for change, he steered Alcoa into closer alignment with the prevailing economic and cultural winds of post-1960 America.

Changing patterns of growth

It has been all too easy for nostalgic aluminum managers to view the first quarter century following World War II in a single descriptive frame of reference, as an unbroken era of steady growth when "the ups and downs of business cycles were not hard to live with and the industry itself, rather than the marketplace, set prices."[3] In fact, this widely shared, telescoped vision of the past is misleading. When brought into tighter focus, we can see that Alcoa's experience from the war through the 1960s was marked by four distinct phases of growth, each with its own set of problems as well as opportunities.

The first two phases of post-war growth fell during the period discussed in the last chapter, when Alcoa adjusted to its new, oligopolistic industry environment. The years 1946 to 1950 were a difficult time of readjustment, as Alcoa's management learned to cope with new rules of competitive behavior amidst uncertainty about the final disposition of Learned Hand's antitrust ruling. Yet, at the same time, the company increased its net income by about fifty-one percent on an increase in gross revenues of sixty-three percent. The second phase began with the Korean War, when Government defense programs provided a powerful new impetus for industry growth. Though not as direct a beneficiary of Government programs as some of its competitors, Alcoa could rely on having a substantial share of its metal going into the stockpile. This enhanced an otherwise prosperous industry environment in which stable patterns of oligopolistic pricing prevailed. Alcoa's strategies were inhibited by lingering pressures of antitrust (the company remained subject to court supervision until 1956); nonetheless, the company embarked on major investments in new facilities that increased revenues by sixty-two percent, between 1951 and 1957, during which time growing capacity was almost constantly pushed to the limits.[4] The book was finally closed on the great antitrust case just when profitable growth was becoming more difficult to achieve. The recession of 1957–8 brought prices tumbling, retarding a $600-million expansion program that had been launched in 1956. With the general economic recovery, Alcoa moved into a third phase of its postwar development, which was characterized by loose, ad hoc, and opportunistic strategies and by the erosion of oligopolistic price discipline. A fourth phase of growth between the war and 1970 was based in large part on high-volume, high-margin strategies attended by organizational reforms.

The recession of 1957–8 had been a shock, coming as it did at a time when all the North American primary producers were in the midst of aggressive capital expansion programs. The recession's aftermath was an extended period of excess capacity in the aluminum industry with downward pressure on prices. But having weathered the company's adjustment to the loss of its monopoly and previous cycles of hard times, Frank Magee remained optimistic. "The next 10 years," he said in 1960, when the company's profits had plunged to their worst level in a decade, "can be the best in the 43 years I've spent with this company."[5] Magee was determined that Alcoa continue to grow as aggressively as possible, and he followed almost every means within his ken to do so, including acquisition.

In 1959–60, Alcoa acquired three new subsidiaries in strategically important markets. Two of them, Rome Cable and Cupples Products, were undone by Alcoa's old nemesis, antitrust, but such initiatives marked a strong departure from the more inhibited strategies of his predecessors. "Building and construction" was the most important domestic market for aluminum and would continue to be so for several years, a fortuitous by-product of which business was Alcoa's entry into urban real estate development. All markets were fair game under Magee, and during his tenure, Alcoa continued to expand into finished and semifinished products of all kinds. And it was on Frank Magee's watch that Alcoa once again moved overseas.

Constraints on growth

Frank Magee's attempts to keep Alcoa moving forward were beset with problems. Some inhibitors to growth were simply matters of corporate competence. In 1959, the company moved more broadly into finished-product markets aimed at specialized users through its acquisition of companies in building, insulated cable, and magnet wire, and through internal diversification into such end products as aluminum siding, irrigation pipes, food packaging, telephone booths, and printed foil. The company's participation in most of these markets was unremarkable, if not unsuccessful. Sparked by competition from Kaiser and Reynolds, the development of "value-added" end markets had become a popular cause in the Sales Department, but Alcoa was never able to master consumer advertising and promotion. For example, its most visible, branded consumer good – apart from Wear-Ever utensils – was Alcoa Wrap, which had never been a strong competitor to the Reynolds' brand, so powerful was the latter company's identification with the product. Stories are legion about some of the more problematic aspects of Alcoa's brand name recognition. One of the funnier variants recalls a customer's complaint about the quality of "Alcoa's Reynolds Wrap."[6]

Consider the case of printed foil, which was fairly typical of Alcoa's desire to make money on value-added processes and which was also typical of Alcoa's chronic inability to develop downstream applications beyond the semifinished stage. In the 1950s, Reynolds sold printed foil directly to food companies, whereas Alcoa sold its industrial foil to other fabricators, who in turn laminated it, printed it, and then resold it for substantial profits. In 1959, Alcoa struck an agreement with R. R. Donnelley Company to run an eight-color rotogravure press, which Alcoa installed at Donnelley's plant in Chicago, and a small division was created to market the printed foil. After receiving a crash course in cellophane, paints, and inks, the company's salesmen discovered that the competition was fiercer and the profit margins lower than anticipated. Substantial losses in printed foil forced the wholesale abandonment of the project.[7]

A more fundamental problem lay in the structural position of Alcoa in the industry. Alcoa's moves downstream brought it into direct competition with too many of its own customers. Alcoa had been lured into many finished markets by the apparent success of its competitors, but the thrust forward was also defensive, a response to the activities of customers who were beginning to integrate backward.[8] But in those markets where technologies were simple and economies of scale unimportant, Alcoa simply could not compete. Smaller fabricators with lower labor and overhead costs could produce finished goods more cheaply. Moreover, the company's moves downstream exacerbated the price wars that were becoming endemic to the fabricating sectors of the industry. Even in those areas where technological sophistication and production economies were important, it was better for Alcoa to stick to its normal practice of working with customers to develop new end uses rather than trying to enter consumer markets directly. Alcoa wisely adhered to this tried-and-true strategy when it cooperated with the major can companies and breweries to develop markets for beverage cans, with General Electric to develop aluminum appliance components, and with auto manufacturers to develop engine parts and wheels, to all of which it could then sell its semifabricated sheet, extrusions, rod, wire, bar, forgings and castings in volume.

By the early 1960s, it was clear that many of the domestic markets for aluminum were maturing; prices were softening; margins on existing products were narrowing. Attempts to extend its product lines into end-user markets were, as we have already seen, not very successful. Monumental architecture was the one area in which Alcoa could hope to make substantial profits, based on high-margin sales of customized orders involving large quantities of metal. Aside from that, until the development of RCS, there was no grand strategy for large-scale growth. During Frank Magee's presidency, steps were taken toward diversification through the acquisition of companies with complementary technologies, but these steps were more opportunistic than strategic, more reactive than planned.

Magee's most expensive acquisition was Rome Cable and Wire Company, which was bought in March 1959 for 355,226 shares

Table 7.1. *Major markets for aluminum produced in the United States, 1960 and 1970 (in thousands of pounds)*

Market	1960 Pounds	% of Total	Rank	1970 Pounds	% of Total	Rank	1960–70 Annual rate of growth
Building and construction	1,325	26.7	1	2,768	26.6	1	7.6
Transportation	1,002	20.2	2	1,790	17.2	2	6.0
Containers and packaging	351	7.1	6	1,514	14.5	3	15.7
Electrical	614	12.3	3	1,428	13.7	4	8.8
Consumer durables	556	11.2	4	969	9.3	5	5.7
Machinery and equipment	374	7.5	5	642	6.2	6	5.6
Exports	326	6.5	—	567	5.5	—	5.7
Other	422	8.5	—	728	7.0	—	5.6

Source: The Aluminum Association, *1970 Aluminum Statistical Review* (New York, 1971).

of Alcoa common. This was an initiative of Fritz Close and Ralph Davies, the vice president of sales, who saw that in addition to its main line of products in copper wire and cable, Rome had small but good capabilities in the production of aluminum bare and insulated cable. In fact, Magee was a reluctant acquirer, not in principle but rather out of fear that Alcoa might try to manage businesses for which it had no competence. Despite his misgivings that the acquisition might take Alcoa too far afield into the copper business, the board approved the purchase. Rome, located in upstate New York, had done much of the insulating work for Alcoa's wire operations at Massena, and its aging CEO had wanted to sell it to Alcoa for some time. A second acquisition, that of Rea Magnet Wire Company, Inc., in Fort Wayne and Lafayette, Indiana, was made in January 1960 for 180,480 shares of common; it took Alcoa into more exotic, specialized applications of copper wire for use in electrical and electronic equipment. Cupples Products Corporation, also acquired in January 1960 for 64,209 shares of common, was another pet project of Close's. With plants in St. Louis, Dallas, and Dowagiac, Michigan, specializing in the manufacture, sale, and installation of aluminum curtain-wall, windows, and doors, Cupples would enable Alcoa to leverage its sales in architectural applications by offering high-volume customers a more integrated set of products and service.[9]

Rea Magnet Wire proved to be a reasonably profitable ancillary line of business for Alcoa until its sale in 1985, but Rome (which proved to be a bad investment almost from the beginning) and Cupples (which proved to be a good one) swept Alcoa back into the jaws of antitrust. Both companies were divested after adverse rulings in court. Alcoa had not sought advance advice on the acquisitions on the assumption that neither of these acquisitions would result in the kind of market share that should cause legal concern. That was a mistake, however, in the legal climate of the 1960s, when the Government was becoming ever more worried about the potential "anticompetitive" effects of mergers. Alcoa was to be rudely reminded that its size, power, and historic reputation as a monopoly were beacons to the Justice Department.[10]

The judicial reasoning in the Rome case seems, by modern standards, draconian. After winning in the District Court in 1962, Alcoa lost the Government's appeal to the Supreme Court in 1964, when that body, by six to three, rejected Alcoa's contention that copper should be included in the definition of the electrical cable market and took a hard line on any tendency toward the reduction of competition in the aluminum conductor business. For example, it was calculated that Rome had only about 1.3 percent of the aluminum conductor wire and cable market, but that by adding Rome's share to Alcoa's 27.8 percent, an industry that included a large number of small producers would suffer a "substantial lessening of competition" within Section 7 of the Clayton Act.[11] If anything, the court's ruling on Rome was an implicit attack on oligopoly framed in terms of its mere *potential* to lessen competition.

As for Cupples, Alcoa lost its case in the Missouri District Court in 1964,[12] after which the company decided not to appeal. Cupples had well under twenty percent of the market for curtain-wall, but here, Alcoa was foiled by a "smoking-gun" letter from Fritz Close to two of his subordinates that enthusiastically predicted that Cupples' business could be built up until Alcoa controlled forty percent of the market. That, according to Hickman, was "just a salesman's boast; there was no plan or anything." But the judge, focusing on Alcoa's deep pockets, took it seriously and ordered the company to divest. It was hard, lamented Hickman, to win an antitrust case in the 1960s. "I think a job was done on us both times."[13]

That Alcoa ran so quickly into legal problems with its new acquisitions justified, in retrospect, the extreme caution the company had taken since the war to avoid even the appearance of overly aggressive market strategies, however much such caution might have inhibited the company's growth. That concern, about market share and the protection of small producers that would be framed by the courts in even more stringent terms than they had been two decades earlier, meant simply that even Alcoa, with all its experience and all its caution, was still highly vulnerable to antitrust. Not until the early 1970s, when the Department of Justice abandoned an investigation into sheet pricing, was the cloud of antitrust finally lifted.

Antitrust aside, Alcoa was beset in the early 1960s by growing worries about capacity and pricing, as the North American oligopoly began to lose control over those basic factors of industry economics. Selling aluminum was a brisk business, but making money on it was becoming more difficult. Four years passed before a healthy equilibrium between supply and demand was restored (not until late 1962 did the American aluminum industry begin to absorb the fifty-six percent increase in capacity brought on stream between 1956 and 1961). Not until 1966 did Alcoa's net income exceed the high the company had set a full decade earlier (even though gross revenues had swelled from $870 million to $1.4 billion).[14] Meanwhile, Alcoa struggled not only to maintain its profitability, but also its market in primary aluminum in the more competitive environment that took shape after the recession. Even though it continued to grow, building its assets to $1.05 billion in sixteen states and eleven foreign countries by 1964, Alcoa's share of the domestic market was dwindling. In 1965, Alcoa had 29.4 percent of American aluminum capacity to Reynolds' 22.4 percent and Kaiser's 20.1 percent. More problematic were the balance sheet numbers: Alcoa's swelling revenues were simply not generating corresponding increases in net income. A surfeit of fabricators in the industry was depressing the margins of the large integrated producers. Even when the price of ingot began to recover by 1963, competition among fabricators became ever more gritty. In 1964, when nearly 100 percent of its theoretical ingot capacity was in operation, "it was a commonplace, not wholly accurate, that there wasn't an independent in the industry that could make a penny on fabricating."[15]

Alcoa's attempts to stabilize fabricating prices could not overcome these harsh realities. The company's annual reports blamed mainly "deteriorating price structures" for its poor returns on assets. A good measure of Alcoa's difficulty stemmed from an industry-wide practice of "commodity" pricing of fabricated goods at heavy discounts from the Alcoa list. Alcoa had touched off this unhealthy situation in 1958, when it introduced special discounts on products with high-volume potential as a way of encouraging demand for its excess capacity. Promotional pricing to create markets for selected products was not new, of course. But as it spread throughout the industry, it was done on such a wide scale, with such regularity, across so many product lines that price cutting, even below cost, became chronic. Lowered prices for selected sheet items, for example, spread to other kinds of sheet, and "in time," noted *Forbes*, "the industry evolved significant commodity prices for nearly every significant market it had." While Alcoa executives cried publicly for a return to price discipline, Alcoa salesmen "cheerfully went along with the crowd." By 1965, John Harper admitted the reality, saying, "We do not intend to hold an umbrella over our competitors while they cut prices."[16]

Still, no one in the industry wanted to prolong a price war, and it was in the process of trying to restore price discipline in the fall of 1965 that Alcoa stumbled inadvertently into one of its more embarrassing crises: President Lyndon Johnson's "aluminum price roll-back." Johnson had just marched the country into Vietnam and had promulgated voluntary wage-price "guideposts" to mitigate the inflation that would surely be exacerbated by war. Over a period of twelve days in October and November, John Harper became the victim of Johnson's desire to find a scapegoat for mounting inflation, lest it become too serious a political liability for his then still popular administration.

The entire affair revolved around the disposition of the Government stockpile, which was coincidentally at issue. Having outlived its original strategic purpose, the stockpile (which, remember, had originated during the Korean War) now bulged with such a surplus of primary metal that it gave the Government great leverage with which it could attempt to control aluminum prices. Alcoa's management had always known that, sooner or later, it would be up to the aluminum companies to buy back the Government surplus, perhaps at a disadvantageous time. Now, in 1965, there was the immediate possibility that the Government, which had been eating some of the American industry's "excess" primary production for several years, might disgorge large quantities of ingot in an attempt to control producer prices in an inflationary economy. The President's Council of Economic Advisers was concerned that an aluminum price increase might reverberate throughout American heavy industry, igniting a "war-boom inflation psychology."[17]

Alcoa's chief counsel, Leon Hickman, had already suggested to the Office of Emergency Planning in March 1965 that the industry draw down the entire stockpile surplus (which amounted to more than 1.8 million tons in excess of the estimated 450,000 the Government actually required) in three-year blocks at market prices. Each aluminum company was to be committed to buy back in proportion to its input with some flexibility as to the time of repurchase, as long as the three-year aggregate amounts were met. But negotiations had become stalled by "maneuvering within the aluminum companies," each wanting to put "the burden on the other fellow as much as possible." Negotiations were still in progress, when, on October 19, Olin Mathieson, a small producer with less than four percent of the nation's primary capacity, announced a half-cent-per-pound increase in its primary and fabricated aluminum products. Reynolds and Kaiser, eager for an opportunity to restore some semblance of orderly administrative pricing in the industry, went along immediately. Alcoa waited. Harper was on his way home from Japan as rumors were already circulating that President Johnson was "sputtering mad," threatening to dump 500,000 surplus tons of metal from the Government stockpile on the market.[18]

After checking with administration officials, Hickman thought he had obtained approval of Alcoa's proposal on the stockpile. Accordingly, Alcoa announced, on November 5, that it would match the industry's price increase. Johnson lowered the boom and issued a call for an immediate price rollback. Government stockpile negotiators had no choice then but to link their agenda to the President's. They informed the aluminum companies that they would have to buy back surplus metal at a much faster rate than the companies claimed they could absorb. Meanwhile, in Congress, Senator Philip Hart, head of the antitrust and monopoly subcommittee, issued a call for an investigation of aluminum industry market behavior. Then on November 7, Secretary of Defense Robert McNamara announced that the Government would offer 200,000 tons of primary metal to the market at whatever price the traffic would bear. Rumors began to circulate that the Government was actually prepared to dump 300,000 tons, enough, surmised *The New York Times*, to "scramble up markets all over the free world."[19]

Hickman flew to Washington and held a press conference, declaring Alcoa's intention to stand by its price increase and let the market determine the winner. This served further to infuriate the President, whose feelings then Harper attempted to assuage, in vain, with a little executive diplomacy. After failing to reach the President by telephone, Harper flew to Washington to meet with the Defense Secretary. On November 10, Harper and McNamara agreed that Alcoa would roll back its price increase on primary metal, if the Government would call off its threat to unload the stockpile. McNamara held a press conference in which he made some astonishing remarks about the wonderful workings of the "free-enterprise market system" while praising the aluminum industry for its "patriotic act" of recission and its willingness to buy back the entire stockpile surplus.

Embarrassing as it was to Alcoa, the upshot of the entire affair was favorable to the industry. The politics surrounding the price rollback virtually forced industry and Government negotiators to settle quickly on a formula for an orderly disposal of the stockpile on a flexible schedule over a period of seven to fourteen years.[20] The orderly purchase of stockpiled metal might inhibit primary expansion to some extent, but, as Hickman took pains to explain it to Alcoa employees, the agreement "does not appear to be a present threat to production . . . operating at full capacity in a booming domestic market."[21] In other words, Harper swallowed his pride in exchange for a satisfactory resolution to the stockpile problem, which in the long run was more important than the anticipated $28 million in revenues that would have accrued to the industry from a price increase.[22]

A new strategy

In fact, Harper was less concerned about growth in primary capacity than he was to focus Alcoa on lines of fabricated products, where the company stood to earn the best returns. Unlike his predecessors, who pursued growth on all fronts as a means to expanding primary capacity, he concentrated on the development of markets in which Alcoa's size, financial power, and unique technological capabilities gave it a special advantage. Even though he was not known as a strategic thinker, it was Harper who made the critical and successful move toward high-volume and technologically sophisticated semifinished goods.

For too long, Harper felt, Alcoa had sold the bulk of its value-added mill products on a kind of project or "job-shop" basis. Most of Alcoa's fabricating plants were multipurpose facilities that had been turning out low-volume, special-order products at higher and higher cost. In the process, Alcoa had become bogged down in too many markets where it had no competitive advantage. If we look at the markets for building products, we can see the problem a bit more clearly. Alcoa had been more successful in developing aluminum for monumental architecture, a specialized project-based market, than in capturing a strong share in residential construction materials, a mass market. To move its metal into the home construction market more effectively, Alcoa would have to compete with many of its own customers in making siding, gutters, downspouts, roofing, shutters, and windows. A subsidiary, Alcoa Building Products, Inc., was set up to sell home construction products, but by 1965, Building Products was running "a poor second" to Alside, Inc., an independent manufacturer, and had "a long way to go before reaching its goal of 25 per cent of the residential market."[23]

Harper understood that Alcoa would fare better overall if it could establish outlets for its metal analogous to some of the steel industry's mass markets for high-volume, continuous runs of semifabricated goods. With this in mind, Alcoa developed a three-pronged strategy: (1) to move beyond its historic concentration on "job-shop" operations in fabricating in order to develop products, such as RCS for the aluminum can market, which could be manufactured on high-volume, low-cost runs in large mills that enjoyed huge economies of scale; (2) to expand its business in high-margin specialty items in highly technical sectors of the market, such as aerospace, for which the company, with its strong research and engineering staffs, had a decisive edge over less-sophisticated producers; (3) to cut its costs of production through large-scale process improvements, plant modernization, organizational reforms, and more systematic planning. Success would then depend on whether Alcoa could bring to high-tonnage, mass markets and high-margin, specialized markets the capital and technical resources necessary to meet those markets quickly and efficiently.

As mentioned earlier, this new strategic formula brought Alcoa into a fourth phase of postwar expansion. Between 1966 and 1970, annual profit levels were restored to their pre-1958 norms of ten percent, and higher. The company, as we shall see next, was also reaping the benefits of its international ventures, which enabled it to invest in facilities abroad wherever material inputs, labor, or markets made it advantageous to do so. Despite a sharp recession in 1970–1, Alcoa would post new records in shipments and revenues during the following year, and profits once again would begin to rise.[24]

International expansion

In 1957, Alcoa was still a domestic enterprise. Its "offshore" operations were limited mainly to the extraction of bauxite, principally from the Dutch colony of Surinam, to freight and passenger operations of ore-bearing steamships, and to a modest export trade. Judge Knox's severing of the joint ownership of Alcoa and Alcan in 1950 had triggered little interest among Alcoa executives in exploring opportunities abroad, despite the apparent potential of foreign markets. In response to competition for ore from other major producers, Alcoa established foreign bases to develop bauxite deposits in the Dominican Republic, Panama, and Costa Rica during the mid-1950s.[25] Otherwise, with the exception of small fabricating operations in Mexico (1953) and Venezuela (1956) – initiatives taken by two Alcoa subsidiaries, The Alcoa Steamship Company and The Aluminum Cooking Utensil Company – Alcoa made no serious attempts to develop foreign factories.

The indifference to international opportunities had strong historical roots, dating back to the company's divestiture of Aluminium Limited in 1928. The interest that the Hunts, the Mellons, and A. V. Davis continued to hold in Limited, which had blossomed into a full-blown multinational enterprise, was a key factor in keeping Alcoa focused on the United States market. Another factor was Roy Hunt's lingering belief that Alcoa was best managed as a domestic enterprise. Wilson and Magee harbored more imperial aspirations than the other directors, but they found little support from Hunt, who had been an advocate of retrenchment from foreign operations in the 1920s and had remained convinced ever since that Alcoa was simply not competent to undertake a foreign business.

Hunt's aversion to overseas expansion was so strong that it extended even to the realm of raw materials for which Alcoa was abroad by necessity. In 1957, Alcoa had already passed up an invitation to participate in Kaiser and Reynolds' development of ore deposits in Ghana, when Lawrence Litchfield, as head of Alcoa's bauxite operations, contracted to enter into a consortium with the French, Swiss, and Canadians to exploit a high-grade deposit in Guinea. When informed of this, Hunt was so irate that he "took Chief and Larry apart in front of a lot of other people in a very miserable way," an event which so outraged Frank Magee that he tendered his resignation in protest.[26] After that, Hunt's active opposition appears to have waned.

Magee and Wilson were not to be denied. At first, they concentrated on those areas of foreign business that were most familiar. In the winter of 1956–7, Alcoa's export business was reorganized and placed in the hands of John Mitchell, who became head of Alcoa International, Inc., which subsumed the operations of the Pan-Ore Steamship Company, which had been handling much of the company's foreign sales. That same year, Alcoa began negotiations with the government of Surinam for the joint development of a $150 million hydroelectric project and smelter. The project, known as the "Brokopondo Development," was sealed in the following year and marked Alcoa's first large-scale venture into foreign aluminum production since the divestiture of Aluminium Limited.

The Brokopondo venture signified a new determination on the part of less-developed nations to demand investment in production facilities in exchange for concession rights to raw materials. The hydroelectric installation was designed to supply a city of two million people in that small nation of 350,000, and it entailed the construction of a forty-five-mile road from the dam site at Afobaka to Paranam, where an 80,000-ton smelter was planned for the end of the decade. In the typical manner of Alcoa's integrated, domestic engineering projects, Brokopondo was to become Alcoa's first major mine-to-metal venture offshore, a progressive departure from reliance on domestic energy and labor in the production of aluminum.[27]

From that point, Alcoa moved quickly into a wider range of foreign ventures. In 1958, the aircraft manufacturer Lockheed, via its representatives at the Mellon Bank, arranged a meeting between Alcoa and the Furukawa Electric Company in Japan to discuss taking a position in the latter's aluminum operations. Lockheed had been dissatisfied with the quality of hard-alloy sheet it was getting for its Japanese assembly plant from Furukawa. The Japanese producer, in turn, recognized its own need for American fabricating know-how. Out of the negotiations emerged Furalco, in which Alcoa took a one-third interest. Furalco was to produce sheet, extrusions, and castings for which Alcoa would provide technical advice on a royalty basis, an unusual step for Alcoa, which had always closely guarded its technology through the semifabricated stages of production.[28]

Less fortunate was Alcoa's thwarted attempt to buy a stake in British Aluminium Company. British Aluminium had never fully recovered from World War II, and by the late 1950s, it was woefully short on financial and smelting capacity. It did have about $112 million in assets, which included low-cost hydropower and smelting

Fig. 7.1. The dam and powerhouse at Afobaka, Surinam.

facilities in Norway and Canada, and it had important, though weakening, distribution channels into European and African markets at a time when American aluminum products were in oversupply. It also had a strong position in the vast, as yet undeveloped Weipa bauxite deposit in Northeast Australia, which had been discovered just two years earlier. According to Magee, British Aluminium had been trying to interest Alcoa in taking a position in it for some time. After its managing director hectored Alcoa executives at a party at Fox Chapel, Viscount Portal of Hungerford, Britain's chief of Air Staff in World War II and now British Aluminium's chairman, came to the United States. He prevailed upon Alcoa to take a position in his company. Lord Portal's motives were simple enough; he was seeking an infusion of cash to complete a hydropowered smelter in Quebec. But his company was a poorly managed business with some strong assets that were, in today's language, undervalued in the market. By November 1958, it became apparent that someone, no one knew who, was attempting a quiet takeover of British Aluminium's stock, and Alcoa was inadvertently sucked into a distasteful competition.[29]

The struggle for control of British Aluminium was a dramatic story. Following Portal's invitation, Chief Wilson had gone to London and took up residence in the Savoy Hotel, where he became embroiled in what was at the time the most sensational takeover battle in the history of British finance. A gentleman every bit as proper and conservative as the "Old Freddies" of the City of London's financial establishment, Wilson was dismayed to find himself locked into a bidding contest against a British industrial concern, Tube Investments, which among its diverse interests owned an aluminum rolling mill.

It was widely suspected that Tube had a secret partner who in fact turned out to be Reynolds Metals. That company's president, Richard Reynolds, was harboring expansionist visions of his own and had long coveted British Aluminium's Canadian facilities and its European outlets. Wilson was, at first, blissfully unaware that a Reynolds vice president had also been working out of the Savoy under the cover of S. G. Warburg & Co., the City of London's most unconventional merchant bank. When the struggle became public in late November, the mainstream British investment community, not yet reconciled to the shifting realities of the City's business decorum and world economic power, howled at the twin spectacles of an unconventional, hostile takeover and of two foreign concerns vying for control of British assets. Merchant bankers working on Alcoa's behalf appealed to the Treasury, for sake of the "national interest," to put a stop to what Fleet Street was already calling "The Great Aluminium War."

Lord Portal had already tried to forestall a takeover of British Aluminium by announcing that he had signed a contract to sell one-third of its common stock to Alcoa for $12.6 million. Acceptance of a more generous Tube–Reynolds tender offer would have placed two-thirds of his company in their control. The Treasury, which would have to approve any deal with a foreign concern, refused to intervene, and the bidding went on. Late in December, a syndicate of fourteen British banking concerns led by Lazard Frères made a bid for 50 percent of British Aluminium's common in support of Alcoa, but it was too little, too late. Reynolds, not rich in cash, floated a new stock issue in the United States in order to finance an all-out takeover effort. While Tube made its generous tender offers to British Aluminium shareholders, Reynolds continued to buy its target's stock on the open market until January 10, when it was announced that the Tube–Reynolds partnership had taken control of eighty percent of British Aluminium (the amount increased to ninety percent in a matter of days).[30]

But Lord Portal had irreparably damaged his cause by failing to consult with major shareholders before striking his deal with Alcoa at a per-share price substantially less than the Tube–Reynolds tender offer. While the British press took Portal and his bankers to task for their "authoritarian" assault on "shareholder's democracy," major institutional shareholders, mostly pension funds and insurance companies, dumped their British Aluminium stock, and brokers for Tube and Reynolds cheerfully bought it.

The British bankers who had tried to intervene on Alcoa's behalf were mortified by their defeat in this rare breach of British business decorum: a hostile raid. It was all the more humiliating because Fleet Street positively reveled in a story that had all the elements of a David and Goliath struggle. The emigré Siegmund Warburg, whose family had been well-established on the Continent with a banking tradition that extended back to the sixteenth century, was nonetheless regarded as an upstart in London, where he had established himself just after the war. News commentators made much of Warburg's defiance of the conventions of the City of London and of the triumph of the daring outlanders who managed Tube over the stuffy conservatives of British Aluminium. The press further chided the pro-Alcoa banking consortium for its desperate appeal to "national interest," an appeal which, in any case, had failed to persuade the Treasury.

Of course, many benefitted from the result; institutional holders of British Aluminium, including the Church of England, realized handsome profits.[31] But in the end, the loss of British Aluminium to American control marked another step in the erosion of Britain's economic power and prestige. As for Alcoa, it was a smaller-scale embarrassment, which was little consolation to Chief Wilson, who was chagrined by the entire ungentlemanly business.[32]

Actually, Wilson might have won British Aluminium had he been prepared to be more aggressive. Alcoa, as Frank Magee pointed out, "had the resources and the ability to go in there and fight for this thing but the taste wasn't there at that time apparently for this international venture."[33] But even more than its lack of aggressiveness, the British episode exposed Alcoa's lack of coherent strategy when it came to international matters. Alcoa had not yet formulated any strong rationale for international expansion beyond its traditional interest in foreign bauxite. While it had been eager enough to respond to Lord Portal's invitation, it had not been prepared to pursue a contested opportunity to the finish.

On the other side, Richard Reynolds had been both aggressive and well-focused. His choice of Warburg as mediary had proven to be an apt alliance between America's most unconventional aluminum producer and Britain's most radical merchant banker. More important, Reynolds had been clear and precise about his motives. British Aluminium offered Reynolds a low-cost smelter in Canada and more direct access to foreign markets at a time when the American market was saturated and when the rest of the Western world was ripe for higher aluminum consumption. Thus, in one bold stroke, Reynolds Metals catapulted itself into a leading position among American producers in the quest for foreign markets. As it happened, Reynolds promptly sold the valuable Weipa bauxite deposit to Comalco, a joint venture of Kaiser and Rio Tinto Conzinc. This, we now know, was a great mistake; Weipa was the best British Aluminium had to offer. But for the moment, Reynolds' stock soared, exceeding Alcoa's per-share price for the first time in its history on May 1, 1959.[34]

As awful as it seemed at the time, the British Aluminium fiasco brought Alcoa back into the European arena. When Lazard (perhaps, in part, as a gesture of atonement)[35] presented Alcoa with an offer to purchase half interest in an Imperial Chemical Industries fabricating plant at Waunarlwydd, near Swansea, in Wales, the board of directors snatched it up. ICI and Alcoa entered an agreement to create a joint-venture corporation known as Impalco (the Imperial Aluminum Company), in which Alcoa took a forty-nine-percent stake. By 1962, Impalco operated four fabricating plants and one secondary aluminum facility in Britain.[36]

Alcoa's most impressive new venture abroad – its entry into Australia – was yet another response to an invitation. As Krome George told it, Lindsay Clark and a group of managers from Australia's Western Mining Corporation arrived in Pittsburgh in the summer of 1960 and revealed their plan to exploit a huge bauxite deposit in Western Australia. One of three major deposits to be discovered on the island continent in the mid-1950s, Western Australia's bauxite had been judged as very low-grade by aluminum company engineers on account of its high silica content (better than twenty percent). But Clark (who was in the process of putting together a large consortium to develop the bauxite) brought with him an amazing revelation. "What nobody had ever bothered to check out," explained George (who at that time was involved in the planning and analysis of foreign prospects) "was the fact that the silica was quartzite and didn't react in the [beneficiation] process and what you had was a shovel full of inert sand and a shovel full of very high-grade bauxite that were easily separated...." A bauxite specialist who was dispatched to examine the ore reported back favorably on the potential

Fig. 7.2. Bauxite conveyer and alumina plant at Pinjarra, Western Australia.

economies. Alcoa and Western Mining agreed to form a company, and George went to Australia in the spring of 1961 as part of a team of negotiators to set the terms of the agreement.[37]

It was no easy business for Alcoa to come to terms with the Australian interests. There was considerable resistance to Alcoa's desire to get a majority interest in Western Mining's bauxite concession. Another problem was that the Japanese company, Mitsubishi, had already been offered a twenty-percent stake in the concession, an offer that took the Alcoa representatives entirely by surprise. Reynolds and Kaiser were also on the scene, and contending rivals chummed like foreign correspondents at the Menzies Hotel bar in Melbourne, where they drank and played bridge while "the Bauxite Derby" raged behind the scenes. Alcoa's representatives, fearing that their tentative agreement with Western Mining could unravel at any moment, operated in secrecy. George communicated with Pittsburgh via his parents in Florida using a nine-digit code based on the surname of Pittsburgh's 1960 World Series hero, Bill Mazeroski. Speed was essential. "It was a precarious situation," George remembered. "We didn't have all this stuff nailed down . . . , and we were up to our ears in Japanese." But somehow ("I made up antitrust law like it was going out of style"), George persuaded Mitsubishi to forego its interest. Finally, according to Frank Magee, John Mitchell, the company's most experienced hand in international business, was able to negotiate a fifty-one-percent interest in an Australian joint-venture company, which was to be funded mainly by Alcoa at a projected cost of about $ 100 million.[38]

The primary mission of Alcoa Australia was to mine and refine bauxite for the world market, but the agreement also called for the building of a power station and smelter at Geelong, Victoria. Western Mining had no plans to do any more than that, while Alcoa wanted to integrate forward to establish markets for the Geelong ingot. In 1962, George negotiated with Alcoa's British partner, ICI, for the development of fabricating operations in Australia. These negotiations were unsuccessful, but the situation was salvaged when Alcoa's partner, Western Mining, decided that it would be prepared to invest in fabricating operations after all.[39]

The formation of Alcoa Australia was decisive in Alcoa's emergence as a multinational; it committed the company almost irrevocably to long-term, large-scale international involvement in all phases of production and marketing. By the time all the elements of the Australian venture were in place, Alcoa's management was thinking of overseas investment as an integral part of the company's growth. Projected Australian smelting capacity was almost equal to that country's current consumption, which had been amply supplied by imports from Aluminium Limited, British Aluminium, and Kaiser. Comalco, too, was building new plants. Alcoa was thus committing itself to a very long-term strategy based not only on

Fig. 7.3. Alcoa–Elektrokemisk Soderberg smelter at Mosjoen, Norway.

projections for the Australian market, but also on the prospects for an even greater Pacific Basin market. "There's a possibility of over-capacity in Australia for a while," Litchfield told *Fortune*, "but these trolley cars come along only once and you've got to get on them."[40]

By the time Magee retired from the chairmanship, Alcoa had expanded its foreign operations well beyond its traditional interests in raw materials. In 1963, aside from its wholly owned mining operations in Surinam, the Dominican Republic, and Jamaica, Alcoa was involved in eight joint ventures in five countries: Mexico (three joint ventures in fabricating, one in smelting), Venezuela, Japan, the United Kingdom and Australia.[41] It would soon enter into a fifty-fifty joint venture with Elektrokemisk in Norway, in order to gain a better foothold in the European market while also supplying the British fabricating plants with lower-cost aluminum. While the company struggled to maintain its profit margins in the competitive markets at home, its annual reports glowed with news of rising volume abroad – foreign sales were up ten percent in 1962, twelve percent in 1963, twenty percent in 1964, and 12.4 percent in 1965. Indeed, Magee's successors amplified his achievement by increasing investment abroad on all fronts, expanding operations on every continent. Overall, between 1962 and 1970, Alcoa's international sales increased from $56 to $164.3 million, the latter figure representing 10.7 percent of the company's total sales.[42]

To recapitulate, there had been no grand strategy driving Alcoa's moves overseas. In retrospect, Magee himself observed that Alcoa's reentry into international operations happened as a series of opportunistic responses, "except in the bauxite end of it where we [always] knew we had to be abroad." But by responding to joint-venture opportunities with increasing vigor, Alcoa developed a broad-based multinational business. By the early 1970s, in addition to the ventures already cited, Alcoa had established smelting operations in Brazil and fabricating plants in Colombia, El Salvador, France, The Netherlands, West Germany, Morocco, Tunisia, and Libya. The company also had four regional sales headquarters in Lausanne for Europe, Africa, and the Middle East; Hong Kong for the Far East; Toronto for Canada; and Coral Gables, Florida, for Latin America and the Caribbean.[43]

Still, without a coherent strategy in which foreign expansion could be treated not only as an integral part of its long-term development but also as a process with its own structural characteristics, Alcoa had difficulty learning how to behave like a true multinational. Instead, Alcoa remained, at heart, an American firm with overseas operations. Charles Parry, who spent nearly five years in Australia from 1962 to 1966, recalled his frustration with Alcoa's corporate management in Pittsburgh during that time. "[W]e tried to run it [Australia] as a division," which, he reflected years later, "created a lot of problems" with the Australian partners rather than "running it as a separate international company.... We still aren't over that totally," he said in 1985, testifying that change in Alcoa's domestic mind-set was and remains a slow and difficult process. "We still don't run [international] partnerships well."[44]

Frank Magee and centralization

If Alcoa's strategy under Frank Magee can be described as loose, ad hoc, and, at best, opportunistic, his approach to management was far more deliberate. By the time he became president, Alcoa's scale and complexity had made it virtually impossible for him to cope with all the decisions that reached his office. He had inherited very little in the way of central office resources. "I'll admit," Magee recalled with a characteristic modesty, "I considered myself not completely adequate for a corporation of this size.... My brain wasn't that big."[45] Judged by those who knew him to be a brilliant executive manager, Magee's problem was hardly a problem of competence. The problem was structural. There was no top-level staff for the systematic analysis of information required to run the kind of huge complex that Alcoa had become since the war. The president and chairman had to assimilate vast amounts of data filtered up though numerous general managers, vice presidents, and executive vice presidents across many diverse lines of business in markets with different characteristics. I. W. Wilson apparently had felt comfortable with the situation, old hand that he was, but Magee, who had been concerned with problems of corporate administration ever since the war, thought there were more efficient ways to organize the decision-making process. One way, he thought, was to expand the numbers of senior officers in Alcoa's corporate office.[46]

Magee had served as an executive vice president under Wilson, but as the new president, all department heads reported directly to him. This was clearly an unsatisfactory situation, so in 1959, he appointed three executive vice presidents, each with responsibility for a group of corporate functions. Magee himself assumed the title of chief executive officer (the first in Alcoa's history) and became a step removed from administrative responsibilities. To Lawrence Litchfield reported all the production functions – departments for Raw Materials, Refining, Smelting, Fabricating, Engineering, Purchasing, Personnel, and Industrial Relations. Leon Hickman took charge of all the legal and financial functions, including the corporate secretary, Alcoa's Washington office, the Steamship Company, and the newly acquired Rome Cable. Minton M. Anderson became responsible for Sales, Public Relations and Advertising, all research and development activities, Alcoa's new international operations, and Wear-Ever.[47]

The board, however, remained small; that is to say, the number of policy makers remained small. Along with Wilson and Hunt, who remained active in the business (Hunt as chairman of the Executive Committee and Wilson as chairman of the board), Hickman and Anderson had long been members. Collegial customs of discourse and behavior at the top continued much the same as they always had.[48] What Magee achieved was a better allocation of functional responsibilities among the top managers, and, more important, the creation of the executive vice presidencies reduced the number of people reporting to the president, whose burdens for overseeing day-to-day operations were lightened substantially.

At the same time, real as well as apparent authority for decisions over all areas of the business became even more highly concentrated at Pittsburgh headquarters. Magee, remember, had long been concerned, as head of Production, with coordinating the "little fiefdoms" that had made Pittsburgh's management of the enterprise difficult. Now that he was president, he finally had the authority, in the words of Krome George, to "bring his people in."[49]

After 1960, the central office staffs were enlarged further to improve coordination among the plants in the company's two main operating divisions, Fabricating and Smelting. The Fabricating Division had become too large for management by one general manager, and so the tasks of the division head were broken out for assignment to several "manufacturing managers," each with his own metallurgist, product planner, and staff assistants. By mid-1963, the Fabricating Division had five such manufacturing managers at a level below the division manager. The Smelting Division was similarly reorganized, and three new staff posts were created to coordinate production, administration, and engineering as problems in those areas arose between Smelting and Fabricating (the latter being the principal customer of the former).

More central office control was designed to prevent local managers from "optimizing" their own production at the expense of the company as a whole. This was as true of Sales as it was of Production. The district sales managers, who had already given up much of their freedom in pricing since the war, were forced to cede much of their power over other kinds of decisions to central office marketing managers.[50] Meanwhile as central office managers increased in number, administrative functions at the plant level were consolidated into the hands of fewer managers. Local works managers with responsibilities for more than one kind of operation reported to the appropriate manufacturing managers for each of the products under his supervision. The consolidation of local administrative tasks and the proliferation of corporate managers brought the process of centralization at Alcoa to its apogee by the end of 1963. At that point, Hugh Morrison, the vice president to whom both Fabricating and Smelting reported, said that it was possible to conceive of the two organizations as a single, consolidated manufacturing entity at the corporate level.[51]

Centralization had a mixed impact on research and development

functions. Magee tried to restore some of the "top-down" management of R&D that had been tried at the end of World War II, but
which had in fact become diluted by the evolution of the subcommittee system. In 1958, the old Technical Committee, which had
become a weak body, was replaced by a Research and Development
Committee headed by the company's chief metallurgist, T. W. Bossert. The new R&D Committee was designed to oversee the activities
of Alcoa's proliferating technical subcommittees. A Technical Policy
Committee, consisting of corporate officers responsible for Marketing, Production, Raw Materials and Personnel along with the Director of Research, set the overall strategic direction for innovation.
Kent Van Horn, as head of the Research Laboratories, was nominally equal in authority to that of the two committees, though in
fact, he was held responsible to them.[52]

The reorganization of R&D at the corporate level reflected Magee's
belief that in a competitive environment, the coordination of innovative activities required more direct executive control. He informed
the Laboratories that there was to be more stringent corporate-level
oversight, more careful budgeting of projects based on market-driven
needs. "There is no thought of reducing the research effort," he
explained in 1960, "but emphasis should be placed on confining
efforts to projects of major importance that promise to produce dividends in a reasonably short time."[53] It was especially important, in
Magee's thinking, that the overall direction of Research be more
closely coordinated with Marketing, and after 1960, all project proposals were funneled through the Commercial Research Division of
the Sales Department.[54]

Further attempts to rationalize and centralize R&D proceeded
under Litchfield and then Harper. The former, in 1962, brought Van
Horn into Pittsburgh as vice president of Research and Development. The technical committees and the new Director of Research
reported to Van Horn, who, in turn, reported to the executive vice
president for production functions, H. C. Erskine. In 1964, the Technical Committee was abolished, further concentrating both R&D
policy and execution under a single central office. During Harper's
tenure, the company's various development groups were consolidated. The idea was to bring operations that had been separated
geographically and administratively into a single Development Department so that the marketing of new Alcoa products and services
could be coordinated from a central point.

It was largely marketing considerations that led to the decision
to build a new, centralized R&D facility that enabled Alcoa for the

first time to house most of its traditionally scattered R&D operations on a single campus. Van Horn, whose own reasons derived from more purely technological considerations, persuaded management of the need for consolidation, because the whole concept fit so nicely with salesman's perspective of Frank Magee, who initially approved the project in 1958 when Alcoa announced its intention to develop a 2,300-acre site at Merwin, Pennsylvania, not far from New Kensington and, more important, close to corporate headquarters. Customers could be better served, Magee reasoned, if they had a central place to visit and discuss their technical needs. A new facility would also enable Alcoa to set up experimental production facilities without disrupting plant activities. Plans moved along slowly until May 29, 1962, when the Alcoa executive committee met on the morning after a "disastrous" plunge in the stock market and voted nonetheless to authorize $30 million for a new Alcoa Technical Center. The development activities were moved into the new facility first, in 1968, but it would take years to complete the process of consolidating most of the research operations from New Kensington, East St. Louis, and Cleveland.[55]

The centralization and geographical consolidation of Alcoa's R&D operations obscured an important reality: the underlying weakness of corporate management in setting research priorities and technical directions for the business as a whole. Instead, the technical subcommittees, which were in effect networks of middle managers and lower-level engineers who served on a rotating basis, continued in effect to set research agendas. The subcommittees, as many as a hundred, considered and proposed new projects and monitored existing ones without strong corporate guidance on long-term priorities regarding overall technical direction or budgets.[56] This had worked well enough at a time when what the management demanded most of R&D was short-term development of new products and processes. (And no one could deny that Alcoa had been very successful in developing important major new products [such as curtain wall and the easy-open can] and in responding quickly to technological threats since World War II.) But in such cases, major developments required a strong corporate champion, such as Fritz Close, to assure the commitment of money and manpower necessary to carry projects to completion. Left to its own devices, the subcommittee system was a poor vehicle for mounting or sustaining long-term programs, especially ones involving more fundamental research that had no immediately foreseeable market results. That would continue to be a problem, and ongoing attempts to impose a more rational corporate-level planning and control system from the top were generally unsuccessful.

Long after his retirement, Magee recalled that as president he had "preached like hell" on the virtues of managerial autonomy and local decision-making. Yet the thrust of his administration made that hard to achieve. In time, it would become apparent that centralization had proceeded too far, that for Alcoa to plan and manage its various products and markets effectively, decision-making authority would have to be granted more and more to "local" sectors of the corporation. Instead, more authority devolved upon corporate department heads, and traditionally powerful, corporate-wide managerial "fiefdoms" continued to flourish in such important areas as engineering and raw materials. Given the growing scale of the company's operations, the widening scope of its business, and the increasing complexity of its technologies and markets, the pressures for greater control by the central office were overriding, and would remain so, as long as the company remained organized around functional principles of organization. In only one sector of the company, R&D, was top–down centralization significantly offset by the existence of semiautonomous, lower-level centers of power: the technical subcommittees. And R&D was one function of the company that could have used more, not less, centralized coordination in the planning and management of its affairs.[57]

Fritz Close: high-volume salesman

On January 1, 1966, Fritz Close became chairman of the board. John Harper, Alcoa's president, might well have taken the title for himself but preferred to wait. Close was diffident about the whole thing. He had little taste for the plotting of strategy and policy, claims not to have understood finance, and cared not a whit for the problems of administration. "I think they just didn't know what to do with me," he said, "so they made me chairman."[58]

Close did have at least one surpassingly important credential. He was, in his words, "an aluminum peddler," but that was a fine thing to be at Alcoa, especially if one were the best in the business. For more than a decade, Close had been Alcoa's answer to the Reynolds brothers in his tireless promotion of new aluminum applications. The salesman most responsible for Alcoa's success in monumental architecture, he had just recently led the company's penetration into what would become its most important market, aluminum cans.

Ebullient, energetic, zealous, he never stopped thinking of aluminum as anything but a miraculous element with nearly boundless potential: "the metal practically sells itself," he declared in his best salesman's pitch.[59]

Today, the mention of Fritz Close's name around older Alcoa managers evokes fond memories of a less formal, "people-oriented" firm, of a simpler, more stable world in which the bright future of aluminum was taken for granted. Close was the exemplary son of the "Alcoa family," the heroic figure of the golden years. To him, working as "an aluminum peddler" was a joyful calling, and he conveyed this attitude to everyone he met. His views of management were simple and entrepreneurial. He liked to think of Alcoa as a spirited clan of loyal managers, engineers, and salesmen whose talents could be mustered and combined at will from one venture to the next. Aluminum was "a people business," he said time and again, and he was always uncomfortable with the trappings and procedures of bureaucratic management, which for the most part he tried to ignore. None of this was lost on John Harper, whose regime would do much to hasten Alcoa's progress toward more formal management, and who had the sense to realize that Close could do much to help sustain company morale amidst cost-cutting and reorganization. He could also maintain the good will of the old guard – Mellon, Hunt, and Wilson – on the board of directors. And he could wine and dine major customers, champion aluminum's prospects in the press, and preside over the company's public relations and R&D programs with an authority befitting his relentless enthusiasm.[60]

Frederick J. Close had come to Alcoa in 1929. At Penn State, he had been a sometimes mischievous student whose academic performance was decidedly undistinguished. Yet he managed to take a degree in engineering, after which he went to work in the Oklahoma oil fields for a year. He then returned to Pennsylvania, where he became active in local politics before joining the company. During his first nine months with Alcoa, he toured its various plants in order to study the gamut of aluminum products and production techniques. His first job assignment was New York City. After reporting to Alcoa's sales office above Grand Central Terminal, Close was indoctrinated into the Alcoa Sales Department's rules of etiquette and management by a hard-boiled district sales chief named Sam Simmons. "Shave every day whether you think you need it or not," Close recalled his boss's instructions. He was also told to wear a white shirt, dark tie, and a vested suit; to address the receptionists by their last names; and to avoid profanity. Armed with $20.00 worth of nickels for use on buses and subways, he was ordered to get off at all stops, walk a half-mile around, and to introduce himself to every possible aluminum customer. It did not take long for the gregarious, aggressive young man to collar some of the leading principals of the New York architectural community. He sold 750,000 pounds of aluminum to the designers of the Empire State Building and another 3 million pounds to the builders of Rockefeller Center. In 1936, he was reassigned to the Edgewater Plant as an assistant manager for screw machine products, press forgings, foil, and collapsible tubes. Far from becoming a victim of the "Peter Principle," he was being well prepared for higher responsibilities for which he would need a wider experience in manufacturing.[61]

Close spent most of the war managing forging operations in Cleveland, where his "walk-around" style of management earned him a reputation as a motivator. After the war, he was brought to Pittsburgh to work in the architectural division of the Sales Department, where, among other things, he conceptualized the Alcoa building. His geniality, intense loyalty to the firm, and knack for sizing up new markets won him acceptance into the inner circles of senior management. He soon became a favorite of A. V. Davis, for whom he ran errands, and of General Mellon, Roy Hunt, and Chief Wilson, all of whom appreciated the unique strengths of his personality and, not incidently, his proven ability to move aluminum out the factory door and into the hands of customers.

At corporate headquarters, Close carved out for himself a role as a champion of new product ideas. By 1950, he was responsible for coordinating the Laboratories' research activities with the Sales Department's marketing plans. He interpreted this role as one that effectively put him "in charge of the research laboratory," which was probably true enough from the Sales Department's perspective. Wilson, he said, had enjoined him to refocus the Laboratories on "things we can sell."[62] Armed with a mandate and a budget to promoté his own agenda at the Laboratories, he spent a good part of the rest of his career in New Kensington badgering, cajoling, pleading with R&D scientists and engineers to join their energies on what he deemed to be marketable products. Some major, as well as minor, efforts he championed did not work out: aluminum bridges proved too costly; aluminum two-by-fours were too conductive, too difficult to join, and too hard to distribute; aluminum violins fell too short of their most important function, the production of good sound. Nevertheless, in 1958, Close became vice president of both the Sales Development and Commercial Research Divisions and was made general sales manager a year later. Promoted to vice president of marketing in 1962, he became executive vice president and took a seat on the board of directors in the following year. By then, it was clear to everyone just how completely Marketing had come to dominate R&D, and Close personified that relationship at the highest level of the corporation.[63]

Close always seemed to be at the center of Alcoa's most important high-volume marketing efforts. In 1959, as the company began to predict a promising future for aluminum in the can industry, the building and construction market was the single largest outlet for Alcoa's aluminum and would remain so into the mid-1970s. During the 1960s, aluminum became more popular for use in industrial buildings, especially for those in corrosive environments, and in large-scale government and commercial structures. By 1972, Alcoa aluminum had been used to sheath such architectural landmarks as the Vehicle Assembly Building at Cape Canaveral, Pittsburgh's Hilton Hotel, Chicago's John Hancock Center, and the World Trade Center in New York, where aluminum also adorned the headquarters of Chase Manhattan Bank and Time, Inc. Multicolored aluminum siding, windows, gutters, and downspouts found growing acceptance in private residences. In the late 1960s, Alcoa promoted residential applications through corporate–civic programs for urban redevelopment. The first major effort along these lines was the establishment of the Allegheny Housing Rehabilitation Corporation "to buy up [90,000 units of deteriorated] housing, renovate it, and rent it or sell it at minimum cost." In 1968, the company joined the JOBS (Job Opportunities in the Business Sector) Program and the Urban Coalition (on which Close served as a director), and established a subsidiary known as the Housing Corporation of America "which will bid to build and sell low-rent housing to public housing authorities."[64]

It was through Close's contacts in the construction industry that Alcoa inadvertently backed into what was to become an extensive real estate business. In 1959, William Zeckendorf found himself short of the founds he needed to exercise an option he had on the 20th Century Fox studios in Los Angeles, which were for sale as a building site. Within forty-eight hours of being called for the $2.5 million he owed, Zeckendorf rushed to Pittsburgh, where he wheedled a loan from Alcoa in exchange for a one-third interest in what was to become a grand complex of offices, dwellings, a shopping center, and a 20-story hotel, all laid out on 180 acres of prime urban land. A few Zeckendorf financial crises later, Alcoa found itself in full possession of the Los Angeles property, which had become widely publicized as Century City. From that point, real estate was pursued more deliberately. By the end of 1962, Alcoa had taken positions in seven major urban developments in Indianapolis, San Francisco, Pittsburgh, Philadelphia, and New York, most of which were Zeckendorf developments organized in 1962 under a wholly owned subsidiary headed by Leon Hickman. Alcoa's real estate activities were subsequently reincorporated in 1963 as Alcoa Properties, Inc.[65]

Indeed, there was, and is, no particularly strong strategic rationale for an aluminum producer to diversify into real estate. The initial justification (and it was largely *ex post facto* reasoning) held that the direct development of properties might be useful for demonstrating the feasibility of aluminum for large-scale structural applications. Fritz Close, at heart a frustrated architect, recruited the best building designers he could find (all of Alcoa's New York properties were designed by I. M. Pei) to create architectural masterpieces out of aluminum. Projects, such as the Kratter Corporation's high-rise housing development on the abandoned Ebbets Field (for which Brooklynites are still in mourning), would take huge orders of aluminum windows, while others, such as the World Trade Center, were luxuriously swathed in aluminum curtain wall. However, it did not take long for Leon Hickman to conclude that if the company's real estate business was "going to do something worthwhile, these buildings would have to go up on their own merits." Government seed money for urban redevelopment and favorable tax provisions for accelerated depreciation made the business even more attractive. By 1963, Alcoa was deep in the building and construction business.[66]

From Century City forward, aluminum became less a factor in the development of Alcoa's real estate operations. The metal was employed selectively in accordance with architects' judgments as to cost and aesthetics. Alcoa properties quickly evolved into a distinct, and hopefully countercyclical, line of business. Hickman said that "if we had known at the beginning" that Alcoa would become awash in real estate properties, "I don't think we would have done it." But the upshot of this historic "accident" proved to be a very profitable business. In 1972, Alcoa reported a $68-million equity investment in real estate operations generating $38.6 million in net income, which was equivalent to thirty-eight percent of the company's net income as reported on its consolidated income statement.[67]

Just as Alcoa was entering the real estate business, Close was also at work on a development that would propel aluminum into its most important mass market. In 1958, virtually all beverage cans

Fig. 7.4. Century City real estate development in Los Angeles in the early 1970s.

in the United States were made with tinplate steel. With production units in the billions, any use of aluminum in cans could provide Alcoa with an important mass outlet for its metal. Close already had fostered some development of aluminum ends for citrus fruit juice containers, a market comprising some eight million pounds of metal in 1961, when Alcoa decided to enter it. Although Reynolds took an early lead in the manufacture of aluminum juice cans, Alcoa responded with a foil and fiberboard composite can that was to become the standard for frozen juice and automotive oil. The most promising market for aluminum packaging was in beer and soft drink cans, for which the technical requirements were stringent because the contents were under pressure. There was already some evidence in 1961 that the presence of aluminum on just one end of a can extended the shelf life of beer. There was considerable interest among brewers in aluminum can ends, but success in this area would require aluminum–magnesium alloys that were exceptionally strong yet light, and amenable to rolling at very high speeds.[68]

It was in 1962 that Alcoa moved into the design of aluminum ends for tinplate cans in the beer industry. The marketing premise was simple enough: Alcoa hoped to capitalize on the brewers' constant need to differentiate an essentially commodity product in the relentless battle for market share. From the consumer's standpoint, the beneficial feature of the aluminum end was a pull-tab that eliminated the need for a special tool, or "church key." Dayton Reliable Tool Company, which had years of expertise in the forming of aluminum, designed an integral rivet that formed the basis for the conventional "Easy-Open" end. The first such ends resulted in many a cut finger, until Continental Can devised a safer, ringed pull-tab, but the aluminum pull-tab was from its inception a powerful transformer of the consumer market.[69] Also important (though less immediately obvious to the consumer) was that the aluminum end virtually doubled the shelf life of canned beer by altering the galvanic reaction between the product and the steel in the container.[70]

Despite these apparent advantages, and despite the interest of brewers in the potential of aluminum-end cans, Alcoa's first sales calls were inauspicious. Alcoa's marketing managers had been running rigorous studies and contended that the easy-open aluminum end, though a more costly element in production, would actually increase beer consumption in the United States. But the major can companies, already doing a banner business with their existing technology, still had to be persuaded, and even such a large brewer as Anheuser Busch was selling all the beer it could produce, packaged in its own steel cans. As one story goes, Fritz Close and Cliff Sands, a marketing manager who was instrumental in the implementation of RCS strategy, took some sample six-packs with aluminum ends made by the Laboratories to St. Louis to show them to Augustus Busch. According to Close, after they had discussed the costs of production (Close quoted Busch a price of $2.00 per thousand over the base price for steel), the Alcoa salesmen were sent packing. Better luck was had with Pittsburgh Brewing, a regional producer, which tested and marketed an aluminum end in 1962, and soon afterward with Schlitz, where Close won a hearing after telling its president that he had already been conducting discussions with Busch. The successful adoption of the aluminum "pop top" by Schlitz through an intensive advertising campaign brought Busch and other major beer producers into the fold.[71]

By the end of 1963, the aluminum top had been adopted by most brewers and was used on forty percent of all U.S. beer cans. By 1968, cans with aluminum ends had more than eighty percent of the canned beer market.[72] A more ambitious program was underway to make an all-aluminum can. Throughout the decade, Close urged his superiors to take the risk necessary to develop RCS facilities on a grand scale – a big risk in that it was by no means a foregone conclusion that the technology would prove out or that aluminum could take the market from tinplate steel. At one point, in 1964, Close wrote that the steel industry had already "awakened" to the threat posed by aluminum, which meant that Alcoa would have to become not only more aggressive in its R&D and marketing, but also more efficient in its operations. He urged that Alcoa move quickly to develop production facilities to meet the "man minutes per unit" of U.S. Steel's new six-stand mill for rapid production of thin sheet.[73] If aluminum could win a major portion of the can market, the entire present world's aluminum capacity would be insufficient to service that single market.[74]

John Harper was persuaded, and committed more than $100 million, between 1963 and 1968, to the installation of light-gauge sheet mill facilities that would be integrated into the company's new smelter at Warrick, Indiana. The stakes were high, but RCS for aluminum cans was exactly the kind of technologically sophisticated, high-volume, continuous-run product that suited Harper's strategy for Alcoa's next generation of growth. At Warrick, a hot reversing mill was installed to roll twenty-two inch thick ingots into slabs that were then rerolled by a continuous hot mill before further processing by one of two cold mills that could produce sheet of thirty-six and forty-eight inches in width.[75] Warrick's integrated primary metal and sheet mill operations achieved a scale and speeds of production that approached those of the steel industry and provided Alcoa with its most impressive high-volume line of business. It was also a high-technology business, insofar as the engineering requirements of coiled container sheet in the required alloys are rigorous. At high speeds, imperfections in the metal will often shut down an entire production line. No one else in the industry was developing facilities that could match Alcoa's production of container sheet.

The challenge, as Alcoa saw it, was to persuade can manufacturers to invest two or three million dollars per can line in order to convert from steel to aluminum cans, each of which required substantially different production techniques. Alcoa initially tried an impact-extrusion process based on a technology developed earlier by the Coors Brewery in Golden, Colorado. In 1963, a developmental can line for extruding aluminum slugs was built near Busch's Budweiser Brewery in St. Louis. Reynolds concentrated on a draw-and-iron technique, which could form cans from circular stamps cut from coiled sheet on a continuous-process basis. Beginning in 1966, at the behest of corporate headquarters, Alcoa's development engineers turned their attention to draw and iron and then pursued parallel

Fig. 7.5. Alumina is unloaded on the Indiana shore of the Ohio River for Alcoa's integrated aluminum smelting and fabricating operations at Warrick.

Fig. 7.6. A coal-fueled power plant provides energy for the entire range of operations at Warrick.

Fig. 7.7. Carbon anodes for Warrick's smelting operation are baked in a ring furnace.

Fig. 7.8. Giant aluminum ingots for sheet rolling at Warrick are made by an unusual horizontal, direct-chill, continuous-casting process.

Fig. 7.9. After scalping and heating, an ingot is passed back and forth through Warrick's hot reversing mill, which reduces the metal to a 1½-inch slab.

Fig. 7.10. Workers monitor Warrick's giant six-stand continuous cold mill where sheet is rolled to final gauge.

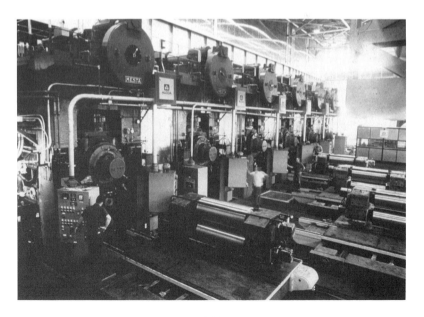

Fig. 7.11. In the finishing area at Warrick, coils of rolled container sheet are inspected and packed for shipping.

Table 7.2. *U.S. beer and soft drink glass and metal can shipments,*
1963–72 (billions of units)

Year	Glass	% Glass	Steel	% Steel	Aluminum	% Aluminum
1963	6.7	36.0	12.0	64.2	—	—
1964	7.3	34.6	13.5	64.0	0.3	1.4
1965	8.1	34.2	15.1	63.7	0.5	2.1
1966	9.5	33.6	18.2	64.3	0.6	2.1
1967	11.9	35.3	20.1	59.6	1.7	5.1
1968	12.8	32.5	24.3	61.7	2.3	5.8
1969	15.5	34.0	27.1	59.4	3.0	6.6
1970	17.6	34.4	28.9	56.6	4.6	9.0
1971	17.5	33.1	29.1	55.1	6.2	11.8
1972	18.3	33.3	29.0	52.1	8.4	14.6

Source: Internal Alcoa estimates based on Department of Commerce data.

tracks of development toward the development of a very lightweight can.[76] Ultimately, the draw-and-iron process, which produced cans at higher rates of speed, prevailed.

Reynolds and Kaiser moved quickly into the manufacture of all-aluminum cans, while Alcoa, true to form, remained strictly a producer of the intermediate products: sheet for "tab stock" (the most profitable sector of the market), for "end stock," and, now, for "body stock" as well. Rather than build its own can production lines, Alcoa put its money in high-volume sheet mills at one end and in R&D at the other, pursuing a long-term strategy of working with the major producers of metal cans. With Close as corporate champion for R&D, funds flowed into Alcoa's product development laboratories for the ongoing design and testing of improved, lighter-weight end products; but at no time did Alcoa's management intend to manufacture cans, except for demonstration purposes. Instead, Alcoa was to play the role of technical consultant and supplier, cultivating the end markets through campaigns of demonstration and education while providing engineering and technical assistance to can manufacturers who would buy aluminum sheet once the demand for aluminum cans was well established. As Cliff Sands explained emphatically, it was Alcoa's policy not to compete with its customers in the container markets.

> Alcoa is not in the can business [he wrote in 1968] nor do they intend to enter the can business either directly or through en-

couragement to packers of any kind. However, Alcoa has conceived a concept of a drawn and ironed can which can be produced
as economically and possibly more economically than any com-
merical container on the market today. Since this concept has
many radical innovations, it is necessary for us to design, develop and sometimes build equipment to produce a [demonstra-
tion] can layout.... It is our intent to recommend this line
to commercial can makers, captive can manufacturers, and
those companies who recently have entered the container
market.... [77]

The strategy worked. From 1965 to the end of 1970, Alcoa's share
of total RCS shipments, measured by weight, increased from twenty-
five to fifty-eight percent.[78] Even as competition increased to "cutthroat" proportions by the end of that period, Alcoa salesmen were
able to attract increasing orders by touting the superiority of its
research, equipment development, and process development that
"have been contributing substantially to the development and therefore the commercial success of many of our customers."[79]

Even though it took considerable effort over a period of years to
persuade beer producers to convert their production facilities, the
tide had clearly turned by 1970. It was just a matter of time before
aluminum would take virtually the entire beverage can market from
steel. Already, between 1965 and 1972, the number of aluminum
cans shipped in the United States increased from half a billion to
nearly 8.5 billion, twenty-two percent of all metal beverage containers shipped in the United States. Despite some efforts by the
steel companies to improve the properties of tinplate (and to develop
"black plate steel"), the all-aluminum can proved to have unassailable advantages. In addition to its greatly prolonged shelf life, it
chilled more quickly, it was lighter, it wouldn't rust, and it was easy
to recycle. The potential for recycling, which Alcoa was slow to see
at first, was multifaceted. Not only did recycling delight environmentalists (which translated into political pressure on the aluminum producers to do so), it attracted customers and lowered the
overall costs of production. Aluminum recycling centers, it was said,
were like "mines above ground," from which every used beer can
became a low-energy input into the production of a new can.[80] Meanwhile, the steel companies – having some potential to counter
with technological innovations of their own (such as lower-cost,
lighter-weight, better-coated, or even tin-free cans) – were slow
to move, and once can producers had converted their can lines, the
game was up.

Money for the expansion of can sheet production was no object in bad times as well as good. RCS, while certainly not immune to economic downturns, was less cyclical than aluminum's other major applications. And beyond the aluminum can lay markets for packaging of all kinds. Alcoa shipped more than half a billion, pilfer-proof closures for bottles and other containers in the late 1960s, by which time aluminum had become a familiar component in both flexible- and rigid-foil applications, in collapsible tubes, and composite containers for all manner of consumer goods. In 1972, "packaging and containers" accounted for 15.5 percent of domestic aluminum sales, third in volume to "building and construction" and "transportation." This was an important trend; Alcoa's growth in the building markets would taper off sharply in the years to come, and despite great progress in the application of aluminum in automotive and aerospace industries, containers and packaging would become the industry's largest market in the short span of a decade. By the 1980s, packaging and containers would produce more revenues for Alcoa than its other major markets in transporation, electrical equipment, and construction combined.[81]

John Harper and the "public corporation"

In 1968, an Alcoa official was quoted to the effect that John Harper had aged ten years during the first five years of his presidency. Harper, it was said, was running himself ragged from just trying to keep up with a vast range of self-ordained responsibilities.[82] A workaholic whose grasp of social and political contexts of business surpassed that of any Alcoa executive who preceded him, Harper seemed to be everywhere, playing to the hilt his roles as both chief executive and chief operating officer to which was added a heavy dose of public relations. He went to work early, got home late, and traveled more frequently than his predecessors – to Washington, to extracorporate board meetings, and to national and overseas business conferences. In the process, Harper brought Alcoa into the public limelight as never before, determined to make his company a model of socially responsible corporate capitalism.

John Dickson Harper was fifteen and lied about it when he got his first summer job in 1925, driving an electric truck at Alcoa, Tennessee, for $12 a week. Later, as a cooperative student in electrical engineering at the University of Tennessee, he continued to work at Alcoa, where he became full-time in 1933, "a hell of a time to get a job," he remembered. "At that time I was the only engineer hired." He was carried on the books as an hourly employee for several months until it became more apparent that he had the makings of a good young manager. He was appointed junior staff engineer for the Alcoa Works' power division, where over the next several years he gained experience designing and operating power stations. During the war, he served as assistant power manager for the company's extensive hydroelectric operations in Tennessee and North Carolina, participating in the design of new power plants and in the development of improved systems of networking between southern and northern utilities, negotiating power agreements with other utilities, and organizing central load dispatching in coordination with the TVA. Harper was also made responsible for his division's labor relations at a time when union organization was in its early, militant stages. To cope with this part of his job, he enrolled in night classes on personnel relations. It was out of his combined experience dealing with public authorities and unions that he developed an abiding taste for the political side of corporate management.[83]

In 1951, with eighteen years of experience under his belt, he was transferred to Rockdale, Texas, to build and manage Alcoa's new lignite-powered smelter. Rockdale, which grew from less than 2,000 to 6,000 inhabitants in two years, was a hothouse of higher education for Harper in corporate community relations. There, Harper's talent for politics ("... drop him in the middle of the Sahara Desert," said Krome George, "and he'd know the guy that ran the nearest oasis in ten minutes") came into full bloom. Sensitive to the human turmoil involved in "changing the nature" of "a rural community which had no industry at all ... into a full-fledged industrial operation," he spent his first year courting local politicians, ranchers, farmers, and businessmen whose hospitality was vital to accommodate the hundreds of workers Alcoa was bringing in and whose cooperation was crucial for gaining Alcoa access to mineral and water rights and favorable tax and infrastructure arrangements. Harper pledged Alcoa's taxes in advance for the extension of basic municipal facilities and schools and donated the land for a new community swimming pool. He organized the Texas Chemical Society to lobby for favorable tax treatment on metals and chemicals corporations and became deeply involved in Texas state politics. "My job," he recalled, "was as much community and state really as it was operations, because we had to make our way in the community and get by without being taxed to death and make our way in the state without being fresh meat for them to pick on." Within a year of ground-breaking, Rockdale poured out its first aluminum. By 1954, it was the company's most productive smelter.[84]

Having earned his spurs as a plant manager, Harper was brought to corporate headquarters to become assistant general manager of Smelting. He caught Frank Magee's attention, who moved him quickly up the ranks to become vice president of both Smelting and Fabricating in late 1960. In a company of specialists, he displayed a strong command of all areas of the business, including marketing and sales, and was especially appreciated by the company's R&D managers for his keen sense of technology. Kent Van Horn maintained that "no other vice president understood what the hell we were doing in New Kensington. He [Harper] understood research."[85] Thus, in an age of mounting external and internal pressures on the corporation, there may have been no one better to lead Alcoa. The social and political activism of the 1960s as well as the growing complexity of Alcoa's markets and technologies demanded someone with the breadth of outlook and experience of a man like Harper. It was almost a foregone conclusion that Harper would head the company when he went on the board in late 1962. He was elected president in April of 1963, when Lawrence Litchfield, at sixty-five, stepped up to the chairmanship.

Harper took the helm at Alcoa just as big business was once again under fire. A new age of social protest was in full swing, and the spirit of reform swept through most sectors of the body politic in one form or another. Corporations, sitting at the center of the established order, were being asked to conform to higher standards of social responsibility than ever before in American history by politicians, union leaders, environmentalists, and consumer advocates alike. No less mainstream a national spokesman than Dwight D. Eisenhower had already neatly articulated the public's abiding fear of corporate power in his farewell address when he coined the term "military–industrial complex." President John F. Kennedy had just made great political capital in his rollback of steel prices, and in the wake of Kennedy's assassination, Lyndon Johnson was able to mobilize widespread popular and congressional support for his "Great Society" agenda, which involved unprecedented levels of Government regulation of the society's economic activities. At the same time, the trend in Government regulation of manufacturing was extending well beyond conventional constraints on pricing and competitive behavior. In the administration of Johnson's successor, Richard M.

Nixon, new federal agencies would be established for the monitoring of corporate hiring practices, occupational safety, and environmental pollution.

Alcoa came under this array of new "social" regulatory controls and was subject to heightened expectations for corporate social responsibility. Harper was sympathetic to these expectations. Though he bristled at the prospect of more regulation of business (he was a traditional conservative Republican in this regard), he had also developed a keen sense of managerial stewardship that stressed the ethical interconnectedness of business and society. His thinking on this subject was more intuitive than analytical, more political than sociological, and he certainly never set down his views in systematic fashion. But he did, at least, deliver a series of lectures at Carnegie–Mellon University in 1976, from which we can glean the basic principles that guided his administration of Alcoa.

The American corporation, Harper declared, was threatened by an increasingly interventionist Government whose best intentions might result in actions that, rather than rendering business more responsible to society, might actually undermine its basic social purpose. That purpose he defined as "the return of an adequate profit," which was vital for "putting into place the necessary base to feed, clothe, house and usefully employ peoples everywhere." On the other hand, he chided American business for its provincialism, for its fear of social and political change, for its chronic indifference to the social aspirations of economically deprived peoples. Business leaders "must recognize," he said, "that the corporation no longer functions solely as an economic institution.... It functions, at least equally, as a social institution. The standards of management – and of individual managers – must take this clearly into account." Harper had little patience with businessmen who merely resisted Government pressure and social criticism. "Unless the emerging values of the society became the controlling values of the corporation," he warned, "change would be imposed from without." Cooperation between business and Government was as necessary as Government control would be inevitable in the absence of such cooperation.[86]

Harper's understanding of the "public corporation" was historical, progressive, teleological. The corporation's obligation to stay attuned to the changing values and needs of society stemmed from its very nature as a "public" institution, the evolution of which was subject to a general historical process that verged toward the "democratization" of business and the more humane and efficient governance of its operations by a managerial meritocracy. This had important implications for the way in which companies should be run. Management, he said, had become more "democratic" (the more apt word would have been "bureaucratic") in that successful corporations were best run by "managers chosen and advanced on the basis of ability, rather than on the basis of ownership or ancestry." It was through the dispersion of stock and the displacement of control of the corporation from the hands of autocratic owners into the hands of professional managers that the corporation had become not only more productive but also more open, "closer to the pulsebeat of the society itself." Likewise, it had become more responsible to its employees out of an evolving "respect of human labor" that had not always been "part of the values dominant in the industrial community," where life in the factory had all too often been "grim, demeaning and hazardous."[87] It was under Harper that Alcoa's plants began to move, at least tentatively, away from the authoritarian paternalism that had characterized shop–floor management.

But even more important, in Harper's scheme of things, was that the modern corporate chief executive understand his role as a quasi-public responsibility. In 1966, the Alcoa house organ reported on a survey that revealed Alcoa, though traditionally a publicity-shy company, to be one of the country's best-known corporations, ranked twenty-fourth in name recognition.[88] This was the way Harper liked it. More than any Alcoa executive before him, Harper saw himself as a capitalist leader standing at the nexus of society and its means of production with a responsibility to be accountable to both.

Harper was convinced that corporate good works was good business and that large-scale capitalist enterprise – openly conducted and rigorously managed – could coexist with the aspirations of an equitable, safe, and democratic society. To prove it, he committed Alcoa to programs designed to alleviate urban unemployment, housing shortages, and racial tensions. In this way, Alcoa became an important factor in the business–Government partnership that revitalized Pittsburgh in the 1970s. There and in other cities, much of Alcoa's real estate development was devoted to the building of low- and middle-income dwellings. Alcoa also participated in the federal Job Opportunities Program and other efforts to stimulate minority participation in business.[89] By the end of the decade, the company reported regularly on its fair employment efforts, on the development of its environmental control systems, and on its programs for improving working conditions in the plants – all well in advance of potential Government injunctions to do so.[90] Harper was especially concerned to open Alcoa to minority workers (although, to be sure, the corporation achieved little in that regard by the time he retired.)[91]

Hunt, Wilson, and Magee before him had devoted time and money to local and regional institutions, but Harper's outside interests were global. His defined his own job explicitly in terms of a community of business interests that extended beyond Alcoa's own parochial business concerns.

> The CEO's first responsibility [he explained] is to be certain the organization is right: staffed right, running right, planning right. He must be sure that there is proper financing, adequate machinery and a prudent supply of the raw materials required ..., that the corporation is properly fulfilling its mission [and] that a high standard of ethics is promulgated and enforced.... These things are basic. On beyond ..., it is not enough for him merely to hire others to cope with the outside influences and concerns. [He] must be able to relate complex concerns, one to another, and to understand the interrelationships of those concerns within his company [and] the commonality of interests between his company and other companies.[92]

With this in mind, he participated in national associations of business leaders and, departing from Alcoa practice, served enthusiastically as a director of other major corporations, among them Metropolitan Life, Goodyear, Procter & Gamble, and COMSAT (a business–Government partnership in communications satellites). He was a prime mover in the Business Round Table, which was established in response to mounting social criticism of capitalism and hostility toward big business, to bring the collective views of big business to bear on public issues. He sat on the Conference Board, on the Committee for Economic Development, and on the Committee for Constructive Consumerism, all emerging forums for the social responsibility of business.[93]

Reforming corporate governance

Harper's view of the CEO as a member of a larger community of business leaders conflated with his view of the progressive evolution of corporate "democracy" to transform the governance of Alcoa. At the top, he opened up the board of directors to outsiders. Magee had already made some attempt to expand the board, but had been unsuccessful. Not until 1965 did Alcoa get its first "outside" member, Paul Miller, president of the First Boston Corporation, in which the

Fig. 7.12. Five generations of corporate chiefs, circa 1965. From left to right are I. W. Wilson, Lawrence Litchfield, Frank Magee, Roy Hunt, and John Harper.

Mellons owned a substantial interest. But as the topics of discussion increased year by year, pressures continued to mount toward making the board's meetings more than mere occasions for "keeping General Mellon informed."[94]

A reconstituted board became possible after both Hunt and Mellon had passed away and other old-timers had run their course to retirement. Only then was Harper able to remake the board in keeping with its evolution into a more "public" corporation. Hunt, who had resigned his position as chairman of the Executive Committee in 1963, continued to attend board meetings and to go to his office daily, despite deteriorating health. He suffered a fatal heart attack on his way to lunch at the Duquesne Club on October 21, 1966. In 1967, John Mayer, chairman of the Mellon National Bank, became the board's second outside member. Mellon died on June 3, 1970. Neither Hunt nor Mellon was succeeded by a new family member, and after the latter's death, a large portion of the Mellon family holdings in the company was dispersed. Alfred Hunt, the corporate secretary, was the sole living legacy of the founding families on the board of directors. (Alfred's younger brother, Torrence, was serving a middle management career in Public Relations and Advertising.) Then in 1970, Fritz Close retired from the chairmanship, which Harper assumed for himself. The retirements of other Alcoa executives (including Wilson, Magee, and Hickman), would leave Harper with a board by 1972 that was overwhelmingly his own creation. By then, of ten directors, five were outsiders, all of whom had become directors since 1965. The other four (not counting Harper himself) were corporate officers, two of whom were Harper appointees: Krome George, who became president in 1970, and Eric Walker, former president of Pennsylvania State University, who had come to Alcoa in 1970 to be vice president for Science and Technology with a mandate to bring more corporate direction and longer-range planning to Alcoa's R&D activities.

The new board structure would transform the CEO's relationship to the directors. The result (and no doubt a large part of the intent) was to give the CEO greater control over strategic decisions. It was probably not coincidental that Harper was by temperament less comfortable than his predecessors with the kind of collegial board-level decision-making that had been Alcoa's hallmark. The proper function of a board, in his view, was to offer critical advice and to evaluate management, but not to make managerial decisions. In 1970, his assumption of the chairman's office as CEO was a novelty at Alcoa, although it followed the general trend in American corporate governance. Thereafter, agendas for the board would become more formal and substantive, and meetings would serve increasingly as forums for strategic review by directors with a wider range of experience. Strong outside directors, used wisely, according to Harper, would keep management from becoming too narrow in its thinking and helped prevent the sort of "strategic mistakes" more likely to be made by an ingrown group of decision-makers.[95]

As the head of Alcoa, Harper tried to run a tight ship. Though less collegial than Wilson or Magee, he delegated more decision-making responsibility to his subordinates from whom he expected, in turn, rigorous efficiency in personal performance, a subject on which he never tired of preaching. Harper also brought Alcoa up to a more sophisticated level of management by introducing systematic principles and practice to corporate planning and administration.

We have already seen that the widenening scope of the CEO's activities by the 1960s required greater delegation of tactical deci-

Fig. 7.13. "Harper's board" in 1971. From left to right (with positions held at the time) are Alcoa directors E. D. Brockett, former chairman of Gulf Oil Corporation; John Mayer, chairman of the board of Mellon National Bank and Trust Company; George Wyckoff, director emeritus; Russell De Young, chairman and CEO of Goodyear Tire & Rubber Company; Paul Miller, president of The First Boston Corporation; John Harper, chairman and CEO: John Mitchell, executive vice president of Primary Products; Frederick "Fritz" Close, former chairman of the board; Nathan Pearson, Investment Management (representing Paul Mellon's estate); J. S. "Jack" Harrison, executive vice president of Mill Products; I. W. Wilson, director emeritus; W. H. Krome George, president; Alfred M. Hunt, secretary; Frank Magee, former chairman and CEO. Not present was Eric Walker, vice president of Science and Technology, who was elected to the board at the end of the year.

sions. But the postwar trend toward centralization had made it "tougher to manage," Harper complained, especially in an era of rapidly rising costs and competition. The sheer complexity of the business demanded more effective, and more authoritative decision-making management at lower levels in the corporation, which in turn required better, more efficient systems of communication. To achieve this, attitudes would have to be changed up and down the corporate hierarchy.

Harper, therefore, encouraged reforms in both the structure and style of management. "Organizational analysis" and "management by objective" (jargon that could not have been used in polite company in the days of Davis and Hunt) became serious undertakings under his regime. From 1963 to 1968, Harper and his executive vice presidents, John Mitchell and John Harrison, redefined managerial responsibilities at all levels to improve cross-divisional communications, and to trim – through firings, attrition, and reassignment – "thick layers of management fat [that] had grown around the corporate middle during the booming 1950s." It was at first hard to get agreement on perceived goals and jobs, but, observed Harrison, simple insistence that plant operations managers "get commitments from their submanagers on their plans for the year – plans to improve performance, training of new managers, ways to automate and to expand" had been a useful way to "give shape to specific areas of responsibility."[96]

But how could responsibilities be better defined across departmental boundaries at appropriate levels? Coordination between production and marketing had weakened considerably as the company had grown larger. The Sales Department was especially problematic, organized as it was into seven industry–market groups – aerospace and defense, building products, consumer durables, electrical, machinery and equipment, packaging, and transportation. Each group had responsibility for its own product planning, development, promotion, and distribution. However, industry sales managers reported to one vice president, who then had to make decisions about prices and serve as arbiter for all manner of problems, large and small. The sales managers were hampered by lack of authority to make field decisions in timely fashion, and they compared their situation unfavorably to that of their counterparts at Reynolds, where marketing managers seemed to enjoy greater autonomy.[97] This problem and others like it were addressed in September 1968, when the first fundamental administrative reform of Harper's regime was implemented.

The 1968 reform divided the company into two "profit centers," a move, albeit limited, toward organizing major lines of business around products rather than functions. Mill Products – all shapes sold to industrial customers for further fabrication – became one major division, or profit center, under Harrison. Mitchell became head of Primary Products, which included all stages of production from mining to the production of aluminum ingot as well as alumina chemicals, aluminum powder, and paints. Mitchell also oversaw all international operations and a varied group of subsidiaries that made end-use products. The subsidiaries, including Wear-Ever, Alcoa Wrap, Alcoa Building Products, and others, were grouped under a vice president for "Allied Products."[98]

The most quickly realized advantage of the new structure was that operating and marketing decisions in the Mill Products division were brought together at levels of the organization below the president's office. Six industry sales groups were organized under two general managers (three each), and tactical decisions could be expected within twenty-four hours.[99] Outside observers liked what they saw; in an opinion poll of industry analysts taken in 1969, Alcoa was seen as having the most promising growth prospects of all the nonferrous metals producers in North America, largely as a consequence of its managerial and structural reforms.[100]

Though the new structure remained highly centralized in its outline, much of the pressure on the central office had been alleviated. The reform also established the principle of an executive office supported directly by the corporation's staff functions. Staff and line functions, which had never been sharply delineated in Alcoa's functional organization, were now made clearer. The profit centers had their own staff groups concerned more with the support of operational and marketing issues, while corporate staffs concerned with "overall planning, strategic direction and control" were attached to the chairman and the president as follows. Public Relations and R&D were organized as staff departments reporting to the chairman, an arrangement, of course, that capitalized on the particular strengths of Fritz Close. The Corporate Secretary, Legal, Personnel, Engineering and Finance reported to Harper – Finance, which included Treasury, Control, and Real Estate departments, was administered by Krome George as executive vice president. George also oversaw the company's new Corporate Planning Department. Planners were coming into vogue in American corporations during the 1960s, and Harper especially liked people who could provide him more precise, more scientific bases for understanding the business, its component parts, its prospects in the marketplace. As computerized management information systems, cost analysis, and forecasting tools swept through American industry in the 1960s, the more intuitive strategies of A. V. Davis, Roy Hunt, and Frank Magee no longer seemed adequate to Harper. Thus, Harper, intuitive manager though he himself was, placed great faith in subordinates of a more analytical disposition.[101]

Headed by Theodore H. Kerry, the Planning Department consisted of two major groups: one for economic analysis and forecasting; the other for management information systems (organized as a subsidiary) and the analysis of internal production and management costs. The planners functioned as a kind of personal staff to the CEO in examining major investment problems. Armed with elaborate mathematical forecasting techniques, they guided Alcoa's facilities planning. For example, a 220-inch rolling mill, the world's largest, was projected for the company's plant at Davenport based on the planners' long-range forecasts for aluminum plate. Five- and ten-year forecasts of industry and Alcoa shipments indicated a need for a nearly $5–billion investment for the industry as a whole just to meet primary aluminum demand in the United States, leading Krome George, then the vice president for Finance, to advocate a policy of targeted investment consistent with Harper's desire to eliminate small, duplicative operations in favor of high-volume facilities dedicated to particular or closely related markets.[102]

It was in the Planning Department's more introspective function, the analysis of internal production costs, that some of the most important developments had taken place since 1963, when George and Kerry had begun to employ computerized methods. For the first time in Alcoa's history, a product's margin could be assessed by going into its true production costs measured element by element. Cost analysis of the production cycle could reveal, for example, that a higher-margin item might actually have underlying, hidden costs that would make it less profitable than a lower-margin substitute that flowed more smoothly through the manufacturing process. Through advanced cost-accounting techniques, many products that the company had been carrying for a long time could be shown to be unprofitable, indicating the need for either elimination of the product lines or improvement in the processes of production.

Partly as a consequence of improved analysis of costs, process innovation acquired a new glamour at the Laboratories, as well as in the plants. The company's basic business of smelting, which still required a high degree of manual operation in the early 1960s, was being computerized in order to eliminate many direct labor functions, improve electrical power efficiency, and maintain more accurate controls over the chemical composition of the bath. The introduction of a continuous-casting process for making large, ready-to-roll ingots and the installation of a high-speed, single-product mill for container sheet at Warrick, Indiana, spelled just the kinds of process-improvement payoffs that Harper's high-volume, mass-production strategy called for. Process technology became targeted for substantial new R&D investment. And though it would not be announced until 1972, Alcoa was developing a radical alternative to the Hall–Héroult Process, at a cost of $25 million over fifteen years.[103]

As planning became the height of fashion, efficiency and productivity became the bywords of the Harper years. Not so far afield was the object lesson of Reynolds, which, despite its brisk sale of aluminum, had seen its earnings and stock price plunge – victims, it was said, "of an expensive and ill-timed expansion, cutthroat competition, a late start in its cost-cutting program, and inbred management." Careful planning and cost-conscious management were at a premium in an industry where the tendency toward overcapacity had become endemic.[104] At Alcoa, Harper was determined to fashion a new management ethos around strategic thinking, computerized automation, and sensitivity to cost-effective methods of manufacture.

Taming costs was increasingly an issue in an inflationary economy. Prior to the energy crisis of the 1970s, management was most concerned about labor costs, subject as they were to ever more successful demands of unions in the triennial collective bargaining process. Between 1946 and 1968, the hourly cost of labor per employee, payroll and benefits included, had swelled from $1.29 to $4.89. But higher wages and benefits were largely offset by increased productivity through automation and scaled-up processes, as the business became more capital-intensive. From 1956 through 1968, nonlabor inputs became an increasing charge against every dollar of revenue relative to labor. Nonlabor inputs in the latter year accounted for 41.58 percent of revenues compared with 35.38 percent thirteen years earlier.[105] Within the same time frame, as shipments nearly doubled from about 755,000 tons, to 1,336,000 tons, the number of employees was reduced from 58,500 to 46,500. Despite the favorable trend, Harper called for even more improvement in productivity.

Neither sound plans nor improved efficiency could be achieved without highly skilled and talented managers. Harper realized that Alcoa could no longer expect to breed strong general managers through the kinds of informal mentorship that had long paved the way to Pittsburgh. In the huge complex that Alcoa had become, the best prospects could too easily get lost in distant operations, only to be overlooked without well-connected patrons. Promotions must be based all the more on objective measures of skill and merit, which in turn required more precise evaluations based on commonly recognized standards. A larger number of middle managers were to be given greater exposure to a wider range of corporate experience, which meant that local works managers, who might have once expected to remain in their plants for entire careers, now looked to moving from job to job, from one location to another, with a much higher frequency. At Pittsburgh, the Personnel Department kept watch for particularly talented young managers who might be sent back to school to acquire specific analytical tools or to study the latest academic wisdom on corporate management. Plant-level seminars were launched to augment a longer-standing program of Pittsburgh Management Conferences that were held twice yearly. The most important and successful of these was the Advanced Management Program, which was first held in 1965, offering select groups of young managers exposure to problems and perspectives of other parts of the corporation as well as opportunities to work on real problems of current interest. In 1966, Fritz Close set up a twenty-three-man "Future Planning Committee," an assembly of "young, intelligent, energetic men" to discuss such fundamental questions as diversification, social responsibility, and organization structure. Many today recall some of the classroom efforts as just so much window dressing. Yet the efforts reflected a more determinedly systematic approach to management development in accordance with more purely bureaucratic – meritocratic – standards of corporate governance.[106]

If one looked for an ideal type in the reformed Alcoa management structure, it might well have been Krome George, a planner who had made a career out of the formal, systematic analysis of costs and opportunities. Indeed, when it came time to groom a successor, Harper tapped George to become president. This was made official in June 1970, as Harper stepped up to the chairmanship, still retaining his authority as CEO.

W. H. Krome George was the first Alcoa president not to have high-level operating experience. An MIT graduate, George had joined the company's alumina refining operations in East St. Louis in 1942 at $180 per month. He was then assigned to the DPC refinery in Baton Rouge (which was later sold to Kaiser) until 1944, when he was sent back to East St. Louis, where he joined other excess DPC refining engineers who "loafed around for three or four years, completely bored because there wasn't all that much to do." He was eventually pulled away from his chemical engineering responsibilities in order to do cost analysis on alumina manufacture.

In 1951, George was called to Pittsburgh, where he helped develop new corporate cost-accounting systems "to more properly reflect what we felt we wanted as engineers than what the accountants felt." Within five years, he rose to become Alcoa's chief cost accountant. He later recounted how, as a cost accountant in the 1950s, he had been part of a "subversive" little "planning unit" in the con-troller's office that found it difficult to introduce the idea of corporate planning under the *ancien regime*. The very word "planning," he said, ignited the rage of the "old guys" who were afraid "that some-body was going to start telling them what to do." At the time, Alcoa had no strong financial organization at all. The corporate treasurers of the era were caretakers ("Chief Wilson . . . didn't need a treasurer to tell him how to go to New York and borrow money. . . . [He] could handle that with one hand tied behind him.") It was only after Frank Magee had decided that he needed more formal economic analysis to manage the business that George got his license to push for more systematic planning and control. In the early 1960s, he waged a successful campaign for cost-cutting programs in the plants based on close analysis of plant overhead requirements.[107]

Under Harper, George shot up through the ranks. After a stint as manager of Economic Analysis and Planning (he had already, according to Frank Magee, been recognized as top-management tal-ent), George became vice president of Finance in 1965, overseeing all planning, accounting, and treasury functions. In 1967, he was promoted to executive vice president, from which perch he was able to push for the corporate-wide implementation of computer-based planning and accounting systems. As president (he would be offi-cially designated chief operating officer in 1972), George would carry the basic thrust of Harper's strategic and structural reforms into the next decade.

The world industry circa 1970

Alcoa, remember, had once held a monopoly in the United States on the production of primary aluminum. It sustained its monopoly for more than half a century because of its ability to exploit factors inherent in refining and smelting technologies. Aluminum had very high capital requirements, and all the stages of its production were functionally interdependent. That is why when Alcoa's directors created Aluminium Limited in 1928, they endowed it with resources at all stages of primary production. Thereafter, until the Govern-ment became involved in World War II, no one else in North America dared even hope to operate a smelter without a captive source of alumina, which, in turn, depended on a reliable source of high-grade bauxite. It also helped to have captive fabricating facilities that would take a substantial portion of the smelter's output. The capital requirements of entry were thus compounded by the desirability, if not absolute necessity, of entering all stages of the business at once and by the additional requirement of having a reliable and inexpensive source of energy to fuel the power-hungry electrolytic Hall Process. Personnel requirements were also high; it took considerable managerial and technical expertise to operate production efficiently.

At the end of World War II, Alcoa's economies of scale, its experience, its well-established supplies of ore, its prime hydropower sources, and its controlling patents on the refining process, made it impossible for even such powerful concerns as Kaiser and Reynolds to enter the field without an intervening force. For those companies to become fully integrated producers after the war, there had to be some positive action on the part of the Federal Government. Subsequently, when Harvey, Anaconda, and Ormet brought their smelters onstream, they too required Government assistance in the form of subsidies and favorable tax policies. All the new producers, large and small alike, benefitted from ongoing antitrust pressure directed against Alcoa by the Department of Justice and the Federal Court of Appeals.

The industry's prosperity was a strong lure to new entry well into the 1960s. Several more primary aluminum ventures emerged in the United States, even though it was a daunting task to finance and build an aluminum smelting business. In the absence of Government incentives, new ventures were typically supported by major aluminum companies. Of the six companies formed to smelt primary aluminum in the United States between 1966 and 1972, only one, a joint venture of the National Steel Corporation and Southwire Corporation, was established outside the existing structure of the aluminum industry and without benefit of Government subsidy. (National Southwire's smelter in Hawesville, Kentucky, which came onstream in 1969, was also the first aluminum venture ever attempted by a steel company.) All the other new North American smelters were affiliated with established major world producers. In 1963, Consolidated Aluminum Corporation, a postwar sheet and foil fabricator owned by Swiss Aluminium Limited, built a smelter in New Johnsonville, Tennessee. In 1966, American Metal Climax and Howmet, the latter controlled by Pechiney, joined forces to found Intalco, a Ferndale, Washington, based venture that employed Pechiney's high-capacity and highly automated potlines rated at 260,000 tons. Four years later, the same alliance formed Eastalco to begin construction of a smelter in Frederick, Maryland. Revere

Copper and Brass, part owner of Ormet, brought its own reduction plant on line in Scottsboro, Alabama, in 1970, and in 1971, Noranda Aluminum, a subsidiary of Noranda Mines, Ltd., of Canada, completed construction of a smelter in New Madrid, Missouri.[108]

Most of the new companies had downstream operations through which they could market their primary output. They found it far more difficult to integrate backward into alumina and bauxite. Whereas Alcoa, Reynolds, and Kaiser were fully integrated, new producers had to rely for the most part on long-term purchasing agreements to obtain reliable, competitively priced sources of supply, an undesirable situation. Harvey's 1962 *Annual Report* informed its stockholders that because control of all operations from mine to metal was so crucial to improving profitability, even "without a corresponding increase in sales volume," that integration had become the prime focus of that company's long-range planning.[109]

Attempts by the newer producers to integrate upstream proved insufficient to propel them into the ranks of the established majors. In 1971, according to the Aluminum Association, the combined capacity of the nonmajor American producers was to stand at about 1,506,000 tons as compared with the combined 3,160,000 tons of Alcoa, Reynolds, and Kaiser, of which Alcoa's 1,475,000 tons comprised about thirty-two percent of the total. If we expand our sights to take in Alcan and the Reynolds-controlled Canadian British Aluminium (which had been founded in 1957 as a partnership of British Aluminum and a Quebec paper producer before falling under the control of Reynolds), total North American capacity stood at more than 5,500,000 tons. The four major producers accounted for about 4,000,000 tons, or seventy-three percent.[110] Thus, even though the North American industry was now comprised of a growing number of players, it remained highly concentrated.

This was true of the world industry, as well. In the industrialized capitalist economies, regional aluminum monopolies, each of which had operated for decades in fairly well-contained geographical markets, had given way during the 1960s to a multinational industry of competitive producers. But these competitors were few in number. Despite the entry of many smaller enterprises since World War II, one could still speak of an industry dominated by the "Big Six," which comprised the four North American majors and two old-line European firms, Pechiney and Alusuisse. Together, the Big Six controlled about sixty-one percent of the total noncommunist world capacity of 11,445,000 tons through their own domestic smelters and through their financial participation in foreign smelters. The re-

Table 7.3. *U.S. primary aluminum capacity, 1971 (thousands of short tons)*

Company	Capacity	% of total
Alcoa	1,475	31.6
Reynolds	975	20.9
Kaiser	710	15.2
Ormet	240	5.1
Howmet	217.5	4.7
Martin Marietta	201	4.3
Anaconda	180	3.9
National Southwire	180	3.9
Consolidated	175	3.7
Amax	130.5	2.8
Revere	112	2.4
Noranda	70	1.5
Total	4,666	100.0

Source: The Aluminum Association, *1971 Aluminum Statistical Review* (New York, 1972).

maining thirty-nine percent of capacity was scattered throughout the habitable regions of the earth, almost entirely in industrial and in advanced "industrializing" countries of the "Third World."

Most Third World production involved the participation of the major aluminum producers. Only five percent of the noncommunist world capacity was Government-owned. Another ten percent of the rated noncommunist capacity belonged to nine private non-North American firms that had been established after World War II in Norway, India, Japan, France, West Germany, South Korea, and Italy. Though events would unfold otherwise, sophisticated observers of the industry anticipated that additional development of aluminum capacity would continue to depend mainly on the expansion of the established major international companies, either through direct investment or through joint ventures.[111]

Joint ventures played a crucial role in the maintenance of the major producers' market shares by reducing competitive pressures. Through joint ventures, established producers could spread their available investment capital over larger spheres of productive capacity while alleviating political problems of entry into protected markets. Vertical joint ventures made it easier for supplier and buyer to exchange technical and managerial know-how and ensured

Table 7.4. *Noncommunist world primary aluminum capacity, 1971*
(thousands of short tons)

Company	Capacity[a]	% of total
Alcoa (U.S.)	1,717	15.0
Alcan (Canada)	1,582	13.8
Reynolds (U.S.)	1,276	11.1
Kaiser (U.S.)	1,021	8.9
Pechiney (France)	886	7.8
Alusuisse (Switzerland)	476	4.2
Other	4,487	39.2
Total "Big Six"	6,958	60.8
Grand Total	11,445	100.0

[a]Figures represent companies' equity share.
Source: Spector, *Aluminum Industry Report* (1975).

aluminum smelters more reliable sources of supply than would be the case in free-market transactions. Horizontal arrangements were useful for "socializing" newer producers into the pricing and supply policies of the industry, which enhanced the ability of the majors to sustain a semblance of the long-term, stable price patterns in a global market that had served them so well in their regional markets. Alcan, Pechiney, and especially Alusuisse had relied heavily on joint ventures to establish their international positions. Of the three major United States firms, Alcoa was most heavily involved in joint ventures, which enabled it to establish mining, refining, and smelting operations in many more countries than did Kaiser and Reynolds.[112]

Just how difficult it remained for entrepreneurs without ties to the aluminum establishment to enter the smelting business is borne out by contemporary calculations of economists on the capital and technical requirements of plants at all three stages of primary production. Alumina refineries, in particular, enjoyed enormous physical economies of scale in their continuous-process operations of up to 330,000 metric tons of annual capacity and could reap substantial administrative economies in managerial units involving duplicate facilities. The optimal size of smelters was smaller, though still large, at about 100,000 metric tons per annum. There were wide variations in optimal economies for smelters depending on a host of siting, climatic, and technical factors (such as degree of automation), but in general, a small plant of 20,000 metric tons was determined to have an average production cost that was ten percent greater than that of a plant five times larger.

In theory, bauxite facilities for mining and beneficiation had much lower "minimum efficient" economies of scale, but the necessity of building shipping and receiving facilities (railways, ocean vessels, ports) made large operations necessary. In a fully integrated primary aluminum operation, the optimal size of an alumina refinery would naturally determine the investment necessary for bauxite and smelting, in order to assure an optimal throughput from mine to metal. Think of it this way: given the basic ratios of approximately four tons of high-grade bauxite to yield two tons of alumina to make one ton of aluminum, a 220,000-ton refinery required mining facilities of 880,000 tons of high-grade (fifty-percent available alumina content) bauxite and a 110,000-ton smelter.[113]

In brief, the costs of entry at efficient scale remained extraordinarily high. The basic investment requirement for aluminum was thought to range from three to seven times what it would take to enter into steel production with equivalent efficient capacity. According to a French analyst (who had published his findings in 1962), the order-of-magnitude investment for an integrated aluminum operation of minimum efficient scale could run as high as $1,000 per ton. Merton Peck had already estimated in 1958 that the total initial investment in an integrated aluminum plant was as much as $800 million.[114] By 1966, the per-ton cost was estimated as high as $1,120 by the Charles River Associates, with a total cost of investment reaching $375 million. A breakdown of investment in facilities (not counting integrated power facilities) would look as follows:[115]

	Cost per ton	Total cost
700,000-ton mine	$8–90	$5.6–6.3 million
330,000-ton refinery	$110–180	$36.3–59.4 million
165,000-ton smelter	$650–850	$149.2–252.7 million

Thus, it should come as no surprise that the primary industry was still dominated by the established, integrated producers.

Alcoa and the other North American majors built plants to larger scale than did European producers, which put the North American companies in a strong economic position to compete in the growing world market for aluminum, provided that barriers to trade were not too high. Producers in every country enjoyed some degree of government protection against the entry of outsiders. Regional economic blocs, such as the British Commonwealth nations, the European Economic Community (EEC), the European Free Trade Association (EFTA), and the Latin American Free Trade Association (LAFTA), maintained discriminatory tariff policies. Japan, along with some less-developed nations, such as Brazil and India, maintained stiff duties on imports. Even so, the trend was toward freer trade. By 1967, according to the best analysis of the situation, "the significance of tariffs in shaping trade in aluminum and its raw materials appears to be diminishing."[116]

By 1972, there had been a marked change in the posture of the United States industry toward tariffs, even though the country had been a net importer of ingot in all but three years since 1950. The shift in the American industry's position had occurred in the early 1960s, when the majors had come to realize that their traditional concern to protect domestic markets was more than offset by their need to ensure unimpeded flow of bauxite and alumina from foreign countries and to find overseas outlets for their increasing output – in both domestic and foreign facilities – of ingot. North American willingness to relax its trade barriers was crucial to the success of the 1967 "Kennedy Round" of the General Agreement on Tariff and Trade (GATT). That year, GATT established a schedule that reduced tariffs in the major industrialized nations, including Japan, by as much as fifty percent, to take full effect in 1972. By 1970, United States duties on bauxite and alumina were virtually nonexistent and on ingot stood at $0.011 per pound, too low to impede imports from Canada and Europe. Tariffs in the two largest markets, Europe and the United States, were not high enough to impede trade, and from 1965–9, exports to Asia (mainly Japan) and to Europe from the United States increased at an annual rate of 11.7 percent, faster than the industry growth rate of eleven percent. Total imports from the United States accounted for over seven percent of American shipments, mostly in the form of ingot.[117]

The decline in tariffs was good news, but Alcoa's executives were more concerned about "*nontariff* barriers,"[118] such as import quotas and exchange controls. Australia, for example, had for all practical purposes stopped granting import licenses by 1963 in order to ensure the consumption of its own swelling domestic production. Many Latin American countries charged premium rates on exchange to pay for imports. Less-developed nations were beginning to build smelters under umbrellas of government protection. Like all the major aluminum producers, Alcoa maneuvered around such barriers so that it could build its own facilities in foreign countries under favorable conditions. But increasingly, investment in underdeveloped nations was becoming inhibited by high costs of construction and by the political risks associated with poor economies and unstable governments.[119]

We have already seen that with its investments in Europe, Africa, Asia, Latin America, and Australia, Alcoa had become a bona fide multinational. Alcoa had gone abroad, for the second time in its history, not simply to expand its base of natural resources – bauxite and power – but to exploit expanding world markets. Its level of investment in new facilities was adequate to ensure that mines, refineries, and smelters comfortably met the standards of efficient scale. New facilities were planned carefully to ensure efficient throughput at all stages of production from mine to metal and even further into a wide variety of semifabricated products serving regional markets. Alcoa was the world's largest producer, controlling about fifteen percent of noncommunist smelting capacity and nearly twenty-four percent of alumina refining capacity.[120]

Alcoa still enjoyed its leading market share in the United States, where most of the world's aluminum was sold. (In 1971, 5,070,000 tons of aluminum were consumed in the United States compared to 4,800,000 tons combined in the next eleven largest noncommunist nations.[121]) But it was becoming clear that the company's future was increasingly linked to demand overseas. In 1972, overseas operations would spur Alcoa to a strong recovery after two years of badly depressed industry conditions. That year, corporate-wide sales of $1.75 billion were a record, as shipments were up 24.5 percent over 1971, about twice the increase for the United States industry as a whole.[122] As international trade barriers and cartel arrangements weakened, as new world markets for aluminum in emerging nations opened up, as new applications for the metal took hold, the world was Alcoa's new frontier.

Alcoa's prospects in 1970

Despite positive signs for global expansion, the experience of recent years taught that while aluminum was still a growth business, stable patterns of administered pricing by a North American oligopoly could no longer be taken for granted. What could be taken for granted, instead, was an inexorable rise in the costs of energy, materials, and labor, all spurred by chronic inflation and by the power of unions to extract liberal wage and benefits from a strike-shy corporation. Alcoa rode out one major strike by the

Aluminum Workers International against eight of its plants for nearly two months in 1968, but only because of extreme pressure to hold the AWI in line with prior agreements struck with the Steelworkers and Autoworkers, the industry's other major bargaining units.[123]

Even more problems were lurking just beneath the surface. The power of the company to adjust to fluctuations in the market while maintaining strong prices was also constrained more than ever by forces beyond its control – not only by the activities of an increasing number of producers in the United States, but also by decisions, political and economic, made around the world. The growing willingness of governments in less industrialized countries to sponsor and subsidize stand-alone smelters loomed as a threat to all major producers. In 1960, about sixteen percent of noncommunist world capacity had been government-sponsored, but by 1970, the proportion had grown to over twenty percent.[124] Thus, as it had happened early in the century, lack of due caution on the part of the world's producers could quickly lead to excess capacity.

Lest we forget, Alcoa's competition came not only from other aluminum companies, but also from producers of other materials. Historically, Alcoa had made a market for its primary aluminum by supplanting other materials by developing an array of aluminum products. When "younger" materials such as magnesium and titanium had threatened parts of Alcoa's business, the company had tried, with modest success, to incorporate them into its own research, development, and production. Whether it could do so successfully in the future remained to be seen. Vast markets held by steel were still ripe for the plucking, although the steel industry was working hard to mount counteroffensives in automobiles, packaging, and even in aircraft.

More serious threats were emerging on less-predictable fronts, where the inexorable advance of science and technology generated new substances that had the potential to challenge aluminum in several well-established markets. Plastics were appearing more and more in construction, transportation, machinery, and packaging, fiberglass in consumer durables, sodium in electrical conductors, and composite materials in specialized, high-margin applications. As industry experts looked toward the future, it seemed likely to some that "the need to become more closely allied with steel and plastics in the marketplace," would bring "major producers ... increasingly under the wings of makers of other materials."[125]

Even within the industry, technology marched ahead, threatening to upset long-standing modes of primary production. The stakes in achieving radical breakthroughs on technological fronts were very high, and the competition very intense. Diminishing hydropower resources in industrial nations and the high cost of developing hydropower in the Third World were driving aluminum producers to develop cheaper alternatives, among which nuclear power seemed the most plausible.[126] All the major producers were also at work on new ways to reduce bauxite directly into aluminum and, alternatively, to find ways to extract aluminum from nonbauxite sources.[127] That these goals had been pursued in vain for more than eighty years made them no less attractive in the present. At Alcoa, development of "The Alcoa Smelting Process" was the company's own attempt at "creative destruction." Employing aluminum chloride electrolysis, the new process would eliminate the need for carbon anodes (which comprised seven percent of the total cost of smelting), operate at lower temperatures, employ higher current densities, eliminate environmental hazards from the use of fluorides, and, possibly, employ nonbauxitic feedstocks. If successful, Alcoa could itself lead a revolution in aluminum production. A technically different but competing program was underway at Alcan.[128]

Coping with increasing competition on both geopolitical and technological fronts was the principal challenge confronting Alcoa in 1970. The company's sources of supply and markets, both, were affected by widening arenas of competition, and, notwithstanding the high degree of concentration in the world industry, the old, stable order of oligopolistic pricing had irrevocably passed. Plastics were cutting into some of aluminum's markets for food packaging, pleasure boats, and automobile trimmings. Yet, as Alcoa assessed its future, its traditional optimism remained intact. The company intended to grow as it had always grown, by promoting aluminum applications, by developing new aluminum products, by finding new markets for existing aluminum products, and by striving for more efficient ways to make aluminum. The formula, refined by Harper's strategy of concentrating on high-volume, high-margin sectors of the aluminum fabricating business, seemed to be working as well as ever. Beyond its already accomplished "diversification" into real estate and titanium forgings and beyond its glimmering interests in desalination, oceanography, and ceramics, Alcoa felt no immediate pressure to rethink its corporate mission.

And why not? Even as the world continued to grow more complex, the industry more crowded, the pressures of technology and competition more uncertain, aluminum was still a young metal with exciting prospects. Having focused its strategies and reformed its structure, Alcoa looked confidently ahead to years of even greater growth and higher profits.

8

Responses to a changing world

In the fall of 1985, Alcoa's ambitious attempt to render the Hall Process obsolete was abandoned. Alcoa's chief executive officer, Charles W. Parry, caught few by surprise when he announced the closing of the Alcoa Smelting Process (ASP) pilot plant in Anderson County, Texas. The write-down of ASP was reported at year-end as part of a $138.8 million after-tax reserve set against the closing of about 25 percent of Alcoa's wholly owned smelting and related refining capacity. This "special charge" was more than enough to plunge Alcoa into its first annual loss in net income since the Great Depression, a loss reported at $16.6 million.[1]

Oddly enough, ASP is not considered to have failed as a technology. It had been conceived as a long-term alternative to the Hall Process in order to reduce smelting costs substantially. The new process had been plagued with chemical problems ever since it had been put into plant-scale operation in 1976, but such technical difficulties were to be expected in the long-term development of a new technology. In 1985, expectations for its technical feasibility remained high. Alcoa was still telling its shareholders that the new process was expected to reduce power consumption alone by a full third less than the 6 kilowatt-hours per pound consumed by the most efficient modern Hall cell. In fact, the decision to discontinue its development came at a time when the company was publicly insisting that the process was "close to success." Why, then, shut it down? "The reason for [the abandonment of ASP]," Parry explained

374

at the time, "frankly, is that early in the twenty-first century, I doubt that aluminum is going to be terribly important to the structure of the company." If anything, aluminum "is going to go the way of copper."[2]

In many respects, aluminum had already gone the way of copper. Like copper, the price of aluminum had once been "administered" by its major producers, and aluminum had since become a commodity item for which the price was determined almost entirely by market forces. The power of the major primary aluminum producers to control base prices had virtually vanished. The world market had become awash in competition at all stages of production. Once regarded as a novelty that its producers struggled to establish in the bailiwicks of "older" materials, aluminum was now threatened by the development of such younger, more exotic materials as plastics, ceramics, and composites. All the North American producers were cutting back on primary capacity. (Reynolds made especially deep cuts in 1985, writing off $380 million for four closed smelters and reducing its capacity by forty-six percent.)[3] By the 1980s, the growth of Alcoa's aluminum business, the rate of which had historically outpaced the Gross National Product, had slipped into a state of secular decline.

Alcoa was being buffeted by the same general economic forces that were affecting most of America's center-industry manufacturers. During the 1970s, growth rates slowed and profits were squeezed by both slackening demand and escalating costs. Energy costs, already on the increase, had surged in the wake of the action taken by the Organization of Petroleum Exporting Countries (OPEC) to induce an oil shortage in 1973 and even more so after 1977, as a result of OPEC's coordinated escalation of prices. The costs of power at Alcoa's seven domestic smelters increased over 400 percent in just a decade. Bauxite supplies came under some pressure from a foreign cartel, and the cost of ore had risen further as a result of increased taxes and royalties levied by host countries.[4] Amid the mounting inflation of the 1970s (the rates of which reached nearly fourteen percent per annum[5]), Alcoa's labor and administrative costs also spiraled. By 1983, master union agreements, which had been tied to automatic cost-of-living adjustments (since 1974), had brought the average total of wages and benefits for hourly employees to $23.50 per hour (compared with a U.S. manufacturing average of $11.95). And as labor costs climbed to "noncompetitive" levels, they stimulated demands for higher salaries among management and technical personnel.[6]

As costs rose, prices became more subject to competitive pressures. Once contained to a large degree by regional oligopolies, price competition had grown rife, making it difficult for a private producer to earn adequate returns in primary production. In 1985, it was estimated that of about fourteen million metric tons of "Western World" aluminum smelting capacity, some thirty percent was subsidized by the ownership or sponsorship of governments. The trend toward government-subsidized smelting was expected to continue growing to more than forty percent by 1990.[7] This was hardly a recipe for the efficient allocation of resources. Most of these smelters were unintegrated facilities. That so many of the smaller producers were badly managed, that they were technologically inferior, and that they usually lacked the economies of scale enjoyed by the smelters of the large producers made no difference; they spilled aluminum onto the world markets, willy-nilly. By 1980, the world's aluminum capacity was (from the perspective of the major producers) in gross excess, and the maintenance of stable ingot prices was no longer even within the realm of wishful thinking.

After more than thirty-five years of a progressive lowering of trade barriers under the General Agreement for Tariffs and Trade, the downstream segments of the aluminum industry had also become internationalized. All types of semifinished and finished aluminum products made abroad were now flowing freely into North American markets, still the largest in the world for aluminum. The challenge from European and Asian producers to the major integrated North American producers was not as great as the threat to, say, automobiles and steel, where American producers not only had disadvantages in labor costs but also in the sophistication of production management and technology. Yet, though there was no great "Japanese threat" in the integrated production of aluminum (power was much too expensive for that to happen), the Japanese, in particular, were establishing toeholds in important markets for semifinished products (such as aerospace and beverage cans) by introducing quality products – often, Alcoa managers complained, at considerable sacrifice in short-term profits in order to achieve long-term gains in market share.[8]

The perception of these phenomena as constituting a new and permanent set of realities prompted a dramatic shift in Alcoa's expectations for the future. Internal studies projecting growth rates of Alcoa's existing aluminum technologies had found them to compare unfavorably to those of "strategically-important, external technologies." The broad conclusion of Alcoa's own analyses was

Table 8.1. *Average aluminum energy and labor costs in noncommunist economies, 1986*

Country	Energy costs (mills per kilowatt-hour)	Hourly wages and benefits (dollars)
U.S.	21.2	19.44
Japan	47.0	16.30
Canada	3.7	16.10
Europe	20.4	13.44
Oceania	11.8	12.20
Asia (except Japan)	35.2	3.70
Africa	14.2	2.40
Latin America	12.5	2.04

Source: Data provided by Alcoa Accounting Department as background for Alcoa's mid-year *Fact Book* (1987).

unsettling, at first resisted, but finally accepted: "advances developing outside of the traditional Alcoa manufacturing world were changing the very basis of future competition.[9]

In early 1983, on the eve of his retirement as chairman, Krome George made his own perceptions of Alcoa's problems explicit in the company's *1982 Annual Report* in which he challenged traditional assumptions about the future of the aluminum industry. His successor, Charles Parry, then led the company through a profound reordering of its corporate mission and structure. This was by no means the first time Alcoa had to respond to a major change in its environment. Nor was it the first time the company had to alter its strategic assumptions. The expiration of its controlling patents, the divestiture of Aluminium Limited, the Great Depression, the demand pressures of World War II, and the advent of Kaiser and Reynolds had all been significant tests of creative adaptation for Alcoa, which had proven its ability, time and again, to survive and grow in a changing world. But through all the changing circumstances, Alcoa's basic mission had remained constant: to sustain its position as the world's leading producer of aluminum. Even though the scale and complexity of its business increased dramatically over the years, there was no fundamental difference in the mission of the modest little enterprise established by Alfred Hunt and Charles Martin Hall and the giant corporation of Frank Magee and John Harper. But now, as it approached the end of its tenth decade of business, the world's largest producer of aluminum and its products

Table 8.2. *Distribution of noncommunist world aluminum capacity, 1982–8 (thousands of metric tons)*

Year	U.S.	Japan	Canada	Western Europe	Australia and New Zealand	Asia (ex. Japan)	Africa	Latin America	Total
1982	5,000	1,132	1,234	3,750	655	827	543	1,029	14,170
1984	4,603	711	1,374	3,649	1,067	1,006	631	1,169	14,183
1986	3,765	240	1,462	3,645	1,282	1,006	632	1,565	13,597
1988 (projected)	3,765	64	1,577	3,580	1,432	1,480	632	1,865	14,395

Source: Data provided by Alcoa Accounting Department as background for Alcoa's midyear *Fact Book* (1987).

was struggling to cope in a world that had changed so profoundly that the very perception of that change had triggered a revolution in strategy and structure.

Krome George and corporate strategy in the 1970s

We have been running ahead of our story, if only to point toward its conclusion. Yet neither the pressures for Alcoa to change nor the changes themselves arose full-blown in the 1980s. We have already seen in the last chapter that the oligopolistic pattern of the aluminum industry was already eroding before 1970. Alcoa had itself contributed to this development as it became a multinational corporation, penetrating regional barriers to competition that had long shaped the international structure of the industry. Alcoa had also made some significant changes in its strategy, most notably in its move into the continuous-production, high-volume, rigid-container sheet market, and in its administration, by moving toward a more market-centered corporate structure. Still, the operative assumption at Alcoa was that it would succeed, as it always had, by being a self-contained system of sourcing, production, and distribution in which the control of primary aluminum was the vital center. In time, Krome George would come to think differently about that.

As we pick up our story in 1971, George was president of Alcoa, and would be designated "chief operating officer" in the following year. To some degree, George was playing the kind of role under John Harper (who remained CEO until 1975) that Frank Magee had played under Chief Wilson some fifteen years earlier. But the comparison ends there. George was of a distinctly new breed of top manager. Though schooled as an engineer, and beginning his career as one, he became a self-made expert in financial and strategic planning, raising himself up on the exquisitely fine details of cost accounting. More of a technocrat than any of his predecessors, he brought with him to the top of the corporation more "scientific," more formally analytical approaches to management. A sailor by avocation, he was to steer, trim, and maneuver Alcoa through some of its brightest and stormiest seas.

If style goes with substance, then by all outward appearances, George was the man for the time. In the 1970s, Alcoa was a far more bureaucratic, less "familial" enterprise than it had been in the days of Roy Hunt and Chief Wilson. The traditionally intimate ties between ownership and management unraveled to the verge of extinction. After Roy Hunt and General Mellon followed A. V. Davis to the grave, the combined Hunt and Mellon common-stock holdings dwindled to less than ten percent by 1975, as institutional holdings (stock owned by insurance companies, mutual funds, retirement plans, educational institutions, and so forth) increased to sixty-five percent of Alcoa's total outstanding common. Alfred M. Hunt, John Mayer, and Nathan Pearson continued to represent "old family" interests on the board, but the ownership of Alcoa was now primarily in the hands of institutional portfolio managers just as the executive management of the company was firmly in the hands of bureaucratic managers.[10]

Moreover, out of the structural reforms of Magee and Harper had emerged a company that was far more technocratic in character and more bureaucratic in form than it had been a generation earlier. That corporate life had also become less mannered, less formal in its protocols (a fact made obvious to older managers by the more common usage of first names between superiors and subordinates and between men and women) could not disguise the fact that Alcoa had become increasingly rule-bound, systematic in its planning, careful about its controls, and meritocratic in the development and promotion of personnel. Thus, not just the structure but the atmosphere had changed as well. George knew that if the much smaller, more paternal company he had joined in the 1940s had been more like the Alcoa of the 1970s, he would probably have been fired early in his career as a redundant refining engineer.[11]

When George later reflected on the change in managerial atmospherics, he explained his view that the modern Alcoa was no longer managed by "gentlemen," no longer lead by executives with the kind of patrician "touch of class" that made Hunt, Wilson, Magee, and Litchfield seem more like paternal heads of a large and loyal "Alcoa family."[12] George himself counted the passing of the older generation as a lamentable loss of style, but he did not share the more sentimental longings of many of his colleagues for the old, less bureaucratic firms. In bygone days, personalities and political loyalties played a relatively larger role in corporate governance and in the grooming and promotion of managers. If anything, George said, the company had remained too familial, too paternal for too long.

> Paternalism is the other side of having these little fiefdoms. Now that was the old Alcoa.... You were loyal to your department, to your immediate superior, your works manager, and he to his division guy.... There was a lot of power fighting.... There was a disparity of treatment of people in those days that doesn't

exist today because of the internal controls our personnel programs employ. We may have been paternalistic in those days,
but we were also arbitrary as hell. . . . So some of this family stuff
is really a by-product of living in little protective houses. . . .
That's over with and I'm damn glad.[13]

Such changes, of course, were relative, not absolute, and George
himself exhibited a number of personal traits that were distinctly
nonbureaucratic. He has been described by subordinates who saw a
great deal of him as a good-humored man for whom personal relationships were vital and personal loyalties important. Sometimes
hot-tempered, and often as blunt and outspoken in public as he was
in private, he is remembered as a leader under whom day-to-day
life could be funny, exciting, and often unpredictable. His occasional
and unpredictable lapses in diplomacy gave his public relations managers fits. It was widely perceived that he had a high degree of
sensitivity to his managers as people, which leavened the more impersonal tendencies of bureaucracy and helped sustain among his
large corporate staff the sense of open and informal communication
between superiors and subordinates in which Alcoa managers, even
to this day, take special pride.[14]

Like Harper, George found that leaders of major corporations became, by necessity, public relations officers. At first, when he became
CEO in 1975, he was not as active as Harper had been in government
relations but, in time, he too became a lobbyist and spokesman for
the industry, as well as for the firm. In keeping with the changing
mood of the times, George was less busy promoting the corporation's
role as a progressive social institution and more concerned with
defending Alcoa's interests vis-à-vis the emerging economic and political issues of the 1970s, becoming in the process a vocal advocate
of nuclear power.

George invested heavily in the modernization and automation of
Alcoa's production facilities. During his regime, Alcoa continued to
computerize the smelting process and the rolling mills at Davenport
and Warrick (all which had begun under Harper in 1964). He introduced modern information systems into many operations that had
been controlled by considerably less-precise, labor-intensive means
since the turn of the century. Aluminum production became much
more a science and less an art, subject now to more precise mathematical modeling, measurement, and control. Determined to make
Alcoa more efficient in every respect, he was nonetheless criticized
by his contemporaries for being too much the accountant, too focused
on "bottom-line" issues, too quick to cut costs, too reluctant to com-

Fig. 8.1. The view from the "pulpit" of the automated, giant 220-inch mill at Davenport, Iowa.

Fig. 8.2. A partial view of a modern Hall-Process smelter showing an automated siphon in operation. At the upper right are vacuum ducts for the control of potline hazardous emissions.

mit to risky, long-term technological departures. On the last count, one can say in retrospect that the weakest part of Alcoa's strategy during the 1970s was an underemphasis on fundamental research across a wider spectrum of technology (George began to restore long-overdue funding for more entrepreneurial, long-term research programs relatively late in his regime), just as the strongest part was a more persistent inculcation of efficient values and systems.

Overall, George had a good command of the financial details of aluminum operations, an extended view of the horizon, and an exceptional ability to relate the particular details of his business to the larger forces at work in the industrial environment. He was also able to look at strategic problems without undue regard to entrenched orthodoxies. It was perhaps that ability that enabled him to conclude so emphatically, by the end of his career, that Alcoa could no longer expect to grow on the basis of its traditional strength in primary aluminum.

As we look at Alcoa's strategic development during the 1970s in a bit more detail, we can see that in the early part of the decade, the company moved along the paths already charted by Magee, Litchfield, and Harper. George accelerated Alcoa's moves overseas and invested heavily in expanding Alcoa's high-margin, high-volume fabricating technologies. He remained committed to defending Alcoa's strength in the mine-to-metal sectors of the business. It was, he later claimed, his own projections for the ASP process that helped launch it in the first place, and it was his desire to sustain Alcoa's position in smelting technology that made him such a strong advocate of cheap nuclear power.[15]

But as he extended the paths laid out for him by his predecessors, George found the terrain more uneven than expected. The highs were high; the lows deep; the pattern increasingly unpredictable. From 1972 through 1982 – a period of intense inflation – Alcoa's sales and operating revenues grew from $1.8 billion to $4.6 billion (in nominal terms), but its operating profits stated as a percentage of sales were generally well under those of the 1960s. The economics of the business remained cyclical but seemed more volatile and less predictable. Alcoa enjoyed record years in shipments in 1973 and then in net income and revenues in 1974, but profits and revenues fell sharply in 1975. Thereafter, the company steadily improved its revenues and profits through 1979, when its net income reached $504.6 million and operating profit $928.7 million. From 1978 through 1980, Alcoa reported higher returns on average invested capital – 11.5 percent in 1978; 16.3 percent in 1979; 13.6 percent in

1980 – than for any time since 1941, while its returns on equity and income per share shot up dramatically. But then, earnings skidded once again, substantially in 1981 and then precipitously in 1982, a very bad year, when Alcoa reported its first loss in nearly fifty years.[16]

Overall, the company struggled to sustain an efficient performance in an era of declining growth rates for most of its traditional common-alloy products, rising costs, and increasing uncertainty. Sudden jumps in the costs of energy and bauxite and the implementation of federally mandated environmental pollution controls (directed mainly toward curbing potline emissions) had further cut into corporate earnings, exacerbating the need to raise new funds from external sources. Achieving the fruits of new investment without "leveraging" the firm to the hilt was a big problem, especially in an era of sharply rising interest rates. In the late 1960s, Alcoa had shown more willingness than usual to finance expansion through debt. By the mid-1970s, Alcoa found it increasingly difficult to finance expansion amidst growing inflation, rising interest rates, and Government attempts at price controls. As CEO, George made it his policy to drive down the company's long-term debt, which he then reduced from 44.7 percent of invested capital in 1975 to 26.3 percent in 1980. That, combined with good earnings at the end of the decade, put Alcoa in reasonably good shape for a new program of major capital expansion over the next five-year period.[17]

A more volatile business, along with rising costs of capital, material, and human resources were accompanied by another reality that had not been of great concern to George's predecessors. The "friendly" holdings of Alcoa's stock by the old families were rapidly dissipating, while Alcoa's perennial presence as a bellwether on the Dow-Jones industrial average was making the company's stock more and more attractive to large institutional holders. By 1975, most of Alcoa's common stock was in the hands of institutional investors,[18] the accounts of which were managed by disinterested professionals who were more attentive than owner–managers or individual shareholders to short-term, bottom-line performance. Alfred M. Hunt and Mellon-related directors may have had an influence on the board of directors out of proportion to their holdings, but their continuing presence provided a sense of long-term interest between owners and managers of the corporation. Nevertheless, Alcoa was under increasing pressure to keep its income and balance-sheet reports looking as strong as possible from quarter to quarter. And George did just that. Alcoa's percentage returns on equity and invested capital

– important conventions in determining the market value of a stock – were stronger from 1976 through 1980 than for any five-year period since World War II, despite a diminishing performance (by historic standards) in operating ratios.[19]

Cost-cutting was a crucial, ongoing aspect of corporate policy in the inflationary years of the 1970s, and systematic cuts took a heavy toll on Alcoa's domestic operations. Alcoa became more hardened toward plants and lines of business that were not generating targeted returns. This had an especially great impact on smelting. Energy costs were the most problematic, but they were less controllable than the cost of human resources. Decisions to modernize older facilities put negotiating relations between management and unions under increasing strain. The continuing viability of many of Alcoa's U.S. operations had come to depend on arriving at agreements on a plant-by-plant basis that deviated in work-rule or financial particulars from the triennial master agreements. For example, the Vancouver, Washington, smelter suffered a sharp rise in energy costs following the expiration of a long-term supply contract with the Bonneville Power Authority. The historic availability of cheap power had retarded the replacement of old smelting technology, and continuing operations would depend largely on concessions from labor. Elsewhere, fabricating operations were discontinued at Cressona, Pennsylvania, in 1977 and at Marshall, Texas, in 1983. Refining operations at Mobile, Alabama, were suspended in 1982 (the facility would be closed officially in 1984). All of these closings followed unsuccessful attempts by the company to obtain wage or work-rule modifications from the unions.[20]

Costs, more than markets, stimulated Alcoa's growing investment in overseas ventures. Domestic labor costs were but one potent factor in a complex web of considerations. Alcoa's overseas strategy was also driven by a desire to develop (in addition to bauxite, of course) refining and smelting operations in countries where – in addition to labor – energy and materials could be obtained at lower cost than in the United States and where new markets for regionally produced aluminum could be exploited. But the most pressing motive, at least of the moment, was the desire to bypass the high cost of electrical energy. Just a glance at the rate at which energy costs were rising relative to materials and labor costs helps make the point even more sharply.

However driven, Alcoa's international business was becoming a far more important component of the corporate balance sheet and income statement. Alcoa had spread extensively over the world in

Table 8.3. *Cost index data for Alcoa's major cost elements,*
1970–86 (1970 = 100)

Year	Salaries, wages, and benefits	Purchased materials	Energy costs
1970	100.00	100.00	100.00
1971	108.84	103.11	105.27
1972	119.77	102.85	109.72
1973	131.27	107.22	125.56
1974	146.88	157.58	173.99
1975	165.42	183.88	235.44
1976	189.84	190.65	261.31
1977	210.97	206.66	309.39
1978	235.35	218.15	341.07
1979	260.67	233.55	384.22
1980	290.62	267.65	465.21
1981	321.22	294.15	535.46
1982	344.80	296.33	592.21
1983	361.01	297.31	600.50
1984	360.87	299.00	586.76
1985	356.76	274.51	502.21
1986	383.98	269.79	399.43

Source: Data provided by Alcoa Accounting Department as background for Alcoa's midyear *Fact Book* (1987).

the 1960s, but its overseas investment remained small as a portion of Alcoa's total investment. In 1980, Alcoa's U.S. capital expenditures were $554 million, as compared with $83 million in foreign countries. However, the trend throughout, especially in refining and smelting, was decidedly shifting abroad. It had become the custom for new refining capacity to be linked to ore and/or smelting facilities in the host country, and the pilot plant for the Alcoa Smelting Process (ASP), which began pilot operations in 1976, was the company's last new smelter in the United States.[21]

By the time George retired, on March 31, 1983, the bulk of Alcoa's overseas investment was in two countries: Brazil and Australia, both joint ventures in which Alcoa owned a majority interest. In Australia, where Alcoa owned fifty-one percent of Alcoa of Australia, Limited, construction of a refinery at Wagerup began in 1979 and of a smelting complex at Portland in 1980. In Brazil, Alcoa launched a joint venture between Alcoa Aluminio and Shell/Billiton in 1981, in which Alcoa took a sixty-eight percent interest. Alcoa committed $1.4 billion to a refining and smelting complex in Sao Luis, which many Alcoa managers viewed then and now as a a high-risk venture. (Alcoa Aluminio, S.A., showed losses in three of its first six years.) That notwithstanding, Alcoa's equity investment in joint ventures overseas began to contribute heavily to Alcoa's equity earnings, which were growing relatively less dependent upon real estate operations. In 1982, Alcoa Aluminio and Alcoa of Australia alone accounted for $45 million of $51.7 million in the company's total equity earnings from unconsolidated subsidiaries.[22]

Downstream, Alcoa's strategy went through two (though to some extent overlapping) phases from the early 1970s to 1983. Early on, a score of common-alloy products were dropped, as long-term strategic considerations drove management toward "product rationalization," favoring the development of fewer but proven high-margin aluminum applications. Following the retirement of Fritz Close, in 1970, top-management interest in a variety of new end-use applications, particularly in the home construction market, waned, and whole lines of business were jettisoned. In 1973, for example, a heavily promoted program for "Alumiframe" was scuttled after comparative calculations showed long-term prospects for residential construction to be comparatively less profitable than for such applications as aluminum parts in automobiles. The Alcoa Wrap foil business was abandoned in 1975; and in 1982, Alcoa divested its oldest corporate relative, Wear-Ever, along with two smaller subsidiaries. Certainly, in some cases, as with Alcoa Wrap, the company had simply been outdone by superior marketing. In others, it had become evident that some perfectly sound, albeit mature, businesses would fare better if liberated from Alcoa's labor and overhead structures. Such decisions were painful and hotly debated, regarded by many middle managers as admissions of defeat, as Alcoa shied away from the risks of new end-market development. The fact that Alcoa made these decisions reflected management's heightened concern to maximize overall returns within shorter time periods and its declining faith in the potential for common-alloy products.[23]

Accordingly, George concentrated his company's resources on products for which margins and/or economies of scale were high, with an emphasis on container sheet, transportation (especially in aerospace applications and in the development of containers for shipping liquefied natural gas), and electrical applications. Flat-rolled products led Alcoa's business, and during the 1970s, heavy investments were made for the expansion of mill capacities at Warrick for RCS, and at Davenport (where the world's largest rolling mill was installed) for aircraft sheet and plate. Advanced forging technologies were installed at Alcoa facilities in Cleveland and California. Such major capital improvements were preemptive competitive strategies that along with constant innovation in production techniques helped sustain Alcoa's market positions in RCS and in many aircraft products. At Davenport, for example, Alcoa maintained a virtual monopoly in the lucrative polished aircraft skin-sheet market, largely on the basis of a rigorous program of empirical production improvements.[24] The sheer productive capacity of Alcoa's container-sheet technology at Warrick, despite serious labor problems, enabled the company to maintain a leading share of the total RCS market, which in 1977 stood at about sixty percent.[25]

Not until the latter part of the decade, as it became increasingly clear that the RCS market was beginning to mature, did Alcoa significantly turn once again to new applications (in some instances in nonaluminum materials) as a major component of strategy. In 1981, for the first time since World War II, a major investment was made to develop a new generation of high-strength aerospace alloys. Interest in pursuing several exotic, high-technology applications accelerated so that by 1983, when George retired, Alcoa was moving on several fronts, forming some joint-venture partnerships in new areas of development, looking at potentially interesting high-technology acquisitions, and preparing to go to market in a variety of such new products as alumina chemicals, satellite antennas, lithoplate, and computer memory discs. Nonaluminum applications, such as the smelting and processing of magnesium and silicon were underway at Addy, Washington, beginning in 1976.[26]

One radical new departure was the decision, in 1972, to make "major sales" of proprietary technology and "analytical and technical training" to other aluminum companies.[27] This was an important reversal in policy. Since World War II, Alcoa had grown ever more secretive about its proprietary technology; its managers might well have gone to the gallows, lips sealed, rather than reveal any of their company's specialized technical expertise. As recently as 1968, Harper had issued a warning to Alcoa's technical personnel to "protect their proprietary technology against both outright and subtle" inquiries, noting that it was not desirable for Alcoa to indulge in the "free exchange of information" as appeared to be the case in the steel industry.[28] But a "conversion" in Harper's and

George's thinking subsequently cleared the way for the company to capitalize on sharing of proprietary information, hardware, and systems. By 1971, a task force was making an inventory of all Alcoa's "saleable know-how," as enthusiasm grew for the prospect of using Alcoa's store of expertise for "making money with little investment." Initially, most of the technology to be sold was in smelting. Within a few years, several of Alcoa's competitors were outfitted with advanced Hall pots and the "Alcoa 398 Process" potline emission control, a process that has since become widely adopted to recycle gas effluent from potrooms and to trap potentially harmful dust particles.[29]

The sale of technology was more than a case of doing well by doing good. The decision was, in effect, forced by circumstances beyond the company's control. By the early 1970s, the Hall–Héroult Process had become a highly dispersed, competitive technology for which few secrets were left. Pechiney, for instance, had already put its own technology on the market. Much of Alcoa's proprietary smelting technology was, in any case, streaming out the door as a consequence of joint-venture relationships and, on occasion, via chicanery.[30] Alcoa could afford to sell, or license, five-year-old smelting technology if it could keep lowering its internal costs of production. And should the ASP prove successful, Alcoa would have a fresh, long-term technological advantage over its Hall–Héroult Process-bound rivals. The sale of technology became an especially important new source of demand for Alcoa's Engineering Department at a time when internal construction power and smelting facilities were declining. A Technology Marketing Division was established in 1972, and quickly began to broaden its offerings and services. By the end of the decade, Engineering was offering extensive services in the licensing of proprietary processes and patents, in engineering design and construction, in testing, and in contract research and development on a selective basis.[31]

An especially bright spot on the technological horizon was aluminum's recyclability. No sooner had aluminum entered the beverage can market than recycling of cans became a prominent environmental and political issue as well as an economic opportunity. Were recycling to become a more significant part of aluminum production, it would significantly lessen the industry's dependence on more energy-intensive smelting. Initially, Alcoa took a public posture that favored recycling (Alcoa was actually slower than Reynolds to come around to this view) while opposing Government legislation requiring it. Later, as recycling legislation was passed in a

Figs. 8.3 and 8.4. A worker removing a burnt piece of anode from a modern 2500-pound (per-diem) smelting pot at Badin, North Carolina (top), and a rooftop view of Badin's Alcoa's 398-Process potline emission-control system in which fluoride gas and alumina dust are trapped in a fluid bed of alumina (bottom).

number of states, Alcoa, already embarrassed by Reynolds' initiative, began to develop new recycling technologies. By 1978, three billion pounds of easily recoverable aluminum were being thrown away each year, which as David Reynolds was quick to point out, was "equal to the entire U.S. output in 1958." Spiraling smelting costs spurred Alcoa to step up its own efforts, and by 1979, Alcoa was processing 110 million pounds of scrap metal. That amount increased fivefold in seven years, so that by 1985, recycling accounted for a full nineteen percent of Alcoa's aluminum ingot capacity.[32]

By most immediate standards of performance, Alcoa's strategies seemed to be working, especially if sharply improved earnings from 1977–80 were any indication. But as the company moved into the 1980s, Alcoa was worried. In 1981, tight-money policies of the Federal Reserve Bank, intended to brake persistent rates of "double-digit" inflation, induced a sharp downturn in the economy. Industrial investment slowed to a trickle and demand for aluminum plunged. By year end, Alcoa had reached a "turning point." According to Charles Parry, "We had just come off the two best years in the company's history. We found ourselves in a deep recession, and we began to sense that something fundamental was wrong."[33]

Why? Alcoa had weathered economic downturns time and again. But this time it was different. The timing of this particular crisis focused the attention of Alcoa's management on some fundamental changes in the industry that had been gathering force for several years and which could no longer be ignored. It had already become obvious that the business cycle for aluminum had become so chronically erratic that it was no longer possible to plan with any degree of certainty. Moreover, there was a real danger that aluminum, having barely kept pace with the GNP in the 1970s, may have permanently lost its luster as a growth industry. As we shall see, Alcoa's research into new products and processes had already been dampened by a presumption that the market for aluminum was rapidly maturing. And the outlook for the 1980s was not bright. During the grim years of 1981–82, when unemployment soared to its highest level since the Great Depression, Alcoa closed its gas-fueled smelter at Point Comfort, idled its ASP plant in Anderson County, and undertook a fundamental reassessment of its business.

That reassessment set the stage for a reformulation of Alcoa's strategy as well as a radical reorganization of its administrative structure designed to impel Alcoa's growth into a more broadly based

Fig. 8.5. Recycling aluminum cans at Alcoa, Tennessee.

"materials company." But before moving to that phase of the story, we must first turn to a brief history of administrative developments in the late 1970s that were already establishing the organizational premises for a new strategy.

The rise of the business-unit structure

Normally, we think of business strategy as a systematic response to perceived opportunities in the marketplace and of corporate structure as the administrative accommodation to strategy. In the main, this is true, although the dynamic relationship between strategy and structure might better be described as reciprocal. Appropriately designed administrative bureaucracies have enabled corporations to do business on a large scale, but as markets, technologies, and the large economy evolve, existing structures and the cultural assumptions that sustain them may constrain an organization's ability to respond. In the late 1970s, Alcoa's view of itself, its very identity as an institution, was deeply rooted in its origin as a primary aluminum producer and predicated on its long history as a tightly integrated, self-contained system of production. Even as the major sources of its profits had moved downstream, its strategic center of gravity remained upstream.[34] Only through an evolving consideration of structural reforms could new organizational premises be established for the more radical change in strategic outlook that would occur in the next decade.

We have already seen that under John Harper, Alcoa had begun to reorganize its corporate structure around its major markets, a reform that was designed to provide greater decision-making flexibility to product and marketing managers than had been possible under a more functionally based administrative hierarchy. The underlying logic of the first stage of the reforms, in 1968, had been to replace an almost purely functional organization (not counting some of Alcoa's more or less autonomous subsidiaries), in which manufacturing and sales were brought together only at the top, with a structure that organized the corporation around its major core businesses.[35]

By the end of 1975, Krome George and his new president, William Renner, presided over an elaborated version of the 1968 structure. Reporting to George were all corporate financial and public relations staff, while production-related staffs for personnel, labor, engineering, and R&D reported to Renner. The major line functions, production and marketing, were organized under executive vice presidents for Mill Products, Allied Products, Primary Products, with a separate department for international business.[36] Organizing production and marketing functions into three major groups left a number of problems unresolved. The evolving market-oriented

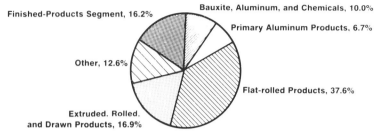

Total Revenues = $2,305.9 million

Key: • BAUXITE. ALUMINUM. AND CHEMICAL: Various aluminas, nonmetal-grade bauxite, and aluminum-related chemicals for industrial applications.
 • PRIMARY ALUMINUM AND CHEMICAL: Various types and grades of aluminum ingot.
 • FLAT-ROLLED PRODUCTS: Plate, sheet, and foil products.
 • EXTRUDED. ROLLED, AND DRAWN PRODUCTS: Extrusions, tubular products, electrical transmission products, wire, rod and bar.
 • OTHER: Forgings, castings, powders?, and pigments, and other miscellaneous manufactured products.
 • FINISHED-PRODUCTS SEGMENT: Closures, screw machine parts, building industrial products, nonaluminum forgings, scrap, tolling, recycling, oil and power generation, and railroads.

Chart 8.1. Alcoa's principal products, 1975 (percent sales and operating revenues). *Source: Facts About Alcoa, 1975.*

structure was so gross in its main outline that Alcoa remained a highly centralized corporation, albeit one in which marketing and production decisions had been broken down into slightly smaller chunks. General management decisions for a large number of product/market areas were still aggregated at very high levels in Pittsburgh, where a senior management Operating Committee convened regularly to monitor the enterprise. Managers from the vice-presidential level on down were still highly specialized operatives in a basically functional, vertically integrated organization, their performance measured on the narrow basis of disciplinary expertise.

In other words, Alcoa's structure neither adequately reflected the company's multiple lines of business nor brought together production and marketing functions at levels where their coordination was most needed. The Harper reforms had carried decision-making authority down to heads of major core businesses that were still very large aggregations of many products and markets. C. Fred Fetterolf described his own view of the situation from his vantage point in Mill Products, where he rose to become head of operations in 1978. By then, he explained:

Fig. 8.6. One manager's view of the shortcomings of Alcoa's corporate planning in the 1970s.

Mill products was a generic term for forging, extrusions, sheet and plate, fasteners, premium castings, wire, rod, and bar and then Ron Hoffman [vice president of sales, Mill Products] was the marketing guy. [We] came together at the Marv Gantz level [executive vice president, Mill Products]..., and there was a tendency to treat all those as one business; that was the Mill Products business. Well, there wasn't a Mill Products business.[37]

Indeed there was not. But members of the Corporate Planning Department had taken a close look at the company's structure, and they had already come to the same conclusion.

The role of the Corporate Planning Department in helping instigate a new round of structural reforms is interesting, if only because at the outset the department seemed so ill-suited for the task. In 1977, the Corporate Planning Department reported to an executive vice president, Theodore Kerry. It was located on a line with the company's production functions, which was consistent with the department's emphasis on year-to-year economic forecasts, financial planning and cost analysis. The main focus of the department's activities was on year-to-year capital planning, analyzing, and coordinating divisional requests "from a corporate point of view." Harry Goern, who was manager of corporate planning services, explained a growing awareness that the entire planning process had become a procedural exercise, too immersed in numbers, and not qualitative enough to provide clear insight into fundamental changes taking place in the industry and the company. Armed with the tools of quantitative analysis that it adopted in the 1960s and honed to greater and greater degrees of precision ever since, the planners were better equipped to deal with short-term financial issues than with fundamental long-term strategy and structure. The planners were determined to change that as they embarked on an ambitious review of the company's structure.

Consultants from Arthur D. Little helped Alcoa develop a procedure for reviewing the competition in its various lines of business. In the first instance, a group of Wear-Ever managers spent two days considering the competitive structure of their markets. Out of the exercise emerged a surprising picture of Wear-Ever as not one, but three, distinct "business units." The exercise was repeated with Flat-Rolled Products and Forgings with similar results. A more complex picture of markets began to take shape. Alcoa was operating in far more diverse competitive arenas than anyone had imagined. Corporate Planning then internalized and expanded the exercise, making a systematic review of the competitive structure of every Alcoa business.[38] That done, the planners concluded that Alcoa had become far too diversified in its operations and markets to continue operating under a system in which decision-making remained concentrated in a few division heads under a relatively centralized structure. It was no longer reasonable to expect a small cadre of corporate top managers to cope with all the strategic decisions required to run all of Alcoa's enterprises. The chief executive, in particular, could no longer be expected to pay close attention to the unique strategic problems of each of a large variety of operational and marketing efforts, each with different sourcing, technical, and marketing requirements. More decentralization of decision-making authority was essential.[39]

The basic outline and rationale for a more decentralized structure can be summarized as follows. A new division of labor that devolved decision-making upon lower-level division managers would relieve top managers of shorter-term burdens, enabling them to concentrate on more general strategic and entrepreneurial concerns. Primary responsibility for the formulation of strategy for each of Alcoa's products would be placed in the hands of business units, each with its own general manager, whose products and markets could be analyzed and whose performance could be assessed more efficiently at microcosmic levels. Then, Goern explained, the central executive office "could do corporate-level planning so that the portfolio could be modified either through divestiture, acquisition, or modification of the divisions."[40] Though the language sounds almost as if the planners were suggesting a conglomerate model for strategy and structure, that is not what they meant. Alcoa could not be defined as a mere collection of businesses tied together only by common ownership. It remained a highly "concentric" enterprise, the heart of which was its vertically integrated aluminum technology. That simple fact was an overriding constraint on even the most imaginative plans for decentralization.

But implementing a more decentralized business-unit organization required Alcoa's top management to delegate more authority to lower-level managers, granting them enough control over their resource and output decisions to run their business units in nontraditional fashion. Politically, there was the obvious problem of assuring corporate executives that their power would not be diminished. How, for example, was the chief executive officer's role to be defined? Strategy was still the CEO's primary responsibility, and the advocates of decentralized planning had to be very careful to take this into account.

Thus, it became a central message of their campaign to insist that business-unit management "does not mean abdication by the CEO," who would retain final authority over business-unit plans that would always be subject to modification in accordance with "broader Corporate considerations." It was left to the CEO to set overall corporate objectives and to provide overall direction and management of business units through a centralized planning and control system. To ensure adherence by business-unit managers to overall corporate objectives, while allowing for the uniqueness of strategic and performance criteria for each unit, required improved corporate information systems and strong, functionally specialized corporate staffs in such areas as engineering, accounting, human resource development, and technology.[41]

The business-unit concept represented a challenge, of sorts, by a younger group of vice presidents to more senior top managers who had spent their best years in a centralized, highly integrated corporation. Corporate executives were intrigued by, though skeptical of, the business-unit concept. Decentralization was for many a highly emotional issue, and discussions about it tended to divide along generational and departmental lines. Bill Renner, the company president, had already been fostering discussions of a fundamental nature in the company's advanced management conferences, and he was supportive. As for George, he is credited with having allowed the "educational process" that was percolating up beneath him to proceed, though at times he appeared to be less than enchanted by its implications. Nevertheless, between 1977 and 1980, a business-unit plan unfolded and implementation of it began.[42]

Meanwhile, the planning staff had charted some sixty-one different Alcoa "strategy centers" cutting across eleven basic types of products and services. A vice president of Flat-Rolled Products was appointed, the first step toward bringing business-unit organization into being. Major business groupings along aggregate product lines had been identified not only for Flat-Rolled Products but also for Raw Materials and Smelting, Chemicals, Ingot, and Engineered Products. Within the general divisions, a number of smaller business units were established. For example, Engineered Products embraced Forgings, Castings, Wire, Rod and Bar, the Stolle Corporation, Tifton (soft alloy extrusions), and Powder and Pigments.[43]

By 1980, business units were up and running in the downstream sectors of the corporation. But many of Alcoa's facilities were built around an interrelated chain of operations, a fact that posed some logistical problems. And because of the high degree of technological integration of aluminum production, the business-unit concept also posed a conceptual problem. It was hard to formulate, in business-unit terms, an organizational concept for upstream operations in a way that differed materially from Alcoa's existing structure. For example, how and at what points were costs to be determined for intermediate products as they were transferred along the vertical chain from mine to metal? Was it feasible, or desirable, to assign costs to bauxite, alumina, and aluminum at market prices, when most of those materials were consumed internally? How, too, were the planning and control of upstream resources and assets shared by downstream business units to be coordinated? The seeming inextricability, the lumpiness, of Alcoa's "core business," which extended from Raw Materials to Flat-Rolled Products, was a high hurdle placed in the way to an effective process of decentralization, and it would remain so for years to come. Later, in 1983, when the company's main operating groups were redefined and expanded to five – Raw Materials, Alumina and Chemicals; Primary Metals; Flat-Rolled Products; Engineered Products; International – it was hard to disaggregate the management of Flat-Rolled Products, the dominant core of Alcoa's business, which accounted for more than half the company's revenues and profits.[44]

It was difficult to arrive at a more decentralized structure on the basis of a single organizational principle. Nowhere was this more evident than in Alcoa's international operations, where economic, cultural, legal, and political differences of foreign countries and joint-venture partners necessarily had to be managed separately from domestic operations. Integrating international plans with those of domestic business units could not always be coordinated directly at lower levels. International operations retained a structure that was basically geographic in its outline under the general direction of a senior corporate officer who coordinated the planning and administration of foreign business within Pittsburgh's corporate objectives.[45] Otherwise, the new business-unit structure was designed to push strategic decision-making for particular products and markets as far down as possible, while the corporate office maintained authority over what might more appropriately be called "grand strategy." To coordinate strategy at the corporate level, George established a new "Office of the Chairman," a response to "the greater complexity of managing the company." Instituted in September 1981, the Chairman's Office initially served a dual purpose: to allocate top-executive responsibilities among a greater number of people and to prepare for the next chief executive succession.[46] This particular organization proved to be a highly protean institution, expanding, contracting and changing rapidly over the ensuing years as senior-level personnel changed and as the definition of roles of the chairman and president kept on evolving.

The allocation of greater strategic and operating responsibility to managers at lower levels was given a boost in late 1982 during the early rounds of implementing a program for reallocating corporate overhead. Though widely perceived by middle managers as little more than a cost-cutting exercise, the process, known as the Overhead Valuation Analysis (OVA), helped in "shifting the center of gravity toward the operating units." It was both timely and important, explained an interim OVA report, "to redefine the role of the corporate center to both increase the cost effectiveness of administration and establish greater latitude and accountability for profit within the operating units."[47] In broad terms, OVA became one method for reconstituting staff groups more as advisory rather than the "full-service" functions they had become. The corporate hierarchy was made "flatter," by eliminating layers of middle managers both at the center and the periphery through reassignment, early retirements, and layoffs. Although corporate as well as plant staffs were sometimes trimmed to excess, business-unit managers, especially in the "noncore" areas, acquired even more power to chart their own market strategies and production requirements and enjoyed substantial increases in local capital-approval limits.[48]

Progress toward that end was glacial in the eyes of its more ardent advocates. But enough lip service was given to the notion that business units should have flexibility to tailor policies to their markets and production needs, and by 1983, plant and business-unit managers had won substantially increased authority to run their operations and manage their personnel in accordance with local conditions. The new business-unit structure began to resemble, in many of its aspects, the kind of autonomous management of operations that had existed in Alcoa's earlier years, as more decision-making responsibility was restored to managers located well down the corporate hierarchy and away from central headquarters at Pittsburgh. At Massena, the operations manager was not only responsible for that site's smelting and fabricating plants, he was also business-unit manager for Wire, Rod and Bar, having corporate-wide responsibility for the planning and implementation of its product and market strategies. When the works manager at the Cleveland forge plant and foundry became a corporate vice president for Engineered Products in the fall of 1983, he was permitted to remain in Cleveland. In some cases, local managers were given new opportunities to try to restore ailing facilities. In June 1983, the operations manager at Alcoa, Tennessee, received a large commitment of funds with which he could modernize smelting and fabricating operations that had come within a hair's breadth of being shut down.[49]

That there was more room for entrepreneurial activity under the business-unit structure can be illustrated by events at Bauxite, Arkansas. Bauxite was Alcoa's oldest extant mining operation, and had also been producing alumina since 1951. When Ronald Kuerner, a second-generation Alcoa chemical engineer, took over the operations in 1976, he was dismayed by what he found. Unprofitable operations at Bauxite had been masked for years by a central accounting system that averaged the costs of feedstock over all Alcoa refining plants. Neither the mine nor the refinery at Bauxite was in any position to compete efficiently with the superior ores and more modern facilities Alcoa had developed overseas to make smelting-grade alumina. The only possible future for the Arkansas Operations lay in the efficient production of specialized alumina-based chemicals. During the economic downturn of 1981–2, when energy costs and demand for alumina products were moving rapidly in opposite directions, it would have been easy to shut down the entire operation. But Kuerner was instead given both time and leeway to reorganize local management through layoffs and job reassignments, to develop his own staff, to deal with local officials on tax and rate matters, to negotiate with union officials on reforming work rules, and even to spend money much as if he were running his own business. He had, under the new structure, the power to commit expenditures in the hundreds of thousands of dollars without having to consult his corporate superiors, a far cry from the $2,000 allowed his predecessor. In 1982, Bauxite lost $28 million, "by our own measure," but in the following year, largely as a consequence of reorganization, Bauxite was restored to financial health.[50]

Crucial to the progress of decentralization, so that it would not degenerate into managerial chaos, was further refinement of the planning process. By the end of 1982, central corporate planning was still bound up in short-term financial and tactical problems and had to be further distinguished in its function and purpose from business-unit planning. What was needed was more careful coordination of unit planning with corporate-level technology, market, and capital goals. At the same time, the development of a high-level staff for science and technology planning was becoming seen as ever more important to the corporate development of new business ventures. RCS had been Alcoa's last great new product and market development, and that sector of the business, though still growing, was attracting a lot of competition. RCS accounted, in 1983, for about twenty-five percent of the company's shipments, but Alcoa's market share, according to the head of Corporate Planning, had slipped badly from a high of around sixty percent to about forty percent in a decade.[51] Moreover, the long-term future of RCS was made increasingly uncertain by even newer packaging technologies, just as other areas of aluminum were growing more vulnerable to plastics and composite materials. It had become clear that only the adoption and mastery of new technologies, whether they were in aluminum or other materials, would carry Alcoa into a new generation of growth.

Realigning R&D

Mastering new technologies would require a strong performance from Alcoa's centralized R&D organization – particularly from the Laboratories, which had become a problematic area in Alcoa's structure. The problem was summed up, in 1983, by G. Keith Turnbull, an outspoken titanium metallurgist who had recently been appointed to a new corporate post as head of Technology Planning. It was Turnbull's opinion that Alcoa had been suffering from a loss of "sensitivity to technology," and that this in turn had impacted unfavorably on Alcoa's formal systems for technology planning and execution. In the company's adoption of business-unit planning, there was, he complained, still no overall "strategic thrust" for technology; corporate plans were not keyed to innovation. Part of the problem, too, lay in the incentives of the new business-unit organization. While business-unit representation on technical subcommittees and task forces had grown stronger, unit managers were too often driven by short-term financial considerations, which had an unhealthy effect on R&D budgeting. The subcommittee system, moreover, had long been too conservative, too reliant on consensus decision-making to sustain exploratory programs through thick and thin. More funding for R&D was not, in and of itself, sufficient. What was needed was a sharper definition of business-unit commitments to utilize specific technologies at specified points in the not-so-near future.[52] Such commitments could be shaped only by top management and would rely heavily on improving Alcoa's capability for scientific research.

Turnbull's was no isolated view. He spoke to a widely shared perception among Alcoa managers that the central R&D organization, specifically the weakness of its integration into operations, had become one of the most troublesome issues for corporate management. Physical consolidation of many of Alcoa's R&D functions during the 1970s had not led to an improved corporate integration of technology planning and implementation. Moreover, there was such heavy emphasis on smelting technology that R&D managers working outside the primary-products area were complaining about lack of support for the development of high-technology aluminum fabrications and for exploration into nonferrous metals and even nonmetals technologies.[53]

Indeed, much seemed to have changed since the Frary era, when Alcoa's R&D community had enjoyed independent status and high reputation in corporate management and the outside world alike. Kent Van Horn had established himself as a scientist of distinction in international circles. Like Frary before him, he had directed the publication of a new textbook collection on aluminum technology. And he had become a vice president, a title Frary had never held. Yet, the consolidated organization he had brought together at Alcoa Technical Center lacked the critical components – a strong program of fundamental research and productive relationships with technical personnel in the plants. In the minds of many operating managers, the Technical Center and the Alcoa Laboratories in particular had grown isolated and aloof from their concerns, becoming a corporate backwater that was failing to innovate in areas that were relevant to the rest of the company.[54]

The origins of the Laboratories' problem, as it was defined in the early 1980s, actually had their roots in the 1950s, when the rise of Reynolds and Kaiser had driven Alcoa to pay more attention to short-term applications engineering. Over time, planning through the subcommittee system became ever more tightly lashed to the needs of production and marketing managers who wanted quicker results in an increasingly competitive environment. By the mid-1960s, corporate management was expressing concern that its investment in R&D be devoted to projects that were most likely to yield quick returns. In the process, the Laboratories became conditioned to the management of short-term incremental improvements. This was not a problem so long as Alcoa could rely upon an accumulated store of fundamental science and technology. But over time, the storehouse was depleted, and after the development of RCS (which as a triumph of applications engineering was the last R&D effort to bring forth major results), remarkably little of breakthrough technological significance occurred at Alcoa's new Technical Center. By the 1970s, just when the Technical Center was beginning to forge an identity as a single technical community (as distinct from the scattered research-and-development operations that had traditionally existed), the reputation of the organization within the company was approaching its lowest point. Even before his retirement in 1970, Van Horn evinced some concern that the corporation was investing too little in long-term work. Fears that Alcoa was missing out on advanced approaches to fabricating led some plants to create their own development facilities; others turned to technology from outside sources. What some plant engineers saw was that the only important innovations at Alcoa occurred on the production line.[55]

Lest we draw too simple a picture, it is important to note that in some areas, the Laboratories achieved dramatic results. Case literature on the study of "stress-corrosion cracking" demonstrates how well, in its aircraft alloy development programs, Alcoa's central R&D organization could coordinate the insights of basic research efficiently with applications development, production, and marketing. Alcoa remained dominant in the development of new alloys, and aircraft alloys in particular required, and got, some of the most creative sustained research efforts.[56] But in other areas, researchers often had to pursue their longer-term research interests quietly, almost *sub-rosa*. Many of the company's officially mandated long-term research efforts were sustained through their early stages by Government funding. Only when what was perceived to be a high-payoff project, with potential for enormous-scale economies (such as RCS applications, liquid-nitrogen-gas tankers, autobody sheet, or ASP) found vigorous champions in top management, could a risky long-term program be mounted and sustained. And there was ever-increasing pressure from corporate management to bring the fruits of research to the market "quicker and more efficiently."[57]

When Van Horn departed, none of his inbred successors were to have the influence in management circles he had enjoyed. An outsider was grafted onto the top of Alcoa's technical community when Harper recruited Eric Walker, a former president of Pennsylvania State University, to become a member of the board of directors and a company vice president and chief scientist. This was an attempt to provide higher corporate status and more coherent coordination of R&D, which continued to have a vice president, J. Howard Dunn. Under Walker and Dunn, a new Alcoa Laboratories was constituted to bring together the research and development organizations at the Technical Center, thereby eliminating what had long been considered an artificial distinction.[58] Then Walker moved to reform the subcommittees, which were still largely controlled by the short-term needs of market and product managers. He challenged Alcoa to extend its research horizons, to liberate research and development from the prevailing corporate "sales mentality," to invest substantially beyond popular short-term projects geared to large-volume applications of aluminum, to look more to outside sources for ideas and expertise, and to support longer-term cutting-edge research.[59] Walker sowed the seeds for future reforms, but at least partly because his views could be dismissed as those of an outsider, he was unable to complete his program by the time he retired in 1975.[60]

The trend away from fundamental research accelerated when budgets were cut in 1976, as Krome George grew apprehensive about Alcoa's ability to recapture increasing manufacturing costs through revenues.[61] Long-term efforts suffered the most. For 1977, Robert

Hampel, vice president for technical development, calculated that two percent of Alcoa's R&D budget was devoted to basic research and that only ten percent of all R&D projects were programmed for more than five years, as opposed to fifteen percent a decade earlier. New product and process development received fifteen percent, declining toward ten percent, of the total R&D budget as compared with around twenty-five percent in the 1960s.[62] Subcommittees for new materials and geology were abolished, and with the decision in 1978 to allocate R&D costs to the business units, the program became increasingly short-term and less concerned with new products and processes. A 1983 consulting report described the company's R&D as a high-caliber engineering organization, hierarchical, bureaucratic, and secretive – so much so that its programs had become overly insulated from creative influences. This was deemed to be true despite the articulated values of the Laboratories that portrayed it as a research science organization. Although it was a matter of proud tradition that Alcoa had pioneered in metallurgical and electrochemical science, the prevailing behavior of the company's research management had become more that of applications engineering.[63]

The Alcoa Smelting Process was a case in point. The ASP project had to struggle to overcome several basic institutional weaknesses: a depleted fundamental knowledge base; excessive secrecy, which prevented consulting openly with appropriate outside experts; and undue time pressure, which forced too rapid a movement from bench- to pilot-scale production before fundamental scientific issues had been fully researched and resolved. The persistence of ASP's technical problems with the intermediate step of aluminum chloride production, problems which were never fully resolved, could be at least partly attributed to the foregoing factors.[64]

Yet, on the other hand, through the development of an elegant, highly efficient electrolytic cell that was at the heart of ASP, researchers had gained insights into the Hall–Héroult Process that enabled them to lift it off the discouragingly flat curve of improvement that the traditional smelting process had been on since the 1940s. By the mid-1980s, Alcoa's Hall pots were substantially improved in unit output and kilowatt-hours per pound. The improved Hall Process thus became a prime example of Alcoa's best efforts in process research and development, but it would not have been possible without the fundamental research that had been carried out under the umbrella of ASP. As a high-priority project that had the backing of top management essential to protect it from the scrutiny of more cash-flow-conscious line managers, ASP demonstrated the value of long-term investments in fundamental research, the fruits of which could be bountiful, even though unpredictable.[65]

Still, dramatic improvements in smelting were occurring at a time when smelting aluminum was fading in importance as a central component of the company's strategy. And there remained the question of Alcoa's overall competence to plan and manage fundamental work on a long-term basis. By 1983, apart from a few enclaves of fundamental research, most of Alcoa's R&D organization was driven by an emphasis on activity rather than reflection, on the meeting of milestones, and on lowering costs in the near term. The overriding emphasis on short-term, low-risk project development had weakened the Laboratories as an innovative force. It was, from an extended historical perspective, easy for consultants to see what had happened: "there had evolved a wide disjunction between self-image and behavior, one rooted in a pre-World War II tradition, the other in a postwar structure." It was an observation that struck Peter Bridenbaugh, the new head of the Alcoa Laboratories, as accurate.[66]

Fortunately, circumstances had already begun to change. Internal efforts to reform the Laboratories had been kept alive, even after Walker's departure. In the late 1970s, as the corporate planning process became more concerned with long-term issues, so did top management's interest in the exploration of new technologies. Growing interest in new ventures, along with a desire to bring R&D into better alignment with the new business-unit structure, focused the attention of corporate management more sharply on mechanisms for achieving longer-term technology planning. In 1982, a board-level Science and Technology Advisory Committee was established to set "strategic R&D direction and gross distribution of the R&D budget." Business-unit organization, meanwhile, was making it feasible to push many shorter-term process developments out to the operating entities, enabling the Laboratories to be more explicitly identified with longer-term and more basic research efforts.

Thus, the R&D organization was brought into alignment with the corporate quest for new technologies on a wider front. After a brief round of reorganization, in which the Technical Center lost some 200 people, a new director was placed in charge of the Laboratories with a mandate to restore science to its center. Almost immediately, new personnel with high-technology research skills began streaming into the Technical Center to support a broad-based resurgence of fundamental research underlying a diverse array of new ventures with breakthrough potential.

Changing conditions of labor relations

No less a problem for Alcoa in this period was the management of its labor relations. For years, at the corporate level, Alcoa's dealings with the major national aluminum unions had been stable, if not entirely amicable. In the relatively high-growth environment of the 1950s to the early 1970s, Alcoa had enjoyed a good measure of labor peace sustained largely through good wage and benefits packages in triennial rounds of pattern bargaining. Aluminum workers, whose compensation had been normally keyed to settlements in auto and steel, were among the highest paid in the nation. Aside from the 1968 Aluminum Workers Union strike (which, incidentally, the local union at Vancouver had refused to join), Alcoa had suffered no extended strike since World War II. With union control of its plants divided among three major unions (in addition to several smaller specialized unions and trades councils), Alcoa had never had to endure a corporate-wide shutdown.

Beneath the relatively calm corporate surface ran troubled waters. It is true that local units of the national aluminum unions were, by and large, politically moderate. Not since the early 1950s had the company contended with such aggressively ideological organizations as the communist Mine, Mill Workers in the Cleveland foundry, a union that eventually was ousted by the United Auto Workers. However, labor relations varied greatly from one location to the next, and some local units were far more militant than others. For example, among plants organized by the Aluminum Brick and Glass Workers (the Aluminum Workers had merged with Brick and Glass in 1971), the Warrick Operations suffered a more consistently adversarial relationship between management and labor than was the case in the more placid environs of Massena or Vancouver. But overall, in too many instances, petty hostilities on the factory floor made work in the plants unpleasant and dampened productivity.[68]

Locally tailored responses to the demands and problems of labor might well become more feasible as the corporation decentralized, but only if good programs enjoyed strong corporate backing. One of the most debilitating effects of Alcoa's modern habit of moving its managers from one place to another had been a breakdown of continuity between local labor and company leadership, precluding any sense of loyalty on the part of workers to company leaders. Older workers at Tennessee remembered "growing up" with particular plant managers who strolled daily through the plants, taking a personal interest in their lives and labor. They criticized younger managers for their remoteness and lamented the corporation's modern recent practice of rotating managers through top plant jobs and of rewarding them, so it seemed, more for technical competence than for their skills in managing people. Massena had five operations managers in six years, leaving local labor officials (and community leaders) to wonder just who exactly represented the company.[69]

The growing pressures of competition, inflation, and cost constraints had caused increasing tension in the plants during the 1970s. Variants of the general problem are the cases of Warrick, Cleveland and Alcoa, Tennessee, three operations chronically plagued with grievances, absenteeism, and declining productivity. In each case, management had to change its ways of dealing with workers in order to prevent the decline or even extinction of operations. At Warrick, management was confronted by a labor force that was steeped in regional labor traditions that bore a sad legacy of bitter strife in the coal-mining industry going back to the 1920s. After more than a decade of deterioration in shop-floor governance, local management was finally able to restore some semblance of order through incremental approaches to work discipline. At Cleveland, the grievances of an an inner-city workforce were pacified by a charismatic works manager. At Tennessee, local management experimented with modern methods of "participative management."

Alcoa, Tennessee, Operations had experienced declining profitability ever since World War II. In the 1970s, its rolling-mill operations operated as a "swing plant," supplementing production for orders taken first by newer, more productive facilities. By the end of the decade, Tennessee was the highest-cost, lowest-quality producer in the corporation. The closing of some facilities and corporate intentions to build a new mill in Brandenburg, Kentucky (which never came to fruition), exacerbated a decline in local morale already damaged by several years of adversarial conflict between labor and management, conflict that manifested itself in personal and psychological battles between front-line supervisors and workers on the plant floor. Tennessee degenerated into a hotbed of grievances and absenteeism, where labor relations suffered more than its share of problems that had become endemic in the corporate labor relations: transient management, inadequately trained supervisors, and poor communications.

Specific to Tennessee was the historic independence of its largely rural workforce, a folk tradition of labor strife (dating from the 1937 shooting), and a clash of styles between outside, typically northern managers and indigenous, southern workers. For the local union, money was rarely the main issue; Alcoa was the best-paying employer in the area. Dignity and quality of life in the workplace were central to the concerns of workers, who regarded Alcoa, for all its faults, to be a basically good employer.[70]

In 1979, when corporate management was considering shutting down a large part of Tennessee Operations, the operations manager called in consultants to provide advice on productivity reforms. By enlisting the support of Local 309, the consultants developed a "Trust and Cooperation [T&C] Program," a joint labor–management effort to plan the long-term future of facilities in Tennessee. This cooperative effort led to significant increases in product output and quality, as grievances and absenteeism declined. New protocols for worker–management conflicts were established to help defuse normal tensions in the workplace, while quality of work issues were treated in joint labor–management meetings. Late in 1982, a progress report noted that "relationships between managers, union officials, and workers ... have gone through a profound transformation over the last two years. Friendships have developed; mutual respect and understanding have grown; and suspicion of the motives of 'the others' has significantly decreased." Workers liked to talk about their personal encounters with Dick Ray, who had become a popular operations manager. The participation of workers in long-range "survival" planning disproved at Tennessee a long-held belief by management that workers could not, or would not, participate in decisions affecting the business.[71]

Regarded as a model program by corporate managers in Pittsburgh, the Tennessee T&C program was paralleled by similar kinds of efforts elsewhere in the Alcoa system. But full-blown programs in "participative management" were more than some managers and local union leaders felt they could support. At Warrick, for example, the challenge was to instill labor–management cooperation where there had been no history of it. The huge plant complex, which began operating in the 1960s, had become the dominant producer of can sheet in the world. It blossomed into a booming, profitable production machine that, nevertheless, as far as labor relations were concerned, was a mess. Featherbedding, slowdowns, absenteeism, drinking, gambling, and sleeping on the job had flourished over a period of years. During peak operations, people went home early after meet-

Figs. 8.7 and 8.8. A giant 50,000-ton Mesta forging press (top) and an automated manipulator for a hydraulic forging press (bottom) at Alcoa's Cleveland Works.

ing self-imposed production quotas only to return, later in the day, to earn overtime-rate hours. Housekeeping and maintenance deteriorated to the point where the operations manager became "ashamed" even to show "the pride of [Alcoa's] fleet" to visitors. Grievances mounted over trivial matters, while supervisors were either ill-suited or ill-trained to cope with situations rife with confrontation. The entire operation, according to one manager, became "hostage to the union," while union officials blamed the problem on supervisors who were unable to manage workers with fairness and effectiveness.[72]

Warrick was also a prime training ground for Alcoa's managers and engineers, and as a consequence, turnover was too brisk to achieve much continuity in approach to labor relations. That, from the perspective of supervisors, was a debilitating factor. More significant was the hapless situation of the floor-level supervisors. With RCS demand rising as fast as Alcoa could supply it, supervisors were told to "get the metal out the door" and were bluntly discouraged from taking any action that might result in a job action or walkout. By the mid-1970s, normal work routines had broken down almost completely. It was far easier for a beleaguered supervisor to cook production figures, to ignore clocking workers in and out, or even to stage a fine show for the benefit of visiting corporate officials than it was to do anything substantive about shop-floor discipline.[73]

Things began to change at Warrick only after corporate Mill Products management signaled its growing concern with costs and productivity in a maturing market for RCS. It was not until 1978 that Ronald Coleman (who had taken over Warrick Operations in 1975) felt that he had the corporate support he needed to make some reforms. When in the late summer of 1979, nearly 200 workers in the cold mill finishing plant staged a walkout over a disciplinary dispute, one worker was fired and scores of others were suspended. (Nothing, it was said, could have done more to stiffen the spines of the supervisors.) But that and other efforts to restore orderly work routines would not improve labor relations and productivity over the long term. "Quick-fix" productivity programs, the likes of which had come and gone over the years, were rejected; everyone was too skeptical for that. Improved training of supervisors, better flow of communications from management to the union, and appeals to worker's pride all became part and parcel of general and persistent efforts toward "raising expectations." In this effort, a heightened awareness of competition helped. Speeches on the subject were useless, but at times an opportunity could be seized for effect. In the economically depressed summer of 1982, managers rolled a coil of Japanese can sheet into Warrick for inspection by the production crews. The coil was "the most beautiful package, the most beautiful metal" anyone at the plant had ever seen. "That," said one supervisor, "hit home."[74]

At Cleveland, labor problems were addressed with older-fashioned methods of benign paternalism. Clyde Gillespie was transferred from Cressona to Cleveland in 1975, where it was expected by some that he would preside over an "orderly shutdown." Cleveland had long been plagued with productivity problems, antagonism between management and the union, and a pattern of violent incidents between workers as well as between workers and managers, including arson. Gillespie had no intention of closing Cleveland and after receiving a corporate commitment for financial backing, he arranged his schedule to overlap three shifts, installed a vigorous maintenance program, and paid assiduous attention to every detail of the plant and its operations. He was everywhere, bypassing the formalities of management–labor protocols, making friends of his workers and in the process overcoming any organized resistance to his programs. He jotted down what he heard, making a list with "eight to ten items on it every day." And according to the Cleveland personnel manager, "we cleaned off that 'people list' every day."

> This is the way Clyde wanted the place run. There wasn't an item left – we paid it a lot of attention. Not just because of the humanitarian aspect, which is what we ought to be doing anyway, whenever we can help it – but there is a practical end of that too – you get a good man out there who is stuck with a problem and he doesn't know where in hell to go, and you fix it, you've got a friend for life.[75]

Gillespie infused his staff with his own relentless optimism, and when he reshuffled the plant's managerial personnel and streamlined operations, he took care to avoid violating the sense of security of the hourly workforce. The introduction of robots and other labor-saving machinery in forging operations reduced the crew size of some jobs by half, but workers were persuaded (as one union member indeed wrote) that improvements in the plant's business capacity would result in an increase in the total number of jobs.[76] The charismatic regime of Clyde Gillespie was, for all its strengths, a hard one on which to build a general model, but at Cleveland it worked. By 1983, the plant had become the platform for the Engineered Products Group, a renaissance production facility driven by humane as well as economic values.

At Cleveland, as elsewhere, there remained the problem of how to sustain supervisory training and strong worker–manager communications over the long run. The future of Alcoa's labor relations was threatened somewhat by a long tradition of rising expectations for automatic increases in economic benefits (made even more "automatic" by the inclusion of cost-of-living indexes in the adjustment of pension benefits after 1974), the long-standing adversarial nature of labor–management organization, and, in some cases, a complete lack of interest on the part of workers to assume a role in making day-to-day decisions. On management's side, there had been a long-standing tendency to ignore problems on the plant floor in prosperous times. Money had too long papered over less than harmonious conditions on the plant floor. For good labor practices to endure across the corporation, managers and workers alike would have to find ways to make permanent the flashes of cooperative spirit that were sparked by more desperate circumstances. Wherever trust may have formed on the basis of personal relationships, it would have to be institutionalized.[77]

There also remained the problem of how to reform the larger corporate relationship between Alcoa and the national labor organizations. In the collective bargaining process, Alcoa could no longer afford to do business as usual every third year. In the 1970s, management had been unable to stem the rising tide of wages and benefits in master contract negotiations. Instead it tried, wherever it could, to improve output by revising work rules in the plants through interim agreements with local unions. For example, local units at the closure facilities at Richmond, Indiana, and Lancaster, Pennsylvania, had been willing to accept adjustments of the economic provisions of the master agreement. At Vancouver, nearly 200 workers had accepted substantial wage cuts to save jobs in the extrusion business. But, as we have noted, other facilities were sold or closed in the face of union resistance. In the bargaining round of 1983, the major unions yielded some economic and work-rule concessions, but management was not able to gain the principle it wanted. What Alcoa wanted was to change the very structure of its relationship with the unions, to transform, somehow, the unitary pattern of bargaining that did not take into account the variety of competitive pressures on different businesses operating in different markets under different conditions of manufacture and cost.[78]

This structural problem was still unresolved when on May 31, 1986, Alcoa's two largest unions struck the company in unison for the first time in history. This time, however, management was determined to wait out the strike, unwilling and indeed, perhaps, unable to buy labor peace, demanding instead that the unions make concessions on existing benefits packages. Alcoa operated production in fifteen plants with managerial, technical, and clerical personnel gathered from headquarters, sales offices, and research facilities. Evidence of improved local labor relations was the considerable measure of good will and courtesy that was shown between unionized workers and plant officials. Strikers did not interfere with the comings and goings of temporary labor, and at several locations, managers and strikers cheerfully fraternized. One plant manager went out of his way to provide shade for the picket line; others provided coffee and doughnuts. Striking workers at a smelting facility took time out to fix an electrical transformer lest production become crippled by a frozen potline. But such cordiality in local arenas of conflict did not go far to resolve the basic structural problem. The 1986 strike ended in early July, after the Steelworkers made some important concessions on benefits and work rules, but basic issues were left to the future. Nonetheless, the national unions discovered that they could no longer extract major concessions from the company facing increasing competition in a mature market for its basic product. More importantly, ongoing organizational reforms at Alcoa were perforce altering the institutional configuration between labor and management. By 1986, relatively centralized labor organizations were negotiating with a relatively decentralized corporation, and Alcoa's general managers were less able as well as less willing to place all the corporation's parts under the constraints of settlements made for the whole.[79]

George's farewell report and the dawn of a new strategy

Nineteen eighty-two was a year in which the morale of Alcoa managers had been badly shaken by the worst economic depression (it was called a "recession," in accordance with modern tendencies of public officials to euphemize) since the 1930s. It was a year in which Alcoa sold off many of its assets, including its ancient franchise, Wear-Ever, and shut down production facilities at Mobile, Alabama, and at Point Comfort and Marshall, Texas. Then in 1983, despite the improving economy, scores of managers expressed fears that their careers, which had once seemed so secure, now seemed constantly at risk. What else should they think when cost-cutting was rampant and when so many of their superiors in Pittsburgh were muttering aloud about the "maturity" of the industry and the demise of aluminum as a growth industry?[80]

Contributing to the gloom was the ongoing Overhead Valuation Analysis. OVA, which had begun in the previous year, was a detailed, "bottoms-up" exercise for evaluating of administrative functions at all levels of headquarters management by the users of those functions. This was in large part necessitated by the ongoing decentralization of operations into business-unit management, but it was generally regarded as a cost-cutting exercise. Like most large American corporations, Alcoa was vulnerable to one of the prevailing contemporary criticisms of American big business – that it had allowed overhead costs to rise and administrative productivity to decline without regard for the most efficient allocation and use of personnel. It was estimated that Alcoa's gross margin on its total shipments had fallen from levels well above thirty percent in the 1960s to about twenty percent in the 1980s and that the trend would continue, despite expected increases in shipments, unless costs were lowered. Administrative and selling costs were a particularly attractive target, and by the end of the year, some $118 million had been cut from a total of $760 million in administrative expenses.[81] In the ensuing three years, hundreds of salaried personnel were induced into early retirement, were reassigned, or were permanently laid off. Alcoa's job-elimination policy was financially attractive to those with long service (among whose number were people the company could ill afford to lose). The central corporate staffs were hit the hardest. Beginning as it did, during hard times, the OVA program was widely interpreted by many managers to be a sign more of corporate weakness than strength, and morale plunged.

That (and indeed much of everything else that was happening at Alcoa) was happening to American heavy industry generally. As stated above, there had been a sea change in the industrial environment that had its origins in the globalization of industrial markets in the 1970s, a change that was as irresistible and irreversible as it was profound in its effects on the capital-intensive manufacturers that formed the heart of the American economy. After a long series of palpable shocks, ranging from the first OPEC oil embargo of 1973, through several years of spiraling inflation exacerbated by sharp increases in petroleum costs after 1977 and mounting unemployment to the recession of 1981–2, a consensus formed among business leaders that the American center industries had somehow grown stagnant. American industry was at a crossroads, and had to reform.

There is no better description of the crossroads arrived at by the aluminum industry than Alcoa's *Annual Report for 1982*. Normally, Alcoa's annual report (like most companies') was a glossily produced state-of-the-company message delivered in the most positive terms – an expensive public relations effort to impress investors with the company's latest products, outline its best hopes for the future, and offer reasonable rationalizations for events or circumstances that might have dampened earnings. It would have been easy enough to attribute Alcoa's poor performance in 1982 to the economic downturn and let it go at that. But this time Krome George took an unusually active role in the preparation of the yearly ritual and made it his swan song. His final annual report bore a subtitle, *Responses to a Changing World*, and in it was a remarkably frank exposition on the prevailing winds in the aluminum industry. Considering the entire sweep of the industry's history from World War II, George's main point was simply this: that global competition and a secular deceleration in the rate of demand had finally transformed aluminum from one of the great growth industries of the twentieth century into one with a far less certain future.

George focused attention on one particular event of high symbolic (as well as substantive) importance: the appearance of primary aluminum as a commodity item on the London Metals Exchange in 1978. The trading of aluminum on the LME was not a cause but an effect of the growing competition in ingot production. Previously, the price structure of aluminum had maintained a fair degree of stability in constant-dollar terms and had held up nicely through the recession of 1974–5, when it also appeared "that the pricing of aluminum mill products had become sufficiently differentiated to be less cyclical in the face of short-term swings in demand."[82] But the ability of the industry to sustain stable prices had weakened substantially since then, especially after 1978. With the advent of commodity trading, ingot prices had become unhinged from the costs of production, at least in the near term, and were thus rendered "overly sensitive to short-term swings in the balance between supply and demand." This sensitivity then reverberated downstream into fabricating prices. Exacerbated by the post-1977 escalation in petroleum prices, costs rose to meet declining prices, and by 1982, it was clear that the industry could no longer expect "to maintain profitability in the face of a prolonged worldwide recession."

The strategic implication of George's analysis went beyond Alcoa's worries for a recession. On the one hand, it was reasonable to expect that new smelters would be built overseas wherever cheaper power and bauxite and developing regional markets justified the investment. But on the other hand, Alcoa (and other producers) had to look forward to shutting down substantial amounts of its primary capacity. Even though projected growth in demand portended better years ahead, Alcoa simply could no longer afford to commit itself to building new smelters "simply to sell metal into the open commodity market." Instead, George declared, "we will prefer to purchase our peak requirements rather than have smelting capacity in excess of our average fabricating needs." Investment would necessarily shift further downstream. Aluminum, George argued, still had high-technology potential. New product developments in aluminum food cans, aluminum-intensive vehicles, aluminum dish antennas, aluminum-lithium alloys, and alumina-based chemicals held out great prospects for the continuing profitability of "a remarkably versatile basic material," whose "flexibility is matched by the flexibility of the company's resources, markets and product lines which are widely distributed around the world."[83]

George's message had a blunt impact. Despite his optimistic outlook for new developments, he had delivered a painful and sobering message. It came at the right time, however, because middle managers at Alcoa had been impatiently awaiting some clarification of a corporate viewpoint. The gradual implementation of business-unit planning had occurred in a manner that left men and women down the ranks confused about the drift of Alcoa's strategy and structure. In the words of a 1982 OVA report:

> . . . a clear and compelling vision is lacking [at Alcoa]. Managers are unclear as to whether the desired Alcoa of 1990 will be larger or smaller, more focused or more diversified, or more centralized or decentralized in its organizing philosophy. Equally, we find no shared understanding as to whether the corporation's fundamental success will be measured by volume, by geographic reach, by degree of integration, or by a financial goal. . . . [Middle-level] managers were wrestling with decisions for which it was hard to identify the objective or end result that senior management desired.[84]

Responses to a Changing World at least established a common set of premises for a corporate-wide discussion of Alcoa's dilemmas.

As the recession faded and economic conditions began to improve, only the most tentative sort of optimism began to form in the ranks.

Not atypical was the business-unit manager for Rod, Bar, and Wire, Dennis Falls, who recounted how he had joined Alcoa in 1966 as a young industrial engineer, confident that he had hitched his career wagon to the best of America's growth industries. That confidence had turned to discouragement in the late 1970s, though he now took some comfort in the observation that the problems of aluminum were "not even close to some of the other major industries like steel." Aluminum was maturing, but with the right product focus, he thought, aluminum might recover.[85] There were others, to be sure, who thought that the alarms were unnecessary. At corporate headquarters, retiring vice chairman Marvin Gantz summed up the feelings of many of the older hands in the business when he told consultants that he felt it was a serious miscalculation for Alcoa to "accept the concept of the maturity of the aluminum industry." Aluminum not only retained all the properties that had made it an almost universally applicable metal, but with modern, low-energy recycling technologies, it had become infinitely reusable. As ever, he said, "God is on our side."[86]

But those at corporate headquarters who would in fact lead Alcoa into its next phase of development were far from sanguine. According to their analysis, Alcoa's basic business was deep in the throes of secular decline. For too long, the success of RCS had masked a decelerating rate of growth in other fabricated product markets where "second-tier" producers were becoming stronger, operating under the price umbrella of the major American producers. In its major broad category of business, Flat-Rolled Products, which had accounted for seventy-five percent of company shipments in 1982, Alcoa was beginning to face vigorous competition from competing materials. This was coming at a time when labor costs for aluminum products were thirty to forty percent higher than those for plastics and glass. Alcoa could no longer count simply on doing what it had always done so well, substituting aluminum for other products. To a reformer such as Charles Ligon, the head of corporate planning, aluminum was in imminent danger of becoming "just another smokestack industry" in which Alcoa was merely "the best of a bad lot."[87]

The above sample of views reflects the range of sentiments expressed by Alcoa managers in the summer of 1983, as problems were being defined but directions were still unclear. It was hard for veteran managers to accept the evidence that Alcoa's traditional strategy of expanding primary aluminum capacity by seeking lower-cost sources of supply and improved means of production was availing

Table 8.4. *Aluminum's share of total beverage can shipments,*
1973–86 (in billions of units)

Year	Aluminum cans	Total metal cans	Aluminum cans as % of total metal cans
1973	10.6	41.7	26
1974	13.8	44.0	31
1975	16.3	42.6	38
1976	20.9	46.4	45
1977	25.8	51.2	50
1978	30.1	54.4	55
1979	33.7	54.4	62
1980	41.5	55.2	75
1981	47.7	56.3	85
1982	51.7	57.9	89
1983	56.7	61.4	92
1984	61.5	65.7	94
1985	65.9	70.3	94
1986	70.0	74.0	95

Sources: Can Manufacturers Institute, *Metal Can Shipments Reports* (1973–86); Alcoa estimates for 1973–4.

them so little in the present day. And it was easy for Alcoa managers to take solace in the comparative misfortunes of their big brothers in steel. Unlike the great American steel companies (whose decline in the early 1980s was really precipitous), Alcoa had expanded its international resource base, cultivated new markets for its basic products, devoted large expenditures to research and development, upgraded its basic processes of production, and watched its costs with increasing care. Nonetheless, there was a nagging fear that not even the company's best efforts could sustain its growth on the basis of its traditional business. Best efforts would not matter if Alcoa had simply become, in a quip managers attributed to Charles Parry, "the low-cost producer of a product that nobody wants."[88]

The new company president, Fred Fetterolf, put it best, when he described the unsettling sense of foreboding that gripped Alcoa in the wake of George's report:

> [T]his great thing that our forefathers gave us, which was low-cost power, great diversity of bauxite..., low-cost refineries, isn't working very well for us today, nor do we see it being that way in the future. For us to come to grips with that, most of us

Fig. 8.9. W. H. Krome George, chairman and chief executive officer, 1975–82.

Fig. 8.10. Charles W. Parry, chairman and chief executive officer, 1982–7.

Fig. 8.11. C. Fred Fetterolf, president and chief operating officer, 1982–

who lived a lifetime believing that the strength of our company is in its underlying facilities, [it] is just a hell of a change.

For management to accept that the vital center of Alcoa's business had grown soft, said Fetterolf, required a giant leap over a "cultural hurdle." And that hurdle was nothing less than Alcoa's own historic success.[89]

New mission; new structure: Alcoa in 1986

A dramatic series of changes unfolded rapidly after 1983 and, by the time our story concludes, were still in progress. It is difficult to draw more than a basic outline of those changes pending a more thorough debriefing of the decision-makers, the release of relevant documents, and the perspective of time. We shall see, however, that at 100 years after Charles Martin Hall made his great discovery, the giant corporation built on his invention was busy carving out a radical new identity for itself. Alcoa's new CEO, Charles Parry, was committed to a fundamental rethinking of Alcoa's business. He had participated for several years in debates over corporate strategy and structure, and he and his corporate planning staff were well-prepared for a major departure. It was based on his broadening definition of Alcoa as a "materials company" that he and Fred Fetterolf would engineer a major transformation of corporate structure.

Parry had joined the company as a metallurgical engineer, in 1948. He was sent to Massena, but, in 1952, when it had become apparent that his daughter would require special schooling for a disability, he was allowed to transfer to Pittsburgh, where, in reality, he was not needed. "That's the kind of company we were," he said. Then, he "tended to drift over a period of the next couple of years into becoming the accounting and cost expert in the Smelting Division."[90] Like George before him, Parry refined and elevated his expertise and eventually moved from cost accounting into Alcoa's new planning function, spending time along the way doing financial planning for the company's international as well as domestic operations. He did a stint as Alcoa of Australia's financial director, and in 1974, after serving briefly as vice president for Corporate Planning, he was moved into Primary Products, where he centralized and integrated the managements of raw materials, refining, and smelting. In December 1979, he was promoted to executive vice president for Primary Products and in 1981, he became president.

Fig. 8.12.   The NASA Space Shuttle sheathed in an aluminum alloy is borne aloft by a more conventional aircraft sheathed in polished aluminum skinsheet.

Both Harper and George nurtured Parry's career, and he reflected their influence. Like Harper, he brought a spacious point of view to strategic and social issues. Like George, he placed high value on formally analytical approaches to problems. Within Alcoa, he was both praised and criticized as a "visionary" strategist. He was popular and well-liked, seen as a friendly, avuncular presence in trying times. Large, round, easy-going, and genial, he was a cheerful "shirt-sleeve manager" who, according to a Steelworker official, was certainly not a man who would immediately strike anyone as the chairman of a major corporation. (That was meant by the speaker as a compliment.[91]) Not overly enamored with the trappings of corporate power, Parry could be found, on any given day, eating lunch at the coffee-shop counter just off the Pittsburgh headquarters lobby. Charles Parry could wax nostalgic on the good old days at Alcoa, but when the time came, he proved willing enough to abandon its old ways of doing business.

In June 1983, Alcoa's senior management Policy Committee convened at Rolling Rock to consider a new corporate "mission statement" as Alcoa began to plot a future in which it would develop, produce, and market "advanced materials." This meeting, which was one of a series of ongoing discussions on strategic and structural matters, can usefully serve as a proxy for the entire process. In the materials prepared for the occasion, Alcoa was defined afresh, though somewhat ungracefully, as "a worldwide manufacturer/supplier of differentiated products and services which have a material orientation, high technological content, and a high value added. . . . " Alcoa's traditional strategy was no longer a viable path to growth. A monolithic conception of the business – "integrated aluminum, from the mines through fabricated products" – had become increasingly untenable. Downstream, Alcoa was "not one business but many businesses," serving many markets. Upstream, aluminum and ingot had become commodities with dim prospects for acceptable rates of return. Alcoa's "core business," the cluster of fabrications known as flat-rolled products – which included RCS, plate and heated sheet, sheet and foil, and aluminum closures – and its vital backward linkages into aluminum and alumina still accounted for most of the corporation's shipments and profits, but most of Alcoa's core products were sold in maturing, domestic markets. For long-term growth and survival, diversification was imperative. The diversity of Alcoa's markets, the commoditization of unalloyed aluminum ingot, and the maturing of major aluminum product markets all compelled a redefinition of the corporation as a more variegated, less aluminum-bound enterprise.[92]

The Policy Committee considered recommendations for a new "two-prong" strategy, which would deemphasize alumina and ingot and invest more resources in high-technology flat-rolled products (such as aerospace applications) while modernizing domestic mills to ensure their long-term competitive positions. Domestic sales of flat-rolled products could then be used as a source of cash for fostering the growth of new, noncore businesses through internal expansion, creation, or acquisition. Existing lines of business in chemicals, engineered products, and international sales of flat-rolled products were readily identified as promising areas for development. On the horizon were business opportunities in "strange new high-growth markets," the pursuit of which would take Alcoa far afield from its traditional approach to the development of aluminum as a product substitute. Key to a new approach was the reorientation of research toward "breakthrough" technologies that would reduce the company's dependence on metal and open entirely new areas of commercial potential.[93]

This new strategy was turned largely into reality, at least in the attempt, during the next three years. By 1986, Alcoa had become, variously in the rhetoric of its management, "a packaging company," "an engineering company," and "a materials company." The development of plastic food containers proceeded concurrently with attempts to make economical aluminum food containers. A joint venture with Fujikura had been launched in 1984 to develop fiber-optic electrical systems. Aluminum- and magnesium-lithium alloy development were responses to the threat of new materials. The company also began testing a structural laminate of aluminum sheet and aramid polymers, known as ARALL 1, developed in conjunction with the 3M Company. Metal-matrix and ceramic-matrix composites were on the horizon.[94]

Alcoa's pursuit of high-technology businesses on a wide front was backed by research-and-development expenditures of unprecedented amounts. Between 1983 and 1986, Alcoa's R&D budget increased from $81.5 million per annum to $148.2 million. More significant than the level of expenditures was the pronounced shift in their allocation toward fundamental research into new materials – aluminum-based materials and also nonaluminum metals, chemicals, ceramics, composites, polymers, laminates, and advanced manufacturing systems. It was from the fruits of such research that Parry hoped to established Alcoa's "technological leadership in advanced materials."[95] In order to restore the substance as well as the spirit of fundamental inquiry, the director of the Laboratories was authorized to hire more research scientists from a variety of disciplines, to enhance the career tracks of nonmanagerial technical personnel, and to broaden the channels of communication to the outside scientific community.

A brief review of the agenda of the Laboratories reveals a striking shift in priorities. The thrust of a new technology strategy—"the discovery, design, characterization, and cost-effective manufacture of highly engineered laminates, and composite materials," focusing "primarily on metals, ceramics, and polymers" is apparent in a comparison of allocations of research expenditures for 1983 and 1986. In the latter year, only forty-four percent of budgeted R&D expenditures were categorized as "aluminum-related." The rest were devoted to the development of "advanced materials," "new businesses and processes," "technical consultation and discretionary research," and "factory automation and computer integration." Major R&D activities for 1986 were categorized as follows: Advanced Metals, such as aluminum-lithium and magnesium-lithium alloys for aerospace and energy applications; New Packaging Systems, including

Table 8.5. *Alcoa's research-and-development expenditures,*
1974–86 (millions of dollars)

Year	R&D expenditures	R&D as % of sales and operating revenues
1974	43.0	1.6
1975	48.1	2.1
1976	48.0	1.6
1977	52.0	1.5
1978	56.9	1.4
1979	57.9	1.2
1980	72.8	1.4
1981	83.9	1.7
1982	87.9	1.9
1983	81.5	1.5
1984	95.4	1.7
1985	119.7	2.3
1986	148.2	3.1

Source: Annual Reports.

"aseptic and flexible packages, microwavable formed containers and high barrier composite containers;" Advanced Computing "that integrates mathematics and human experience;" Ceramics, for use in computers, telecommunications systems, and military armor; Engineered Materials, including "powder metal alloys, structural laminates, and metal matrix composites;" Separations Technology and Systems, to separate valuable or harmful components of gases and liquids; and Aluminum Intensive Vehicles (AIV). The very language suggests how far Alcoa was prepared to travel from its traditional research base in aluminum metallurgy and engineering.

In expanding Alcoa's scientific and technological purview, Parry envisioned the manufacture of products, components, and systems that were neither bound by aluminum nor limited to semifinished output. Rather than sell aluminum aerospace alloys to an aircraft builder, Alcoa would sell entire aircraft parts made from new materials produced in revolutionized manufacturing facilities. In new applications of aluminum, the idea now was not simply to look for ways to replace other materials in existing products but to invent new products. The AIV development program, for example, looked at first glance like another attempt to develop a set of high-tonnage product substitutes. But AIV was not conceived as a straightforward

Table 8.6. *Focus of Alcoa's research-and-development expenditures,*
1980 and 1986

Category	1980	1986
Aluminum-related	78%	44%
Advanced materials	3	21
New businesses and new processes	3	20
Technical consultation and discretionary research	16	11
Factory automation and computer integration	—	4

Source: Facts About Alcoa (1986).

substitution of aluminum for steel; it was predicated on an assumption that there would be a market for an entirely new kind of vehicle that would require, at the outset, radically new principles of design and manufacture. These were heady prospects, visionary but exemplifying a revivified faith in the power of science and technology to move the corporation into new market frontiers.[96]

The new strategy was to be supported by Alcoa's ongoing administrative reforms, which if taken to their logical conclusion would support more diverse entrepreneurial efforts at the business-unit level. Indeed after 1983, the decentralization of Alcoa's operations proceeded apace. This trend had great impact on the size and functions of the Pittsburgh headquarters, as corporate staffs were trimmed back to the bare bones. One extreme example of the effects of this process was the decline of the central Engineering Department, which illustrated the changing nexus between Alcoa's headquarters and its operating entities.

Ever since the days of Edwin Fickes, the Engineering Department had been an important bastion of corporate power, a crucial cog at the very center of Alcoa's vertically integrated structure. Engineering had been responsible for the management of large-scale projects in power generation, refining, and smelting construction, which had given the company a powerful long-term competitive advantage in capital costs. On that basis, Engineering had acquired prestige, authority and a high degree of autonomy, offering its members a distinctive professional identity within Alcoa and a strong, organizationally based *esprit de corps*. In the pre-World War II era of strong local plant autonomy, Engineering's huge capital responsibilities had made it one centralized corporate department that could dictate to local operations managers. The department's corporate power increased with centralization after the war, and as late as 1978, Engineering remained the keystone of Alcoa's edifice of corporate self-sufficiency.[97]

Undaunted by growing signs of overcapacity, Engineering kept itself busy with projects in energy management and was committed to adding or selling one new smelter every eighteen months and one new refinery every twenty-four months. All that changed abruptly in the early 1980s, when the decline of refining and smelting activity in the United States became accepted as a permanent fact of life. With the rise of the business units, operating managers became freer to go outside the corporation to purchase their requirements, and so Engineering lost its "lock" on the provision of support services. Accordingly, the number of engineers at Pittsburgh began to shrink, and between 1981 and year-end 1985, the central engineering staff was cut from 322 to 64. Many were laid off as a result of job elim-ination (for example, most drafting work was put on an outside contracting basis). Others were transferred to Flat-Rolled Products, Refining, Chemicals, and Primary Metals business-unit organiza-tions. Still others were lodged in a new systems engineering group located outside the city. In 1986, apart from Construction, Engi-neering had ceased to be a corporate-level staff function. The process of dismantling Engineering was disruptive, and there was a serious question as to how Alcoa could maintain a strong sense of profes-sional belonging and high standards among a more dispersed corps of engineers. The morale of those remaining at corporate head-quarters also plunged (in 1984, the department's head resigned to seek greener pastures). Other central departments (with the notable exception of R&D) were pared back as well. As Fetterolf trimmed and reallocated personnel, anxiety spread throughout the ranks. Parry and Fetterolf worried, privately as well as publicly, about the impact of Alcoa's reorganization on managerial loyalties, but stock analysts generally saw the cuts as a sign that Alcoa was eliminating wasteful overhead, becoming "leaner" and more competitive in its structure.[98]

Still, amidst all this activity, there was little overt indication that Alcoa's diversification had proceeded much beyond the research-and-development stages. As late as September 1985, Fetterolf insisted that substantial diversification beyond aluminum was but one view of the company's future, while Parry took pains to remind everyone that while Alcoa was a "materials company," it remained one with a dominant "aluminum core."[99] And Alcoa's structure, though more decentralized, remained bound by the broad categories of aluminum

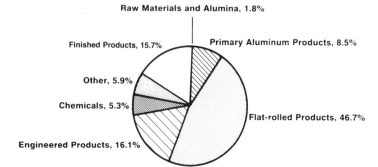

Total Revenues = $5,162.7 million

Key: • Raw Materials and Alumina: Bauxite, metal-grade alumina, caustic soda.
      • PRIMARY ALUMINUM PRODUCTS: Various types and grades of aluminum and
        magnesium ingot.
      • FLAT-ROLLED PRODUCTS: Plate, sheet, and foil products.
      • ENGINEERED PRODUCTS: Forgings, extrusions, drawn tube, castings, and wire.
      • CHEMICALS: Various aluminas, nonmetal grade bauxite and related chemicals for
        industrial applications, including ceramics.
      • OTHER PRODUCTS: Overhead transmission and covered electrical products, powders,
        and pigments, scrap sales, and ingot tolling.
      • FINISHED-PRODUCT SEGMENT: Finished products made principally by Alcoa
        Subsidiaries, such as Stolle Corp., Alcoa Defense Systems, Rae Magnet Wire, and the Precision Products
        Division at Lancaster, Pennsylvania.

Chart 8.2. Alcoa's principal products, 1985 (percent sales and operating revenues). *Sources: Alcoa, 1985 Annual Report. Facts About Alcoa, 1986.*

products, reflecting still the dominant influence of vertically integrated technologies. In the spring of 1986, Alcoa's corporate organization chart was a slightly consolidated version of the 1983 plan, with all operations aggregated under the following corporate-level groups: Primary Metals (which had subsumed Alumina and Raw Materials), Flat-Rolled Products, Engineered Products, and International.[100]

Then in the summer of 1986, just when the process of reducing the corporate staffs seemed to have run its course, Parry unveiled a new structure for the corporation. Three of the five new corporate groups combined broad market segments that would be served by diversified technologies. An Aerospace and Industrial Products group comprised aircraft, automotive, and other transportation markets as well as industrial markets for forgings, castings, extrusions, rod and bar, and sheet and plate products. To Packaging Systems reported all businesses in beverage and food packaging employing aluminum and nonaluminum materials alike. A group for Metals

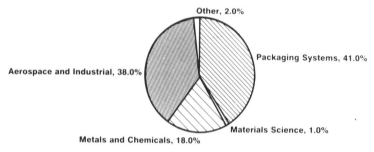

Other, 2.0%

Packaging Systems, 41.0%

Aerospace and Industrial, 38.0%

Materials Science, 1.0%

Metals and Chemicals, 18.0%

Total Revenues = $4,667.2 million

Key:
• PACKAGING SYSTEMS: Minimum sheet, foil and laminate materials, closures, recycling and packaging, machinery and equipment.
• AEROSPACE & INDUSTRIAL: Aluminum bar, castings, extrusions, plate, rod, sheet and tube, and forgings made of aluminum, magnesium, steel, and titanium. Also includes Stolle Corp., manufacturer of building, automotive, and appliance products.
• METALS AND CHEMICALS: Bauxite, alumina, industrial chemicals, and magnesium.
• MATERIALS SCIENCE: Advanced ceramics, fiber optics, defense materials systems, and separations technology.
• OTHER: Primarily revenues of subsidiaries sold during the year.

Chart 8.3. Alcoa's principal product groups, 1986 (percent sales and operating revenues). *Source: Alcoa, 1986 Annual Report.*

and Chemicals included Alcoa's upstream aluminum operations – bauxite, alumina, domestic smelting – as well as magnesium and a variety of industrial chemicals. Alcoa's overseas aluminum business remained segregated under a group vice president for International, who was to oversee Alcoa's smelting and fabricating operations in Europe, Asia, Australia, Latin America, and the Middle East.[101] A small fifth group, Materials Science, was charged with more entre-preneurial responsibilities. It was to serve as an "umbrella under which Alcoa will find, nurture, and grow new businesses in existing and nontraditional materials and markets." Materials Science em-braced Alcoa Defense Systems, which had been formed in 1985, to make advanced materials for military applications, and all oper-ating entities for the production and marketing of high-performance ceramics, separations technology, fiber optics, and the AIV. Mate-rials Science was given a mandate to make acquisitions in nonalumi-num areas, and by the end of 1986, Alcoa purchased companies with expertise in metallic and composite structures for aerospace and marine applications and in separation, purification, and filtration materials and systems. Though its revenues were but a tiny portion of Alcoa's total business (Materials Science generated less than $50

Fig. 8.13.   Ceramic powders and forms made in the Alcoa Laboratories.

million in 1986, mostly from companies acquired late in the year), its mandate to make acquisitions and to enter into joint ventures on a wide front placed it at the leading edge of Alcoa's technological diversification.[102]

Gone in the new structure was any vestige of direct corporate responsibility for production and marketing functions. At the corporate level, the principle of decentralized management had triumphed over the constraints of Alcoa's integrated aluminum business, which was in the future to be coordinated at lower levels of the organization. In contrast to the days when Alcoa had few middle managers with broad management skills, several years of experience with the development of business units had made it more feasible to allocate executive authority to a wide array of divisional managers. More responsibility for marketing and production could now be pushed down to business-unit managers and divisional heads, who in turn reported to the group vice presidents. Each group vice president had become in effect a chief executive of a cluster of related business activities that drew on a larger pool of corporate resources in technology and money. It was left to the corporate CEO and his staff to manage the overall financing and strategic planning of a portfolio of businesses, while the duties of the president included the implementation of corporate plans; the allocation of human resources and the direction of employee relations; and the planning and coordination of research and development (a responsibility that was to be shared with the chairman).

Parry's program for aggressive diversification had thus crystallized in a radical new structure. Alcoa was poised to move into a postaluminum age. The implementation of Parry's program was to be left to others; he would announce his retirement in the spring of 1987. But before retiring, he made bold assertions to the effect that Alcoa could expect to derive but half its revenues from aluminum within ten years. "We are," he told his employees in December 1986, "square in the midst of the greatest change this company has ever undergone."[103]

Afterthoughts

By the end of 1986, Alcoa had run full course in its strategic and structural evolution. It had been founded to produce aluminum, capitalizing on an invention that held out great promise for low-cost production of a potentially useful metal. Under the protection of patents, the company grew by reinvesting its earnings, by acquisition, and by achieving crucial economies of scale in the production of aluminum through the building of large production facilities. Alcoa also supported its "horizontal" expansion through "vertical integration," establishing its control over critical sources of raw materials and energy while moving into the production, marketing, and distribution of semifinished and, on occasion, finished products. By these strategies, Alcoa managed to sustain an almost unassailable North American monopoly in primary aluminum long after its controlling patents expired in 1909. To cope with the increasing scale and complexity of its operations, the company rationalized its internal affairs by creating a centrally governed bureaucracy administered by functionally specialized departments. By 1920, Alcoa was so large (and efficient in terms of economies of scale), so thoroughly integrated, so competent in its basic technology, and so self-sufficient that it was able to sustain an American monopoly on its basic business in primary aluminum production until political and economic events of World War II enabled competition to gain a foothold.

Alcoa's functional organization was to endure for decades, becoming ever more centralized in its governance – well into the 1960s –

even as its markets and products grew more diverse. That process of centralization began to reverse in the late 1960s, as the company began to restructure its bureaucracy around lines of business instead of technological functions. In the meantime, a large internal research capability had become established as a centralized, science-based function in the pre-World War II era. Initially, the main purpose of Alcoa's research organization was to establish a knowledge base that would enable the corporation to improve its basic processes and to develop new fabricating processes and alloys. As competition increased after World War II, research became ever more intertwined with development, and both were more directed toward cost-reduction and the creation of new products. In the 1950s and 1960s, the development of high-volume and/or high-margin products for markets in electrical transmission, ground and air transportation, construction, and packaging sustained and increased Alcoa's aluminum business at a high rate of growth. But by the 1980s, when it became apparent that growth by these means could no longer be sustained at high rates in the face of increasing competition and newer technologies, Alcoa began to prepare for the possibility of a post-aluminum age.

Alcoa also became an international corporation, at first in the quest for bauxite and later to obtain lower-cost power and labor for products to be sold in the United States. The company also invested in facilities abroad to produce and sell aluminum in foreign markets. After one abortive experience trying to manage foreign operations in the 1920s, Alcoa went overseas again, in the late 1950s, and has since become a substantial multinational enterprise. By the end of 1986, Alcoa's operations were spread throughout fifteen nations, and a full third of Alcoa's 55,000 employees worldwide worked outside the United States.[104] Alcoa's moves abroad coincided with and contributed to the globalization of the aluminum markets, a process that at first aided the destabilization of the oligopolistic pattern of the world industry and eventually destroyed it. One interesting domestic side effect has been that antitrust – once so central to the concerns of Alcoa's management and for so long a time a constraint on corporate strategy – has been rendered irrelevant in most aluminum markets.

Not so irrelevant but also changing is another major historic constraint on Alcoa's management: the power and authority of national labor organizations. The rise of industrial aluminum unions by World War II effectively separated most of the hourly workforce's economic interests and working conditions from the arbitrary con-

Location	Bauxite	Alumina, chemical products	Primary aluminum	Power	Steel plate	Foil	Extrusions	Tube products	Wire, rod, bar	Forgings	Castings	Closures, closure machinery	Electrical products	Finished products[1]	Can recycling	Other[2]
Australia																
Geelong, Alcoa of Australia Limited			•		•	•										
Kwinana, Alcoa of Australia Limited	•	•														
Pinjarra, Alcoa of Australia Limited	•	•														
Portland, Alcoa of Australia Limited*			•													
Wagerup, Alcoa of Australia Limited	•	•														
Belgium																
Hemiksem, †Lamitref Aluminium N.V.									•				•			
Brazil																
Cotia, Alcoa Aluminio S.A.													•			
Itapissuma (Recife), Alcoa Aluminio S.A.					•	•	•									
Pindamonhangaba, Alcoa Aluminio S.A.							•				•			•		
Pocos de Caldas, Alcoa Aluminio S.A.	•	•	•	•									•			
Sao Luis, Alumar Consortium		•	•													
Sorocaba, Alcoa Aluminio S.A.							•									
Tubarao, Alcoa Aluminio S.A.							•									
Guinea																
Sangaredi, †Halco (Mining), Inc.	•															
France																
Bologne, Forges de Bologne										•						
Jamaica																
Clarendon, Alcoa Minerals of Jamaica, Inc.	•	•														
Japan																
Iwakuni City, Moralco, Limited			•													
Tokyo, Shibazaki Seisakusho Limited												•				
Mexico																
Acuna, Arneses Y Accesarios De Mexico, S.A. de C.V.													•			
Mexico City, Alcomex, S.A.							•	•								
Puebla, Almexa Aluminio, S.A. de C.V.					•	•	•									
Tulpetlac, Almexa Aluminio, S.A. de C.V.					•	•	•								•	
Veracruz, †Aluminio, S.A. de C.V.				•												
The Netherlands																
Drunen, Alcoa Nederland B.V.							•	•	•							
Rotterdam, Alcoa Chemie Nederland B.V.			•													
Norway																
Lista, †Mosal Aluminum Elkem a.s & Co.			•													
Mosjoen, †Mosal Aluminum Elkem a.s & Co.			•													
Spain																
Barcelona, Capsulas Metalicas S.A.												•				
Surinam																
Moengo, Suralco Aluminum Company	•															
Paranam, Suralco Aluminum Company	•	•	•													
United Kingdom																
Swansea, Alcoa Manufacturing (G.B.) Limited						•		•	•							

*Under construction
†Minority interest
[1] Includes finished products such as building products and containers
[2] Includes operations such as secondary ingot, hydroelectric power, ocean transportation, caustic soda and manufactured products

Chart 8.4.   Alcoa worldwide operations, 1986.

trol of paternalistic management. Thereafter, workers' interests across Alcoa's major operating facilities were more or less uniformly advanced and defended through adversarial rituals of negotiation, grievance procedures and, when things went badly, strikes. Alcoa's corporate relations with its unions followed the patterns set by such larger industries as autos and steel, and only recently, under the

	Bauxite	Alumina chemical products	Primary aluminum	Powder	Sheet, plate	Foil	Extrusions	Tube products	Wire rod, bar	Forgings	Castings	Closures closure machinery	Electrical products	Finished products /	Can recycling	Other?
United States																
Addy, Wash., Northwest Alloys, Inc.															●	
Alcoa, Tenn.			●		●	●								●		
Atlanta, Ga., Universal Adsorbents, Inc.		●														
Badin, N.C.			●		●											
Bauxite, Ark.	●	●														
Bridgeville, Pa., Pakco Industrial Ceramics, Inc.		●														
Cleveland, Ohio										●	●					
Conover, N.C. AmericanPowdered Metals Co.													●			
Corona, Calif.											●					
Davenport, Iowa					●	●										
Delhi, La., Tifton Aluminum Company, Inc.							●									
Evansville, Ind.		●			●									●		
Fort Meade, Fla.		●														
Fort Smith, Ark., Norton/Alcoa Proppant Co.		●														
Franklin, N.C. Nantahala Power and Light Co.																●
Graham, N.C. Permatech, Inc.		●														
Houston, Miss., Alcoa Fujikura, Ltd.													●			
Lafayette, Ind.										●	●					
Lancaster, Pa.											●					
Latrobe, Pa., Pakco Industrial Ceramics, Inc.		●														
Lebanon, Pa.					●	●										
Massena, N.Y.			●						●	●						
Massena, N.Y., Alcoa Conductor Products Co.													●			
Nashville, Tenn., Alcoa Fujikura, Ltd.													●			
New York, N.Y., Alcoa Steamship Company, Inc.																●
North Haven, Conn., American Powdered Metals Co.													●			
Olive Branch, Miss., Advanced Closures, Inc.												●				
Point Comfort, Texas		●														●
Princeville, Ill., H C Products Co.													●			
Richmond, Ind.											●					
Ripley, Miss., Alcoa Fujikura, Ltd.													●			
Rockdale, Texas			●	●					●							
San Diego, Calif., Alcoa Defense Systems, Inc.																●
Sidney, Ohio, The Stolle Corporation													●			
Spartanburg, S.C., Alcoa Fujikura, Ltd.													●			
Tifton, Ga., Tifton Aluminum Company, Inc.							●									
Vancouver, Wash.									●							
Vancouver, Wash., Alcoa Conductor Products Co.																
Vernon, Calif.							●						●			
Vidalia, La.			●				●	●		●						
Wenatchee, Wash.				●												
Zelienople, Pa., Lancy International, Inc.		●														
West Germany																
Ludwigshafen, Alcoa Chemie GmbH		●														
Tellig, Alcoa Deutschland GmbH												●				
Viernheim, Alcoa Deutschland GmbH												●				
Worms am Rhein, Alcoa Deutschland GmbH												●				

Chart 8.4. Alcoa worldwide operations, 1986. (cont'd)

twin pressures of competition and diversification, does that pattern seem to be breaking.

In all, Alcoa has followed what historians have identified as a general pattern of evolution in capital-intensive corporations, moving successively – and successfully – through strategies for horizontal and vertical integration, investment in research and development, expansion overseas, and, all along the way, continuing investment in new products. Until the 1980s, the strategies Alcoa pursued built one upon the other in more or less cumulative fashion over the years and included all but one of the basic strategic options open to any industrial enterprise. That one untried option was diversification into new lines of business. There had been times when Alcoa had attempted to develop and produce alternative technologies in basic metals, such as magnesium and titanium, and in nonaluminum products, such as copper wire and plastic closures. But diversification into nonaluminum areas was never a significant component of Alcoa's strategy until the 1980s, and then only after management had already established an organizational basis for diversification and had concluded that the enterprise could no longer expect to sustain a high rate of growth on the basis of its traditional aluminum technologies. Still, diversification could not simply build on older strategies; it required backing away from some of the corporation's conventional assumptions about the focus of its technology and the integration of its operations. Looked at this way, the recent effort to move into nonaluminum materials appears to be a profound historic departure for the corporation.

* * *

How, then, can we assess this apparently momentous development, having duly considered the longer passage of Alcoa's history? Does a more informed knowledge of the corporate past provide any insight into its future? Certainly, we cannot extrapolate from the past how successfully the company will fare under its new strategy. Nor can we foresee how far Charles Parry's successors will march down the path he and his staff have charted. Outcomes will be revealed only in time; any attempt to anticipate them is speculation. Management, of course, will speculate; it must. The historian can simply try to pose some useful questions.

How far can Alcoa's attempts at technological diversification be reasonably expected to go? Alcoa has succeeded historically by establishing new products and markets out of the creative exploitation of a unified technological base. The current thrust of Alcoa's research and development implies a corporate competence across a range of related scientific disciplines far broader than those traditionally brought to bear on aluminum metallurgy, electrochemistry, and engineering. Setting priorities, staffing, and managing research and development in aluminum have always been difficult. Will conducting a broader range of scientific and engineering programs prove to be too difficult?

How far can decentralization go? Alcoa, like all complex corporations, has faced ongoing challenges in managing the structural relationship between the center and peripheries of its operations. Alcoa has traditionally been managed by executives who remained closely attuned to the "nuts and bolts" of the company's operations long after the business had achieved gigantic scale and complexity. In a more diversified, decentralized corporation, will corporate management become so detached, so removed in its understanding of operations that its ability to plan and allocate resources for the enterprise as a whole will dissipate into a rarefied exercise in quantitative abstraction? And if that is not the desired outcome, can a company that has a weak bureaucratic tradition implement and sustain the kinds of formal channels of communication and authority that will effectively integrate the complementary resources of a diversified enterprise *in the absence of the kind of overwhelming technological imperative for integration that held together its traditional aluminum business?* The long-term thrust toward decentralization is clear and even desirable, but at some point, Alcoa's corporate management might be in danger of becoming a mere conglomerate shell.

Will Alcoa and its major unions be able to resolve the principal structural dilemma that has undermined more than four decades of bureaucratic accommodation? A once-integrated, relatively unitary organization has broken down in the processes of diversification and decentralization so that the legitimate basis for uniform agreements between the corporation and national labor unions is undermined by the very logic of market diversity. By 1986, the question of how centralized unions were going to deal with a decentralized corporation was largely unresolved. Neither Alcoa nor its unions have been inclined to undertake basic reforms for decades. Can they do so now?

And finally: Has aluminum really had its day? More specifically, will Alcoa's aluminum business be largely displaced by new technologies within the near future, say, by the end of the century? Of course the rate and extent to which aluminum-based technology will decline as a portion of Alcoa's total business is impossible to predict. Chief Wilson thought that the aluminum business had peaked when he joined the company in 1911. Magnesium was the great threat after World War I, and Alcoa researchers were worried about plastics after World War II. A remarkable series of unexpected applications for aluminum have been extracted over decades of development. It may yet be that the light, versatile, and still somewhat mysterious "metal of clay" retains some surprises.

In the sweep of history, such questions may seem to reflect only temporal concerns. In the long run, Alcoa's continuing success will be subject, as always, to the imagination and skill of its management, the competence and dedication of its employees, the constraints of technology, the availability of financial and material resources, the vicissitudes of the economy, and luck – the fortuitous event or circumstance over which the company has no control. For a century, Alcoa's managers and employees have proven their ability to adapt creatively to virtually every major opportunity and threat presented to them, through good times and bad, through fortunes ill and kind. In the process, they have built a vast and powerful institution – a complex corporate mechanism for the conversion of energy, labor, and raw materials into a wonderful array of useful products and technologies, generating enough wealth along the way to enrich its owners, sustain the livings of its employees, and to renew its own existence on an ever-increasing scale. If that historical record counts for anything, then Alcoa's chances for the future are better now than they were a century ago, when Charles Martin Hall's homespun invention was capitalized with twenty thousand dollars and an entrepreneurial dream.

Appendix A

Comparison of Alcoa's growth and Gross National Product, 1929–1986

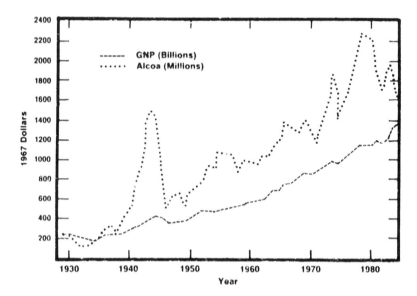

Chart A.1. Comparison of Alcoa's growth (sales and operating revenues) and U.S. Gross National Product, 1929–1986.

Appendix B

Aluminum Company of America:
selected historical financial data

.

Table B.1. *Alcoa's earnings and stockholders equity, 1889–1926*
(*in thousands*)

End of year	Average equity ($thousands)	Pretax earnings after interest charges ($thousands)	Pretax earnings as a percentage of equity (%)	Dividends and cash paid to stockholders ($thousands)	Retained earnings ($thousands)
1889[a]	10				
1890	510	(0.6)	(0.1)		(0.6)
1891	991	(18)	(1.8)		(18)
1892	970	(23)	(2.4)		(23)
1893	1,029	140	13.6		140
1894	1,136	74	7.1		74
1895	1,186	66	5.6	40	26
1896	1,201	65	5.4	60	5
1897	1,197	(14)	(1.2)		(14)
1898	1,233	87	7.1		87
1899	1,632	181	11.1	68	113
1900	2,084	322	15.5	131	191
1901	2,345	446	19.0	116	330
1902	2,702	520	19.2	136	384
1903	3,074	476	15.5	116	360
1904	3,419	424	12.4	96	328
1905	4,640	1,228	26.5	222	1,006
1906[b]	6,655	2,331	35.0	408	1,923
1906[c]	7,923	746	9.4	124	622
1907	9,505	2,949	31.0	408	2,541
1908	11,378	1,242	10.9	36	1,206
1909	14,537	5,964	41.0	315	5,649
1910	18,901	4,413	23.3	765	3,647
1911	22,651	4,634	20.5	749	3,884
1912	26,460	4,502	17.0	758	3,744
1913	30,043	4,182	13.9	749	3,433
1914	33,974	5,554	16.3	1,124	4,430
1915	40,058	8,955	22.4	1,217	7,737
1916	55,664	25,349	45.5	1,873	23,476
1917	76,124	19,688	25.9	2,247	17,441
1918	91,366	15,383	16.8	2,341	13,042
1919	102,511	11,122	10.8	1,873	9,250
1920	109,300	6,668	6.1	2,341	4,326
1921	107,851	(5,914)	(5.4)	1,311	(7,225)
1922	100,700	(5,968)	(5.9)	1,124	(7,092)
1923	102,348	12,354	12.1	1,966	10,388
1924	112,408	11,981	10.7	2,344	9,636
1925	135,805	22,334	16.4	3,455	18,879
1926	159,711	15,191	9.5	4,432	10,759

[a]Fiscal year ended August 31 until 1906.
[b]Last four months of 1905.
[c]In 1906, the fiscal year began to run concurrently with the calendar year.
Source: based on *US v. Alcoa*, Equity 85–73, Exhibit 1709.

Table B.2. *Selected Alcoa financial data, 1927–86*

Year	Sales and operating revenues ($millions)	Operating profit ($millions)	Net income[a] ($ millions)	Oper. profit as % of sales and oper. revs. (%)	Common shares outstanding[b] (thousands)	Net income per common share[b] ($)
1927	83.0	20.2	13.4	24.3	53,015	0.11
1928	100.8	27.8	20.0	27.6	53,015	0.17
1929	108.0	32.9	24.9	30.5	53,015	0.30
1930	80.3	15.1	8.8	18.8	53,015	(0.001)
1931	56.7	9.3	3.7	16.4	53,015	(0.10)
1932	37.0	3.6	(2.3)	9.7	53,015	(0.13)
1933	43.2	7.6	1.7	17.6	53,015	(0.015)
1934	59.1	9.6	2.9	16.2	53,015	0.01
1935	76.1	14.3	7.1	18.8	53,015	0.06
1936	102.5	31.9	21.6	31.1	53,015	0.08
1937	127.8	36.4	23.5	28.2	53,015	0.12
1938	90.9	25.8	15.7	28.4	53,015	0.15
1939	156.5	52.6	36.1	33.6	53,015	0.48
1940	215.2	81.9	45.8	38.1	53,015	0.73
1941	296.3	105.7	40.1	35.7	53,015	0.62
1942	457.2	127.4	32.0	27.9	53,015	0.47
1943	689.3	170.0	35.5	24.7	53,957	0.53
1944	673.4	152.0	27.8	22.6	53,958	0.38
1945	490.6	90.0	21.0	18.3	53,958	0.26
1946	298.2	35.4	24.3	11.9	53,689	0.33
1947	381.6	59.6	29.4	15.6	53,689	0.46
1948	436.8	80.6	40.6	18.5	53,689	0.65
1949	344.4	52.7	20.9	15.3	53,689	0.31
1950	476.2	110.3	46.9	23.2	53,689	0.76
1951	534.5	138.7	39.9	25.9	53,689	0.64
1952	577.8	126.3	47.4	21.9	58,768	0.76
1953	707.5	162.4	60.5	23.0	59,053	0.99
1954	708.3	160.1	61.9	22.6	60,330	0.99
1955	845.0	222.0	87.6	26.3	61,146	1.40
1956	864.4	225.3	89.6	26.1	61,660	1.42
1957	869.4	202.3	75.6	23.3	61,822	1.18
1958	753.1	140.0	42.9	18.6	61,935	0.65
1959	858.5	169.3	55.6	19.7	63,115	0.84
1960	861.2	134.0	40.0	15.6	63,942	0.59
1961	853.3	148.6	43.0	17.4	64,017	0.63
1962[f]	938.7	168.0	56.4	17.9	64,109	0.84

Net worth or stockholders equity ($millions)	% return on average net worth (%)	Working capital^c ($millions)	Total long-term debt^d ($millions)	% return on avg. invested capital^e (%)	Year
173.2	7.9	64.3	61.3	8.1	1927
161.4	11.9	61.9	40.9	10.3	1928
177.4	14.7	54.4	41.7	12.6	1929
177.4	5.0	54.9	44.0	4.9	1930
172.2	2.1	53.2	60.7	2.7	1931
165.2	(1.4)	45.0	62.1	0.3	1932
164.5	1.0	47.7	57.9	2.2	1933
164.7	1.8	33.4	48.9	2.6	1934
167.2	4.3	30.3	35.3	4.5	1935
160.7	13.2	20.2	36.6	12.3	1936
165.7	14.4	22.5	36.3	13.2	1937
172.6	9.3	42.1	52.2	8.6	1938
178.0	20.6	52.3	34.1	18.6	1939
201.8	24.1	39.3	27.1	21.7	1940
225.9	18.8	33.6	104.1	15.3	1941
241.9	13.7	47.0	132.5	10.1	1942
261.5	14.1	118.8	162.1	9.8	1943
273.2	10.4	147.4	118.8	7.6	1944
278.0	7.6	222.3	84.0	6.2	1945
286.9	8.6	129.1	0.6	8.0	1946
271.7	10.5	122.8	100.7	9.5	1947
300.6	14.2	130.1	140.5	10.8	1948
306.4	6.9	107.7	160.3	5.3	1949
341.0	14.5	126.4	161.4	10.6	1950
360.6	11.4	68.4	143.6	8.6	1951
391.3	12.6	98.7	346.0	8.7	1952
435.3	14.6	89.7	323.7	9.0	1953
486.3	13.4	182.7	370.4	8.7	1954
555.1	16.8	224.5	308.4	11.0	1955
621.1	15.2	189.6	273.3	10.7	1956
670.5	11.7	187.8	359.2	8.6	1957
687.1	6.3	293.0	468.5	4.7	1958
733.0	7.8	319.3	437.7	5.5	1959
759.2	5.4	303.8	413.0	4.1	1960
774.9	5.6	312.1	398.7	4.3	1961
811.8	8.1	303.7	373.2	6.1	1962

Table B.2. (*continued*)

Year	Sales and operating revenues ($millions)	Operating profit ($millions)	Net income[a] ($ millions)	Oper. profit as % of sales and oper. revs. (%)	Common shares outstanding[b] (thousands)	Net income per common share[b] ($)
1963	972.1	170.0	51.1	17.5	64,161	0.76
1964	1,036.9	186.8	57.7	18.0	64,240	0.86
1965	1,165.6	219.4	75.2	18.8	64,271	1.13
1966	1,373.0	288.1	107.1	21.0	64,440	1.62
1967	1,360.8	306.9	108.4	22.6	64,470	1.64
1968	1,352.8	293.4	104.7	21.7	64,496	1.58
1969	1,545.2	317.6	122.4	20.6	64,511	1.86
1970[g]	1,522.4	295.3	114.3	19.4	64,519	1.73
1971	1,441.2	213.8	52.9	14.8	65,029	0.78
1972	1,753.0	262.2	100.9	15.0	65,614	1.51
1973	2,157.3	309.7	100.3	14.4	66,149	1.49
1974	2,727.3	450.5	174.6	16.5	66,764	2.59
1975	2,305.9	218.8	64.8	9.5	67,724	0.93
1976	2,924.4	384.5	143.8	13.1	68,658	2.07
1977	3,416.5	457.9	195.2	13.4	69,381	2.79
1978	4,051.8	672.0	312.7	16.6	70,110	4.45
1979	4,785.6	928.7	504.6	19.4	70,340	7.15
1980	5,147.6	898.1	469.9	17.4	73,065	6.54
1981	4,977.5	624.7	296.2	12.6	74,458	3.97
1982[h]	4,647.6	118.9	(9.1)	2.6	78,925	(0.15)
1983[i]	5,263.4	501.0	164.5	9.5	80,939	2.03
1984	5,750.8	717.0	256.0	12.5	81,141	3.13
1985	5,162.7	244.6	(16.6)	4.7	81,372	(0.23)
1986[j]	4,667.2	438.5	264.0	9.4	87,051	3.08

[a]Includes income from equity investments, as well as from operations, since 1964.
[b]Giving effect to a 3 for 1 common stock split in 1943, a 2 for 1 split in 1953, a 2 for 1 split in 1955, a 3 for 2 split in 1973, and a 2 for 1 split in 1981.
[c]Same as net current assets.
[d]Includes portion of long-term debt due in current year.
[e]Invested capital equals long-term debt plus net worth. The % return on invested capital was calculated by dividing average invested capital by net income plus interest expense on an after-tax basis.
[f]1962 amounts do not include a special gain on the sale of investment amounting to $7.88 million, equal to $0.12 per share of common stock.

Table B.2. (*continued*)

Net worth or stockholders equity ($millions)	% return on average net worth (%)	Working capital[c] ($millions)	Total long-term debt[d] ($millions)	% return on avg. invested capital[e] (%)	Year
834.2	6.2	277.8	402.9	4.9	1963
863.6	6.8	324.0	503.9	5.2	1964
907.0	8.5	304.2	505.9	6.3	1965
981.1	11.3	442.6	655.2	8.1	1966
1,049.0	10.7	470.0	684.3	7.4	1967
1,113.0	9.7	448.0	710.1	6.8	1968
1,194.5	10.6	446.0	792.8	7.4	1969
1,249.0	7.8	455.4	904.4	5.9	1970
1,266.2	4.2	520.1	976.3	3.8	1971
1,335.0	7.8	564.9	931.8	6.0	1972
1,400.6	7.3	597.9	902.1	5.8	1973
1,540.2	11.9	569.8	963.1	8.6	1974
1,575.4	4.2	644.2	1,272.6	4.1	1975
1,665.6	8.9	581.6	1,178.8	6.8	1976
1,829.6	11.2	667.1	1,182.4	8.3	1977
2,089.5	16.0	735.6	1,148.9	11.5	1978
2,505.6	22.0	859.0	1,037.1	16.3	1979
2,933.8	17.3	820.0	1,048.6	13.6	1980
3,136.7	9.8	950.4	1,412.2	8.3	1981
3,112.5	0.3	965.8	1,741.4	2.2	1982
3,227.5	5.5	939.4	1,683.1	5.8	1983
3,343.6	7.8	985.9	1,634.9	7.3	1984
3,307.9	(0.5)	876.5	1,606.1	1.6	1985
3,721.6	7.2	607.5	1,392.4	6.9	1986

[g]1970 amounts do not include an extraordinary item charge of $14.8 million, equal to $0.29 per share of common stock.
[h]1982 amounts do not include an extraordinary gain of $19.89 million, equal to $0.26 per share of common stock.
[i]1983 amounts do not include an extraordinary gain of $9.68 million, equal to $0.12 per share of common stock.
[j]1986 amounts do not include an extraordinary charge of $9.90 million, equal to $0.12 per share of common stock.
Source: Data provided by the Alcoa Accounting Department, which has recalculated early figures provided by *Annual Reports* in accordance with modern accounting standards.

Table B.3. *Contribution of equity earnings[a] to Alcoa's net income,*
1964–86

Year	Equity earnings ($millions)	Net income ($millions)	Equity earnings as % of net income (%)
1964	(2.5)	57.7	(4.3)
1965	(3.3)	75.2	(4.4)
1966	(0.1)	107.1	(0.01)
1967	(1.0)	108.4	(0.9)
1968	4.4	104.7	4.2
1969	14.6	122.4	11.9
1970[b]	13.5	114.3	11.8
1971	1.1	52.9	2.1
1972	32.1	100.9	31.8
1973	1.3	100.3	1.3
1974	10.5	174.6	6.0
1975	10.8	64.8	16.7
1976	25.6	143.8	17.8
1977	38.6	195.2	19.8
1978	57.2	312.7	18.3
1979	93.1	504.6	18.5
1980	84.2	469.9	17.9
1981	58.7	196.2	29.9
1982[b]	51.7	(9.1)	568.1
1983[b]	59.2	164.5	36.0
1984	38.6	256.0	15.1
1985	3.4	(16.6)	(20.1)
1986[a]	220.5	264.0	83.5

[a]Includes equity earnings from Alcoa's real estate operation, from unconsolidated foreign operations, and from other entities in which Alcoa owned at least a 20% interest.
[b]Does not include extraordinary gains or charges for that year.
Source: Data supplied by the Alcoa Accounting Department.

Appendix C

Aluminum, copper, and steel: price per pound, 1907–1978

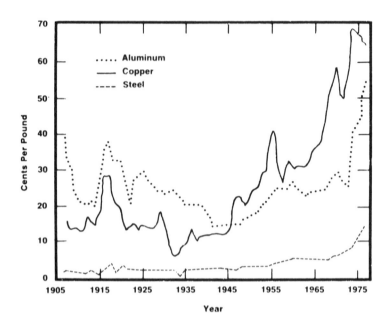

Chart C.1. Aluminum, copper and steel prices, 1907–1978.

Appendix D

Aluminum Company of America:
selected organization charts, 1918–1986

Chart D.1. Alcoa corporate organization, 1919.

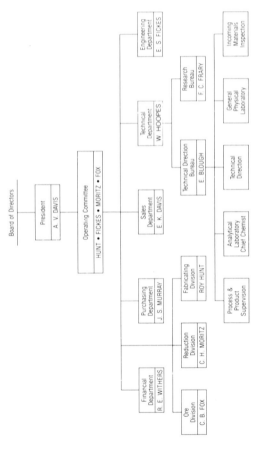

Board of Directors

President
A V DAVIS

Operating Committee
HUNT • FICKES • MORITZ • FOX

Financial Department
R E WITHERS

Purchasing Department
J S MURRAY

Sales Department
E K DAVIS

Technical Department
W HOOPES

Engineering Department
E S FICKES

Ore Division
C B FOX

Reduction Division
C H MORITZ

Fabricating Division
ROY HUNT

Technical Direction Bureau
E BLOUGH

Research Bureau
F C FRARY

Process & Product Supervision

Analytical Laboratory Chief Chemist

Technical Direction

General Physical Laboratory

Incoming Materials Inspection

457

Chart D.2   Alcoa Badin Smelting Works organization, 1919.

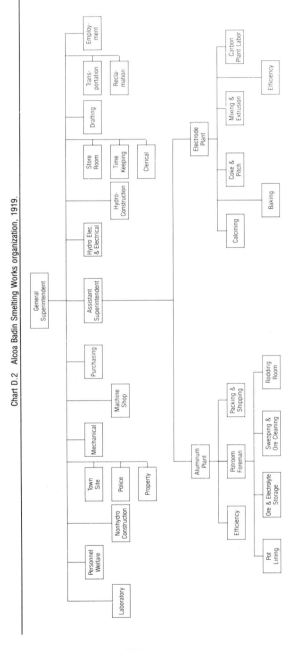

458

Chart D.3 Alcoa, U.S. Aluminum Company — Fabricating Division, New Kensington Works organization, 1919.

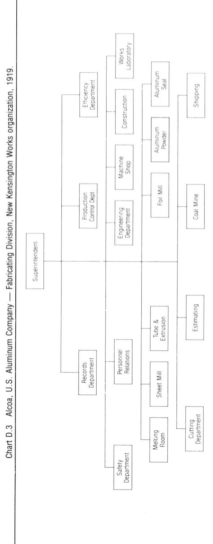

Chart D.4. Alcoa corporate organization, 1929.

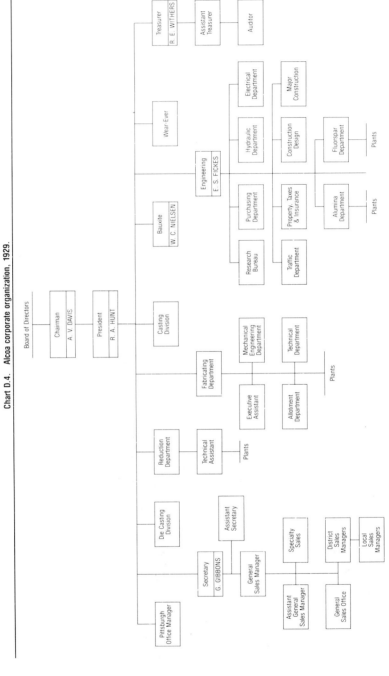

Chart D.5. Alcoa corporate organization, 1959.

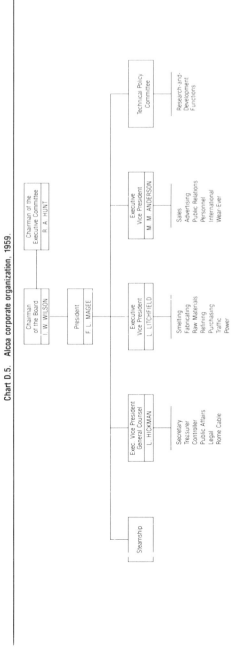

461

Chart D.6. Alcoa corporate organization, 1968.

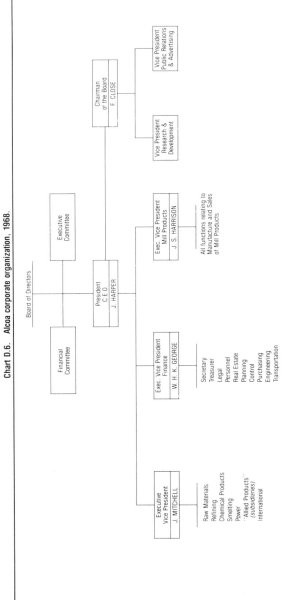

Board of Directors

Financial Committee

Executive Committee

President
C E O
J HARPER

Chairman
of the Board
F. CLOSE

Vice President
Research &
Development

Vice President
Public Relations
& Advertising

Executive
Vice President
J. MITCHELL

Raw Materials
Refining
Chemical Products
Smelting
Power
"Allied Products"
(subsidiaries)
International

Exec. Vice President
Finance
W. H. K. GEORGE

Secretary
Treasurer
Legal
Personnel
Real Estate
Planning
Control
Purchasing
Engineering
Transportation

Exec. Vice President
Mill Products
J. S. HARRISON

All functions relating to
Manufacture and Sales
of Mill Products

462

Chart D.7. Alcoa corporate organization, 1975.

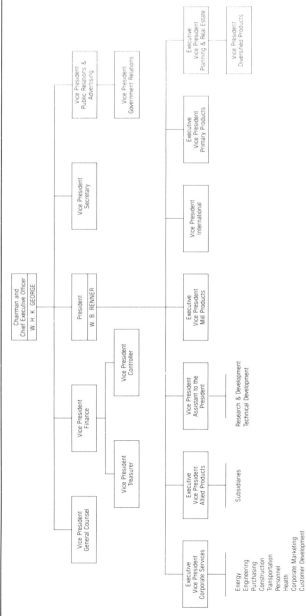

463

Chart D.8. Alcoa corporate organization, 1983.

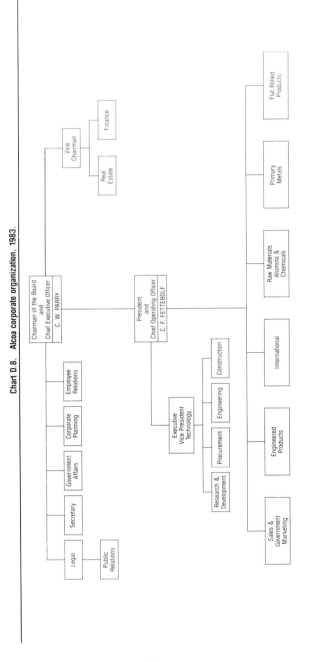

464

Chart D.9. Alcoa corporate organization, 1986.

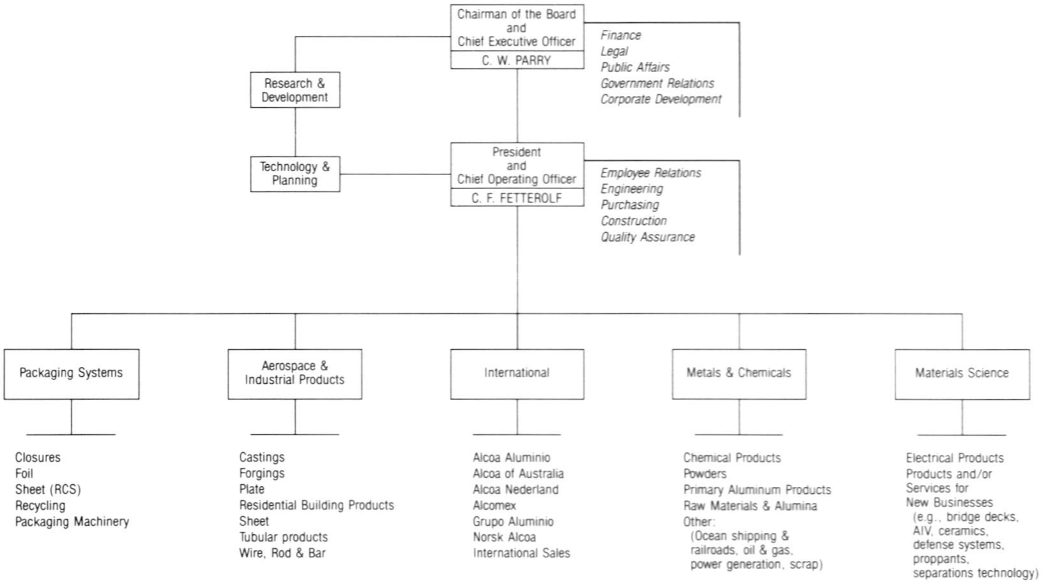

Chairman of the Board and Chief Executive Officer
C. W. PARRY

Finance
Legal
Public Affairs
Government Relations
Corporate Development

Research & Development

President and Chief Operating Officer
C. F. FETTEROLF

Employee Relations
Engineering
Purchasing
Construction
Quality Assurance

Technology & Planning

Packaging Systems

Closures
Foil
Sheet (RCS)
Recycling
Packaging Machinery

Aerospace & Industrial Products

Castings
Forgings
Plate
Residential Building Products
Sheet
Tubular products
Wire, Rod & Bar

International

Alcoa Aluminio
Alcoa of Australia
Alcoa Nederland
Alcomex
Grupo Aluminio
Norsk Alcoa
International Sales

Metals & Chemicals

Chemical Products
Powders
Primary Aluminum Products
Raw Materials & Alumina
Other:
(Ocean shipping &
railroads, oil & gas,
power generation, scrap)

Materials Science

Electrical Products
Products and/or
Services for
New Businesses
(e.g., bridge decks,
AlV, ceramics,
defense systems,
proppants,
separations technology)

465

Appendix E

Interviews cited

Because the written record on key events and decisions is scrappy at best, this history of Alcoa rests heavily on interviews with current and former managers and employees of the company. The author has had countless conversations with Alcoa managers, employees, and consultants over a three-year period, as well as with "outsiders" who, for one reason or another, have followed Alcoa or the aluminum industry. Many of these conversations were recorded as formal interviews, which are listed below. Most of the formal interviews, which were undertaken between 1983 and 1986, were recorded on tape and were subsequently transcribed. A few were conducted without the benefit of sound recording and are listed separately.

The interviews were not intended to be "oral histories." Most were focused on particular issues of interest to the author and his associates, whose immediate task was not to prepare for this publication, but to undertake a proprietary study of Alcoa's corporate culture, the main outline of which was reported publicly in *Across the Board* (September 1986). Nonetheless, Alcoa has recognized the value of the interviews as an important record of aspects of the corporate history. Therefore, notes of untaped interviews and raw (unedited) transcripts of taped interviews have been placed in the custody of the Alcoa Archives as of this writing.

All interviews cited were conducted by the author and/or his colleagues at The Winthrop Group., Inc.

Table E.1. *Cited interviews taped and transcribed*

Interviewee	Position at time of interview	Date of interview
William Arnold	Manager, Human Resources, Alcoa Corporate Headquarters	Aug. 15, 1983
Paul Cantanzerite	Labor Relations Supervisor, Cleveland Works	Apr. 13, 1984
Frederick "Fritz" Close	Former Chairman of the Board	Aug. 24, 1983
Tom Clausen	Process Development and Control Unit Supervisor, Davenport Works	Mar. 29, 1984
Ronald Coleman	Operations Manager, Warrick Operations	July 21, 1983
Brad Dina	Hydraulic Press Operator, Cleveland Works	Apr. 16, 1984
Jerry Duncan	Ingot Area Supervisor, Warrick Operations	July 21, 1983
Marty Fackelman	Manager, Wheel Plant, Cleveland Works	Apr. 13, 1984
Dennis Falls	Operations Manager, Massena Operations; Director, Wire, Rod, and Bar Business Unit	July 6, 1983
Dan Farrish	Press Operator, Cleveland Works	Apr. 16, 1984
Al Favre	Former Titanium Project Manager, Cleveland Works	Apr. 16, 1984
C. Fred Fetterolf	President and COO	Sept. 10, 1985
Ben Fischer	Former Assistant to the President, United Steelworkers of America	July 2, 1986
Michael Gambill	Manager, Human Resources and Industrial Relations, Alcoa, Tennessee, Operations	June 16, 1983
Marvin Gantz	Vice Chairman of the Board	July 7, 1983
Clyde Gillespie	Vice President, Engineered Products	Apr. 14, 1984
John D. Harper	Former CEO and Chairman of the Board	Aug. 25, 1983

Table E.1. (*continued*)

Interviewee	Position at time of interview	Date of interview
Leon Hickman	Former Executive Vice President and General Counsel	Mar. 8– Apr. 6, 1984
William Hoffman	Manager, Organizational Planning, Alcoa Corporate	Aug. 25, 1983
Alfred M. Hunt	Corporate Secretary	Dec. 22, 1983; July 10, 1984
Arthur Johnson	Former Carbon Plant Engineer, Niagara Works and Massena Operations	Apr. 15, 1985
Donald Johnson	Former Plant Manager Alcoa and Reynolds Metals	Dec. 31, 1984
Harvey Johnson	General Manager, Alcoa International	July 1983
Frank Jones	Vice President, Government Affairs	July 2, 1984
J. Tyson Kennedy	Pittsburgh District Sales Manager	Aug. 19, 1986
John Kane	Manager, Public Relations, Alcoa Laboratories	June 1983
Charles Kopatich	Finishing Area Supervisor, Warrick Operations	July 21, 1983
Ronald Kuerner	Operations Manager, Arkansas Operations	Aug. 9–10, 1983
Irving Lipkowitz	Former Department of Justice Economist	Apr. 10, 1985
Frank Magee	Former CEO and Chairman of the Board	Jan. 18–19, 1984
Paul Mara	Senior Vice President, Aluminum Association	Mar. 25, 1985
Jack Morber	Vice President, Industrial Relations	June 14, 1983
John Moritz	Mining Production Manager, Arkansas Operations	Aug. 17, 1983
Charles Parry	CEO and Chairman of the Board	Aug. 22, 1985
Don Paro	Manager, Public Relations, Warrick Operations	July 20, 1983

Table E.1. (*continued*)

Interviewee	Position at time of interview	Date of interview
Bob Rand	Chief Industrial Engineer, Arkansas Operations	Aug. 9, 1983
Chet Recko	Manager, Advanced Manufacturing, Cleveland Works	Apr. 16, 1984
Bob Rushbolt	Production Supervisor, Cleveland Works	Apr. 16, 1984
Allen Russell	Former Vice President, Alcoa Laboratories	Jan. 8, 1985
Bob Schell	Former Mining Production Manager, Arkansas Operations	Aug. 17, 1983
Ed Smith	Manager, Human Resources, Warrick Operations	July 20, 1983
John Stephenson	Public Relations Coordinator, Local 104, Aluminum, Brick and Glass Workers, Warrick Operations	July 21, 1983
Philip Stroup	Former Chief Chemist, Alcoa Laboratories	Aug. 1983
Larry Thibault	Group Benefits Supervisor, Warrick Operations	July 21, 1983
Bruce Thrasher	District Director, United Steelworkers of America	Aug. 18, 1983
Henry Todys	Production Manager, Cleveland Works	Apr. 16, 1984
G. Keith Turnbull	Manager, Technology Planning, Alcoa Corporate	July 8, 1983
Kent Van Horn	Former Vice President, Research and Development	June 1984
Eric Walker	Former Director and Vice President, Science and Technology	May 10, 1985
Jerry Whicker	Process Development Superintendent and Control Supervisor, Davenport Works	Mar. 29, 1984
Ed Yakamavage	Personnel Manager, Cleveland Works	Apr. 13, 1984

Table E.2. *Cited interviews not taped*[a]

Interviewee	Position at time of interview	Date of interview
Cyrus L. Bass Charles L. Bell Woodrow Bell John Brazil Tom Garlington Ernest Lee Kesterson	Retired Employees, Arkansas Operations	Aug. 8, 1983
Harry Goern	Vice President and Regional Manager, Europe	Aug. 30, 1985
Marshall Hurst and John Morris	Officials, Local 309, United Steelworkers of America, Alcoa, Tennessee	June 16, 1983
Frank Kramer	Manager, Industrial Relations, Alcoa Corporate	June 14, 1983
Lee O'Nan	Manager, Corporate Planning, Alcoa Corporate	Sept. 11, 1985; Jan. 7, 1986

[a]Summaries of notes are in Alcoa Archives.

Notes

Chapter 1

1. The standard source on the company's early history is Charles C. Carr, *Alcoa: An American Enterprise* (New York: Rinehart & Co., 1952).
2. Minutes of the board of directors of The Pittsburgh Reduction Company (at first called The Pittsburgh Aluminium Company), July 31 and August 8, 1888 (hereafter cited as *Minutes*), on file in the Office of the Corporate Secretary, Aluminum Company of America, Pittsburgh, PA.
3. Much of the evidence on the cost of aluminum before 1855 is anecdotal. Alfred Cowles, *The True Story of Aluminum* (Chicago: Regnery, 1958), p. 8, gives a range for 1852 between $500 and $700 per pound. For some data on other metals, see the U.S. Department of Commerce, Bureau of the Census, *Historical Statistics of the United States, Colonial Times to 1970* (Washington, DC, 1975), pp. 209, 606. Note, by comparison, that copper was valued at about $0.60 per kilogram.
4. A standard source on the technical and chemical history of aluminum is Junius David Edwards, Francis C. Frary, and Zay Jeffries, *The Aluminum Industry*, 2 vols., I, *Aluminum and its Production* (New York: McGraw-Hill, 1930), chap. 1. See also the earlier American text, Joseph W. Richards, *Aluminum: Its History, Occurrence, Properties, Metallurgy and Applications, Including its Alloys*, 2d ed. (Philadelphia: Baird, 1890), chap. 1. A recent survey of the technical and market history is Marie Boas Hall, "The Strange Case of Aluminium," in A. Rupert Hall and Norman Smith (eds.), *History of Technology*, I (London, 1976), pp. 143–57.
5. Ibid. Lavoisier is quoted through Philip Farin, Gary G. Reibsamen, and

the *Metals Week* editorial staff, *Aluminum: Profile of an Industry* (New York: McGraw-Hill, 1969), p. 10.

6. Ibid.

7. Oersted is quoted from his *Oversigt over der Konelige Danske Videnska-bernes Selskabs Fordhandlinger* (1824–5) in Edwards et al., *Aluminum and its Production*, pp. 2–3. Wöhler is quoted in Farin et al., *Aluminum*, p. 10.

8. Deville explained his discovery in *De l'Aluminium, ses Propriétes, sa Fabrication et ses Applications* (Paris, 1859), which became the standard text on aluminum for most of the rest of the nineteenth century.

9. Edwards et al., *Aluminum and its Production*, pp. 5–7.

10. Ibid. See Robert Friedel's unpublished manuscript, "The Psychology of Aluminum" (1975) in the Alcoa Archives, Aluminum Company of America, Pittsburgh, Pennsylvania (hereafter referred to as AA), env. 1202, which discusses Deville's understanding that no significant market for aluminum could be found without first lowering its price substantially.

11. Edwards et al., *Aluminum and its Production*, pp. 7–11.

12. Richards, *Aluminum*, pp. 37–8; "Price of Aluminum," AA, uncatalogued.

13. Hall, "The Strange Case of Aluminium," p. 149; Edgar H. Dix, Jr., "Aluminum Cap-Piece on Washington Monument," *Metal Progress* (December 1934), reprint, n.p.

14. Cowles, *The True Story of Aluminum*, p. 8; Edwards et al., *Aluminum and its Production*, pp. 12–13; *Metal Statistics, 1913* (6th ed., [1913]), p. 239.

15. On the "crude empiricism" of metallurgy and the advance of the discipline, see the good, brief discussion in Nathan Rosenberg, *Technology and American Economic Growth* (Armonk, NY: M. E. Sharpe, Inc., 1972), pp. 75–83, 119–23. See also Cyril Stanley Smith, "Materials and the Development of Civilization and Science," *Science* (May 14, 1965), p. 911, who implies that the development of the discipline over the centuries preceded fundamental scientific understanding of the behavior of metals under different conditions of working and alloying.

16. Edwards et al., *Aluminum and its Production*, ch. 1; Donald H. Wallace, *Market Control in the Aluminum Industry* (Cambridge, MA: Harvard University Press, 1937), app. A; Richards, *Aluminum*, p. 24. It was Richards's view that "advances made in dynamo-electric machinery...led to the revival of the old methods of electrolysis discovered by Deville and Bunsen [who had electrolyzed barium, chromium, and magnesium], and to the invention of new methods of decomposing aluminum compounds electrolytically."

17. Little has been written about Charles Martin Hall, a private, secretive man, who left only a small body of scientific correspondence. The standard biography is the account by Junius Edwards, *The Immortal*

Woodshed: The Story of the Inventor who Brought Aluminum to America (New York: Dodd, Mead, 1955).

18. Jewett made these remarks at his fiftieth class reunion at Yale. They are quoted in Emily Nunn, with the assistance of Norman C. Craig, *The Centenary of Hall's Discovery* (Oberlin, OH: Oberlin College, 1986), p. 6.

19. Carr, *Alcoa*, p. 10; Edwards, *Immortal Woodshed*, pp. 37ff; Cowles, *The True Story of Aluminum*, p. 65.

20. Ibid.; Martha Moore Trescott, *The Rise of the American Electrochemicals Industry, 1880–1910: Studies in the American Technological Environment* (Westport, CN: Greenwood Press, 1981), pp. 312–31, speculates, perhaps stretching the evidence, on Julia Hall's participation in her brother's work.

21. For the sequence of experiments, I have relied upon Norman C. Craig's, "Charles Martin Hall—The Young Man, His Mentor, and His Metal" (text of a lecture provided by the author, 1986).

22. Except where noted, the quoted material in this and the next paragraphs are from the text of the inventor's description of his discovery as printed in "The Perkin Medal, Remarks in Acknowledgement by Mr. Hall," *Industrial and Engineering Chemistry*, III (1911), reprint, n.p.

23. In the 1880s, German scientists, Grätzel and Kleiner, patented electrolytic aluminum processes in Germany. Those processes, however, attempted to decompose aluminum from molten aluminum salts, such as aluminum chloride and cryolite. Trescott, *Rise of the American Electrochemicals Industry*, p. 60.

24. Norman C. Craig, who has replicated Hall's experiment at Oberlin College, also concludes that within the limits of his resources, Hall "followed a path of very good science." I am indebted to Professor Craig for providing me with relevant details of his own research into Hall's records (private correspondence with the author, April 29, 1986.)

25. Richards, *Aluminum*, 3d ed. (1896), pp. 25–6, explained the scientific basis of Hall's discovery, as follows. "The principle involved is the electrolytic decomposition of alumina, dissolved in a bath of fluorides of aluminum and others based, the current reducing the dissolved alumina without affecting the solvent. This method is essentially different from any of the preceding electrical processes, which contemplated and operated simply the decomposition of a molten aluminum salt, such, for instance, as the *solvent* used by Mr. Hall. The knowledge that the fused fluorides dissolve large quantitites of alumina, and that the electric current will act on this dissolved alumina without decomposing the solvent, was the essence of Hall's invention. . . . "

26. Ibid., p. 36. Héroult did not become involved in commercial aluminum manufacture until late in 1889.

27. Neither Edwards, *The Immortal Woodshed*, pp. 83–5, nor Carr, *Alcoa*,

p. 13, are reliable sources on this matter. They miss the nub of Héroult's problem, which was that he did not provide a "Preliminary Statement" (as had Hall), which under patent law forced the court to rely on the date of his American application, which was May 22, 1886. I thank Edward B. Foote of Oakmont, Pennsylvania, for pointing this out to me. Trescott, *Rise of the American Electrochemicals Industry*, pp. 322–6, argues that Julia Hall's memory and record-keeping habits were crucial to Hall's case, but in fact her testimony does not appear to have been a decisive factor in the court's decision.

28. *Centenary of the Hall & Héroult Processes, 1886–1986* (London: International Primary Aluminium Institute, 1986), pp. 17–40; Edwards et al., *Aluminum and its Production*, pp. 13–14.

29. *Memoire Déscriptif* of French patent no. 175,711, April 23, 1886, translation from International Primary Aluminium Institute, "Proposed IPAI Publication for the Centenary of the Hall and Héroult Processes in 1986," AA, uncatalogued.

30. The contemporary diagnosis was Banti's disease (Edwards, *The Immortal Woodshed*, p. 228).

31. See Nunn, *Centenary of Hall's Discovery*, pp. 10–11. Copies of Hall's Last Will and Testament are in the Oberlin College Archives, Mudd Learning Center, Oberlin, Ohio (hereafter referred to as OCA). I have used the copy in record group 7/1/4, box 17.

32. On Hall's personality, see Edwards, *Immortal Woodshed*, p. 202 and passim; interview with Arthur Vining Davis, chairman of board of directors, Aluminum Company of America, circa 1938, pp. 5–6, AA, env. 167. See also the letters from W. A. Thomas to Junius Edwards, June 15, 1951, copy on file at AA, and John R. Rogers to Lord, Day, & Lord, December 7, 1928, OCA, 2/7/1, box 128.

33. Deville, *De l'Aluminium*, p. 140.

34. Paul Héroult, speech to the Metallurgical Congress in Paris, 1900, quoted in Adolphe Minet, *The Production of Aluminum and its Industrial Use*, 1st ed., rev., trans. Leonard Waldo (New York: Wiley, 1905), pp. 115–16.

35. Ibid. On the progress of Héroult's efforts to bring aluminum into production, see Edwards et al., *Aluminum and its Production*, pp. 35ff.; Cowles, *True Story of Aluminum*, pp. 91–96.

36. Edwards, *Immortal Woodshed*, passim, provides a very gentle description of Hall's apparently repressed personality. On the contributions of Julia Hall, see Trescott, *Rise of the American Electrochemicals Industry*, pp. 312ff.

37. Edwards, *Immortal Woodshed*, pp. 60ff; Wallace, *Market Control*, pp. 509–12.

38. Electrothermic methods of production involve the use of electricity as a source of heat in electric furnaces, whereas in electrolysis, electricity

becomes part of the chemical reaction. See Trescott, *Rise of the American Electrochemicals Industry*, pp. 3–4.

39. Edwards, *Immortal Woodshed*, pp. 73–9. See also the correspondence of Edwin Cowles, President of Cowles Electric Smelting & Aluminum Company, for July 20, 1877 and August 4, 1877, which form part of the exhibits in *Cowles v. Pittsburgh Reduction Company*, U.S. Circuit Court, Northern District of New York. In his letter of August 4, Edwin Cowles wrote that Hall's process was seen to have "great merit." The Cowles brothers feared that "If some parties were to get hold of his process, there might be great danger of its killing our process."

40. Accounts vary on the circumstances of Hall's leaving, but the most complete, though somewhat antagonistic treatment is Cowles, *True Story of Aluminum*, pp. 70ff.

41. A. V. Davis (Davis interview, p. 2) quipped that Hunt "was the outstanding metallurgist in the United States at the time. With all respect to . . . Hunt, I must add that . . . he was probably the only metallurgist in the country." That was not quite true, but Hunt's rare education and experience proved important to the early development of aluminum.

42. David B. Houston, "A Brief History of Capital Accumulation in Pittsburgh: A Marxist Interpretation," *Pittsburgh–Sheffield, Sister Cities*, Joel Tarr (ed.) (Pittsburgh: Carnegie Mellon University, 1986), pp. 36–7.

43. Franklin K. Toker, "Reversing an Urban Image: New Architecture in Pittsburgh, 1890–1980," in ibid., p. 2.

44. On Hunt and his career, see the privately printed work by Junius Edwards, *A Captain in Industry* (New York: privately printed, 1957); "Alfred Ephraim Hunt," *Dictionary of American Biography* (New York: Scribners, 1932), IX, pp. 381–2. A grandson, Richard Hunt, informs me that Alfred Hunt had planned to run for political office.

45. *Minutes*, July 31 and August 8, 1888. A contract was made with Hall and Cole on the day of the first meeting ("Article of Agreement . . . between Romaine C. Cole . . . and Charles M. Hall . . . and Alfred E. Hunt and George H. Clapp et al.," dated July 31, 1888, AA, env. 251). The agreement stated that Hall and Cole were to receive 5,416 and 2/3 shares of common stock, while the directors were to receive 1,500 shares (presumably each) for $20,000. Obviously, this did not happen right away.

46. Ibid.; "Twenty Years of Aluminum Manufacture," *The Metal Industry*, 7 (January 1909), p. 8; George Gibbons, "Talk to Research Department, 11/2/31," AA, env. 583, p. 7.

47. A. V. Davis, "The Early Beginnings of the Aluminum Industry," undated ms. on file in AA, env. 21. The early stockholding arrangements are outlined in Carr, *Alcoa*, chap. 1–3, passim.

48. "Article of Agreement," July 31, 1888; *Minutes*, October 2, 1889. The growing personality conflict between Hall and Cole appears in a letter from the former to his sister, Julia, September 16, 1888, AA, env. 251. Cole, according to Edwards (*Captain in Industry*, pp. 49–50), was somewhat peripatetic by temperament and quit work in the plant after a few weeks, professing rheumatism as an impediment to labor. After lack of success in selling aluminum, Cole sold the last of his shares in the business by January 1893.

49. Charles Martin Hall to Julia Hall, December 18, 1888, January, 12, 18, 1889, and February 3, 1889, in ibid; Edwards, *Captain in Industry*, pp. 41–3; address delivered by Mr. Arthur V. Davis at the Memorial Service in honor of Charles Martin Hall at Oberlin, Ohio, January 22, 1915, AA, env. 87.; Davis, "Early Beginnings of the Aluminum Industry"; Carr, *Alcoa*, p. 37.

50. See the copy of the testimony of A. V. Davis in *Pittsburgh Reduction Company v. Cowles Electric Smelting Company*, May 11–12, 1898, pp. 178, 192, 197, AA, env. 6. For greater technical detail on the early process, see Edwards et al., *Aluminum and its Production*, pp. 23–4.

51. Extracts from a talk before the Pittsburgh Chamber of Commerce by A. V. Davis, February 13, 1927, AA, uncatalogued; Davis, "Early Beginnings of the Aluminum Industry."

52. Ibid.; *Pittsburgh Reduction Company v. Cowles*, Davis testimony, p. 188. No records were kept on early employees.

53. "Supplemental Brief Submitted by the Aluminum Company of America," U.S. Congress, House Committee on Ways and Means: *Tariff Hearings*, 60th Congress, 2d Session, Document No. 1505, Schedule C., 1908–1909, p. 4111.

54. *Minutes*, June 5, September 18, and October 16, 1889.

55. Ibid., October 2, 1889; Carr, *Alcoa*, pp. 40–2.

56. Alfred E. Hunt to William Thaw, Jr., February 15, 1892, AA, env. 754.

57. In 1891, for example, the company reported a heavy shortfall of $21,146.33 in cash. Shortly thereafter, the Mellons joined the board of directors and provided a substantial loan to the company. See the *Minutes*, March 23, 28, and April 7, 1892.

58. Charles J. V. Murphy, "The Mellons of Pittsburgh," reprinted from *Fortune* (1967), pp. 5–7.

59. Ibid., p. 12.

60. *Minutes*, March 28, 1892. On the impact of the Mellon connection, see Carr, *Alcoa*, pp. 40–7.

61. An extended treatment of the Mellons' financial and business activities is David E. Koskoff, *The Mellons* (New York: Crowell, 1978). Still useful, also, is the brief biography by Allen Nevins, "Andrew William Mellon," *Dictionary of American Biography*, XXII, Supplement 2, pp. 446–52.

62. *Minutes*, 1891–1893.

63. Charles Martin Hall to Romaine C. Cole, November 10, 1891, *Cowles Electric Smelting and Aluminum Co. v. The Pittsburgh Reduction Company*, U.S. District Court, Northern District of New York, complainant's exhibits, p. 118, AA, env. 1060.

64. Carr, *Alcoa*, p. 39.

65. Edwards et al., *Aluminum and its Production*, pp. 24–5; Carr, *Alcoa*, pp. 52–3.

66. Seabury C. Mastick, "Lectures on Patents," *Industrial and Engineering Chemistry*, VII (October 1915), p. 881. Mastick's series of lectures, including extended treatment of the aluminum litigation, are printed in the same journal and volume from September through December 1915.

67. Cowles, *True Story of Aluminum*, pp. 98–9. On the Davis incident, I have relied on the copy of his testimony given in *Pittsburgh Reduction Company v. Cowles Electric Smelting and Aluminum Company*, April 11, 1891, pp. 57ff, AA, env. 6.

68. Wallace, *Market Control*, p. 530.

69. Cowles, *The True Story of Aluminum*, p. 20 and chap. VII.

70. Mastick, "Lectures on Patents," p. 1072; Wallace, *Market Control*, p. 532; Edwards et al., *Aluminum and its Production*, p. 28.

71. Hall to Cole, December 9, 1891, quoted in Cowles, *True Story of Aluminum*, pp. 101–2.

72. Hall to Thomas W. Bakewell, January 15, 1898, Alcoa Laboratories Archives, Alcoa Technical Center, Merwin, Pennsylvania (hereafter referred to as ALA); Wallace, *Market Control*, p. 533.

73. Wallace, *Market Control*, pp. 534–5.

74. Ibid.; copy of Davis testimony, *Pittsburgh Reduction Company v. Cowles*, p. 946. See also the commentary by J. W. Richards in *Aluminum World*, April 1902, p. 132; Edwards et al., *Aluminum and its Production*, pp. 29–30. Edwards et al. argue that the decision was highly unjust, that Bradley "was not even sure that fusion could be maintained by the electric current alone, for he described the use of an auxiliary heating device, such as the flame of a blowpipe, directed upon the surface of the electrolyte." For an opposing view of the merits of the Coxe decision, see Cowles, *True Story of Aluminum*, esp. chap. VIII and IX.

75. *Engineering News*, L (1903), p. 390.

76. District Court of the United States for the Southern District of New York, *United States v. Aluminum Company of America*, Equity No. 85–73, exhibit 265; A. V. Davis, Statement Regarding Settlement of Patent Litigation with Electric Smelting and Aluminum Company in "Statements of A. V. Davis, Department of Justice—Consent Decree, June 26 and 27, 1911," pp. 73–7, AA, env. 7.

77. Equity No. 85–73, exhibit 198; Cowles, *True Story of Aluminum*, pp. 106–7.

78. The U.S. Patent Office poll, conducted in honor of its 150th anniversary, is cited in Carr, *Alcoa*, p. 59. The list included: Whitney's cotton gin; Fulton's steamboat; McCormick's reaper; Morse's telegraph; Goodyear's vulcanization of rubber; Howe's sewing machine; Sholes's typewriter; Westinghouse's air brake; Bell's telephone; Edison's phonograph and motion-picture projector; Tesla's induction motor, Hall's aluminum process; Merganthaler's linotype; the Wright brothers' airplane; DeForest's three-electrode vacuum tube; Baekeland's thermosetting plastics (bakelite); Burton's oil cracking.

Chapter 2

1. The definitive work on the rise and evolution of the modern "managerial" enterprise is Alfred D. Chandler, *The Visible Hand: The Managerial Revolution in American Business* (Cambridge, MA: Harvard University Press, 1977). Among Chandler's numerous writings on the structure of American industry, see esp. *Strategy and Structure: Chapters in the History of American Enterprise* (Cambridge, MA: MIT Press, 1962), chap. I. A good, brief primer is Glenn Porter, *The Rise of Big Business, 1860–1910* (Arlington Heights, IL: AHM Publishing, 1973). Except where some specificity of citation is deemed necessary, the notes in this chapter are intended to serve as guides to further reading for those not familiar with the literature of business history.
2. In 1840, the Census placed about eighty-nine percent of the nation's population in "rural territory," that is, in communities of less than 2,500 inhabitants. Only twelve cities had populations exceeding 25,000. See U.S. Department of Commerce, *Historical Statistics of the United States: Colonial Times to 1970, Part 1* (Washington, DC: U.S. Government Printing Office, 1975), Series A 43–56, A 57–72.
3. Alexis de Tocqueville, *Democracy in America*, Phillips Bradley (ed.) (New York: Vintage Books, 1945), vol. 2, p. 166.
4. A comprehensive discussion of antebellum American factory production is David A. Hounshell, *From the American System to Mass Production, 1800–1932: The Development of Manufacturing Technology in the United States* (Baltimore, MD: Johns Hopkins University Press, 1984).
5. On antebellum market structure, see Glenn Porter and Harold C. Livesay, *Merchants and Manufacturers: Studies in the Changing Structure of Nineteenth-Century Marketing* (Baltimore, MD: Johns Hopkins University Press, 1971).
6. See Chandler, *Visible Hand*, esp. chap. 3 and 6 on the impact of the infrastructure industries and pp. 316–19 on trends toward association to control prices and output.

7. Ralph W. Hidy and Muriel E. Hidy, *Pioneering in Big Business, 1882–1911* (New York: Harper and Row, 1955), esp. pp. 40–6.

8. On the merger wave, see Thomas K. McCraw, *Prophets of Regulation: Charles Francis Adams, Louis D. Brandeis, James M. Landis, Alfred E. Kahn* (Cambridge, MA: Harvard University Press, 1984), pp. 97–8; Ralph Nelson, *Merger Movements in American Industry, 1895–1956* (Princeton, NJ: Princeton University Press, 1959); Naomi Lamoreaux, *The Great Merger Movement in American Business, 1895–1904* (New York: Cambridge University Press, 1985).

9. Chandler, *Visible Hand*, p. 320; Alfred S. Eichner, *The Emergence of Oligopoly: Sugar Refining as a Case Study* (Baltimore, MD: Johns Hopkins University Press, 1969).

10. On the rise of capital markets in the postbellum era, see John A. James, *Money and Capital Markets in Postbellum America* (Princeton, NJ: Princeton University Press, 1978) and on investment banking, Vincent P. Carosso, *Investment Banking in America: A History* (Cambridge, MA: Harvard University Press, 1970).

11. Adam Smith, *The Wealth of Nations* (New York: Modern Library Edition, 1957 [1st ed., 1776]), p. 7; Andrew Carnegie, *The Gospel of Wealth and Other Timely Essays*, Edward C. Kirkland (ed.) (Cambridge, MA: Harvard University Press, 1962), p. 62.

12. Ibid. and Karl Marx, *Capital*, Frederick Engels (ed.) (New York: International Publishers, 1967 [1st ed., 1867]), vol. 3, p. 79.

13. For a more technical discussion of the various consequences of physical economies of scale, see F. M. Scherer, *Industrial Market Structure and Economic Performance* (Chicago: Rand McNally, 1970), pp. 72ff.

14. The ill-fated attempts of labor-intensive firms to grow large are outlined in Chandler, *Visible Hand*, chap. 10; Porter, *Rise of Big Business*, pp. 79–80.

15. Carnegie's discussion of capital-intensive industry appeared in the *North American Review* (1899), quoted in Porter, *The Rise of Big Business*, p. 11.

16. Technical problems involved in the continuous, integrated operation of the smelting process are discussed in detail by Edwards et al., *Aluminum and its Production*, pp. 307–15.

17. Chandler, *Visible Hand*, pp. 292–312; Mary Yeager, *Competition and Regulation: The Development of Oligopoly in the Meat Packing Industry* (Greenwich, CT: JAI Press, 1979); Harold C. Passer, *The Electrical Manufacturers* (Cambridge, MA: Harvard University Press, 1955); Andrew B. Jack, "The Channels of Distribution for an Innovation; The Sewing Machine Industry in America," *Explorations in Entrepreneurial History*, 9 (February 1957), pp. 113–41.

18. Marx, *Capital*, I, pp. 448–51.

19. The concept of "transactions cost" savings in its historical setting is

discussed by Oliver E. Williamson, "Emergence of the Visible Hand: Implications for Industrial Organization," in Alfred D. Chandler, Jr., and Hermann Daems (eds.), *Managerial Hierarchies* (Cambridge, MA: Harvard University Press, 1980), pp. 182–202.

20. George David Smith, *The Anatomy of a Business Strategy: Bell, Western Electric and the Origins of the American Telephone Industry* (Baltimore, MD: Johns Hopkins University Press, 1985), chap. 5.

21. For the emerging structure of the steel industry, see Peter Temin, *Iron and Steel in Nineteenth-Century America* (Cambridge, MA:, 1964). James H. Bridge, *Inside History of the Carnegie Steel Company* (New York, 1903) is quoted in Porter, *Rise of Big Business*, p. 54.

22. Chandler, *Visible Hand*, pp. 321–5.

23. Ibid., introduction and passim.

24. A class interpretation of the rise of management is advanced by David F. Noble, *America by Design: Science, Technology, and the Rise of Corporate Capitalism* (New York: Oxford University Press, 1977). Noble focuses on the nexus of the engineering profession, institutions of higher education, and large-scale corporate development.

25. Joseph A. Schumpeter, *Capitalism, Socialism and Democracy*, 3d ed. (New York: Harper and Row, 1950).

26. A good history of the industrial laboratory in the United States is Leonard S. Reich, *The Making of American Industrial Research: Science and Business at GE and Bell, 1876–1926* (New York: Cambridge University Press, 1985).

27. Noble, *America by Design*, p. 118.

28. See the comprehensive works on this subject by Mira Wilkins, *The Emergence of Multinational Enterprise: American Business Abroad from the Colonial Era to 1914* (Cambridge, MA: Harvard University Press, 1970), esp. chap. III; and *The Maturing of Multinational Enterprise: American Business Abroad from 1914 to 1970* (Cambridge, MA: Harvard University Press), esp. chap. I.

29. U.S. Steel had nearly $2.4 billion in assets in 1919, while General Motors, as the fifth largest industrial had $447 million. Alcoa in 1919 was valued at about $125 million. See A. D. H. Kaplan, *Big Enterprise in a Competitive System* (Washington, DC: The Brookings Institution, 1954), p. 147.

30. *Historical Statistics of the United States, Part 1*, Series A 6–8, 57–72; Series F 1–5; Series D 11–25.

31. The historical literature on the public response to the rise of big business is vast. Some good surveys offering varied interpretations are Robert Wiebe, *The Search for Order, 1877–1920* (New York: Hill & Wang, 1977); Samuel P. Hays, *The Response to Industrialism: 1885–1914* (Chicago: University of Chicago Press, 1957); Richard Hofstadter, *The Age of Reform* (New York: Knopf, 1955); Louis Galambos, *The Public Image of Big Business in America: 1880–1940* (Baltimore, MD:

Johns Hopkins University Press, 1975); Gabriel Kolko, *The Triumph of Conservatism: A Social Reinterpretation of American History, 1990–1916* (New York: Free Press, 1963).

32. McCraw, *Prophets of Regulation*, p. 166, cites the testimony of the sugar trust magnate, Louis O. Havermeyer, before Congress' ad hoc Industrial Commission in 1899. When asked if he seriously thought that the public had no right to know about the financial condition or affairs of publicly chartered, publicly held corporations, Havermeyer replied: "Yes; that is my theory. Let the buyer beware; that covers the whole business."

33. *The Bankers Magazine* (1901) is quoted through Thomas C. Cochran and William Miller, *The Age of Enterprise: A Social History of Industrial America*, rev. ed. (New York: Harper and Row, 1961), p. 201. On Roosevelt, see John Morton Blum, *The Republican Roosevelt* (New York: Atheneum, 1954), pp. 115ff.

34. McCraw, *Prophets of Regulation*, chap. 2, offers a brief survey of the period.

35. Ibid., chap. 4; William Letwin, *Law and Economic Policy in America: The Evolution of the Sherman Antitrust Act* (Chicago: University of Chicago Press, 1965).

36. Edwin S. Fickes to C. B. Fox, May [illegible], 1913, AA, env. 108. The specific issue had to do with fear of possible liability arising from the use of X-ray machines for in-house medical examinations for employees.

37. Equity No. 85–73, Arthur Vining Davis testimony, stenographer's minutes p. 14541.

38. *Standard Oil Co. of New Jersey v. United States*, 221 U.S. 1 (1911).

39. Arthur S. Link (ed.), *The Papers of Woodrow Wilson*, Vol. 25 (Princeton, NJ: Princeton University Press, 1978), p. 153. Wilson tried to distinguish between corporations that had achieved great size through efficiency from those that achieved size and power through "monopoly."

40. McCraw, *Prophets of Regulation*, chap. 3.

41. Walter Lippmann, *Drift and Mastery: An Attempt to Diagnose the Current Unrest* (Englewood Cliffs, NJ: Prentice-Hall, 1961), pp. 42–3. The trend toward the separation of ownership and managerial control of the corporation was set forth later in great detail in a classic treatise by Adolph A. Berle, Jr., and Gardiner C. Means, *The Modern Corporation and Private Property* (New York: Macmillan, 1933).

42. *United States v. U.S. Steel Corporation*, 251 U.S. 417 (1920).

43. A general history on the evolution of labor's legal status is Stephen J. Mueller, *Labor Law and Legislation* (Cincinnati, OH: Southwestern, 1949). On the organization of labor to establish and maximize its property rights, see Mancur Olsen, *The Logic of Collective Action: Public Goods and the Theory of Groups* (New York: Schocken Books, 1971), chap. 3.

44. Useful histories of the rise and development of the modern labor movement and union organization are Foster Rhea Dulles and Melvyn Dubofsky, *Labor in America: A History*, 4th ed. (Arlington Heights, IL: Harlan Davidson, 1984); Selig Perlman, *A History of Trade Unionism in the United States* (New York: Macmillan, 1922); Phillip Taft, *Organized Labor in American History* (New York: Harper and Row, 1964); David Brody (ed.), *The American Labor Movement* (New York: Harper and Row, 1971); Brody, *Workers in Industrial America: Essays on the 20th Century Struggle* (New York: Oxford University Press, 1980); David Montgomery, *The Fall of the House of Labor* (New York: Cambridge University Press, 1987) (through World War I).

45. The Bureau of Labor Statistics studied families of Ford Motor Company Workers in 1929 and found that while most were living at the margins of their incomes, they were spending less than a third of their earnings on food, as compared to half (by average workers) in 1900. (Ford workers were earning slightly above the national average for workers that year). *Monthly Labor Review*, 30 (1930), pp. 11–54.

46. On "welfare capitalism," see Brody, *Workers in Industrial America*, chap. 2. A more detailed history of the vicissitudes of organized labor between the war and the New Deal is Irving Bernstein, *The Lean Years: A History of the American Worker, 1920–1933* (Boston: Houghton Mifflin, 1960).

47. Prior to Norris–LaGuardia, Congress had granted such rights only to railway workers. The Railway Labor Act of 1926 protected the organization of railway workers against "interference, influence or coercion" by employers and set up a National Mediation Board. This national legislative triumph of the railway workers, due largely to their unequivocal status as workers in an interstate commerce industry, did not immediately apply to workers in other industries.

48. The best discussion of the development of "internal labor markets" is Sanford M. Jacoby, *Employing Bureaucracy: Managers, Unions and the Transformation of Work in American Industry, 1900–1945* (New York: Columbia University Press, 1985).

Chapter 3

1. Address delivered by Arthur Vining Davis at the Memorial Service in honor of Charles Martin Hall, AA, uncatalogued.

2. Arthur V. Davis to the Hon. H. D. Flood, Chairman, Committee on Foreign Affairs, House of Representatives, June 11, 1917, OCA, 5/1/2, Box 8.

3. Some of the flavor of the early operations at the New Kensington Works is conveyed in Otto Kaiser, "Scraps of History," a typescript dated April 1929, ALA.

4. Arthur V. Davis to Alfred E. Hunt, October 15, 1891, AA, env. 1287.

5. Hall explained that at New Kensington, the company would enjoy "free land, cheap coal and $10,000 in cash [source not specified] to move our works." The availability of tax-free land left ample room for expansion. Hall believed New Kensington would save $15,000 to $20,000 in annual operating expenses. See his letter to Julia Hall, May 10, 1890, ALA, env. 251.

6. Alfred E. Hunt to William A. Thaw, Jr., February 15, 1892, AA, env. 754.

7. *Minutes* for May and June 1893 and September 18, 1894.

8. Trescott, *Rise of the American Electrochemicals Industry*, passim, is a comprehensive treatment of the Niagara industrial complex.

9. Ibid., September 1897, September 15, 1898, September 21, 1899, and October 23, 1900.

10. *Minutes*, September 17, 1895 and September 18, 1898; Charles M. Hall to Alfred E. Hunt, September 27, 1898, ALA.

11. *Minutes*, February 6, 1893, September 18, 1894.

12. The company's purchase of power from Niagara Falls and its impact is noted in Trescott, *Rise of the American Electrochemicals Industry*, p. 124 and passim.

13. Profit rates – defined as net earnings after interest charges and taxes as a rate on capital plus owners' equity – were calculated from Equity No. 85–73, exhibits 1709, 1735–37, by Charlotte Muller, *Light Metals Monopoly* (New York: Columbia University Press, 1946), p. 63.

14. Davis, "Early Beginnings of the Aluminum Industry."

15. Edwards, *Captain in Industry*, p. 72.

16. In *The Aluminum World*, February 1900, aluminum applications were cited for kitchen and dining utensils, bottles, watches, book trimmings, wagon frames, equipments for soldiers, marine and aeronautical devices, surgical equipment, scientific instruments, wire (nonelectrical applications), foil, bottle caps, aluminum powder and paint, lithographs, and reduction processes.

17. Edwards, *Captain in Industry*, pp. 67–79.

18. On the company's entry into the utensil business, see J. H. Spicer and W. H. Smith, "History of the Origin, Growth & Development of the Aluminum Cooking Utensil Company" (March 1939) in "Histories of the Manufacturing Properties of the Aluminum Company of America, Affiliated Companies and Defense Corporation Plants" (hereafter known as "Plant Histories"), Vol. 18, pp. A–1 ff., AA. See also, Carr, *Alcoa*, pp. 112–14.

19. Testimony of Arthur Vining Davis in Equity No. 85–73, stenographer's minutes pp. 18658–65, 21176. See also, Wallace, *Market Control*, pp. 408–9. Some thirty-seven distinct American companies made aluminum cooking utensils in 1914. That number would increase to more than fifty by 1930.

20. The proliferation of aluminum products can be readily seen in a quick scanning of early promotional materials in the AA. See also Charles Martin Hall to The Jury of Awards, Pan-American Exposition, July 16, 1901, ALA, uncatalogued. In 1901, when aluminum sold as low as thirty cents a pound, it was "when price and specific gravity are both considered a cheaper metal for construction purposes than either brass or copper." The metal remained more expensive per pound than iron, zinc and lead, but its lightness and other properties often compensated for the difference in price.

21. Richards was writing for *Metals Industry*, which I have quoted through Wallace, *Market Control*, p. 14.

22. Davis himself recounted this story at some length in his testimony in Equity No. 85–73, stenographer's minutes, pp. 18647–58.

23. AKL [Alvah K. Lawrie] to S. S. Stadtler, Secretary, American Electrochemical Society, October 7, 1904, AA, env. 119. On the development of the electrical transmission market, see also Wallace, *Market Control*, pp. 14–16.

24. Ibid.; Fickes, "History," pp. 9–10.

25. Magee interview. See Appendix E for full citations of interviews.

26. Ibid; "Massena Works Fabricating Division, 1904 to 1956, inclusive," in "Plant Histories," Vol. 9B–1; Fickes, "History," p. 10.

27. Ibid., p. 34.

28. Wallace, *Market Control*, pp. 20–21; A. V. Davis to Joseph W. Richards, March 12, 1909; Magee interview. According to Magee, the loss of the auto body market to steel "was sort of an ironic thing because it was the aluminum that was thrown into the big steel ingot molds; it cured the oxygen bubbles in the steel and allowed the production of deep drawn steel for automobile bodies." An aluminum body, moreover, "was made by hand, pretty much, and the steel body could be put in a big press and drawn."

29. "Plant Histories," passim.

30. *Minutes*, September 17, 1895.

31. "Plant Histories," Vol. 10A; *Minutes*, September 17, 1895; Statement of A. V. Davis, Department of Justice – Consent Decree, July 26–27, 1911, AA, env. 7. See also Edwards at al., *Aluminum and its Production*, pp. 301–4, for technical detail.

32. Alfred E. Hunt to Charles M. Hall, June 7, 1897, AA, uncatalogued. The shift in the political climate re tariff protection was explained by Hunt as a consequence of the maturation of "many of the large industries in the country, which industries were the bone and sinew of the protective tariff of the past.... They have been protected until they have gotten into position where they are able to compete with foreign manufacturers and are independent of the tariff. Therefore the influence of these same strong, large concerns is to have the tariff for revenue only; so that the policy of the Republican party will be to shift

to the Democratic position of a few years ago – 'Tariff for Revenue only....' "

33. Trescott, *Rise of the American Electrochemicals Industry*, p. 65; Stevenson, "Historical Expansion," p. 4.

34. *Minutes*, September 17, 1896.

35. Gibbons, "Talk to Research Department," pp. 15, 21.

36. Carr, *Alcoa*, chap. 7, offers a good survey of early waterpower development. See also James W. Rickey, "Hydro Power for the Production of Aluminum," *Transactions of the Electrochemical Society*, Seventh General Meeting (Niagara, New York, October 8, 1936), 183–93.

37. A good general treatment of the subject is Lawrence Litchfield, Jr., "Bauxite," *Chemical Industries* (February and March 1941). I have used a reprint in the AA, 1135. See also, Carr, *Alcoa*, chap. 5; Kaiser, "Scraps of History," p. 5.

38. "Plant Histories," Vol. 19. Copies of the contracts, which were to cause Alcoa problems in subsequent antitrust proceedings, are reprinted as Exhibits 121–3, Equity No. 85–73.

39. Statement of A. V. Davis, Department of Justice – Consent Decree, July 26–27, 1911, pp. 20–21; Fickes, "History," pp. 128, 135, 153; "Plant Histories," Vol. 19.

40. Hunt to Hall, June 7, 1897.

41. "Plant Histories," Vol. 19; Carr, *Alcoa*, chap. 5; Stevenson, "Historical Expansion," p. 8.

42. Litchfield, "Bauxite," pp. 4, 11; Edwards et al., *Aluminum and its Production*, pp. 118–19, 125–6.

43. See especially three letters written by Hall on August 3, 1910 to A. V. Davis, to E. S. Fickes (the chief engineer), and to C. B. Fox (the East St. Louis plant superintendent) in the Hall file, AA, env. 251. In the elided words, Hall mentioned that the Bayer patent had expired "five or six years ago" (letter to Fox), but in fact Bayer's American patent had been granted on March 6, 1894 (see Edwards et al., *The Aluminum Industry*, p. 127, fn. 1).

44. Charles B. Fox to Edwin S. Fickes, July 14, 1911, and Fox to Charles H. Moritz, July 23, 1915 in a bound collection of Fickes's correspondence, AA, env. 116.

45. Edwards at al., *Aluminum and its Production*, pp. 281–5.

46. On the Calderwood railway, see Richard M. Bruckner, "A History of Calderwood, Tennessee," copy of manuscript on file at the public relations office, Alcoa Works, Alcoa, Tennessee, pp. 15–16. On the company's barge fleet and engineering capabilities generally, see Fickes, "History," p. 157 and passim. See also A. V. Davis to Fickes, February 27, 1906, Fickes's correspondence, for Davis's worry that he would have to put salesmen in charge of managing construction jobs because of a shortage of construction personnel.

47. Fickes, "History," pp. 66–7; Wallace, *Market Control*, p. 397.

48. Ibid., p. 396–7; Fickes, "History," pp. 76–7; testimony of Isadore C. Freud, March 2, 1939, Equity No. 85–73, stenographer's minutes, pp. 12215–19, 12232–50.

49. Wallace, *Market Control*, pp. 182–8, 202. Alcoa managers and engineers offered paeans of praise for the company's vertically integrated structure in testimony in the 1937 antitrust proceedings. See, for example, testimonies of A. V. Davis, I. W. Wilson, G. R. Gibbons, R. A. Hunt, and C. F. Nagel in Equity No. 85–73.

50. Muller, *Light Metals Monopoly*, p. 63. See, above, note 13.

51. Wallace, *Market Control*, pp. 29–30; Davis to Flood, June 11, 1917.

52. Wallace, *Market Control*, pp. 31ff.

53. Ibid., p. 29; Tariff Hearings – Statements by A. V. Davis, Nov.–Dec. 1908, p. 2305, and Testimony of A. V. Davis – Tariff Schedules, Ways and Means Committee, January 14, 1913, AA, env. 8.

54. Wallace, *Market Control*, p. 29; Tariff Hearings – Statements by A. V. Davis, Nov.–Dec. 1908, pp. 4111–15, 2305–7.

55. A former director of the International Aluminum Cartel, Louis Marlio, provides a useful treatment of the subject in *The Aluminum Cartel* (Washington, DC: The Brookings Institution, 1947), esp. chap. II. Alcoa's participation in the early cartels is detailed in the testimony of A. V. Davis, July 11, 1939, Equity No. 85–73, stenographer's minutes, pp. 19548–750.

56. Davis admitted to Alcoa's own excess in this regard (see his letter to Joseph W. Richards, April 6, 1908, AA, env. 119). In general, Alcoa was able to find demand for its growing capacity. In only three of the first thirty-one years of its history did the company suffer from an "excess" of capacity. During the 1908 depression, the firm tried to tailor its growth more cautiously toward short-term demand. In a letter to Charles H. Moritz, October 10, 1908, AA, uncatalogued, Davis referred to a modest expansion of sheet rolling capacity at Niagara as a trade-off of economies of scale for more modest investment.

57. Marlio, *Aluminum Cartel*, pp. 13–15. The French producers were adamant about lowering prices from the cartel price and precipitated the formal dissolution of the association on April 9, 1908. By then, "production of the competing companies amounted to about 7,300 tons a year, while the sales of the Aluminum [the cartel] reached only 4,700 tons."

58. Ibid., p. 15.

59. Joseph W. Richards to A. V. Davis, April 9, 1908, AA, env. 119.

60. Testimony of A. V. Davis, Tariff Schedules, January 14, 1913, AA, env. 8. When asked if he could accept a reduction of the tariff to an ad valorem rate of about twenty-five percent on foreign aluminum prices of ten to fourteen cents per pound, Davis replied: "We would either have to meet the foreign price or go out of business. Probably

the result would be that we would first meet the foreign price and then go out of business."

61. Carr, *Alcoa*, pp. 100–2; "Plant Histories," Vol. 25A; Fickes, "History," pp. 143ff.

62. Petition in Equity in the U.S. District Court of Western Pennsylvania, *United States v. Aluminum Company of America* (Washington, DC, 1912).

63. There is a brief allusion to the company's antitrust problem in the *Minutes* of June 22, 1911, noting that the company would open all its records and books for the investigation. The quoted phrase is from U.S. District Court of Western Pennsylvania, 159 session, 1912, Decree.

64. Ibid.; U.S. Patent Office Hearing, *A. H. Cowles v. Franz A. Rody*, October 23, 1916, p. 3, cited in Cowles, *True Story of Aluminum*, pp. 112–13.

65. Western District of Pennsylvania, 159 Session, 1912, Decree.

66. Fickes, "History," pp. 143–4.

67. The quote is cited through the Aluminum Price Fixing and Court of Claims (War Industries Board), December 21, 1934, A. V. Davis testimony, p. 1871, copy on file in the AA, env. 10.

68. Between 1904 and 1935, the Mellon family holdings in Alcoa increased from 28.78 to 37 percent of the total outstanding voting stock. See J. R. D. Huston to Roy A. Hunt, May 17, 1935, AA, env. 83.

69. See Mellon's corespondence on his desire to seize control of the company attached to a letter from J. R. D. Huston to Roy A. Hunt, May 17, 1935, in ibid.

70. Rogers to Lord, Day & Lord, 7 December 1928, OCA, 2/7/1, box 128.

71. Freeman Lincoln, "The Man Who is Buying Up Florida," *Fortune* (November 15, 1961), p. 149ff., offers a useful, compact portrait of Davis in his later years. Overall, I have relied on scraps of written information, occasional speeches, and oral recollections of Alcoa executives who knew Davis for my impressions of his character.

72. On Edward K. Davis's early career, see Duncan C. Campbell, *Global Mission: The Story of Alcan: Volume I to 1950* (Ontario: Ontario Publishing Limited, 1985), pp. 6–9.

73. Ibid.

74. See Hall's Last Will and Testament and Fauver & Fauver, Attorneys at Law, "Re: Aluminum Company of America," circa January 1929, OCA, 7/1/4, box 17. Johnson, of course, shared the power of voting the stock in trust at Alcoa stockholder's meetings, but is appears that he deferred to Davis's judgment on matters relating to the company.

75. Rogers to Lord, Day & Lord, 7 December 1928.

76. *Minutes*, 1910–1916. Roy Hunt's career is outlined in a brief "Personality – Biographical Sketch," AA, env. 462.

77. A. V. Davis testified that after the first decade of development, the company became highly profitable, but that the policy was to limit dividends. Dividends were issued only twice in the first decade (Davis to Flood, June 11, 1917). Throughout the patent period, earnings were largely left in the business. In 1909, the owners took out profits from the patent period, as the company's approximately $24,000,000 in assets were "declared . . . out to our stockholders" (Testimony, Tariff Schedules, 1914, pp. 1847–8). According to Wallace, *Market Control*, pp. 226, 544–5, dividends were paid out at a rate of one percent on common and three percent on preferred stock on total net earnings of $61,763,000, between 1909 and 1916, as average annual rates of return on assets ranged between 14.1 percent and 30.6 percent.

78. *Minutes*, 1916.

79. "Plant Histories," Vol. 17B.

80. The move to Pittsburgh "had the merit of affording better working quarters . . . and assisting the office force to an understanding that the factory at New Kensington was not the company's major and dominant activity." The move also pleased those who simply preferred the city life and disliked the commute to factory. Fickes, "History," p. 99.

81. No single source defines a job description for a plant superintendent. The paragraph is inferred from a wide reading of contemporary materials.

82. Compare Davis's testimony in *Tariff Hearings*, 1908, p. 4112 and C. H. Fox to E. S. Fickes, May 12, 1913, Fickes Correspondence, AA, env. 106. See also A. V. Davis – Testimony, Hearings before the Committee on Finance, United States Senate, February 12, 1913, AA, env. 8.

83. Fickes, "History," p. 94.

84. Four scholarly treatments on community and labor relations in various Alcoa plants are Carl I. Meyerhuber, Jr., "Organizing Alcoa: The Aluminum Workers' Union in Pennsylvania's Allegheny Valley, 1900–1971," *Pennsylvania History*, 48 (July 1981), pp. 195–8; Sammy E. Pinkston, *The History of Local 309, United Steelworkers of America, AFL–CIO–CLC, Alcoa, Tennessee, 1933–1977* (Knoxville, TN: Keith Press, 1976); Russell D. Parker, "Alcoa, Tennessee; The Early Years, 1919–1939" in the East Tennessee Historical Society, *Publications* 48 (1976), pp. 84ff; Gordon Scott Bachus, *History of Bauxite* (North Little Rock, AR: Heritage, 1968), chap. 2–4. I have also relied on Kaiser, "Scraps of History," pp. 8–9, and Lamar Taylor, "History of the Alcoa Aluminum Workers Union," ms. on file at USWA Local 309, Alcoa Tennessee, p. 3.

85. Carr, *Alcoa*, p. 196.

86. Parker, "Alcoa, Tennessee," pp. 88–9; letters from Fox to Fickes for 1913, Fickes Correspondence, AA, env. 106.

87. Interview with Arthur V. Davis, undated, AA, env. 167; *Aluminum World*, 6 (1896), p. 119.

88. Francis C. Frary to John J. Beer, July 23, 1962, ALA.
89. "Plant Histories," Vol. 2A and 11; Fickes, "History" and corespondence, passim; Earl Blough to Roy A. Hunt, October 9, 1915, ALA; Edwards, *Immortal Woodshed*, pp. 228–9.
90. See the often amusing exchange of letters among Richards, Hall, and Davis in the Dr. Joseph W. Richards Correspondence, 1891–1901, AA, env. 119.
91. Fickes, "History," passim.
92. These experiments, according to Norman C. Craig, may not have been as bizarre as they may seem in retrospect to modern contemporaries. "Hall had long had an interest in developing ... fuel cells ... as potentially efficient sources of electrical energy for use in the electrochemical industry. Early on he recognized that a critical problem was finding an inexpensive source of catalytic metals for the electrodes. It is likely that his belief in his early findings of evidence for iron metals being converted into platinum metals by the action of intense electrical sparks was encouraged by the revolutionary work being carried out on the radioactive elements in the same time period. Rutherford, Soddy, the Curies, and others were finding that radioactive elements underwent transmutation and that these changes were associated with large energies. Evidently Professor Chandler of Columbia University, a major figure in American science at the time, encouraged Hall in these activities." (Craig to author, April 29, 1986).
93. See W. A. Thomas, "Notes on Niagara Works History," in "Plant Histories," Vol. 11; W. A. Thomas to Junius Edwards, June 15, 1951 (italics mine).
94. Fickes, "History," pp. 78–80. George Gibbons verified that "no important acts were carried out" at Alcoa without Hall's approval ("Talk to Research Department," p. 4).
95. Fickes "History," pp. 78–80.
96. Carr, *Alcoa*, p. 147ff., devotes a chapter to the growth of aluminum demand and applications during the war.
97. Ibid., pp. 157–8. Carr cites a list of products "prepared in alphabetical order shortly after the war ... as follows: airplane parts, ammonia converters, automobile parts, bimetallic tubing, auto bodies, bolts and nuts, brewery equipment, brush guards, buoys, bus-bars, cameras, cans, canteens, cathode plates, caul plates, crank cases, deodorizing apparatus, dials, electrical supplies, explosive manufacturers' equipment, fan motor housings, electrical feeders, film-roll spindles, fireworks, funnels, fuse wire, gas-mask fittings, gasoline tanks, gasoline-pump cylinders, gear-housings, helmets, identification tags, lens housings, lightning arresters, artificial limbs, magnet wire, magneto covers, mess kits, meter bases, motor housings, nitrate fixation equipment, oil floats and pans, optical supplies, reels, reflectors, retorts, rubber molds, patterns, periscope caps, pistons, explosive pow-

der, pump cylinders, scientific apparatus, screens, screw machine products, signals, splints, starter cables, tanks, dry battery terminals, thermit, trolley bows, tubing, U-tubes, vats, welding wire, auto wheels, windshield frames, wire cloth, yokes."

98. Ibid., p. 148; *The New York Times*, July 3, 1981.
99. Thomas Crepar to Alfred M. Hunt, January 11, 1898; Andrew Johnson to Pittsburgh Reduction Company, March 7, 1898, AA, env. 304. This and the following paragraphs follow closely from an article by Bettye Pruitt and George David Smith, "The Corporate Management of Innovation: Alcoa Research, Aircraft Alloys, and the Problem of Stress Corrosion Cracking," in Richard Rosenbloom (ed.), *Research on Technology Management and Policy* (New York: JAI Press, 1986) pp. 33–81.
100. Orville Wright to Frederick C. Pyne, December 9, 1939, AA, env. 304.
101. Robert J. Anderson, *The Metallurgy of Aluminum and Aluminum Alloys* (New York: Baird, 1925), pp. 274–5.
102. John W. Hood, "History of Alcoa Aluminum in Aircraft, Alcoa Contributions Toward Aluminum Alloy and Structural Developments in Aircraft" (unpublished ms.), pp. 90–1, ALA, env. 1008.
103. Pruitt and Smith, "Corporate Management of Innovation," pp. 41–2.
104. Memorandum, Earl Blough to Roy Hunt, June 23, 1953, cited in Hood, "History," p. 90.

Chapter 4

1. Wallace, *Market Control*, app. C; Aluminum Company of America, Annual Reports to the Stockholders, 1927–1937. Alcoa did not publish annual reports until 1927, from which time they appeared yearly, usually printed about three months after the close of the fiscal year, which was also the calendar year. All annual reports will hereafter be referred to as *Annual Report*.
2. See the investment report by the firm Van Cleef and Jordan, "Introductory Survey of Aluminum" [1932], Oberlin College Archives, 5/1/2, box 8.
3. Ibid. The automobile industry consumed only a third of total output of new aluminum during the years 1924–9 and only 15.75 percent in 1931.
4. Product histories can be gleaned from many sources. A convenient compendium is a large manuscript of assembled facts, policies, and sentiments titled "Aluminum Company of America, 1888–1942" (circa 1947), AA. Internally, this manuscript, the work of many hands, was known as the "Alcoa Bible," and so it will be cited hereafter. See also the Close interview.
5. Carr, *Alcoa*, pp. 165–78; Equity No. 85–73, *Brief of Aluminum Com-*

pany of America and other Defendants ... (hereafter referred to as *Alcoa Brief*), 2 vols., I (1941), pp. 203–8.

6. According to Carr, *Alcoa*, p. 157, the company had feared the coming of a depression all during the war, as it expanded its productive capacity. I have seen no direct evidence of this, although the leaders of many large firms prepared themselves for postwar production cutbacks. The cancellation of orders in 1920–1 apparently caught the company by surprise, however, after two years of strong sales (see the Magee interview).

7. According to Campbell, *Global Mission*, p. 103, Alcoa was "short of 55 million pounds of aluminum in 1925, 42 million in 1926 and 22 million in 1927, forcing [Davis] to buy what he could from the Germans, a practice he didn't particularly enjoy."

8. Magee and Close interviews.

9. *Annual Reports*, 1930–40. There was one brief downturn in earnings in the recession of 1937–8.

10. Wallace, *Market Control*, p. 243.

11. *Alcoa Brief*, II, p. 589. The consent decree of 1912 had enjoined "any contract or agreement, either verbal or written, the purpose or effect of which would be to restrict the importation into the United States, from any part of the world, of aluminum, or alumina, or bauxite, or any other material from which aluminum can be manufactured, or to fix or illegally affect the prices of such aluminum, alumina, bauxite, or other material, when imported." See Equity No. 85–73, exhibit 1009.

12. Equity No. 85–73, testimony of A. V. Davis, stenographer's minutes, pp. 18735–9; 19677–8; 19765–7; 18739–78, and exhibits 21011, 1013–15.

13. Ibid., stenographer's minutes, pp. 18552–6. See also the testimony of other officers at pp. 21482, 22540, 33241, 40353. Though Alcoa was accused by would-be competitors and the Government of having secret agreements with European producers, no evidence was ever presented. Wallace, *Market Control*, p. 158, fn. 13, after interviewing knowledgeable sources concluded that there were no understandings between Alcoa and the postwar cartel. See also, Marlio, *The Aluminum Cartel*, pp. 20–6.

14. David E. Koskoff, *The Mellons* (New York: Crowell, 1978); Wallace, *Market Control*, p. 82.

15. Ibid., pp. 143, 159, and passim; Campbell, *Global Mission*, p. 103. Alcoa was short fifty-five million pounds in 1925, forty-two million in 1926, and twenty-two million in 1927.

16. Wilkins, *Maturing of Multinational Enterprise*, chap. II and III.

17. Equity No. 85–73, Davis testimony, stenographer's minutes pp. 19128–9; 19200–4, 20576–7; 21244–5, and exhibits 12, 21, 41, 892, 984. The potential effect of an Alcoa presence in Europe on exports to the United States formed part of the antitrust allegations against Alcoa.

18. *Alcoa Brief*, I, pp. 625–32.
19. Edwards et al., *Aluminum and its Production*, pp. 220–6. The commercial feasibility of leucite depended on the recovery of marketable potassium salts in addition to the alumina.
20. On leucite, see Equity No. 85–73, Davis testimony, stenographer's minutes, p. 18423–32; Fickes, "History," pp. 276–7; Campbell, *Global Mission*, pp. 222–6. Campbell has made a close study of this episode and notes that Davis himself had been skeptical of the process before entering into the arrangement.
21. Equity No. 85–73, Davis testimony, stenographer's minutes, pp. 20717–24. The Soderberg Process today is much as it was then, involving the continuous feeding of coke and pitch into a hopper suspended above the aluminum smelting bath. Heat from the bath causes an anode to solidify in the hopper into a continuous mass extending down to the bath. As the carbon is consumed in the electrolytic process, more carbon can be lowered from the hopper in a regulated manner. The classic prebaked anode method requires separate anode furnaces and separate rodding facilities and the anodes must be replaced individually as they are consumed. Prebaked anodes involve more labor but are more efficient in the cell operation and emit fewer gases.
22. *Alcoa Brief*, I, pp. 607–25.
23. Ibid., pp. 638–9; Equity No. 85–73, Davis testimony, stenographer's minutes, p. 18647.
24. Campbell, *Global Mission*, p. 78.
25. Ibid., pp. 97–100; Wallace, *Market Control*, pp. 131–5.
26. Equity No. 85–73, Davis testimony, stenographer's minutes, pp. 20114–76.
27. Campbell, *Global Mission*, pp. 106–7.
28. That the Duke investment was passive became an important element in the final remedy to the antitrust case in later years when the Duke interests were exempted from the requirement of major stockholders in both Aluminium Limited and Alcoa to divest their holdings in one company or the other. See below, Chapter 6.
29. Fickes, "History," pp. 255–66; Campbell, *Global Mission*, pp. 125–33.
30. Campbell, *Global Mission*, pp. 2–3, 16–18; *Annual Report*, 1929.
31. Equity No. 85–73, Davis testimony, stenographer's minutes, pp. 19039–46. Mejia is quoted in Campbell, *Global Mission*, p. 8.
32. Equity No. 85–73, testimonies of Roy Hunt and George Gibbons, stenographer's minutes, pp. 21766–7, 22527–36.
33. For Ronald Graham, *The Aluminum Industry and the Third World: Multinational Corporations and Underdevelopment* (London: Zed Press, 1982), the avoidance of antitrust was the only reason, but it is unlikely that the cartel alone would have provided the impetus for divestiture without added pressure from other causes.
34. Equity No. 85–73, Davis testimony, stenographer's minutes, pp. 19039–46.

35. Ibid., pp. 21770–3.
36. Wilkins, *Maturing of Multinational Enterprise*, chap. III.
37. Ibid., testimony of E. K. Davis, pp. 16121–7, 16137–43.
38. See above, chap. III.
39. Chandler, *Strategy and Structure*, esp. pp. 326–37.
40. Ibid., pp. 333–4. The quote is from John Moody, *The Truth about Trusts* (New York: Moody Press, 1904), p. 195.
41. Only a few partial organization charts for 1919 are extant, and those relate to Badin, New Kensington, and Toronto Works for 1919 in the AA, env. 1059B. The outline of the central office structure and the relation of its departments to operations are revealed in "Functional Organization Chart of the U.S. Aluminum Co. New Kensington Works Showing the Relation of Alcoa and Aluminum Cooking Utensil Company." A convenient way to track the formation of new subsidiaries is through Fickes, "History," which gives the reasons for their creation or acquisition.
42. Ibid.
43. Ibid.
44. Ibid.; Aluminum Company of America – List of Officers, by Year, AA, env. 481.
45. "Organization Chart for 1929," AA, env. 1059B.
46. "Aluminum Company of America, Organization Chart," April 19, 1938, AA, env. 1059B.
47. Fickes, "History," p. 294.
48. This point is generally agreed to by veterans of the era. See, for example, the Hickman and Lipkowitz interviews.
49. See above, chap. III.
50. This account is based on records at Oberlin College, which were called to my attention by Geoffrey Blodgett, who is at work on a book on the architect Philip Johnson, the son of Homer H. Johnson, who was Charles Martin Hall's attorney.
51. Arthur Vining Davis to the Trustees of Oberlin College, May 5, 1925, OCA, 7/1/4, box 17.
52. Ibid.
53. Ibid.; resolution of the Board of Trustees of Oberlin College [May 6, 1925], copy in ibid.
54. Homer H. Johnson to the Board of Trustees of Oberlin College, May 5, 1925 and Fauver & Fauver, "Re: Aluminum Company of America," [ca. January 1929], in ibid.
55. Ibid.; "Statement in Regard to the Settlement of the Estate of Charles M. Hall," unsigned memorandum [ca. August 1925], in ibid.; George B. Siddall, "Trustees of Hall Estate to Turn Over Bequest Funds to Oberlin," *The Oberlin Alumni Magazine* (December 1925), pp. 9–10, OCA, 5/1/2, box 6.
56. John R. Rogers (Oberlin trustee) to H. C. King (Oberlin president), March 26, 1926, copy in OCA, 2/7/1. box 28; Goerge B. Siddall (Oberlin

trustee) to Homer H. Johnson, May 27, 1927, OCA, 7/1/4, box 17; Fauver & Fauver, "Re: Aluminum Company;" C. K. Fauver (Oberlin trustee), memorandum, July 31, 1929, OCA, 5/1/2, box 6. Davis claimed repeatedly that the prices quoted on the Curb Exchange were "exorbitant," "absurd," "fantastic," and "fictitious," and could not be substantially supported. The book value of the stock in July 1929, he said, was but $12.00 and that earnings per share for 1928 were $7.00 See Guy W. Mallon (Berea trustee), memorandum, July 30, 1929, OCA, 5/1/2, box 6.

57. Fauver & Fauver, "Re: Aluminum Company;" Lord, Day & Lord to Guy Ward Mallon, Chairman, Special Committee on the Charles M. Hall Bequest to Berea College, Nathan L. Miller to Mark L. Thomsen, July 23, 1929, and supporting correspondence, 2/7/1, box 128.

58. Conference at the Office of George W. Schurman, November 12, 1929, OCA, 5/1/2, box 6.

59. W. F. Bohn (assistant to Oberlin president) to Ernest H. Wilkins (Oberlin president), February 11, 1919; Thurston (Oberlin treasurer) to Amos C. Miller, February 18, 1929; Ernest H. Wilkins to Mark L. Thomsen, March 11, 1929, all in OCA, 2/7/1, box 128.

60. Draft of a letter to Arthur Vining Davis and Homer H. Johnson (ca. May 1929) and Guy W. Mallon, memorandum, July 30, 1929, Oberlin College archives, 5/1/2, box 7.

61. Davis claimed that many of the shares sold off by the institutions had been distributed to officers and employees of Alcoa and that 20,000 shares had gone to the Mellon brothers (memorandum of a conference in Cleveland, October 15, 1929, OCA, 5/1/2, box 6).

62. C. K. Fauver, memorandum, July 30, 1929; memorandum of a conference in Cleveland, October 15, 1929; C. K. Fauver, memorandum, November 8, 1929; conference at the office of George W. Schurman, November 12, 1929; unsigned memorandum, November 27, 1929; all in OCA, 5/1/2, box 6.

63. Agreement between the Trustees of Oberlin, Berea, and the American Missionary Association, January 21, 1930; Preambles and Resolutions to be Adopted by the Oberlin Trustees, January 25, 1930, OCA, 5/1/2, box 8. Mark Thomsen, a "hard boiled Marine" of a lawyer who had been assigned to negotiate with William Watson Smith, Davis's attorney, was credited with the settlement by Loren N. Wood to Ernest H. Wilkins, January 4, 1930, ibid.

64. Unsigned memorandum of a conference in Cleveland, Ohio, October 12, 1929, October 15, 1929; C. K. Fauver, memorandum, June 7, 1929, both in OCA, 5/1/2, box 7. Johnson, in fact, remained angry for years to come and in his capacity as executor of Hall's estate, appears to have obstructed plans for the erection of Hall auditorium until the late 1940s. See Geoffrey Blodgett, interview with William E. Stevensen, July 18–20, 1979, OCA.

65. Memorandum labeled "Confidential and Return to D. M. Love, 7/1/47" OCA, 30/91, box 7. The memorandum appears to have been written shortly after the conversation, which is suggested by both its tone and recall of detail. Oberlin's archivist, William Bigglestone, informed me that Love was a careful keeper of records. The label on the cover is not in Love's hand and appears to have been added years later when the document may have been circulating in conjunction with discussions over delays in the approval of a design for Hall Auditorium.

66. R. K. Mellon came onto the board in 1930, joining his father, Richard B., who died in 1935.

67. Gibbons, "Talk to Research Department," p. 32. The first "public" annual report appeared in early 1928 (for 1927) and was not much more than a simple balance sheet. The production of annual reports was as much a response to criticism of the company for the secrecy of its operations as it was a service to new stockholders.

68. "Aluminum Company of America, List of Officers"; *Minutes*, 1898 and 1909.

69. The traditional autonomy of local operations is a matter of lore. I was struck especially by this point as it was made by some leading citizens of Massena, New York, to me in casual conversation during a visit there in 1983. See also the Magee interview.

70. Fickes, "History," pp. 211–12.

71. Arthur Johnson interview.

72. Magee interview.

73. Hunt's dream is recounted in *Aluminum by Alcoa* (Pittsburgh: Aluminum Company of America, 1969), p. 94.

74. The company routinely took on debt, usually in the form of long-term debenture gold bonds or mortgage bonds to support expansion projects. The debt to equity (not including surplus) ratio for the firm in 1927, an extreme year for debt was about 1:2.5 and in 1937 was about 1:5. It was the board's policy to retire debt quickly and to issue preferred stock to its principal stockholders in lieu of floating bonds. The ratios of preferred to common stock for the same years is striking: 20:1 in 1927 and 18:1 in 1937, indicating the directors' intention of keeping the voting (common) stock under close control. See the *Annual Reports*.

75. Personality–Biographical Sketch of Irving W. Wilson, AA, env. 643.

76. Carr, *Alcoa*, p. 137. See also above, chap. III.

77. William Hoopes to Joseph W. Richards, May 16, 1917, AA, env. 671.

78. Unpublished biographical materials on Frary are found in the AA, env. 641. See esp. Junius D. Edwards, "The Medalist and His Work" (1939); James G. Vail, "The Personal Side of the Medalist" (1946); Webster N. Jones, "The Scientific Achievements of the Medalist" (1946).

79. Charles H. Moritz to F. C. Frary, May 21, 1917, and Moritz to Hoopes, June 2, 1917, AA, env. 641; Francis C. Frary to John J. Beer, August 8, 1962, ALA.

80. Moritz to Hoopes, October 24, 1917, and Hoopes to Moritz, October 26, 1917, AA, env. 671; Carr, *Alcoa*, p. 136.

81. "History of Alcoa Research Laboratories," "Plant Histories," Vol. 2A, General Introduction. Blough's duties are described as follows: "No. 1 – Supervision of Analytical Laboratories; No. 2 – Supervision of Physical Laboratories; No. 3 – Supervision of processes and products; No. 4 – Inspection of incoming materials."

82. On the organization of the Research Bureau, see Fickes, "History," pp. 206ff; [Francis C. Frary] "History of Early Aluminum Research," undated ms. on file in the AA, env. 671, pp. 8–9.

83. Frary, "History of Aluminum Research," pp. 8–9; Fickes, "History," pp. 205–6.

84. Frary, "History of Early Aluminum Research," pp. 10–11.

85. Edwards et al., *The Aluminum Industry*, I, pp. 323–7; Fickes, "History," p. 207.

86. Ibid., p. 209; Carr, *Alcoa*, pp. 237–8.

87. Ibid.; Van Horn interview.

88. Ibid.; Fickes, "History," pp. 207ff.; Francis C. Frary to Kent R. Van Horn, June 3, 1957, ALA.

89. Frary, "History," p. 15; Francis C. Frary, "Research in the Aluminum Industry," *Journal of Industrial and Engineering Chemistry*, 31 (January 1939); Close and Van Horn interviews; Equity No. 85–73, Davis testimony, stenographer's minutes, p. 19363.

90. Carr, *Alcoa*, pp. 138–9; Fickes, "History," p. 299.

91. During World War II, Alfred M. Hunt, the founder's grandson, worked in the Massena potrooms, and described the work on the "Hall Pots" as follows: " ... everything was done by hand pretty much except lifting the crucibles. The raising and lowering of the anodes was done by a jack on the anode rack and pushed from the anode up or down, depending on which way you thought it should go.... In those days you had to keep the vat in which the whole process revolved around in a certain alkaline or acidity and you couldn't let it get too acid and you didn't want it to get too alkaline. There was just a happy medium there. They do that to some extent today, but it's all done by computers.... In those days you'd take the tongs and you'd dip into the bath and you'd take a small sample and you'd run the sample in the laboratory and determine what needed to be added to the vat so that you could get the proper ongoing of the pots." See the Hunt interview.

92. Campbell, *Global Mission*, pp. 79–80; Carr, *Alcoa*, p. 143.

93. W. T. Ennor, "Processes for Making Ingot for Working, Review and Present Status," transcript of a "metallurgical meeting" dated June 3, 1937, ALA. Ennor explained that the basic idea of the Direct Chill process was "to freeze an outer ingot shell in a mold, continuously withdraw the shell, and directly chill it and this rapidly solidify the entire ingot by means of water spray. A long series of tests involving

the cooling of molten metal from one mold surface only was first made and showed the enormous insulating effect of the small air space between ingot and mold and the extremely rapid freezing that could be obtained by applying cooling water directly to the metal." (Nagel's remarks were made at the same meeting.)

94. E. B. Alderfer and H. E. Michl, *Economics of the Aluminum Industry* (New York: McGraw-Hill, 1942), pp. 94–7.

95. This and the next two paragraphs rely heavily on *Alcoa Brief*, II, pp. 509–64, and on the antitrust testimonies of the Baush principals and customers in Equity No. 85–73, stenographer's minutes, passim.

96. George Haskell admitted that Baush's Duralumin was priced at a loss for several years. See his testimony in Equity 85–73, stenographer's minutes, pp. 2842–4.

97. Haskell testified that the metal department of Baush had failed to turn a profit from 1919–35 (see ibid., stenographer's minutes, pp. 2828–31).

98. Carr's assessment (*Alcoa*, p. 212) was relatively generous given the ill feelings most Alcoa principals harbored toward Haskell.

99. Fickes notes that Alcoa had actually considered buying the Baush facility in 1933, but found all the plant and equipment inadequate for quality work and in terrible disrepair. He concluded that "the Baush people were either superbly ignorant or indifferent as to what was required to make Duralumin satisfactorily or economically." Fickes, "History," pp. 294–5.

100. *Alcoa Brief*, I, pp. 524–5; E. H. Dix, "Application of 'Alclad' Aluminum Alloy Sheet to the Aircraft Industry," *Aviation*, 25 (1926), reprint, n.p.; Junius D. Edwards to D. B. Hobbs, September 27, 1938, ALA.

101. Equity No. 85–73, testimony of C. F. Nagel, stenographer's minutes, pp. 24429–43.

102. See the testimonies of George Haskell and C. F. Nagel, Jr., in ibid., pp. 2773–7; 24338–65.

103. Vail, "Personal Side of the Medalist," pp. 9–10; Jones, "Scientific Achievements," p. 5; Van Horn interview.

104. Van Horn interview.

105. See Table 71 in Nathaniel H. Engle, Homer E. Gregory, and Robert Mosse, *Aluminum: An Industrial Marketing Survey* (Chicago: Irwin, 1945), p. 261.

106. Arthur Johnson interview. Johnson claimed that he was fired by the Massena plant superintendent in 1933 for his display of sympathetic concern for the plight of Depression-era workers in the carbon plant.

107. Meyerhuber, "Organizing Alcoa," pp. 197–98; Russell D. Parker, "Alcoa, Tennessee; The Early Years, 1919–1939," *East Tennessee Historical Society Publications*, 48–1976 (1979), pp. 84ff.; Gordon Scott Bachus, *History of Bauxite*, pp. 18ff.

108. Ibid., pp. 20–37; George D. Smith, "Notes from Conversations with Retired Alcoa Employees, Bauxite, Arkansas, 8/10/83," AA, uncatalogued.

109. Fischer interview.

110. See the report of I. W. Wilson on labor and wage rates in the Aluminum Industry, 1926–33, minutes of the Aluminum Association, September 26, 1933, on file at the Aluminum Association, Inc., 818 Connecticut Ave., Washington, DC.

111. Minutes of the Aluminum Association, August 2, 8, 23, and September 26, 1933.

112. *The New York Times*, September 4, 1933 and December 2, 1933; Sammy E. Pinkston, *The History of Local 309, United Steelworkers of America, AFL–CIO–CLC, Alcoa, Tennessee, 1933–1937* (Knoxville, TN: Keith Press, 1976), pp. 11–12.

113. Meyerhuber, "Organizing Alcoa," pp. 197–205.

114. On the organization of other plants, see Carr, *Alcoa*, chap. 14 and app. The troubled relationship between the locals and the national union is vividly described by Meyerhuber, "Organizing Alcoa," pp. 202ff.

115. Ibid.; *The New York Times*, August 4, 1933.

116. Meyerhuber, "Organizing Alcoa," p. 204; Pinkston, *Local 309*, pp. 14–15; *The New York Times*, esp. August 11–15, 23–28, and September 6–8, 1934.

117. Meyerhuber, "Organizing Alcoa," pp. 208–11.

118. Meyerhuber, "Organizing Alcoa," pp. 208–12; *The New York Times*, March, 7, 14, 21 and April 14, 21, 1937

119. Fickes, "History," pp. 218–19; Pinkston, *Local 309*, pp. 15–22; *The New York Times*, May 20, 1937.

120. No legal responsibility for the shootings was ever assigned, although contemporary news accounts of the event placed the blame squarely on the heads of the police. See Pinkston, *Local 309*, pp. 22–26; *The New York Times*, July 8, 1937; Taylor, "History of the Alcoa Aluminum Workers Union," p. 19.

121. Pinkston, *Local 309*, pp. 28–37.

122. It is interesting to note that salaries and wages as a percentage of the value of aluminum products did not change substantially between 1929 and 1939. In the former year, salaries and wages were 23.1 percent of expenditures as compared with 61.3 percent for materials and energy, and 15.6 percent for other items. By 1939, salaries and wages were 22.2 percent of the total, while materials and energy were 60 percent and other items were 17.8 percent. See Engle et al., *Aluminum*, p. 105 (Table 26) and p. 203 (Table 73).

123. The *Annual Reports* show Alcoa's net income for 1938 at $15.6 million as compared with $27.6 million for 1937. Net income would increase to $36.6 million in 1939.

124. Competition from new metals was the explicit concern of three letters triggered by the fiftieth anniversary of aluminum in 1938. See S. K. Colby to J. D. Edwards, August 31, 1938; Francis C. Frary to Colby, September 13, 1938; Edwards to Colby, September 14, 1938; all in ALA.

Chapter 5

1. *Historical Statistics*, Series Y, 254–7.
2. Graham, *Aluminum Industry and the Third World*, pp. 26–7.
3. The Government's bill of complaint in Equity No. 85–73 was filed on April 23, 1937.
4. Alcoa executives were especially proud of the praise they received in the Third Annual Report of the Truman Committee, which had been established to investigate wartime military contract abuses (Carr, *Alcoa*, p. 255).
5. Gibbons, "Talk to Research Department," p. 27.
6. *The Temporary National Economic Committee*, March 2, 1939, p. 262.
7. The Government's bill of complaint, Equity No. 85–73; *The Pittsburgh Gazette*, October 9, 1924.
8. On the FTC and Alcoa, see Davis G. Cullom, "The Transformation of the Federal Trade Commission, 1914–1929," *Mississippi Valley Historical Review*, 49 (December 1962), pp. 442, 449; *Aluminum Company of America: Report of the Special Assistant to the Attorney General, William R. Benham* (Washington, DC: U.S. Government Printing Office, 1926); *The New York Times*, April 7, 23, 1929 and April 5, 1930.
9. In addition to Baush were suits brought by the Sheet Aluminum Company of Jackson, Michigan, and by Aluminum Industries of Lagrange, Illinois. These firms also filed complaints with the Department of Justice. See the Hickman interview; Wallace, *Market Control*, pp. 375, 480.
10. Wallace, *Market Control*, pp. 480ff.; Carr, *Alcoa*, chap. 16; Hickman interview.
11. For example, from 1890 through 1934, only 9 of a total of 540 antitrust charges levied by the Department of Justice involved vertical integration. Alcoa seems to have been especially vulnerable on this point. See Richard A. Posner, "A Statistical Study of Antitrust Enforcement," *Journal of Law and Economics*, XIII (October 1970), p. 398.
12. Haskell testified later that Davis had settled simply to win peace. Haskell himself was put on an Alcoa retainer as part of the settlement in order to prevent any further legal action. See Haskell's testimony, Equity No. 85–73, stenographer's minutes, pp. 2668–77.
13. The Government's bill of complaint, Equity No. 85–73.
14. Campbell, *Global Mission*, p. 229.

15. Ellis Hawley, *The New Deal and the Problem of Monopoly* (Princeton, NJ; Princeton University Press, 1966), p. 375; *The New Yorker* (January 31, 1942), p. 38.

16. Gibbons, "Talk to Research Department," pp. 34–5.

17. *The Pittsburgh Gazette*, October 17, 1928; *The New York Times*, February 18, 1930; *Fortune* (March 1930), reprint, n.p. *Fortune* was attempting to defend Alcoa's position, praising the company's best efforts to develop the aluminum industry by actively fostering competition in downstream markets.

18. Murphy, "The Mellons of Pittsburgh," p. 15; Keith L. Bryant, Jr., and Henry C. Delthoff, *A History of American Business* (Englewood Cliffs, NJ: Prentice-Hall, 1983), pp. 275–6.

19. As late as November 13, 1940, A. V. Davis was complaining bitterly about the company's continuing reputation for being "controlled by the Mellon interests" (A. V. Davis to Marshall Field, AA, env. 167A).

20. Hickman interview.

21. *Pittsburgh Press*, October 31, 1933. The title of the dispatch was "Flock of Vice-Presidents Support Aluminum Chief."

22. Hawley, *New Deal*, chap. 22.

23. Ellis Hawley, "Antitrust," *Encyclopedia of American Economic History*, p. 780. In the wake of the recession of 1937, New Dealers began to attribute the collapse of recovery "to misuse of business power, to pricing decisions that had negated the effects of monetary expansion, and to the withholding of investment for political reasons."

24. A telling account of the trial's length and Arnold's handling of it appeared in two issues of *The New Yorker* (January 24 and 31, 1942).

25. The *New York Times*' coverage of the trial depicted a company on the defensive against a well-articulated government attack. Writing in *The New Yorker* (January 24, 1942), pp. 25, 28, Alva Johnston deplored Arnold's use of the press as a forum for making a case outside the courtroom with a barrage of innuendo and misreporting of facts that would never have stood up in court. Irving Lipkowitz, a partisan to the Government's case, recalled his own understanding that it was Alcoa's policy to refrain from publicity during the case, leaving the advantage in the media to the Antitrust Division (Lipkowitz interview).

26. Equity No. 85–73, 44 F Supp. 97, at 116–50.

27. On market structure, see *Alcoa Brief*, I, pp. 360ff. Caffey was persuaded by Alcoa's presentation on these points.

28. Equity No. 85–73, 44 Supp. 97, at 168–79.

29. Ibid., at 211–14.

30. Ibid., 308–9; Equity No. 85–73, Haskell testimony, stenographer's minutes, pp. 2668–844.

31. Equity No. 85–73, 44 F Supp. 97, at 150–65; Davis testimony, stenographer's minutes, pp. 20855–6.

32. Equity No. 85–73, 44 Supp. 97, at 230–86.
33. Ibid., at 309.
34. Ibid., at 310; *The New Yorker* (January 24, 1942), p. 30.
35. Lipkowitz interview.
36. Ibid.
37. *The New Yorker* (January 24, 1942), pp. 27–30, (January 31, 1942), pp. 39–41.
38. Carr, *Alcoa*, pp. 229–30.
39. Equity No. 85–73, 148F 2d at 416.
40. *Standard Oil Co. of New Jersey v. United States*, 221 U.S. 106.
41. Equity No. 85–73, 148 F.2d at 416, 431.
42. Ibid., at 425.
43. Ibid., at 427.
44. Alcoa's claim that its earnings over time averaged ten percent of stockholders' equity was based on calculations that expressed earnings as a percentage of capital employed (paid-in capital plus retained earnings). If earnings were expressed as a percentage of capital paid in, as government authorities did, then earnings amounted to fifty-five percent of investment. See Alderfer and Michl, *Economics of the American Industry*, p. 104.
45. Equity No. 85–73, 148 F. 2d at 416, 426–7, 432–4. 439–45.
46. Ibid., at 446.
47. Robert H. Bork, *The Antitrust Paradox: A Policy at War with Itself* (New York: Basic Books, 1978); A. D. Neale, *The Antitrust Laws of the U.S.A.: A Study of Competition Enforced by Law*, 2d edition (London: Cambridge University Press, 1970), p. 112 [emphasis added].
48. George W. Stocking and Myron W. Watkins, *Monopoly and Free Enterprise* (New York: Twentieth Century Fund, 1951), pp. 288–9. Cf. Bork, *The Antitrust Paradox*, pp. 61ff., who emphasizes the intention of the framers of the act to protect consumer welfare.
49. See, for example, the brief treatment of this significant development in Lawrence M. Friedman, *A History of American Law* (New York: Simon and Schuster, 1973), pp. 591ff.
50. Hickman interview.
51. Neale, *Antitrust Laws*, pp. 110 and fn.
52. Richard M. Hunt (a son of Roy Hunt) to John E. Wright and George Smith, January 28, 1987, copy in possession of the author. Richard Hunt relates a charming coincidence in which he was dating the granddaughter of Judge Augustus Hand just after the war: "Through her I met Judge Learned Hand once and he seemed amused about my family relations and also about my questions on his court decision. What I recall specifically was the urgency with which he pursued the distinctions between Alcoa's intentions 'that may have been respectable' and the actual fact that Alcoa had become a *de facto* monopoly that was not in the public interest." Hunt goes on to say that he found

Hand, despite all the trouble he had caused Alcoa, to be "a marvelous, witty and learned (he lived up to his name) man with a twinkle not a glower in his eye."

53. See above, note 43.
54. Hickman interview.
55. "Details of Aluminum Company of America Production and Fabrication Expansions from January 1937 to July 1941," Part II of a draft report written by William White, 1941 [hereafter referred to as "White Report"], AA, env. 141, pp. 1–12; *Annual Reports* for 1937–8.
56. Ibid.; "Alcoa Bible," p. 191; Campbell, *Global Mission*, p. 245.
57. "White Report," p. 23; "Alcoa Bible," p. 191.
58. "Alcoa Bible," pp. 191–2; *Annual Report*, 1939; Muller, *Light Metals Monopoly*, pp. 202–4.
59. Ibid., pp. 196–7, 203–5; U.S. Senate, 77th Congress, 1st Session, *Hearings before a Special Committee Investigating the National Defense Program, Pursuant to S. Res. 71*, part 3, May 12, 14, 15, June 16, 17, 1941, *Aluminum* (hereafter cited as Truman Committee Hearings), pp. 716, 743–4, 817, and part 7, p. 2116. In fact, the price per pound of aluminum had come down to $0.15 only after severe public criticism of Alcoa's attempt to hold the line at $0.17.
60. Reynolds, himself, testified on this in ibid., part 3, p. 752. The story is related in greater detail in I. F. Stone, *Business as Usual, The First Year of Defense* (New York: Modern Age Books, 1941), p. 54.
61. Robert Sheehan, "Look at the Reynolds Boys Now," *Fortune* (August 1953), pp. 106–13.
62. 77th Congress, 1st Session. Sen. Rep. No. 480, Report Mr. Mead, June 26, 1941, p. 3; Truman Committee Hearings, part 3, p. 891.
63. Muller, *Light Metals Monopoly*, pp. 200–1.
64. *Moody's Manual*, 1943, p. 383; Carr, *Alcoa*, pp. 249–50.
65. Campbell, *Global Mission*, p. 298.
66. Harold Stein, "The Disposal of the Aluminum Plants," in Harold Stein (ed.), *Public Administration and Policy Development* (New York: Harcourt Brace, 1952), p. 318; Muller, *Light Metals Monopoly*, p. 200.
67. Carr, *Alcoa*, pp. 250ff.
68. *Annual Reports*, 1941–5; Carr, *Alcoa*, p. 258.
69. "Alcoa Bible," p. 18; *Annual Report*, 1942.
70. John F. Clark to Laurel Hummer, August 14, 1986, copy in possession of the author.
71. Carr, *Alcoa*, app. The quoted phrase is from Engle et al., *Aluminum*, pp. 114–15.
72. Fischer interview.
73. On Zonarich's role in the anti-Communist purge, see Meyerhuber, "Organizing Alcoa," pp. 212–14. On the Cleveland struggles, I have followed accounts in the *The New York Times*, June 3, 10, 11, 12, 13, 1941, September 23, 26, 1942, February 27, and July 25, 1943.

74. I have followed accounts of the strikes in the public press. See esp. *The New York Times*, July 8, 9, 23, 24, 1943, October 3, 1945, and January 12, 1946.

75. Ibid., July 26, 27, August 1, 1940; March 6, 10, 13, 22, 23, 1941; April 18, 19, 21, 23, May 4, and July 8, 9, 23, 1943; October 3, 12, 1945; Lipkowitz interview.

76. In the summer of 1943, starting wages ranged from a low of $0.60 to $0.65 per hour in the Southeast to a high of $0.80 to $0.90 per hour in the Northwest. The NWLB was reluctant to close these differentials too quickly on the grounds that to do so might prove disruptive to local economic and industry conditions. See Engle et al., *Aluminum*, pp. 105–6.

77. *The New York Times*, August 16, 18, 20, 29, 1942.

78. Fishcher and Harper interviews.

79. Engle et al., *Aluminum*, pp. 104–5. In April 1943, the average aluminum worker earned $1.026 compared with $1.019 in iron and steel and $0.998 in nonferrous metals.

80. Ibid., pp. 102–5, 110–11. In 1939, the labor costs per metric ton of bauxite, alumina, and aluminum stood at $8.28, $8.03, and $21.31, respectively. By 1943, the labor costs had increased to $11.34, $9.50, and $31.85, respectively.

81. Pinkston, *Local 309*, p. 44–5.

82. Ibid., pp. 47–9; *The New York Times*, March 12, 17, 22, and December 2, 3, 1946.

83. Subsequent annual reports adjusted these figures downward to account for a shortening of special amortization provisions allowed by the Government for wartime plant and facilities.

84. Carr, *Alcoa*, chap. 18; Muller, *Light Metals Monopoly*, chap. VIII; memorandum from Stanley V. Malcuit to Roy A. Hunt, re: "Germany's Master Plan," February 10, 1959, private copy in the possession of Richard Hunt.

85. "Alcoa Bible," p. 186; Muller, *Light Metals Monopoly*, pp. 202–4.

86. Joseph Barkin and Charles A. Walsh, *Germany's Master Plan: The Story of Industrial Offensive* (New York: Duell, Sloan and Pearce, 1944), pp. 47, 114, 211, and chap. 16, saw the entire arrangement as I. G. Farben's means for limiting American magnesium production while Hitler built his air force. Alcoa, meanwhile, benefitted from a tacit price policy that would keep the general price of magnesium in a 3:2 ratio with that of aluminum. Such arguments, which were aired in Congressional hearings and which were echoed by the DOJ (see Muller, *Light Metals Monopoly*, pp. 190–2; Wendell Berge, *Cartels: Challenge to a Free World* [Washington, DC: Public Affairs Press, 1944], pp. 221–25), underestimated the technical problems in producing magnesium on a cost-competitive basis and ignored the relatively high cost of aluminum in Germany.

87. *Annual Reports*, 1945, 1946.
88. Campbell, *Global Mission*, pp. 251, 374.
89. "Aluminum Reborn," *Fortune* (May 1946, reprint), n.p.; Muller, *Light Metals Monopoly*, pp. 201–2.
90. The history of the disposal of the aluminum plants is chronicled in close detail by Stein, "Disposal." See esp. pp. 320–2.
91. Ibid.; F. R. Darrow, memorandum, "Aluminum Company of America," October 23, 1946, AA, env. 288.
92. Stein, "Disposal," pp. 322–6; Lipkowitz interview.
93. *Fortune* (May 1946), reprint, n.p.
94. Stein, "Disposal," p. 315. In canceling, the RFC invoked a provision in the master lease that gave it a right to terminate Aloca's leases on sixty days' notice, if capacity utilization fell below forty percent in any six-month period. Alcoa felt that the Government had done some creative accounting in demonstrating an across-the-board decline in capacity utilization for all DPC plants since their peak production in 1943, but the company's objections were unavailing.
95. Carr, *Alcoa*, p. 268; Stein, "Disposal," pp. 331–6.
96. Ibid., pp. 322, 325, 332. Symington's confirmation was delayed for a month because of his reputation for hostility to antitrust lawyers as "impractical theoreticians." But, as is often the case with confirmation hearings, a statement made in the defense of candidacy became a pledge for future action, and Symington soon proved to be a stout antimonopolist when it came to settling the Government's business with Alcoa.
97. The WSB and the RFC jointly sent a letter to companies soliciting their interest in the DPC aluminum plants on August 30 in conjunction with the termination of Alcoa's leases on the plants.
98. Stein, "Disposal," pp. 336ff.; *The Aluminum Industry*, letter from the Attorney General referred to the Committee on Military Affairs, 19th Congress, 1st Session, Washington, DC, 1945, pp. 9–11.
99. *The New York Times*, October 17, 1945.
100. Hickman interview.
101. Ibid. This view is corroborated by the Hunt interview.
102. *The New York Times*, January 6, 1946; Stein, "Disposal," pp. 345–7.
103. Ibid.; *Fortune* (May 1946), reprint, n.p.
104. Lipkowitz interview.
105. *Fortune* (May 1946), reprint, n.p.
106. Stein, "Disposal," pp. 347–52.
107. "The Arrival of Henry Kaiser," *Fortune* (July 1951), p. 68.
108. Subcommittee on the Study of Monopoly Power of the House Judiciary Committee, *Aluminum Hearings*, 82d Congress, 1st Session, 1951, Part 1, pp. 902–5.
109. Stein, "Disposal," pp. 352–6; Equity No. 85–73, 91 F Supp. 333.
110. Darrow memorandum, "Aluminum Company."

111. Ibid.; *Annual Report*, 1946; *Modern Metals* (December 1950), p. 23.
112. Ibid.; Nathaniel H. Engle, Homer E. Gregory, and Robert Mosse, *Aluminum: An Industrial Marketing Survey*, (Chicago: Irwin, 1945), pp. 172–8.
113. Ibid.; Davis to Field, November 13, 1940; Engle et al., *Aluminum*, pp. 129–30.
114. Close interview.
115. Interview with William E. Stevenson, July 18–20, 1979, by Geoffrey Blodgett; transcript on file at the OCA.
116. This and the following two paragraphs are based mainly on the Magee, Hickman, Hunt, and Harper interviews.
117. Interviews with Magee, Hickman, Harper, and Hunt; *Alcoa News*, January–February 1978, pp. 2–4; *The New York Times*, October 17, 1977.
118. Hunt interview. A copy of the organizational chart of 1942 is included with a memorandum from one of its drafters, Raynal W. Andrews, which was sent to the AA ca. January 1984.
119. Magee interview.
120. I have found no record of the number of managers who left the company, although anecdotal evidence suggests that in both quality and number, the defection was substantial. Alcoa's total number of employees declined from a peak of more than 90,000 at the height of the war to less than 40,000 at the end of 1946.
121. Donald Johnson interview. Johnson was impressed by the company's ability to hold its more senior supervisors. He said that they "had a built in loyalty" that was hard to crack. "Old Alcoa people wouldn't even talk."
122. "Alcoa Bible," pp. 6ff., 113ff., and passim.
123. *Annual Report*, 1946.

Chapter 6

1. Close interview.
2. Growth in real GNP is taken from U.S. Department of Commerce, Bureau of Economic Analysis, *The National Income and Product Accounts of the United States, 1929–74*, p. 6.
3. Merton J. Peck, *Competition in the Aluminum Industry, 1945–1958* (Cambridge, MA: Harvard University Press, 1961), chap. IX, is the fullest expression of the view that aluminum expansion was a creature of government stockpiling and amortization policies.
4. George J. Stanley, "Postwar Aluminum Marketing Revolves Around Cost and Volume," *Iron Age* (September 6, 1945), p. 129.
5. Harper and George interviews.
6. *Annual Reports*, 1948 and 1957.

7. William B. Harris, "The Splendid Retreat of Alcoa," *Fortune* (October 1955), p. 122.

8. Stanford Research Institute, *The Impact of the Aluminum Industry on the Economy of the Pacific Northwest* (Vancouver, WA: 1954), n.p.; Cowles, *True Story of Aluminum*, chap. I and app. A.

9. Ibid.; *Modern Metals* (December 1950), 23; *Annual Reports*, 1946–49.

10. Department of Commerce, Business and Defense Services Administration, *Materials Survey: Aluminum*, (Washington, DC, 1956), VII–14; *Annual Reports*, 1950–6.

11. Hickman interview. The *Alcoa News*, January 1966, explained that the initial requirements for the stockpile "were calculated to serve the country through a five-year atomic war. Later the five years was cut to three. Today... requirements are set... for brush-war emergencies only...."

12. Charles E. Silberman, "How Much Can Business Borrow," *Fortune* (January 1956), p. 131, noted that Alcoa's debt was conservatively managed by contemporary standards.

13. Peck, *Competition in the Aluminum Industry*, pp. 150–4; *Fortune* (October 1955), pp. 120, 244.

14. Ibid.; *Modern Metals* (December 1950), p. 28; *Business Week* (1962), reprint, n.p.

15. *Annual Reports*, 1951–7.

16. Peck, *Competition in the Aluminum Industry*, pp. 151–2, notes that at the end of the third quarter in 1955, "the weighted average effective rate of interest to maturity for Alcoa's debt was 3.03 percent compared to 4.335 percent for Reynolds and 3.776 percent for Kaiser." See also Equity No. 85–73, 153 F. Supp. 132 at 152.

17. Peck, *Competition in the Aluminum Industry*, Table 27, p. 163.

18. *Fortune* (October 1955), p. 118.

19. Ibid.

20. Hersh, *The Mellons*, p. 383, writes that Wilson was elevated over Roy Hunt's objection and cites "Leon Higby" (presumably Hickman) as his source. Though possible, I have no confirmation of this or any other conflict over the succession.

21. Contemporary accounts of Wilson's importance to the company appear in *Fortune* (October 1955), pp. 118–20; *Modern Metals* (December 1950), pp. 22–33; *Forbes* (August 15, 1951), pp. 13, 15; *Pittsburgh Press*, March 6, 1955.

22. The data on shareholders was supplied by the Corporate Secretary's Office at Alcoa.

23. *Annual Reports*, 1946–51. Only one vice president, Thomas D. Jolly, had been a corporate officer before the end of the war.

24. Hunt interview.

25. Hickman interview.

26. *Business Week* (February 4, 1956), pp. 42–5; Magee interview.

27. Van Horn interview.
28. Margaret B. W. Graham, "Alcoa R&D and the Loss of Monopoly," paper delivered at the convention of the Organization of American Historians, April 12, 1986.
29. This line of interpretation was first developed in The Winthrop Group, Inc., "Alcoa's Corporate Culture: Enduring Strengths and Embedded Constraints" (October 1983), a report prepared for Alcoa's management.
30. Ibid.; Van Horn and Stroup interviews.
31. Graham, "Alcoa R&D and the Loss of Monopoly;" Parry interview.
32. Favre, Recko, and Gantz interviews.
33. See the Close and Gantz interviews. The quoted phrase comes from Wilmot's testimony in *Hearings, Aluminum Industry* (1958), p. 41.
34. *Business Week* (December 19, 1953), p. 118. I have not been able to locate a copy of the reported 1949 survey.
35. *Modern Metals* (December 1950), p. 34; *Forbes* (August 15, 1951), pp. 12–16.
36. *Annual Report*, 1952. The Foundation did not mark the beginning of Alcoa's corporate contributions, but offered the company an opportunity to "satisfy such obligations at a minimum cost to shareholders."
37. Shelby Stewman and Joel Tarr, "Public–Private Partnerships in Pittsburgh: An Approach to Governance," in *Pittsburgh–Sheffield, Sister Cities*, pp. 150ff.
38. *Fortune* (October 1955), pp. 118–20.
39. *Annual Reports*, 1952, 1956. Alcoa also enjoyed growing markets in bridge and highway structures, containers, and chemicals.
40. A. M. Sperber, *Murrow: His Life and Times* (New York: Freundlich Books, 1986), p. 357.
41. *Business Week* (December 19, 1953), p. 115.
42. Sperber, *Murrow*, pp. 453–4.
43. *The New York Times*, May 3, 1955. Sperber, *Murrow*, pp. 483–4, cites Richard Salant of CBS and Charles Mack, a veteran network cameraman and friend of Murrow's, as sources.
44. *Forbes*, (August 15, 1951), p. 15.
45. Equity No. 85–73, 91 F. Supp. 333 (S.D.N.Y., 1950); Equity No. 85–73, 153 F. Supp. 132.
46. Theodore Kovaleff, *Business and Government Policy During the Eisenhower Administration: A Study of the Antitrust Policy of the Antitrust Division of the Justice Department* (Athens, OH: Ohio University Press, 1980), pp. 10–11, 71ff. U.S. House of Representatives, Subcommittee No. 3 on Minerals and Raw Materials, *Report* (Washington, DC, 1956), pp. 44ff.
47. Equity No. 85–73, 91 F. Supp. 333 (S.D.N.Y. 1950), at 364, 415, 416.
48. Ibid., at 347 [emphasis added].
49. Ibid.

50. George interview.
51. Ibid.
52. Simon N. Whitney makes this point in *Antitrust Policies: American Experience in Twenty Industries*, 2 vols., I (New York: The Twentieth Century Fund, 1958), p. 100.
53. Hunt interview; Campbell, *Global Mission*, pp. 413–17.
54. Equity No. 85–73, 91 F. Supp. 333, passim; Whitney, *Antitrust Policies*, I, p. 100.
55. Equity No. 85–73, 91 F. Supp. 333, passim.
56. Ibid.
57. The quote is from George Stocking, *Workable Competition and Antitrust Policy* (Nashville, TN: Vanderbilt University Press, 1961), p. 143. See also Walter Adams, "The Aluminum Case: Legal Victory—Economic Defeat," *American Economic Review* (December 1951), pp. 915–22.
58. Equity No. 85–73, 153 F. Supp. 132 (S.D.N.Y., 1957).
59. Judge Hand's Decision 15 Years Later," speech by Lawrence Litchfield, Jr., President Aluminum Company of America at the Graduate School of Industrial Administration, Carnegie Institute of Technology (April 28, 1961) in the General Speech File, Alcoa Headquarters. Simon Whitney noted that the per-share value of Alcoa's stock was ten times greater than it had been in 1941 just after its first-round antitrust victory (*Antitrust Policies*, I, p. 115).
60. See, for example, the interviews with W. H. Krome George, Charles Parry, Alfred Hunt, Frederick Close, and Leon Hickman.
61. Lipkowitz interview.
62. Peck, *Competition in the Aluminum Industry*, pp. 27–8. Peck's analysis of the industry was the first significant scholarly economic study of the industry to appear since 1937, when Wallace's *Market Control* had been published.
63. Stanley Malcuit, "The Broad Aspects of Competition and Its Effects on Alcoa," Edited . . . from Extemporaneous Talk Given at Education and Training Conference, Tapoco Lodge, NC (December 2, 1959), AA, uncatalogued, pp. 7, 10; Malcuit, "Economics of the Aluminum Industry," unpublished manuscript, ALA; House Select Committee on Small Business, Subcommittee No. 3, *Hearings, Aluminum Industry* (Washington, DC, 1958), p. 57.
64. The economic literature on price leadership is extensive. Useful summaries of the problem are provided by F. M. Scherer, *Industrial Market Structure and Economic Performance* (Chicago: Rand McNally, 1970), esp. chap. 6; A. D. H. Kaplan, J. B. Dirlam, and R. F. Lanzillotti, *Pricing in Big Business: A Case Approach* (Washington, DC: The Brookings Institution, 1958).
65. Malcuit, "The Broad Aspects of Competition," p. 12; Peck, *Competition in the Aluminum Industry*, pp. 41–2.

66. Pig aluminum was distinguished from unalloyed ingot until August 2, 1960, when the term "pig" was dropped in industry discussions of prices. By that time, the quality of pig and ingot had converged. Before 1960, ingot was marked up from pig as follows:

Year	Markup
1944–53	$0.01
1953–5	$0.015
1955–6	$0.0019
1956–60	$0.0021

Charles River Associates, *An Economic Analysis of the Aluminum Industry*, prepared for the Property Management and Disposal Service, General Services Administration, Washington, DC (March 1971), p. 4.

67. *Hearings, Aluminum Industry* (1957), pp. 136–8.

68. Charles River Associates, *The Economic Effects of Pollution Controls on the Nonferrous Metals Industry: Aluminum*, prepared for the Council on Environmental Quality (December 1971).

69. R. S. Reynolds, Jr., and Dusty Rhoades (of Kaiser) testified in 1955 that aluminum prices were too low, but that they could not sell at a higher price than Alcoa. See *Hearings, Aluminum Industry* (1955), pp. 243–4, 314.

70. *Monopoly Power Hearings* (1951), pp. 632–4, 678. This kind of pricing behavior corresponds to Herbert A. Simon's model of "satisficing" behavior, a perfectly rational acceptance of an adequate, though not maximum, level of current profits keyed to expectations of achieving higher long-term gains. See "A Behavioral Model of Rational Choice," *Quarterly Journal of Economics*, 69 (February 1955), pp. 99–118.

71. Ibid.

72. Malcuit, "Economics of the Aluminum Industry," p. 422; Peck, *Competition in the Aluminum Industry*, chap. IV. Of course, secondary smelters most often served an "overflow market" in which their aluminum was available at market prices, but the overflow character of their market caused great instability in secondary prices (Peck, p. 78).

73. Ibid., p. 42. The industry's weighted mill cost of producing primary aluminum pig increased from $9.58 to $13.50 between 1947 and 1955 due mainly to increased power and manufacturing costs (Malcuit, "Economics of the Aluminum Industry," p. 386). The surge in prices between 1955 and 1957 was explained by Alcoa as reflecting a substantial increase in costs of production, especially labor costs, which had increased during that time by $0.46 per hour (*Hearings, Aluminum Industry* [1958], p. 65).

74. Malcuit, "The Broad Aspects of Competition," p. 24.

75. In 1957, for example, it was reported that Alcoa consumed about 69% of its own primary output; Reynolds, 58%; Kaiser, 46% (*Hearings,*

Aluminum Industry [1958], pp. 47–8). This was sharply down from the 80–5% that had been consumed internally in times of greater shortages.

76. Cf. Peck, *Competition in the Aluminum Industry*, pp. 62–72.

77. *Hearings, Aluminum Industry* (1955), p. 266.

78. Peck, *Competition in the Aluminum Industry*, p. 82. The "paradoxical" effects of the antitrust problem were nicely described in a different context by *Business Week* (February 1, 1964), p. 21.

79. Ibid., chap. IX.

80. Ibid., pp. 173–81.

81. Ibid., p. 437; "The Light Metals Industry," pamphlet published by *Modern Metals* (Chicago, 1955).

82. Alfred E. Kahn, "A Legal and Economic Appraisal of the 'New' Sherman and Clayton Acts," *Yale Law Journal* (January 1954), p. 304.

83. Hickman Interview. There is some question as to how much influence primary producers could exercise over those margins in any case. Any narrowing of margins between flexibly priced extrusions and rigidly priced ingot might just as likely be a result of highly competitive conditions in the extrusion markets as a manifestation of the ability of primary producers to control ingot prices.

84. *Fortune* (October 1955), p. 118. Ironically, Alcoa came to rue this agreement in the 1957–8 recession, when the company had to cut back its own production even further than it might have in order to honor its commitment to purchase ingot from Aluminium Limited.

85. See the testimony of R. S. Reynolds, Jr., on this point in *Hearings, Aluminum Industry* (1955), pp. 245–6; *Business Week* (February 4, 1956), pp. 132–3.

86. *Iron Age* (March 1946), p. 126. Aluminium Limited had more than a $0.03 per pound cost advantage in smelting in 1949 (First Boston Corporation, *Aluminum: The Industry and the Four North American Producers* [Boston, MA, ca. 1951], p. 37). The aluminum tariff was reduced from $0.03 to $0.02 per pound in 1948 and then to $0.015 in 1951 (Whitney, *Antitrust Policies*, II, p. 105).

87. Peck, *Competition in the Aluminum Industry*, pp. 47–51. Nathaniel Davis of Aluminium Limited demurred from the Soviet dumping theory espoused by American producers, citing instead excess domestic capacity.

88. The tenacity with which the company clung to this point of view is expressed well by E. B. Wilber, "Research and Resources," a speech delivered to the Los Angeles Society of Securities Analysts, November 17, 1958, AA, uncatalogued.

89. *Iron Age* (March 1946), p. 128; Robert Sheehan, "Look at the Reynolds Boys Now," *Fortune* (August 1953), pp. 110, 172; *Fortune* (October 1955), p. 120; Robert Sheehan, "Kaiser Aluminum – Henry J.'s Marvelous Mistake," *Fortune* (July 1956), pp. 81–2.

90. *Business Week* (April 30, 1955), pp. 42–4.

91. Ibid.; *Annual Reports*, 1949–57.

92. Peck, *Competition in the Aluminum Industry*, chap. XI. Advances in many fabricating techniques, such as welding and finishing, came from smaller, specialized producers or from customers of end products for whom the payoffs in those areas were more immediately felt. But, although Peck credits smaller producers with most of the innovation in those areas on the basis of patents, not all techniques were likely to have been patented, especially in cases where the primary producers may have wanted to treat techniques as proprietary secrets.

93. *Fortune* (October 1955), p. 120.

94. See Alcoa and Reynolds testimonies in *Hearings, Aluminum Industry* (1955), pp. 44, 229, 237–8.

95. Peck, *Competition in the Aluminum Industry*, p. 148.

96. Meyerhuber, "Organizing Alcoa," pp. 216–19.

97. *Agreement Between the Aluminum Company of America and the International Union, United Steelworkers of America*, May 8, 1947 (Knoxville, TN, n.d.); *Annual Report*, 1949; Pinkston, *Local 309*, pp. 53ff.

98. This and the following paragraphs are based largely on interviews with Jack Morber, a former industrial relations vice president at Alcoa, and Frank Kramer, his successor, and both recorded interviews and unrecorded conversations with union officials and rank-and-file workers in Massena, New York; Alcoa, Tennessee; Bauxite, Arkansas; Cleveland, Ohio; and Warrick, Indiana.

99. Morber Interview.

100. In 1952, "there was no standardized method at arriving at a wage rate for a new job or a changed job. It was strictly a negotiating process." By 1956, that had changed through the development of "joint procedures." See ibid.

101. Lyle R. Mercer, "Worker–Management Communications – A Key to Improved Employee Relations" (1948), AA, env. 531.

102. Ibid.

103. Fischer interview.

104. The *Annual Reports* of the 1950s complained about the problem of high labor costs while generally ignoring the problems of labor–management conflict.

105. *The New York Times*, October, 17, November, 10, December 8, 1949; January 21, 26, 27, and 30, April 18, July 10, 17, 18, 20, 26, and 28, 1952; August, 1 and 14, 1956.

106. Kramer interview; Pinkston, *Local 309*, pp. 54–5.

107. Ibid., p. 60. The concept of guaranteed wages was an old one, dating back to the late nineteenth century when the National Wallpaper Company agreed to guarantee members of the Machine Printers and Color Mixer's Union eleven months' employment.

108. The Alcoa base wages were provided by the company's Accounting Department.

109. Farrish interview.

110. Fischer interview.

111. For this and the following paragraphs, I have relied on background information provided by already cited interviews with Frank Magee, Leon Hickman, Alfred M. Hunt, and Kent Van Horn. I have also followed Chandler, *Strategy and Structure*, pp. 326ff.

112. *Business Week* (June 6, 1953), pp. 71–80.

113. *The New York Times*, October 17, 1977; *Alcoa News*, January–February, 1978, pp. 2–4.

114. *Pittsburgh Press*, March 6, 1955.

115. *Fortune* (October 1955), p. 119.

116. See Aluminum Company of America, Partial Organization, May 1957, AA, env. 1059A.

117. *Fortune* (October 1955), p. 119.

118. The Harper, George, and Parry interviews all offer some support for the interpretation of organizational problems I have offered in this paragraph, which was confirmed by informal conversations I have had with other managers who worked at Alcoa during the 1950s.

119. Chandler, *Strategy and Structure*, p. 339.

120. Chandler makes the point about the importance of informal lines of authority at Alcoa in ibid., pp. 339–41.

121. The quoted phrase is from a paper by Bettye H. Pruitt, "Alcoa Laboratories: Impetus and Direction in Incremental Innovation" (unpublished ms., The Winthrop Group, Inc., 1986).

122. For this and the next paragraph, see ibid., pp. 24ff. The relevant correspondence is E. H. Dix to C. F. Nagel, Jr., March 26, 1953; T. W. Bossert to J. H. Alden, E. V. Blackmun, and H. J. Rowe, April 21, 1953; E. H. Dix to C. F. Nagel, Jr., November 19, 1954; T. W. Bossert to Division and Department Heads, April 20, 1960, ALA.

123. Chandler, *Strategy and Structure*, pp. 338–41.

124. *Annual Report*, 1957.

125. Chandler, *Strategy and Structure*, pp. 339–40.

Chapter 7

1. Kennedy interview.

2. Magee and Hickman interviews. Litchfield's election as president in September 1960 was recognized by the board as a "holding operation" until younger candidates for top management, such men as John Harper, head of production, and John Mitchell, head of Alcoa's international business, became more seasoned.

3. *Insight* (November 10, 1986), p. 42.

4. *Annual Reports.*
5. *Modern Metals* (June, 1959), p. 2; *Business Week* (April 16, 1960), p. 168.
6. The proliferation of product lines is easily traced through the *Annual Reports.* From informal conversations with Alcoa managers, I have been struck by differences in opinion as to whether Alcoa was really committed to developing end-use finished products in the 1950s. Some have told me that products, such as Alcoa Wrap, were developed more for the sake of public relations without much concern for their profitability. My own conclusion, based on my reading of the marketing dilemmas posed by the postwar competitive environment, was that Alcoa entered end-use markets in earnest but found that such markets were neither as attractive nor as manageable as anticipated.
7. Fetterolf interview.
8. Frank Magee tried to justify Alcoa's departure from its customary reluctance to compete with its fabricator–customers, pointing out that many fabricators were integrating backward into semifinished operations, thus competing with the traditional core of Alcoa's own value-added operations (*Business Week* [April 16, 1960], pp. 168–176).
9. Magee and Hickman interviews; *Annual Report*, 1959.
10. Leon Hickman explained that these acquisitions were truly regarded by the company as "innocuous" expansions of some of its operations and that he was reluctant to approach the Republican Antitrust Division during the late 1950s because "the Republicans were always on the defensive, anti-trust-wise. . . ." He relied instead on advice from Herbert Bergson, former antitrust chief of the Truman administration, who had been hired by Alcoa's Washington office. Bergson, Hickman said, warned him that the Eisenhower antitrust division would not likely "grant approval of anything unless it is so clear that you needn't have taken it there" and pronounced Alcoa's plans as "defensible." See the Hickman interview.
11. 214 F Supp 501; 1964 SCT 1283. The climate during these proceedings was certainly not improved by Alcoa's indictment on charges of having attempted to fix prices on aluminum conductor cable in the late 1950s, a charge to which the company pleaded *nolo contendere* in 1964.
12. 233 F. Supp. 718.
13. Ibid. Close's memorandum, dated February 11, 1960, is cited in the court's decision. The relevant passage reads as follows: "I am completely aware of the financial situation confronting us but in view of what is going on in the building trades, I believe . . . that it is essential that we move rapidly to establish ourselves as the leader in this business with the ultimate objective of getting at least 40 percent of all the business in those items which we would manufacture in the Cupples set-up."
14. Ibid.

15. *Annual Reports; Forbes* (April 1, 1961), p. 15; *Steel* (August 13, 1962), pp. 61–3; George Bookman, "Alcoa Strikes Back," *Fortune* (November 1962), p. 116.

16. *Forbes* (September 1, 1965), pp. 20–1. Alcoa had learned a hard lesson in 1960–1, when, in an attempt to hold the line in conduit and rod, wire, and bar markets, it lost market share to lower-priced competitors.

17. *The New York Times*, February 13, 1966.

18. Leon E. Hickman to Buford Ellington, Director, Office of Emergency Planning, March 17, 1965, AA, uncatalogued; Hickman interview.

19. Ibid; Hickman interview. In truth, Hickman noted, much of the stockpile was of inferior quality and that outdoor storage had oxidized the metal so that it would cost "a cent or two to clean it up." "Who would buy it? It was a white elephant, really. But I think, undoubtedly, it demoralized our market."

20. Memorandum of Understanding: Part I. – Government Program for Use of Excess Stockpile Aluminum to Fill Government Orders and Contract...between the United States of America...and Aluminum Company of America, November 23, 1965, AA, uncatalogued. Alcoa was scheduled to take 29.4 percent of the total, based on its estimated share of installed primary aluminum capacity in 1965.

21. *Alcoa News* (January 1966), p. 7.

22. Alcoa executives, who believed that they had acted in good faith from the beginning, were left to puzzle over Lyndon Johnson's "irrational" behavior. Hickman continued to feel years after the event that Johnson had "booby-trapped us into going ahead," considering that he "could have put up a warning to John Harper very easily not to do it [follow Olin's price increase]." Still, he added, "I don't think the lesson is to look out for hot-tempered Presidents. The lesson basically is don't let the Government into the aluminum business." (See the Jones and Hickman interviews.)

23. *Fortune* (November 1965), p. 118.

24. *Annual Reports.*

25. Magee interview.

26. Ibid.

27. *Annual Report*, 1957. The Brokopondo agreement provided that Alcoa build a 150,000-kilowatt hydroelectric station on the Surinam River, which it would operate for seventy-five years. In addition to powering a smelter, originally projected as a 60,000-ton facility in Paranam, the hydroelectric station was to serve broader national needs. Surinam, for its part, was to provide land and basic infrastructure facilities and was to remove the population and buildings from the area of construction.

28. Magee interview; *Annual Report*, 1958.

29. Magee interview. The decision was made casually enough. As Magee

told it: "I remember we had a big party at Fox Chapel and he [one Bill Thomas of British Aluminium] kept hammering away at us.... He said, 'You goddam Yankees. You indicated you were interested, but I'm flying tonight to England and I'm going to talk to Lord Portal tomorrow morning. I'm going to call you tomorrow morning. Are you going to say yes or are you going to say no?' Well, he called and we talked it over with Chief and the rest of the people and we agreed to it." Krome George (interview) remembered that Lord Portal came to confer with Alcoa executives before the decision was finally taken. Magee and George differed as to Alcoa's interest in British Aluminium: Magee stressed the importance of the Weipa deposit; George recalled that Alcoa had not yet grasped the significance of Australia's bauxite potential.

30. George interview; *The New York Times*, December 1, 6, and 9, 1958, January 7 and 10, 1959. In the end, Reynolds had reportedly spent $45 million in cash, while Tube had exchanged its own stock for its share of British Aluminium.

31. For fuller accounts of this episode, see Freeman Lincoln, "The Hottest Thing in Aluminum," *Fortune* (June 1959), pp. 112ff.; Joseph Wechsberg, *The Merchant Bankers* (New York: Pocket Books, 1968), pp. 128–62.

32. The 1958 *Annual Report* stated blandly that "the directors of the British Aluminium Company, Limited, offered to sell 4.5 million shares of authorized, but as yet unissued, common stock of their company to Alcoa in order to obtain capital funds for future expansion.... Before the purchase was completed, however, the control of British Aluminium changed hands, and Alcoa thereupon withdrew, believing this course of action to be in the best interests of its shareholders."

33. Magee interview.

34. Ibid; *The New York Times*, January 25, 1959; *Fortune* (June 1959), p. 111. Reynolds' stock price had normally traded at $20 to $40 per share lower than Alcoa's. On May 1, 1959, it closed at 83¾ to Alcoa's 81⅝.

35. George interview. "They [Lazard Freres] were hurting. They felt they owed us something so they looked around and they brought us the ICI deal."

36. *Annual Reports*.

37. George interview.

38. Ibid; Magee interview; *Annual Report*, 1961.

39. George interview. The negotiations with ICI may have foundered on a clerical blunder. Three sets of estimates were drawn up in Pittsburgh: optimistic, middle-of-the-road, and pessimistic. The worst estimate was clipped in the upper right-hand corner so that copies of it would be identified by a clear black triangle. George's plan was to show ICI board members meeting in Australia the best estimate and

to reveal the middle estimate if necessary. But when he arrived at the ICI House in Melbourne, he "detected a little coolness in the air," and soon discovered to his horror that a copy of the low-end estimate (the triangle was plainly visible) had been sent to his counterparts at ICI. "They had more polite reasons for putting their money in the fertilizer business," said George. (ICI did, in fact, invest in the phosphate business.)

40. *Fortune* (November 1962), p. 160.
41. *Annual Report*, 1962.
42. "International Department, Aluminum Company of America," a memorandum dated May, 1981, AA, uncatalogued, p. 3.
43. *Aluminum by Alcoa* (1969), pp. 101–5; *Annual Report*, 1972.
44. Parry interview.
45. Magee interview.
46. Ibid.; *Annual Reports*.
47. Chandler, *Strategy and Structure*, pp. 337–9.
48. *Fortune* (November 1962), p. 114, observed that Alcoa was still managed by a kind of committee of "veterans" who "still answer their own telephones, still get to work before 9:00 a.m., still eat lunch at the Duquesne Club, and still generally pass up a midday cocktail – all Alcoa traditions of long standing."
49. George interview.
50. *Alcoa News* (December 1963), pp. 4–5.
51. Fetterolf interview.
52. Ibid; Van Horn interview.
53. Frank L. Magee, remarks cited in an R&D subcommittee budget review meeting, August 15, 1960, quoted in Pruitt, "Alcoa Laboratories," p. 27.
54. John H. Alden to members of the Research and Development Committee, October 5, 1960, ALA.
55. Van Horn interview; *Annual Reports*; *Alcoa News* (July 1964), pp. 9–10.
56. This characterization of the subcommittee system is based largely on my reading of drafts of a work in progress on Alcoa R&D by Margaret B. W. Graham and Bettye Pruitt. Their view of the subcommittee system is supported by extensive interviews of managers responsible for R&D from the 1950s through the 1970s.
57. Magee interview. That the trend toward centralization of corporate decision-making was as pronounced as I have interpreted it rests largely on anecdotal evidence from conversations with a wide range of managers who were with the company in the 1950s and 1960s. The organizational charts, read in the absence of other sources of information, do not necessarily support interpretations of trends in either direction.
58. Close interview.

59. *Business Week* (January 18, 1969), pp. 38–46.
60. Gantz, Harper, Hickman, and Close interviews.
61. Ibid; *Close-up: F. J. Close: A Kind of Biography* (1970), on file in the Public Affairs Department, Alcoa headquarters.
62. Close interview.
63. Ibid.; Magee, Hickman, Harper, Van Horn, and Close interviews. Close himself related a story about an instance when Chief Wilson called him on the carpet for his inability to stay within a budget while handing him "$160,000 for my own personal account."
64. *Aluminum by Alcoa*, pp. 50–2; *Annual Report*, 1968.
65. Hickman and Close interviews; *Annual Reports*. In 1972, Alcoa Properties, Inc., owned all or part of Allegheny Center, Washington Plaza Apartments, and the William Penn Hotel in Pittsburgh, Century City and Century Plaza Hotel in Los Angeles, Golden Gateway in San Francisco, East Lake Apartments in Grand Rapids, United Nations Plaza, Staten Island Docks, and Westview Apartments in New York, and Washington Plaza Hotel in Seattle. Alcoa Florida, Inc., was co-developer of a "planned community" near Palm Beach. Century Malibu, Inc., was developing residential real estate in California. Challenge Developments, Inc., was developing single-family dwellings and shopping centers. And the Housing Corporation of America was designing and developing public housing for sale to public-housing authorities.
66. Hickman interview; *Fortune* (November 1962), p. 117. It was rare for Alcoa to serve as its own contractor; virtually all the company's contracting was conducted through partnerships. Reynolds Metals was also moving into real estate and, as usual, did business differently. Reynolds acted as its own developer.
67. Ibid.; *Annual Report*, 1972. Hickman said that Alcoa enjoyed far less success in managing shopping centers and apartment buildings relative to its greater returns from office buildings.
68. Cliff Sands to S. J. Simmons, Jr., September 20, 1961, ALA.
69. *Annual Reports*; Kennedy interview.
70. The shelf life of an all-steel can was about thirty to sixty days, after which the chemical action of the beer, which slowly dissolved the iron in the tinplate, began seriously to affect the flavor and color of the product. See the discussions in the Minutes of the Task Force on Rigid Containers of the Subcommittee on Packaging, passim, ALA; *Brewer's Digest*, November 1963, n.p.
71. Close interview.
72. *Annual Report*, 1962; *Aluminum by Alcoa*, p. 42.
73. F. J. Close, memorandum, "The Steel Industry," April 22, 1964, ALA.
74. Ibid.: *Modern Metals* (June 1959), p. 21.
75. "Warrick Operations Chronological History," AA, uncatalogued.
76. My discussion of the development of can sheet is supported by the Close and Kennedy interviews and *Annual Reports* and is informed

by details made available to me by Alcoa's Rigid Packaging Division Marketing Office.

77. Cliff Sands, "Statement of Policy," July 22, 1968, ALA.
78. According to Alcoa's Rigid Packaging Division's estimates, Alcoa shipped about 67 million pounds of rigid container sheet in 1965, as compared with an industry total of 265 million pounds. In 1970, the shipments for Alcoa and the industry had increased, respectively, to 524 million and 905 million pounds.
79. Cliff Sands, memorandum, "Alcoa Capabilities," November 19, 1968, ALA.
80. Kennedy interview. Five hundred million pounds of recycled aluminum cans, considered to be a reasonable return by the 1980s, could support two optimum-size domestic smelters.
81. *Annual Reports*, 1972, 1980.
82. *Dun's Review* (July 1968), p. 40.
83. John D. Harper, *A View of the Corporate Role in Society* (Pittsburgh: Carnegie-Mellon University Press, 1976), introduction; *John Dickson Harper, Businessman and Leader: An Informal Chronicle* (1976), on file in the Public Affairs Department, Alcoa headquarters; Harper interview.
84. Ibid.; George interview; George Sessions Perry, "How to Get Along with Texans," *The Saturday Evening Post* (March 5, 1955), p. 25.
85. Magee, Hickman, and Van Horn interviews.
86. Harper, *A View of the Corporate Role*, pp. 42–3. He went on to say, "Government is not the enemy. Society is not the enemy. Environmentalists, consumerists, unionists, youth – these are not the enemy. For the corporation, as for all our institutions, the enemy is within. It is in our own narrowness and parochialism, in our own complacency and isolation, that the real enemy lies. It is against this enemy that the manager must exert the greatest effort" (p.55). See also Harper's interview in *Business Today* (Spring 1975), pp. 6–7.
87. Harper, *A View of the Corporate Role*, pp. 23, 38–9, and passim.
88. *Alcoa News*, November 1966, pp. 8–9.
89. Alcoa was part of a larger coalition of corporate and community leaders who coordinated investments in time and money to alleviate slum conditions and to provide new housing for Pittsburgh's urban poor, movement that reached its height during the years 1968 through 1974. See Stewman and Tarr, "Public-Private Partnerships in Pittsburgh," pp. 163ff.
90. *Annual Reports*.
91. By the end of 1975, only two percent of all technical and management personnel in Alcoa's domestic operations were classified as minorities (including black females). Women were also rare. White females constituted only 2.4 percent of all technical and managerial positions. The numbers would improve to 7.6 percent and 10.8 percent, re-

spectively, by 1986. (Information supplied by the Accounting Department, Alcoa headquarters.)

92. Harper, *A View of the Corporate Role*, pp. 52–3.
93. Ibid., pp. 10–11; Harper interview.
94. Hunt interview. On one occasion, when General Mellon suggested the addition of a director from his own intimate circle of corporate connections, Roy Hunt demurred. (Mellon himself had once interceded to prevent Wilson from bringing in a senior executive of the Mellon Bank.) At the end of Magee's term as chairman, the directors consisted of nine Alcoa officers, Mellon, and George W. Wyckoff, representing the Paul Mellon family interests. Alfred Hunt spoke of Mellon and Wyckoff, who went on the board in 1957, as "outsiders," but noted, too, that Wyckoff and Miller were really "Alcoa-oriented individuals." It was not until Mellon's death that "outsiders" in the more commonly used sense of the term joined Alcoa's Board.
95. Harper interview.
96. Ibid.; *Dun's Review* (July 1968), p. 41.
97. Ibid.; *Business Week* (January 18, 1969), pp. 38–46.
98. Memorandum, John D. Harper to Dr. J. W. Newsome, August 23, 1968, re: Company Reorganization, AA, uncatalogued.
99. Ibid; *Annual Report*, 1968; *Alcoa News*, January 1965, pp. 4–5.
100. *Non-ferrous Metals Analysts Appraise...Aluminum Company of America* (Princeton, NJ: Opinion Research Corporation, 1969). A similar poll of industry analysts taken six years earlier had been much less favorable.
101. Close and George interviews. Fritz Close, not surprisingly, hated the computers, the despised tools of a new generation of cost accountants and financial specialists who were exercising more and more influence over executive decisions.
102. *Alcoa News* (August 1966), pp. 10–11; Goern interview. Goern, incidentally, attributed much of the planning department's fascination with new forecasting techniques to George Haymaker, a member of the group who had returned from MIT's Sloan School where he had been exposed to mathematical modeling.
103. *Annual Reports*; Van Horn interview.
104. *The New York Times*, September 10, 1972.
105. *Annual Reports*.
106. *Annual Reports*; *Alcoa News* (April 1966), p. 8, April 1967, pp. 13–14, and October 1968, pp. 8–9.
107. W. H. Krome George, *Executive: An Informal Chronicle* (1983), on file in the Public Affairs Department, Alcoa headquarters; George interview.
108. The *Metals Week* survey of the industry in 1969 (Farin and Reibsamen, *Aluminum*, pp. 140–5) offers good summary profiles of the world's aluminum producers. I have supplemented this with the his-

torical information on producers in Rhea Berk, Howard Lax, William Prast, and Jack Scott, *Aluminum: Profile of the Industry*, (New York: *Metals Week*, McGraw-Hill, 1982), pp. 173–86.

109. Harvey is quoted by John A. Stuckey, *Vertical Integration and Joint Ventures in the Aluminum Industry* (Cambridge, MA: Harvard University Press, 1983), p. 2.

110. The Aluminum Association, *1971 Aluminum Statistical Review* (New York, [1972]); Farin and Reibsamen, *Aluminum*, pp. 16–24, 140.

111. Spector, *Aluminum Industry Report* (1975); Brubaker, *Trends in the World Aluminum Industry*, pp. 99–117; Charles River Associates, *Economic Analysis of the Aluminum Industry*, pp. III–36–45. Total Sino–Soviet bloc capacity, which output did not trade in the so-called "free-world" market, approached 2,500,000 tons, or about twenty-seven percent of the total world capacity.

112. Cf. Stuckey, *Vertical Integration and Joint Ventures*, chap. 4, esp. pp. 176–9; Charles River Associates, *Economic Analysis of the Aluminum Industry*, p. III–45.

113. A discussion of the capital requirements of aluminum plants is in Brubaker, *Trends in the World Aluminum Industry*, chap. 4. Specialized studies, all pointing to the same general conclusion are United States Secretariat, *Pre-Investment Data on the Aluminum Industry*, by Jan H. Reimers, ST/ECLA/Conf.11/L.24 (January 28, 1963); United Nations, *Studies in Economics of Industry 2: Pre-Investment Data for the Aluminum Industry*, ST/CID/9 (New York, 1966); Alexander Karin, "Economic and Directional Growth in the Aluminum Industry," *Proceedings of the Council of Economics*, American Institute of Mining, Metallurgical and Petroleum Engineers, Inc., Annual Meeting (New York, February 25–29, 1968), pp. 256–97.

114. Philippe Leurquin, *Marché Commun et Localizations* (Louvain, France: Editions Nauwelaerts, 1962), p. 226; Peck, *Competition in the Aluminum Industry*, p. 170.

115. Charles River Associates, *The Economic Effects of Pollution Controls on the Nonferrous Metals Industry: Aluminum*, prepared for the Council on Environmental Quality (December 1971), pp. 21–7.

116. Brubaker, *Trends in the World Aluminum Industry*, pp. 129–33. See also Farin and Reibsamen, *Aluminum*, pp. 110–11.

117. Charles River Associates, *Economic Analysis of the Aluminum Industry*, p. I–6; Brubaker, *Trends in the World Aluminum Industry*, p. 131; Farin and Reibsamen, *Aluminum*, pp. 94, 110.

118. *Annual Report*, 1967.

119. Brubaker, *Trends in the World Aluminum Industry*, esp. pp. 113–40.

120. MIT Sloan School and Harvard Business School, *The World Aluminum Industry*, Case No. 9–375–351 (Cambridge, MA, 1975), pp. 17, 19.

121. Ibid., p. 14.

122. *Annual Report*, 1972.
123. *Annual Report*, 1968; Kramer interview.
124. *Annual Report*, 1983.
125. Farin and Reibsamen, *Aluminum*, p. 164.
126. Ibid., p. 164. "If, perhaps, two-thirds of the smelters built after 1976 turn to nuclear, then by 1984 as much as thirty to forty percent of the capacity of the world industry would be nuclear-based. If, for one of many reasons . . . , nuclear should become unpopular, it's still a safe bet that about ten percent of capacity would be nuclear-based anyway by 1984."
127. As always, the problem was to find economically sound alternatives to the Hall and Bayer Processes. Only the Soviet Union and Poland were producing alumina from nonbauxitic ore during peacetime, which would not have been economically competitive with bauxitic alumina on the world market. See ibid., p. 154.
128. Allen S. Russell, "Pitfalls and Pleasures in New Aluminum Process Development," *Metallurgical Transactions B*, 12 B (June 1981), pp. 207–8; Stroup interview.

Chapter 8

1. *Annual Report*, 1982.
2. *Facts About Alcoa* (1984); *Annual Report* 1986; Parry interview.
3. *Insight* (November 10, 1986), p. 43.
4. Comprised mainly of the Caribbean bauxite-producing countries, the International Bauxite Association was formed in 1974. According to Stuckey, *Vertical Integration*, p. 102, Jamaica taxes and royalties increased from $1.70 to $15 per ton during the 1970s. Surinam taxes and royalties increased from $2 to $12.50 per ton in the same period. But uniform prices proved hard to devise and difficult to enforce in recessionary years. By virtue of a shift in its bauxite dependence away from the Caribbean to Guinea, Australia, and Brazil, Alcoa mitigated the impact of the cartel countries' levies.
5. The consumer price index, using 1967 as the base year (1967 = 100), increased from about 116 to 281 between 1970 and 1980. The wholesale price index ran up from about 112 to 305 in the same period.
6. *Annual Report*, 1982.
7. *Annual Report*, 1985.
8. Whicker and Clausen interview; Kopatich, Duncan, and Thibault interview.
9. A brief summation of the impact of this exercise in self-critical revelation appears in the *Alcoa News*, March/April, 1987, p. 6. Specifically, the "outside technologies" studied for comparison were computers, polymers, and advanced manufacturing systems, all high-growth sectors of the international economy.

10. Gross estimates provided by Alcoa's Office of the Corporate Secretary reveal the following: in 1975, the Hunt family held approximately four percent of Alcoa common, the Mellon interests about six percent. By 1985, the Mellon interests' stake would fall to around one percent, while institutional holdings would increase to seventy-five percent. Alcoa employee stock plans accounted for about four percent of the total in both 1975 and 1985.

11. See especially the Close and George interviews.

12. Ibid. The notion of a corporate family is common to many businesses, indeed to institutions of all kinds. I have learned, over the course of four years of consulting with the company, that the idea of an "Alcoa family" has multiple origins, stemming from associations in different arenas and at different levels of corporate life: in the social life of the old company towns, in the normal affinities of employees for fraternal association in the workplace, and in the shared sense of professional and functional identity of technicians and managers across geographic and organizational boundaries. The Alcoa family permeates decades of internal company literature and was implicitly promoted at the very top of the corporation by the company's leading stockholders and their close associates in senior management, so many of whom were dedicated to the company's growth, preservation, and integrity as an institution and to the well-being of its personnel over an exceptionally long period of time. Even under the more bureaucratic regimes of the 1960s and 70s, even after Davis, Wilson, Hunt, and Mellon were gone, the ideal of the Alcoa family persisted, becoming a way of referring to the sense of loyalty career managers felt for the firm. For a pointed reference to the binding power of this notion of corporate family, see "Alcoa's Corporate Culture: Enduring Strengths and Embedded Constraints," a report prepared by The Winthrop Group, Inc., Cambridge, MA, October 10, 1983, AA, uncatalogued.

13. George interview.

14. This and other characterizations of contemporary Alcoa directors and executives are based on a wide range of interviews, (many of them informal) of Alcoa managers and employees. See also "Alcoa's Corporate Culture," which discusses the nonbureaucratic tenor of Alcoa's modern administration.

15. George and Jones interviews.

16. See App. B, Table B.2; *Annual Reports*.

17. Ibid.

18. See above, note 10.

19. App. B, Table B.2.

20. *Annual Reports*, esp. 1979 and 1985; Parry, Morber, and Kramer interviews.

21. *Annual Report*, 1980; *Forbes* (January 5, 1981), p. 84.

22. *Annual Reports*, 1980–3.

23. Ibid., 1970–82; O'Nan interview.
24. Whicker and Clausen interview.
25. Estimate provided by Alcoa's Rigid Packaging Division Marketing Office.
26. Gantz interview; *Annual Reports*, 1981 and 1982.
27. W. H. Krome George to R. C. Sharp, January 26, 1972, ALA; *Annual Report*, 1973.
28. John D. Harper to J. W. Newsome, September 9, 1968, ALA. This memorandum was circulated throughout the company. Harper went on to say: "At virtually every operation we have some technique or piece of equipment developed by Alcoans which provides a competitive advantage for Alcoa and thus a more secure future for us all. But the advantage is ours so long as the technical capacity we develop is known and used only by Alcoa. Keeping this advantage is a job for all of us— a job that grows more important (and more difficult!) every day as the competition grows stronger."
29. See the George interview and various memoranda and correspondence on file at ALA, including Robert N. Wagner to Dr. Eric A. Walker, November 27, 1970; C. F. Billhardt to W. L. Crawford, October 5, 1970; J. W. Newsome to Director, Division Chiefs, and Department Heads, March 3, 1971; Verne C. Koch to D. J. George, August 13, 1971; R. G. Hampel to Task Force on Sale of Know-How, October 15, 1971 and November 11, 1971.
30. Ibid. George explained the inevitability of leaks of technological information with an anecdote. He recalled being taken to an expensive lunch in New York by a competing aluminum executive. That executive's company had a problem with a smelter, the design of which had been based on Alcoa engineering prints long thought to have been expropriated by an independent electrical contractor. George explained that he had asked his host, "Why are you buying me this million-dollar lunch? He said, 'Well, you know, we stole the technology for a plant that we have and I've got a theory that if you steal something that big from somebody, they've got an obligation to kind of help you make it work!' That was such a disarming viewpoint that we sent a fellow with a half trailer down there and fixed it for him."
31. Ibid; *Annual Reports*.
32. Thomas Y. Canby, "Aluminum, the Magic Metal," *National Geographic* (August 1978), p. 204; *Annual Report*, 1985.
33. Charles Parry, remarks to senior management at Pittsburgh, July 30, 1986, transcript provided by the Alcoa Public Relations Department.
34. "Alcoa's Corporate Culture," pp. 18–19 and passim.
35. See above, chap. VII; Harper and Hoffman interviews.
36. See App. D, Chart D.7.
37. Fetterolf interview.
38. Ligon, Goern, and O'Nan interviews.

39. This and the following paragraphs to the end of the section are based largely on documents made available to me by Alcoa's Planning Department. A good summary view of the essence of the matters discussed here is a memorandum from Harry Goern to W. B. Renner, D. R. Whitlow, and W. M. Quackenbush, November 15, 1979, regarding "Organizational Planning," AA, uncatalogued.

40. Ibid.

41. Ibid.

42. Cf. Fetterolf, Parry, Goern, and O'Nan interviews. The younger group of vice presidents, including Ronald Hoffman and Fred Fetterolf from the Mill Products Group (where Renner, himself, had served as executive vice president), were strong proponents of business-unit organization. George Haymaker, who had gone from the planning function to become managing director of Alcoa Australia, was another supporter. Charles Parry, then the vice president of operations in Primary Products, was, according to some accounts, more aloof, reportedly concerned about an adverse impact of uncoupling the management of aluminum and alumina. Among the more senior managers, Marvin Gantz, head of Mill Products, and James McGowan, head of Primary Products, were described as much more conservative about the prospects for decentralization.

43. Memorandum: "Organizational Planning"; Goern interview.

44. O'Nan, Fetterolf, and Hoffman interviews; App. D, Chart D.8.

45. Johnson interview.

46. *Alcoa Digest* (September/October 1981), p. 1; Parry and Gantz interviews. At first, Bill Renner (who would retire in 1982) became vice chairman overseeing "general corporate services," while the new president, Charles Parry, became responsible for the day-to-day operations of the major production and marketing groups (Primary, Mill and Allied Products, and International Operations). Another vice chairman, Marvin Gantz, had been promoted from Mill Products to take on specific responsibility for corporate technical activities.

47. McKinsey & Company, Inc., memorandum to Alcoa OVA Steering Committee, "Reflections on Alcoa" (December 1982), copy provided to the author by the Corporate Planning Department.

48. Ibid.

49. "Alcoa's Corporate Culture," p. 17; Falls, Gillespie, and Gambill interviews.

50. Rand and Kuerner interviews.

51. Ligon interview. In fact, Alcoa's share of the total RCS market was closer to forty-two percent in 1983 (estimate provided by Alcoa's Rigid Packaging Division Marketing Office).

52. Turnbull interviews.

53. "Alcoa's Corporate Culture," pp. 34ff.

54. Ibid. The problems affecting Alcoa's R&D are being developed at length in a work in progress by Margaret B. W. Graham and Bettye Pruitt.
55. Ibid.; Whicker and Clausen interview.
56. See my extended, more technical discussion in "The Corporate Management of Innovation: Alcoa Research, Aircraft Alloys, and the Problem of Stress-Corrosion Cracking," with Bettye Pruitt, in Richard S. Rosenbloom (ed.), *Research on Technological Innovation, Management, and Policy*, (Greenwich, CT: JAI Press, 1986), pp. 33–81.
57. Evidence of the perception among R&D managers that corporate management was exerting pressure on the Laboratories to focus on high-tonnage applications appears in a letter from J. H. Dunn to W. W. Binger and R. L. LaBarge, June 21, 1968, ALA, in which Dunn reports that "Mr. Close [Alcoa's chairman and principal R&D champion] continuously emphasizes the need for Alcoa to be forward looking in areas which will absorb large tonnages of aluminum." Dunn enclosed a sample form on which projects could be reported to management on which the project name was followed immediately by the tonnage per annum it would sell. See also J. D. Harper to Staff Meeting Attendees, February 2, 1971, and T. R. Gauthier to J. W. Newsome, November 30, 1971, ALA.
58. E. A. Walker and J. H. Dunn, "R&D Organization," April 23, 1973, ALA.
59. See, for example, Eric Walker to J. H. Dunn, R. G. Hampel, J. W. Newsome, May 25, 1971; T. R. Gauthier to J. W. Newsome, November 30, 1971; Gauthier to Members of Research and Development Committee, March 10, 1972, ALA.
60. From informal conversations, I have learned that there are substantial differences of opinion about Walker's experience, competence, and impact, which are not easily reconciled. But it is clear that Walker was regarded by some as an outsider or worse, a heretic who questioned the prevailing management orthodoxy.
61. W. H. Krome George, memorandum, "Research and Development," April 16, 1975, and George to Staff Meeting Attendees, September 22, 1975.
62. R. G. Hampel, memoranda to subcommittees, February 17, and March 4, 1976, ALA.
63. "Alcoa's Corporate Culture," pp. 37–8.
64. Allen S. Russell, "Pitfalls and Pleasures in New aluminum Process Development," in American Society for Metals and the Metallurgical Society of AIME, *Metallurgical Transactions B*, 12B (June 1981), pp. 203–15, offers a candid view of Alcoa's problems with ASP. See also Margaret B. W. Graham, "Corporate Research and Development: The Latest Transformation," *Technology in Society* 7 (1985), p. 186.

65. Ibid. See also letters on file at ALA: G. T. Holmes to P. T. Stroup, March 21, 1962; Stroup to Holmes, April 4, 1962; Holmes, memorandum, "New Hall Cell," February 1, 1963; Holmes to Members of Smelting Subcommittee, May 13, 1963; C. C. Cook to Holmes, October 28, 1966; Holmes to Potroom B Task Force, December 12, 1966; J. W. Dyer to Task Force on Potrooms, July 29, 1968; J. G. Kaufman, "Minutes of Joint Meeting," May 17, 1979.

66. "Alcoa's Corporate Culture," p. 37. The quoted phrase is from George David Smith and John E. Wright, "Alcoa Goes Back to the Future," *Across the Board*, XXIII (September 1986), p. 27.

67. J. Lee O'Nan to H. M. Goern and R. G. Hampel, April 28, 1978; M. Mohajery to J. Lee O'Nan, April 25, 1978; William B. Renner, "Technical Planning – Major Projects Search," August 6, 1979; Roger C. Haddon, memorandum, "R&D Budgeting and Planning through the Subcommittee System," May 12, 1980; J. W. Evancho to Members of the Subcommittee for Corporate R&D, February 12, 1982; A. C. Sheldon to Subcommittee Chairmen, Secretaries, and Technical Coordinators, April 5, 1982. ALA.

68. "Alcoa's Corporate Culture," pp. 28ff.

69. Ibid., p. 27; Arnold and Smith interviews. Alcoa's Human Resource Department was concerned about the effects of job rotation and had begun to slow the trend by the early 1980s.

70. The Busch Center, The Wharton School, "Whatever Happened to Alcoa in Tennessee?" a report prepared for the Alcoa, Tennessee, Operations, June, 1980, on file at Alcoa Operations, Alcoa, Tennessee; Gambill interview.

71. Ibid; Russell L. Ackoff and William Deane, "The Revitalization of Alcoa's Tennessee Operations" (December 1982), 5ff., on file at Alcoa Operations.

72. Smith and Stephenson interviews.

73. Kopatich, Duncan, and Thibault interview. Charles Kopatich, an area supervisor in the finishing department, recalled how unprepared he had been to work in Warrick's adversarial environment when he transferred there from Davenport in 1971. He remembered that in the day-to-day turmoil, his stomach became "just absolutely eaten up," while other supervisors melted to tears in the evening when they gathered together for mutual support. But for the money (Alcoa paid the best salaries and wages in the region), he would have stayed home. It is fair to say that workers at Warrick and other trouble spots with whom I talked informally said much the same thing: but for the money, they would have stayed home.

74. Ibid; Smith and Coleman interviews.

75. Gillespie interview; Yakamavage and Cantanzarite interview. Cleveland's labor problems are discussed in a disguised Harvard Business School case, *LVI Allentown Works* (A), case number 0–682–046. At

this writing, access to thé case is restricted, subject to approval from Aluminum Company of America.

76. Ibid; Farish and Dina interviews; Joel P. Vujevich, "The United Automobile, Aerospace & Agricultural Implement Workers of America: Local Union 1050: Past & Present," undated manuscript on file at Alcoa works, Cleveland, Ohio.

77. "Alcoa's Corporate Culture," pp. 32–3.

78. Ibid.; Kramer, Morber, Thrasher, and Fischer interviews.

79. Fischer interview; Smith and Wright, "Alcoa Goes Back to the Future," p. 31.

80. "Alcoa's Corporate Culture," p. 4ff.

81. "Reflections on Alcoa"; OVA Summary Presentation to Alcoa Steering Committee, December 2, 1982, copy provided to the author by Alcoa's Corporate Planning Department.

82. On p. 8, George recalled that aluminum officials were "called on the carpet" in 1975 by senior administration economic officers who were concerned that aluminum was not behaving according to classic economic models of supply and demand.

83. See also the George interview.

84. "Reflections on Alcoa," p. 4.

85. Falls interview.

86. Ligon and Gantz interviews.

87. "Overview: Past, Present & Future," prepared for Policy Committee Use at Rolling Rock Meeting, June 21–2, 1983, a memorandum provided to the author by the Corporate Planning Department, Alcoa headquarters; Ligon interview. It was fine, said Ligon, "to be the best aluminum company in the world . . . when it was a high-growth business, but when it's not a high-growth business, it's just another smokestack industry."

88. The remark attributed to Parry was repeated to me in more or less the terms quoted in the text by several Alcoa managers. See, for instance, the Ligon interview.

89. Fetterolf interview.

90. Parry interview.

91. Thrasher interview.

92. "Overview: Past, Present, & Future."

93. Ibid.

94. *Annual Report*, 1985.

95. *Insight* (November 10, 1986), p. 42.

96. Ibid., p. 44; *Facts About Alcoa* (1986), p. 11.

97. I have discussed this a bit more fully in "Edwin Stanton Fickes and the Rise of Alcoa Engineering," *Alcoa News* (March/April 1987), pp. 16–19.

98. T. L. Carter to R. D. Hornbeck, June 18, 1986, copy provided to the author.

99. Parry and Fetterolf interviews; *Annual Reports*, 1984–5.
100. App. D, Chart D.9.
101. "Draft Remarks by Charles W. Parry . . . Meeting on Reorganization," July 30, 1986, copy provided by the Alcoa Public Affairs Department; *Alcoa News* (August 1986), pp. 12–13.
102. Ibid.; *Annual Report*, 1986. See also App. D, Chart D.9.
103. *Alcoa News* (December 1986), p. 10. Parry did not necessarily anticipate "a significant shrinking of the aluminum business." He was hoping instead for strong growth in other areas.
104. Ibid.

Index

References to charts, tables, and photographs do not appear in this index. Please refer to Table of Contents.

531

sition to diversified multinational, 309 (*see also* international expansion); vice-presidents, 152, 153, 159, 258, 430, 526n42; vulnerability to antitrust, 196–7

Aluminum Cooking Utensil Company (Wear-Ever), 85–6, 152, 153, 204, 288, 305, 321, 331, 358–9, 396; divestiture of, 387, 414; semiautonomous entity, 298

Aluminum Employers Association, 187–8

Aluminum Goods Manufacturing Company, 86, 102, 112, 204

aluminum industry, 1, 106, 191, 212; Alcoa dominance of, 59–60, 111 (*see also* monopoly); Alcoa's structural position in, 78, 313; changes in, 264, 391; circa 1970, 363–70; concentration of, 365, 372; and control of capacity and pricing, 316; at crossroads, 416–19; cyclical nature of, 256, 277, 296, 308, 383, 391; decline in, 418–19; effect of Alcoa antitrust decision on, 213–14; effect of world wars on, 191; employment levels in, 178; in Europe, 106–8, 109; Federal Government relations with, 217, 218, 232–3; Federal Government restructuring of, 233–42; future of, 377–79, 436; as growth industry, 133, 136, 175, 308, 391, 415; integrated producers in, 241–2; international structure of, 379; labor rivalry in, 74; maturity of, 418 (*see also* markets, mature); as monopoly, 196; new producers in, 284–5; protectionism and, 139; secular decline in, 418; and tariffs, 369; and threat to dissolve Alcoa, 209–10; wages in, 188; *see also* oligopoly

Aluminum Intensive Vehicles (AIV), 425–6, 429

Aluminum Ore Company, 305

Aluminum Research Laboratories, 163, 167–9, 170, 171, 175, 176; *see also* Alcoa Research Laboratories

Aluminum Rolling Mills Corporation, 194

aluminum science: Alcoa knowledge base in, 42, 261–2

Aluminum Screw Machine Product Company, 151

Aluminum Seal Company, 153, 305

aluminum siding, 312, 338

aluminum workers, 29, 119; communism as issue among, 225; organization of, 75, 176–89 (*see also* unions)

Aluminum Workers International (AWI), 291–2, 294, 295, 371

Aluminum Workers of America (AWA), 224–5, 229, 290

Alusuisse (co.), 21, 365, 367

American Bell Telephone Company, 52–3

American Body Company, 159–60, 161

American Electrochemical Society, 18, 89, 122

American Federation of Labor (AFL), 70, 73–4, 224, 225, 291; conservatism in labor organization, 182, 184, 224; and unionization of Alcoa, 119, 181–2, 183, 184, 186, 187, 188

American Magnesium Corporation, 151, 167, 230–2, 305

American Metal Climax, 364–5

American Missionary Association, 18, 154–7

American Tobacco, 50, 60, 66, 112

ammonal, 127

amortization, accelerated, 253, 254, 284

Anaconda Aluminum Company, 251, 284, 364

Anderson, Minton M., 227, 260–1, 299, 331

Anheuser Busch, 341

annual reports, 222, 229–30, 258, 262, 316, 329, 377, 492n1; 1982, 416–21

antimonopolists, 200–1, 211, 274

antitrust, 60–8, 146, 264, 432; and Alcoa expansion, 256–7; Alcoa's problems and concerns with, xx, 67–8, 76, 78, 189, 251–2, 277, 283, 303, 311, 312, 364; Alcoa's new acquisitions and, 314–16; and competition, 274–5; market control and, 111–13; as political tool, 199; as regulatory weapon, 68

antitrust case (*U.S. v. Alcoa*), 193–214, 233; costs of, 201; Duke investment and, 494n28; effects of, 213–14, 245, 246, 257; penalty for successful free enterprise in, 208–9, 210, 212; remedy in, 237, 238, 269–76, 311

antitrust law: effect of Hand's decision on, 207–10, 213; tacit collusion and, 278

antitrust policy (U.S.), 274

antitrust suits, 201; rule of reason in, 210

Apex Smelting Company, 242

applications (aluminum), 41, 78–9, 93, 133; new, 42, 83–93, 133–5, 250, 335–6, 387, 425, 436; in corporate strategy, 388; research and development and,